# HUDSONS

The definitive guide to heritage in the United Kingdom

# HUDSONs

## The definitive guide to heritage in the United Kingdom

Published by Visit Heritage Ltd,
26 Eldon Business Park, Chilwell, Nottingham NG9 6DZ
Email: info@visitheritage.co.uk www.visitheritage.co.uk



*Front cover:* One of two bronze lions outside the north entrance to Holkham Hall commissioned by the 2nd Earl of Leicester in 1871 from Joseph Boehm.

2019

# KEY TO SYMBOLS

*Hudson's is organised by region according to this map. We use the symbols on this key to include as much information as possible. We indicate ownership so if you are a member of a heritage organisation, you know if you can have privileged access, but please check first.*

- Information
- Toilets
- Baby Changing
- € Accepts Euros
- Open All Year
- Parking Available
- Suitable for Disabled People
- Cycling Routes
- Dogs Welcome
- Accommodation
- Audio Tours
- Guided Tours
- Educational/School Visits
- Café / Tearoom / Refreshments
- Restaurant
- Shop
- Plant Sales
- Private or Corporate Venue
- Special Events
- Weddings
- In the Movies

- Member of Historic Houses but does not give free access to Friends
- Ⓕ Member of HH giving free access under HH Friends Scheme
- Owned by National Trust
- Owned by National Trust Scotland
- In the care of Historic Scotland
- In the care of English Heritage
- In the care of Cadw, the Welsh Government's historic environment service
- Royal Horticultural Society Partner Garden
- NIEA In the care of Northern Ireland Environment Agency
- In the care of the Landmark Trust
- Churches Conservation Trust

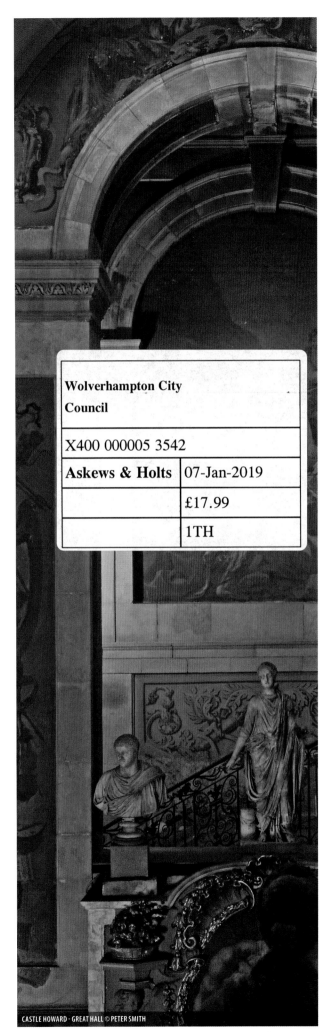

CASTLE HOWARD - GREAT HALL © PETER SMITH

On behalf of Visit Heritage

*Welcome to*

# HUDSONS

We are the only totally independent representation of all that is Heritage in the United Kingdom. We aim to encourage people of all ages to explore our heritage and help keep these amazing buildings, gardens and fascinating landmarks alive for the generations to come.

We want to encourage you to explore our unrivalled history as well as visit and get close to places which helped form the world we know. Not only will this expand your mind, but it also helps the hundreds of people and organisations that are working to maintain our Heritage.

We hope that you enjoy looking at the beautiful places to visit, and some of the amazing photos we have selected to share with you in this edition. This year we have chosen to also emphasise weddings and in particular the wonderful opportunities that can be had from holding a wedding in some of these fantastic places. We have even attempted to provide tips in planning your wedding and have called on experts from various disciplines to contribute articles for you.

If you want to be a Member of Visit Heritage you can become a Time Traveller and receive updates and other opportunities from us. Our quarterly magazine has loads of tips, news, updates, as well as a fun section to encourage children to become involved. Please go to our website, visitheritage.co.uk - join us page for more information about how you can become a Time Traveller.

Finally, I encourage you to go to the Visit Heritage website and see what is on offer. It will keep you informed of events and opportunities that you can visit or take the whole family to. Please spend a little bit of your valuable time this year in visiting and appreciating the wonderful Heritage on offer in these beautiful lands.

*Paul Bridle*

We want Hudson's to make discovering Britain's heritage easy for you but please check opening times before you visit to avoid disappointment. Many heritage places open regularly but others only occasionally or only for special events.

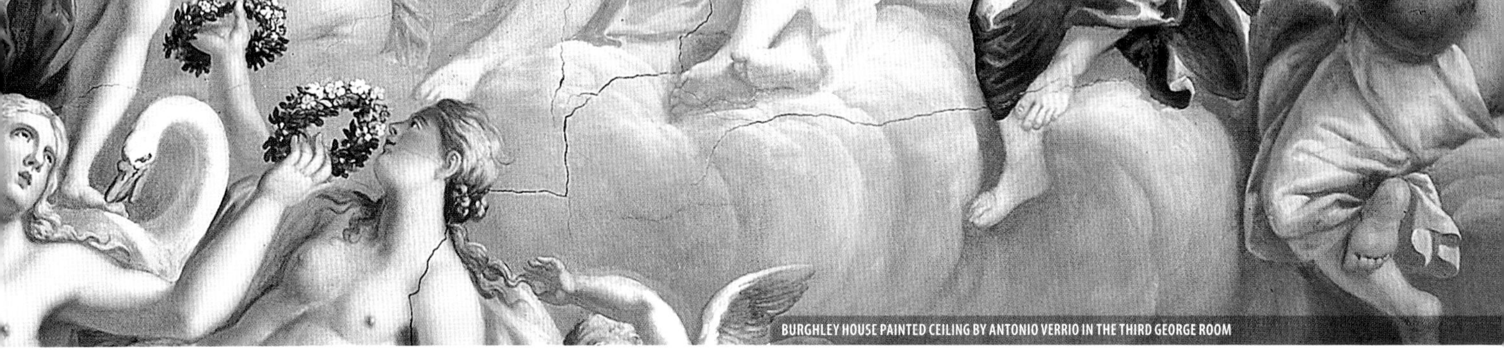
BURGHLEY HOUSE PAINTED CEILING BY ANTONIO VERRIO IN THE THIRD GEORGE ROOM




Publisher: Visit Heritage

Editorial: Antonia Buxton; Rachel Price-Hood, Sarah Greenwood Derek Tarr, Sue Hodgson, Gary Swarbrooke, William Sitwell, Siobhan Craven-Robins, Carol Barnes, Rebecca Koziak.

Publishing & Production Managers: Gary Swarbrooke, Neil Jones

Creative team: Neil Jones

Cover Photography: Richard Clark OMNI42

Bookings: Antonia Buxton; Rachel Price-Hood

Web team: Antonia Buxton; Rachel Price-Hood

Social media: Edwina Holmes

Printer: Biddles, King's Lynn, Norfolk PE32 1SF

Distribution: Compass International Publishing Services, Brentford TW8 9DF

Address: Unit 26 Eldon Business Park, Chilwell, Nottingham NG9 6DZ Tel: 020 3880 5059
email: info@visitheritage.co.uk

Thanks to all private owners, local authorities, English Heritage, Historic Royal Palaces, Historic England, Historic Environment Scotland, the National Trust, the National Trust for Scotland, the Royal Collection, the Landmark Trust, Heritage Open Days for their information and for keeping Hudson's accurate and up-to-date.

HUDSON'S

TIME TRAVELLER

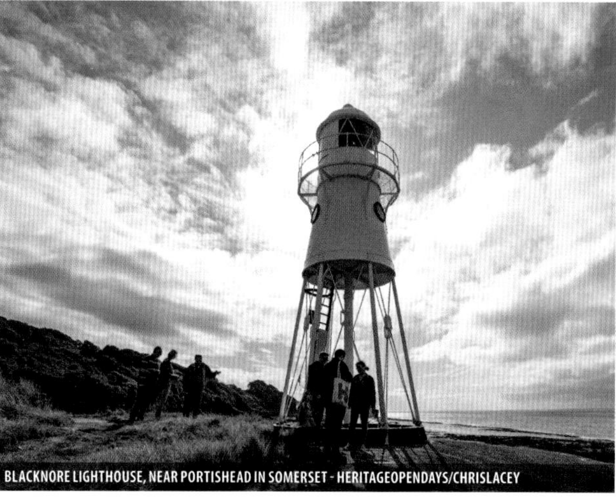
BLACKNORE LIGHTHOUSE, NEAR PORTISHEAD IN SOMERSET - HERITAGEOPENDAYS/CHRISLACEY

BADDESLEY CLINTON, A NATIONAL TRUST PROPERTY IN WARWICKSHIRE - HERITAGEOPENDAYS/CHRISLACEY

# HERITAGE OPEN DAYS

The nation's biggest festival of history and culture will be back and bigger than ever in 2019. From 13-22 September places of every description across Britain will welcome two million visitors to over 5000 events. Doors - actual and metaphorical - across the country will be flung open. From cathedrals, castles and nature reserves to microbreweries, private homes and recycling plants, Heritage Open Days is a unique snapshot of 21st century Britain. A dizzying array of walks, tours, events, performances and one-off happenings make the festival a treasure trove of compelling, unique and inspiring experiences. What other festival allows you to experience an escape room in the oldest pub in England, visit the IBM headquarters and archive, learn about the history of cider (with tasting) and have a go at making medieval tiles, all in the same town?

Our theme for 2019 is **PEOPLE POWER,** a celebration of the myriad ways that people across time have taken action to change our world. We'll share stories of community and civic work, marches, sit-ins, peaceful protests, rebel songs and revolutionary ideas - exploring the social history of our places, built and natural - how people have shaped them and been shaped by them.

2019 also marks Heritage Open Days 25th birthday, providing a fantastic opportunity to celebrate 25 years of people across the country sharing the stories and places that make us who we are. We'll be looking at our own history and how far we've come and use the occasion to reflect on the impact our thousands of organisers have had on their communities over the past quarter-century.

Thanks to support from players of People's Postcode Lottery and the National Trust, Heritage Open Days continues to grow each year with 2019 promising to be more exciting, fascinating and fun than ever!

HILLSBOROUGH COURTHOUSE

## HRP ANNOUNCE PLANS FOR HILLSBOROUGH COURTHOUSE AND FORT

Independent charity, Historic Royal Palaces has announced that they will be taking over the management of Hillsborough Courthouse and Fort.

A grand re-opening is planned for spring 2019 following a programme of repair and conservation which will transform Hillsborough Castle into a major visitor destination.

The Fort which was built in the mid-17th century commanded the chief roads from Belfast to Dublin before being transformed a century later into the distinctive Georgian 'gothic' style seen today.

A tree-lined path with a set of late 18th century wrought iron gates at each end leads you to The Courthouse. Completed in 1810 and located in the town square the building was originally a covered market.

The renovation will include a new learning facility hosting a range of learning and engagement activities for schools and families as well as community events.

Patricia Corbett, Head of Hillsborough Castle, said: *'We are delighted to take on the long-term management of Hillsborough Courthouse and Fort. Both buildings are intrinsically linked with the history of Hillsborough Castle and its original residents the Downshire family and will continue to play an important role for the village of Hillsborough. As a charity, our aim to open up these spaces for everyone to enjoy, whilst preserving them for future generations.'*

## Write a story about the loveliest Castle in the World!

To celebrate the Castle's 900th anniversary, Leeds Castle, near Maidstone in Kent are inviting children all over Britain to enter an exciting story writing competition; *'Leeds Castle's 'Big 900'* Story Writing Challenge'.

Stories should be based around the themes of castles and time travel, and be no more than 900 words. Entries will be separated in two age brackets, 5 - 9 years and 10 - 13 years.

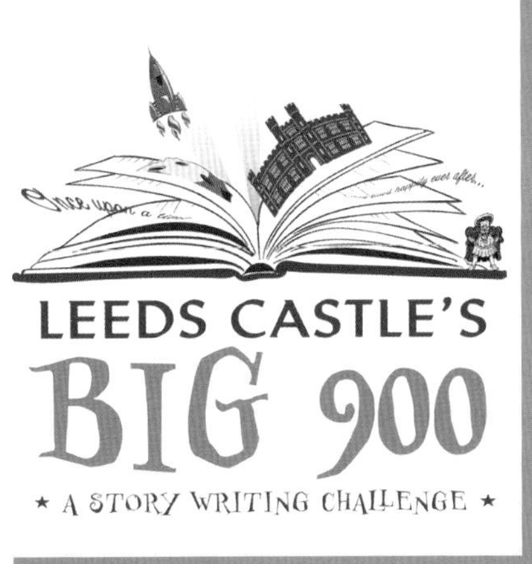


The competition will be judged by renowned broadcaster and author Clare Balding, along with Sir David Steel, the Chief Executive of Leeds Castle and Helen Ellis, Head of Education.

One of Britain's leading and BAFTA winning broadcasters, Clare Balding is also a best-selling and award-winning author of five books. Clare has released two children's books titled *'The Racehorse Who Wouldn't Gallop'*, and *'The Racehorse Who Disappeared'*, in addition to a short novel named *'The Girl Who Thought She Was a Dog'* for World Book Day in 2018.

Finalists from each age category will be invited along with their families to an Awards Day at Leeds Castle on 30th May 2019.

Two lucky winners will receive fantastic prizes including fun hampers, a stay at Knight's Glamping; a private tour of the Castle; and family tickets to the Fireworks Spectacular 2019.

The two winning stories will go into a time capsule to be buried by the winning children and HRH Princess Alexandra and only opened again in 100 years' time.

Entries should be submitted before 12pm on 5th March 2019, see www.leeds-castle.com for further information.

# V&A DUNDEE

The V&A Museum, Dundee opened its doors on 15th September 2018 and welcomed 27000 visitors in its first week. Scotland's first dedicated design museum, embracing the countries design heritage and future whilst highlighting its fabulous achievements.

The building situated on Dundee's Riverside Esplanade was designed by award-winning Japanese architects Kengo Kuma & Associates, the vison, a *'living room for the city'.*

The striking curved 8,000m$^2$ building has no exterior straight lines and was created to give the appearance of a Scottish cliff face.

The Scottish Design Galleries include around 300 beautiful and innovative objects front the V&A's collections and other lenders, representing a wide range of design disciplines from the decorative arts – including furniture, textiles, metalwork and ceramics - to fashion, architecture, engineering and digital design.

The galleries, which are free to enter, explore what is unique about Scotland's design landscape, historically and today.

At the centre of the galleries is the Charles Rennie Mackintosh Oak Room. A partnership between V&A Dundee, Glasgow Museums and Dundee City Council, giving visitors the opportunity to see a complete Charles Rennie Mackintosh tearoom interior from the 1950's.

**V&A Dundee is free to enter and open daily from 10.00 to 17.00.**

V&A, DUNDEE, SCOTLAND ©HUFTON+CROW

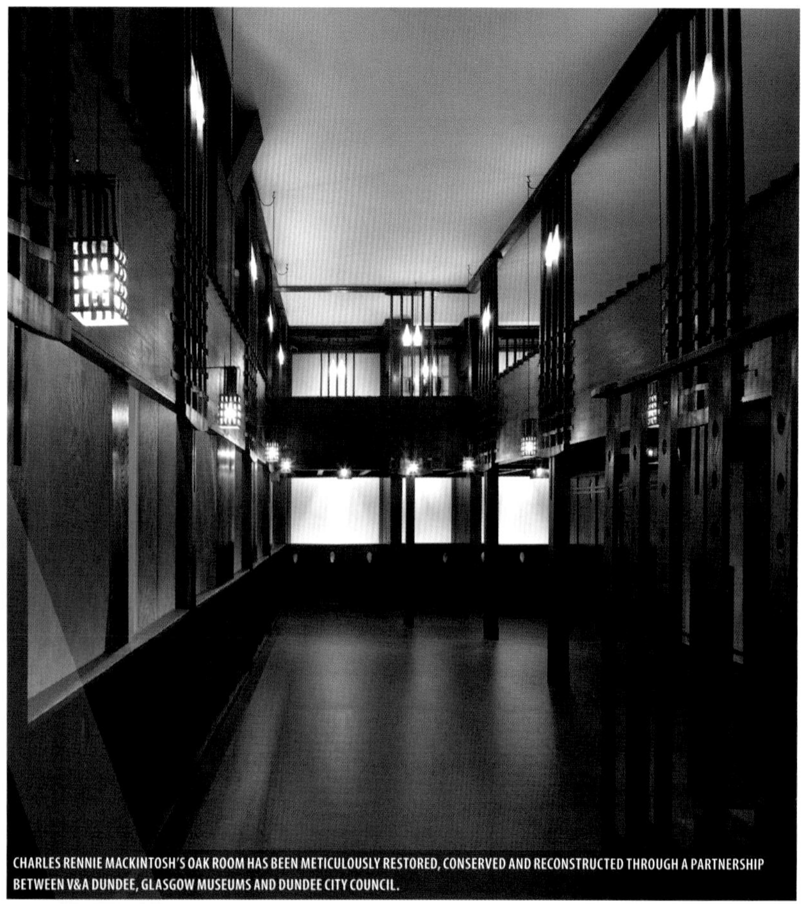

CHARLES RENNIE MACKINTOSH'S OAK ROOM HAS BEEN METICULOUSLY RESTORED, CONSERVED AND RECONSTRUCTED THROUGH A PARTNERSHIP BETWEEN V&A DUNDEE, GLASGOW MUSEUMS AND DUNDEE CITY COUNCIL.

DILLAN MARSH AND ELEANOR CLARE WOODS - UPPER LAKE COURTESY THE ARTIST COURTESY OF YSP

# YORKSHIRE SCULPTURE PARK

**Yorkshire Sculpture Park's new £3.6million visitor centre will open to the public on Saturday 30 March 2019.**

The open-air gallery in West Bretton near Wakefield welcomed over 480,000 people in 2017, its 40th anniversary year and the addition of the new Visitor Centre will increase essential capacity and enhance the visitor experience.

Designed by architects Feilden Fowles and built on the site of a quarry within the 500 acre Bretton Estate, the centre will be known as The Weston, acknowledging the significant support from family grant-maker, The Garfield Weston Foundation.

The Weston Foundation's Director, Philippa Charles, said; *'The Weston Family was delighted to support this project to enable more people to enjoy the Park and contribute to the Park's long-term financial sustainability'.*

The project is supported by Arts Council England, Wakefield Council, The Garfield Weston Foundation, Dunard Fund, The Foyle Foundation, The Sackler Trust, The Wolfson Foundation, B&M Retail Plc, The Arnold Burton Charitable Trust, The John S Cohen Foundation, Mtec, The Holbeck Charitable Trust, Catkin Pussywillow Charitable Trust, and other funders who wish to remain anonymous. Visitors to the Park have also contributed over £50,000 in donations to the project.

Gemma Shahjahan, Business Development Director of William Birch said: ***'Yorkshire Sculpture Park is a huge asset to the arts and leisure scene in the Yorkshire region and construction of The Weston has allowed us to be part of the next exciting phase in the journey of the Park. The project has also been a great opportunity for our apprentices to work on such a prestigious and much-loved visitor attraction local to them. We all very much look forward to unveiling the new facilities.'***

The parks artistic programme for 2019 features major indoor and open-air exhibitions and ambitious interventions in the landscape.

THE WESTON UNDER CONSTRUCTION © JONTY WILDE

THE MONA LISA BY THE ITALIAN RENAISSANCE ARTIST LEONARDO DA VINCI - 'THE BEST KNOWN, THE MOST VISITED, THE MOST WRITTEN ABOUT, THE MOST SUNG ABOUT, THE MOST PARODIED WORK OF ART IN THE WORLD.

## DEATH OF LEONARDO DA VINCI
### 500 YEARS

Widely recognised as one of the best painters ever to have lived Da Vinci died at the age of 67 *(a very good age for the era)* in 1519 in France.

Considered by many to be a genius, a one-off, Da Vinci is credited with advances and inventions in the fields of not just art, but literature, nature, architecture, medicine, sculpturing, anatomy, mechanics and engineering.

He was commissioned by Kings Louis XII and Francois I and around 15 surviving paintings are credited to him the most famous being The Mona Lisa (permanently housed at the Louvre in Paris) and The Last Supper (displayed in the Santa Maria Delle Grazie in Milan). None of his works were signed making new discoveries extremely difficult. As well as the artworks, there are also notebooks of sketches and scientific diagrams

The Royal Collection owns over 500 drawings by Da Vinci which were originally acquired by King Charles II.
The Queen's Gallery at Buckingham Palace and the Palace of Holyroodhouse in Edinburgh will be showcasing these in February 2019, as well as smaller collections being displayed at cities throughout the UK between February and May 2019. For more information visit The Royal Collection Trust website.

## CONCORDE'S FIRST FLIGHT
## 50 YEARS

Concorde was a joint venture between England and France and planes were bought by British Airways and Air France.

Its first test flight took place from Toulouse on March 2nd 1969 with scheduled passenger flights commencing in 1976 after some 7 years of testing. The planes reached speeds of up to 1320mph, twice the speed of sound, and travelled at an altitude of 60,000 feet. Passengers could cross the Atlantic in under 3 hours.

Passengers were usually wealthy and/or famous due the huge costs involved in this method of travel *(up to 30 times more than the cheapest alternative).*

The final flight of a Concorde took place on November 26th 2003 after the decision was made by both airlines to retire the planes due to falling passenger numbers and outdated technology. The announcement was made in the aftermath of a fatal crash in France of a Concorde flying to New York.

In 2015 Club Concorde announced plans to return one of the planes to service after securing financial investment to facilitate this.

In the meantime, visitors can step aboard Concorde Alpha Foxtrot which was the last Concorde to fly and is now on display at the Aerospace Museum in Bristol.

## THE BIRTH OF QUEEN VICTORIA
## 200 YEARS

Born Alexandrina Victoria at Kensington Palace on 24th May 1819 Queen Victoria came to the throne in June 1838 and went on to rule until her death in 1901. She was Britain's longest reigning monarch *(with 63 years 7 months and 2 days on the throne)* until the current monarch Queen Elizabeth II surpassed this on September 9th 2015.

In 1840 Victoria married Prince Albert of Saxe-Coburg and Gotha and they had nine children together.

Osbourne House was built on the Isle of Wight between 1845 and 1851 for Queen Victoria and Prince Albert as a summer home and rural retreat. Prince Albert designed the house himself in the style of an Italian Renaissance palazzo. It was where Victoria died in 1901. Balmoral was also purchased as a royal residence by Prince Albert.

Queen Victoria's reign was characterised by great social, political and industrial change and the British Empire expanded to its most far-reaching and powerful during the Victorian era. New technology included the telephone, the sewing machine, the electric light bulb and electric street lighting in London.

Advances in transportation saw the first paddle steamer invented by Isambard Kingdom Brunel, the opening of the steam powered London underground and the first tarmac road.

In medicine the discovery by John Snow that bacteria could be passed through the water supply and not just through the air led to advances in hygiene and cleaning up of the sewage systems. The invention of anaesthetic came about in the mid 1800's and the queen herself used chloroform to ease labour pains during the birth of two of her children.

Also in the year of Victoria's birth the South Shetland Islands are discovered by William Smith, Birmingham's streets are illuminated for the first time by gas, and romantic poet Keats writes his famous ode 'To Autumn'.

## THE TREATY OF VERSAILLES
### 100 YEARS

2019 marks 100 years since the formal end of World War I. Although the armistice was declared on November 11th 1918, the peace process was made official by the signing of the Treaty of Versailles on June 28th 1919.

The treaty was the result of the Paris Peace Conference which began in January 1919, its purpose being to assign responsibility to Germany for the war and to arrange reparation of damage. The treaty also put in place measures to make it difficult for Germany to start similar conflicts in the future. In pursuit of this aim a lot of territory previously held by Germany was taken away by the allies.

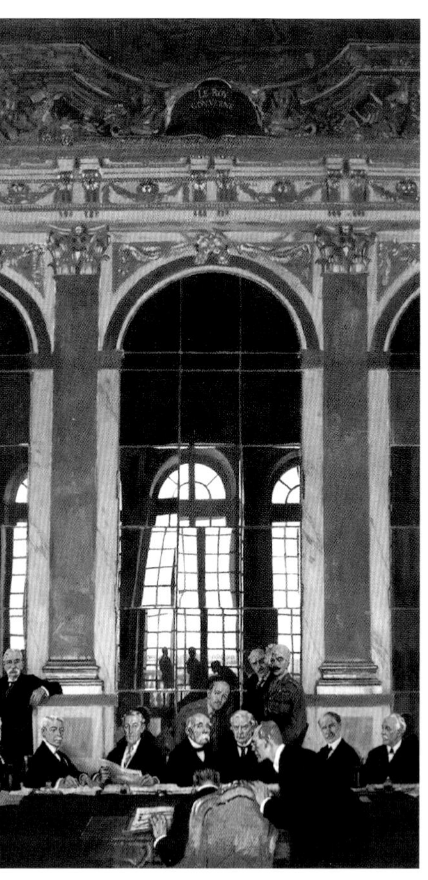

Some viewed the restrictions and financial punishments as overly harsh. When seen with hindsight they may be considered as being contributory factors to the taking back of territories and rearmament that led up to the outbreak of WW2 and the reason for many Germans being receptive to the rule of Hitler at this particular point in history.

The treaty remains an important historical document however the original was destroyed on the orders of Hitler during the German occupation of France. There is a copy in the UK which is stored at The National Archives in London.

## FIRST U.K. FORESTRY ACT
### 100 YEARS

The first Forestry Act passed in 1919 created the Forestry Commission in the UK. At its inception tree coverage in the UK was below 5% and complete de-forestation was a very real threat mainly down to the depletion of timber stocks during the First World War. The first trees planted by the Commission were planted at Eggesford Forest in Devon on December 8th 1919.

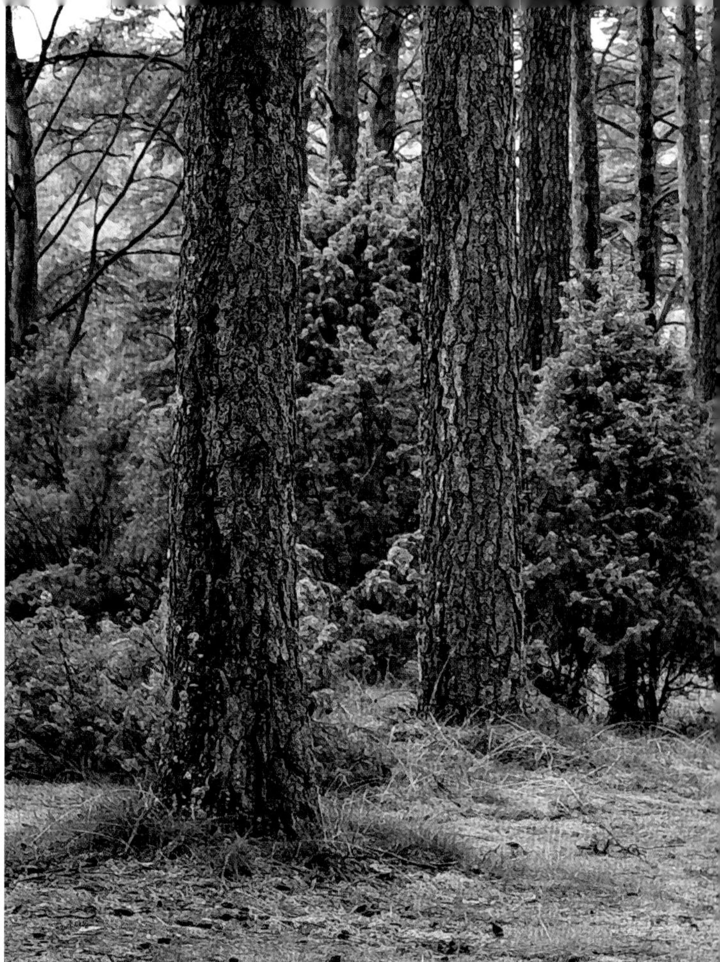

At the onset of the Second World War the commission could more efficiently control and record timber stock and make re-forestation a priority at the end of the war.

The technological revolution in the 1960s meant that timber could be extracted more efficiently and also that new trees could be planted in areas that previously were not possible. Increased awareness meant that the forestry industry grew into a business-like organisation

In 2011 aerial monitoring showed that the tree-covered areas of the UK were approximately 13%, a substantial increase from the less than 5% before the work of the commission started. Today the commission works in close conjunction with other conservation groups to help preserve wildlife and address agricultural issues.

## CLEVELAND WAY
### 50 YEARS

The Cleveland Way is situated within the North Yorkshire Moors National Park and stretches for 109 miles taking in coast, castles, villages and moorland along the way.

The campaign for the route, which stretches from Helmsley to The Brigg at Filey, was started in the 1930s by the Teeside Ramblers Association. The formal proposal to create the route was submitted in 1953 and the route eventually opened in 1969. As well as walks and hikes for all abilities the trail welcomes cyclists, horse riders and marathon runners.

Notable landmarks along the way include Whitby Abbey, Helmsley Castle, the site of the old Hambleton Down Racecourse and the famous White Horse of Kilburn at the Southern end of Sutton Bank. There is an abundance of birdlife on the trail.

The Othmotherley to Clay Bank section of the trail crossed through five different sections of breath-taking moorland and beyond Claybank you will reach Urra Moor the highest point of the North Yorkshire Moors. If the coast is more your thing visit the seaside towns of Scarborough, Filey, Whitby and Robin Hoods Bay.

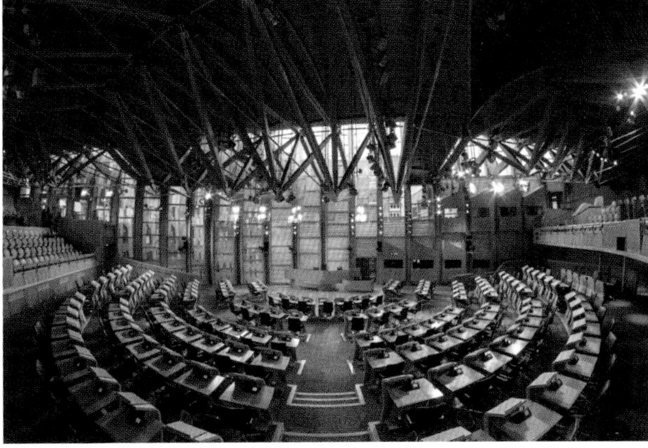

## SCOTTISH PARLIAMENT
## 20 YEARS

The first meeting of Scottish Parliament took place on 12th May 1999. This historic day marked the devolution of legislative power from Westminster to the Scottish Executive after the Scottish Devolution Referendum in 1997.

From its formation in 1999 parliament was housed temporarily in the General Assembly Hall of the Church of Scotland. In 2004 parliament moved to the Scottish Parliament Building in Holyrood, Edinburgh.

## THE STAFFORDSHIRE HOARD
## 10 YEARS

2019 marks 10 years since the Staffordshire Hoard was discovered at Hammerwich, near Lichfield, the biggest find of its kind on record anywhere in the world. Gold items were initially discovered by Terry Herbert on farmland owned by Fred Johnson. Subsequently English Heritage and Staffordshire County Council were called in to undertake the excavation work leading to the complete hoard being discovered.

The find included over 3,500 from the Anglo-Saxon period, many of which are currently displayed by Birmingham Museums Trust. A lot of the objects are thought to be of military rather than domestic origin and include ornate silver and gold sword decorations and gold strips inscribed with biblical quotations. The items are thought to date back to the 7th century. ■

# Meet Our 2019 Cover Star

## HOLKHAM HALL

**Here in the UK we really are spoilt for choice with our Heritage Houses; stunning design and architecture, gardens landscaped by some of the most highly skilled gardeners in the world and fabulous collections of furniture and artwork.**

With this in mind, the question of who to feature on the cover of Hudsons is always a hotly debated topic here at Visit Heritage - it only happens once a year, and we want to get it right!

With such a tough decision to make we decided to ask our Heritage Houses to give us their own views on why they should feature as our cover property in 2019.

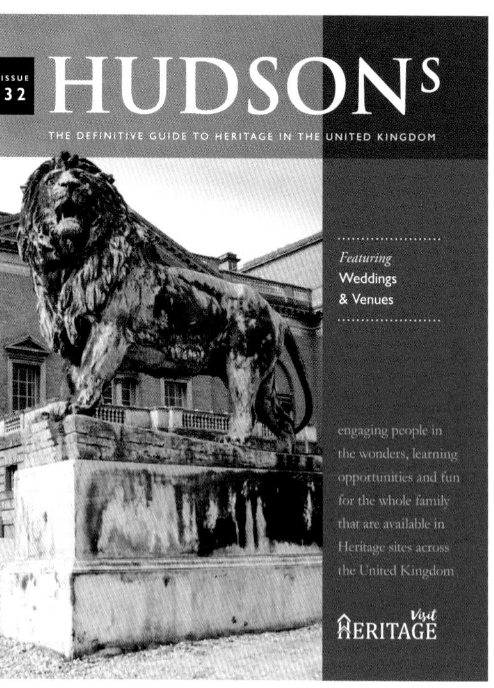


Entrants were asked to tell us in no more than 100 words why they should feature on the cover with up to four images which they believe illustrate what UK heritage stands for. You can see a selection of the entries overleaf.

After careful consideration, we decided that our winner was... Holkham Hall. Here is the statement they submitted as part of their entry:

***Holkham Hall is an 18th century Palladian-style house, based on designs by William Kent and built by the 1st Earl of Leicester. Even during the build in the 1740s curious visitors came to inspect progress and once finished and occupied, Tuesday was specified as 'the day they show the house'. Today, the stunning grandeur of the architecture and the magnificence of the state rooms displaying superb collections of ancient statuary, original furniture, tapestries and paintings have made the hall a popular tourist attraction. Sir Simon Jenkins, in his book 'England's Thousand Best Houses' comments 'It is the perfect English house from the Golden Age of the Grand Tour, surviving intact in its original setting and with the founding family still in custodianship... there is none finer.'***

The lion statue featured on the front cover is one of two bronze statues located at the rear of Holkham, commissioned by the 2nd Earl of Leicester in 1871. They were designed and constructed by Joseph Boehm.
The image was selected because we wanted to recognise that our heritage can be represented by many things in addition to a historic house or garden.

Our photographer, Richard Clark - OMNI42, travelled to Holkham where he received a warm welcome and spent the day shooting pictures of the house and grounds, nature reserve and wider estate. The selection of images *(opposite)* give a taste of the diversity on this vast 25,000 acre estate on the North Norfolk Coast, which we think encapsulates everything UK Heritage has to offer.

# THE HUDSONS 2019 COVER COMPETITION

*There could be only one winner of the Hudsons 2019 cover competition, however we received a number of entries, here's a selection of the runners-up...*

## Boconnoc
*Cornwall*

Boconnoc in Cornwall was painstakingly restored by owners Mr and Mrs Anthony Fortescue over a period of 12 years after it had fallen into disrepair following the second world war. Their devotion to the preservation of this historic estate, and commitment to the local area has meant that they now have a flourishing business and thriving community. Their efforts were recognised in 2012 when they were awarded the Sotheby's Historic House Association Restoration Award. Since then, the family continue to innovate and conserve this historic estate for future generations to appreciate.

## Capesthorne Hall
*Cheshire*

2019 Capesthorne Hall will celebrate its 300 anniversary with ongoing celebrations throughout the year. To coincide with the opening of eco-lodges on site providing a significant new source of income for the upkeep of the Hall and Chapel and significant repair work. Capesthorne Hall, built between 1719 and 1732 and set in 100 acres of picturesque Cheshire parkland, has been touched by nearly 1,000 years of history.

The Hall has a fascinating collection of fine art; marble sculptures; porcelains; tapestries and English, European, Far Eastern and American antique furniture.

A family Chapel, and beautiful lakeside gardens.

## Otley Hall
*Suffolk*

We believe that Otley Hall is a sublime example of a 15th/16th century moated Hall but with a unique historical twist.

The little known story of Bartholomew Gosnold's voyages to America in 1602 and again in 1607 *(before the Pilgrim Fathers)* are fascinating.

He founded Jamestown and named Martha's Vineyard for his infant daughter who later sadly died young.

The journeys made were planned and mapped out around the hearthside of the Great Hall. They peak interest not only from British visitors but from the many American tourists that visit our shores hoping to trace their family ties. What better way to build our special relationship, than to feature a property that is key to our joint heritage.

## Thirlestane Castle
*Scotland*

Family home of the Duke of Lauderdale, Thirlestane Castle is one of the oldest and finest castles in Scotland. Built in 1590, this national treasure and the Maitland family played an important role in history. In the 1980s, Gerald Maitland-Carew was the first private owner of a historic house to give his home to a charitable trust and open it as a visitor attraction so more people could enjoy it. Since then, there's been an uphill battle with dry rot leading to extensive renovations, the most recent in 2014 when the Castle had to close to the public.

## Chartwell
*Kent*

Chartwell is one of the flagship properties within the National Trust, opened by The Trust to the public over fifty years ago it continues to be one of the most iconic and visited properties. Chartwell was the beloved family home of one of Britain's greatest leaders Sir Winston Churchill. In 1946 the house was presented to the National Trust as a permanent memorial to Churchill's achievements. The house remains much as it was when the Churchill's lived here, filled with treasures and personal belongings from every aspect of his life. Preserving his legacy for future generations.

## Markenfield Hall
*Yorkshire*

Markenfield is one of a handful of mediaeval manor houses that could still be recognised by its original owner. It has survived religion and politics, royalty and confiscation, tenancy and near-ruin. Despite all of this it had maintained its sense of tranquillity - a remarkable atmosphere that visitors frequently comment upon. Under the loving care of its owners (past, present and future) the Hall has - and will - stand as a testament to its builders, to determination, loyalty and the abiding love that can develop for a house that is more than just bricks and mortar.

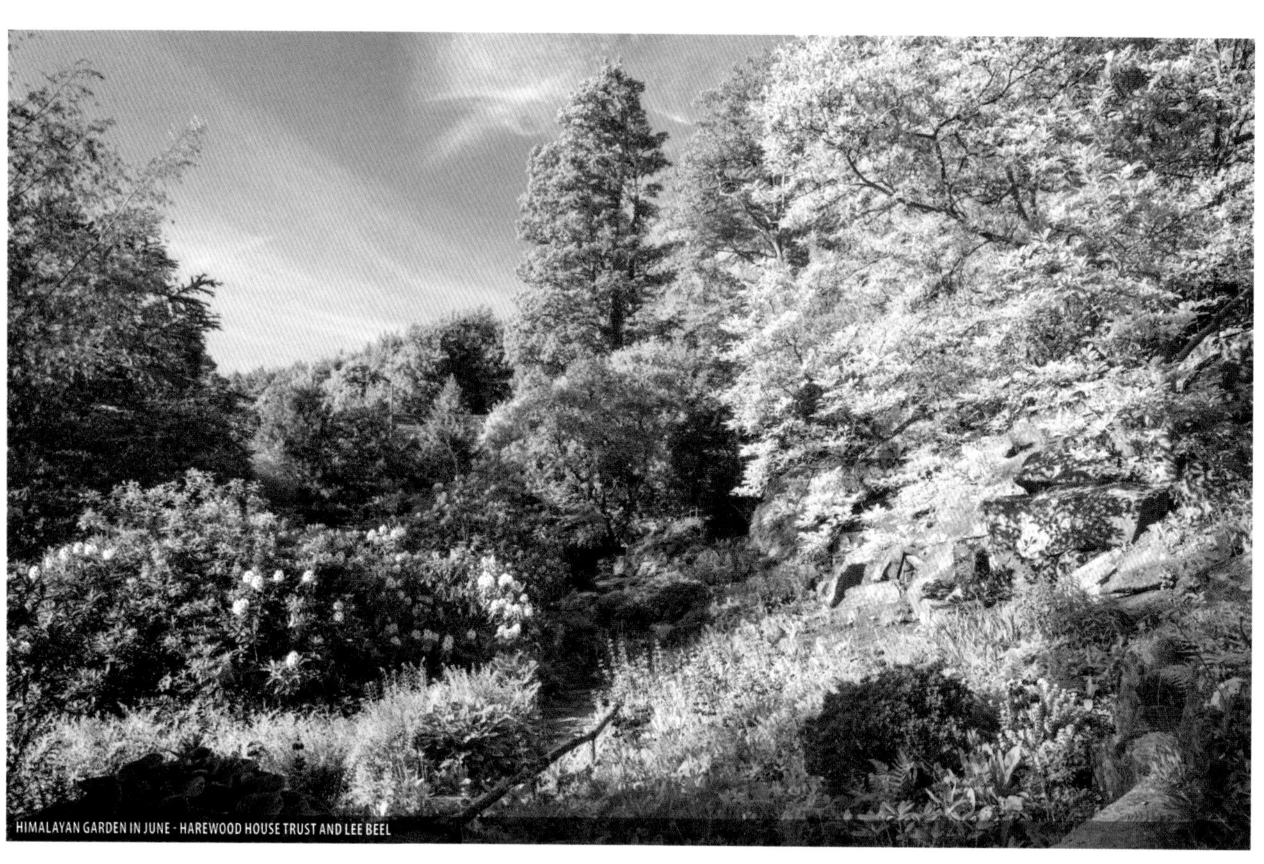
HIMALAYAN GARDEN IN JUNE - HAREWOOD HOUSE TRUST AND LEE BEEL

# HERITAGE GARDENS

*Gardens are an inextricable part of our heritage, as settings for buildings and as treasuries of design, lifestyle and plants...*

*In these pages, we've explored some of our favourites*

HERITAGE GARDENS

# Parham House & Gardens

PARHAM HOUSE VEGETABLE GARDEN - ELIZABETH ZESCHIN

Parham's magnificent gardens are a series of interlocking pictures, woven into each other with a tapestry-like effect, designed to excite for a long season, peaking in summer and late autumn. The beautiful four-acre 18th century Walled Garden includes herbaceous borders of Edwardian opulence, a rose garden artfully filled with mixed planting, a wonderful 1920s Wendy House and a majestic vegetable parterre, creating a haven of peace and tranquillity.

Its opulent mixed borders provide flowers and plants to decorate every room in the House, an old Parham tradition. A magical teak glasshouse is fit to burst with delicious displays of aromatic and tender plants.

The seven acres of Pleasure Grounds include a lake set among native trees and heathers, and even a delightful turf maze.

Parham's own plant nursery offers a wide range of carefully selected and interesting plants for sale.

ALUIM

PARHAM HOUSE GARDEN - ELIZABETH ZESCHIN

# Raveningham Gardens

*by Sir Nicholas Bacon*

Before the 1950s Raveningham had a typically Edwardian style garden - the South front was dominated by a long path, terraced onto the lawn and ending to the East with a thatched Summer House. This was the influence of the Arts and Crafts movement at the turn of the last century. A Victorian walled garden with an 1890's Boulton and Paul Conservatory and the usual melon pits and backhouses provided produce for the House. All these features survive today after a significant programme of renovation.

Like so many other good gardens, they are primarily the inspiration of one person, in this case it was my mother Priscilla, who transformed the garden over 50 years, from the early 1950's.

The walled kitchen garden has been brought back to working order in the last 20 years having been the commercial growing area for 26,000 chrysanthemums until the 1970's and is once again producing vegetables and fruit for the House, the Tea Room and also for sale.

The Garden is predominantly neutral to alkali soil, and the climate is fairly brutal and thus choices of trees and shrubs were made accordingly. In 1987 we suffered from the hurricane which destroyed the wood behind the garden. That gave us the opportunity of replanting with a large variety of trees and shrubs. The eminent plantsman Roy Lancaster was instrumental in creating the design. The new arboretum replaced a 19th century pleasure ground wood known as the Icehouse Plantation, and more than 40 varieties of oak have been planted in this area. Beyond the arboretum is a newly created stumpery with many different types of fern having been introduced amongst the 200 stumps which make up the Victorian 'throwback'. A small collection of polypodiums have been introduced and a gradually increasing collection of magnolias is beginning to make an impact.

RAVENINGHAM MYTHIC BEAST SCULPTURE AND BORDER

My wife, Susan, is a sculptor and her work is placed around the Garden. In 1999 she devised the idea of a Time Garden based on Francis Bacon's ideas for a garden for all seasons ('An Essay on Gardening'). This is adjacent to the greenhouse and features a viewing mound as favoured by Sir Francis.

In the Spring the garden is filled with drifts of snowdrops and spring bulbs. My Mother's legacy has been the plants named after her - a fuchsia, a snowdrop and agapanthus: and of course, the herbaceous borders which spill over the paths and lawns. The important aspect for us is to develop Priscilla's legacy as well as adding various features including the Herb Garden and Bacon's Garden. Her vision for a garden was to ensure that the planting of exciting and rare plants would provide interest throughout the year by dint of their flowers, shape and foliage. That is a tough call sometimes!

The garden covers approximately 10 acres and surrounds the 18th century Raveningham Hall.

RAVENINGHAM HERB GARDEN

RAVENINGHAM STUMPERY

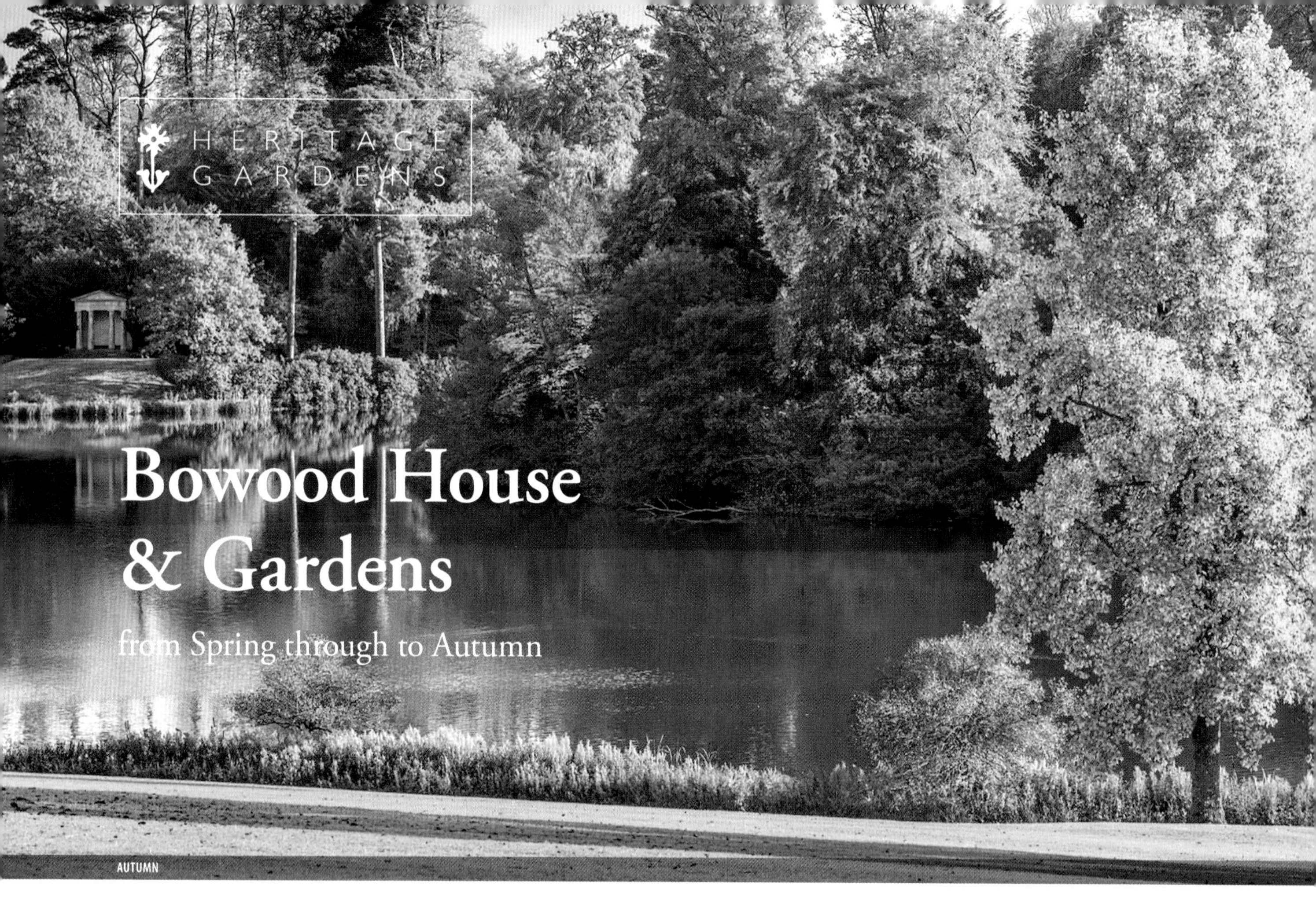


# Bowood House & Gardens

## from Spring through to Autumn

AUTUMN

Within 2,000 acres of Grade I listed Capability Brown parkland, the Bowood visitor has much to discover across the 100 acres of Pleasure Grounds that open from spring through to autumn - and also within the Woodland Garden (late April - early June), elsewhere on the Estate where the Lansdowne family has lived since 1754.

Virtually every period of English garden design, from the Georgian period onwards, is now represented at Bowood, named the Historic Houses Association/Christie's 'Garden of the Year 2014'. Here the scenery is peppered with an incredible range of highlights that include Italianate Terraces, rock landscapes, cascades, grottoes, a Hermit's Cave and a lakeside Doric Temple.

In 1762, the 2nd Earl of Shelburne *(later to become the 1st Marquess of Lansdowne)* commissioned Lancelot 'Capability' Brown to design the parkland at Bowood. A sinuous lake was formed by damming two streams and the western side sculpted for great vistas to sweep down to the water's edge. The levelling of the ground was a massive undertaking and the project also involved the creation of a ha-ha, planting the trees and shrubs, sowing grass seed and forming the Great Plantations. Once Brown's work was completed, Bowood House was set 'naturally' into its landscape with belts of trees encircling the Pleasure Grounds beyond the House's Walled Garden. Today, Bowood is considered as one of the finest examples of Capability Brown's work.

The tulips are one of the first signs of new life as Bowood House and Gardens re-opens to the public each spring (on 30th March in 2019) with some 13,000 planted each year around the House and in the Walled Garden's borders.

From spring, midweek guided tours of the Walled Garden run through into autumn. The four-acre plot is made up of four distinct, one-acre squares comprising formal borders, a picking garden, glass houses and a working kitchen garden packed with fruit and vegetables. These 60-minute tours (to be booked in advance) are angled around the season and what is in bloom at the time. Additionally, tours can be tailored to private groups of 15+ visitors.

Another 'must' is Bowood's 30-acre Woodland Garden - with its own dedicated entrance, two miles from the House and Gardens within the Estate's western corner. Its six-week season from late April is not to be missed! Unique to Wiltshire, its positioning on a narrow strip of green sand - running between Poole and the Wash - explains why this outstanding display of rhododendrons, magnolias and azaleas is so very special. Originally laid out in 1854 by the 3rd Marquess of Lansdowne, some of the earliest known rhododendron hybrids in the UK are featured. A passionate gardener, Charlie Lansdowne (the 9th Marquis) has - since 1972 when he took the helm at Bowood - continued planting in the spirit of the generations preceding him. The Woodland Garden is his particular pride and joy.

WHISTERIA BORDERS

From late April and into May, wisteria drapes the front of Bowood House and the Walled Garden with the roses then a highlight in both spots from mid-June through to mid-July. The Walled Garden's 'Bowood Chintz' double borders (reflecting the Colefax & Fowler fabric of the same name) have been planted to be fully in flower from June through to early October. The design for the House's East Border, in turn, ensures the appearances of 'wow' plants from early June through to September.

Come autumn, Bowood's arboretum shows off Capability Brown's trees having achieved maturity - allowing today's visitor full appreciation of what the legendary designer could only have imagined for Bowood.

BLUEBELLS IN THE WOODLANDS

SPRING

RAVENINGHAM STUMPERY

TULIPS ROUND THE FOUNTAIN

# Kiplin Hall

KIPLIN WALLED GARDEN

In the 18th century, the Crowe family created the framework of the gardens and pleasure grounds at Kiplin Hall. There was a serpentine lake, woodland walks, flower gardens and a walled garden with glass houses. The historic library includes a 1779 volume, A Treatise on the Culture of the Pineapple and the Management of the Hot-House, but we don't know whether this prestigious fruit was actually grown at Kiplin. In Arthur Young's A Six Months Tour through the North of England of 1770, he describes Christopher Crowe the Younger's agricultural experiments and developments, and praises his innovative rotation of crops and use of manure.

Robert Crowe's daughter, Sarah, and her husband, the 4th Earl of Tyrconnel, owned Kiplin from 1818 until her death in 1868. The Earl was proud of the fruit produced on the estate – peaches, apricots, figs, grapes – and delighted in the latest technology. In October 1851, his journal reports that the sight of his new steam threshing machine made Lady T nervous and giddy! Lady Tyrconnel had her own garden beside the orchard, with flower beds, stone urns and a pond surrounded by tufa rocks from Italy. Her conservatory on the outer south-facing wall of the walled garden was well-stocked with hothouse plants by the gardeners. She planted wildflowers in the woodland, including many shades of pink primroses which still grow there today.

Kiplin Hall's once-flourishing gardens almost disappeared during the 20th century. By the 1990s, grass grew throughout the walled garden and only the yew hedges, with their peacock shapes, survived around the old topiary garden. In 2010, the Trustees employed Kiplin's first head gardener in almost 100 years. Working with about 40 wonderful, all-weather volunteers, Chris Baker has transformed many areas of the gardens.

The Rose Garden is full of beautifully scented old varieties, with pelargoniums planted beneath. Inside the topiary hedge is a formal White Garden filled with hostas, hellebores, astilbe, lilies, campanulas and other plants with white flowers or silvery leaves. The Sensory Garden includes a rustling hornbeam hedge, the scent of camomile and thyme, and the gentle sound of wind-blown grasses among a delicate palette of colours and mixture of textures. Near the Hall, there are geometrically shaped Parterres and a Perennial Garden, close to colourful Herbaceous Borders, a Hot Border and a Laburnum Arch. The old Orchard was replanted with heritage apple trees in 2017, funded by an American descendant of George Calvert, who built Kiplin and founded Maryland.

The greatest transformation has been in the Walled Garden, where the paths have been recut, the gardeners' dipping pool and greenhouse restored, and the garden areas brought back to full production. Vegetables, salads, herbs, fruit and soft fruits are all used in our Tea Room and sometimes sold on our Produce Cart. Cutting flowers provide gorgeous colour and scent.

Plans for 2019 include a metal structure to support exotic planting on the old Conservatory site, a Wisteria Arch, and colourful planting around Christopher Crowe's venerable oak. Kiplin's gardens are once again a very special place for visitors to enjoy. ■

KIPLIN - IRISES

KIPLIN ORCHARD 2018

*'In this feature, I share some of my tips and advice to help you enjoy planning your wedding, and hopefully make it a little easier!'*

Siobhan Craven-Robins

# TIPS FOR A PERFECT WEDDING

SIOBHAN CRAVEN-ROBINS AT THE RITZ

BRIGHT COLOURS LOOK DYNAMIC AGAINST A PLAIN BACKGROUND

## *Planning your wedding is an exciting, creative and hugely organisational undertaking!*

If you are planning it without professional help, it is important that you make the process as pleasurable as it can be - and the way to do this is to allow enough time and ensure your budget fits your requirements and wishes. Allowing enough time means that you can pace the planning and enjoy it rather than feeling rushed or trying to cram it into already busy weekends. As a guideline, 8-12 months is an ideal time frame.

In this feature, I share some of my tips and advice to help you enjoy planning your wedding, and hopefully make it a little easier! It is a unique experience and a happy one; it is important that you enjoy the organising of it almost as much as the day itself!

## SET A BUDGET

Your perfect day will not necessarily be dictated by your spending parameters. However, as you start planning your wedding, you may discover expenses that you had not considered such as transport/delivery costs, wedding insurance (always advisable), outmess for your suppliers or a catering service levy.

I suggest that from the outset, you list all the possible expenses and costs. Make a full list of everything you want and under each item, add in the extras. Create a spreadsheet of all your wedding 'items' and their estimated costs and this will help you create a realistic budget.

Here are some of the costs that are easy to overlook when first drafting your budget.

## VENUE & CATERERS

Service charge - usually levied if the venue is also providing the catering and isn't just a dry hire.

## VAT

Menu tasting charge, wine tasting charge. Some venues may offer a free tasting for the two of you, but charge for any extra people.

**Corkage** - if you want to supply your own alcohol.

**Set up and breakdown costs** - if you are opting for a marquee, check if the venue charges hire on the days this will be set up and taken down.

**Outmess cost for your suppliers on the day** - they all need feeding and watering! Don't forget them!

## PHOTOGRAPHY & FILMING

Check your packages include all you want e.g. an album or as many copies of the DVD as you require etc.

Check the time allocation is sufficient. Most start at an 8 hour package - ensure that is long enough to accommodate all that is happening at your wedding that you will want captured on film. Remember this 8 hours starts from when they start photographing or filming (usually from when the bride is getting ready) NOT from the start of the wedding ceremony.

## ATTIRE

For the bride, there are extras such as bridal underwear, hair and make-up (including the trial), and possibly a flat pair of shoes for dancing!

## FLOWERS

It's not just the bouquets, buttonholes and décor. There will usually be a charge for transport and for clearing.

Often, during his speech, the groom will present bouquets to the mothers. If you wish to do this, ensure you order them with your florist and add them to your budget.

## STATIONERY

Your invitations (and possibly Save the Dates) will need to be posted, ensure you include postage in your budget. Keep in mind that Order of Service can be shared between two people, so you don't need one for everyone and menus can double as place cards if you have the guest names printed or handwritten on each one. If you are going for place cards or menus with the names handwritten, ensure you include calligraphy in the budget. Similarly, if you plan to have the invitation envelopes handwritten too.

## CEREMONY

There is usually a fee to the choir if you wish to film your religious ceremony.

Some religious properties and/or officiants operate on a donation basis.

## CAKE

You will usually need a cake stand and knife. Check if this is something you must hire or if it is provided by the venue

## ENTERTAINMENT

Prices quoted are usually for 3 hours (with breaks). Ensure that is enough time to cover however long you want them to play or perform for.

Check if they come with lights - not all bands do - in which case you will need to hire in additional lighting

## TRANSPORT

If your ceremony and reception venues are in two locations, you may want to consider supplying transport for your guests, particularly if parking is limited at either of them. You can choose one meeting point for the initial pick up and the end of evening drop off. Or, to keep costs down, guests can rely on taxis to get to the ceremony and home at the end of the night, but you provide transport between the two locations.

## GIFTS

It is customary to give your wedding party gifts for playing a part in supporting you on your special day. Ensure you add these to the budget.

## DELIVERY & COLLECTION COSTS

Whatever furniture, lighting, props etc you hire for your wedding - there will be a delivery, possibly a setup, and a collection cost.

PERSONALISE YOUR WEDDING WITH TABLE NAMES RELEVANT TO THE TWO OF YOU

# TOP TIPS

You may want to tip some of your vendors, particularly if a service charge isn't levied. Allocate a portion of your budget for this.

Your guest list is instrumental in working out an accurate budget. It is essential that you make this list first as you cannot accurately work out costs without knowing how many people you are catering for.

Be realistic from the outset: If you will be travelling on major roads to get to your ceremony location, a horse and carriage is not your ideal mode of transport! Similarly, if you are set on an outdoor wedding ceremony, choose a reliable month for fine weather but ALWAYS have a wet weather contingency plan.

## GIVE YOURSELF ENOUGH TIME

A wedding takes time to organise, a dress can take up to 9 months to be made, popular venues often must be booked a good year in advance and invitations should ideally go out 6-8 weeks prior to the big day. Ensure that you have a realistic time period to plan your wedding and then you can enjoy all the preparation at a steady pace instead of in one mad rush!

As a general rule-of-thumb, there is an order in which to book your wedding suppliers. This timeframe is based on 12 months of planning:

**12 Months**
*Book a Wedding Planner* - if you are hiring one!
Venue & ceremony venue (Do not confirm until you have contacted and confirmed whoever will officiate your ceremony - this particularly applies to venues where they use a registrar or officiant from an official body to conduct the ceremony).

*Bridal gown* - they can take up to 9 months to make.

Photographer, videographer, hair and make-up artist and entertainment. These suppliers can only take one wedding per date and if you have your heart set on someone, then book them early!

**9-10 Months**
*Caterers* (if it's not in-house catering at your reception venue)

**8 Months**
*Florist, props/furniture and production/lighting*

*Transport*

**6 Months**
*Groom, bridesmaid and ushers attire*
*Cake*
*Stationery* (and calligraphy)

**4 Months**
*Wedding rings*

**3 Months onwards**
*Extras such as gifts for wedding party and favours*
The sooner you book everything, the better. There is no definitive time plan, as it all depends on suppliers' availability and how long you have to plan your wedding. This is a practical order to book them in.

# DECIDE WHO WILL ORGANISE YOUR WEDDING

This can be a crucial, and sometimes, political decision! There will be no end of advice and offers, but ultimately it is your special day and the organisation of it should fall upon the best person to realise this. In the event of a possible permanent family rift, hiring a wedding co-ordinator is a sensible option.

It is important to keep in mind that whoever is paying for the bulk of the wedding should be involved in some of the planning. If the two of you are paying for it, then it is down to you two to choose if you wish to involve anyone else. It is considerate to invite parents along to see the venues, perhaps to the menu tasting, and they should certainly be present at the ceremony rehearsal. Brides often opt to involve their mother in the bridal gown and bridesmaids dress shopping. It is also considerate for you both to be involved in helping your parents choose their outfits.

If one set, or both sets of parents are contributing financially to your wedding, they may well expect more involvement in the planning. If you find this a daunting thought, prepare a to do list early on and allocate jobs. This gives them defined roles and tasks which makes them feel valued and helpful, and for you, you know that these tasks are being dealt with by (hopefully) reliable people!

If your family situation is one where you fear over-bearing intervention and opinion, it is wise to hire a wedding planner. The planner then becomes the liaison point and prevents you from having to field unwanted opinions and help.

FIREWORKS ARE AN EXCITING OPTION TO ADD TO YOUR EVENING RECEPTION

YOUR CAKE CAN BE A STAND-ALONE FEATURE - IT CAN PROVIDE AN EXCITING CENTREPIECE THAT ADDS TO THE RECEPTION DECOR

# ENSURE YOUR WEDDING DAY IS NICELY PACED

Although you would like your day to last as long as possible, this does not work in practice. If the day goes on too long, guests will get bored or tired - and leave early. It's best to end the party before it fizzles out. Your drinks reception should be no longer than 90 minutes and dancing for up to 3 hours is plenty. A successful wedding is one that flows with guests never being bored, hungry or thirsty.

We have all been to events, shows or ceremonies and become bored because they have gone on too long and we feel obliged to stay. A wedding is no different!

A guide is to say that the whole occasion from start to finish should be between 8 -10 hours. The variation in time is largely down to a little longer dancing and allowing time for guests to get between the ceremony and reception venue, if they are taking place at different locations.

**Here is an example:**

| | |
|---|---|
| 3pm | *Ceremony* |
| 3.45pm | *Photos* |
| 4pm | *Depart for reception venue* |
| 4.30pm | *Drink reception* |
| 5.30pm | *Group photos* |
| 5.45pm | *Dinner called* |
| 6.15pm | *Bride & Groom announced into the room* |
| 6.30pm | *Dinner served* |
| 8.30pm | *Speeches & cake cutting* |
| 9pm | *First dance* |
| 12am | *Bride & groom depart* |

It is important that speeches are not too long, there is an appropriate amount of time to speak and still maintain everyone's attention and enjoyment. Some people are more adept at speaking and are not at all daunted at making a wedding speech. If this isn't the case, I always say keep it short, sincere, and don't try to be funny. A genuine, heartfelt speech is as well received as a hysterically funny and witty one. Don't feel the pressure to be what you are not. As a rule, father of the bride speaks for 5 minutes, as well as the groom, and the best man for up to 15 minutes. Brides often choose to speak too, and this is usually after the groom and before the best man. Speeches usually take place at the end of the meal, but people often opt to have them take place before or between courses. Again, if public speaking is not something you relish, I always suggest doing them before the meal, that way you can all relax and enjoy the meal with the fearful anticipation removed! ■

# CHOOSING
## A VENUE FOR YOUR
# WEDDING

*We asked Carol Barnes, who is manager of Global Accounts with HelmsBriscoe the world's largest venue finding business, to tell us what advice she gives to her clients about choosing a heritage site for their wedding venue.*

I have always been passionate about history, and even as a child, my favourite school trip was to Dover Castle. It was on our doorstep and many other kids moaned *'not there again'*, but for me, I was in my element. In my dreams I felt I was born a princess, but I somehow got switched at birth. Faced with my reality, I had to make do with visiting all the places I should have grown up in! I would touch the walls and feel the history seeping into my bones, picture the banquets that would have taken place in the great hall, imagine sleeping in a chamber with no glass windows but snug under the furs on my four-poster bed.

Since joining HelmsBriscoe in 2016, the venue searches I find myself getting most excited about, and with a real sense of personal connection, are when a client asks me to look for a historic venue for their very special event. I always want to find the right venue, but finding the right historic venue… *well,* that's special!

DOVER CASTLE AERIAL PANORAMA 2017 - WIKI

**To ensure you don't just get my view, I asked some of my clients what they look for when choosing a historic venue, as well as why they might select a historic location over a standard venue.**
***Below are a couple of the responses I received:***

*'I think a historic location probably needs the whole package, so I want to know it will be a stunning backdrop for my wedding. I want to know that there's a lot of countryside around it; that my guests will enjoy the views. But that said, it needs to be accessible too, somewhere with places close enough to stay.'*

*'It's a feeling for me. It means something to my relationship. We love the countryside, we like exploring and seeing amazing sights. We'd hate to have something conventional and too much like everyone else's wedding. We'd also rather have a great venue over a nice dress or a fancy wedding car.'*

**In their feedback, brides pointed out potential pitfalls of historic venues, which they admitted were personal to them. Some of the points raised are also reasons why other clients love these kinds of venues! These items include:**

**Limited overnight accommodations:** this can be a challenge if the event, such as a wedding, is taking place throughout the day and into the night. However, if the venue has created relationships with nearby hotels, this can help to streamline the process for clients when making their booking choices.

**Price:** if a historic venue is more expensive, there is usually good reason. The upkeep for the building is partially supported by the prices charged, as well as covering actual cost of the catering and trimmings. Also, should anything go wrong, such as a spillage, it may require specialist cleaning.

**Location and size:** some of the most stunning buildings are either tucked away or not local enough. In addition, historic buildings are what they are - the rooms can't be made larger, so they dictate the size of the groups that can come to an event. Many venues add marquees to overcome this, though marquees may tend to look similar across different historic venues, so adding historical decoration could help reintroduce uniqueness to an event.

**Unique design:** historic venues often have design elements that you don't find in standard hotels, which may need to be taken into account. For example, one of my clients told me that, to limit the risk of injury to guests and the building, their invitations asked ladies not to wear heels due to the cobbles and parquet flooring.

**So why would a bride choose a historic venue over a standard hotel ballroom? Some people see hotels as *'soulless'* whereas historic venues have character, such as The Great Hall at Hampton Court Palace, they tell a story that is out of the ordinary, and because of this, at events like weddings or corporate networking where guests don't always know others, the historic talking points make great conversation starters.**

**Many of the clients I spoke to are eager to book historic venues for these very reasons, and they provided me with the following ideas for attracting their event spend:**

*'Think unique like your venue. If a couple are looking at your venue, they probably want something different. For me, this should be a complete package of difference. I probably would compromise on price if I knew that they were putting on street food or craft beer. In fact because I'm so into heritage/countryside that I'd likely pay more knowing that my money went to the upkeep of the place.'*

*'It's helpful to have good imagery on the website showing the room dressed in various ways with the span of numbers that the room caters for. Frequently, I'm shown the room empty and it is hard for someone like me to imagine it full.'*

**People want to choose history. They want it to be accessible, and many Heritage sites that can be used for weddings and corporate events do make it exactly that. My clients have shown me they love history as much as I do, and have awakened in me the renewed spirit of my inner princess! I want to find them beautiful historic venues.**

*'Historic events tend to work best as they add to a sense of occasion. If they can serve dinner, the room looks great, they can do the numbers and the price is good – we are happy. We don't really have to deal with the pitfalls as we trust the venue to manage any of these challenges. So long as we know of any limitations before the event we can work within them.'*

# CONSIDER AN *Historic Venue* FOR **YOUR** WEDDING

BLENHEIM PALACE WEDDING © CHRISWEBBPHOTOGRAPHY@GMAIL.COM

Rebecca Koziak

*Canadian Wedding & Special Events Coordinator*

*High Culture: Weddings & Special Events Inc.*

## There are numerous historic properties throughout the United Kingdom - many of which have become tourist destinations.

At one time all wedding ceremonies would take place in either a church or registrar's office, now, options are plentiful. Although this also means that hotels and conference venues have been erected for such ceremonies, there is considerably more charm in selecting an historic property. As more venues are licensed to host civil ceremonies and civil partnerships, there has also been an increase in the promotion of hospitality services. There are now venues that accommodate either ceremonies or receptions exclusively, and others that offer both services for wedding related events.

WEDDING GREAT HALL AT MARKENFIELD HALL

Historic sites have been preserved for generations and although many are now privately owned and occupied, they continue to greatly influence tourism. These properties have therefore tapped into another market - the hospitality industry. No longer do couples simply peruse the historical artefacts and read stories about the events that once took place within these estates, they can now host their own event.

With no shortage of historic properties throughout the United Kingdom, prospective clients are certainly spoiled for choice. Those who live in the UK have easily attainable options, but there are also couples who travel to these destinations enhancing their sense of wanderlust.

Before saying 'I Do' to an historic property for the wedding venue, there are a number of things to consider. First and foremost, determining an overall budget is necessary. The next most critical factors are selecting the guest list and the venue. For some, the guest list will influence the rest of their selections, while for others the venue itself will outweigh subsequent decisions. As much as a wedding day is focused on the couple, it is also about bringing guests together for the celebration - whether it be an intimate ceremony for 8 at Markenfield Hall, a modest reception for 25 in the woods in Holkham Park, or a grandiose soirée for 2,000 in a marquee at Blenheim Palace, all events require ample consideration.

Regardless of the size and grandeur - a quaint cottage nestled in the countryside or a magnificent stately home situated amongst thousands of acres of English parkland - all historic properties are representative of quintessential English architecture which spans many eras and styles. However, there is more to think about than just choosing a venue and a date. Venues often have availability restrictions, due to seasonal accessibility, or the fact that they are run as a tourist destination or family home, meaning events can only run on specific days of the week. Many of these venues are also non-religious; however, some, such as The Woburn Estate, promote the accommodation of different faiths and multi-day events. It is also important to note that, although many properties can accommodate wedding ceremonies, these venues must have a specific licence in place and not all spaces within the property will be licensed.

In many churches, ceremonies are only offered for couples with a family or residential connection, or who are regular worshippers - this is true of St. Withburga's Church situated near Holkham Hall, one of a few historic properties with an affiliated church. There can be more flexibility for couples who opt for a ceremony at a non-religious venue, as long as the ceremony does not include anything religious, such as hymns or biblical readings. However, with a private chapel on site, Markenfield Hall, for instance, offers a unique addition to any civil ceremony, where couples are invited to the chapel for a service blessing after the civil ceremony has taken place. All civil ceremonies must be reserved and approved by the local registrar's office prior to confirming the venue - date selection with the registrar's office is done in conjunction with venue selection because details of location must be included; and, while the government states that at least 28 full days' notice must be given at the local office, some venues require these details up to a year in advance. Burghley House, for example, notes that clients may provisionally book the venue; however, a booking is not guaranteed until confirmed with the registrar a maximum of one year prior to the selected date.

HOLKHAM HALL

Now that budget has been determined, date set, and venue options selected, the next step is to consider expectations for the event. Aside from picturesque settings for wedding photography, another benefit to selecting an historic property is that most will host one event per day with exclusive access; thereby providing focused dedication. Before making final decisions, it is important to review all the properties rules and regulations.

None of the above should be seen as insurmountable challenges to booking an historic site for a wedding, but it is essential to consider the following:

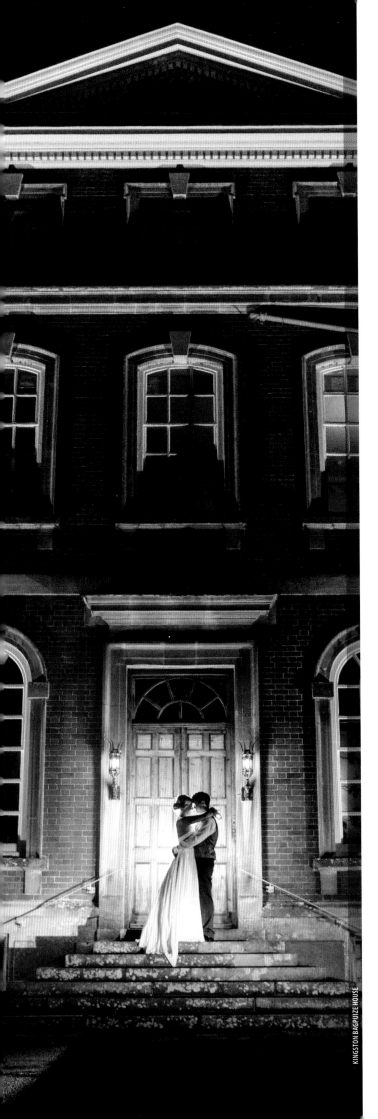

KINGSTON BAGPUIZE HOUSE

**Accessibility plays a key role** - from time restrictions and access guidelines for vendors and guests alike, to parking or taxi routes and ease of entry for guests with limited mobility and close proximity to accommodations. Unlike Holkham Estate and the Woburn Estate, many historic properties will not have on site accommodation, so overnight stays within a reasonable distance at varying prices should be considered.

**Catering requirements** - some venues will provide in-house caterers and many have started to offer package options to include food and beverage components - some of which include décor items or other services making the planning effortless. Those venues that do not offer food and beverage on site will have options for preferred caterers, many of which will offer all food and beverage requirements and will be familiar with the venue and its restrictions.

BURGHLEY HOUSE

**Vendor restrictions** can also affect venue selection: some properties will only allow preferred suppliers to work on site, others will allow a combination of provided and client-chosen suppliers.

**Event insurance** is a necessary item for consideration for both clients and vendors. Burghley House, for instance, requires vendors to hold public liability insurance for five million pounds. It is therefore important to confirm all requirements with the venue prior to selecting additional suppliers. ■

# THE HOLKHAM ESTATE IS AT THE FOREFRONT OF CONSERVATION IN THE UK

Lord Leicester, the 8th Earl of Leicester, speaks to Hudsons about the issues he is passionate about and the challenges he faces.

LORD LEICESTER, THE 8TH EARL OF LEICESTER

## When did Holkham first become environmentally aware and become associated with renewable energy?

Ever since I left the army in 1993 and returned to Holkham. It is something I have always been interested in.

I have always been interested in logistics and how many wasted and unnecessary journeys are made by people who are disorganised. I look at countries such as Switzerland that has very well integrated logistics systems. You land at an airport where you go down one set of escalators into a train and when that drops you at your destination there is a bus waiting for you, and we are not very good at that in this country. Also, just general waste; lights being left on, taps being left on, maybe I inherit that from my parents who brought me up during the Winter of Discontent.

THOMAS COKE'S MAGNIFICENT PALLADIAN FACADE AT HOLKHAM HALL

## Can you outline the various sources of renewable energy used on the estate and any plans for future developments?

- Solar panels for pre-warming water in the Shower Blocks at Pinewoods Caravan Park c. 1999
- 100 Acre Solar Park in c.2003 (20MW)
- 2.5MW Anaerobic Digestion Plant 2013
  *- breaks down animal & food waste to produce bio-gas*
- 1MW of BioMass Boilers x3 in 2014
  *- run on wood rather than oil or gas*
- Ground Source Heat Pumps warming c.25,000sqft of office space

For the future, an aspirational thing would be a district heating scheme, but those are only really good in a new build development. Trying to hook up a whole village of 18th and 19th century houses, could be a bit problematic so at the moment I think no. I think we would always look at ground source heat, because that is a good, cost effective way of heating and indeed refrigeration. If we did another office development, we would probably look at that. You have the luxury, on an estate like this with lots of space that you can put lots of kilometres of water pipes into the surrounding fields and pastures.

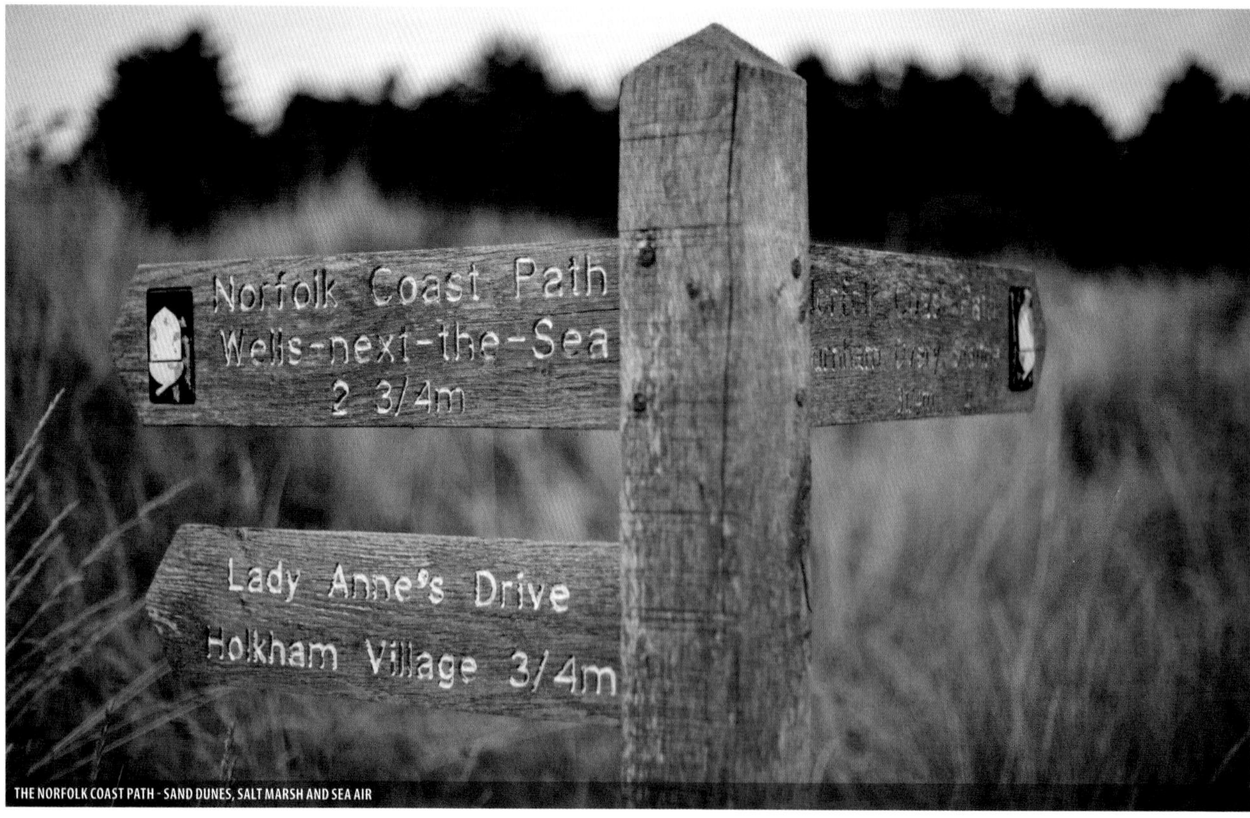

THE NORFOLK COAST PATH - SAND DUNES, SALT MARSH AND SEA AIR

## Have you been involved personally in these installations?

I haven't been involved personally in overseeing the execution of them but my directive ten years ago was that I was responsible for my team looking at all these different types of renewable energy and ways of incorporating them and installing them on the park. Around twenty years ago we installed a few hot water solar panels at the caravan park. That was a very early adoption, but the technology, of course, has moved on so much in the last decade and will continue to move on. The weakness of solar is that it's not producing energy in the night time. Something that we may consider is, as battery technology improves, if one can get a bank of batteries which are charging up during the day and discharging at night. You are then providing much more even energy for the National Grid.

The one thing that I don't do, which you may have noticed is wind. I don't necessarily object to the wind turbines but I know a lot of other people do. I'm looking out of my window now into a nice 18th century parkland and it would be a bit of a shame if there was a great big windmill behind it. They are being put out to sea now which is probably a far better place for them as there is more wind! We have to consider the local community and I think for people that live right next door to them they would not consider it a great thing.

## How do you strike a balance between running a successful farming business while also addressing environmental issues?

I believe good environmental credentials are good for business. If you are trying to be less of a 'consumer' then naturally you are looking after the planet, and saving money, and often being incentivised to do so by central government grants. Here we are in the 21st century and more people, certainly in the Western World, are taking on board the need to be looking after the environment.

We have just opened a new café down on Holkham National Nature Reserve called The Lookout and we have got rid of all single-use plastics. We are looking at completely reducing packaging but what packaging we do have is made from bio-degradable materials. We put things in what looks like a plastic pot but is actually made of starch, and bio-degrades very quickly. We are not selling packets of crisps, we will buy a big packet of crisps and pour them out into the starch pots. We also provide cured ham and boiled eggs this way so the customer doesn't have to throw anything away and litter the nature reserve. Its' been a challenge but I think people really appreciate it. We tell the story about it on a wall in the café and people see it and think that's great that we are doing a lot for the environment. Of course, a lot of our community up here care about it too. We organise beach litter picking days and we get loads of volunteers coming on those, and Holkham beach is almost pristine. Apart from stuff that comes up on the sea, most people take their rubbish away.

## What steps if any do you take to engage the general public regarding conservation of the local area?

- Field to Fork Experience *(exhibition)*, c.40,000 visitors per annum explaining modern farming at Holkham running hand in hand with Conservation
- Full time education officer since 2013 running school visits
- In hand management of Holkham National Nature Reserve, one of the most important NNRs in the British Isles. Interpretive Centre opened August 2018. 800,000 visitors.

In the Lookout Café where we have got rid of single use plastics we are telling people about what we are doing. In the café we are not selling bottled water, which could make us a lot of money. Instead we have got a water fountain, so people can help themselves to free water and we are selling cups for life, or bottles for life, so they might decide to buy one of these, and again that is part of the education of people. Before, every time we wanted a drink we went to a shop and bought a bottle of water,

FIELD TO FORK EXHIBITION

THE PORT AT HOLKHAM

now, more and more people are buying a bottle for life and filling it up. I do it too, if I'm going out I just get an old bottle and fill it with tap water and that's my water for in the car, so I'm not buying all these single-use plastic bottles.

The café also has a lot of interpretative panels, it's done really well because it's a good interesting historical story of the reserve and the countryside around and land management. Of course our website is very detailed and we have a website on the nature reserve and on the conservation on the estate. The Field to Fork museum is a great success too, which is also about educating people.

## What effect has taking back the management of the nature reserve had?

We are able to manage it holistically with other departments on the estate, notably the Farm *(livestock grazing)* and topping of grasses. I think the fact that we are fully responsible for the nature reserve means that many more of our employees have effectively become stakeholders in it, so it's not just a case of saying *'oh that's the nature reserve, they run that'*, everyone is involved. We've got farm men, gamekeepers, education team, marketing, and our café people. Two of the cafés are by the nature reserve so they get lots of questions from visitors.

We have been congratulated by Natural England for the management of the reserve. This is because the smaller an organisation is the quicker it is able to make decisions. We get suggestions made to us by our Conservation Team and we have an Advisory Board. The board often just says *'yes, give it a go'*, as opposed to many larger organisations that might say *'oh well yes, we quite like that but we just need to send it up to another committee to approve it'*, and then they may prevaricate as well, whereas we can get on and do things. I'm sure we make a few mistakes but we make a lot more decisions.

## From a personal point of view, what do you feel is the most valuable contribution you have made that you would like to see continued by your descendants?

Energising the estate, running it with Endeavour. Endeavour is a great word. It's going out there, boldly, and trying things and doing things, and that energises people.

Choosing the right people. I might not be involved for instance in hiring someone to work in one of the cafés, but absolutely I am responsible for hiring all my managers, and as soon as someone joins us I like to meet them.
I want to take a leading role in the country for excellent conservation management, because I think as a private organisation we are able to do that rather more swiftly than the big organisations that prevaricate.

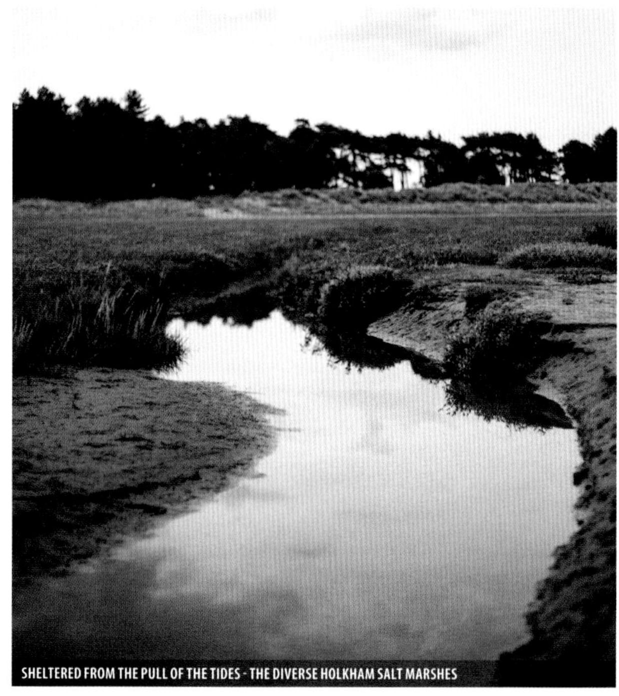
SHELTERED FROM THE PULL OF THE TIDES - THE DIVERSE HOLKHAM SALT MARSHES

## What measures do you take to protect the estate from future flood risks? *[From the sea?]*

We are not allowed to do anything. We put pressure on the Environment Agency to bolster the Sea Walls which they do from time to time. We would like to contribute to these defences if we were, say, given a tax break for doing so. There is talk of the situation changing, for instance some sea walls are going to be strengthened by the Environment Agency over at Burnham Norton, which is part of the estate and Burnham Deepdale which is neighbouring and our contribution will be giving them the soil with which to increase the height of the sea walls rather than them having to buy soil and truck it in from miles away.

## What has been the biggest challenge you have faced during your involvement with conservation at Holkham and how did you overcome it?

I think the biggest challenge is a cultural one. Many *'Conservationists'* are not honest about the need for predator control. Trying to change that, and educate the public about that need is a continuing challenge. People's perception - the general public's perception - of the natural world is a little bit *'touch-feely'*. People do not want to exterminate these species from their land, rather to keep them under control. That is why we undertake predation control and kill things like stoats, rats and corvids that do a lot of damage to young fledgling birds and little mammals. It's about finding a balance and having an honest conversation about that which some conservational organisations find difficult to have.

## There is no doubt that Holkham is at the forefront when it comes to giving back to the local community and environment. What drives you to continue this?

Local support helps you with planning. I always maintain friendly dialogue and communication with the Planning Officers. They have a thankless but important job to do. We have our Corporate Social Responsibility, we give quite a lot of money to local charities, we help fund playgrounds. We still own quite a lot of playing fields and we haven't sold those off for housing like a lot of others, even councils have sold their playing fields off for housing, so we are still providing those facilities for the community. Without your community behind you, life is a great deal harder. ■

THE LOOKOUT CAFÉ IS COMMITTED TO REDUCING WASTE AND WE AIM TO BE FREE OF SINGLE-USE PLASTIC.

# Britain's Country Homes & WW2

1939-45

INVERAILORT HOUSE 28/02/2011 CONTRIBUTED BY MARTIN BRISCOE

## Inverailort Castle

Inverailort Castle, from 18th century a sunless apparition at the head of Loch Ailort, Inverailort has at its core a Georgian box (leadwork dated 1756) with intact interiors looking earlier than its c.1850 remodelling; further alterations 1867 and 1875 by Alexander Ross. Earlier looking range to rear - the original dwelling? *(Ceann a' Chreagain).*

The house's present appearance is the culmination of a century's unsatiated demand for expansion by descendants of Maj. Gen. Sir Alexander Cameron, who bought Inverailort from Clanranald in 1828. More digestible than J Pond Macdonald's somewhat nightmarish baronial addition of c.1891, is Reginald Fairlie's 1912 extension to the right in an Old Scots style.

One curiosity of the interior is the untouched official signage confirming Inverailort's significance as the Special Training Centre established here in 1940, whose operations subsequently combined with other units to form the Commandos, and later as the Royal Marines Commando base. The house was requisitioned in 1940 during World War II for training use by Special Services Units.

The estate and grounds were intensively utilised for training of Special and Commando units. The house was returned to the Cameron-Head family in May 1945. Used by the army at first it was transferred to the Royal Navy for Commando training in August 1942 after which it was called HMS Lochailort.

OVER 60 BROCKET BABIES AT BROCKET HALL

## Brocket Hall

Brocket Hall was handed over to the War Office and it became a Maternity Hospital run by the Red Cross during World War II. Over 8,338 babies were born at Brocket Hall during this period. Lord Melbourne's room became the birthing room and the Prince Regents Suite was the recovery room.

Brocket Babies were born within the safety of the walls of Brocket Hall, and in the peace of the countryside. Over several years of running the Brocket Babies website we have been able to establish contact with over 1,000 of those Brocket Babies spread over 25+ countries around the world. Brocket Hall was used by the City of London Maternity Hospital before and after the destruction of the inpatient section of that hospital in London EC1 by enemy action.

A website was created to allow those who were born, gave birth, or who worked at Brocket Hall to share and read about events of those times, to make contact with each other, and to share stories passed on to them by their families. Whilst many babies have always known they were born at Brocket Hall there is a small but increasing number of those who were born in Brocket Hall and subsequently adopted and only found they are one of the World Famous Brocket Babies when they obtained their original birth certificates.

LEMSFORD - THE VICARAGE

## Lemsford House

Lemsford House, St. John the Evangelist's first vicarage.

Lemsford House, on Brocket Road, was built in 1859 as the vicarage for the church of St. John the Evangelist, Lemsford. It was designed, as was the church, by the architect David Brandon (1813-1897). The Revd. F E Coggin, vicar from 1892-1905, found the house too small and enlarged it. However the Revd. A E Ward, vicar from 1905-1920, found it too large and expensive to run so a second vicarage, now known as *'Church End'* was built further down Brocket Road.

The Brocket Estate, who owned the property, rented out Lemsford House to wealthy tenants, the rental income being used to augment the vicar's stipend.

When Brocket Hall became a Maternity Hospital during World War II some unmarried mothers whose babies were to be put for adoption stayed in Lemsford House until the adoption went through. Between October 17th 1940 and February 15th 1948 the baptism of 133 babies born to single mothers giving their address as Lemsford House are recorded in the parish baptism register. The church has no other information about the inhabitants of Lemsford House.

Lemsford House closed when Brocket Hall ceased to be a Maternity Hospital in 1949 and the house was divided into five self-contained flats. It was sold in 1976 for about £25,000. It has since become a single residence.

WADDESDON NEARING COMPLETION IN 1883, BEFORE THE ADDITION OF THE MORNING ROOM WING

## Waddesdon Manor

Baron Ferdinand (1839-1898), who built Waddesdon, was a typical pan-European Rothschild. Ferdinand left his estate to his youngest unmarried sister, Alice (1847-1922). She was only 12 when their mother died and was raised by their eldest sister, Mathilde, in Frankfurt. Alice moved to England and often acted as Ferdinand's hostess. She lived in a house adjacent to his in London and bought a country estate bordering Waddesdon.

She regarded herself as the protector of Ferdinand's inheritance and is famous for establishing 'Miss Alice's Rules' - guidelines for the care and preservation of the collections which even today form the foundation for those of the National Trust.

She enjoyed collecting, and much of the arms and armour in the collection was bought by her, but her great passion was gardening. The Waddesdon Archives preserve an extraordinary correspondence with her head gardener on all sorts of minute details.

Alice left Waddesdon and her estate at Eythrope to her great-nephew James de Rothschild (1878-1957) of Paris. He was Mathilde's grandson and his mother was Alice's favourite niece. James married an Englishwoman, Dorothy Pinto, and became a naturalised British citizen.

During the Second World War, James and Dorothy de Rothschild moved into the Bachelor's Wing, leaving the main house for children evacuated from London. There were 100 children all under five, the first and last time there were children at the Manor. All but three rooms in the main house were emptied for their use, with James and Dorothy continuing to live in the Bachelors' wing once the war was over.

James's ultimate legacy was to preserve Waddesdon for future generations. Like his predecessors, he died childless. After the war, James was increasingly unwell and he began to consider Waddesdon's fate after his death. Having no descendants, and with the end of the era of grand country house entertaining, he decided to leave the Manor, its collections of national importance and 165 acres of garden and park to the National Trust.

ALDENHAM PARK

## Aldenham Park

Aldenham Park was the home of the Acton family, who were prominent Catholics, and the peaceful atmosphere of the park was interrupted at the beginning of the war by the arrival of sisters and pupils of the Convent of the Religious of the Assumption.

Based in Kensington Square, the convent ran the first Montessori school in Britain. It had catered for girls up to the age of 13, but in the war older girls were educated until they were ready to take their higher certificates.

In 1939 the building in Kensington Square was needed by the ARP (Air Raid Precautions) so the sisters had to find a new home for the school and the teaching nuns.

Various offers of help came, including from Lord Acton, who had served at the altar at the convent's church at Kensington, while two of his sisters had briefly attended the school as teenagers.

Lord Acton invited the school to Aldenham partly in an effort to ensure there would be an income for the estate while he was with his regiment, but also to see that Aldenham would not be requisitioned by the military.

The vanguard from the school, of 10 choir sisters and five lay sisters, arrived on September 1, 1939, with the children soon to follow. Their arrival was a shock to Ronald Knox, a brilliant Catholic scholar and theologian of his time, who had been invited to stay in the peace and quiet of Aldenham Park by Daphne Acton - he had helped her in her conversion to Catholicism - so that he could work on his big project to translate the Old and New Testaments from the original Latin Vulgate. He found himself reluctantly thrust into the role of the school's chaplain.

Within days of arriving at Aldenham the nuns became convinced the house was haunted. There were several ghostly happenings which frightened them and the girls alike.'

Despite the valuable addition of fruit and vegetables from the garden, the food was described as revolting.

'After the food, what the girls remembered most was the cold. The main problem with the house was that it had not been designed for so many inhabitants.

Conditions in their new home were tough, with a leaking roof and no heating. The school uniform was a navy blue dress with a white removable collar. Washing was done on site and according to one pupil they were only allowed to change their underwear once a week and washing was equally infrequent, with the upshot that two girls sent their washing home and it came back in biscuit tins, sometimes with a cake.

The school's complement was 54 teenage girls, 15 nuns, and a nursing mother, for six years the school thrived at Aldenham Park, and on the whole the girls loved life there.

The school moved out after the end of the war in Europe. It did not go back to Kensington Square, as the buildings had been designated to be a new teacher training college, but went instead to another house, Exton Hall in Rutland.

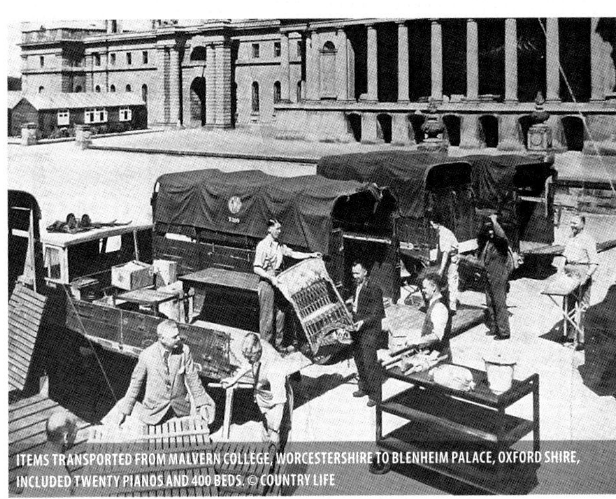
ITEMS TRANSPORTED FROM MALVERN COLLEGE, WORCESTERSHIRE TO BLENHEIM PALACE, OXFORDSHIRE, INCLUDED TWENTY PIANOS AND 400 BEDS. © COUNTRY LIFE

## Blenheim Palace

During the Second World War more than 400 boys were evacuated to the palace from Malvern College.

*'We arrived at Malvern College School House, to find the doors wide open, and the house being inspected by bowler-hatted officials pf the Ministry of Works, who were already giving instructions for work to be carried out. As yet war had not been declared, though Poland had been invaded, and no requisition order had been served.'*
H.C.A Gaunt, headmaster of Malvern College
1st September 1939.

For one academic year the college used the Blenheim Palace State Rooms as dormitories and classrooms - and the boys even had lessons in the bathrooms, according to a spokesperson for the palace.

Meanwhile, Blenheim Park was used by the Home Guard, and the lake for preparation for the D-Day landings. The country house was later used by MI5.

HOWICK HALL GARDENS

## Howick Hall

Howick was the home of the Grey family from 1319 until the death of the 5th Earl Grey in 1963. The Estate then passed to his eldest daughter, Lady Mary Howick, and through her to her son the present Lord Howick of Glendale, grandson of the 5th Earl Grey. Charles, the 2nd Earl Grey, is the most distinguished family member.

As leader of the Whig party he was Prime Minister from 1830 to 1834. During which time the Great Reform Bill of 1832 was passed. This started the process of parliamentary reform which eventually led to our modern democracy. He married Mary Elizabeth Ponsonby in 1794. Their marriage was a happy and fruitful one, having 15 children.

Howick is also the home of Earl Grey tea! The tea was specially blended by a Chinese mandarin for Charles, 2nd Earl Grey. It was created to suit the water from the well at Howick. Using bergamot in particular to offset the taste of the lime in it. Lady Grey used it in London when entertaining as a political hostess. As a result it proved so popular that she was asked if it could be sold to others. Consequently, this is how Twinings came to market it and it is now sold worldwide. Sadly the Greys, being unbusinesslike, failed to register the trademark. As a result they have never received a penny in royalties.

Howick Hall was used as a convalescent hospital for many ranks from 1941-1945. Over 11 different nationalities were treated there including Finnish, Greek, Polish, Czech, Dutch and Commonwealth soldiers, sailors and airmen.

UPTON HOUSE

## Upton House in Warwickshire

Driven by the need to protect bank staff and key assets from the worst of the London air raids, the Bearsteds moved merchant bank M. Samuel & Co to the safety of the Warwickshire countryside when war was declared. The family moved out and 22 bank staff took over the elegant house.

On 31st August, Peter Samuel, a director of his family's London based bank, M Samuel & co. sent a telegram to the staff at the family's country house near Banbury in Warwickshire: *War Imminent STOP CONFIDENTIAL prepare Upton House STOP No Time to Lose Peter Samuel.*

The reply came back : *'Staff Ready'.*

Bank staff slept in shared dormitories and ate meals of rook pie in the Long Gallery, while secretaries typed surrounded by treasured works of art.

The wartime atmosphere continued outside with sand bags piled up and an Anderson shelter in the garden, while heritage vegetables were being grown in an allotment. During the war land girls tended the gardens and lived in the stables while armed servicemen guarded prisoners of war working in the grounds.

By 1941, when an airfield was built near to Upton House, Lord Bearsted no longer felt that his painting collection was safe. As part of the recreation, visitors will discover how 40 of the most precious art works were sent to a special storage facility in a Welsh slate mine with the National Gallery collection.

VOICES FROM THE PAST INSIDE THE GUARD HOUSE AT COLESHILL © NATIONAL TRUST IMAGES, JOHN MILLER

## Coleshill House

What if the Germans had invaded Britain 80 years ago... Who would have co-ordinated the fight back for freedom? Well, wartime Prime Minister, Winston Churchill imagined just this and he set in motion a hush-hush network of spies and saboteurs, weapons and espionage, where brave men lived a secret life to keep their country safe. And it took place here at Coleshill.

In the Second World War, the House had a hidden history. Unknown to villagers, it was requisitioned to become the top secret training headquarters for the British Resistance or Auxiliary Unit.

Who were the Auxiliers?

When war broke out in 1939, most fit and able men were called up for active duty. But for some, the war was not to be so straightforward. They were destined to live a completely secret life, as members of the British Resistance or the Auxiliers.

In peacetime they might have been farmers, mechanics, gamekeepers, butchers, labourers or miners. They were specially selected, very fit and very brave.

Unbelievably, over 3,000 men were trained as Auxiliers at Coleshill. And their model of training - using small cells of six people working independently and in complete isolation from other groups - has been described as the precursor of modern-day warfare.

Was there an Auxilier in your family?

Check out the British Resistance Archive run by the Coleshill Auxiliary Research Team (CART), a not for profit organisation whose volunteers carry out and publish their research on the British Resistance.

ARISAIG HOUSE © JOHNNY_9956 FLICKR

## Arisaig House

The paramilitary schools were based at ten shooting lodges in the Arisaig and Morar areas of Invernesshire, with the Special Operations Executive staff headquarters in Scotland based at Arisaig House. The courses lasted at first for three weeks but were later increased to five weeks. They included physical training, silent killing, weapons handling, demolition, map reading, compass work, field craft, elementary Morse, and raid tactics.

The agents being trained came from a range of nationalities, and each group was housed in separate schools, as security protocol dictated that they should not mix. This policy was applied right up to the final briefing.

The training began with a hard slog over the unwelcoming terrain of Invernesshire. Both men and women had to complete the course, and they would be equally tired, aching and covered in cuts and bruises having crawled on their bellies and trekked up mountains.

Their weapons training and unarmed combat equipped agents for close combat only. William Fairbairn and Eric Anthony Sykes - two ex-Shanghai municipal police officers - taught unarmed combat, or silent killing. The pair gave their name to the FS fighting knife - a small knife used mainly by the Commandos - and their Fairbairn Fighting System was subsequently taught to members of the FBI and CIA.

Weapons training introduced the students to the Colt .45 and .38, and to the Sten gun, which was considered unreliable by some. The students were taught to fire by 'pointing' the gun, tucking their firing arm into their hip, rather than by the more orthodox method of taking aim, and they always fired two shots to be certain of their target. This system was known as the Double Tap system and it was specific to SOE agents. One of the props used to help the students with target practice was a life-sized figure on a winch, set to come at the agents at speed.

Demolition and explosives training was essential, as sabotage was high on SOE's remit. Using dummy explosives, rail sabotage was carried out with the cooperation of the West Highland Line, who also supplied the school with a train. Students were taught how to lay dummy charges and fog signals, then walk away and hide.

ASTON ABBOTS

## Aston Abbots Abbey

In the Second World War from 1940 to 1945 Dr Edvard Beneš, the exiled President of Czechoslovakia, stayed at The Abbey in Aston Abbotts. His advisers and secretaries (called his Chancellery) stayed in nearby Wingrave, and his military intelligence staff stayed at nearby Addington. President Beneš gave a bus shelter to the villages of Aston Abbotts and Wingrave in 1944. It is on the A418 road between the two villages.

BIGNOR MANOR HOUSE, WEST SUSSEX, ENGLAND.

## Bignor Manor

During the darkest days of World War II when France was under Nazi occupation, it was inconceivable to most people that there might be an air service across the Channel. But there was, run by the secret intelligence services in Britain and the French resistance, and the start of the dangerous journey was often this house, Bignor Manor in West Sussex.

Nestled at the foot of the South Downs, it is more a pleasant-looking farmhouse than a manor house. It was rented in the 1940s by Anthony Bertram and his wife Barbara, who lived there with their two young sons and a menagerie of animals. An author and art critic, Tony Bertram had served in the 1914-18 war, and though he was too old for the front line this time, he was recruited into MI6 on account of his fluent command of French. Given the title of Major, he became the liaison officer for the French agents arriving and departing via the moonlight flights run by RAF Tangmere.

Barbara Bertram played a vital role, too. Resourceful and calm, she welcomed these men (and occasionally women) into her home. Often their introduction to her was over a breakfast she had cooked, using eggs from the chickens, at 4am. As the war went on, she found she was effectively running a hostel for spies and saboteurs, with little outside assistance and in conditions of utmost secrecy. No one in the village of Bignor was allowed to know what was happening - and neither, amazingly, did her children. When numbers grew, and the men became impossible to hide, it was put about that she was looking after injured French servicemen.

This led to some amusing episodes of light relief in what was always a tense situation as they passed the hours and days until full moon and the risky ascent in a Lysander plane to their renew fight. The French and others involved in the operations would play darts in a local pub, the White Horse at Sutton. During one match against the regulars, one of the French with an arm in a sling (purely for effect) astonished his adversary by a brilliant performance despite using his 'wrong' arm.

More than two hundred French personnel passed through Bignor Manor during the course of three years. Throughout this time, the Bertrams offered practical assistance and the comfort of being looked after in the atmosphere of a spirited house party. The clandestine flights took place during the nights of full moon; between the moons, Major Bertram trained them in finding landing fields in France and organising operations on the ground there.

When the men wanted calm, they helped in the garden and relied on Barbara's sympathetic ear and understanding. When they wanted company, she would drop everything to make up a four at bridge, or play darts, or go for a walk. Her discretion and gaiety made her immensely popular. 'The ones who were leaving were mostly there for two or three days; but they were nervous, short-tempered, impatient, and let's face it, scared stiff. Difficult guests, but so good was she with them that I have often heard them say, 'Our best memory of England was the time we had to spend in Mrs Bertram's house,' recalled one high-ranking member of the Resistance.

One tiny incident illustrates why Barbara Bertram was so loved. When a group arrived off the night flight from France, their boots were often very muddy from the field where the plane had taken off. Barbara collected this mud and grew mustard and cress on it, to be able to offer the men salad grown on French soil.

VIEW OF AUDLEY END

## Audley End

Audley End was the most ambitious house of its period in England. In form and scale it was a royal palace in all but name, intended to accommodate royal visitors on their progresses around the country (James I visited twice in 1614). It had symmetrically arranged state apartments for the king and queen occupying the first floor of the inner court and linked by a long gallery.

Thomas Howard, 1st Earl of Suffolk, who built the present Audley End had rebuilt the inner court first, working around the footprint of the medieval cloister but making the plan regular and each of the elevations entirely symmetrical. His uncle, Henry Howard, 1st Earl of Northampton, and a Flemish mason, Bernard Janssen, are credited as collaborators with Howard himself in the restrained design.

In a second phase Howard added an outer court of lodgings in an altogether more florid style, drawing on French and Flemish Mannerist sources. This is now best represented in the surviving entrance porches on the west front and was probably to the design of the London surveyor John Thorpe.

All this was surrounded by a formal landscape, approached through a forecourt intended to be flanked by service blocks. These were not completed as intended: only one was built, to the north, probably as lower-status accommodation for the court on a progress, and it was rapidly converted to a stable block.

In World War Two it became part of the General Headquarters Line, the main defence line of the UK. There are many features surviving in the grounds including pillboxes, bridge barriers, mining chambers to blow up bridges, and a loopholed wall made by the Home Guard. Later in the war the house was used as a training centre by the Polish section of the Special Operations Executive.

THE FIRE AT MELFORD HALL

## Melford Hall

Sir Richard Hyde Parker, 12th Baronet, tells us about his time at Melford Hall and his memories of the Second World War.

*'I was born at Melford Hall, followed by my sister two years later, on the day war was declared. The house was then requisitioned and occupied by the army and we moved to a house on the green opposite.'*

*'My strongest early memories go back to 1942, when I was nearly five, watching the house burning in the distance. That afternoon I walked hand-in-hand with my father to the scene, which was comparable, at my age, to a burnt-out box on a bonfire.*

*'The fire gutted the North Wing and destroyed adjoining roofs. Water from the firemen's hoses also caused extensive damage to important interiors and subsequently dry-rot.*

*'Professor Sir Albert Richardson was the only architect prepared to restore the wing without demolishing the surviving structure, and his successful use of an internal concrete frame remains visible today.'*

*'I continued to grow up in a world where the trappings of war, divorced from serious action, were a delight to a small boy living at the hub of military activity.*

*'Until in June 1944 the 1st Battalion of the Royal Hampshire Regiment was inspected by King George VI at Melford Hall before going into action as spearhead troops in the assault on Gold Beach during the D-Day landings.*

*'My final memories of the war are as a child on V.E. Day, standing by the biggest bonfire I had ever seen, on Long Melford Green. There were no fireworks during the war so the army fired endless flares that criss-crossed the sky like searchlights but in red, green and yellow.*

*'There were troops from the camps at Melford Hall and Kentwell Hall, Americans from the aerodromes at Alpheton and Acton and us from Melford with the many evacuees who came from London to live with us.'* ■

# UK Hotel Guides 1935-2018

*Malcolm Orr-Ewing*

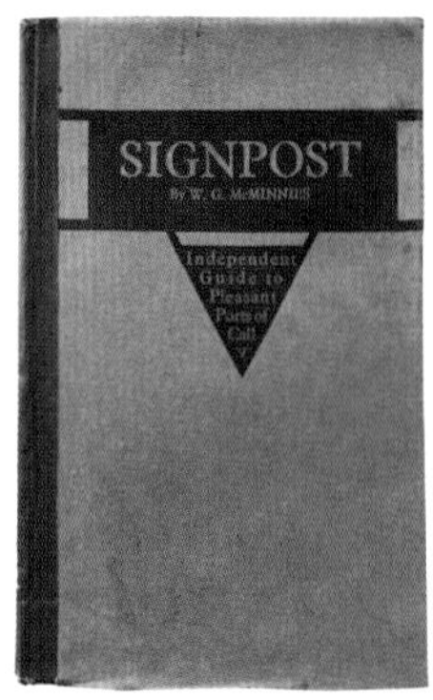


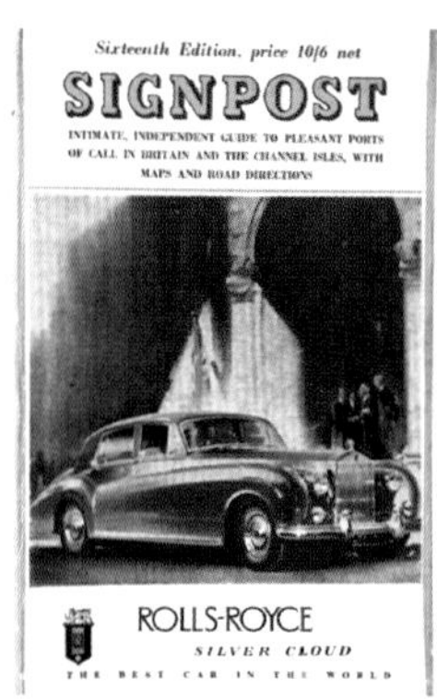

The first UK Hotel Guides by chance were both published in 1935. One was edited by motoring journalist Ashley Courtenay and the second by my maternal grandfather WG ('Mac') McMinnies. Ashley's Guide was sub-titled *'Lets Halt Awhile'* and Signpost was sub-titled *'Pleasant Ports of Call'*. My grandfather was 51 when he started Signpost in 1935. The Sunday Times in 1998 wrote... *'One of the oldest guides, Signpost, was founded by eccentric ex-World War I Flying Instructor, WG McMinnies.'* What they failed to state was that Granpa was only a flying instructor because he had a wealth of knowledge of **car** engines and had never actually flown an aeroplane before! They might have added that he was a Rally Driver, having partnered Amy Johnson in the 1938 RAC Rally, was the first man up Snowdon (the mountain) on a motorbike and raced for the Morgan Car Company at Le Mans three times!

So what else was going on in 1935? There was a drought lasting 22 days and for the fourth consecutive year, temperatures exceeded 90°F. The bank rate stood at 2% and the Archbishops' Commission on the Ministry for Women declared that there was no place for women in the priesthood! 1935 saw the opening of Imperial Airways *(forerunner to BA)* regular service to Australia, taking 12 days. Fred Perry retained his Wimbledon tennis title and Sir Malcolm Campbell broke the world land speed record at 301 miles per hour. The Driving Test was introduced two years later in 1937.

The guide prospered and by 1938 there were over 350 entries - independently owned hotels - and there was an American edition. One hotel, The Petwood in Woodhall Spa, featured in the 1937 and 1938 editions before it became the home of Guy Gibson's 617 Dambusters Squadron in World War II, and is still featured in the 2018 edition. Granpa also founded an Ireland edition, but after the war, this got subsumed into the main book.

WILLIAM GORDON MCMINNIES AFC BA

My grandfather used to visit every single hotel personally each year, take all the photographs and write all the reviews. Surprisingly for an hotel inspector, he was more or less a teetotaler, judging an hotel on whether they served a *'decent Dubonnet'*. He also had half his stomach removed in the 1960s so had a very small appetite!

Petwood Hotel, Woodhall Spa, Lincs.

PETWOOD HOTEL

The Signpost entry for Petwood Hotel from 1938 alongside the 2018 version.

*'One of the oldest guides, Signpost, was founded by eccentric ex-World War 1 Flying Instructor, WG McMinnies.'*

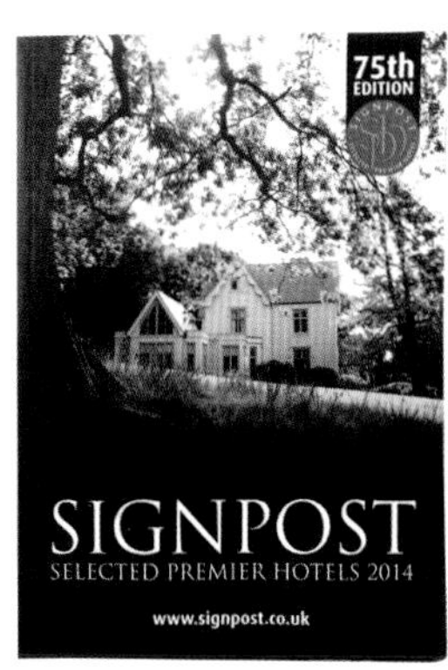


The guide suspended publication during the war years due to paper shortages. After the war both the AA and RAC published guides to inspected hotels, and the AA Hotel Guide continued in printed format until 2012. In the 1990s, Alistair Sawday, a former travel agent, published popular accommodation guides to France and Italy, then Britain, under the title Special Places to Stay. The Red Michelin Guide to Great Britain and Ireland, also started in the 1930s, just listed hotels, with grades. Recently the guide has added 50-word short menu and hotel descriptions and its town plans are still unrivalled. The Michelin guide is popular with hoteliers, as, being financed by the vast Tyre Company, it does not need to ask participants for a contribution towards the cost of entries. Also inspectors are genuinely 'anonymous' and hotels only usually know their rating when the annual guide is published every January.

In the 1980s Derek Johansen started his guides, devoting a full A4 glossy colour page to selected hotels. Johansens Guide was bought by the Daily Mail Group in 2000 and sold to Conde Nast in 2010 who continue to publish it under the print title of European Hotels & Spas (with the lion's share covering the British Isles). Les Routiers published a guide in the 2000s and there was a Rooms for Romance publication and a rival to Johansens Guides in The Best Loved Hotel Guide. This continues as a website only. Other still printed guides include Charming Small Hotels and the English Tourist Board's B&Bs and Hotels. Signpost is the only printed guide which has been published every year since 1935 (except for during the war years). Mr McMinnies sold the title to a friend of his in Birmingham, Christopher Carney-Smith, a solicitor, in 1972. Chris sold the title to the undersigned, Mr McMinnies' maternal grandson, in 1996 and then, upon my retirement, the title was bought by NVG/ Hudsons Media in 2014 and then by Visit Heritage Ltd of Nottingham in 2017. The Signpost member hotels now have the benefit of a wider exposure, thanks to all hotels also being promoted in the sister publication Hudsons Heritage Guide. ■

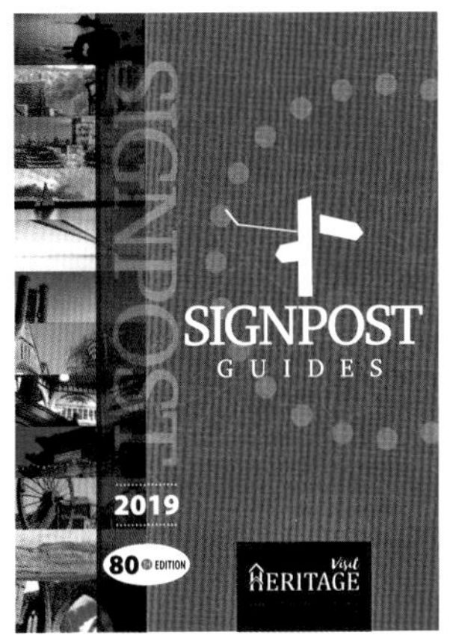

The 80th edition continues the Signpost tradition of presenting a select collection of premier places to stay.

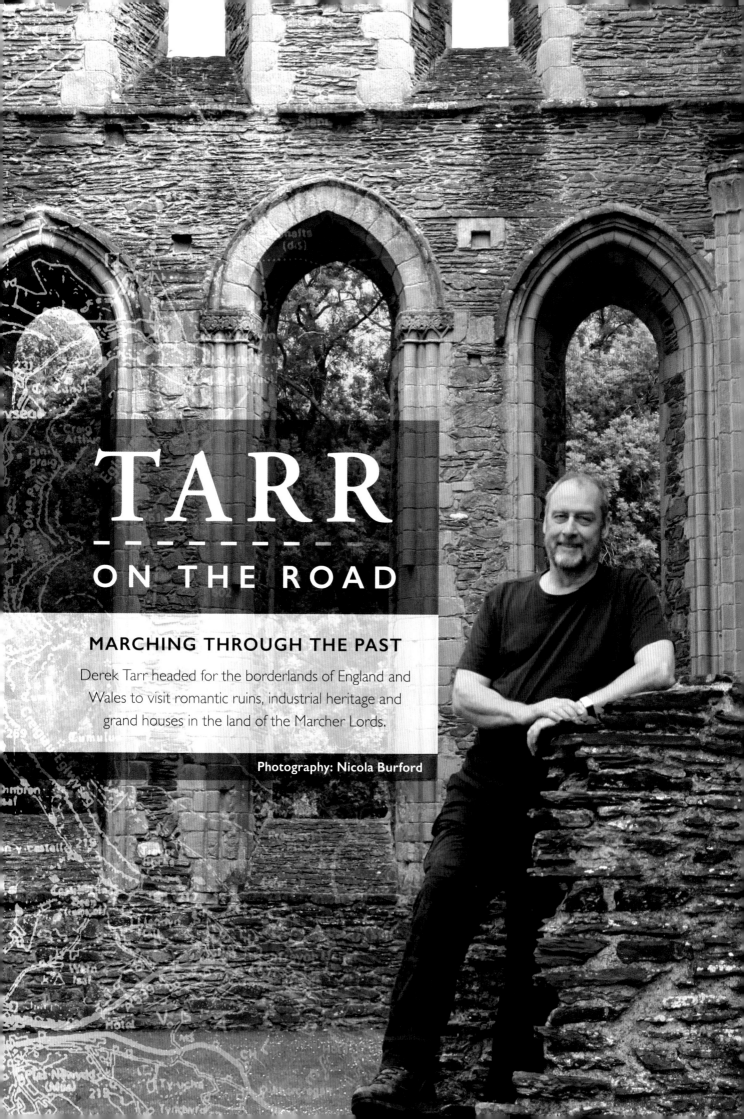

# TARR ON THE ROAD

## MARCHING THROUGH THE PAST

Derek Tarr headed for the borderlands of England and Wales to visit romantic ruins, industrial heritage and grand houses in the land of the Marcher Lords.

Photography: Nicola Burford

*This border region of rolling hills and limestone uplands is part of the area known as the Welsh Marches and a gateway to North Wales. The character of the people and the scenery have been forged by historical conflict, industry and agriculture. My ramble to visit key sites has used part of the Offa's Dyke National Trail as well as local tracks and towpaths with the course of the sparkling River Dee never far away.*

# Walk 1

## ERDDIG TO RUABON

3.7 MILES APPROX.

Nestled beyond the southern outskirts of Wrexham lies the distinguished property of Erddig. It was built in 1684 for the generous and colourful Joshua Edisbury, the High Sheriff of Denbighshire. Such was the excessive overspending on the property that he was declared bankrupt in 1709 and the house was subsequently sold to the barrister John Meller in 1714. Over the next few years he extended and improved the house by adding two wings. Meller died childless and the estate passed to his sister's youngest son Simon Yorke. Erddig remained in the hands of the Yorke family for the next 240 years.

Unlike other historic properties there is an emphasis towards the people that worked on the estate. Upon arrival I was directed to a labyrinth of outbuildings with many exhibits including a workshop, a smithy, a display of carriages and even a stable of donkeys. Unusually, the house is accessed via the staff quarters. In The Servants' Hall there are a number of portraits of estate workers, many painted in the 1790s by the local artist John Walters following a commission by the first Philip Yorke.

The house has a fine array of furniture with the star attraction being the magnificent lit à la duchesse state bed, renovated by the Victoria & Albert Museum in the 1970s. The nineteenth century portable shower in The Bathroom was one of the more quirky items that caught my eye.

For much of the life of the estate, coal mining had been the main form of income. This ended in 1947 with the nationalisation of the industry. Due to the lack of funds for maintenance, along with subsidence caused by the shafts from the nearby Bersham colliery, the house fell into disrepair. In 1973 the National Trust took ownership and started a programme of renovation to save this treasure.

With the heat of the mid-afternoon sun warming me I left Erddig and headed south alongside the Wat's Dyke. This border, constructed in the Dark Ages between Mercia and the Welsh tribes, runs from Maesbury in Shropshire to Basingwerk Abbey on the River Dee estuary.

Just my luck! For weeks Britain had been basking in unrelenting sunshine but this afternoon the ominous sound of thunder rumbled in the near distance. A few miles to my right, the Welsh mountains were covered in threatening clouds. By the time I arrived at Ruabon the rain was torrential and I was drenched to the skin. Fortunately, the staff at the Wynnstay Arms, my stop for the night, were extremely accommodating and I was able to dry my clothes in the boiler room.

Ruabon is a small, pleasant village that once was a hub of heavy industry. It is the birthplace of Mark Hughes, the football manager and former Manchester United, Barcelona and Wales player.

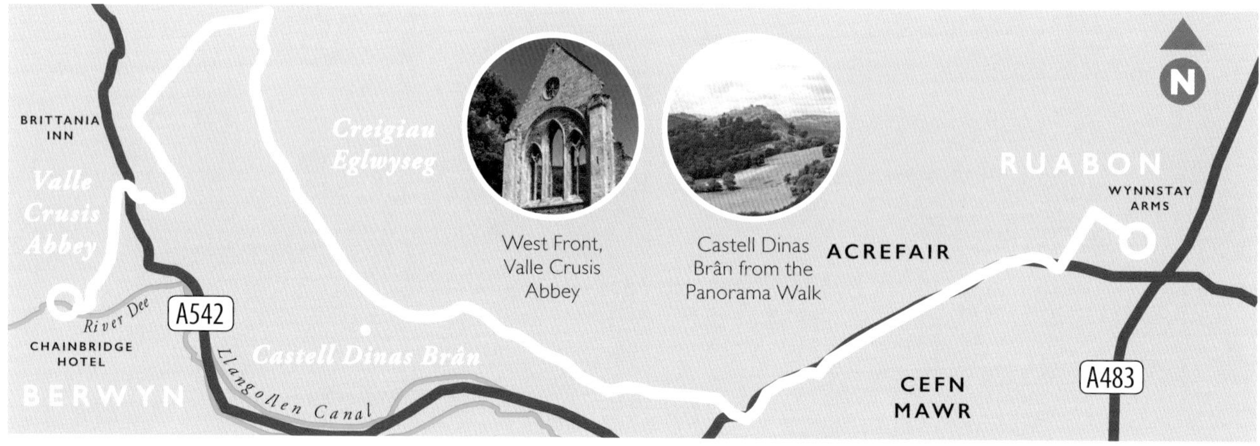


# Walk 2

## RUABON TO BERWYN

10.7 MILES APPROX.

This morning the weather was more clement as I left Ruabon. I followed another more famous ancient earthwork, Offa's Dyke, built in the late 8th century as a border between the kingdoms of Mercia and Powys, before skirting the urban area surrounding Cefn-Mawr and heading towards the rising mountains. Upwards through dense forest along the path known as the Panorama Walk, I eventually arrived at a remarkable vista across the Vale of Llangollen and beyond. From here, the route continued northwards along lanes and through lush green pastures, passing beneath the towering limestone escarpments of the Eglwyseg Mountain before turning south towards the abbey of Valle Crusis. It was here, amongst the romantic ruins, that I enjoyed my picnic lunch.

The Cadw administer this beautifully maintained site. Valle Crusis, or Valley of the Cross, is the remains of an abbey built in 1201 by Madog ap Gruffydd Maelor, a prince of Powys Fadog. By 1535 it was said to be the second richest Cistercian abbey after Tintern. However, like so many, it was dissolved two years later during Henry VIII's Dissolution of the Monasteries. The Tate are in possession of a lovely watercolour painting by J.M.W. Turner made after his visit to these ruins in 1794. Located on a mound nearby is the Pillar of Eliseg, the shaft of a ninth century cross from which the abbey derives its name.

The final mile of the day was over Velvet Hill, which brought me to the delightful Horseshoe Falls and the Chain Bridge at Berwyn on the River Dee. This is the beginning of the UNESCO World Heritage site I was to wander through over the next couple of days. The falls are actually a weir designed by Thomas Telford to draw water from the river into the waterway now known as the Llangollen Canal. The canal was originally a navigable feeder on the Shropshire Union system, but today it exists solely for leisure purposes. The Chain Bridge was installed to transport coal and minerals from the canal to Telford's new London to Holyhead road, now the A5, avoiding paying the toll on the Llangollen Bridge. It has been rebuilt on a couple of occasions.

The Chainbridge Hotel makes a handy place to stay.

EAST RANGE VALLE CRUSIS

EGLWYSEG LIMESTONE ESCARPMENT

DEREK AT ELISEG'S PILLAR

# Walk 3

## BERWYN TO LLANGOLLEN

4.5 MILES APPROX.

A short day in miles is required for the many attractions to experience on the way. I headed towards Llangollen along the side of the canal, passing the Royal International Pavilion, the home of the International Eisteddfod. This world famous music festival is held annually in July. I was accompanied along the towpath by horse-drawn tourist boats and upon arriving at the town was greeted by the shrill whistle of a steam train from the Llangollen Railway, the only standard gauge heritage railway in North Wales.

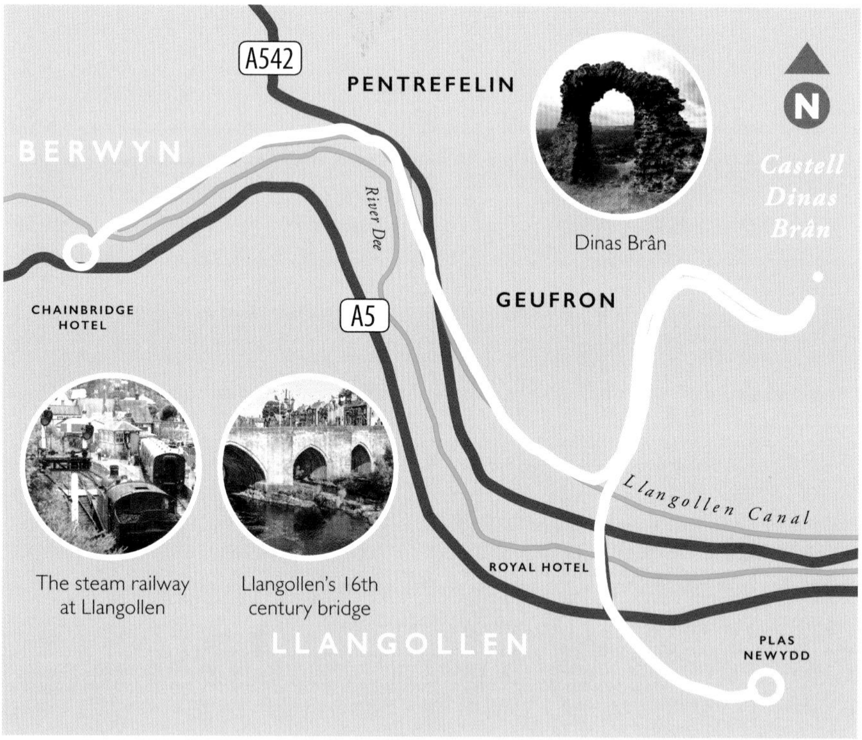

Dinas Brân

The steam railway at Llangollen

Llangollen's 16th century bridge

Before sampling the delights of this attractive and busy town, I decided to climb to the imposing Castell Dinas Brân, a 'Tolkienesque' ruin perched 800 feet above Llangollen with extensive views in all directions. The name roughly translates as 'Crow Castle' and on the ascent I passed through a gate with a metal crow standing sentinel. Located on the site of an Iron Age fort this once mighty castle had a surprisingly short operational life. Built in the 1260s it was a key strategic location in the wars between the princes of Powys Fadog and England. However, following a successful attack by the English it was set on fire and badly damaged. It was never repaired and now stands as a monument to ancient conflicts.

Back in the town I visited the Llangollen Museum, housed in a former library, which contains many fascinating artefacts of local history, before moving on through streets bedecked with bunting and flowers to arrive at the Courtyard Coffee Shop for lunch. My next 'port of call' was a real treat – Plas Newydd, a striking black and white house on the edge of town run by the Denbighshire County Council. Between 1780 and 1831 this was the home to Lady Eleanor Butler and Sarah Ponsonby, along with their servant Mary Caryll. They scandalised their families by eloping from Ireland to live in Wales in 'Romantic Retirement' beneath the ruins of Dinas Brân. The house is embellished with copious wooden carvings culled from churches and old furniture often collected by their many friends and admirers. The intriguing 'Ladies of Llangollen' were visited by many famous people including Sheridan, Sir Walter Scott and on numerous occasions Arthur Wellesley, the future Duke of Wellington. The beautiful and peaceful gardens contain a standing stone circle erected for the 1908 Eisteddfod.

The centrepiece of Llangollen is the 16th century bridge, a Scheduled Ancient Monument, straddling the foaming River Dee. According to an anonymous poem from 200 years ago, the bridge is one of the 'Seven Wonders of Wales'. White water canoeing and kayaking are popular pastimes on this stretch of the river.

After a busy day I savoured a delicious meal of chalk stream trout washed down with a pint of the local Facer's D.H.B. beer at the riverside Corn Mill Restaurant. This former mill has been sensitively restored and retains many old features, including an operating waterwheel. I retired to The Royal Hotel nearby, where a young Queen Victoria once stayed with her mother.

PLAS NEWYDD IN LLANGOLLEN

HORSE-DRAWN BOATS ON THE LLANGOLLEN CANAL

# Walk 4

## LLANGOLLEN TO CHIRK CASTLE

8.7 MILES APPROX.

Following a hearty breakfast I returned to the wharf and set off along the canal for an easy walk to Telford's spectacular 'stream in the sky', the 18 span Pontcysyllte Aqueduct that carries the canal over the River Dee. The star of this World Heritage Site is not for the faint-hearted who have no head for heights! Narrow boats slip across an iron trough with a precarious 126 feet drop to the valley floor below with little to hang on to! Walking is safer, if no less exhilarating, as the entire towpath has a hand rail.

Following a route through rolling countryside I reached Chirk Castle, the guardian of the entrance to the Ceiriog Valley, with its round towers shimmering in the early afternoon light. The last Welsh castle built by Edward I to remain occupied sits on a hill with far-reaching views over the Cheshire and Shropshire Plains. Completed in 1310, it was constructed by Roger Mortimer as part of the chain of castles built to supress the Welsh. There then followed a number of turbulent years as the castle frequently changed hands between numerous warring factions before being bought by Thomas Myddleton in 1595. Although now owned by the National Trust, the Myddleton family have kept rooms for private use.

The West Range is the only part of the castle that survives from the Middle Ages and a climb up old stone stairs is required to access the upper rooms. One of the features here is the exposed workings of the clock that adorns the wall of the courtyard. The newer structure contains a wide range of both medieval and classical styles. The Cromwell Hall has the appearance of an ancient room but in practice was designed in the 1840s. The rest of the house is a mix of neoclassical and Victorian Gothic. The Grand Staircase, built by Joseph Turner in the 1770s, leads to The State Rooms where there is an array of fine furniture, art and plasterwork. The decorative blue and gold ceiling in The Saloon is of particular note. The Bow Drawing Room has an atmosphere of life in the castle in the middle of the 20th century and includes a fan vaulted ceiling by Thomas Harrison, A.W.N. Pugin's original fireplace and paintings by Augustus John. In the South Range the atmospheric, smoke-stained Servants' Hall, used as a dining room for over 200 years until the Second World War, retains the aura of continuing use.

There has been a formal garden at Chirk since 1653 and it is a pleasure to saunter through its herbaceous borders, neat topiary and unusual statues. From here I strolled down to view the beautiful Baroque iron Davies Gates at the exit of the estate.

Like many grand houses, Chirk Castle owes its longevity to the wealth created by centuries of industry on its very doorstep. In 2012 it was designated a Site of Special Scientific Interest as a home to rare species including lesser horseshoe bats, grassland fungi and deadwood beetles.

My ramble took me through a land rich in culture, which throughout history has experienced a constantly changing environment. The arteries of river, rail, canal and road now fuel this tourist destination and there is plenty for the visitor to see and do. This land of scenery, myth and song has a wonderfully broad variety of Welsh heritage to experience. Time has softened the scars of industry and conflict and much of what was once functional is now considered romantic.

I'm sure the Ladies of Llangollen would find it as beautiful today as in 1800. ■

ADAM'S TOWER, CHIRK CASTLE

PONTCYSYLLTE AQUEDUCT

THE DAVIES GATES, CHIRK CASTLE

THE SALOON AT CHIRK CASTLE WITH DECORATIVE BLUE AND GOLD CEILING

# A moveable feast

By William Sitwell

The library at Weston Hall, my home in Northamptonshire, is a tranquil space on the ground floor of a house which variously dates back in parts to the 17th century and earlier.

It's my favourite room in the house. Its green walls are lined with bookcases, whose edges are gilded in gold paint. The books vie for space with a few paintings, a view of the kitchen garden by Rex Whistler, some works by the Italian futurist Gino Severini and above the dark mahogany doors, two views of the Bay of Naples. My grandfather, the writer Sir Sacheverell Sitwell, liked them because they reminded him of where he was born: in Scarborough.

Many of the books date back to the early 19th and 18th century. There are copies of Hansard, records of State Trials, plenty of Latin and Greek texts and various encyclopaedias. At the bottom of one shelf is a collection of old papers, in particular, a scrapbook filled with pages of spidery, neat writing and a number of loose leaves with other various jottings.

These are 17th century *'receipts'* collected by an ancestor of mine, one Lady Anne Blencowe. A printed copy of Lady Blencowe's manuscript was published in the 1920s and a further book edited by a descendant of hers came out in 2004.

Most of Lady Blencowe's recipes are for entertaining. Her husband was a judge and local Member of Parliament and evidently quite prosperous. When his daughter Susanna lost her husband to illness when quite young, he felt sorry for her and her two young children, so he bought her a house as a gift on Valentine's Day in 1714. That house is Weston Hall. It's a property that passed through the female line of the family until my great-grandfather acquired it from an aunt and gave it to my grandfather Sacheverell as present on his marriage to the Canadian beauty Georgia Doble. It was Georgia who showed the original manuscript to her friend George Saintsbury who had it copied and printed in 1925.

The book gives us a good insight into the culinary world of the 1660s. We learn, for instance, that marigold is added when making cheese, to colour it, as indeed many cheeses were coloured until relatively recently (perhaps Red Leicester is a rare exception today). Lady Blencowe credits the recipes she includes to a variety of people. There is *'To do green oranges Lady Stapleton's Way'*, for example, and *'To roast fowl Sir Thomas Perkingses' way'.* (the latter, incidentally, is stuffed with oysters and onions before being roasted on a spit.) She also includes a recipe *'To make Bisketts, Mrs B's way'.*

KITCHEN SCENE WITH A MAID DRAWING POULTRY, THE PARABLE OF THE RICH MAN AND THE POOR LAZARUS, FROM KITCHEN AND MARKET SCENES WITH BIBLICAL SCENES IN THE BACKGROUND - JACOB MATHAM (1571–1631) - WIKI

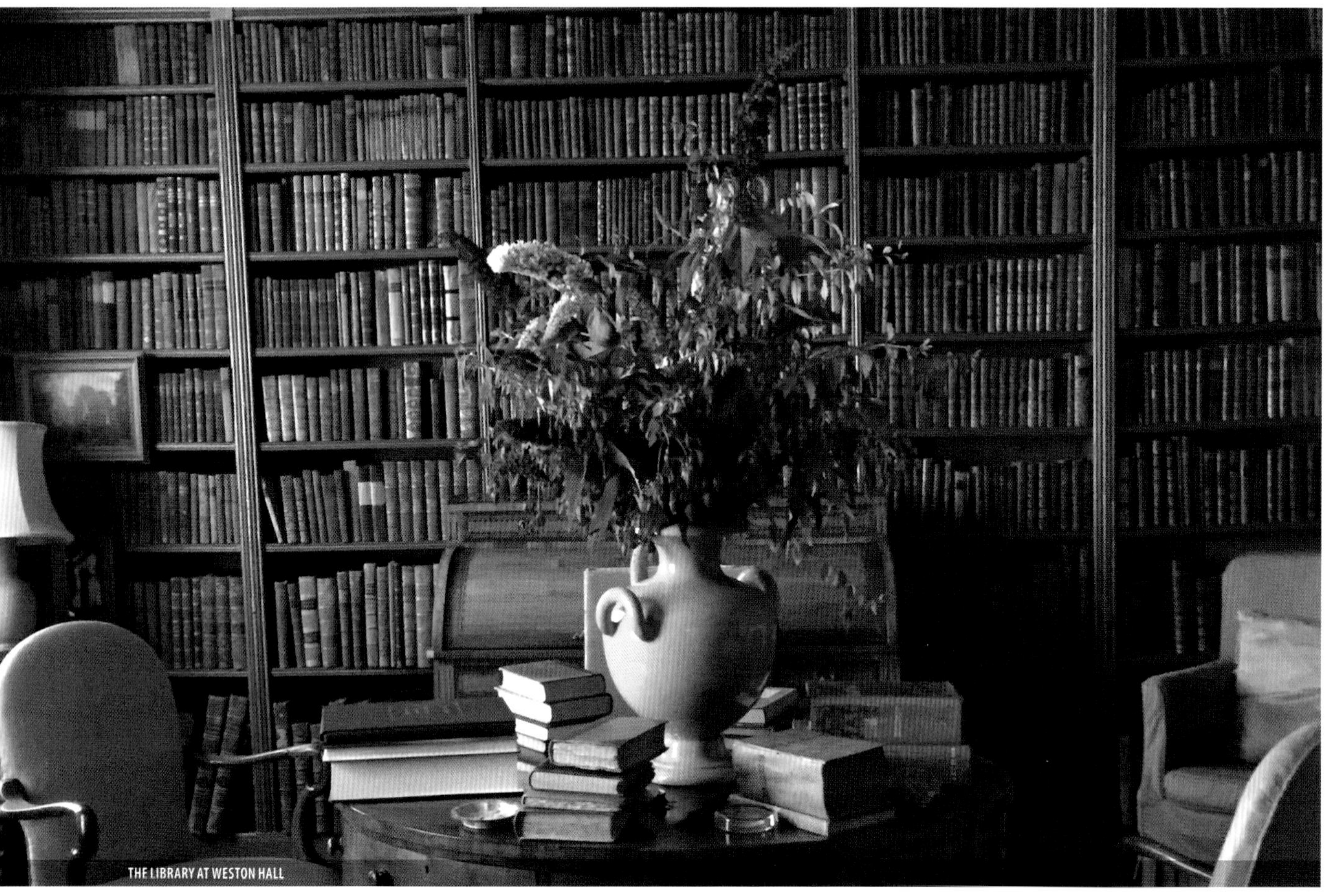

THE LIBRARY AT WESTON HALL

Some recipes would appeal to the modern palate. There is a delicious recipe for Spanish custard, for instance, using ground almonds, orange flower water, eggs, caster sugar, cream and sherry. Other dishes belong more firmly in the past: a *'little pye for Entermess'* is a spectacular interlude for a banquet, being a chicken in a pie with stuffed larks. There is also an alarming recipe for crayfish which includes the instruction to *'bruise'* their legs in a mortar while still alive.

In addition to the recipes, there are the inevitable *'Physical Receipts',* including solutions for giddiness, swollen legs, madness even and several cures for indigestion, suggesting it was a common complaint of the time. A remedy for the *'bite of a mad dog'* sees the patient being drained of 10 ounces of blood, given a mixture of unheard-of dried herbs to be drunk with warm milk before a terrifying programme of cold dips in a river or spring every morning for a month.

She also suggests whitening teeth with burnt date stones, *'to strengthen ye eyes'* by chewing on aniseed and having someone blow on your eyes, and *'to whiten cloth'* by using sheep's dung and then dunking the cloth in a stagnant pond.

I like that these papers are here in this room, because I think it's likely that in the late 17th and early 18th century the room was where the family dined. The house was much smaller then. A pretty two-up, two-down building surrounded by gardens overlooking on one side a courtyard. Across was a further, earlier building that housed – according to old plans for the house - a *'bakehouse'* and a kitchen. There was access also to this building through an underground passage. Steps down into a cellar from the main house led to the dark passage and finally the kitchen. And thus the dining room was located at the furthest point from the kitchen.

This was deliberate of course. And having looked at the beautiful and delicate clothes that we still have at the house that were worn by the ladies and gentleman of the 18th and 17th centuries, one can understand why. Indeed we have spotted no oil-like stains on these costumes!

It is only relatively recently that the antics of the kitchen have become of interest to the squires and their partners of manor houses and grander stately homes. No gentleman, unless cheekily and unusually under-cover, would have been seen down there in the vulgar area of food preparation. And those kitchens of the 17th century would have seemed like a cottage industry.

THE KITCHEN AT WESTON HALL

Households were very self-sufficient: they would not just have produced their own sickness remedies but the likes of toothpaste, soap, rat poison and weed killer. Bread was baked, beer brewed and housekeepers would have been highly tuned in to the seasons. Store-cupboards would be very well stocked and the running of them highly tuned to the kitchen garden. Seeds for herbs and vegetables would be sown like clockwork, always mindful of what would be needed fresh in the summer months, stored, pickled or cured for the winter.

There were no supermarkets. In the days when deliveries came on foot or using horsepower, the delivery man needed feeding, as did anyone passing by on business.

All of which industry was simply so much vulgarity for the owners of the house, although doubtless the lady of the manor would visit the cooks and housekeeper down there from time to time.

And then as time progressed and society changed the kitchen and dining rooms began to move. The Weston dining room became a library as the courtyard was absorbed into the house to make a large dining room. In the mid-20th century a dining room was built a little closer to the kitchen and a pantry and parlour was located in-between. That parlour became a kitchen in the 1970s and in the 1980s my parents turned the old kitchen into a sitting room.

Today the kitchen is where most people live. Their ovens, islands and fridges are status symbols. This dramatic change occurred after the Second World War when households began to invest in fridges and early advertisements show people dressed as if for a cocktail party showing off their new purchases.

I've actually turned that sitting room back into a big old kitchen, and with an Aga and big table, it serves as a wonderfully warm and inviting space. We've popped a discreet TV into the library and my wife and I have *(shhh)* occasional telly-suppers on our laps in there. It's fun to dine in there, but it's a long old trek down to the kitchen if you've forgotten the mustard.

Weston Hall is open for group visits by appointment. The Wing of the house (with the old kitchen) can be rented via Airbnb. William Sitwell also runs a successful supper club also at Weston Hall.

Further details for both via:
**westonsupperclub@hotmail.com**
**www.williamsitwell.com**

# Harvington Hall

# a remarkable survival...

**Steeped in centuries of history, Harvington Hall is a moated manor house of many secrets. It contains the largest surviving series of priest hides in the country, together with an abundance of rare, original Elizabethan wall paintings.**

Originally built in the 1300s and developed magnificently in the late 1500s, Harvington Hall brings to life the fascinating history of the survival of Roman Catholic families and priests during the Reformation of the late sixteenth century. At a time when it became treasonous to practice the Roman Catholic faith in England, Catholic families were forced to hear Mass in secret. Over time, penalties for celebrating Mass increased in severity both for priests and anybody harbouring them, and so Catholic families were forced to hide priests in their houses despite the risk they faced. Special hides were built to conceal priests and any Massing paraphernalia should a search be undertaken on the property. Many such searches occurred, and some were successful.

Harvington Hall brings this fascinating history of survival to life with its array of ingenious hiding places and symbolic wall paintings. Concealing no less than seven hiding places, as well as a cunning chimney escape, the Hall is believed to have been a safe house for secular priests in the late sixteenth and early seventeenth centuries. The hides at Harvington also show the development of priests' hiding places over the period, and in particular highlight the genius of the notorious priest hide maker, St. Nicholas Owen, who was at work from 1588 to 1605 and was eventually arrested at Hindlip, ten miles from Harvington, in a search which altogether lasted for twelve days.

OPPOSITE - SWINGING BEAMS HIDE INTERIOR

DOUBLE HIDE UNDER STAIRCASE

Harvington's two rudimentary hides next to chimney-stacks contrast dramatically with the ingenious concealments built by this master craftsman. All of these are located near to the Great Staircase, which would have acted as a cover for the building works. Owen's hides each have a distinctive character and different methods of concealment. The hide in Dr Dodd's Library, for example, is accessed via a 'swinging beam' at the back of a book cupboard and could be latched shut from the inside. The hide on the Great Staircase is opened by lifting a portion of the staircase itself, and even then there is another large hide secreted behind the small cavity that is revealed; the two would have been separated by a false wall panel. Some carefully placed valuables in the outer hide might tempt an Elizabethan soldier to increase his assets... and keep quiet the little hiding place he stole from, and thus also the capacious hide behind it that might conceal the priest himself.

SMALL CHAPEL

WITHDRAWING ROOM HIDE

Also believed to have been put in place by Nicholas Owen, in one of the upper bedrooms there is a false chimney which enabled a swift escape into the loft space and its hide lurking behind a false wall, the second largest priest hide ever found. The 'fireplace' of this false chimney has been blackened to cleverly reinforce the deception. With such remarkable features surviving, it is very easy to picture the scene: a priest jolted from his sleep by the frenzied rush of soldiers around the building, jumping out of bed, turning his mattress in the hope that its warmth will not betray him, and climbing desperately up the false chimney to crawl along the garrets into the confined safety of a hide, where he must wait indefinitely for the sake of his life.

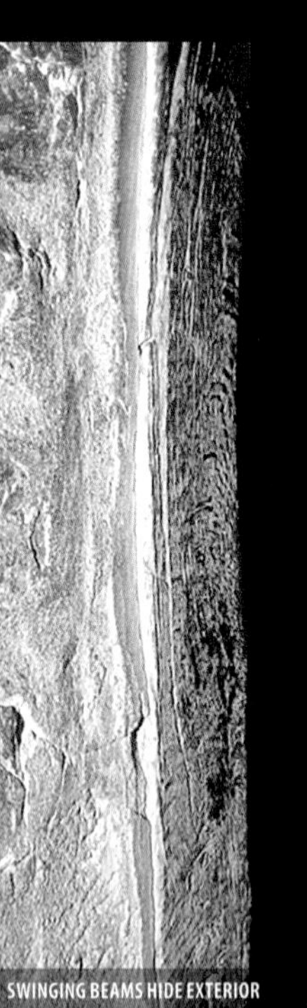

SWINGING BEAMS HIDE EXTERIOR

In addition to its plethora of priest hides, Harvington also boasts a series of contemporary wall paintings, some of which are believed to be symbolic of the Catholic faith. In the Small Chapel, for instance, is a pattern depicting the blood and water of the Passion of Christ. Many of these paintings have been unspoiled since c. 1600, and some were likely to have been part of the decoration implemented after the installation of the hides, and thus a significant part of their story. Perhaps this is what prompted Michael Hodgetts, in his *Secret Hiding-Places (1989)* to say that, 'At Harvington, the southwest wing as a whole is the most outstanding architectural record of the Counter-Reformation anywhere in England.' ■

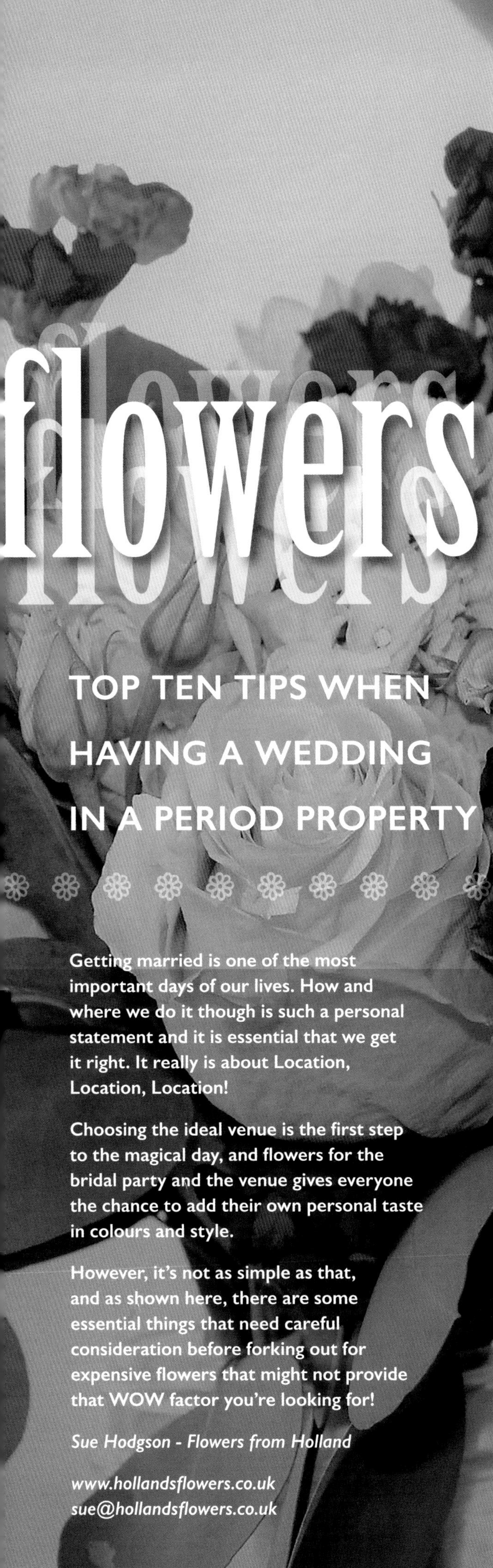

# flowers

## TOP TEN TIPS WHEN HAVING A WEDDING IN A PERIOD PROPERTY

**Getting married is one of the most important days of our lives. How and where we do it though is such a personal statement and it is essential that we get it right. It really is about Location, Location, Location!**

**Choosing the ideal venue is the first step to the magical day, and flowers for the bridal party and the venue gives everyone the chance to add their own personal taste in colours and style.**

**However, it's not as simple as that, and as shown here, there are some essential things that need careful consideration before forking out for expensive flowers that might not provide that WOW factor you're looking for!**

*Sue Hodgson - Flowers from Holland*

*www.hollandsflowers.co.uk*
*sue@hollandsflowers.co.uk*

**1 Geographical Location** Thistles and Heather for Scotland, Lavender for Norfolk, White Rose for Yorkshire, etc.

**2 What was/is the building used for?**
***a.*** A Windmill: Corn and Sunflowers
***b.*** Masonic Halls: Pomegranates, Blue Forget-Me-Nots, Laburnham
***c.*** Historical Importance: symbolic additions to complement this.

**3 Architecture Features** If there are stone or wooden carvings depicting exuberant foliage and flowers or structural/architectural shapes, they could be incorporated within your designs using the actual varieties.

**4 The Season** The grounds themselves can give plenty of foliage throughout the year and depending on the season, the use of conkers, cones and even bare branches can be used to great effect. Replication of woodland Spring bulbs in pots such as Snowdrops, Jonquils and Bluebells can provide beautiful perfume and delicate flowers.

**5 The amount of daylight** you have in the reception room and were your photographs are going to be taken. Receding colours such as purple, blues, dark reds will have poor definition.

**6 Temperature of the room** The wrong flowers can wilt and droop quickly if they are unhappy!
***a.*** If it is cold and drafty, avoid using fine stemmed flowers
***b.*** If you're having roaring log fires and radiators blasting out, avoid using delicate petals, especially woody foliage where the leaves will dry and turn crispy!

**7 Type of room** is it a library or the old kitchens or Stables? Your designs could incorporate something relating to this, such as old books stacked up with flowers on them as table centres.

**8 Staircases** are a great place for pictures. Lights and flowers on each tread looks wonderful as does a simple gypsophila garland on the bannister.

**9 Size of rooms** arrangements need to be in scale. No point having a 3m wide fireplace with a 300mm arrangement on it, it will get lost! - Large rooms will also carry heavy scented flowers spectacular well, so used heady-scented blooms such as Stargazer Lilies, Hyacinths, Narcissi and Winter Jasmin

**10 Age/Period of the Property** if its and Art Deco building this may have a different style of arrangement to that of an Elizabethan Hall.

**Sundays:** *reading the newspaper supplements, roast dinner, ironing the children's school uniforms, settling down in front of the TV in time for the latest period drama.*

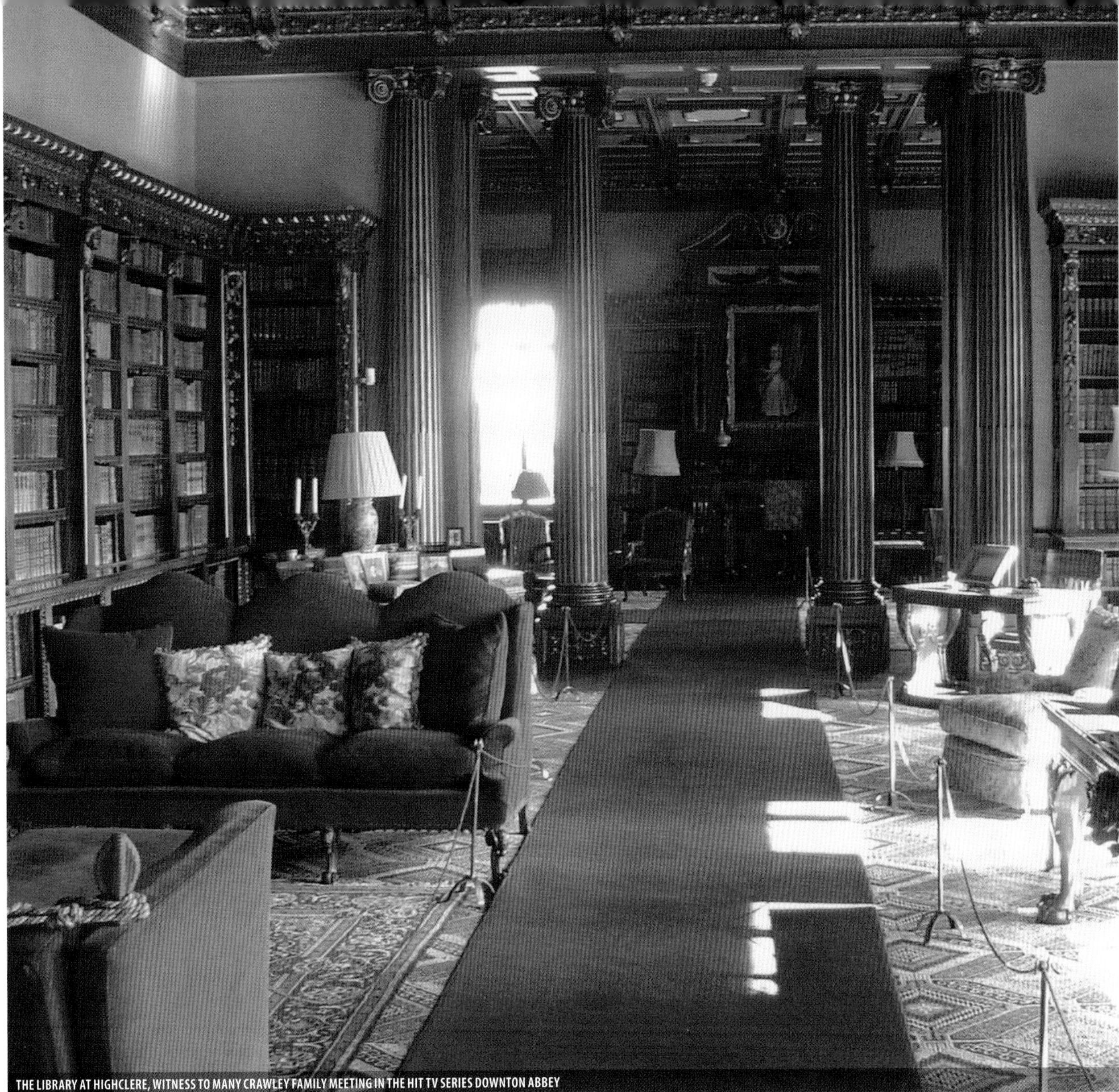

THE LIBRARY AT HIGHCLERE, WITNESS TO MANY CRAWLEY FAMILY MEETING IN THE HIT TV SERIES DOWNTON ABBEY

## DOWNTON ABBEY

Downton Abbey first hit our screens eight years ago and became the most successful British TV series of the 21st century. A worldwide hit and a winner of Emmys, Golden Globes and more, Downton got us hooked on the British costume drama and in turn sparked our interest in the period settings such programmes rely on.

Fans of the show ensure that tours and open days to the real Downton, Highclere Castle in Hampshire, home of The Earl and Countess of Carnarvon are always a huge success. With a release date now announced for the long-awaited film it doesn't look like things will slow down any time soon!

**What is it that makes shows like Poldark and Vanity Fair ideal for Sunday night entertainment?**

**Where do we start?**

**Lavish production, elaborate costumes?**

Escapism, the nostalgia of being transported to a bygone time when ladies wore elaborate gowns, men were gracious gentlemen *(apart from the villains obviously!)* and dreamy romances bubble slowly. Old-fashioned values, the feel of a literary classic.

We are given the opportunity to discover more about significant events in our countries past and appreciate how cultures have changed politically and socially.

While we are drawn to a life that seemed simpler, we are also reminded to appreciate our own era as *Call the Midwife* often prompts us to do.

The costume drama is a British speciality, and the one thing all these dramas have in common is the period setting.

## OUTLANDER

OUTLANDER - GOSFORD HOUSE MARBLE HALL

Time-travelling series Outlander, based on the novels of American author, Diana Gabaldon and filmed on location in Scotland and at Wardpark Studios in Cumbernauld has boosted tourism in Scotland. The series follows the fortunes of Claire Randall as she moves between two lives from the 1940s to the 1740s and takes us on a race through Scottish history at its most turbulent times.

Locations include Clava Cairns, Inverness Historic Environment Scotland as the fictional Craigh na Dun, the location of the time-portal. Hopetoun House appears several times. In series one the Red Drawing Room as the Duke of Sandringham's home and the rear steps the location of the duel between the Duke of Sandringham and the laird of the McDonalds. Gosford House provides interior grandeur for season three while the exterior was used for the Dunsany family's estate of Helwater.

## GUNPOWDER

BBC drama Gunpowder starred Game of Thrones actor, Kit Harrington who can trace his ancestry back to Robert Catesby one of the chief orchestrators of the 1605 Gunpowder Plot against the King in Parliament. He was the driving force behind the production of a 3-part series dramatising the events that led to the arrest of Guy Fawkes, still remembered in England every 5th November. The production made use of a group of medieval and Elizabethan buildings in Yorkshire and Derbyshire that provided an authentic atmosphere. These included Kirkstall Abbey and Ripley Castle in Yorkshire and Haddon Hall in Derbyshire.

***'In Yorkshire and Derbyshire, we were spoilt for choice with a huge array of period country houses, landscapes and historic buildings that worked perfectly.'***

Mandy Sharpe, Location Manager, Gunpowder, courtesy Creative England.

POLDARK – AIDEN TURNER, ROSS POLDARK

## POLDARK

The British-American dramatisation of Winston Graham's 12-volume Cornish family saga Poldark returned to our screens in 2015. Set in the early 19th century, the story tracks the loves, hatreds and intrigues of a Cornish mining family and during the first series hearts across the nation were set aflutter by scenes of the lead actor, Aidan Turner. Poldark has also given us all a new reason to visit Cornwall for the gorgeous coastal scenery against which horsemen ride furiously in nearly every episode.

'Trenwith', the Poldark family home was played by Chavenage House in Tetbury, Gloucestershire. If Chavenage appears familiar that may be because it also provided the backdrop for BBC period dramas Wolf Hall, Lark Rise to Candleford and Tess of the D'Urbervilles.

The Cotswold manor house owned by the Lowsley-Williams family since 1891 attracts fans from all over the world and provides the opportunity to escape to 18th century Cornwall with intimate tours of the property

## VICTORIA

2019 sees the return of Victoria to our screens. The first series was ITV's highest rating drama of 2016 and has also been hugely popular in the US. Written by Daisy Goodwin and starring the endearing Jenna Coleman we continue the heart-warming sometimes heart wrenching tale of the most famous couple of the nineteenth century.

Filmed in North Yorkshire at stunning locations including Castle Howard and Newby Hall in the north and Bramham Park and Harewood House in the West. Interestingly in 1844 Victoria visited the Duke of Atholl at his home, Blair Castle and the Castle appears as itself in series two.

## VANITY FAIR

The recent adaptation of Vanity Fair, the novel by William Makepeace Thackeray is lavish and elaborate as you would expect from Mammoth Screen who also produce Poldark and Victoria but has a sleek modern edge. As soon as the cover of Jimi Hendrix' *All Along the Watchtower* kicked in it was obvious this was going to be a little different. Narrated by Michael Palin as Thackeray we follow the story of witty adventurer Becky Sharp, played by Olivia Cooke as she strives for something which is not worth having! The fabulous carousel scene was filmed at Syon Park, West London standing in as Vauxhall Pleasure Gardens, a popular Georgian night out. When filming at Syon House, the crew were right next to Heathrow Airport and in the flight path planes flying over every 50 seconds! Other locations include Lancaster House, Osterley House and Marble Hill.

PEAKY BLINDERS - THE 17TH CENTURY STABLE BLOCK AT PEOVER HALL

## PEAKY BLINDERS

Another darker drama which proved to be a massive success also by Taboo creator Steven Knight and starring Tom Hardy is the gripping gangster series Peaky Blinders.

Set in the 1920's we were introduced to the brooding Thomas Shelby, played by the enigmatic Cillian Murphy in 2013 and series five is set to return in 2019.

The tale of a Birmingham-based gang named after the real gang's charming trick of stitching razor blades into the peaks of their cloth caps has won accolades including a BAFTA television award for best drama.

With the Black County Museum providing the location for Charlie's scrap metal yard and Admiral Grove, a road of terraces in Liverpool appearing as the street where the Shelby's live in Small Heath, Birmingham.

Newby Hall, Ripon stars in series one setting the scene for cellars, billiards room, gardens and the statue gallery, which doubled as Birmingham Museum.

In series three it's 1924 and the Shelby's have gone up in the world with Tommy moving to a Warwickshire manor house which is actually Arley Hall in Cheshire. The hall as it appears today was built between 1832 and 1845 by Rowland Egerton-Warburton. Designed by George Latham the house features elaborate ceilings and oak panelling, impressive fireplaces.

The library sets the scene for Tommy's office and the gallery the Shelby's dining hall. The stable block which appears in the third series is actually the working stable yard of Tatton Estate's Peover Hall. Dating back to the 17th century the interior and exterior of the yard were used as the setting for numerous scenes in both the first and second episodes.

Filming for the fifth series started in autumn and should grace our screens in spring 2019.

TABOO –THE RAINBOW PORTRAIT AT HATFIELD HOUSE

## TABOO

We were exposed to the darker, supernatural side of the early 19th century as Taboo introduced us to the deeply troubled James Delaney played by Tom Hardy. Presumed dead Delaney returns from Africa to find his Father dead the country at war with the US and the world apparently dominated by the machinations of the East India Company.

Written by Steven Knight, Tom Hardy and his father Chips Hardy Hatfield House, Hertfordshire starred as the Headquarters of the East India Company. Look closely and you can spot the famous Rainbow portrait of Elizabeth I behind Jonathan Pryce's Sir Stuart Strange.

Locations also include Ham House, Surrey and Chenies Manor House, Buckinghamshire while the Delaney house can be found on Stepney Green Gardens in East London.

The gritty drama is set to return to our screens in 2019.

## SO, WHAT'S IT LIKE WHEN THE FILM CREWS INVADE?

# WE ASKED NEWBY HALL TO TELL US.

Historic houses and gardens have been used for the set and backdrop for many a period drama and Newby Hall in Ripon, North Yorkshire is no exception.

The stately home which is owned by Richard and Lucinda Compton has been used as a location for Mansfield Park, Peaky Blinders and Death Comes to Pemberley over the years and in the last year alone filming took place at Newby for the feature film The Little Stranger, ITV's Victoria and Agatha Christie's The ABC Murders starring John Malkovich and Rupert Grint which will air on the BBC at Christmas.

Filming is a massive undertaking and the sheer number of people involved is always surprising. The range of different skills required means that the house can be completely taken over whilst filming takes place, everyone has their own job to do and the logistics of it all coming together is staggering.

The attention to detail is phenomenal, whilst filming recently for Victoria, the light switches at Newby were of the wrong period and considered too 'modern' and had to be covered up with something appropriate to the period

Directors often mention what they like about filming at Newby is that as a private home, apart from the spectacular interiors and gardens is that it can be adaptable, there aren't layers of red tape to go through and can usually give a 'yes' or 'no' as to whether something can be moved, painted or used in filming.

**Asked as to why Newby is chosen so often for filming Stuart Gill, Newby's Commercial Director says:**

*'The mix of Georgian and Victorian Architecture and interiors makes Newby such an appealing prospect for location scouts and the gardens can fit any period as there are several styles and type of gardens within the grounds.*

*Filming has become such a part of life here at Newby. It's great publicity for us as well and it can bring a whole new audience that may not have been aware of us before. Often, the location scouts really love the 'unseen' parts of the house. For the first series of Victoria both the cellars and attics were used as 'below stairs' at Kensington Palace.*

*We always look to weigh up the pros and cons of having filming here at the house as it can be hugely disruptive. For one, it still is a family home and we have to be mindful of that and also the disruption for our visitors as we may have to close the house whilst filming goes on. Our visitors are normally quite interested in the whole experience and the chance of seeing a film set often makes up for any disappointment in not being able to visit the house.'*

# THE UK HERITAGE AWARDS

The UK has more heritage than almost any country in the world.

If you are looking for a good day out, nothing is more rewarding than taking a trip into history.

Once a year, in the opulent setting of Goldsmith's Hall, London, Visit Heritage gathers some of the innovators in the heritage industry together to celebrate what is new, inspiring and enjoyable.

Our distinguished judges are experts in their field and their deliberations each year reveal the vibrancy and freshness of the heritage world.

Thank you to our sponsors Bidwells, New Mind, Lucy Robinson PR and Omni 42. A brand new award, 'Contribution to Heritage' was kindly sponsored by Savills.

Here's a review our recent winners. Join our discussions online at www.visitheritage.co.uk to make your own suggestions.

BIDWELLS
new mind
LRPR
LUCY ROBINSON PUBLIC RELATIONS
ØMNI42
savills

UK HERITAGE AWARDS 2018

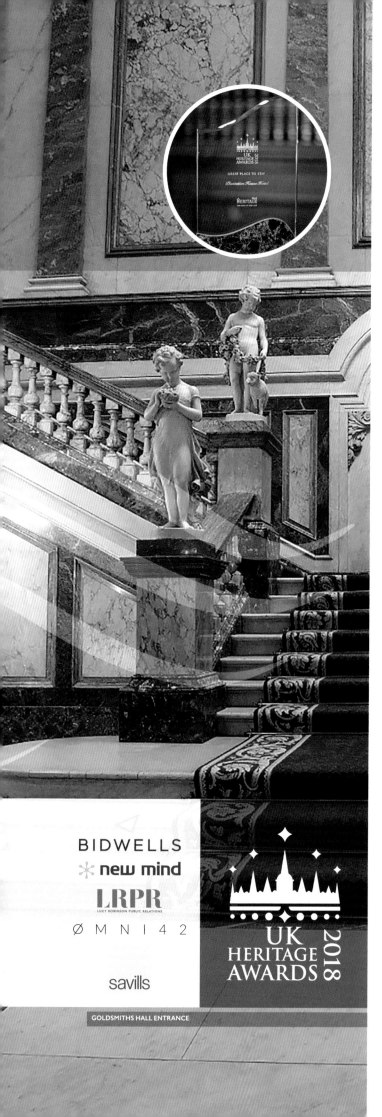

GOLDSMITHS HALL ENTRANCE

WINNER BEST FAMILY DAY OUT - ALNWICK CASTLE

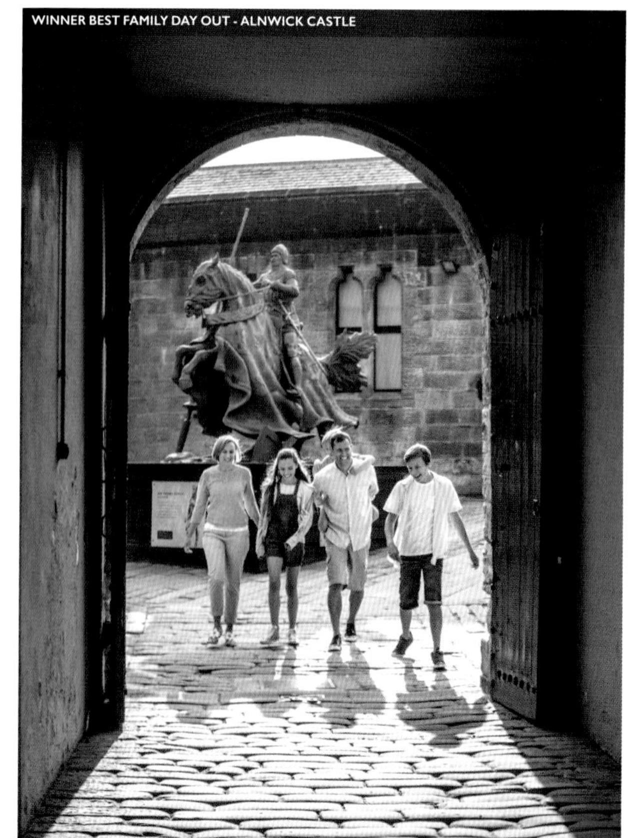

## FAMILY DAY OUT

### Alnwick Castle

The Duke of Northumberland's home at Alnwick Castle has a cornucopia of entertainment on offer to family visitors. Well informed guides lead history and film tours. In the Knight's Quest arena, costumed adults help budding knights and princesses dress up in medieval finery or try their hand at traditional crafts, swordplay and medieval games. The most courageous can brave interactive games and animatronics in the new Dragon Quest.

## GREAT PLACES TO EAT

### Castle Howard

Now offering a special Afternoon Tea in the gracious surroundings of the Grecian Hall, available both in summer and at Christmas.

## SHOPPING EXPERIENCE

### The Queen's Gallery

The exceptional collection of works of art in the Royal Collection maintain an air of prestige for a national and international audience.

## WONDERFUL PLACES TO STAY

### The Victoria at Holkham

With stunning views overlooking Holkham National Nature Reserve and at the gateway to palladian Holkham Hall, The Victoria Inn has a great location.

## BEST EVENT / EXHIBITION

### The Beaulieu International Autojumble

The home of the National Motor Museum, had the innovative idea of hosting a get-together for auto enthusiasts from all over the world.

## BEST WEDDING VENUE

### Myres Castle

The castle dates back to the 1530s with outstanding formal gardens and now offers 10 en-suite bedrooms with additional space in the gate lodge.

## CONTRIBUTION TO HERITAGE

### English Heritage and Google Arts & Culture

In all, detailed images of 2000 objects at 29 sites are now online, photographed with ultra high-resolution Gigapixel and Art Camera technology.

## JUDGES RECOGNITION

### English Heritage, Portchester Castle

To recognise the research into records showing that 2000 black and mixed-race men, women and children arrived as prisoners of war at Portchester Castle.

## HIDDEN GEM

### The Charterhouse

Tudor mansion, almshouse and the former premises of two public schools. The survival of so much of the medieval monastery, the Tudor great house and its continued life as a community is remarkable.

## BEST LOOS

### Hampton Court Palace

Adopting a fun approach, the designers have given visitors a chance to keep learning about Henry and his wives during time spent in the loo.

# SIGNPOST

## GREAT PLACES TO STAY

### Plantation House Hotel

## OUTSTANDING CUSTOMER EXPERIENCE

### Old Rectory Norwich

## GOURMET DELIGHT

### Gilpin Hotel and Lake House

## MUST VISIT

### Milsoms Maison Talbooth

# ABOUT THE WINNERS

## FAMILY DAY OUT

*Winner:*

### Alnwick Castle, Northumberland

A family visit to Alnwick Castle promises a true cornucopia of entertainment. In the Knight's Quest arena, budding knights and princesses can dress up in medieval finery, sample swordplay and try traditional crafts. Courageous kids can brave interactive games and animatronics in the new Dragon Quest, while guides lead entertaining history and film tours. Alnwick Castle was used as the film location for Hogwarts; watch out for Harry Potter-inspired characters and broomstick training sessions – all in one entry fee.

*Commended:*

### Llancaiach Fawr Manor, South Wales

Families visiting the 16th century fortified manor house at Llancaiach Fawr Manor step into a live costumed interpretation of the times of local Civil War leader, Colonel Pritchard - a brilliantly fun day out.

## GREAT PLACES TO EAT

*Winner:*

### Castle Howard, North Yorkshire

Castle Howard's special Afternoon Tea is reason enough to visit Sir John Vanbrugh's baroque masterpiece. Specially created by Head Pastry Chef, Vanessa Wade, afternoon tea is served during the summer and at Christmas for the perfect afternoon out. Meanwhile, Castle Howard's other catering outlets are benefiting from investment in new equipment and the success of 'Castle Howard at Christmas' has expanded into a dedicated Christmas café.

*Commended:*

### Stansted Park, Hampshire

Lunch and tea at Stansted Park is served in the charming restored Edwardian conservatory overlooking the Walled Garden. The judges commended it as a prime example of a local business that is at the heart of the local community.

ALNWICK CASTLE - BEST FAMILY DAY OUT

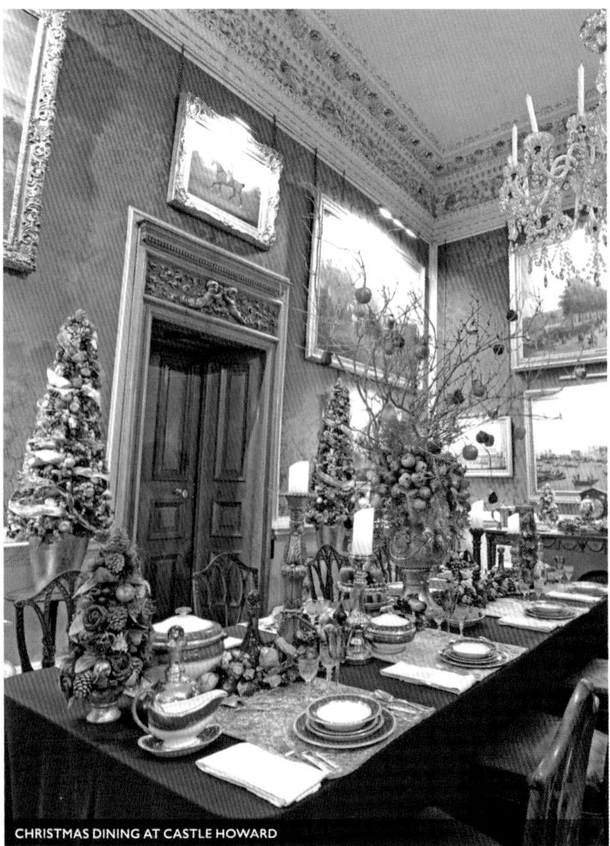

CHRISTMAS DINING AT CASTLE HOWARD

## SHOPPING EXPERIENCE

*Winner:*

### The Queen's Gallery, London

The shop at the Queen's Gallery manages to cope with large visitor numbers, communicate the exceptional collection of works of art in the Royal Collection and maintain an air of prestige in exemplary style. The shop is sophisticated and well arranged, full of bespoke pieces drawn from the collection, while there are plenty of items to appeal to children.

## WONDERFUL PLACES TO STAY

*Winner:*

### The Victoria at Holkham, Norfolk

The Victoria Inn's location couldn't be better; less than a mile from England's best beach, views over Holkham National Nature Reserve and with brilliant access to Holkham Hall. The 20 bedrooms are named after shooting drives on the Holkham Estate and antique touches come from Holkham Hall. Local fish, game and meat from the estate are on the menu, plus there's a warm welcome for dogs.

THE QUEEN'S GALLERY, LONDON

VICTORIA SITTING ROOM AT HOLKHAM

# ABOUT THE WINNERS

## BEST EVENT/EXHIBITION

*Winner:*

### The International Autojumble at Beaulieu, Hampshire

The International Autojumble at Beaulieu, home to the National Motor Museum, has run every year, for 50 years. The idea to host a get-together for motoring enthusiasts from around the world was first realised in 1967; today, the event is Beaulieu's largest annual heritage get-together, with more than 37,000 visitors. Loyal exhibitors love it, look forward to it and often arrange their diaries around it.

*Commended:*

### Whitby Abbey – English Heritage

Whitby Abbey's ILLUMINATED ABBEY event for Halloween bought Bram Stoker's Dracula to life, revisiting the Abbey's history with theatrical characters in a spectacle that could be enjoyed by the whole town.

*Commended:*

### Houghton Hall, Norfolk

Landscape artist Richard Long's 'EARTH SKY' exhibition at Houghton Hall was his largest since a 2009 Tate retrospective; the quality of contemporary artists shown at Houghton Hall is exceptional. Long's work has been added to the Marquess of Cholmondeley's growing collection of contemporary art giving lasting impact.

A MEMORABLE PETROL-FUELLED DAY OUT AT BEAULIEU AUTOJUMBLE

## BEST WEDDING VENUE

*Winner:*

### Myres Castle, Fife

Myres Castle aims to combine impeccable service with the relaxed feeling of staying with friends. The castle dates back to the 1530s with outstanding formal gardens and now offers 10 en-suite bedrooms with additional space in the gate lodge. The Barnquee - a specially designed hybrid between a barn and marquee - built in the gardens with local larch tree supports and is unique to the Castle, offering something away from the norm. There is space to seat 160 guests, a rustic bar, and beautiful light filtering through the canvas roof and the trees above.

*Commended:*

### Hedsor House, Buckinghamshire

Brides and Grooms have exclusive use of the Georgian mansion and country estate at Hedsor House. From the Italianate Central Hall to the 12th century Chapel, the spaces are adaptable, while the bridal suite claims to be one of the largest in Europe.

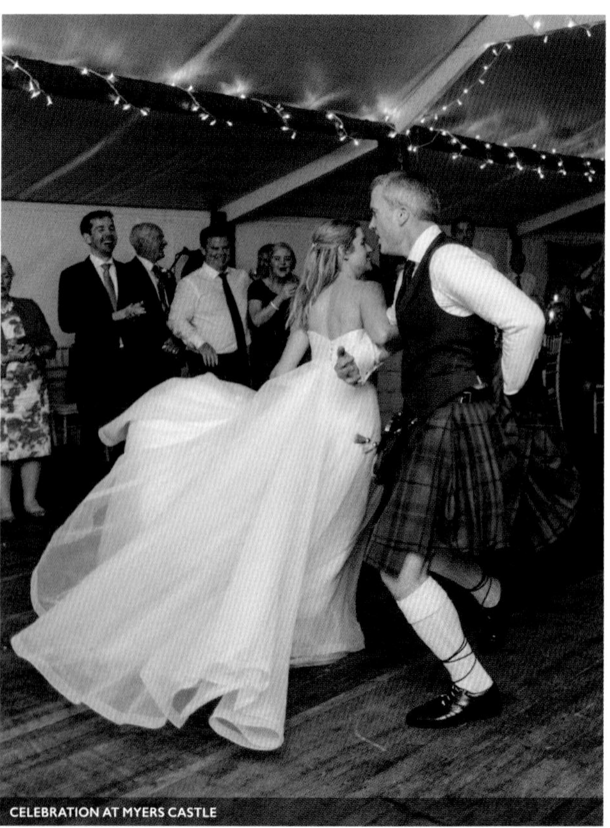

CELEBRATION AT MYERS CASTLE

## CONTRIBUTION TO HERITAGE

*Winner:*

### English Heritage and Google Arts & Culture

2017 marked a ground-breaking collaboration between English Heritage and Google. Detailed images of 2000 objects at 29 sites are now available online, photographed with ultra-high-resolution Gigapixel and Art Camera technology. This was Google's first collaboration across many sites and is the largest amount of content generated with a partner on the platform. The result is free, instant access to treasures not normally available to view, including Frank Wilkins' 1820 painting of the Battle of Hastings or a 360° curator-led tour of Osbourne House.

*Commended:*

### Blenheim Palace, Oxfordshire

Blenheim Palace's new 10-year plan sets out 10 ambitious goals for the evolution of the Palace and estate in the next decade. This includes a £40 million restoration plan, a plan to acquire key items lost from the collection in the past, the establishment of an endowment fund for the Palace, and tripling Blenheim's contribution to the local economy.

ART CAM SET UP AT BATTLE - ENGLISH HERITAGE AND GOOGLE ARTS & CULTURE

## JUDGES RECOGNITION

*Winner:*

### English Heritage - Portchester Castle, Hampshire

The judges wanted to recognise English Heritage for the exemplary research that illuminated this underappreciated aspect of our history, and especially the Curator, Abigail Coppins, who did the research.

In 1796, 2,000 black and mixed-race men, women and children arrived as prisoners of war at Portchester Castle. English Heritage's new creative installation opened in July 2017, telling their story through objects, models, panels and theatre, highlighting an important moment in Black British history; the struggle for emancipation in the Caribbean in the 18th and 19th centuries.

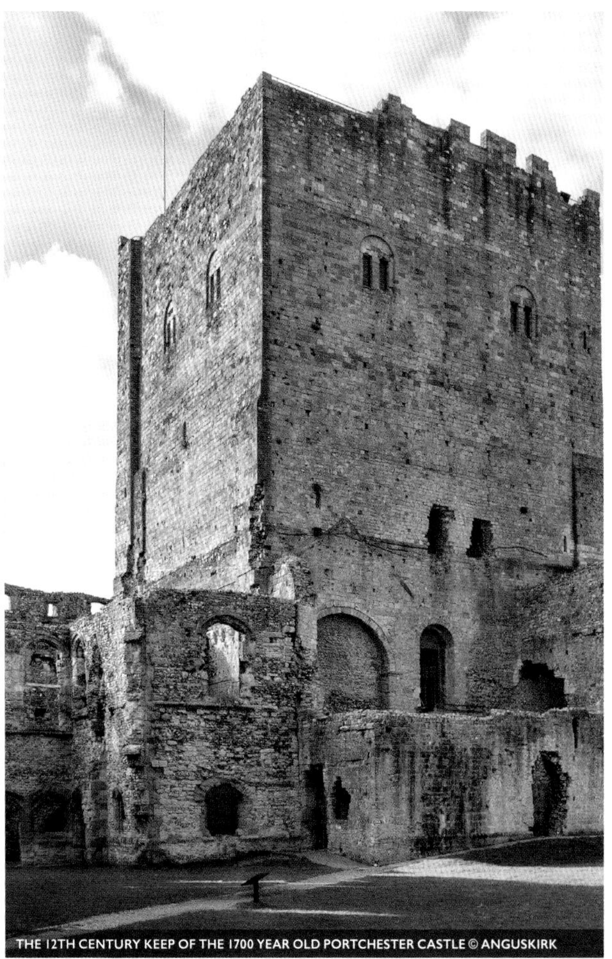

THE 12TH CENTURY KEEP OF THE 1700 YEAR OLD PORTCHESTER CASTLE © ANGUSKIRK

# ABOUT THE WINNERS

## HIDDEN GEM

*Winner:*

### The Charterhouse, London

The Charterhouse is open to visitors for the first time, with a new reception, shop, museum and guided tour. A true hidden gem, The Charterhouse reveals the surviving buildings of a Carthusian priory, the Tudor mansion of the Howard family, an almshouse and the former premises of two public schools. The survival and preservation of so much history - all just moments from Smithfield Market – is extraordinary, and a visit is truly fascinating.

*Commended:*

### Bridge End Gardens, Suffolk

Bridge End Gardens is a total hidden gem, tucked into a corner of Saffron Walden. Planting adheres to Victorian principles, and there is a new Visitor Centre designed as an Orangery and a bed of commercial saffron – demonstrating the town's role in the historic saffron industry - to add to its heritage appeal.

CHARTERHOUSE, WASH COURT

## BEST LOOS

*Winner:*

### Hampton Court Palace, Richmond

The newly-refurbished toilets at Hampton Court reflect the Tudor history of the royal palace. Taking a fun approach, visitors have the chance to keep learning about Henry and his wives during time spent in the loo. Specially designed graphics reveal Tudor beauty tips and silhouette you in costume in the mirror in a unique experience!

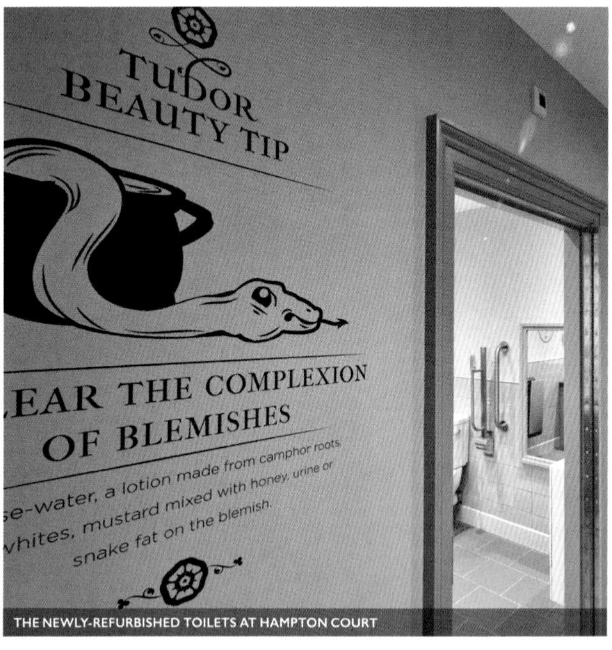

THE NEWLY-REFURBISHED TOILETS AT HAMPTON COURT

Castle Howard

Harewood House

Chatsworth

Holkham Hall

Burghley House

Woburn Abbey

Blenheim Place

Hatfield House

Beaulieu

Leeds Castle

# LONDON

VIEW OF ROOFTOPS ACROSS LONDON ©VISITENGLAND

**COUNTRYSIDE**
Royal Parks
Hampstead Heath
River Thames

**HERITAGE**
Royal palaces
Homes of the Famous
Parliament & Democracy

**FOOD**
Cuisines of the world
Jellied eels
Chelsea Buns

# Dr Johnson's House

## Wit and words

*'When a man is tired of London, he is tired of life'.*

So famously said Dr Samuel Johnson, Britain's most quoted writer after Shakespeare. Duck into Gough Square, a stone's throw from Fleet Street, behind some of modern London's gleaming towers, to find an elegant 18th century house where the famous author made the most of everything the metropolis had to offer. This is the house where Samuel Johnson - wit, raconteur and compiler of the most famous Dictionary of the English language - lived for 11 years in the 1750s.

PASSERS-BY ARE NOT TIRED OF LONDON AT DR. JOHNSON'S HOUSE

It is important to our literary heritage because this is the very spot where Johnson wrote his famous dictionary; there's a facsimile copy in the garret that he used as a workroom. Johnson's Dictionary was the very first to trace the use of words to an original quotation, the format familiar today, and unlike any other, it could be funny. It is Johnson's gift for wit that makes him so appealing. Luckily for us, he was surrounded by other writers who delighted in recounting his conversation so from James Boswell 's biography and the diaries and letters of his friends, Mrs Hester Thrale and Fanny Burney, you can almost feel this entertaining character at work in these modestly furnished rooms.

THE UPSTAIRS GARRET ROOM WHERE SAMUEL JOHNSON'S DICTIONARY WAS COMPILED

Today it's all very calm; you can't help longing for the great man himself to burst through the door, large and loud, full of bombast and Tourette's (of which Syndrome he may have suffered). He'd have sat down to stroke Hodge the cat and had you laughing in a moment. You'll wish that you too were alive in London around 1750. ■

JOHNSON'S COMFORTABLE FIRST FLOOR ROOMS

# London

## Top 3 Venues

SYON PARK - JOSEPH HALL WEDDING PHOTOGRAPHY

### Syon Park, Brentford

Syon Park has it all - a country estate located in a city. Choose the Great Hall or The State Dining Room in Syon House for your wedding ceremony. The Great Conservatory, in the centre of the gardens is perfect for summer entertaining and a great space for your reception. For larger parties, the Garden Room Marquee can seat up to 600. For corporate events, a large selection of rooms are available to suit all party sizes. If you are looking for outside space the 'Capability' Brown landscaped parkland on the banks of the River Thames is great for picnics.

HOUSE OF COMMONS WEDDING © PAUL ROGERS PHOTOGRAPHY

### Houses of Parliament, Westminster

Did you know that you can hold your conference in the historic Houses of Parliament buildings in the Palace of Westminster? The Jubilee Room in The House of Commons is available for weddings and civil ceremonies, accommodating up to 60 people with larger parties more suited to the Members Dining Room. A selection of rooms in both houses are available for functions and celebrations including the Churchill Room, and the Thames Pavilion, a newly renovated marquee with views across the Thames.

BANQUETING HOUSE MAIN HALL - HIRE SPACE

### Banqueting House, Whitehall

Formerly part of the site of the Royal Palace of Whitehall today's Banqueting House was designed and built by Inigo Jones and completed in 1622 for the specific purpose of entertaining. The spectacular gilded ceiling in The Main Hall includes nine oil-on-canvas paintings by Rubens. The Main Hall is accessed by a grand staircase from the Entry Hall, a path taken by the many Kings and Queens that have been entertained here over the centuries.
The Banqueting House is available for exclusive hire for your special occasion.

NTS

**University Boat Race, Oxford v Cambridge, Putney to Mortlake** *Sunday 7th April 2019*

**Virgin Money London Marathon** *Sunday 28th April 2019*

**The RHS Chelsea Flower Show, Royal Hospital Chelsea** *21st-25th May 2019*

## Top 3 Annual Events

### The RHS Hampton Court Palace Flower Show
*1st - 7th July 2019*

Covering over 34 acres of land The Hampton Court Palace Flower Show is the biggest of its kind anywhere in the world. There will be workshops to teach new crafts and skills to use in your own garden, plenty of opportunity to buy plants and gardening products as well as sampling food and drink. One of the themes in 2019 will be health and well-being, and will explore some of the positive effects that plants can have on peoples' mental health.

THE RHS HAMPTON COURT PALACE FLOWER SHOW

### Twilight Tours, Tower of London
*Selected dates November to April*

Experience the Tower of London in a whole new light and take in the unique atmosphere as the sun sets. Enjoy after-hours access to Traitor's Gate, Bloody Tower and The Scaffold Site. Hear stories of prisoners in the Tower, tales of past Royal residents and discover some of the secrets kept behind the Castle walls for centuries. Dates are limited so makes sure you book early to avoid disappointment. Wear warm and practical clothing and be prepared for uneven steps and narrow spaces.

TWILIGHT TOWER TOURS - THE DOTS

### Christmas in Leicester Square
*Early November – Early January*

Leicester Square is transformed in the run-up to Christmas. Buy gifts, decorations and festive food and drink at the many stalls. Visit the Belgian Spiegeltent which hosts a whole range of entertainment to suit all ages. There is also the chance for children to visit Santa in his grotto. Entry to the market is free, so walk around, soak up the atmosphere and maybe treat yourself to a glass of mulled wine! Charges will apply for performances held in the Spiegeltent.

LEICESTER SQUARE - FLICKR

# London

## Places to stay and eat

SAN DOMENICO HOTEL

### San Domenico Hotel

San Domenico House is an intimate, luxurious 'boutique' townhouse hotel located only a few minutes' walk from bustling Sloane Square and the fashionable heart of Chelsea. Behind its Victorian facade, San Domenico House enjoys all the luxuries of a small palace preserving the charm and intimacy of its 19 rooms and suites. With easy access to the city and West End, it is ideally suited to business executives and leisure travellers alike. Free WiFi internet connection is provided in all bedrooms.

An additional feature is a rooftop terrace with far-reaching views across Chelsea. Whether guests want to have an English or Continental breakfast in the charming breakfast room or they wish to enjoy afternoon tea in the antiques-filled lounge, San Domenico House will provide them with the highest standard of service in a comfortable and relaxed atmosphere.

**29-31 Draycott Place, London**
**Greater London SW3 2SH**

**020 7581 5757**

**www.sandomenicohouse.com**
**info@sandomenicohouse.com**

### Twenty Nevern Square
*Hotel*

20 Nevern Square
London SW5 9PD

020 7565 9555

www.twentynevernsquare.co.uk
twenty@mayflowercollection.com

### Batty Langley's
*Hotel*

2 Folgate Street, Shoreditch
London E1 6BX

020 7377 4390

www.battylangleys.com
reservations@battylangleys.co.uk

### The Wine Library
*Restaurant*

43 Trinity Square
London EC3N 4DJ

020 7481 0415

www.winelibrary.co.uk
info@winelibrary.co.uk

## Searcys Roof Garden Rooms

Searcys Roof Garden Rooms at 30 Pavilion Road provides a peaceful haven in the heart of Knightsbridge, convenient for Harrods, Hyde Park, major museums and the West End via the nearby underground station. It offers a relaxed atmosphere and friendly staff with a high level of personal and attentive service. This hotel is a hidden gem in the bustle of London. It is perfect for people seeking an alternative to large hotel chains. All eleven rooms are individually designed to have a country house feel, however now with super king size beds, plasma TVs with a wide option of channels, plus the usual amenities, such as, WIFI, air conditioning and tea and coffee brought automatically to your room. Bathrooms provide luxury touches with bath robes and Molton Brown products.

30 Pavilion Road, London, Greater London SW1X 0HJ

020 7584 4921

www.searcys.co.uk
rgr@searcys.co.uk

SEARCYS ROOF GARDEN ROOMS

## The Thatched House
*Restaurant*

115 Dalling Road, Hammersmith
London W6 0ET

020 8741 6282

www.thatchedhouse.com
connect@thatchedhouse.com

## Newens: The Original Maids of Honour
*Tea Room*

288 Kew Rd, Richmond
London TW9 3DU

020 8940 2752

www.theoriginalmaidsofhonour.co.uk
enquiries@theoriginalmaidsofhonour.co.uk

## The Petersham Nurseries Teahouse
*Tea Room*

Church Lane, Richmond Upon Thames, Surrey, London TW10 7AB

020 8940 5230

www.petershamnurseries.com
info.richmond@petershamnurseries.com

# SYON PARK Ⓕ

www.syonpark.co.uk

SYON PARK - LILY POND

## London home of the Duke of Northumberland with magnificent Robert Adam interiors, 40-acres of gardens, including the spectacular Great Conservatory.

Described by John Betjeman as the 'Grand Architectural Walk', Syon House and its 200-acre park is the London home of the Duke of Northumberland, whose family, the Percys, have lived here for 400 years. Originally the site of a late medieval monastery, excavated by Channel 4's Time Team, Syon Park has a fascinating history. Catherine Howard was imprisoned at Syon before her execution, Lady Jane Grey was offered the crown whilst staying at Syon, and the 9th Earl of Northumberland was imprisoned in the Tower of London for 15 years because of his association with the Gunpowder Plot. The present house has Tudor origins but contains some of Robert Adam's finest interiors, which were commissioned by the 1st Duke in the 1760s. The private apartments and State bedrooms are available to view.

The house can be hired for filming and photo shoots subject to availability. Within the 'Capability' Brown landscaped park are 40 acres of gardens which contain the spectacular Great Conservatory designed by Charles Fowler in the 1820s. The House and Great Conservatory are available for corporate and private hire. The Northumberland Room in Syon House is an excellent venue for conferences, meetings, lunches and dinners (max 60).

The State Apartments make a sumptuous setting for dinners, concerts, receptions, launches and wedding ceremonies (max 120). Marquees can be erected on the lawn adjacent to the house for balls and corporate events. The Great Conservatory is available for summer parties, launches, filming, photoshoots and wedding receptions (max 150).

**OWNER**
The Duke of Northumberland

**CONTACT**
Contact: Estate Office
Tel: 020 8560 0882
Email: info@syonpark.co.uk
Events: events@syonpark.co.uk
Visitors Centre: visitorcentre@syonpark.co.uk

**LOCATION**
Syon House, Syon Park, Brentford, Middlesex TW8 8JFMap Ref: 19:7C
Between Brentford & Twickenham, off A4, A310 in SW London.

**TRANSPORT ROUTES**
Car | Bike | Bus | Train | Tube | Aeroplane

**OPENING TIMES**
Syon House:
13 Mar - 27 Oct 2019
Weds, Thurs, Suns and BHs 11am - 5pm (last entry 4pm)

Gardens only:
11 Mar - 27 Oct 2019
Daily 10.30am - 5pm (last entry 4pm)

House Garden & Great Conservatory:
Closed from 29 Oct 2018 - 10 Mar 2019.

**ADMISSION**
House, Gardens & Conservatory:
Adult £13, Child £6, Conc £11.50,
Family (2+2) £30.
Booked groups (25+):
Adult £11.50, Conc £10.50, School Group £4.

Gardens & Great Conservatory:
Adult £8, Child £4.50, Conc £6.50,
Family (2+2) £18, School Group £3.

**ADDITIONAL**
Syon House Ventures reserves the right to alter opening times. Please phone or check website for up to date details and special events.

No photography in the House.

WC's.

Free parking.

WC's. House - Limited access. Gardens and Great Conservatory - fully accessible.

London Syon Park Hilton Hotel at www.londonsyonpark.com

By arrangement.

By arrangement.

Café in the Garden Centre.

The Garden Kitchen Restaurant in the Garden Centre.

Syon Park Visitor Centre, open daily 10.30am-5pm during the season.

Garden Centre.

Syon House & the Great Conservatory available for exclusive luncheons, meetings & corporate.

Available for formal dinners, ceremonies, receptions & parties.

See website for details.

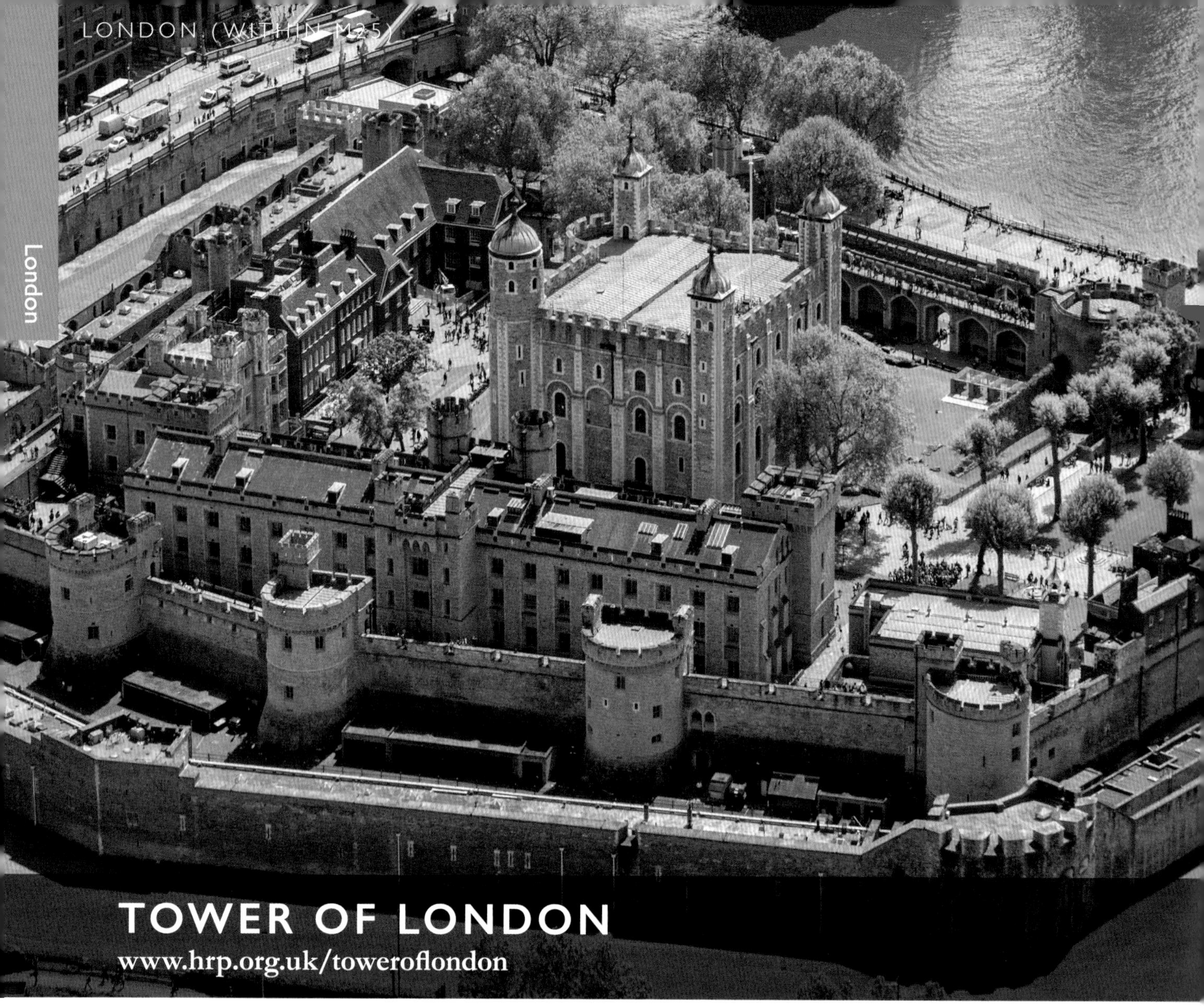

# TOWER OF LONDON

www.hrp.org.uk/toweroflondon

DISCOVER LONDON'S CASTLE - HOME OF THE CROWN JEWELS

THE FAMOUS YEOMAN WARDERS, COMMONLY KNOWN AS BEEFEATERS

©ROYAL COLLECTION TRUST © 2018, HER MAJESTY QUEEN ELIZABETH II

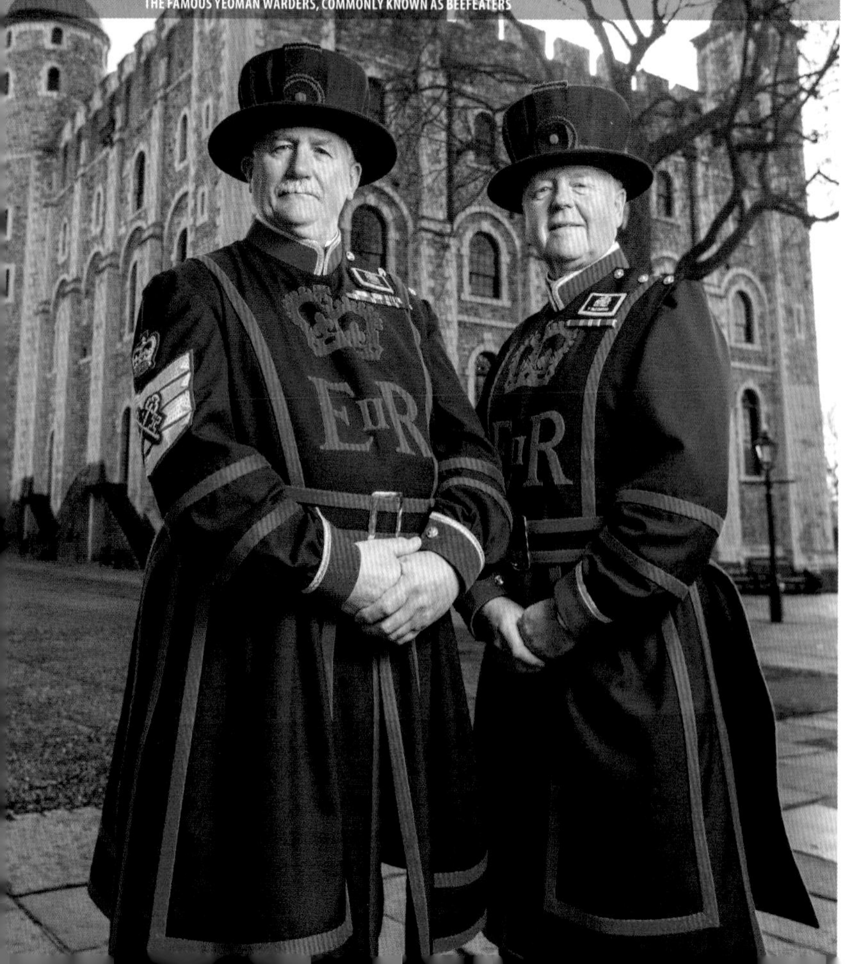

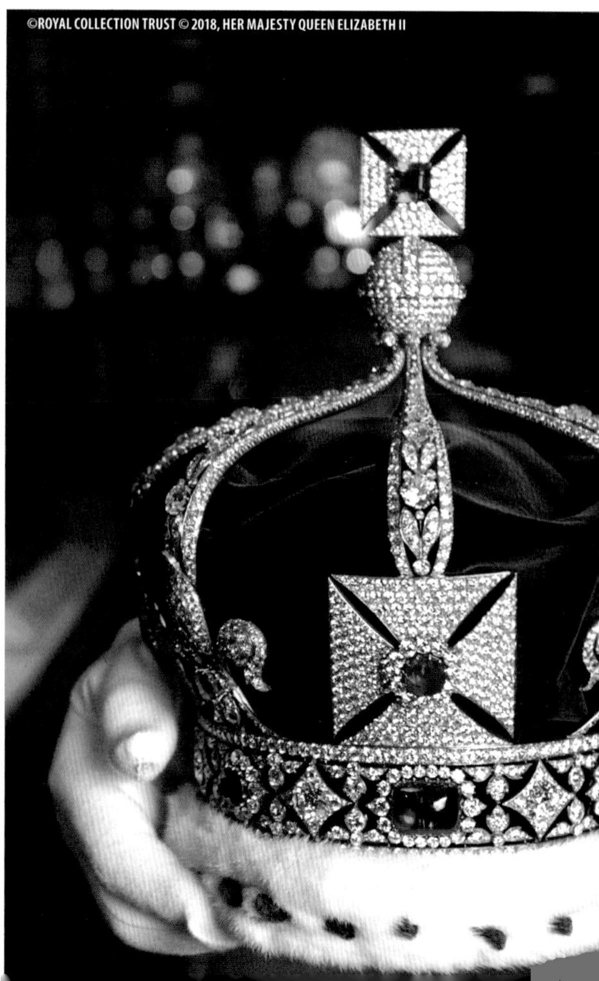

**The Tower of London is a 1,000-year-old castle that protects the Crown Jewels. It was a secure fortress, a royal palace and an infamous prison.**

The Tower of London, founded by William the Conqueror in 1066-7, is one of the world's most famous fortresses, and one of Britain's most visited historic sites. Despite a grim reputation for being a place of torture and death, there are so many more stories to be told about the Tower and its intriguing cast of characters.

This powerful and enduring symbol of the Norman Conquest has been enjoyed as a royal palace, served as an armoury and for over 600 years even housed a menagerie! Don't miss the Crown Jewels in the famous Jewel House, unlocking the story behind the 23,578 gems in the priceless royal jewels. Marvel at the Imperial State Crown and the largest diamond ever found; and see the only treasure to escape destruction in 1649, after the Civil War. For centuries, this dazzling collection has featured in royal ceremonies, and it is still in use today.

Join Yeoman Warder Tours to be entertained by captivating talks of pain, passion, treachery and torture at the Tower. Visit Tower Green and see the memorial to the people who died within the Tower walls. Find out why the last execution at the Tower was in 1941 and see how instruments of torture were used to extract 'confessions' from prisoners. Explore the story of how five coins changed history in the Royal Mint Exhibition, discover what life was like in the surprisingly luxurious Medieval Palace, and explore the stories of Henry II, Edward I and their courts at work.

See one of the Tower's most famous sights, the ravens. Legend has it Charles II believed that if the ravens were ever to leave the Tower, the fortress and the kingdom would fall.

Step into 1,000 years of history every day at the Tower of London.

**OWNER**
Historic Royal Palaces

**CONTACT**
Tel: 0203 166 6000
Email: visitorservices.tol@hrp.org.uk
Venue Hire & Corporate Hospitality:
020 3166 6226

**LOCATION**
London EC3N 4AB
Map Ref: 20:P7
Bus: 15, 42, 78, 100, RV1.
Underground: Tower Hill on Circle/District Line.
Docklands Light Railway: Tower Gateway Station.
Rail: Fenchurch St Station & London Bridge Station.
Boat: From Embankment Pier, Westminster or Greenwich to Tower Pier. London Eye to Tower of London Express.

**OPENING TIMES**
Summer:
Mar-Oct, Tue-Sat 9am-5.30pm.
Last admission 5pm.
Mon & Sun 10am-5.30pm.
Last admission 5pm.

Winter:
Nov-Feb, Tue-Sat 9am-4.30pm
(last admission 4pm).
Mon & Sun 10am-4.30pm
(last admission 4pm).
Closed 24-26 Dec and 1 Jan.

**ADMISSION**
Visit www.hrp.org.uk/toweroflondon
or call 0203 166 6000 for more information.

**CONFERENCE/FUNCTIONS**
Conferences: Up to 150
Meetings: 6 to 200
Receptions: 10 to 300
Lunches: Up to 150
Dinners: 6 to 240

No photography in Jewel House.

Toilet and disabled WC facilities available.

Baby changing facilities available.

Closed 24-26 Dec and 1 Jan.

None for cars. Coach parking nearby.

Dedicated facilities, tours and wheelchair hire are available. Please view the access guide.

Tower audio guides are available (subject to availability).

Yeoman Warder tours are free and leave front entrance every ½ hr.

Offering everything you need for the perfect educational visit. To book 0203 166 6000.

Apostrophe: by the river. New Armouries Café: Light bites. Raven Café: Gourmet sausages.

Licensed. Perkin Reveller: British food, stunning views.

Shop for gifts & souvenirs inspired by this famous royal residence and its iconic Yeoman Warders.

Visit: hrp.org.uk/hireavenue
or call 020 3166 6226.

Please see the 'Explore' website page to see what's on.

# KENSINGTON PALACE

**www.hrp.org.uk/kensingtonpalace**

2019 marks the 200 year anniversary of Queen Victoria's birth at the palace. From 28 May 2019, explore the re-presented rooms where the young princess spent her childhood before discovering that she was queen at just 18 years of age. From princess to empress, then discover what happened once Victoria become queen in a new exhibition which explores the private woman behind the public monarch, re-examining her later life and legacy.

Before Victoria the Georgian kings also called the palace home. Follow in the footsteps of Georgian courtiers in the sumptuous King's State Apartments which show some breath taking examples of the work of architect and painter William Kent.

Visit the Queen's State Apartments, the intimate, private rooms created for Queen Mary II, who ruled jointly with her husband, King William III, in the 17th Century.

**CONTACT**

Owner: Historic Royal Palaces
Tel: 0203 166 6000
Email: kensingtonpalace@hrp.org.uk

Venue Hire & Corporate Hospitality:
Tel: 020 3166 6115
Kensington Gardens, London W8 4PX

Map Ref: 20:18 - In Kensington Gardens.

Underground: Queensway on Central Line, High Street Kensington on Circle & District Line.

**OPENING TIMES**

Summer (1 Mar - 31 Oct) Mon-Sun 10am-6pm
Last admission- 5pm
Winter (1 Nov - 28 Feb) Mon-Sun 10am-4pm
Last admission - 3pm Closed 24 - 26 Dec.

**ADMISSION**

Visit www.hrp.org.uk/kensingtonpalace or call 0203 166 6000 for more information.

**CONFERENCE/FUNCTIONS**

Conferences: Up to 120 Receptions: Up to 300
Lunches: Up to 200 Dinners: 20 to 200

- Information centre.
- Toilet facilities available.
- Baby changing facilities available.
- Closed 24-26 Dec.
- Nearby public car parking.
- Dedicated facilities, tours, carer tickets and wheelchair hire available.
- Assistance dogs only.
- The Pavilion Café is a perfect spot for afternoon tea in the royal grounds
- Shop offering everything from souvenirs and gifts, to fine jewellery.

- Weddings, dinners, receptions and gala celebrations. Visit hrp.org.uk/hireavenue or call 020 3166 6115.

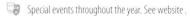

- Special events throughout the year. See website .

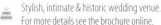

- Stylish, intimate & historic wedding venue. For more details see the brochure online.

BANQUETING HOUSE

# HOUSES OF PARLIAMENT

## www.parliament.uk/visit

Tours of the Houses of Parliament offer visitors a unique combination of 1,000 years of history, modern day politics and stunning art and architecture. See the famous green benches in the Commons Chamber, the gilded throne canopy in the Lords Chamber and the medieval hammer-beam roof in Westminster Hall. Add stylish afternoon tea with a view of the River Thames.

- Photography and mobile phone use in Parliament is limited to certain areas. Please ask for advice.
- Toilet facilities and disabled WC.
- Family friendly with baby changing facilities available.
- When the Houses are sitting, visitors are welcome to watch debates from the public galleries.
- Tour route accessible. Alt route via a lift available if required.
- Assistance dogs only.

 Approx. 60-75 mins.

 Approx. 90 mins.

 Jubilee Café - selection of light meals & drinks.

 Jubilee Shop off Westminster Hall offers an attractive range of gifts, souvenirs & books.

 For seasonal activities and events please see the website.

**CONTACT**
Contact: Bookings Team Tel: 020 7219 4114
Email: visitparliament@parliament.uk

**LOCATION**
Westminster, London SW1A 0AA
Map Ref: 20:M8 - Central London, 1km S of Trafalgar Square.
Underground: Westminster.

**OPENING TIMES**
Tours every Sat throughout the year & most weekdays during parliamentary recesses including the summer, Christmas & Easter.

**ADMISSION**
Check website for tour dates & prices. Discounted group rates for groups of 10 plus if booked in advance.

# KEATS HOUSE

## www.keatshouse.org.uk

Discover the beauty of poetry and place in the former home of the Romantic poet John Keats. Displays of original manuscripts, artefacts and paintings tell the story of how the young poet found inspiration, friendship and love 200 years ago in this stunning Regency villa. Listen to Keats's famous odes, see the engagement ring he gave to his true love Fanny Brawne, or explore our beautiful garden. The House comes alive with regular events, from poetry performances to family fun days.

**CONTACT** Owner: City of London Corporation Tel: 020 7332 3868
Email: keatshouse@cityoflondon.gov.uk

**LOCATION** 10 Keats Grove, Hampstead, London NW3 2RR Map Ref: 20:K3
Hampstead Heath (London Overground): Hampstead or Belsize Park (Northern Line).

**OPENING TIMES** Wed-Sun: 11am-5pm.

**ADMISSION** See website for latest prices and concessions.

- Prams can be left in the covered veranda area outside.
- An accessible toilet is available.
- Toilets located at back of the building and include baby changing facilities.
- Open all year round.
- Disabled parking space.
- Ground floor. Tactile & subtitled AV exhibits. Accessible toilet.
- 1.30pm & 3pm - check before visiting.
- Learning programme.
- Books, souvenirs, vintage items & gifts.
- Available for private hire.
- Poetry performances, talks, walks and special events. 3rd Sun of month Family Day.

# WESTMINSTER CATHEDRAL

## westminstercathedral.org.uk

The Roman Catholic Cathedral of the Archbishop of Westminster. Spectacular building in the Byzantine style, designed by J F Bentley, opened in 1903, famous for its mosaics, marble and music. Tower viewing gallery has spectacular views across London. Exhibition of vestments, rare ecclesiastical objects and sacred relics.

**CONTACT** Owner: Diocese of Westminster
Contact: Revd Canon Christopher Tuckwell
Tel: 020 7798 9055

**LOCATION** Victoria St, London, SW1P 1LT
Map Ref: 20:L9 - Off Victoria Street, near Victoria Station.

**OPENING TIMES** All year: 7am-7pm.

**ADMISSION** - Free.
Tower : Adult £6, Concession £3, Family £12,
Exhibition: Adult £2, Conc £1, Family £4.
Joint Tower and Exhibition: Adult £7, Concession £4, Family £14.

- TripAdvisor 2014 Cert of Excellence.
- Tel. for times at Easter & Christmas.
- Booking required.
- Worksheets & tours.

 Café.

 Products which relate to or echo the art and architecture of the Cathedral.

 Tel. 020 7798 9028 for Tower/Exhibition opening times.

## BANQUETING HOUSE

**hrp.org.uk/banquetinghouse**

This revolutionary structure was the first in England to be built in a Palladian style. It was designed by Inigo Jones for James I, and work finished in 1622. Intended for the splendour and exuberance of court masques, the Banqueting House is probably most famous for one real life drama: the execution of Charles I which took place here in 1649. One of Charles's last sights as he walked to his death was the magnificent ceiling painted by Peter Paul Rubens in 1630-4.

**CONTACT** Owner: Historic Royal Palaces
Contact: Banqueting House Visitor Services
Tel: 0844 482 7777
Email: banquetinghouse@ hrp.org.uk

**LOCATION** Whitehall, London SW1A 2ER Map Ref: 20:M8- Located on Whitehall in central London, a short walk from Westminster, Charing Cross and Embankment stations.

**OPENING TIMES** Mon-Sun 10am-5pm. Closed 24, 25, 26 Dec & 1 Jan. Before visiting, please confirm we are open.

**ADMISSION** See website for prices.

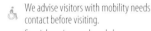

We advise visitors with mobility needs contact before visiting.

Special sessions and workshops designed for pupils of all ages.

Souvenirs and gifts, to fine jewellery.

Weddings, receptions, dinners, award ceremonies.

Please see website for detail.

## KEW PALACE

**www.hrp.org.uk/kewpalace**

Kew Palace was built as a private house in 1631 but became a royal residence between 1729 and 1818. More like a home than a palace, the privacy and intimacy of this smallest of English royal palaces made it the favourite country retreat for King George III and his family in the late 18th Century. Don't miss the chance to climb to the top of the Great Pagoda for breathtaking views over Kew Gardens.

**CONTACT** Owner: Historic Royal Palaces
Tel: 0203 166 6000
Email: kewpalace@hrp.org.uk

**LOCATION** Kew, Richmond, Surrey TW9 3AB Map Ref: 19:C7 - A307. Junction A307 & A205 (1m Chiswick roundabout M4).

**OPENING TIMES** Apr-Sep 10.30am-5.30pm. Last entry 5pm.

**ADMISSION** Free of charge. Admission tickets to Kew Gardens must be purchased to gain access to Kew Palace. (For gardens prices, see website). Extra ticket required for the Great Pagoda.

Toilet facilities available.

Baby changing facilities available.

Parking available.

WC's.

Weddings, receptions, dinners, meetings.

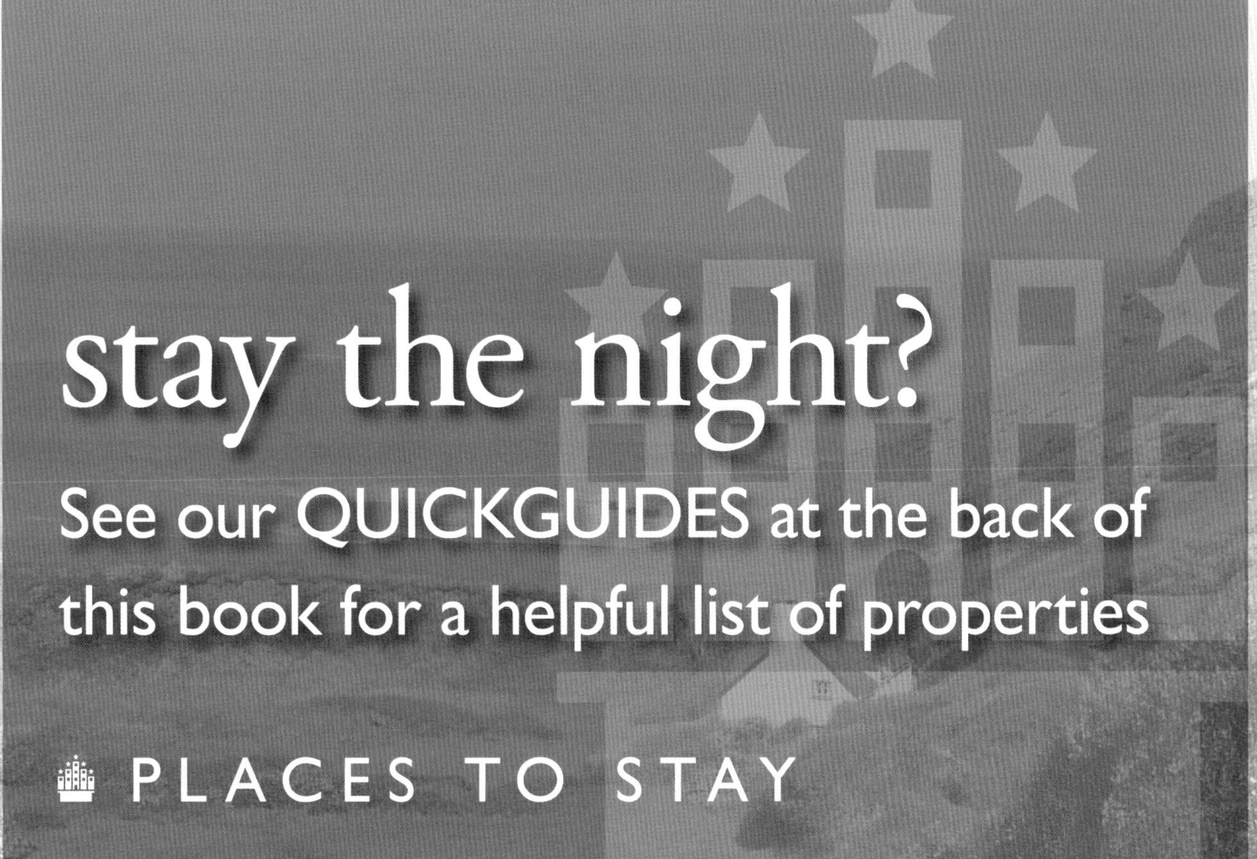
stay the night?
See our QUICKGUIDES at the back of
this book for a helpful list of properties
PLACES TO STAY

**18 FOLGATE STREET**
Spitalfields, East London E1 6BX
**Tel:** 020 7247 4013 **Email:** info@dennisevershouse.co.uk

**18 STAFFORD TERRACE**
London W8 7BH
**Tel:** 020 7602 3316 **Email:** museums@rbkc.gov.uk

**2 WILLOW ROAD**
2 Willow Road, Hampstead, London NW3 1TH
**Tel:** 020 7435 6166 **Email:** 2willowroad@nationaltrust.org.uk

**APSLEY HOUSE**
Hyde Park Corner, London W1J 7NT
**Tel:** 020 7499 5676 **Email:** customers@english-heritage.org.uk

**BENJAMIN FRANKLIN HOUSE**
36 Craven Street, London WC2N 5NF
**Tel:** 020 7925 1405 **Email:** info@benjaminfranklinhouse.org

**BOSTON MANOR HOUSE**
Boston Manor Road, Brentford TW8 9JX
**Tel:** 0845 456 2800 **Email:** victoria.northwood@cip.org.uk

**BUCKINGHAM PALACE**
Brentford SW1A 1AA
**Tel:** 020 7766 7300 **Email:** bookinginfo@royalcollection.org.uk

**BURGH HOUSE & HAMPSTEAD MUSEUM**
New End Square, Hampstead, London NW3 1LT
**Tel:** 020 7431 0144 **Email:** info@burghhouse.org.uk

**CARLYLE'S HOUSE**
24 Cheyne Row, Chelsea, London SW3 5HL
**Tel:** 020 7352 7087 **Email:** carlyleshouse@nationaltrust.org.uk

**THE CHARTERHOUSE**
Charterhouse Square, London EC1M 6AN
**Tel:** 020 3818 8873 **Email:** tours@thecharterhouse.org

**CHELSEA PHYSIC GARDEN**
66 Royal Hospital Road, London SW3 4HS
**Tel:** 020 7352 5646 **Email:** enquiries@chelseaphysicgarden.co.uk

**CHISWICK HOUSE & GARDENS**
Chiswick House, Burlington Lane, London W4 2RP
**Tel:** 020 3141 3350 **Email:** mail@chgt.org.uk

**DR JOHNSON'S HOUSE**
17 Gough Square, London, EC4A 3DE
**Tel:** 020 7353 3745 **Email:** curator@drjohnsonshouse.org

**ELTHAM PALACE & GARDENS**
Eltham Palace, Court Yard, Eltham, London SE9 5QE
**Tel:** 020 8294 2548 **Email:** customers@english-heritage.org.uk

**EMERY WALKER'S HOUSE**
7 Hammersmith Terrace, London W6 9TS
**Tel:** 020 8741 4104 **Email:** admin@emerywalker.org.uk

**FENTON HOUSE**
Hampstead Grove, London NW3 6SP
**Tel:** 020 7435 3471 **Email:** fentonhouse@nationaltrust.org.uk

**FORTY HALL**
Forty Hill, Enfield, Middlesex EN2 9HA
**Tel:** 020 8363 8196 **Email:** forty.hall@enfield.gov.uk

**FREUD MUSEUM**
20 Maresfield Gardens, London NW3 5SX
**Tel:** 020 7435 2002 **Email:** info@freud.org.uk

**FULHAM PALACE & MUSEUM**
Bishop's Avenue, Fulham, London SW6 6EA
**Tel:** 020 7736 3233 **Email:** admin@fulhampalace.org

**HAM HOUSE & GARDEN**
Ham Street, Richmond-upon-Thames, Surrey TW10 7RS
**Tel:** 020 8940 1950 **Email:** hamhouse@nationaltrust.org.uk

**HANDEL & HENDRIX**
25 Brook Street, London W1K 4HB
**Tel:** 020 7495 1685 **Email:** mail@handelhendrix.org

**HOGARTH'S HOUSE**
Hogarth Lane, Great West Road, London W4 2QN
**Tel:** 020 8994 6757 **Email:** john.collins@carillionservices.co.uk

**KENWOOD HOUSE**
Hampstead Lane, London NW3 7JR
**Tel:** 020 8348 1286 **Email:** kenwood.house@english-heritage.org.uk

**LEIGHTON HOUSE MUSEUM**
12 Holland Park Road, London W14 8LZ
**Tel:** 020 7602 3316 **Email:** museums@rbkc.gov.uk

**MARBLE HILL HOUSE**
Richmond Road, Twickenham TW1 2NL
**Tel:** 020 8892 5115 **Email:** customers@english-heritage.org.uk

**OLD ROYAL NAVAL COLLEGE & QUEEN'S HOUSE**
King William Walk, Greenwich, London SE10 9NN
**Tel:** 020 8269 4747 **Email:** boxoffice@ornc.org

**OSTERLEY PARK & HOUSE**
Jersey Road, Isleworth, Middlesex, TW7 4RB
**Tel:** 02082 325050 **Email:** osterley@nationaltrust.org.uk

**RANGER'S HOUSE**
Chesterfield Walk, Blackheath, London SE10 8QX
**Tel:** 020 8853 0035 **Email:** customers@english-heritage.org.uk

**RED HOUSE**
Red House Lane, Bexleyheath DA6 8JF
**Tel:** 0208 303 6359

**SOMERSET HOUSE**
Strand, London WC2R 1LA
**Tel:** 020 7845 4600 **E-mail:** info@somersethouse.org.uk

**SOUTHSIDE HOUSE**
3 Woodhayes Road, Wimbledon, London SW19 4RJ
**Tel:** 020 8946 7643 **E-mail:** info@southsidehouse.com

**SPENCER HOUSE**
27 St James's Place, London SW1A 1NR
**Tel:** 020 7514 1958 **E-mail:** tours@spencerhouse.co.uk

**STRAWBERRY HILL**
268 Waldegrave Road, Twickenham TW1 4ST
**Tel:** 020 8744 1241 **E-mail:** enquiry@strawberryhillhouse.org.uk

**WILLIAM MORRIS GALLERY**
Lloyd Park, Forest Road, Walthamstow, London E17 4PP
**Tel:** 020 8527 9782

# ENJOY HERITAGE

BECOME A

# TIME TRAVELLER

**FREE MEMBERSHIP**

- Regular email offers & updates

**VIP MEMBERSHIP** £27.50 *per year*

- Regular email offers & updates
- Quarterly issues of Time Traveller
- A **FREE** Hudson's Guide *(RRP £17.99)*
- A **FREE** Signpost Premier Selection *(RRP £10.99)*
- A vote in the UK Heritage Awards

UK HERITAGE AWARDS 2019

*join now...* shop.visitheritage.co.uk

Visit HERITAGE
THE HOME OF HERITAGE

020 3880 5059

sales@visitheritage.co.uk

www.visitheritage.co.uk

# SOUTH EAST

OXFORDSHIRE • BERKSHIRE • BUCKINGHAMSHIRE • HAMPSHIRE
ISLE OF WIGHT • SURREY • SUSSEX • KENT

THE SEVEN SISTERS, THE WHITE CLIFFS OF DOVER. ©VISITBRITAIN/CHARLIE WAITE

**COUNTRYSIDE**
Chalk downs
New Forest
The Solent

**HERITAGE**
Mansions & manor houses
Plant collector gardens
Naval heritage

**FOOD**
Apples & cherries
Banoffee pie
Fine English wine

# Belmont House

## Ring time on the Empire

Stop in any room at Belmont House on the hour to capture the melodic chime of the clocks that fill every room. There are 340 clocks and watches here, collected by the late 5th Lord Harris, whose home this was. Today Lord Harris' collection is the finest in private hands in Britain. Fascinating clock tours happen monthly.

BELMONT HOUSE THE EXTERIOR AND ORANGERY © DAVID ARCHER/BELMONT HOUSE TRUST

The atmosphere here is Regency elegance; the house was designed by neo-classical architect Samuel Wyatt in 1793. It originally provided a sanctuary for the 1st Lord Harris when he returned newly wealthy from India in 1801. Harris had successfully led the troops in the defeat of the fabulously wealthy Tipu Sultan of Mysore. It turned him from a career soldier into a landowning 'nabob' (official or governor). The family stuck with the British Empire; his son fought at Waterloo, his grandson was Governor of both Trinidad and Madras and his great-grandson was Governor of Bombay. The house has Louis XV and English Georgian furniture, enlivened by the occasional tiger or elephant's foot, and over 40 watercolours of the celebrated 19th century Trinidadian painter, Michel Jean Cazabon.

LOUIS XV CHAIRS AND SETTEES IN THE DRAWING ROOM © DAVID ARCHER/BELMONT HOUSE TRUST

There is another important reason for making a journey to Belmont. It is one of the homes of British cricket. The 4th Lord Harris was a first class cricketer in the 1880s, rightly regarded as 'the Father of English Cricket'. Book a stay in the Prospect Tower, built as a tea house but converted into a cricket pavilion by the 4th Lord Harris and now a charming Landmark Trust holiday cottage for two.

The house is open for booked tours but the gardens open all year round. There are herbaceous borders, a Walnut Walk and a superb Pinetum. Don't miss the more eccentric delights of the Victorian shell grotto and the family's pet cemetery. ■

THE WALLED GARDEN © DAVID ARCHER/BELMONT HOUSE TRUST

# South East

## Top 3 Venues

KINGSTON BAGPUIZE HOUSE MARQUEE

### Kingston Bagpuize House, Oxfordshire

Set in the beautiful Vale of the White Horse in Oxfordshire, Kingston Bagpuize House and grounds are available for exclusive hire for weddings and corporate events, including the use of the marquee on the West Park during the Summer months. The charm of this 300-year-old house is that it is still lived in today as a family home. Private dinners for up to 40 people, breakfast meetings and presentations can be comfortably hosted within the house itself. The entrance hall and drawing room of the house have featured on the popular television period drama Downton Abbey.

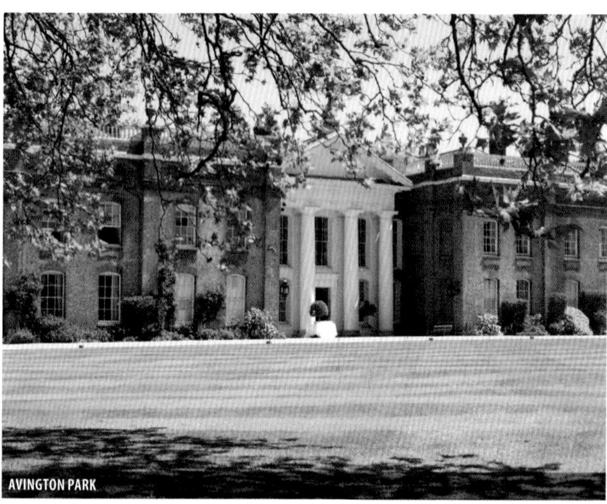
AVINGTON PARK

### Avington Park, Hampshire

Set in acres of parkland bordering the River Itchen in Winchester, the house is available for exclusive hire only so you really have the freedom to tailor your event. The estate is licensed for civil ceremonies and well equipped to host small, private dinners or meetings as well as larger conferences. The surrounding lawns and meadow mean that there is plenty of room for outdoor pursuits. There is also a 9-hole golf course and fishing nearby. Avington has at one time played host to King Charles II and King George IV.

PENSHURST BARONS HALL ©JIGSAW DESIGN AND PUBLISHING

### Penshurst Place, Kent

The team at Penshurst takes care of every little detail for you including recommendations for accommodation for your party if required. They can organise rooms at the Leicester Arms Hotel just opposite Penshurst Place as well as having personally visited other hotels and B&Bs in the area. Also available for Christmas parties and dining, The Baron's Hall and The Sunderland Room are just two of the impressive choice of spaces available for your event. Penshurst was once used by Henry VIII as a hunting lodge and was also visited often by Queen Elizabeth I.

**Henley Royal Regatta, Oxfordshire** *3rd - 7th July 2019*

**Mayday Celebrations, Magdalen Bridge, Oxfordshire** *1st May 2019*

**Cowes Week, Isle of Wight, Hampshire** *10th - 17th August 2019*

## Top 3 Annual Events

### The Beaulieu Autojumble, Hampshire
*April and September*

Perfect for the motor enthusiast, and those working on projects that require parts, these hugely popular events start with the Spring Autojumble in April. Browse through thousands of stalls to find that elusive spare part. The Spring event also includes the Land Rover Rummage, popular with Land Rover enthusiasts. The larger International Autojumble event takes place in September. Look out for a host of other specialist motoring events taking place throughout the year at Beaulieu. Beaulieu is also home to the National Motor Museum.

INTERNATIONAL AUTOJUMBLE

### International Jousting & Medieval Tournament Arundel Castle, West Sussex - *July*

Competitors descend on Arundel from all over the world to take part in this thrilling tournament which takes place over several days. The medieval sport of jousting is a true test of skill and strength, pushing each competitor to their limit before an eventual winner is crowned. The highlight of Arundel's events calendar, there is something to appeal to all ages. As well as jousting there are crafts, stalls, music and displays to entertain all the family. You can even try your hand at archery!

ARUNDEL CASTLE SIEGE 2016 - GOLDFISH PHOTOGRAPHIC

### Christmas at Blenheim Palace, Oxfordshire
*Late November - 1st January*

Walk the spectacular Winter Trail, improved and re-imagined each year, lit with lasers, projections and twinkling pea-lights. See the formal gardens illuminated and take a walk around the Christmas Market. There are Christmas themed events taking place at Blenheim day and night in the run-up to the big day and beyond.

STAFF DECORATE ONE OF THE GIANT CHRISTMAS TREES IN THE GREAT HALL AT BLENHEIM PALACE

# South East

## Places to stay and eat

DRAKE'S HOTEL

### Drake's Hotel

Sitting directly on the sea front with fabulous views of the iconic Palace Pier, Drakes retains its pole position as the most luxurious and romantic boutique hotel in Brighton. Having opened their doors over 12 years ago, the hotel has lost none of its edginess and city chic. Their discreet sign says everything about this place. They're not into flashy displays at this doublefronted listed Georgian townhouse and most people who stay there have been recommended by someone in the know. Rooms are spectacularly stylish, most with freestanding baths in front of large picture windows (the best views from the first floor rooms), with luscious handmade beds dressed with goose down duvets and velvet throws. On request, a bubble bath can be run for your arrival and a selection of fabulous extras can be ordered to enhance your stay. Do remember to book a table in their excellent fine dining restaurant, having enjoyed an aperitif in the slick cocktail bar beforehand.

**43 Marine Parade, Brighton, East Sussex BN2 1PE**

**01273 696934**

**www.drakesofbrighton.com**
**info@drakesofbrighton.com**

### White Horse Hotel & Brasserie

*Hotel*

19 Market Place, Romsey,
Hampshire SO51 8ZJ

01794 512431

www.thewhitehorseromsey.co.uk
thewhitehorse@twhromsey.com

### 4 Canon Lane at Chichester Cathedral

*Hotel*

4 Canon Lane, Chichester,
West Sussex PO19 1PX

01243 813585

www.chichestercathedral.org.uk
events@chichestercathedral.org.uk

### The March Hare

*Restaurant*

2-4 South Hill,
Guildford, Surrey GU1 3SY

01483 401 530

www.marchhareguildford.com
MarchHare.Guildford@
whitebrasserie.com

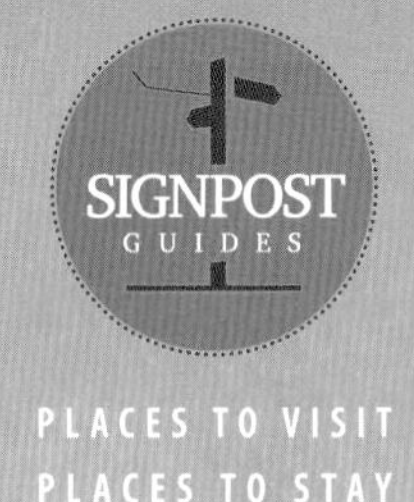


## Powder Mills Hotel

The Powder Mills is a stunning privately owned Listed Georgian country house hotel set in 150 acres of parkland, lakes and woods, adjoining the famous 1066 Battlefield and Abbey. Guests can explore beautiful woodland trails and fish for carp and pike in the 7 acre lake, or enjoy the outdoor swimming pool in season. The hotel has a relaxed, welcoming atmosphere and exudes period charm with rooms full of comfy sofas, antiques, interesting artwork and a selection of good books. Public rooms have wonderful log fires in winter. The hotel is ideally located for exploring Sussex and Kent, with the Channel Tunnel just one hour's drive away.

There are interesting castles and gardens to visit nearby, including Bodiam, Sissinghurst and Batemans and numerous antique shops to explore in neighbouring picturesque villages. Truly a magical spot to while away a few days.

**Powdermill Lane, Battle, East Sussex TN33 0SP**

**01424 775511**

**www.powdermillshotel.com**
**reservations@thepowdermills.com**

POWDER MILLS HOTEL

### The Lamb at Angmering
*Restaurant*

The Square, Angmering
Littlehampton BN16 4EQ

01903 774300

www.thelamb-angmering.com
info@thelamb-angmering.com

### Annie's Tea Room
*Tea Room*

Annie's at Canal Yard, Canal Road
Thrupp, Kidlington OX5 1JZ

07425 621742

www.anniestearoom.co.uk

### The Cobblestone Tea House
*Tea Room*

7 Cobblestone Walk, 74 High Street
Steyning BN44 3RD

01903 366171

www.facebook.com
The-Cobblestone-Tea-House

South East

# DORNEY COURT

**www.dorneycourt.co.uk**

'One of the finest Tudor Manor Houses in England' - *Country Life*. Grade I Listed and noted for its outstanding architectural and historical importance. Home of the Palmers for 400 years, passing from father to son over 14 generations. Highlights include the magnificent Great Hall, oak and lacquer furniture and artwork which combine to tell the story of the House. The stunning Coach House Barn with its landscaped courtyard provides a beautiful space for events.

- Film & photo shoots. Weddings. Events No stiletto heels.
- Loo's equipped with disabled facilities at the House and Kitchen Garden.
- Accepts Euros.
- By special appointment. Min 20
- Plenty of free parking available.
- Welcomes disabled and special needs visitors. Video tour of upstairs rooms.
- Obligatory. A range of flexible options for visiting Dorney Court.
- Guided tour aimed at the curriculum with a focus on the Tudors.

- The Tea Room offers a range of light snacks, homemade goodies, soft drinks & delicious cream teas.

- Licensed. The Palmer Arms - good hearty food in a classic pub setting.

- Gift shop offering stationery, postcards & mementos of a wonderful day.

- Garden centre (www.dckg.co.uk).
- Flexible venue for conferences, meetings and launches.

- For events & activity days please see the 'Events' section of the website.
- Perfect wedding reception venue with landscaped gardens and 12C Church.

- Perfectly suited for filming & photographic shoots; unquestionably unique with stunning backdrops.

**CONTACT** Owner/Contact: Mr James Palmer Tel: 01628 604638
Email: info@dorneycourt.co.uk Twitter: @dorneycourt

**LOCATION** Nr. Windsor, Berkshire SL4 6QP
Map Ref: 3:G2 5 mins off M4/J7, 10 mins from Windsor, 2m W of Eton.

**OPENING TIMES** May Bank Holidays (5,6 May and 26, 27 May) and all Aug - open afternoons 1.30pm - 5pm.

**ADMISSION** Adult £9, Child (10 yrs+) £5.50, OAPs £8.50.
Groups: 10+ £8.50pp when open to public.
Private group rates at other times.

DORNEY COURT HALLWAY

## HUGHENDEN

NATIONAL TRUST IMAGES/MATTHEW ANTROBUS

**nationaltrust.org.uk/hughenden**

Amid rolling Chilterns countryside, discover the hideaway of Benjamin Disraeli, the most unlikely Victorian Prime Minister. Stroll through his German Forest, relax in his elegant garden and imagine dining with Queen Victoria in the atmospheric manor.

**CONTACT** Owner: National Trust Contact: The Estate Office Tel: 01494 755573 Info Line: 01494 755565 Email: hughenden@nationaltrust.org.uk **LOCATION** High Wycombe, Buckinghamshire HP14 4LA Map Ref: 3:F1 - 1½ m North of High Wycombe on the West side of the A4128. **OPEN** 1 Jan-31 Dec, daily. **ADMISSION** House and Garden: Adult £13.00, Child £6.50, Family £32.50, Groups: Adult £11.10, Child £5.55. (Free for NT members).

Prices includes voluntary 10% donation. Closed 24 & 25 Dec. See website for details Parking is available. Partial. WCs. Stableyard café & Dizzy's tea room. Gift shop, with a range of local products and plant stall and a second hand book shop.

## WOTTON HOUSE

The Capability Brown Pleasure Grounds at Wotton, currently undergoing restoration, are related to the Stowe gardens; both belonged to the Grenville family when Brown laid out the Wotton grounds between 1750 and 1767. A series of man-made features on the 3-mile circuit include bridges, temples and statues. Please note that only the Pleasure Grounds are open to the public, not the House.

**CONTACT** Owner: David Gladstone Tel: 01844 238363 Email: davidgladstone@wottonhouse.com **LOCATION** Wotton Underwood, Aylesbury, Buckinghamshire HP18 0SB Map Ref: 7:B11 Either A41 turn off at Kingswood, or M40/J7 via Thame. **OPEN** 3 Apr - 4 Sep, Wed only 2 - 5pm. Also 22 Apr, 27 May, 29 Jun, 3 Aug, 31 Aug. **ADMISSION** Adult £6, Conc £3, Child free. Groups max 25.

Limited parking for coaches. Accessible. Dogs welcome on leads. Guided tours obligatory.

NATIONAL MOTOR MUSEUM - BEAULIEU

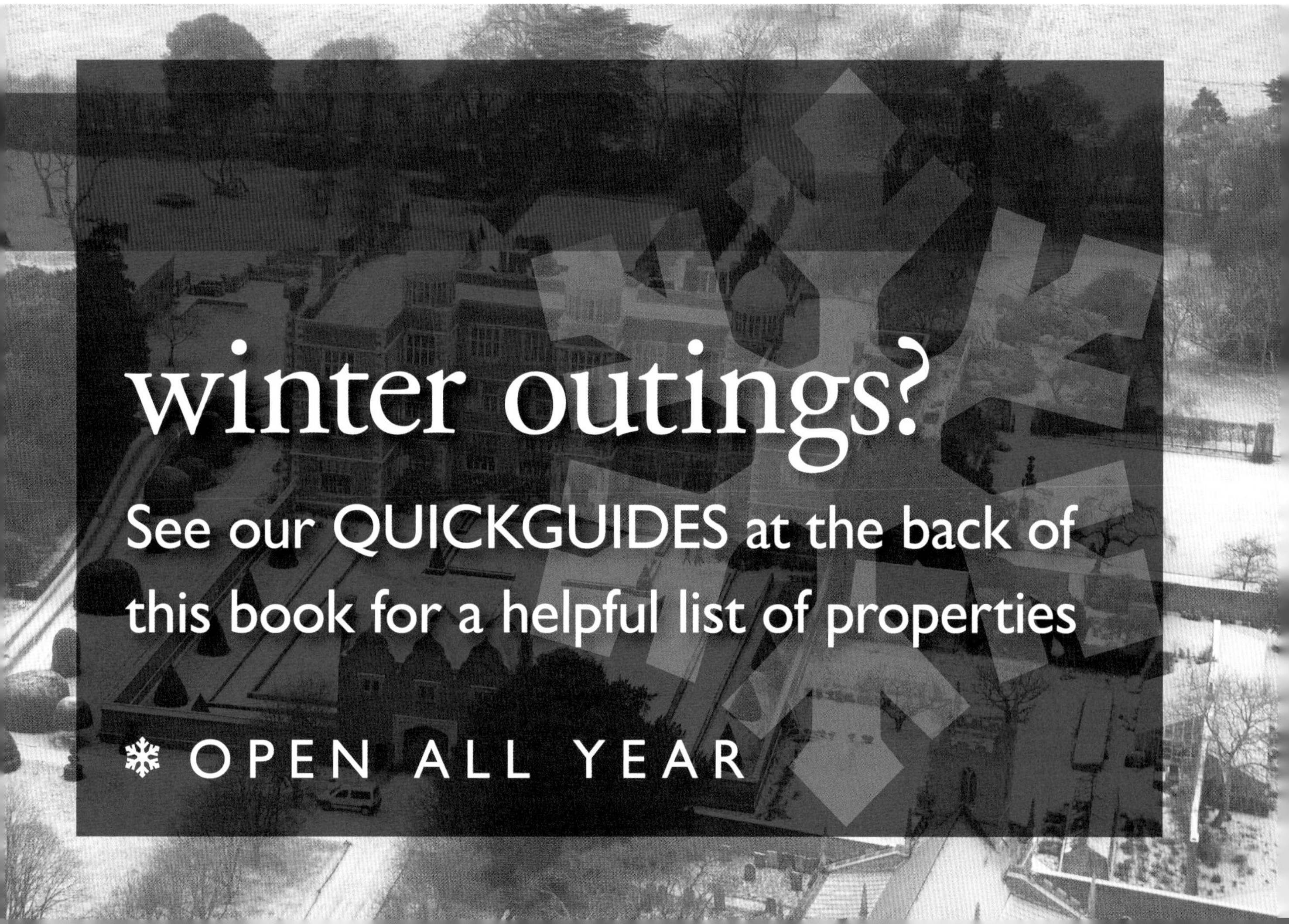

# BEAULIEU

www.beaulieu.co.uk

UK HERITAGE AWARDS 2018

WINNER
BEST EVENT/ EXHIBITION

PALACE HOUSE

BEAULIEU ABBEY

## Beaulieu, in the heart of the New Forest, features a range of heritage attractions

**Palace House**

Once the gatehouse of the medieval Beaulieu Abbey, Palace House has been the Montagu family home since 1538. Explore this gothic styled Victorian country home as costumed guides give you a flavour of life `below stairs' and share with you the fascinating history of the house and the generations who have lived there. Visit the recently restored Victorian Kitchen which has been put back to its original layout with a working range. Plus, enter through a false bookshelf door to the library which formed part of the late Lord Montagu's private apartments. Discover the remarkable story of two women in the Montagu family in 'The Lady and The Rebel' exhibition. Palace House is home to the first dedicated Soviet Russian art gallery in the UK, displaying a selection of paintings and sculptures from the Art Russe foundation.

**Beaulieu Abbey & Exhibition**

Founded on land gifted by King John to Cistercian monks in 1204, Beaulieu Abbey was largely destroyed during the Reformation. The conserved ruins demonstrate the scale of what was once a vast complex. One of the surviving buildings houses an exhibition on the history of the Abbey and the monks that lived and worked here.

**The National Motor Museum**

Over 250 vehicles tell the story of motoring in Britain from its pioneering origins to the present day. From the earliest motor carriages to classic family saloons, displays include historic sporting motors, modern rally cars, F1 racers and a rustic 1930's country garage. The Luxury of Motoring display follows the development, design and social history of luxury motoring, featuring a collection of over 25 Lalique mascots.

**Grounds & Gardens**

Explore the informal Wilderness Garden, fragrant Victorian Flower Garden and the Victorian Kitchen Garden. Enjoy the Mill Pond walk through parkland woods and look out for the Rufus Memorial Cairn – to commemorate the death of King William Rufus who, evidence suggests, was killed by an arrow whilst hunting at Beaulieu in 1100.

**OWNER**

Lord Montagu

**CONTACT**

Visitor Enquiries
Tel: 01590 612345
Email: visit@beaulieu.co.uk

**LOCATION**

Beaulieu, Hampshire SO42 7ZN
Map Ref: 3:C6
M27 to J2, A326, B3054 follow brown signs.
Take the local bus service within the New Forest.
There is a Station at Brockenhurst 7m away.

**TRANSPORT ROUTES**

Car | Bus | Train

**OPENING TIMES**

Summer Whitsun-Sep Daily, 10am-6pm.
Winter Oct-Whitsun Daily, 10am-5pm

Please check website for exact dates.

**ADMISSION**

All year Individual and group rates upon application.

Group Discount: 15+

**REGULAR EVENTS**

Beaulieu hosts a range of family-friendly and motoring themed events throughout the year.

Visit www.beaulieuevents.co.uk for details.

All ticket enquiries to our Special Events Booking Office. Tel 01590 612888.

- Allow 4-5 hours for visits. Helicopter landing point.
- WC's. There are 3 sets of disabled toilets on the site.
- Baby changing facilities available.
- Closed 25 Dec.
- Unlimited. Free admission for coach drivers plus voucher.
- WC. Wheelchairs in Visitor Reception by prior booking.
- Cycle route going through the estate.
- In grounds, on leads only.
- Attendants on duty.
- Professional staff available to assist.
- Part of the Brabazon Restaurant- sandwiches to cooked meals and tea & cold drinks.
- Seats 250.
- Palace House Kitchen Shop & Main Reception Shop.
- Beaulieu offers a versatile & unique venue with a difference. Conferences, meetings or receptions.
- Please see website.
- Please see: beaulieu.co.uk/corporate-and-weddings.

South East

# AVINGTON PARK

**www.avingtonpark.co.uk.**

From the wrought iron gates and long avenue of limes, approach well-tended lawns, bordering the river Itchen and the elegant Palladian facade. William Cobbett wrote of Avington Park that it was 'one of the prettiest places in the County' and indeed it is true today. Dating back to the 11th Century, and enlarged in 1670, the house enjoys magnificent painted and gilded state rooms overlooking lawns and parkland. Over the years Charles II and George IV stayed at various times. St Mary's, a fine Georgian church, may also be visited.

Rooms on show are the Main Hall, Library, Conservatory, Ballroom & Drawing Room.

Toilet facilities available.

Baby changing facilities available.

Parking available within the grounds.

Partial (ground floor only) and WC.

In grounds, on leads. Guide dogs only in house.

Guided tours.

Tea bar open during public openings.

Exclusive use for conferences, films, photoshoot's, private parties, seminars & corporate events.

Open-air theatre, two performances in summer.

Exclusive use for weddings.

**CONTACT** Owner/Contact: Mrs S L Bullen
Tel: 01962 779260 Email: enquiries@avingtonpark.co.uk

**LOCATION** Winchester, Hampshire, SO21 1DB
Map Ref: 3:D4 OS Ref: SU532323
4m NE of Winchester ½m S of B3047 in Itchen Abbas.

**OPENING TIMES** May - Sep: Suns & BH Mons & Mons in Aug, 2.30 - 5.30pm. Last tour 4.30pm. Group visits welcome by appointment all year round. Please contact for details.

**ADMISSION** Adult £12, Child £6.

# STANSTED PARK

**www.stanstedpark.co.uk**

UK HERITAGE AWARDS 2018 COMMENDED GREAT PLACES TO EAT

Stansted House and its Chapel stand in 1800 acres of parkland and ancient forest within the South Downs National Park. The state rooms are furnished as though the 10th Earl was still at home giving the visitor a real sense of a bygone era.

**CONTACT** Stansted Park Foundation, Estate Office Tel: 02392 412265 Email: enquiry@stanstedpark.co.uk

**LOCATION** Rowlands Castle, Hampshire, PO9 6DX Follow brown heritage signs from A3(M) J2 Emsworth or A27 Havant.

**OPENING TIMES** House & Chapel: Easter Sunday - end September; Sun, Mon, Tues & Wed 1pm-5pm (Last admission 4pm).

**ADMISSION** Adult £10, Concession £8, Child £5, Family £25 (5-15 years). Groups/Education visits by appointment.

Toilet and baby changing facilities

The grounds are open all year.

Use Garden Centre car park- disabled next to the Tea Room.

Suitable. WC's. Please download the access statement on the website.

By arrangement. Guided tours min 10.

By arrangement.

The Pavilion Tearoom, breakfast, light lunches, afternoon tea, cakes & beverages.

Shop for locally sourced food and drink.

Garden centre.

Private/corporate hire with 'wow' factor.

Please see website.

A beautiful venue for your ceremony.

## GILBERT WHITE & THE OATES COLLECTIONS

**gilbertwhiteshouse.org.uk**

Explore the lives of three explorers of the natural world. Home of the naturalist Gilbert White, and surrounded by 25 acres of garden and parkland. The Oates Collections celebrates the lives of 19th Century explorer Frank Oates, and Lawrence Oates who travelled on the ill-fated Terra Nova Expedition.

**CONTACT** Tel: 01420 511275 Email: info@gilbertwhiteshouse.org.uk
**LOCATION** High St, Selborne, Alton GU34 3JH Map Ref: 3:E4 Selborne is on B3006 from Alton to A3.
**OPEN** Jan-Feb ½ term Fri-Sun 10:30-4:30, Feb-Mar & Nov-Dec Tues-Sun 10:30-4:30 Apr-Oct Tues-Sun 10:30-5:00, July & August Open 7 days a week.
**ADMISSION** Adult £10, Conc £9, U16 £4.50, U5 Free.
Family Ticket (2A+3C): £24. Pre-booked group of 10+ £7.50. Garden Only: £6.

In village, 2 min walk. Suitable. Assistance provided. Dogs welcome in grounds only. Wonderful café in restored 18th Century stables. Books, local produce and gifts. Buy plants from garden. Provides the perfect British country venue for your wedding.

## GOODNESTONE PARK GARDENS

**www.goodnestoneparkgardens.co.uk**

'The most perfect English garden' 14 acres of beautiful tranquillity including a woodland area, large walled garden and tearoom.

**CONTACT** Francis Plumptre Tel: 01304 840107
Email: enquiries@goodnestoneparkgardens.co.uk
**LOCATION** Goodnestone Park, Nr Wingham, Canterbury, Kent CT3 1PL Map 4:N3. OS Ref TR254 544. 8m Canterbury, 1½m E of B2046 - A2 to Wingham Road, signposted from this road. Postcode of Car Park: CT3 1PJ. **OPENING TIMES** Apr: Sun 12 - 4, May - Aug: Tue, Wed, Thu, Fri 11-5pm and Sun 12-5pm, Sep: Sun 12-4pm.
**ADMISSION** Adult £7, Child (6-16) £2.00, Season Ticket £15.00, Family Season Ticket (2+2) £30.00, Groups (20+) £6.50 (out of opening hours £8.00). When areas of garden closed: £5.00

Suitable. WCs. Licensed. Partial. By arrangement. Parking. Guide dogs only. Plant Sales. Events please see website.

# STRATFIELD SAYE HOUSE

### www.stratfield-saye.co.uk

After the Duke of Wellington's victory against Napoleon at the Battle of Waterloo in 1815, the Duke chose Stratfield Saye as his country estate. The house contains many of the 1st Duke's possessions and is still occupied by his descendants being a family home rather than a museum.

- Toilet facilities available.
- Parking is available.
- WC. Please contact for further details see access statement on the website.
- Camping and caravanning in the country park.
- Access to Stratfield Saye House is by guided tour only.
- Tailored school visit packages, please contact for further details.
- Sourcing the best local ingredients for the farm shop & cafe; simply delicious.
- Farm shop selling cosmetics, home and garden goods.
- Contact for possible Corporate bookings/ packages in the country park
- Please see list of events in the country park section of the website.

**CONTACT** Owner: The Duke of Wellington
Contact: Estate Office Tel: 01256 882694

**LOCATION** Stratfield Saye, Hampshire RG7 2BZ
Map Ref: 3:E2 - Equidistant from Reading (M4/J11) & Basingstoke (M3/J6) 1½m W of the A33.

**OPENING TIMES** Easter: Thur 18 - Mon 22 April 2019
Summer: Thur 1 - Mon 26 Aug 2019

**ADMISSION** Weekdays: Adult £11.50, Child £4, Over 60s/Student £10.50
Gardens only: £4 Weekends: Adult £13.50, Child £5,
Over 60s/Student £12.50 Gardens only: £5
Private group visits by appointment only

# PENSHURST PLACE & GARDENS

### www.penshurstplace.com

Set in the beautiful Weald of Kent, Penshurst Place & Gardens has stood on the banks of the river Medway since the 14th century, when the awe-inspiring medieval Baron's Hall was built. The hall, 11 acres of formal gardens and huge adventure playground are just a snapshot of the many unmissable sights for visitors to the ancestral home of the Sidney family, who have made Penshurst Place their home since 1552.

Now in its 72nd year of being open to the public Penshurst Place is the go-to stately home for horticultural enthusiasts and passionate historians alike, as well as adults and children of all ages!

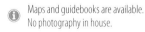

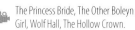

- Maps and guidebooks are available. No photography in house.
- Accessible toilets situated outside the Garden Restaurant and main entrance.
- Seasonal opening times. See website.
- Ample free parking for cars/coaches.
- Partial. See website for further details.
- Sustrans cycle route to Tonbridge across the wider estate parkland.
- Guided tours by appointment only.
- See website for educational information.
- Porcupine Pantry outside the paid perimeter. Open all year.
- Licensed Garden Restaurant.
- Gift Shop outside the paid perimeter. Open all year.
- Plant Centre outside the paid perimeter.
- Conferences and Christmas parties.
- See www.penshurstplace.com/whats-on
- Licensed ceremony and reception venue.
- The Princess Bride, The Other Boleyn Girl, Wolf Hall, The Hollow Crown.

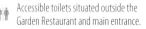

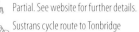

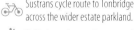

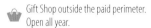

**OWNER** Viscount De L'Isle MBE

**CONTACT** Tel: 01892 870307 Email: contactus@penshurstplace.com

**LOCATION** Penshurst, Nr Tonbridge, Kent TN11 8DG Map Ref: 19:H12
From M25 Junction 5 follow A21 to Tonbridge, leaving at Hildenborough exit; then follow brown tourist signs. From M20/M26 Junction 2a follow A25 (Sevenoaks) A21 for Hildenborough, then follow brown tourist signs.

**OPENING TIMES** Open weekends only from 16 Feb to 24 Mar.
Half Term 18 - 22 Feb. (Gardens only open at this time) From 30 Mar to 27 Oct.

**ADMISSION** Adult (16+): House & Gardens, £12, Gardens only, £10. Child (5-15) House & Gardens, £6.50, Gardens only, £6.00. Up to two under 5's can enter for free per paying adult, charged at £2.50 per child, per visit thereafter.

# IGHTHAM MOTE

**www.nationaltrust.org.uk/ightham-mote**

'Ightham Mote is like an island in time. Within its walls, a single life is only a brief thing and a whole century is little more than a pause.'

Surrounded by a moat, Ightham Mote has a quirky charm of its own. Dating from 1320, it was home to medieval knights, Tudor courtiers, High Society Victorians and an American businessman. It isn't a place of grand avenues and imposing vistas, but a family home, which evokes a deep sense of history throughout its different styles. Surrounding the house are peaceful gardens comprising herbaceous borders, an orchard, lake and pleasure grounds.

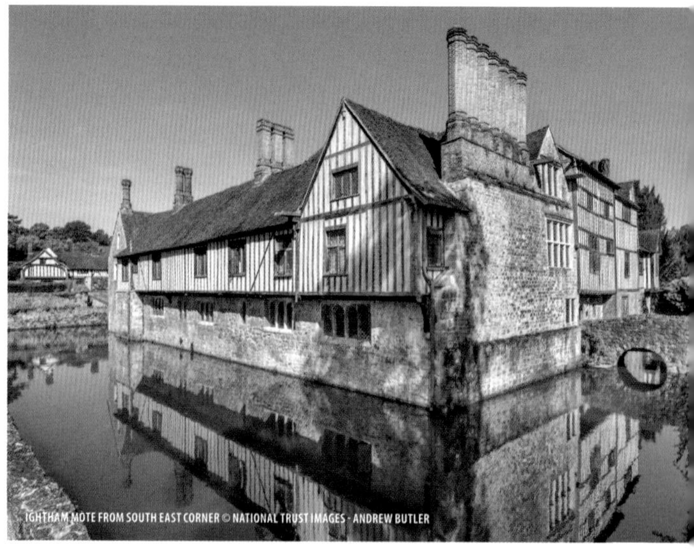

IGHTHAM MOTE FROM SOUTH EAST CORNER © NATIONAL TRUST IMAGES - ANDREW BUTLER

- Steep slope, passenger buggy/lower drop off available.
- Toilet facilities available.
- Baby changing facilities available.
- Open all year.
- Parking available.
- WCs. Wheelchairs ground floor access only
- Guided tours.
- Self-led or workshops available from £5 per person.
- Licensed.
- Gift Shop.
- Plant sales.
- Private or corporate venue.

**CONTACT** Tel: 01732 810378
Website: www.nationaltrust.org.uk/ightham-mote,
Email: Ighthammote@nationaltrust.org.uk

**LOCATION** Mote Rd, Ivy Hatch, Sevenoaks TN15 0NT
OS Ref TQ584 535. 6m E of Sevenoaks off A25.
2½ S of Ightham off A227.

**OPENING TIMES** Open daily all year, excl. 24 & 25 Dec.
10am - 5pm. House: 11am - 5pm, Mar - Oct, and 11am - 3pm, Dec.
Last entry ½ hour before closing. Some areas may be partially closed during winter months. See website for full details.

**ADMISSION** See website for details.

# QUEBEC HOUSE

**nationaltrust.org.uk/quebec-house**

The childhood home of General James Wolfe, Quebec House retains much of its original charm and family feel. Interactive collections and objects belonging to Wolfe are used to explore Georgian family life and Wolfe's most celebrated victory at the Battle of Quebec in 1759. It gives a glimpse into family life in the 1730's and you can have a go at some of the pastimes Wolfe and his family would have enjoyed, such as quill pen writing and we have Georgian style clothes that families can try on.
Every Sunday our volunteer cooks recreate some of Mrs Wolfe's eighteenth century recipes such as lemon drops, King or Queen cakes and macaroons, free tastings are available.

COPYRIGHT NATIONAL TRUST/CHRIS JONAS

- Translated hand held guides in French & German on the history of Quebec House & General Wolfe.
- Accessible toilets on the ground floor.
- Parking approx 80 yards away in the main town car park, free for 3 hours.
- Gravel paths, a ramp at the front of the house. One step on the ground floor and staircase.
- Dogs on short leads welcome in grounds. Guide dogs only in house.
- Guided tours at 12pm & 12:30pm (book on arrival). On Suns Mrs Wolfe's recipes are re-created.
- Groups of children for educational visits by arrangement.
- Tea room selling light refreshments, outside chairs and tables.
- The shop is in the coach house, second hand books area in the tea room.
- See the 'What's on' section of the website for all upcoming events.

**CONTACT** Owner: National Trust
Contact: Marketing & Development Manager Tel: 01959 567430
Email: quebechouse@nationaltrust.org.uk

**LOCATION** Quebec Square, Westerham, Kent, TN16 1TD Map Ref: 4:M3

**OPENING TIMES** House open Wed 27 Feb – Sun 3 Nov,
Weds - Suns, private tours at 12pm and 12.30pm, free flow around the house from 1 - 5pm. Coach house, refreshment area and exhibition open from 11am - 5pm, last entry 4.30pm.

**ADMISSION** Adult £5.90, Child £2.90, Family £14.50
Groups +15: Adult £5.50, Child £2.75.

# LEEDS CASTLE

www.leeds-castle.com

Leeds Castle, 'the loveliest Castle in the world' is celebrating its 900th anniversary in 2019.

Open daily, discover the glorious gardens and grounds, spiralling yew maze, free-flying falconry displays, leisurely punting trips and the unique Dog Collar Museum.

Children will enjoy riding on Elsie the Castle Land Train, taking a trip on the ferry boat and the adventure playgrounds. Leeds Castle is set in 500 acres of beautiful Kent parkland with something new to discover every day.

With an exciting programme of events planned for this landmark year in the Castle's history, keep an eye on the website for dates and further information.

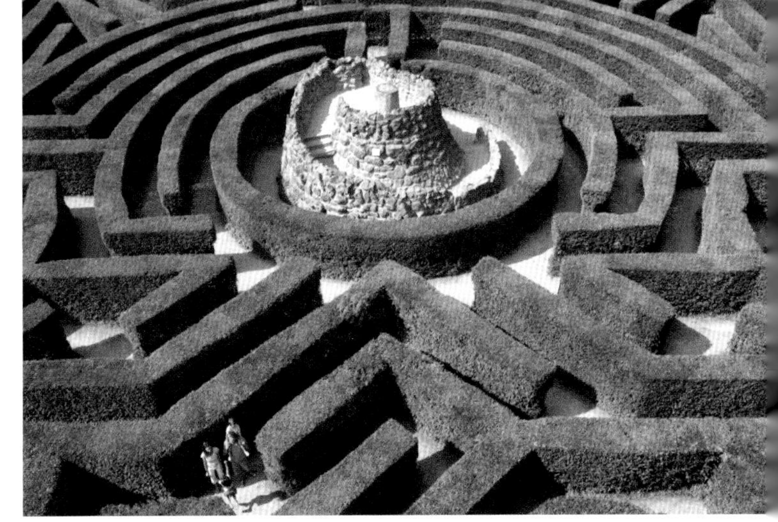

**CONTACT**

Owner: Leeds Castle Foundation
Tel: 01622 765400 Fax: 01622 735616
Email: enquiries@leeds-castle.co.uk

**LOCATION**

Maidstone, Kent ME17 1PL
Map Ref: 4:L3 From London to A20/M20/J8, 40m, 1 hr.
7m E of Maidstone, ¼m S of A20.

**OPENING TIMES**

Summer:
1 Apr-30 Sep Daily, 10.30am-4.30pm (last adm).
Winter:
1 Oct-31 Mar Daily, 10.30am-3pm (last adm).

**ADMISSION**

Annual Tickets (prices valid until 31 Mar 2019).

Adults £25.50
Senior Citizen £22.50
Student £22.50
Visitor with disabilities £22.50
Child (4-15yrs) £17.50
Infants (under 4yrs) Free

Toilet and disabled toilet facilities available.

Baby changing facilities available.

Accepts Euros.

Closed on the first weekend of November for fireworks and Christmas Day.

Free parking. Hard standing spaces reserved for visitors with disabilities.

Please ask for assistance and information. Wheelchairs are available on loan free of charge.

B&B, Holiday Cottages & Glamping.

An audio tour can be collected from the Castle Shop at a reduced rate for visitors with disabilities.

Restaurant available for lunch and evening dinner bookings.

Banquets, meetings, seminars, presentations and conferences.

For the latest events please see the 'What's On' section of the website.

# RESTORATION HOUSE

www.restorationhouse.co.uk

Fabled city mansion deriving its name from the stay of Charles II on the eve of The Restoration. This complex ancient house has beautiful interiors with exceptional early paintwork related to decorative scheme 'run up' for Charles' visit. The house also inspired Dickens to create 'Miss Havisham' here. 'Interiors of rare historical resonance and poetry', Country Life.

Fine English furniture and strong collection of English portraits (Mytens, Kneller, Dahl, Reynolds and several Gainsboroughs). Charming interlinked walled gardens and ongoing restoration of monumental Renaissance water garden A private gem. 'There is no finer pre-civil war town house in England than this' - *Simon Jenkins, The Times.* 'Deserves a medal' - *Jools Holland.*

Make sure to visit the Renaissance Water garden, including access to oculus domed gazebo, dramatic tiered terracing with presiding Matthew Darbyshire Farnese Hercules and other compelling antique statues.

**CONTACT**

Owner: R Tucker & J Wilmot
Contact: Robert Tucker Tel: 01634 848520
Email: robert.tucker@restorationhouse.co.uk

**LOCATION**

17-19 Crow Lane, Rochester, Kent ME1 1RF
Map Ref: 4:K2
In Historic centre of Rochester, off High Street, opposite the Vines Park. 5 minutes' walk from Rochester Station with high-speed to St Pancras and regular services to Victoria and Charing Cross.

**OPENING TIMES**

30th May to 27th Sept Thur - Fri 10am - 5pm
Plus Sat 1st June 12 - 5pm, 12-5pm. Photographer's hour Fridays 10 - 11am during opening times.
Tea Shop: Open same days as house.

**ADMISSION**

Adult £8.50 (includes 36 page illustrated guidebook)
Concession £7.50
Child £4.25
Groups +8 - Tours £11 per person.

No stilettos.
No photography in house except Fri 10-11am.

Antique privies with lavender strewn floors.

 To Tea Shop and half of garden.

By appointment £11per person, minimum 8 people.

Charity run Tea Shop. Open when house is open.

# BELMONT HOUSE & GARDENS

**www.belmont-house.org**

Belmont is an elegant 18th Century house, home to six generations of the Harris family. It contains many mementoes of the family's history and travels; including, fine paintings, furniture, Indian silverware and perhaps the finest private clock collection in the country. The gardens contain a Pinetum complete with grotto, a walled ornamental garden, specimen trees and a large kitchen garden with Victorian greenhouses, all set in parkland.

- No photography in house.
- Disabled toilet facilities available.
- Gardens. See opening times.
- Limited for coaches.
- Partial. WC's. Please see the access statement for further details.
- In the gardens, on lead only.
- Spend a relaxing week or two on the Belmont Estate in one of our delightful holiday cottages.
- The interior of the House can only be viewed by guided tour.
- Tea Room open from 1pm on Sat & Sun for cream teas & cakes. Self-service Mon-Fri.
- In the kitchen garden.
- For corporate event please contact.
- Spring Fair, NGS Days, Outdoor Theatre, Bushcraft, Woodfest, Xmas Events & Meet the Head Gardener Tours.

**CONTACT** Owner: Harris (Belmont) Charity Tel: 01795 890202
Email: administrator@belmont-house.org

**LOCATION** Belmont Park, Throwley, Faversham, Kent ME13 0HH
Map Ref: 4:M3 - M2 Jct 6 - 4½m SSW of Faversham, off A251

**OPENING TIMES** Open Apr - Sep. Please visit our website for opening hours, tour times & special events. Gardens open daily, 10am-6pm or dusk if earlier. Groups Tue & Thu by appointment. Pre-booked specialist clock tours 1.30pm last Sat of the month.

**ADMISSION** House & Garden: Adult £10 (Garden: £5), Child £5 - Under 12's FREE (Garden: 12-16yrs £2.50), Concs £8 (Garden £4)
Groups £8pp. Clock Tour £20

# CHARTWELL

**www.nationaltrust.org.uk/chartwell**

Chartwell was a home and a place that truly inspired Sir Winston Churchill. The house is still much as it was when the family lived here, with pictures, books, gifts from around the world and personal mementoes. The studio contains the largest collection of Churchill's paintings and offers insight into Churchill the painter. The garden reflects Churchill's love of the landscape and nature, including the lakes he created. The woodland offers family walks, trails, a treehouse, Donkey Jack caravan, swings, see-saws, a Canadian camp and much more to explore.

© NATIONAL TRUST/CHRIS LACEY

- Entry to the house is by timed ticket, available from the visitor centre.
- Toilets behind shop and in garden. Accessible toilet next to visitor centre.
- Adjacent to the visitor welcome centre.
- The garden, shop and café open daily from 10am - 5pm (closed 24,25 Dec).
- Open all year 250m from house. £3 all day parking for non-members.
- Steps and steep slopes leading to the house. Mobility bus available.
- On short leads permitted in the grounds, water bowls outside the café.
- Private tours available, contact the property for more details.
- Reinforce your classroom work with our creative learning sessions.
- Landemare café serves a selection of hot/cold meals, cakes scones and beverages.
- Gift shop offers Churchill memorabilia and items for the house and garden.
- Selling the same varieties of roses that can be found in the garden.
- Conference & function facilities. The Mulberry Room can accommodate 80.
- Please see the 'What's On' section of the website to see all upcoming events.

**CONTACT** Owner: National Trust
Contact: Marketing & Development Manager
Tel: 01732 868381 Email: chartwell@nationaltrust.org.uk

**LOCATION** Mapleton Road, Westerham, Kent TN16 1PS
Map Ref: 19:F11 - 2m S of Westerham, forking left off B2026.

**OPENING TIMES** House: 1 Mar -3 Nov, daily, 11.30-5pm (last entry 4pm).
Garden, Shop, Café, Exhibition & Studio: Daily, 10am - 5pm.
Times vary please call for further details.
Studio: Closed in Jan, by tour only in Feb.

**ADMISSION** House, garden and studio:
Adult £15.50, Child £7.75, Family £38.75
Garden, exhibition, studio and winter season:
Adult £9.00, child £4.50, family £22.50

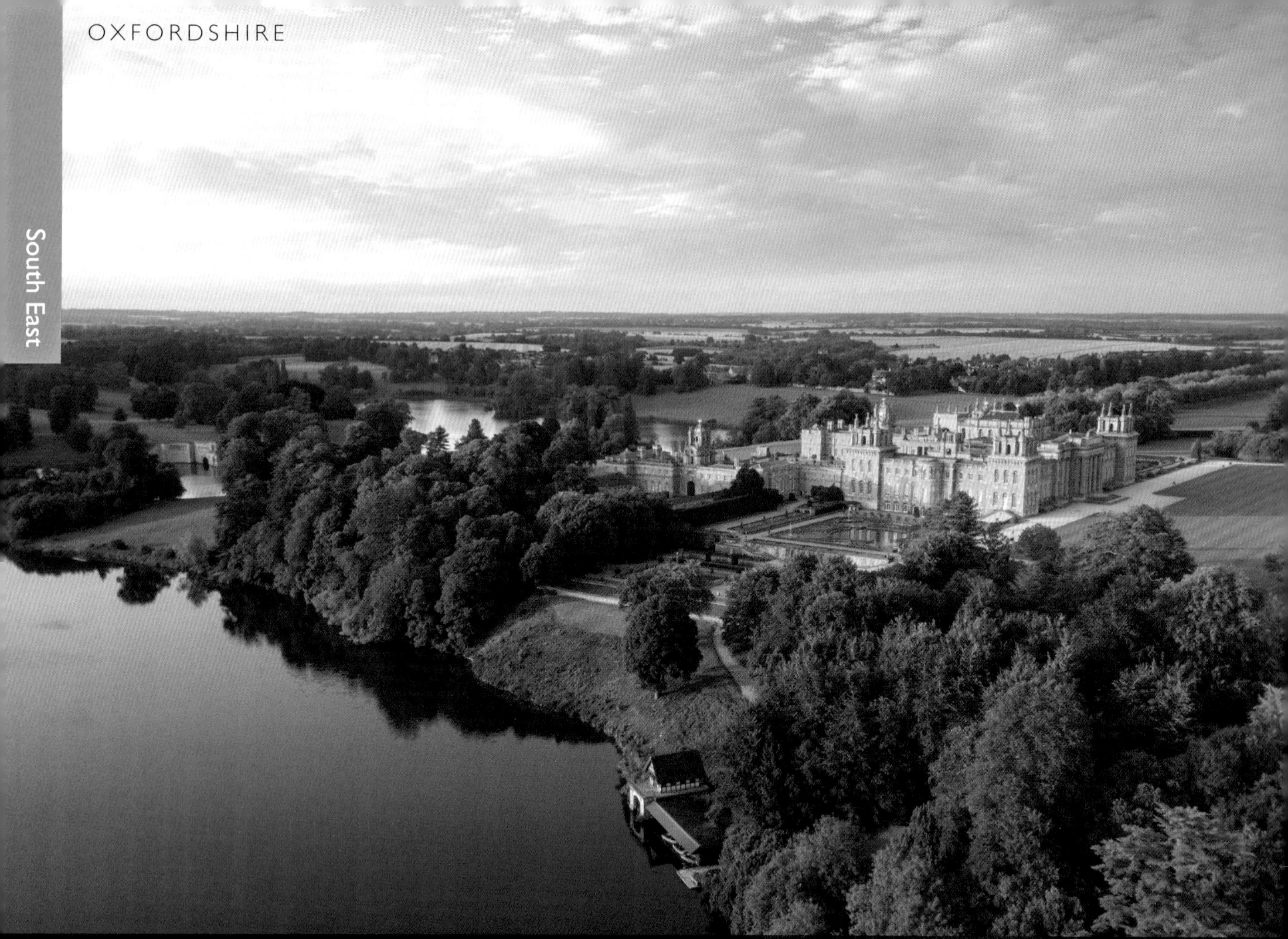

# BLENHEIM PALACE

www.blenheimpalace.com

COMMENDED
CONTRIBUTION TO HERITAGE

BLENHEIM PALACE ROSE GARDENS

BLENHEIM PALACE GREAT HALL

# Britain's Greatest Palace

Receive a warm welcome into the home of the 12th Duke and Duchess of Marlborough and the birthplace of Sir Winston Churchill.

Wonder at this masterpiece of 18th Century Baroque architecture, which houses some of the finest antique collections in Europe. Take a tour of the State Rooms and admire the portraits, tapestries and exquisite furniture while learning about the 300-year history of this National Treasure.

Explore this World Heritage Site amongst over 2000 acres of 'Capability' Brown landscaped Parkland. Take a stroll and admire some of the finest views in England.

Discover the array of Formal Gardens, including the Rose Garden, Water Terraces and Secret Garden. A short miniature train ride away from the Palace is the Pleasure Gardens, which boast a Giant Hedge Maze, Butterfly House, Lavender Garden and Adventure Playground.

Blenheim Palace hosts a wealth of events, exhibitions and tours throughout the year. From firm favourites to new experiences, there is something for everyone to enjoy. Relax in one of the on-site cafés and restaurants, serving everything from informal coffee and cake to luxury Afternoon Teas, fine dining and more. Spend some time in the award-winning East Courtyard shop and find locally produced crafts and gifts with many ranges that are exclusive to Blenheim Palace.

**OWNER**
The 12th Duke and Duchess of Marlborough

**CONTACT**
Contact: Customer Service
Tel: 01993 810530
Email: customerservice@blenheimpalace.com

**LOCATION**
Blenheim Palace, Woodstock,
Oxfordshire OX20 1PP
Map Ref: 7:A11
By car: From London, M40, 144 (1.5 hours), 8 miles North West of Oxford. London 63 miles, Birmingham 54 miles.
By bus: No.S3 from Oxford.
By coach: From London Victoria to Oxford.
By rail: Oxford Parkway Station.

**OPENING TIMES**
Park: 9.00 - 18.30 Palace: 10.30 - 17.30
Formal Gardens: 10.00 - 18.00 (or dusk if earlier)
Last admission to all areas is 45 minutes before closure.

Open throughout the year, although closed on 7th January and Christmas Day. Opening times vary during the winter season, please check the website before your visit.

**ADMISSION**
Palace, Park & Gardens: Adult £27, Concession £25.00 Child £16, Family: £67.50

Park & Gardens: Adult £17, Concessions £14, Child £7.60, Family £44.50.

Annual Pass Offer: Buy one day get 12 months free!* Enjoy entry to our World Heritage Site throughout the year for the price of one day.
Discounts available on group bookings (15+ visitors), contact our Groups Sales Team on 01993 815600 or email groups@blenheimpalace.com

For hospitality enquiries, contact our Sales & Events Team on 01993 813874 or email sales@blenheimpalace.com

*Terms & Conditions apply

- Commercial photography or filming is not permitted without prior permission.
- Toilet facilities available.
- Baby changing facilities available.
- Open throughout the year except 7th January and Christmas Day.
- Free parking for cars and coaches.
- Toilet facilities & lift access to the Palace. Blue Badge Holder parking & carers go free.
- The opportunity to cycle around the Parkland is available once per year on our Family Cycling Day.
- Dogs on leads may enter the Park only. Assistance dogs welcome.
- Options available in our local area.
- Audio Guide available in 9 languages.
- Guided tours available from Mon-Sat year-round.
- Talks and tours for school groups are available.
- Three cafés serving snacks, light meals and drinks are available on site.
- The Orangery Restaurant serves Afternoon Tea and delicious seasonal lunches.

- Two shops selling a range of gifts and souvenirs.

- Plants are available seasonally at our shops.
- Weddings, corporate hospitality and private events are available.
- Please see the 'What's On' section of the website to discover our year-round event calendar.
- Wedding ceremonies available.
- Popular filming location and also available for photoshoots.

# BROUGHTON CASTLE Ⓕ

www.broughtoncastle.com

**'About the most beautiful castle in all England... for sheer loveliness of the combination of water, woods and picturesque buildings.'** *Sir Charles Oman (1898).*

Broughton Castle is essentially a family home lived in by Lord and Lady Saye & Sele and their family. The original medieval Manor House, of which much remains today, was built in about 1300 by Sir John de Broughton. It stands on an island site surrounded by a 3 acre moat. The Castle was greatly enlarged between 1550 and 1600, at which time it was embellished with magnificent plaster ceilings, splendid panelling and fine fireplaces. In the 17th Century William, 8th Lord Saye & Sele, played a leading role in national affairs. He opposed Charles I's efforts to rule without Parliament and Broughton became a secret meeting place for the King's opponents. During the Civil War William raised a regiment and he and his four sons all fought at the nearby Battle of Edgehill. After the battle the Castle was besieged and captured. Arms and armour from the Civil War and other periods are displayed in the Great Hall. Visitors may also see the gatehouse, gardens and park together with the nearby 14th Century Church of St Mary, in which there are many family tombs, memorials and hatchments.

**Gardens**

The garden area consists of mixed herbaceous and shrub borders containing many old roses. In addition, there is a formal walled garden with beds of roses surrounded by box hedging and lined by more mixed borders.

**OWNER**
Lord Saye & Sele

**CONTACT**
Contact: Manager, Mrs James
Tel: 01295 276070
Email: info@broughtoncastle.com

**LOCATION**
Broughton, Nr Banbury, Oxfordshire OX15 5EB
Map Ref: 7:A10
Broughton Castle is 2½m SW of Banbury Cross on the B4035, Shipston-on-Stour - Banbury Road. Easily accessible from Stratford-on-Avon, Warwick, Oxford, Burford and the Cotswolds. M40/J11.
Rail: From London/Birmingham to Banbury.

**TRANSPORT ROUTES**
Car | Bus | Train

**OPENING TIMES**
Apr-Sep inclusive, 2-5pm Weds, Suns & Bank Holiday Mons.
Open all year for groups - by appointment only.

**ADMISSION**
Adult £10
Child (5-15yrs) £6
Concession £9
Garden only £6
Groups:
Adult £10
Child (5-15yrs) £7
Garden only: £7

(There is a minimum charge for groups - please contact the manager for details).

Photography allowed in house.

Toilets open from 2pm, when the castle is open. Disabled toilets in car park with other toilets.

Open all year on any day, at any time, for group bookings - by appointment only.

Limited parking. Disabled parking available.

Partial, please see the 'Disabled Access' section of the website for further details.

Guide dogs only in house. On leads in grounds.

Available for booked groups.

Available by prior arrangement. Primary and secondary school groups are welcome.

Teas on open days. Groups may book morning coffee, light lunches and afternoon teas.

The small gift shop is open on all open days from 2pm until 5pm.

Available for corporate events, small conferences and promotional events.

Selected for a wide range of film shoots, including feature films, TV dramas and TV commercials etc.

# BUSCOT PARK

www.buscotpark.com

Buscot Park is the home of the Henderson Family and the present Lord and Lady Faringdon, with their eldest son James and his wife Lucinda. They look after the property on behalf of the National Trust as well as the family collection of pictures, furniture, ceramics and objects d'art, known as the Faringdon Collection, which is displayed in the House. Built between 1780 and 1783 for a local landowner, Edward Lovedon Townsend, the estate was purchased in 1889 by Lord Faringdon's great-grandfather, Alexander Henderson, a financier of exceptional skill and ability, who in 1916 was created the 1st Lord Faringdon. He greatly enlarged the House, commissioned Harold Peto to design the famous Italianate water garden, and laid the foundations of the Faringdon Collection. Among his many purchases were Rembrandt's portrait of Pieter Six, Rossetti's portrait of Pandora, and Burne-Jones's famous series, The Legend of the Briar Rose. His grandson and heir, Gavin Henderson, added considerably to the Collection, acquiring important furniture designed by Robert Adam and Thomas Hope, and was instrumental in returning the House to its late 18th Century appearance. The family, together with their fellow Trustees, continue to add to the Collection, to freshen its display, and to enliven the gardens and grounds for the continuing enjoyment of visitors.

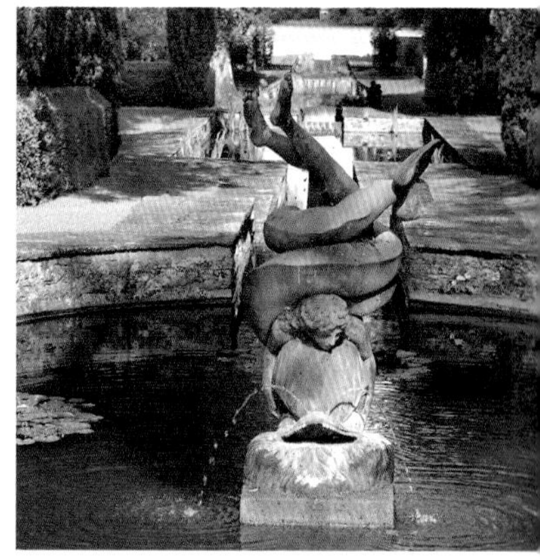

**CONTACT**

Owner: The National Trust
(Administered on their behalf by Lord Faringdon)
Contact: The Estate Office Tel: 01367 240786
Info Line: 01367 240932 Email: estbuscot@aol.com

**LOCATION**

Faringdon, Oxfordshire SN7 8BU Map Ref: 6:P12
Between Faringdon & Lechlade on A417.

**OPENING TIMES**

House, Grounds & Tea Room:
1 Apr - 30 Sep
Wed-Fri & BH weekends as listed on website.

**ADMISSION**

House & Grounds: Adult £10, Over 65s £8, Child (5-15) £5, Under 5 Free.

Grounds only: Adult £7, Over 65s £5, Child (5-15) £3.50, National Trust members: Free.
Groups - Advance booking only.

No photography in house.

Toilet and disabled WC's facilities available.

Ample car parking, 2 coach spaces.

Partial. Ramps & motorised PMVs. Please contact prior to visit for more information. Steps to House.

Not permitted - Guide dogs only. They may be exercised in the Paddock Field (the overflow car park).

Open the same days as the House, offering cream teas, cakes & slices, cheese scones, hot & cold drinks.

Small shop selling peppermint products, local cider, honey, guide books & a selection of postcards.

A selection of plants and surplus kitchen garden produce available when in season.

## STONOR PARK

www.stonor.com

Home to the Stonor family for over 850 years. The warm brick façade conceals medieval buildings dating back to the 12th century.

**CONTACT** Neil Scott General Manager 01491 638 587 enquiries@stonorpark.com

**LOCATION** Henley on Thames, Oxfordshire RG9 6HF M4 – junction 8/9 M40/6 Map Ref: 3:E1

**OPENING TIMES** House, chapel, gardens and wonderwoods adventure play park for the younger folk. Group bookings open all year by appointment. Other openings times please visit the website

For public events and festive openings please refer to website.

**ADMISSION** For up to date admission prices visit the website.

- No photography in house.
- Parking 100 yards away.
- Partial access.
- Beautiful walking and cycling routes.
- On leads. Guide dogs only in House.
- Private guided tours by appointment.
- Please contact the Manager for details.
- A selection of hot & cold lunches.
- Shop with local crafts and honey.
- Please contact the Manager for details.

STONOR PARK

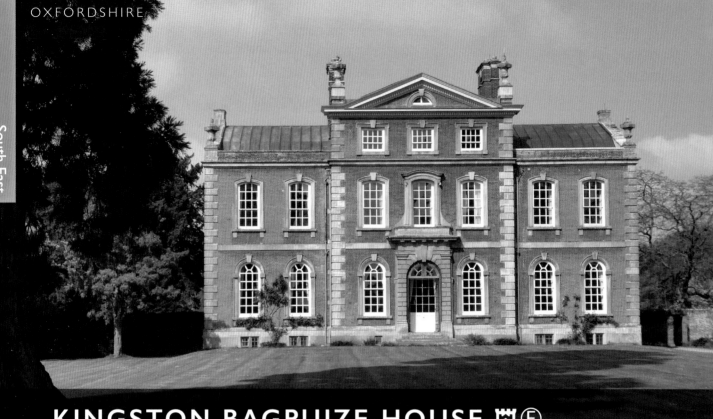

# KINGSTON BAGPUIZE HOUSE

**www.kbhevents.uk**

This lovely family home built in circa 1660 was remodelled in the early 1700's for the Blandy family. With English and French furniture in the elegant panelled rooms the entrance hall is dominated by its handsome cantilevered staircase. The surrounding mature parkland and gardens contain an interesting collection of cultivated plants giving year round interest including snowdrops and magnolia in spring, flowering trees and shrubs in summer and autumn colour. The 18th Century panelled pavilion overlooking the gardens is reached from the raised terrace walk.

A venue for civil marriages, wedding receptions and small conferences. Available for filming and photo shoots. Featured as Lord Merton's home in Downton Abbey series 5,6 and the 2016 Christmas finale.

**CONTACT**

Owner: Mrs Francis Grant Contact: Virginia Grant
Tel: 01865 820259 Email: info@kbhevents.uk

**LOCATION**

Kingston Bagpuize, Abingdon, Oxfordshire OX13 5AX
Map Ref: 7:A12 - Kingston Bagpuize village, off A415 ½ mile south of the A415/A420 intersection. Abingdon 5m, Oxford 9m.

**OPENING TIMES**

Gardens only (snowdrops): 3, 10, 17 & 24 Feb.
House & Gardens: March 10, 11, 24 & 25
April 7, 8, 14, 15, 28 & 29, May 12, 13, 26 & 27
June 9, 10, 23 & 24, July 7-9 & 21-23
August 4-6 & 18-20, Sept 1, 2, 15 & 16
All days 2-5pm (last entry to house 4pm).
Free flow visit to ground floor.

**EVENTS 2019:** 24 Feb Sun Kingston Bagpuize Snowdrop Fair see website, 26 May Sun Rare Plant Fair - www.rareplantfair.co.uk, 29 Jun Sat Village Fete Garden open

**ADMISSION**

House & Garden: Adult £9, Child/Student (11-21) £5.50.
Garden: Adult £6, Child/Student (11-21) £4.
See website to confirm open dates & times, Group Rates 20+ by written appointment weekdays all year.

- Restricted photography in house on open days.
- Toilet and disabled WC facilities available.
- Baby changing facilities available.
- Open days: Feb -Sep. Pre-booked group visits all year.
- Free parking is available.
- Disabled access in the garden, but restricted to house.
- For pre-booked group visits 20+. Self guided tours with notes on open days.
- By arrangement.
- Afternoon teas available. Morning coffee for pre-booked groups.
- Pre-booked lunches available for 20+.
- Cards & pottery in the tearoom.
- Rare Plant Fair Sun 26 May www.rareplantfair.co.uk.
- Please see 'Corporate' section of the website.
- Please see the 'Visiting' section of website for events.
- Available on an exclusive basis, for civil ceremonies & wedding receptions. See website.
- Featured in Downton Abbey 2015/16.

# ROUSHAM HOUSE

www.rousham.org

Rousham represents the first stage of English landscape design and remains almost as William Kent (1685-1748) left it. One of the few gardens of this date to have escaped alteration. Includes Venus' Vale, Townsend's Building, seven-arched Praeneste, the Temple of the Mill and a sham ruin known as the 'Eyecatcher'. The house was built in 1635 by Sir Robert Dormer. Don't miss the walled garden with it's herbaceous borders, small parterre, pigeon house and espalier apple trees. A fine herd of Longhorn cattle are to be seen in the park. Excellent location for fashion, advertising, photography etc.

## CONTACT

Owner/Contact: Charles Cottrell-Dormer Esq
Tel: 01869 347110
Mobile: 07860 360407
Email: ccd@rousham.org

## LOCATION

Nr Steeple Aston, Bicester, Oxfordshire OX25 4QX
Map Ref: 7:A10
E of A4260, 12 miles North of Oxford, South of B4030, 7 miles West of Bicester.

## OPENING TIMES

Garden: All year, daily, 10am-4.30pm (last admission).
House: May-Sep, Pre-booked groups.

## ADMISSION

House & Garden: £12
Garden: £6
No children under 15 years.

## REGULAR EVENTS

Events are held in the park, immediately next to the house. Please see website for more information.

Open access to the house and garden can be arranged for events.

Open all year.

Parking available.

Partial.

Local accommodation: The Holt Hotel, Hopcrofts Holt (about 1 ½ miles, special rates for visitors.)

Please see website. Available for photographic shoots.

Car rallies, The Bentley, MG & Aston Martin owners clubs have all held rallies at Rousham.

Ideal Oxfordshire venue for wedding receptions, offering a site to pitch a marquee.

The gardens, park & exterior are available as a location for television and feature films.

# HAMPTON COURT PALACE

www.hrp.org.uk/hamptoncourtpalace

UK HERITAGE AWARDS 2018

WINNER
BEST LOOS

WEST FRONT, HAMPTON COURT PALACE

EAST FRONT GARDENS

CHAPEL ROYAL

## Immerse yourself in the greatest and most authentic Tudor experience in the world.

Explore the home of Henry VIII, his wives and children, experiencing their public dramas and private lives in the unique world of the Tudor court. Learn how Henry's marriages changed the course of history, in the same rooms where his family affairs became international crises. Discover atmospheric corridors, where Tudor ghosts are said to still wander. Marvel at the grandeur of the magnificent Great Hall, see the stunning vaulted ceiling of the Chapel Royal and explore the enormous kitchens, the most extensive surviving 16th Century kitchens in Europe today.

Then experience a second palace – a Baroque masterpiece by Sir Christopher Wren built for William II and Mary II – its spectacular views and ornamental gardens providing a fascinating glimpse of Stuart and Georgian privilege.

Equally stunning inside and out; the palace is surrounded by formal gardens and sits in 60 acres of parkland gardens, including the 18th Century Privy Garden and world famous maze. Don't miss the Magic Garden, our interactive play garden for families. Populated by mysterious mythical beasts, with battlements to storm, towers to besiege, and even a secret grotto to discover, the Magic Garden is a unique way for your family to explore the palace's past.

**OWNER**
Historic Royal Palaces

**CONTACT**
Tel: 0203 166 6000
Email: hamptoncourt@hrp.org.uk
Venue Hire & Corporate Hospitality:
020 3166 6507 / www.hrp.org.uk/hireavenue

**LOCATION**
Surrey KT8 9AU
Map Ref: 19:B9
Car: From M25/J15 or M25/J12 or M25/J10.
Rail: 35 mins from Waterloo, zone 6 travelcard.
Boat: From Richmond, Kingston or Runnymede.

**OPENING TIMES**
Summer (25 Mar - 27 Oct)
Mon-Sun 10am-6pm Last admission - 5pm
Last admission to Magic Garden and Maze- 5:15pm

Winter (28 October - 31 March)
Monday-Sunday- 10am-4.30pm
Last admission- 3.30pm Last entry to Maze- 3.45pm

Closed: 24-26 Dec.
The Magic Garden is closed during the winter.
Please check our website before visiting for details.

**ADMISSION**
Visit www.hrp.org.uk for admission prices, or call 0203 166 6000.

**CONFERENCE/FUNCTIONS**
Conferences: Up to 250
Receptions: Up to 400
Lunches: Up to 220
Dinners: Up to 270
Marquees: Up to 3000

- Information Centre.
- Toilet and disabled WC's facilities available.
- Baby changing facilities available off Base Court & in the Tiltyard Café.
- Closed 24-26 Dec.
- Ample for cars, coach parking nearby.
- Dedicated facilities, tours, carer tickets & wheelchair hire available. Accessibility guide available.
- Assistant dogs only.
- Audio tours available.
- Private guided tours are available (subject to availability).
- Rates on request 0203 166 6000.
- The Privy Kitchen Café: Traditional food. Fountain Court Café: Afternoon teas, restaurant setting.
- Licensed. The Tiltyard: self-service restaurant, children's meals.
- Shop offer everything from souvenirs & gifts, to fine jewellery.
- Weddings, dinners, receptions.
- Special events all year round, visit website for details.
- One of the most stunning wedding venues in Surrey. Download the wedding brochure for more details.

# LOSELEY PARK

**www.loseleypark.co.uk**

Loseley Park, built in 1562 by Sir William More, is a fine example of Elizabethan architecture. The rooms contain fascinating works of art, furniture from the 17th Century and many unique features. The Walled Garden is compared favourably to gardens of national renown.

- No photographs that are taken at Loseley may be sold commercially except with written permission.
- Toilet facilities available.
- Baby changing facilities available.
- For weddings, private and corporate functions.
- Plentiful parking and free of charge to visitors. 150 cars, 6 coaches.
- Ground floor of house accessible to non-motorized wheelchairs only. Full Access Statement available.
- Obligatory: 45 mins. Pre-booked Garden tours available.
- Please contact for further details on educational visits.
- Light lunches and teas available.
- Plant sales available.
- The outstanding range of facilities cater for an array or functions.
- Please see the 'What's On' section of the website for all upcoming events.
- The perfect venue for Civil Ceremonies and wedding receptions. Please see website for full details.
- For filming location enquires please contact.

**CONTACT** Owner: Alexander More-Molyneux
Tel: 01483 304440 / 01483 405119
Catering enquiries: 01483 457103
Email: enquiries@loseleypark.co.uk Web: www.loseleypark.co.uk

**LOCATION** Guildford, Surrey GU3 1HS Map Ref: 3:G3 - 30m SW of London, leave A3 S of Guildford on to B3000. Signposted.

**OPENING TIMES** House: May-Jul Mon-Thu 12pm-4pm. Sun & BHs: 1pm-5pm Gardens & Grounds: May-Jul: Sun-Thu: 11am-5pm & BHs

**ADMISSION** House & Gardens: Adult £10-£15, Child (5-16yrs) £0-£5, Under 5yrs Free, Concs £5-£10, Family (2+3) £25-£30.
Gardens & Grounds only: Adult £5-£10, Child (5-16yrs) £0-£5, Concs £5-£10
Groups: 10+ Please contact for group bookings.
Prices are a guide only; please refer to the website.

the whole family?

See our QUICKGUIDES at the back of this book for a helpful list of properties

DOGS WELCOME

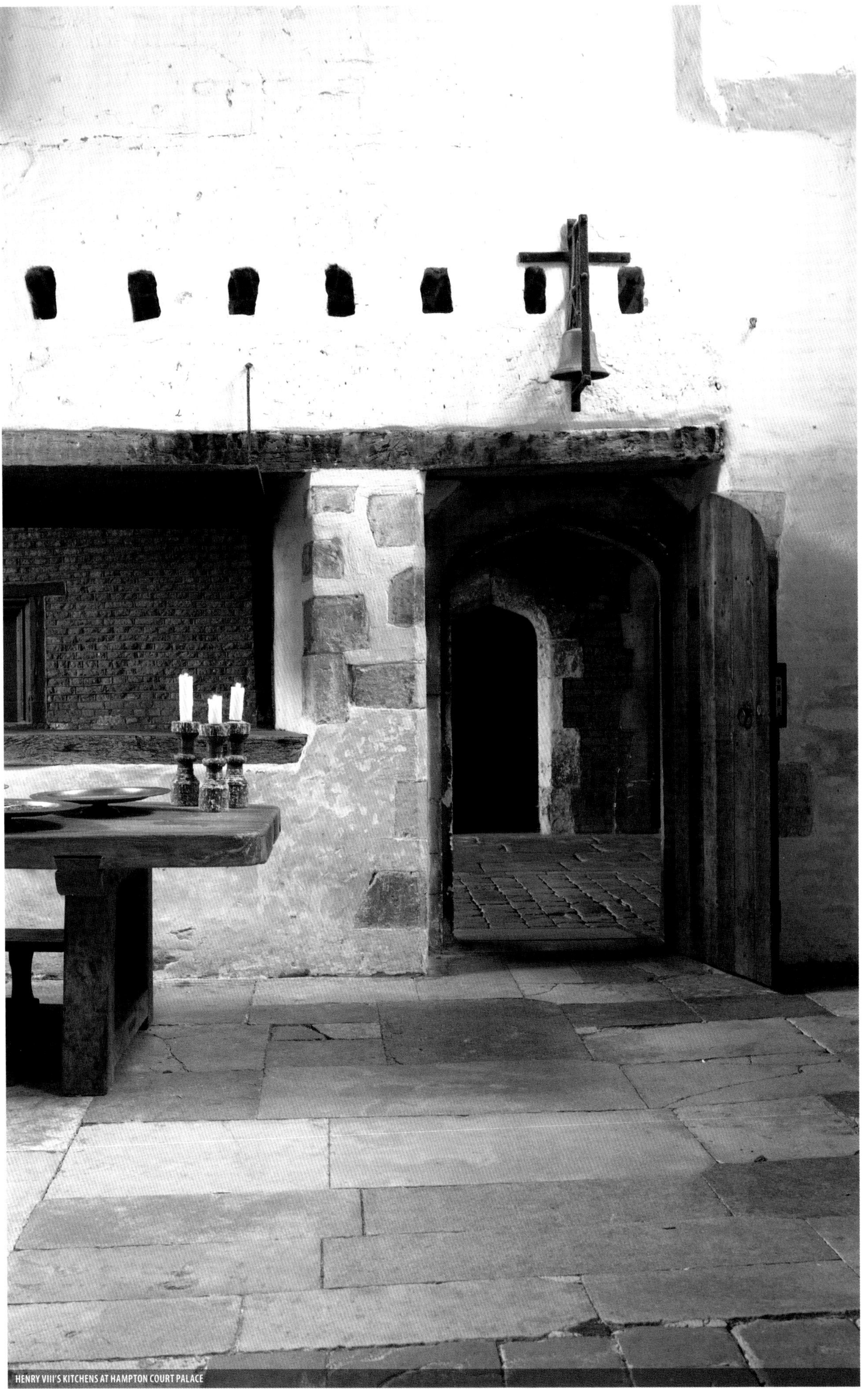

HENRY VIII'S KITCHENS AT HAMPTON COURT PALACE

# ARUNDEL CASTLE & GARDENS

www.arundelcastle.org

Overlooking the Sussex Downs and the River Arun, the magnificent Arundel Castle has commanded the West Sussex landscape since the 11th century.

Constructed during the reign of William the Conqueror, visitors will see the splendid Norman Keep, along with its fine medieval Gatehouse and Barbican. Today, Arundel Castle is one of England's greatest inhabited stately homes and the ancestral home of the Dukes of Norfolk.

The Gardens are both beautiful, fascinating and surprising. The Collector Earl's Garden, a tribute to avid art collector Thomas Howard, 14th Earl of Arundel, was conceived by the Duchess of Norfolk and offers a unique take on the traditional walled garden. Each spring, the Gardens are home to a breath-taking display of tulips. The White Garden, the Rose Garden, the Stumpery and the Organic Kitchen Garden are all open to visitors.

The 14th century Fitzalan Chapel offers an exceptional example of Gothic architecture; its carved stone tombs are of major artistic interest. Inside the Castle, the majestic Barons' Hall, the Regency Library and the magnificent drawing room - are among the twenty historic rooms available to explore.

Arundel Castle has a busy events calendar during its open season. This includes the International Jousting and Medieval Tournament, the longest of its kind in the world, open-air performances of Shakespeare in August and family-friendly history days that run throughout the summer.

From the Norman conquest of England to the turbulence of the Civil War to the advent of electricity, Arundel Castle has played a unique and important role throughout British history.

**OWNER** Arundel Castle Trustees Ltd

**CONTACT**

Stephen Manion, Castle Manager
Tel: 01903 882173
Email: visits@arundelcastle.org

**LOCATION**

Arundel Castle, Arundel, West Sussex BN18 9AB

Map Ref: 3:G6

Central Arundel, N of A27. Brighton 40 mins, Worthing 15 mins, Chichester 15 mins. From London A3 or A24, 1½ hrs. M25 motorway, 30m. Bus: Bus stop 100 yds. Rail: Station 1½m. Air: Gatwick 25m.

**OPENING TIMES**

2 Apr - 3 Nov 2019, Tues to Suns, Good Fri & Easter Mon. May BH Mons, and Mons in Aug.
Fitzalan Chapel, Gardens & Grounds, Gift Shop: 10am - 5pm. Castle Keep, Restaurant & Coffee Shop: 10am - 4.30pm. Castle Rooms: 12 noon - 5pm. Last entry 4pm.

**ADMISSION** Please contact us or see website for up-to-date admissions rates. Group rates available.

Lavatories / WC are located adjacent to The Collector Earl's Garden and on the ground floor of the Castle.

Ample car & coach parking in town car park. Free admission & refreshment voucher for coach driver.

WCs, ramps and lifts. Please see website.

On special event days admission prices may vary.

By prior arrangement. Tour time 1½-2 hrs. Tours available in various languages - please enquire.

Norman Motte & Keep, Armoury & Barons' Hall. Special rates for school children (5-16yrs) & teachers.

Licensed coffee shop offer refreshments including hot & cold drinks, light lunches, cakes and pastries.

Licensed counter service restaurant.

Discover the distinctive & exclusive gift range in the Castle Shop.

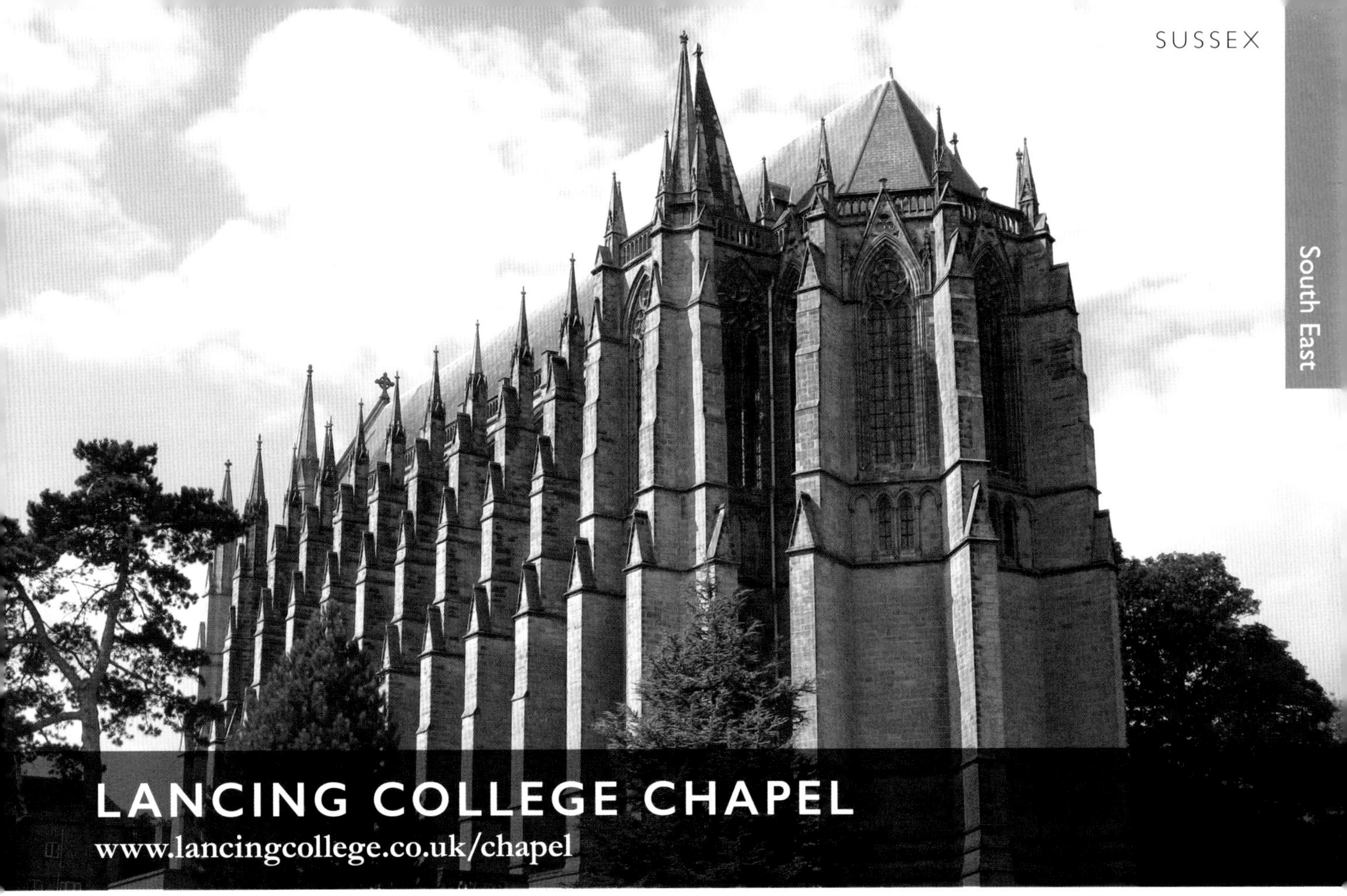

# LANCING COLLEGE CHAPEL

**www.lancingcollege.co.uk/chapel**

Lancing College Chapel is the place of worship for the community of Lancing College, the central minster of the Woodard Schools and a well-loved Sussex landmark. The Chapel stands prominently on the South Downs. The exterior, with its pinnacles and flying buttresses, is a testament to Victorian structural bravado. Designed by Herbert Carpenter in the 13th Century French gothic style, it is the fourth tallest ecclesiastical building in England.

The foundations were laid in 1868 and the atmospheric crypt came into use in 1875. The upper chapel was dedicated in 1911 but the west wall and rose window were added in the 1970s. There is now a plan to complete the building with a west porch. A beautiful war memorial cloister was built in the 1920s.

**OWNER**
Lancing College Chapel Trust

**CONTACT** The Verger Tel: 01273 465949
Email: verger@lancing.org.uk
Reception, Lancing College Enquiries Tel: 01273 452213.

**LOCATION**
Lancing, West Sussex BN15 0RW Map Ref: 3:H6
Car: North of the A27 between Shoreham-by-Sea & Lancing at the Coombes Rd/Shoreham Airport traffic lights. Filter right if coming from the East. Turn off Coombes Rd at sign for Lancing College and proceed to the top of Lancing College drive, then follow signs to the Main Car Park.

Rail: Train to Shoreham-by-Sea or Lancing on the London-Littlehampton & Portsmouth line & take a taxi.

Bus: The nearest bus routes are Brighton & Hove Buses 2A, Compass Buses, 106 & Coastliner 700.

**OPENING TIMES**
10am - 4pm Mon - Sat. 12 noon - 4pm on Sun. Every day of the year except for Good Friday, Easter Sunday, Christmas Day, Boxing Day and New Year's Day.

**ADMISSION**
Free. Donations are requested for the Friends of Lancing Chapel. Visitors are asked to sign in for security purposes as they enter the Chapel. The other College buildings are not open to the public.

Guide books, information leaflets and a DVD.

Toilet facilities available.

Every day of the year except for Good Friday, Easter Sunday, Christmas Day, Boxing Day and New Year's Day.

Please follow signs to the Main Car Park.

The upper chapel (but not the crypt) is easily accessible for those with mobility issues.

Guide dogs only in Chapel.
Dogs on leads welcome in College grounds.

Guided tours & brief talks can be booked with the Verger. Groups should be booked in advance.

School & other educational groups are welcome & may request guided tours & other information.

Stall with guide books and postcards at entrance to the Chapel.

Please see website for special events.

# GREAT DIXTER HOUSE & GARDENS

www.greatdixter.co.uk

Great Dixter, built c1450, is the birthplace of the late Christopher Lloyd, gardening author. Its Great Hall is the largest medieval timberframed hall in the country, restored and enlarged for Christopher's father (1910-12). The house was largely designed by the architect, Sir Edwin Lutyens, who added a 16th Century house (moved from elsewhere) knitting the buildings together as a family home. The house retains much of the collections of furniture and other items put together by the Lloyds early in the 20th Century, with some notable modern additions by Christopher. The gardens feature a variety of topiary, ponds, wild meadow areas and the famous Long Border and Exotic Garden. Featured regularly in 'Country Life' from 1963, Christopher was asked to contribute a series of weekly articles as a practical gardener - he never missed an issue in 42 years. There is a specialist nursery which offers an array of unusual plants of the highest quality, many of which can be seen in the fabric of the gardens.

Light refreshments are available in the gift shop as well as tools, books and gifts. The whole estate is 57 acres which includes ancient woodlands, meadows and ponds which have been consistently managed on a traditional basis. Coppicing the woodlands, for example, has provided pea sticks for plant supports and timber for fencing and repairs to the buildings. There is a Friends programme available throughout the year. Friends enjoy invitations to events and educational courses as well as regular newsletters.

**CONTACT**
Owner: The Great Dixter Charitable Trust
Contact: Perry Rodriguez Tel: 01797 252878
E-mail: office@greatdixter.co.uk

**LOCATION**
Northiam, Rye, East Sussex TN31 6PH
Map 4:L5 Signposted off the A28 in Northiam.

**OPENING TIMES**
30 Mar - 27 Oct: Tue - Sun,
House: 2 - 5pm. Garden: 11am - 5pm.

Specialist Nursery Opening times:
Please see our website for details.

**ADMISSION**
House & Garden: Adult £10.50, Child £1.50
Garden only: Adult £8.50, Child £1.00
A Gift Aid on admission scheme is in place.

**REGULAR EVENTS**
Study days on a wide range of subjects available.
Please check the website for details.

No photography in House.

Shop.

Plant sales.

Tours obligatory.

Parking limited for coaches.

Educational visits available.

Guide dogs only.

Events.

©PARHAM PARK LIMITED, PHOTOGRAPHY E ZESCHIN

# PARHAM HOUSE & GARDENS

**www.parhaminsussex.co.uk**

One of the top twenty in Simon Jenkins's book *'England's Thousand Best Houses'*. Idyllically set in the heart of an ancient deer park below the South Downs, the Elizabethan House contains an important collection of needlework, paintings and furniture.

The magnificent Long Gallery, 158ft (48m) long, is the third longest in an English private house. The spectacular gardens include a four-acre Walled Garden with stunning herbaceous borders and extensive Pleasure Grounds.

Parham has always been a well-loved family home; only three families have lived here since its foundation stone was laid in 1577. It is now owned by a charitable trust, and lived in by Lady Emma and Mr James Barnard and their family.

Parham's tranquillity and timeless beauty have changed little over the centuries.

©PARHAM PARK LIMITED, PHOTOGRAPHY E ZESCHIN

**CONTACT**

Owner: Parham Park Ltd
Contact: Estate Office Tel: 01903 742021
Email: enquiries@parhaminsussex.co.uk
Facebook: /ParhamHouseAndGardens
Twitter: @parhaminsussex
Instagram: /parham_house_gardens

**LOCATION**

Parham Park, Pulborough, West Sussex RH20 4HS
Satnav and GPS: RH20 4HR
Midway between Pulborough & Storrington on A283.
Map Ref: 3:G5.

**OPENING TIMES**

April - October. Please see website for more details.

**ADMISSION**

Please see website for more details.

Toilet facilities available.

Ample free parking. Designated parking for coaches and disabled visitors is within 50 metres.

Disabled access in the gardens & ground floor of the house. Full accessibility statement on website.

In gardens only, on leads.

Open on house & garden open days only.

Licensed.

Gifts including Parham's own jams and preserves.

Plants selected and grown by our own garden team.

House & Garden tours are available by arrangement, led by Parham guides & the gardening team.

Please see the 'Events' page on the website for what's on.

# PETWORTH

## www.nationaltrust.org.uk/petworth

Inspired by the Baroque palaces of Europe, Petworth House is an extraordinary and surprising ancestral seat created by just one family over 900 years. The 17th-century building you see today comprises grand state rooms which form the centrepiece of your visit. Designed to display the taste, lifestyle and artistic patronage of generations, the state rooms offer an infinity of paintings and sculpture, including major works by Van Dyck, Turner, Reynolds and Gainsborough. A particular highlight is the earliest English globe in existence dating back to 1592 . This remarkable collection reflects a journey of survival and success through the Tudor Reformation, Gunpowder Plot and the Napoleonic Wars. Separate Servants' Quarters offer a glimpse of life 'below stairs', featuring domestic rooms and Historic Kitchen with a 1000 piece copper batterie de cuisine while the 700 acre Capability Brown landscaped deer park offers panoramic views.

- Photography without flash allowed.
- Adapted mobility toilets.
- Changing facilities, pushchairs.
- Closes 24 and 25 Dec.
- 700 meters from mansion - NT Members free. Non- members £4
- Mobility vehicle runs between car park and mansion. Wheelchairs to borrow.
- Allowed in Petworth deer park only, guide dogs have full access.
- Guided tours, check website.
- Educational visits by arrangement.
- Café and coffee shop.
- Two shops with range of gifts & plants.
- For special events, please see website.

**CONTACT** Owner: National Trust Contact: The Administration Office
Tel: 01798 342207 Email: petworth@nationaltrust.org.uk

**LOCATION** Petworth, Church Street, West Sussex GU28 0AE
Map Ref: 3:G5 - Both mansion & park car parks located on A283;
Follow signs from centre of Petworth (A272/283). SatNav: GU28 9LR

**OPENING TIMES** House: 1 Jan-24 Feb, 11am-4pm. 25 Feb-3 Nov, 11am-5pm.
4 Nov-31 Dec, 11am- 4pm.
Pleasure Grounds Café and Gift Shop: 1 Jan-3 Feb, 10am-4pm.
4 Feb-3 Nov, 10am-5pm. 4 Nov-31 Dec, 11am-4pm.

**ADMISSION** Adult £15.60, Child (5-17yrs) £7.80, Family £39,
Groups £13.50 (pre-booked).

PAINTED ROOM - ST MARY'S HOUSE

# ST MARY'S HOUSE & GARDENS

www.stmarysbramber.co.uk

Enchanting medieval house and family home, winner of Hudsons Heritage 'Best Restoration' award in 2011. Features in Simon Jenkins' book 'England's Thousand Best Houses'. Fine panelled interiors, including unique Elizabethan 'Painted Room'. Magnificent Victorian Music Room. Interesting family memorabilia and other fascinating collections.

Charming cottage-style tea room. Five acres of grounds. Formal gardens with amusing topiary, and exceptional example of prehistoric tree Ginkgo biloba. 'Secret' Garden, with Victorian fruit-wall and rare pineapple pits, Rural Museum, Jubilee Rose Garden, Terracotta Garden, King's Garden, unusual circular Poetry Garden, woodland walk and Landscape Water Garden with island and waterfall. A haven of tranquillity and beauty.

**CONTACT**

Owner: Mr Peter Thorogood MBE & Mr Roger Linton MBE
Tel: 01903 816205
Email: info@stmarysbramber.co.uk

**LOCATION**

Bramber, West Sussex BN44 3WE

Map Ref: 3:H6

Bramber village off A283. From London 56m via M23/A23 or A24. Buses from Brighton, Shoreham and Worthing.

**OPENING TIMES**

May-end Sep: Suns, Thur & BH Mons, 2-6pm. Extra Weds in Aug, 2-6pm. Last entry 5pm.

Groups at other days and times by arrangement.

**ADMISSION**

House & Gardens:
Adult £10, Conc £9, Child £5, Groups 20+ £10.
Garden only:
Adult £6, Child £3, Groups 20+ £6.

No photography in house. Printed room guides for visitors on open days.

In main house and the tea rooms. Disabled toilets available.

Car park for visitors. 20 cars or 2 coaches.

Partial. Welcoming visitors with disabilities; please see access statement on the website.

Obligatory for groups (max 55).Visit time 2½-3 hrs.

Contact to organise a school visit for an educational experience.

A wide selection of refreshments are available in the cottage-style Orchard Tea Rooms.

Well-stocked gift shop selling souvenirs, collectables, books and music.

Plant sales in restored 19th Century glasshouse.

Surrounded by formal and topiary gardens with fountains, perfect for private functions.

For events and concerts, see website and sign up to the mailing list for updates.

Elegant Victorian Music Room licensed for 90. Exclusive use of reception rooms & gardens.

## ARUNDEL CATHEDRAL

**www.arundelcathedral.org**

French Gothic Cathedral, church of the RC Diocese of Arundel and Brighton built by Henry, 15th Duke of Norfolk and opened 1873.

**Mass Times** Tue, Wed, Fri, Sat: 10am
Mon & Thu: 8.30am at Convent of Poor Clares
Sat: 6.15pm Vigil Mass at Convent of Poor Clares
Sun: 9.30am & 11.15am

**CONTACT** Owner: Diocese of Arundel & Brighton Contact: Rev. Canon T. Madeley Tel: 01903 882297 Email: aruncath1@aol.com **LOCATION** London Road, Arundel, West Sussex BN18 9AY Map Ref: 3:G6 - Above junction of A27 and A284.
**OPEN** Summer: 9am-6pm. Winter: 9am-dusk. **ADMISSION** Free

Open all year round. Accessible. By arrangement. Shop open Mon-Fri, 10.30am - 12.30pm & 1.30pm - 4.30pm and after services, on special occasions and on request. For all upcoming Cathedral events please see the website.

## HIGH BEECHES WOODLAND & WATER GARDEN

**www.highbeeches.com**

A beautiful woodland and water garden which has been sensitively planted with many rare trees and shrubs. A suburb wildflower meadow and spectaucular autumn colour.

**CONTACT** Contact: Sarah Bray
Tel: 01444 400589
Email: gardens@highbeeches.com
**LOCATION** High Beeches Lane, Handcross, West Sussex RH17 6HQ Map Ref: 4:I4
**OPENING TIMES** Everyday (except Weds) 1 pm to 5pm.
**ADMISSION** Adult £8.50, Concessions £8.00, Children (5-16) £2.00

# CLINTON LODGE GARDEN

**www.clintonlodgegardens.co.uk**

A formal but romantic garden, around a Caroline and Georgian house, reflecting the gardening fashions throughout its history. Tree lined lawn and parkland, double blue and white herbaceous borders between yew and box hedges, a cloister walk swathed in white roses, clematis and geraniums.

**CONTACT** Owner/ Contact: Lady Collum
Tel: 01825 722952
Email: garden@clintonlodge.com
**LOCATION** Fletching, Uckfield, East Sussex TN22 3ST Map Ref: 4:I5 In centre of village behind tall yew and holly hedge.
**ADMISSION** Private Visits: £12-£14.

Homemade teas available.
Lunch by arrangement for groups of 10-30. No Sundays.
NGS Entrance: £6, Child: Free.
Sunday, 28th April, Monday, 10th June
Monday, 24th June, Monday, 5th August

For more information see website.
WC not suitable for disabled access.
Limited. Off road parking on NGS open days.
Partial. Please contact for further details.
By arrangement.
Vinery: Homemade cakes and tea.
Vinery: Postcards and preserves.
NGS days only.

# FIRLE PLACE

**www.firle.com**

The family's 500 year old history at Firle Place commenced when Sir John Gage (1479-1556) completed his manor house c.1543, in the lee of the chalk folds of the Sussex South Downs. The house was remodelled in the 18th Century, providing its present Georgian façade, including the rare Serlian window on the entrance front. The celebrated works of art now housed at Firle, comprising Old Master paintings, furniture and Sèvres porcelain, reflect the taste of successive generations of collectors and familial relationships, significant additions arriving in the mid-1950s from the Cowper collection at Panshanger House, Hertfordshire and the Grenfell collection from Taplow Court, Berkshire.

No photography in house.

Wheelchair access will be to the ground floor and Tea Room only, and can be provided if required.

In grounds on leads.

Home to a wide range of accommodation for parties of any size.

Exclusive out-of-hours guided tours: 25+ people £8.50pp. -25 people £9pp (minimum £215).

Tearoom, please see website for details.

Shop.

Available for private hire.

Please see website for special events.

For details on weddings at Firle, please contact Bryony at weddings@firle.com or 07788 446621.

**CONTACT** Owner: The Rt Hon Viscount Gage
Tel: 01273 858567 Email: enquiries@firle.com

**LOCATION** Firle, Nr Lewes, East Sussex BN8 6LP Map Ref: 4:J6
4m SE of Lewes on A27 Brighton/Eastbourne Road.

**OPENING TIMES** Jun-Sep. Please see website for 2019 opening days & times. Tea Room opens, without charge on House opening days only.

**ADMISSION** Please see the website or contact for 2019 admission prices. Private group tours can be arranged by prior appointment. Call 01273 858307 or see website for details.

# HAMMERWOOD PARK

## www.hammerwoodpark.co.uk

The best kept secret in Sussex, with house and park preserved 'untouched by a corporate plan'. Built by White House architect Latrobe in Greek Revival style in 1792 as a temple to Bacchus, left derelict by Led Zeppelin, painstakingly restored by the Pinnegar family over the last 30 years and brought to life with guided tours, concerts (some including ex-Finchcocks' instruments) and filming.

- Helipad (see Pooley's - prior permission required).
- Toilet facilities available.
- Accepts Euros.
- Small groups by appointment all year round.
- Parking spaces are available.
- Bed & Breakfast.
- In grounds only.
- Obligatory.
- Educational visits by arrangement.
- Tea is served in the Elgin Room.
- Conferences.
- Please see the 'Concerts' section of the website to see brochure.

**CONTACT** Owner: David and Anne-Noelle Pinnegar
Tel: 01342 850594 Email: antespam@gmail.com

**LOCATION** East Grinstead, Sussex RH19 3QE Map Ref: 4:J4
3.5 m E of East Grinstead on A264 to Tunbridge Wells, 1m W of Holtye.

**OPENING TIMES** 1 Jun - end Sep: Wed, Sat & BH Mon, 2 - 5pm.
Guided tour starts 2.05pm. Private groups: Easter-Jun. Coaches strictly by appointment. Small groups any time throughout the year by appointment.

**ADMISSION** House & Park: Adult £8.50, Child £2.
Private viewing by arrangement.

# NYMANS

## www.nationaltrust.org.uk/nymans

One of the National Trust's premier gardens, Nymans was a creative retreat for the artistic Messel family. The garden contains rare and unusual plant collections of national significance, including a stunning collection of subtly fragranced magnolias in springtime. The Rose Garden, created by Maud Messel in the1920s, is scented by hints of old fashioned roses. In autumn dramatic shows of native tree colour precede the winter's structural form. Discover hidden corners through stone archways, walk along tree-lined avenues, all the while surrounded by the lush countryside of the Sussex Weald. The comfortable yet elegant house, a partial ruin, reflects the personalities and stories of the talented Messel family. The adjoining woodland has plenty of opportunities to spot wildlife.

- Information available from the Welcome Hub.
- Closed Christmas Eve & Christmas Day. Please see website for opening arrangements.
- All weather parking suitable for all year round.
- Toilet facilities available.
- Baby changing facilities available.
- Disabled access in Car Park and Cafe toilets
- Kiosk and Horse Box open at busy times. Tea garden.
- Daily in the garden.
- Plant sales available.
- Shop.
- Weddings.

**CONTACT** Owner: National Trust Contact: Nymans
Tel: 01444 405250 E-mail: nymans@nationaltrust.org.uk

**LOCATION** Handcross, Haywards Heath, West Sussex RH17 6EB
Map Ref: 4:I4 - 30m At Handcross on B2114, 12 miles south of Gatwick, just off London-Brighton M23.

**OPENING TIMES** Gardens: Open all year 10-5*
(*4pm closure from 1st Jan - 3rd Feb and 4th Nov - 31st Dec)
House and Gallery: Open 4th Feb - 3rd Nov 10am - 4pm
(will close for short periods to change exhibitions)
Closed 24th and 25th Dec
For more information and any other changes please see the website.

**ADMISSION** Adult £14 (S) £15.40 (GA) Child £7 (S) £7.70 (GA)
Family (2 adults) £35 (S) £38.50 (GA) Family (1 Adult) £21 (S) £23.10 (GA)
Group Adult £12.00 Group child £6.00 Groups must pre book.

ASHDOWN HOUSE
Lambourn, Newbury, Berkshire RG17 8RE
**Tel:** 01494 755569 **Email:** ashdown@nationaltrust.org.uk

BASILDON PARK
Lower Basildon, Reading, Berkshire RG8 9NR
**Tel:** 0118 984 3040 **Email:** basildonpark@nationaltrust.org.uk

ENGLEFIELD HOUSE GARDENS
The Estate Office, Englefield Road, Theale Berkshire RG7 5DU
**Tel:** 0118 930 2221

THE SAVILL GARDEN
Wick Lane, Englefield Green, Surrey TW20 0UU
**Tel:** 01784 485400 **Email:** enquiries@windsorgreatpark.co.uk

SHAW HOUSE
Church Road, Shaw, Newbury, Berkshire RG14 2DR
**Tel:** 01635 279279 **Email:** shawhouse@westberks.gov.uk

WASING PARK
Aldermaston, Reading, RG7 4NB
**Tel:** 0118 971 4140 **Email:** info@wasing.co.uk

WINDSOR CASTLE
Windsor, Berkshire SL4 1NJ
**Tel:** 020 7766 7304 **Email:** bookinginfo@royalcollection.org.uk

ASCOTT
Wing, Leighton Buzzard, Buckinghamshire LU7 0PR
**Tel:** 01296 688242 **Email:** info@ascottestate.co.uk

BLETCHLEY PARK
The Mansion, Bletchley Park, Milton Keynes MK3 6EB
**Tel:** 01908 640404 **Email:** info@bletchleypark.org.uk

CHENIES MANOR HOUSE
Chenies, Buckinghamshire WD3 6ER
**Tel:** 01494 762888 **Email:** macleodmatthews@btinternet.com

CLAYDON HOUSE & GARDENS
Claydon House, Middle Claydon, Buckinghamshire MK18 2EY
**Tel:** 01296 730349 **Email:** claydon@nationaltrust.org.uk

CLIVEDEN
Taplow, Maidenhead SL6 0JA
**Tel:** 01628 605069 **Email:** cliveden@nationaltrust.org.uk

NETHER WINCHENDON HOUSE
Nether Winchendon, Nr Thame, Buckinghamshire HP18 0DY
**Tel:** 01844 290101 **Email:** contactus@netherwinchendonhouse.com

STOWE HOUSE
Stowe House, Stowe, Buckingham MK18 5EH
**Tel:** 01280 818002 **Email:** Houseinfo@stowe.co.uk

STOWE LANDSCAPE GARDENS
New Inn Farm, Buckingham MK18 5EQ
**Tel:** 01280 817156 **Email:** stowe@nationaltrust.org.uk

WADDESDON MANOR
Waddesdon, Nr Aylesbury, Buckinghamshire HP18 0JH
**Tel:** 01296 820414 **Email:** enquiries@waddesdon.org.uk

WEST WYCOMBE PARK
West Wycombe, High Wycombe, Buckinghamshire HP14 3AJ
**Tel:** 01494 513569 **Email:** westwycombe@nationaltrust.org.uk

BREAMORE HOUSE & MUSEUM
Breamore, Fordingbridge, Hampshire SP6 2DF
**Tel:** 01725 512858 **Email:** breamore@btinternet.com

**BROADLANDS**

**Romsey, Hampshire SO51 9ZD**
Broadlands is the historic home of the Mountbatten family.
**Map Ref:** 3:C5
**Tel:** 01794 505080
**Website:** www.broadlandsestates.co.uk
**Open:** Jun-Sep. Please see our website for details.

EXBURY GARDENS & STEAM RAILWAY
Exbury, Southampton, Hampshire SO45 1AZ
**Tel:** 023 8089 1203 **Email:** info@exbury.co.uk

HARCOMBE HOUSE
Park Lane, Ropley, Alresford, Hampshire SO24 0BE
**Tel:** 07796 195550 **Email:** vjeswani@k-capital.net

HIGHCLERE CASTLE, GARDENS & EGYPTIAN EXHIBITION
Highclere Castle, Newbury, Hampshire RG20 9RN
**Tel:** 01635 253210 **Email:** theoffice@highclerecastle.co.uk

HINTON AMPNER
Bramdean, Alresford, Hampshire SO24 0LA
**Tel:** 01962 771305 **Email:** hintonampner@nationaltrust.org.uk

**HOUGHTON LODGE GARDENS**

**Stockbridge, Hampshire SO20 6LQ**
The best surviving example in England of an 18th Century Cottage Orné, overlooking the River Test.
**Tel:** 01264 810502 **Email:** info@houghtonlodgegardens.co.uk
**Map Ref:** 3:C4 **Website:** www.houghtonlodge.co.uk
**Open:** 30 Mar-30 Sep, 11am-5pm. Weekends & BHs 10am-5pm.
**Admission:** Adult £7.50, Child £3.50, Under 3 yrs Free.

JANE AUSTEN'S HOUSE MUSEUM
Chawton, Alton, Hampshire GU34 1SD
**Tel:** 01420 83262 **Email:** enquiries@jahmusm.org.uk

KING JOHN'S HOUSE & HERITAGE CENTRE
Church Street, Romsey, Hampshire SO51 8BT
**Tel:** 01794 512200 **Email:** info@kingjohnshouse.org.uk

MOTTISFONT
Mottisfont, Nr Romsey, Hampshire SO51 0LP
**Tel:** 01794 340757 **Email:** mottisfont@nationaltrust.org.uk

PORTCHESTER CASTLE
Portsmouth, Hampshire PO16 9QW
**Tel:** 02392 378291 **Email:** customers@english-heritage.org.uk

SIR HAROLD HILLIER GARDENS
Jermyns Lane, Ampfield, Romsey, Hampshire SO51 0QA
**Tel:** 01794 369318 **Email:** info@hilliergardens.org.uk

TUDOR HOUSE & GARDEN
Bugle Street, Southampton SO14 2AD
**Tel:** 023 8083 4536 **Email:** museums@southampton.gov.uk

THE VYNE
Sherborne St John, Basingstoke RG24 9HL
**Tel:** 01256 883858 **Email:** thevyne@nationaltrust.org.uk

WINCHESTER CATHEDRAL
9 The Close, Winchester SO23 9LS
**Tel:** 01962 857200 **Email:** visits@winchester-cathedral.org.uk

WINCHESTER CITY MILL
Bridge Street, Winchester SO23 9BH
**Tel:** 01962 870057 **Email:** winchestercitymill@nationaltrust.org.uk

ST AUGUSTINE'S ABBEY
Longport, Canterbury, Kent CT1 1TF
**Tel:** 01227 767345 **Email:** customers@english-heritage.org.uk

BOUGHTON MONCHELSEA PLACE
Boughton Monchelsea, Nr Maidstone, Kent ME17 4BU
**Tel:** 01622 743120 **Email:** mk@boughtonplace.co.uk

CHILHAM CASTLE
Canterbury, Kent CT4 8DB
**Tel:** 01227 733100 **Email:** chilhamcastleinfo@gmail.com

COBHAM HALL
Cobham, Kent DA12 3BL
**Tel:** 01474 823371 **Email:** enquiries@cobhamhall.com

COBHAM WOOD & MAUSOLEUM
Cobham DA12 3BS
**Tel:** 01732 810378 **Email:** cobham@nationaltrust.org.uk

DEAL CASTLE
Victoria Road, Deal, Kent CT14 7BA
**Tel:** 01304 372762 **Email:** customers@english-heritage.org.uk

DODDINGTON PLACE GARDENS
Doddington, Nr Sittingbourne, Kent ME9 0BB
**Tel:** 01795 886101

DOVER CASTLE
Castle Hill, Dover, Kent CT16 1HU
**Tel:** 01304 211067 **Email:** customers@english-heritage.org.uk

DOWN HOUSE
Luxted Road, Downe, Kent BR6 7JT
**Tel:** 01689 859119 **Email:** www.english-heritage.org.uk/darwin

EMMETTS GARDEN
Ide Hill, Sevenoaks, Kent TN14 6BA
**Tel:** 01689 859119 **Email:** visits@winchester-cathedral.org.uk

GODINTON HOUSE & GARDENS
Godinton Lane, Ashford Kent TN23 3BP
**Tel:** 01233 620773 **Email:** info@godinton-house-gardens.co.uk

THE GRANGE
St Augustine's Road, Ramsgate, Kent CT11 9NY
**Tel:** 01628 825925 **Email:** bookings@landmarktrust.org.uk

GREAT COMP GARDEN
Comp Lane, Platt, Borough Green, Kent TN15 8QS
**Tel:** 01732 886154 **Email:** info@greatcompgarden.co.uk

GROOMBRIDGE PLACE GARDENS
Groombridge, Tunbridge Wells, Kent TN3 9QG
**Tel:** 01892 861444 **Email:** carrie@groombridge.co.uk

HALL PLACE & GARDENS
Bourne Road, Bexley, Kent DA5 1PQ
**Tel:** 01322 526574 **Email:** info@hallplace.org.uk

HEVER CASTLE & GARDENS
Hever Castle, Hever, Edenbridge, Kent TN8 7NG
**Tel:** 01732 865224 **Email:** info@hevercastle.co.uk

HOLE PARK GARDENS
Hole Park, Benenden Road, Rolvenden, Cranbrook, Kent TN17 4JA
**Tel:** 01580 241344 **Email:** info@holepark.com

ST JOHN'S JERUSALEM
Sutton-at-Hone, Dartford Kent DA4 9HQ
**Tel:** 01732 810378 **Email:** stjohnsjerusalem@nationaltrust.org.uk

KNOLE
Sevenoaks, Kent TN15 0RP
**Tel:** 01732 462100 **Email:** knole@nationaltrust.org.uk

LULLINGSTONE CASTLE & WORLD GARDEN
Eynsford, Kent DA4 0JA
**Tel:** 01322 862114 **Email:** info@lullingstonecastle.co.uk

LULLINGSTONE ROMAN VILLA
Lullingstone Lane, Eynsford, Kent DA4 0JA
**Tel:** 01322 863467 **Email:** customers@english-heritage.org.uk

MOUNT EPHRAIM GARDENS
Hernhill, Faversham, Kent ME13 9TX
**Tel:** 01227 751496 **Email:** info@mountephraimgardens.co.uk

NURSTEAD COURT
Nurstead Church Lane, Meopham, Kent DA13 9AD
**Tel:** 01474 812368 **Email:** info@nursteadcourt.co.uk

OWLETTS
The Street, Cobham, Gravesend DA12 3AP
**Tel:** 01732 810378 **Email:** owletts@nationaltrust.org.uk

PAINSHILL PARK TRUST LTD.
Portsmouth Road, Cobham KT11 1JE
**Tel:** 01932 868113 **Email:** info@painshill.co.uk

PROVENDER HOUSE
Provender Lane, Norton, Nr Faversham, Kent ME13 0ST
**Tel:** 07773 790872 **Email:** info@provenderhouse.co.uk

QUEX PARK
Birchington, Kent CT7 0BH
**Tel:** 01843 841119 **Email:** www.quexpark.co.uk

RIVERHILL HIMALAYAN GARDENS
Sevenoaks, Kent TN15 0RR
**Tel:** 01732 459777 **Email:** sarah@riverhillgardens.co.uk

ROCHESTER CASTLE
The Lodge, Rochester-Upon-Medway, Medway ME1 1SW
**Tel:** 01634 402276 **Email:** customers@english-heritage.org.uk

SCOTNEY CASTLE
Lamberhurst, Tunbridge Wells, Kent TN3 8JN
**Tel:** 01892 893820 **Email:** scotneycastle@nationaltrust.org.uk

SISSINGHURST CASTLE
Sissinghurst, Cranbrook, Kent TN17 2AB
**Tel:** 01580 710700 **Email:** sissinghurst@nationaltrust.org.uk

SMALLHYTHE PLACE
Smallhythe, Tenterden, Kent TN30 7NG
**Tel:** 01580 762334 **Email:** smallhytheplace@nationaltrust.org.uk

TONBRIDGE CASTLE
Castle Street, Tonbridge, Kent TN9 1BG
**Tel:** 01732 770929 **Email:** tonbridge.castle@tmbc.gov.uk

TUDOR HOUSE
King Street, Margate, Kent CT9 1QE
**Tel:** 01843 577577 **Email:** visitorinformation@thanet.gov.uk

WALMER CASTLE & GARDENS
Deal, Kent CT14 7LJ
**Tel:** 01304 364288 **Email:** customers@english-heritage.org.uk

ARDINGTON HOUSE
Wantage, Oxfordshire OX12 8QA
**Tel:** 01235 821566 **Email:** info@ardingtonhouse.com

CHASTLETON HOUSE
Chastleton, Nr Moreton-In-Marsh, Oxfordshire GL56 0SU
**Tel:** 01608 674981 **Email:** chastleton@nationaltrust.org.uk

GREYS COURT
Rotherfield Greys, Henley-On-Thames, Oxfordshire RG9 4PG
**Tel:** 01491 628529 **Email:** greyscourt@nationaltrust.org.uk

MAPLEDURHAM HOUSE & WATERMILL
Mapledurham, Reading RG4 7TR
**Tel:** 0118 9723350 **Email:** sissinghurst@nationaltrust.org.uk

MILTON MANOR HOUSE
Milton, Abingdon, Oxfordshire OX14 4EN
**Tel:** 01235 831287

MINSTER LOVELL HALL & DOVECOTE
Minster Lovell, Oxfordshire, OX29 0RR
**Tel:** 0870 333 1181 **Email:** customers@english-heritage.org.uk

NUFFIELD PLACE
Huntercombe, Henley on Thames RG9 5RY
**Tel:** 01491 641224 **Email:** nuffieldplace@nationaltrust.org.uk

SULGRAVE MANOR
Manor Road, Sulgrave, Nr Banbury, Oxfordshire OX17 2SD
**Tel:** 01295 760205 **Email:** enquiries@sulgravemanor.org.uk

WATERPERRY GARDENS
Waterperry, Nr Wheatley, Oxfordshire OX33 1JZ
**Tel:** 01844 339226 **Email:** office@waterperrygardens.co.uk

CLAREMONT LANDSCAPE GARDEN
Portsmouth Road, Esher, Surrey KT10 9JG
**Tel:** 01372 467806 **Email:** claremont@nationaltrust.org.uk

GODDARDS
Abinger Common, Dorking, Surrey RH5 6TH
**Tel:** 01628 825925 **Email:** bookings@landmarktrust.org.uk

GREAT FOSTERS
Stroude Road, Egham, Surrey TW20 9UR
**Tel:** 01784 433822 **Email:** reception@greatfosters.co.uk

HATCHLANDS PARK
East Clandon, Guildford, Surrey GU4 7RT
**Tel:** 01483 222482 **Email:** hatchlands@nationaltrust.org.uk

LEITH HILL PLACE
Leith Hill Lane, Coldharbour, Dorking, Surrey RH5 6LY
**Tel:** 01306 711685 **Email:** leithhillplace@nationaltrust.org.uk

LIMNERSLEASE AT THE WATTS GALLERY
Down Lane, Compton, Guildford, Surrey GU3 1DQ
**Tel:** 01483 810 235 **Email:** info@wattsgallery.org.uk

POLESDEN LACEY
Great Bookham, Nr Dorking, Surrey RH5 6BD
**Tel:** 01372 452048 **Email:** polesdenlacey@nationaltrust.org.uk

RHS GARDEN WISLEY
Nr Woking, Surrey GU23 6QB
**Tel:** 0845 260 9000 **Email:** wisley@rhs.org.uk

VANN
Hambledon, Godalming, Surrey GU8 4EF
**Tel:** 01428 683413 **Email:** vann@caroe.com

1066 BATTLE OF HASTINGS
Battle, Sussex TN33 0AD
**Tel:** 01424 775705 **Email:** customers@english-heritage.org.uk

ALFRISTON CLERGY HOUSE
The Tye, Alfriston, Nr Polegate, East Sussex BN26 5TL
**Tel:** 01323 871961 **Email:** alfriston@nationaltrust.org.uk

ANNE OF CLEVES HOUSE
52 Southover High Street, Lewes, East Sussex BN7 1JA
**Tel:** 01273 474610 **Email:** anne@sussexpast.co.uk

BATEMAN'S
Burwash, Etchingham, East Sussex TN19 7DS
**Tel:** 01435 882302 **Email:** batemans@nationaltrust.org.uk

BODIAM CASTLE
Bodiam, Nr Robertsbridge, East Sussex TN32 5UA
**Tel:** 01580 830196 **Email:** bodiamcastle@nationaltrust.org.uk

CHARLESTON
Firle, Nr Lewes, East Sussex BN8 6LL
**Tel:** 01323 811626 **Email:** info@charleston.org.uk

CHICHESTER CATHEDRAL
Chichester, West Sussex PO19 1PX
**Tel:** 01243 782595 **Email:** visitors@chichestercathedral.org.uk

FAIRLIGHT HALL GARDENS
Martineau Lane, Fairlight, Nr Hastings East Sussex TN35 5DR
**Tel:** 01424 814132 **Email:** admin@fairlighthall.co.uk

FARLEY HOUSE & GALLERY
Muddles Green, Chiddingly, Nr Lewes, East Sussex, BN8 6HW
**Tel:** 01825 872856 **Email:** tours@leemiller.co.uk

FISHBOURNE ROMAN PALACE
Salthill Road, Fishbourne, Chichester, Sussex PO19 3QR
**Tel:** 01243 785859 **Email:** adminfish@sussexpast.co.uk

GLYNDE PLACE
Glynde, East Sussex BN8 6SX
**Tel:** 01273 858224 **Email:** info@glynde.co.uk

HASTINGS CASTLE
Castle Hill Road, West Hill, Hastings, East Sussex TN34 3AR
**Tel:** 01424 444412 **Email:** bookings@discoverhastings.co.uk

LEWES CASTLE & MUSEUM
Barbican House, 169 High Street, Lewes, East Sussex BN7 1YE
**Tel:** 01273 486290 **Email:** castle@sussexpast.co.uk

LEWES PRIORY
Town Hall, High Street, Lewes, East Sussex BN7 2QS
**Tel:** 01273 486185 **Email:** enquiries@lewespriory.org.uk

MICHELHAM PRIORY
Upper Dicker, Hailsham, East Sussex BN27 3QS
**Tel:** 01323 844224 **Email:** adminmich@sussexpast.co.uk

BORDE HILL GARDEN
Borde Hill Lane, Haywards Heath, West Sussex, RH16 1XP
**Tel:** 01444 450326 **Email:** info@bordehill.co.uk

COWDRAY HERITAGE TRUST
Cowdray Estate, Cowdray Park, Midhurst, W Sussex, GU29 0AQ
**Tel:** 01730 812423 **Email:** enquiries@cowdray.co.uk

GOODWOOD HOUSE
Chichester, West Sussex, PO18 0PX
**Tel:** 01243 755055 **Email:** info@goodwood.com

PALLANT HOUSE GALLERY
9 North Pallant, Chichester, West Sussex
**Tel:** 01243 774557 **Email:** info@pallant.org.uk

PASHLEY MANOR GARDENS
Pashley Manor, Ticehurst, Wadhurst, East Sussex TN5 7HE
**Tel:** 01580 200888 **Email:** info@pashleymanorgardens.com

PEVENSEY CASTLE
Pevensey, Sussex BN24 5LE
**Tel:** 01323 762604 **Email:** customers@english-heritage.org.uk

PRESTON MANOR
Preston Drove, Brighton, East Sussex BN1 6SD
**Tel:** 03000 290900 **Email:** visitor.services@brighton-hove.gov.uk

THE ROYAL PAVILION
Brighton, East Sussex BN1 1EE
**Tel:** 03000 290900 **Email:** visitor.services@brighton-hove.gov.uk

SACKVILLE COLLEGE
High Street, East Grinstead, West Sussex RH19 3BX
**Tel:** 01342 323414 **Email:** admin@sackvillecollege.org.uk

SAINT HILL MANOR
Saint Hill Road, East Grinstead, West Sussex RH19 4JY
**Tel:** 01342 334171 **Email:** info@sainthillmanor.org.uk

SHEFFIELD PARK & GARDEN
Sheffield Park, Uckfield, East Sussex TN22 3QX
**Tel:** 01825 790231 **Email:** sheffieldpark@nationaltrust.org.uk

STANDEN
West Hoathly Road, East Grinstead, West Sussex RH19 4NE
**Tel:** 01342 323029 **Email:** standen@nationaltrust.org.uk

UPPARK HOUSE & GARDEN
South Harting, Petersfield, West Sussex GU31 5QR
**Tel:** 01730 825415 **Email:** uppark@nationaltrust.org.uk

WAKEHURST PLACE
Ardingly Road, North of Ardingly, West Sussex
**Tel:** 01444 894004 **Email:** wakehurst@kew.org

WEALD & DOWNLAND OPEN AIR MUSEUM
Town Lane, Singleton, Chichester, West Sussex PO18 0EU
**Tel:** 01243 811363 **Email:** office@wealddown.co.uk

WEST DEAN COLLEGE & GARDENS
West Dean, West Dean, West Sussex PO18 0RX
**Tel:** 01243 818210 **Email:** enquiries@westdean.org.uk

WILMINGTON PRIORY
Wilmington, Nr Eastbourne, East Sussex BN26 5SW
**Tel:** 01628 825925 **Email:** bookings@landmarktrust.org.uk

WOOLBEDING GARDENS
Midhurst, West Sussex GU29 9RR
**Tel:** 0844 249 1895 **Email:** woolbedinggardens@nationaltrust.org.uk

CARISBROOKE CASTLE
Newport, Isle Of Wight PO30 1XY
**Tel:** 01983 522107 **Email:** customers@english-heritage.org.uk

NUNWELL HOUSE & GARDENS
Coach Lane, Brading, Isle Of Wight PO36 0JQ
**Tel:** 01983 407240 **Email:** info@nunwellhouse.co.uk

OSBORNE HOUSE
East Cowes, Isle of Wight PO32 6JX
**Tel:** 01983 200022 **Email:** customers@english-heritage.org.uk

VENTNOR BOTANIC GARDENS
Undercliff Drive, Ventnor, Isle of Wight PO38 1UL
**Tel:** 01983 855397

# SOUTH WEST

CORNWALL • DEVON • DORSET
SOMERSET • WILTSHIRE • GLOUCESTERSHIRE

BRIDGE OVER THE RIVER DART NEAR POSTBRIDGE, DEVON ©VISITENGLAND/DIANA JARVIS

## COUNTRYSIDE

Jurassic Coast
Dartmoor, Exmoor, Bodmin Moor
Atlantic surfing beaches

## HERITAGE

Drake & Raleigh
King Arthur
Tin mining heritage

## FOOD

Seafood
Cornish pasties
Clotted cream

# Cadhay

## Rise and fall

Cadhay has needed charm to survive a ding-dong history of neglect and salvation. The house is having a good period in it's history. The present owner is a designer of contemporary furniture and a descendant of the family who lived here under the Tudors. He has turned this 16th century manor house into a comfortable home available for a wedding, a big weekend away or a summer afternoon's visit on a Friday.

THE ELIZABETHAN EXTERIOR OF CADHAY

The story this house tells is of the aspirant Tudor gentry who profited from the Dissolution of the Monasteries under Henry VIII. In this case, it was John Haydon and his great-nephew Robert. John married the heiress of Cadhay and built the house in the 1540s. His heir Robert married Joan Paulet, a woman with great connections at court since both her father and cousin were Privy Councillors to the Tudors. Robert added a bit of grandeur in 1617, enclosing a courtyard at the heart of the house with a new Long Gallery. The Court of the Sovereigns, embellished with statues of the Tudor Kings and Queens, is now Cadhay's glory. There is Henry VIII's familiar square jaw with his stomach cinched into ceremonial robes that look like a big dress while Henry, Mary, Edward and Elizabeth each wear a crown as big as a cushion.

THE MEDIEVAL ROOF OF THE ORIGINAL GREAT HALL AT CADHAY

By 1737 Cadhay was in disrepair. Its new owner 'Georgianised' the house, creating a Dining Room from the Great Hall and adding panelling, new fireplaces and sash windows. By the late 19th century Cadhay was again in decline and home to several farming families. Luckily, an Edwardian academic, Dampier Whetham, came to the rescue in 1910, restoring the interiors and revealing the Tudor fireplaces. Since his death, the house has been home to descendants of its Elizabethan mistress, Joan Paulet, and they have engineered the latest revival in Cadhay's volatile history. ■

CONTEMPORARY PLANTING AROUND THE MEDIEVAL FISH PONDS IN THE CADHAY GARDENS

# South West

## Top 3 Venues

PRIDEAUX PLACE

### Prideaux Place, Cornwall

Situated on the North Cornish Coast, Prideaux Place has been owned by the same family since 1592. Prideaux Place can host a range of events in its Great Hall, Elizabethan panelled dining room, or the Susannah room which features a 16th century vaulted plasterwork ceiling. The Deer Park is home to what is thought to be one of the oldest fallow deer herds in the country. The estate is also available for hire as a film and tv location, for car rallies, concerts and exhibitions. Prideaux Place is also home to large collection of Teddy Bears which have been collected from all over the world.

MINTERNE GARDENS © DAN ROADS

### Minterne Gardens, Dorset

Minterne Country House and Gardens are set in 1600 acres of parkland which make it perfect for outdoor pursuits and team building activities. There are facilities for clay-pigeon and game shooting, 4 wheel-drive and more. There is also a go-karting track nearby. There are rooms to suit small and intimate weddings as well as larger parties and exclusive hire is also available. The stunning Trafalgar Hall can cater for up to 400 guests with the addition of a marquee. Between 1840 and 1947 plant hunters scoured the world for new species and the seeds of some of these expeditions were planted at Minterne as the sub-tropical shrubs that are seen today in the Himalayan Gardens.

USHERS OUTSIDE BOCONNOC HOUSE

### Boconnoc, Cornwall

The Boconnoc estate really does have something to suit all needs. For civil and humanist ceremonies there are various venues, including the Garden room in the house itself, the Stable Yard and the Georgian Bathhouse, all providing stunning backdrops for your special day. The 800 year old Boconnoc Church set in the centre of the estate features a stunning vaulted ceiling and stained glass windows. King Charles I once spent the night here and the room he slept in is now called 'The King's Bedroom'. Exclusive hire is available to accommodate family holidays, summer getaways and Christmas breaks.

**Summer Solstice, Stonehenge, Wiltshire** *21st June 2019*

**Glastonbury Music Festival, Worthy Farm, Somerset** *26th - 30th June 2019*

**Exeter Festival of South West Food and Drink, Devon** *May 2019*

## Top 3 Annual Events

### Festival of Lights, Longleat, Wiltshire *from November*

See Longleat illuminated with hundreds of Chinese Lanterns in what has become an ever-popular annual event. Each year has a different theme and visitors will be treated to spectacular illuminated storytelling.
Ride the Santa Train, and visit Santa in his grotto. The train runs daily during the festival, but make sure you pre-book to avoid disappointment. Take the safari drive-through route and see the big cats, zebras and monkeys. Don't forget to visit Longleat House itself. Check out the website for up to date information on the festival.

LONGLEAT FESTIVAL OF LIGHTS

### Boconnoc Steam Fair, Cornwall *July*

Run by the Liskeard Steam and Vintage Club this annual event attracts visitors from all over the world.
The fair showcases steam vehicles from old tractors and motorcycles to classic cars and military vehicles. There are trailer and tractor rides so that visitors can see more of the Boconnoc Estate, including the lakes and gardens. There are craft stalls, a fun fair, live-music and a fully licensed refreshments area.

BOCONNOC STEAM FAIR

### Frampton Country Fair, Frampton Estate, Gloucestershire *September*

One of only a few traditional country fairs in the UK the annual fair is set in over 30 acres of countryside, and includes over 400 stalls and three main showground rings. There is a craft marquee and a farmer's market as well as numerous refreshment stands. Celebrate everything the countryside has to offer with dog and equestrian displays, shooting and fishing demonstrations.

FRAMPTON COUNTRY FAIR © STROUD NEWS AND JOURNAL

# South West

## Places to stay and eat

NORTHCOTE MANOR

### Northcote Manor

Northcote Manor is a manor house of 18th century origins, hidden in the heart of the North Devon countryside in a milieu of timeless tranquility, reflecting its monastic origins. It sits in 20 acres of mature woodlands, lawns and gardens, including a walled secret garden and apple orchards. There is an aura of quiet relaxed sophistication throughout which makes award winning Northcote ideal for a short break. Guests leave with their batteries recharged and ready to face the world again after a bit of self-indulgent escapism. The focus is on real comfort, excellent cuisine and attentive yet discreet service. Local attractions abound: the River Taw and nearby National Trust houses as well as RHS Rosemoor and the foodie heaven of Barnstaple covered market. The little hill town of Chumleigh with its ruined castle and 1633 Barnstaple Inn is also nearby, as well as the sandy beaches of Croyde Bay and Morte Bay.

**Burrington, Umberleigh, North Devon EX37 9LZ**

**01769 560501**

**www.northcotemanor.co.uk**
**rest@northcotemanor.co.uk**

### Plantation House Hotel

*Hotel*

Totnes Road, Ermington,
Ivybridge, Devon PL21 9NS

01548 831100

www.plantationhousehotel.co.uk
info@plantationhousehotel.co.uk

### Alexandra Hotel & Restaurant

*Hotel*

Pound Street, Lyme Regis
Dorset DT7 3HZ

01297 442010

www.hotelalexandra.co.uk info@
hotelalexandra.co.uk

### Cotswold House Hotel & Spa

*Hotel*

The Square, Chipping Campden
Gloucestershire GL55 6AN

01386 840330

www.bespokehotels.com
reservations@cotswoldhouse.com

## Berry Head Hotel

The Berry Head Hotel is set in a superb water's edge position in six acres of its own gardens and woodland, in the seclusion of the Berry Head Country Park, which is noted for its bird life and rare wild flowers. The hotel is steeped in history. It was built as a military hospital in the Napoleonic Wars and was later the home of the Reverend Francis Lyte, who wrote the famous hymn Abide With Me at the hotel, no doubt inspired by the glorious sunsets. The historic fishing port of Brixham, where William of Orange first landed to claim the English crown, is only a short walk away. The comfortable lounge and the restaurant, which overlooks the terrace, enjoy spectacular views of Torbay and the Devon coast. The two restaurants, Bonapartes à la carte restaurant and The View brasserie with wonderful sea views and offering a varied selection of local seafood fresh from the fish market in Brixham; and other locally sourced produce.

Berry Head, Brixham TQ5 9AJ

01803 853225

www.berryheadhotel.com
stay@berryheadhotel.com

BERRY HEAD HOTEL

## The Hawkins Arms
*Restaurant*

Fore Street, Probus
Truro TR2 4JL

01726 882208

hawkinsarms@gmail.com
thehawkinsprobus.co.uk

## The Plantation Tearooms
*Tea Room*

The Plantation, The Coombes
Polperro PL13 2RG

07889 241097

tripadvisor.co.uk - search:
The Plantation Tea Rooms

## Madame Butterfly
*Tea Room*

16 Maristow Street
Westbury BA13 3DN

01373 228512

www.madamebutterfly.biz
info@madamebutterfly.biz

# PRIDEAUX PLACE Ⓕ

www.prideauxplace.co.uk

**Tucked away above the busy port of Padstow, the home of the Prideaux family for over 400 years, is surrounded by gardens and wooded grounds overlooking a deer park and the Camel estuary to the moors beyond.**

Completed by Sir Nicholas Prideaux in 1592 this stunningly beautiful Elizabethan manor house, home to fourteen generations of Prideaux, overlooks the Camel Estuary 'An Area of Outstanding Natural Beauty', and the bustling picturesque fishing port of Padstow to Bodmin Moor beyond.

The Prideaux family have been prominent in Cornwall for longer than that, being recorded as Lords of Prideaux Castle at Luxulyan at the time of the Norman Conquest in 1066, indeed Peter Prideaux-Brune is a direct descendant of William the Conqueror.

Prideaux Place has changed little in the last two centuries. The house as seen today is almost entirely the work of three members of the family, Sir Nicholas Prideaux in the 16th Century, Edmund Prideaux in the 18th Century and the Revd. Charles Prideaux -Brune in the early 19th Century. It now combines its traditional Elizabethan architecture with the exuberance of fine Horace Walpole Style Strawberry Hill Gothic with later Georgian additions. No Victorian fashion spoils this very Cornish house.

The topographical drawings by Edmund Prideaux, who travelled extensively, are some of the most treasured documents in the house and they are of huge historical value often helping with research, more recently with the detailed restoration of a window at Blickling Hall in Norfolk.

When Peter and Elisabeth arrived in 1988 a huge challenge lay before them. With dry rot, wet rot and most of the rooms under scaffolding there was also a large garden which had become completely overgrown. Today with the on-going restoration the house and the surrounding gardens are once more beginning to flourish.

The house, whilst still remaining very much a family home, opened to the public in 1987 and is now an internationally renowned film and television location. Visitors are enchanted by its cornucopia of Cornish history from tales of the Civil War, the 16th Century plasterwork ceiling of the Great Chamber, fine panelling, paintings and porcelain to its part leading up to the D-Day landings and a Japanese mother of pearl Namban chest, one of only three to survive from the time of the Armada.

From the house one overlooks the park with its fine herd of fallow deer. It is thought to be the oldest deer park in the country dating back to the 5th Century and its enclosure by the Romans. Legend has it that if the deer die out so does the Prideaux family.

Most recently the stunning and completely unspoilt cliff scenery on Estate land between Trevone Bay and Stepper Point at the mouth of the Camel Estuary has been used for the filming of Poldark.

**CONTACT**

Owner: Peter Prideaux-Brune Esq
Contact: The Administrator
Tel: 01841 532411 Fax: 01841 532945
Email: office@prideauxplace.co.uk

**LOCATION**

Padstow, Cornwall PL28 8RP
Map Ref: 1:E8 - 5m from A39 Newquay/Wadebridge link road. Signposted by Historic House signs.

**OPEN**

House:
Easter Sun 21 Apr - Thur 25 Apr, then Sun 12 May - Thur 3 Oct
(Sun - Thur 1.30pm - 4pm last tour)

Grounds and Terrace Café:
Open daily 10.30am - 5pm
7 Apr - Fri 25 Oct
Closed on Sats and 1 May

**ADMISSION**

Adults £10.00, Children (age 12-16 years) £5.00
Grounds only: £4
Children 12 - 16 years: £2.

Group Rate: price on application

No picnics.

- Open air theatre, open air concerts, car rallies, art exhibitions, charity events.
- Toilet and Baby changing facilities available.
- By arrangement.
- Parking available.
- Partial. Ground floor and grounds.
- Dogs welcome on leads.
- Obligatory.
- By arrangement.
- Terrace Café situated in what was once the Old Schoolroom. Fully licensed.
- Gift shop.
- By arrangement.
- Please see website for upcoming special events.
- Wedding ceremonies and receptions.
- The historical context & architecture of Prideaux Place makes it one of the most sought after film locations.

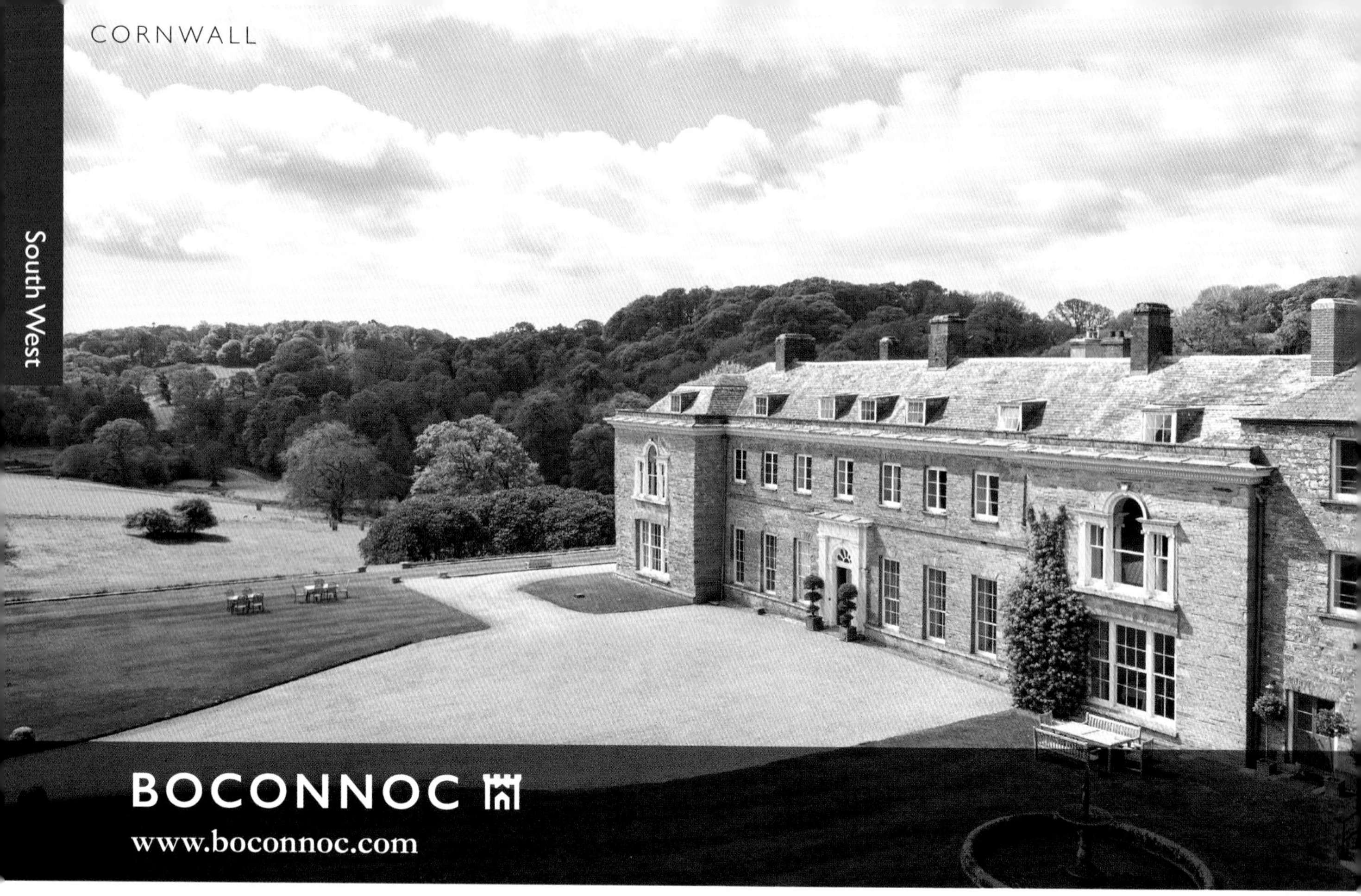

# BOCONNOC

www.boconnoc.com

Boconnoc House, the winner of the 2012 HHA/ Sotheby's Award for Restoration and the Georgian Group Award, was bought with the proceeds of the Pitt Diamond in 1717. Three Prime Ministers, a history of duels and the architect Sir John Soane play a part in the story of this unique estate. The beautiful woodland garden, the Georgian Bath House, Soane Stable Yard, 15th Century Church and naturesque landscape tempt the explorer.

Exclusive weddings with onsite accommodation for up to 40 people, private hire, film and fashion shoots and corporate days are part of Boconnoc today. Other regular events include the Boconnoc Music Award concert by the Royal College of Music and the Boconnoc Steam Fair.

TIM CHARLES PHOTOGRAPHY

**CONTACT**

Owner: Boconnoc Trustees
Contact: Sima Hill
Tel: 01208 872507
Email: office@boconnoc.com

**LOCATION**

Boconnoc, Lostwithiel, Cornwall PL22 0RG
Map Ref: 1:G8 - A38 from Plymouth, Liskeard or from Bodmin to Dobwalls, then A390 to East Taphouse and follow signs.

**OPENING TIMES**

Garden: 6, 19, 26 May 2 - 5pm.
Private Tours: By appointment only.

**ADMISSION**

House & Gardens: £18 Child (under 12) Free.
Groups by appointment.

**SPECIAL EVENTS**

Endurance GB Ride 22 & 23 June,
Boconnoc Music Award concerts with the Royal College of Music 16 & 18 July,
Steam Fair at Boconnoc 26 - 28 Jul.

Toilet facilities available.

Baby changing facilities available.

Parking available.

Partial.

In grounds, on leads.

18 doubles (9 en suite).
Holiday and residential houses to let.

By appointment during May - Sep.

By appointment.

Please see website for conferences with accommodation available.

Please see the events calendar on the website.

Church or civil ceremony.

Perfect film and photography location.

# ST MICHAEL'S MOUNT

**www.stmichaelsmount.co.uk**

This beautiful island has become an icon for Cornwall and has magnificent views of Mount's Bay from its summit. The church and castle, whose origins date from the 12th Century, have at various times acted as a Benedictine priory, a place of pilgrimage, a fortress, a home to the St Aubyn family, and is now a magnet for visitors from all over the world.

Striding the causeway or crossing by boat. Treading medieval pathways or exploring tropical gardens. Climbing to the castle or uncovering stories of harbour, legend and family home.

Marvel at the views, hear the islanders' tales and unearth a history that lives on in every step - through time and tide the Mount creates moments to remember.

- Please refer to website for up to date information for events and activities.
- WC's and disabled toilets on the island.
- Baby changing facilities available.
- Coach/car parking on mainland. Not National Trust - charges apply.
- Partial - see website for access statement. Assistance dogs allowed in the castle & garden.
- Dogs permitted in the village/harbour area, not in the castle or garden.
- By prior arrangement.
- By prior arrangement.

- Island Cafe offers expansive sea views from its garden. Pasties, sandwiches, cream teas.

- Sail Loft serves fresh Newlyn fish specials, homebaked cakes, cream teas and local ales.
- Visit the Island Shop or Courtyard Shop for unique product ranges, accessories and gifts.

- Plant sales available.

- Events throughout the year - see website for details.

**CONTACT** Owner: National Trust Contact: St Aubyn Estates
Tel: 01736 710265 Additional Tel: 01736 710507
Email: enquiries@stmichaelsmount.co.uk

**LOCATION** Marazion, Nr Penzance, Cornwall TR17 0EL
Map Ref: 3:G5 - Marazion, Near Penzance.

TRANSPORT ROUTES - Car | Bike | Bus

**TYPICALLY OPEN** Castle Opening times: (Sun-Fri) Sun 24 March - Fri 28 Jun 10:30 - 17:00, Sun 30 Jun - Fri 30 Aug 10:00 - 17:30, Sun 1 Sept - Fri 1 Nov 10:30 - 17:00. Garden Opening times: Mon 15 Apr - Fri 28 Jun 10:30 - 17:00 (Mon - Fri only) Thur 4 Jul - Fri 30 Aug 10:00 - 17:30 (Thu and Fri only) Fri 5 Sep - Fri 27 Sep 10:30 - 17:00 (Thu and Fri only)

Please note that there are limited opening times during the winter. Please check the website for full opening times.

**ADMISSION** Please see website for all admission prices.

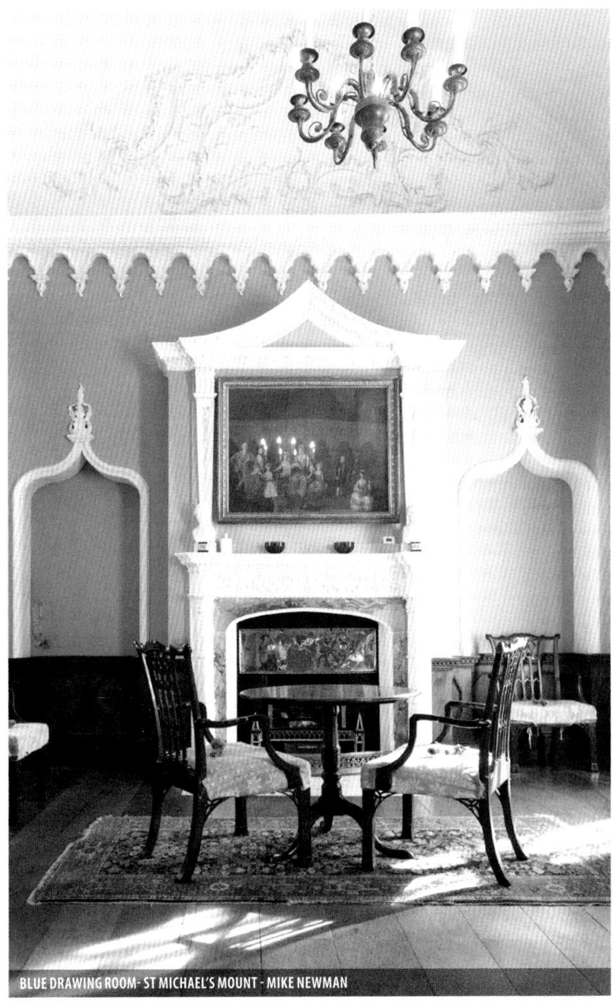

BLUE DRAWING ROOM - ST MICHAEL'S MOUNT - MIKE NEWMAN

# TREWITHEN GARDENS & PARKS

**trewithengardens.co.uk**

Trewithen means 'house of the trees' and the name truly describes this early Georgian house in its wood and parkland setting. The 30 acre garden is an International Camellia Society Garden of Excellence (1 of only 5 in the UK) and is also renowned for its rhododendrons, magnolias and Champion Trees.

**CONTACT** Owner: Mr S T J Galsworthy Contact: Liz White Contact: Gary Long Tel: 01726 883647 Email: secretary@trewithenestate.co.uk

**LOCATION** Grampound Road, Nr Truro, Cornwall TR2 4DD Map Ref: 1:E9 - On the A390 between Truro & St Austell.

**OPENING TIMES** Gardens: Mar 1-Jun 30 daily 10am-4.30pm. House: Mar-Jun Mon & Tue afternoons 2pm-4pm (guided tours only - booking advisable).

**ADMISSION** Adult £8.50, Child U12 Free. Combined entry, group rates & concessions available.

- No photography inside.
- Toilet & disabled toilet.
- Parking available also for coaches.
- Partially, mostly level gravel paths.
- Dogs welcome on leads at all times.
- Please contact for guided tour details.
- The Tea Shed, shop & plant centre.

# CADHAY 🏰 Ⓕ

**www.cadhay.org.uk**

Cadhay is approached by an avenue of lime-trees, and stands in an extensive garden, with herbaceous borders and yew hedges, with excellent views over the original medieval fish ponds. The main part of the house was built in about 1550 by John Haydon who had married the de Cadhay heiress. He retained the Great Hall of an earlier house, of which the fine timber roof *(about 1420-1460)* can be seen. An Elizabethan Long Gallery was added by John's successor at the end of the 16th Century, forming a unique courtyard with statues of Sovereigns on each side, described by Sir Simon Jenkins as one of the 'Treasures of Devon'.

Parking available.

Ground floor and grounds.

Luxury self-catering holiday accommodation for 22 in an historic Elizabethan manor.

Obligatory.

The Apple Store is now a Tea Room.

Venue to celebrate a landmark birthday, anniversary, reunion or other special occasions.

Please see the news section of the website for all events.

A unique venue for a Devon wedding; atmospheric & individual.

**CONTACT** Owner: Mr R Thistlethwayte
Contact: Jayne Covell Tel: 01404 813511

**LOCATION** Ottery St Mary, Devon EX11 1QT
Map Ref: 2:L6 1 mile North West of Ottery St Mary. From West take A30 & exit at Pattesons Cross, follow signs for Fairmile & then Cadhay.
From East, exit at the Iron Bridge & follow signs as above.

**OPENING TIMES** May - Sep, Fri 2pm-5pm. Also, late May & Summer Bank Holiday Sat - Sun-Mon. Last tour 4pm.

**ADMISSION** House (Guided tour) & Gardens: Adult £8, Child £3.
Garden only: Adult £4, Child £1. Groups 15+ by prior arrangement.

---

# HARTLAND ABBEY 🏰 Ⓕ

**www.hartlandabbey.com**

Built in 1160, Hartland Abbey is a hidden gem on the stunning North Devon coast. Passing down generations from the Dissolution, it remains a fascinating, lived-in family home: architecture from 1160 to 1850 by Meadows and Sir George Gilbert Scott; murals, important paintings and furniture, porcelain, early photographs, documents and family memorabilia. Exhibitions: 'Filming at Hartland Abbey since 1934' and 'William Stukeley-Saviour of Stonehenge'. Woodland gardens and walks lead to the Jekyll designed Bog Garden and Fernery, restored 18th Century Walled Gardens of flowers, fruit and vegetables, the Summerhouse, Gazebo and the beach at Blackpool Mill. Location for BBC's 'Sense and Sensibility', 'The Night Manager' and 'Guernsey' in 2017. Beautiful daffodils, bluebells and tulips in spring. Delicious home cooking in The Old Kitchens Tea Room. One mile from Hartland Quay. 2016 Winner 'Best Garden and/or Country House in N Devon'. Coaches very welcome. Special Events - see website. Daffodil Day.

Parking adjacent to house.

Partial. Disabled WC.

Dogs in grounds, on leads.

Conducted tours by arrangement.

Homemade lunches & cream teas.

Small shop in the museum selling a wide range of gifts.

Plants for sale produced in our gardens.

Wedding receptions. Corporate events.

Five separate venues.

**CONTACT** Owner: Sir Hugh Stucley Bt Contact: Theresa Seligmann
Tel: 01237 441496/234/01884 860225 Email: ha_admin@btconnect.com

**LOCATION** Nr Bideford, North Devon EX39 6DT Map Ref: 1:G5
15m W of Bideford, 15m N of Bude off A39 between Hartland and Hartland Quay on B3248.

**OPENING TIMES** House, Gardens, Grounds & Beachwalk: 31 Mar - 30 Sept, Sun-Thu 11am-5pm. (House 2pm-5pm - last adm 4pm). Tearoom, Light lunches & cream teas: 11am-5pm.

**ADMISSION** House, Gardens, Grounds & Beachwalk: Adult £12.50, Child (5-15ys) £5, Under 5 Free, Registered disabled £10.50, Family (2+2) £30. Gardens, Grounds, Beachwalk & Exhibition: Adult £9.50, Child (5-15ys) £4.50, Under 5 Free, Registered disabled £6.50, Family (2+2) £24. Groups & coaches: Concs 20+. Open at other dates & times. Booking essential.

# FURSDON HOUSE & GARDENS

## www.fursdon.co.uk

Fursdon House is at the heart of a small estate where the family has lived for over 750 years. Set within a hilly and wooded landscape the gardens and grounds are attractive with walled and open areas with far reaching views. Family memorabilia with fine costumes and textiles are displayed on informal guided tours.

A restored Victorian cottage offering stylish holiday accommodation is available on the estate.

- Caters for conferences. No photography or video.
- Toilet facilities available.
- Baby changing facilities available.
- Ample parking but limited for coaches.
- Partial. Please see our access statement for all access details.
- Dogs on leads are allowed in the gardens.
- 1 self-catering holiday property.
- Obligatory.
- Coach Hall Tea Room serving cream teas & selection of cakes, when the gardens & house open.
- Coach Hall suitable for small meetings & conferences. Max 40 seated.
- See the 'News & Events' section of the website for all the upcoming events.
- Fursdon hosts a very small number of unique and special wedding receptions each year.

**CONTACT** Owner: Mr & Mrs E D Fursdon Contact: Mrs C M Fursdon Tel: 01392 860860 Email: admin@fursdon.co.uk

**LOCATION** Cadbury, Nr Thorverton, Exeter, Devon EX5 5JS Map Ref: 2:K6 - Off A3072 between Bickleigh & Crediton. 9 miles North of Exeter signposted through Thorverton from A396 Exeter to Tiverton Road.

**OPENING TIMES** Gardens & Tea Room: Easter - Sep Weds, Thus & BH Mons. House: Open for guided tours Jun - Aug, Weds, Thus & BH Mons 2.30pm & 3.30pm. Group tours at other times by arrangement. Some special openings on Suns. See website for details.

**ADMISSION** House & Garden: Adult £9 (Garden only: £4.50) Child Free.

# TIVERTON CASTLE

## www.tivertoncastle.com

The wooden motte and bailey castle built in 1106 by the de Redvers Earls of Devon was on an ancient fortified Saxon site owned by King Alfred, high above the River Exe. When the Courtnays inherited in 1293 they rebuilt in stone with four towers in a courtyard style with a large outer bailey. The building has altered down the ages due to changing fashions, climate, Civil War damage and old age. Princess Katherine Plantagenet, Countess of Devon, lived here until her death in 1527 and is buried in St Peter's Church next door. General Tom Fairfax captured the Castle in 1645 when a lucky shot hit the drawbridge chain. Some rebuilding followed, and then in the 18th century the Carews inherited, then sold the Castle in 1922/3.Now the Castle is a peaceful private house with a fine collection of armour - some pieces can be tried on, interesting furniture and pictures, and a beautiful garden among the romantic ruins.

- Excellent loo facilities.
- Limited for coaches. Free parking for visitors in the drive. 20 spaces.
- Partial. Please see website for further information.
- Make a castle your home, stay in one of our 5 self-catering holiday properties.
- Private house within the courtyard, by arrangement. Tour parties welcome all year when not open.
- Great fun for children; welcoming school parties, specially if the children come in period costume.
- Tiny shop selling inexpensive, good quality souvenirs mainly relating to Castle.
- Plant sales available.
- Please see the 'What's on' section of the website to see all local attractions.

**CONTACT** Owner: Mr and Mrs A K Gordon Contact: Mrs A Gordon Tel: 01884 253200 Alt Tel: 01884 255200 Fax: 01884 254200 Email: info@tivertoncastle.com

**LOCATION** Park Hill, Tiverton, Devon EX16 6RP Map Ref: 2:K5 - 7 miles from J25 on M5 along A361 towards Tiverton follow Castle signs.

**OPENING TIMES** Easter - end Oct: Sun, Thu, BH Mon, 2.30pm-5.30pm. Last admission 5pm. Open to groups (12+) by prior arrangement all year outside opening hours.

**ADMISSION** Adult £8, Child (7 - 16yrs) £3, Under 7's Free. Garden: £2

## CASTLE HILL GARDENS

castlehilldevon.co.uk

Set in the rolling hills of Devon, Castle Hill Gardens offers a tranquil visit. Stroll through the spectacular gardens, dotted with mystical temples, follies, statues, vistas and a sham castle. The path through the Woodland Gardens, filled with flowering shrubs, leads you down to the river, the magical Satyr's temple and Ugley Bridge.

**CONTACT** Owner: Mr James and Lady Laura Duckworth-Chad. Contact: Crystal Andrews Tel: 01598 760421/01598 760336 option 2 Email: gardens@castlehill-devon.com **LOCATION** Filleigh, Barnstaple, Devon EX32 0RQ Map Ref: 2:I14 - A361, take B3226 to South Molton. Follow brown signs to Castle Hill. **OPENING TIMES** Daily except Sats. Apr-Sep 11am-5pm. Oct-Mar 11am-dusk. **ADMISSION** Please see website for prices.

Daily except Sats. Free parking. Partial. WC's. On leads. Groups and coach parties welcome at all times by prior arrangement. Refreshments available Apr-Sep.

## HEMERDON HOUSE

hemerdonhouse.co.uk

Built in the late 18th Century by the current owners' ancestors, Hemerdon House is a trove of local history, containing naval and military mementos, books, paintings, furniture, china and silver collected through many generations. Family members offer tours of the interior on certain days of the year - please see website for details.

**CONTACT** Tel: 07704 708416 Email: hemerdon.house@gmail.com **LOCATION** Plympton, Devon PL7 5BZ Map Ref: 2:I9 SatNav directions may be misleading so please see website for directions. **OPENING TIMES** See website for dates. **ADMISSION** HHA Member: £5 Adult, £7.50 Child, Free (Under 12)

Parties of 6 or more please contact us in advance; parties of 10 or more by prior arrangement only. Toilet facilities available. Free parking. Partial access - please see website for details. Dogs on leads are permitted in the grounds while the house is open. Two tours, approximately 1 hour 15 minutes each, starting at 2.30pm and 4pm.

## SAND

sandsidbury.co.uk

Sand is one of East Devon's hidden gems. The beautiful valley garden extends to six acres and is the setting for the lived-in Tudor house, the 15th Century Hall House, and the 16th Century Summer House. The family, under whose unbroken ownership the property has remained since 1560, provide guided house tours.

**CONTACT** Caroline & Diana Huyshe Tel: 01395 597230 Email info@sandsidbury.co.uk

**LOCATION** Sidbury, Sidmouth EX10 0QN Map Ref: 2:L7 Well signed, 400 yards off A375 between Honiton and Sidmouth. Don't use SatNav postcode.

**OPENING TIMES** BH Suns & Mons, June 1st & 2nd. Open 2pm-6pm last tour 5pm. Groups by appointment. For other dates see website.

**ADMISSION** House & garden: Adult £8, Child/Student: £1. Garden only: Adult £3, Accompanied Child U16: Free

No photography in house.
Toilet facilities available.
Parking available.
Partial.
Dogs welcome on leads.
Guided tours obligatory.

## DEANS COURT

www.deanscourt.org

An historic private house and garden that has been lived in for 1,300 years. Guided Tours: 10am, 11.30am, 1pm. (approx. 80 mins) Meet at gate on Deans Court Lane.

**CONTACT** Owner: Sir William & Lady Hanham Contact: Jonathan Cornish Tel: 01202 849314 Email: info@deanscourt.org

**LOCATION** Deans Court Lane, Wimborne, Dorset BH21 1EE , Map Ref: 3:B6 Follow signs to Wimborne Town Centre; pass through the Square, at the end of the High St. cross the junction (opp. Holmans TV shop) into Deans Court Ln.

**OPENING TIMES** May 5, 6, 9, 16, 23, 26, 27, 30. Jun 2, 6, 13, 20, 23, 27, 30. Jul 4, 7, 11, 18, 25. Aug 1, 4, 8, 11, 15, 18, 25, 26.

**ADMISSION** Adults £8, Senior & Disabled £6, Child (under-16) & HHA Friends Free

- Parking available only on NGS open days.
- Contact for further details.
- Dogs welcome on NGS open days only.
- Holiday houses sleep from 4-26.
- Tour times: 10am, 11:30am & 1pm. Meet at the gate on Deans Court Lane.
- 20 pers. max.
- Healthfood Café.
- Homestore.
- Beautiful venue for licensed weddings.

## LULWORTH CASTLE & PARK

www.lulworth.com

Impressive 17th Century Castle & historically important 18th Century Chapel set in extensive parkland, with views towards the Jurassic Coast. Built as a hunting lodge to entertain Royalty, the Castle was destroyed by fire in 1929. Since then it has been externally restored and internally consolidated by English Heritage.

**CONTACT** Owner: The Weld Estate Tel: 01929 400352 E-mail: info@lulworth.com

**LOCATION** East Lulworth, Wareham, Dorset BH20 5QS Map Ref: 2:P7 In E Lulworth off B3070, 3m NE of Lulworth Cove.

**OPENING TIMES** Castle & Park: Typically open Sun-Fri from Mar-Dec. Dates & times check website or call before visiting.

**ADMISSION** Pay & Display parking £3, allowing access to Park walks, Play & Picnic areas, Castle Tea Room. Admission applies for Castle & Chapel - please see website. EH & HHA members Free entry.

- Open Mar-Dec.
- WCs. Lift access to Upper Ground floor.
- Parking available.
- Guide dogs only in buildings. Dogs on leads welcome in the park.
- By arrangement.
- Concerts, corporate & private hire/ events, weddings by arrangement.
- Licensed.
- Events held throughout year.

## MINTERNE GARDENS

www.minterne.co.uk

Landscaped in the manner of 'Capability' Brown, Minterne's unique garden has been described by Simon Jenkins as 'a corner of paradise'. 20 wild, woodland acres of magnolias, rhododendrons and azaleas providing new vistas at each turn, with small lakes, streams and cascades. Private House tours, dinners, corporate seminars, wedding and events. As seen on BBC Gardeners' World. Voted one of thc ten Prettiest Gardens in England by The Times.

- Gardens open daily from 10am - 6pm, Feb - Nov.
- Toilet facilities available.
- Parking is free for visitors in the car park opposite St Andrews Church. Picnic tables in car park.
- Features various steep and uneven surfaces and are therefore NOT advised for wheelchairs.
- In grounds on leads.
- By arrangement, with a minimum of 20 in the party. Tours personally guided by Lord Digby.
- Café on East Terrace open from 10.30am, Apr - Oct (weather permitting) Light lunches & cream teas.
- Serves as a spectacular venue for guests seeking a private dining experience.
- Seminars/Team Building/ Away Days.
- Please see website for details on plant sales .
- Offering a small & intimate wedding venue for licensed civil ceremonies or large reception for your wedding.
- Minterne has been featured in films, television, radio, broadsheet newspapers and books.

**CONTACT**
Owner/Contact: The Lord & Lady Digby
Tel: 01300 341370 Email: enquiries@minterne.co.uk

**LOCATION**
Minterne Magna, Nr Dorchester, Dorset DT2 7AU
Map Ref: 2:06
On A352 Dorchester/Sherborne Road, 2 miles North of Cerne Abbas.

**OPENING TIMES**
1 Feb - 9 Nov: daily, 10am - 6pm.

**ADMISSION**
Adult £6, Child (accompanied by an adult) Free.
RHS members: Free entry from 1 Feb - 31 Mar & 1 Jun - 9 Nov.
Not free Apr - May.

South West

## ST GILES HOUSE
**www.stgileshouse.com**

This beautiful family home has been brought back to life following an award winning restoration and now hosts unique weddings, festivals and bespoke events. A beautiful 400 acre park surrounds the house and provides a stunning backdrop to one of Dorset's most prestigious venues. Exquisite rooms, a state of the art nightclub and a 17th century Riding House that has been converted into a luxury 8 bedroom accommodation, makes coming here an unforgettable experience. Please contact us to find out more.

**CONTACT** Owner: The Earl of Shaftesbury Nick Ashley-Cooper Tel: 01725 517214 E-mail: emanuel@stgileshouse.com

**LOCATION** Wimborne St Giles, Dorset BH21 5NA Map 3:A5. - Wimborne St Giles, 4mls SE of A354, past almshouses and church.

**OPENING TIMES** By appointment for groups and for bespoke events. Book Riding House accommodation online.

Parking.
Dogs on leads.
Corporate functions.
Weddings.
By appointment only.
Events.

## SHERBORNE CASTLE & GARDENS
**sherbornecastle.com**

Built by Sir Walter Raleigh in 1594. Home of the Digby family since 1617. View magnificent staterooms, nationally important collections of art, furniture and porcelain, Raleigh's kitchen, a museum and a 'Capability Brown' exhibition. The 'Great Stories' bring the Castle to life. 42 acres of English landscape gardens by 'Brown', a 50 acre lake, herbaceous borders, specimen trees and sweeping vistas.

**CONTACT** Owner: Edward Wingfield Digby Contact: Robert Smith Tel: 01935 812072 Email: castleoffice@sherbornecastle.com

**LOCATION** New Road, Sherborne, Dorset DT9 5NR Map Ref: 2:05 - ¼m from town station. Follow signs from A30 or A352.

**OPENING** Castle, Gardens, Gift Shop & Tea Rooms: Good Friday 19 Apr - 27 Oct 2019; daily except Mon & Fri (Open BH Mon); Gardens from 10am, Tearoom from 10.30am, Castle & Gift Shop from 11am.

**ADMISSION** Castle & Gardens: Adult £12, Senior £11.50, Child Free (max 4 per adult). Gardens only: Adult/Senior £6.50, Child Free (max 4 per adult). Groups: 15+ discount options available on application.

Visitors can use the picnic tables provided.
Facilities for wheelchairs and baby changing.
Unlimited free parking for coaches/cars.
Access to the ground floor only. A slide show runs showing inaccessible rooms.
Dogs welcome in the gardens on short leads.
Pre-booked private & self-guided tours of the castle available for groups.
Private/self-guided tours for students.
Tea Room for light lunches & teas.
Gift Shop offers a variety of unusual gifts.
Wonderful venue for Ceremonies & Receptions.
Available as a filming location.

## SANDFORD ORCAS MANOR HOUSE

Tudor manor house with gatehouse, fine panelling, furniture, pictures. Terraced gardens with topiary and herb garden. Personal conducted tour by owner.

**CONTACT** Owner/Contact: Sir Mervyn Medlycott Bt Tel: 01963 220206

**LOCATION** Sandford Orcas, Sherborne, Dorset DT9 4SB Map Ref: 2:05 2½m North of Sherborne, Dorset 4m South of A303 at Sparkford. Entrance next to church.

**OPENING TIMES** Easter Mon, 10am-5pm. May & Jul-Sep: Suns & Mons, 2pm-5pm.

**ADMISSION** Adult £5, Child £2.50. Groups (10+) Adult £4, Child £2.

Parking is available.
Unsuitable.
Dogs welcome in grounds,on leads.
Person conducted tours are obligatory.

### WOLFETON HOUSE

A fine medieval and Elizabethan manor house lying in the water-meadows near the confluence of the rivers Cerne and Frome. It was embellished around 1580 and has splendid plaster ceilings, fireplaces and panelling. To be seen are the Great Hall, Stairs and Chamber, Parlour, Dining Room, Chapel & Cyder House.

**CONTACT** Owner: Capt N T L L T Thimbleby Contact: The Steward Tel: 01305 263500 Email: kthimbleby.wolfeton@gmail.com **LOCATION** Nr Dorchester, Dorset DT2 9QN Map Ref: 2:06 1½m from Dorchester on the A37 towards Yeovil. Indicated by Historic House signs. **OPENING TIMES** Jun-end Sep: Mon, Wed & Thu, 2pm-5pm. Groups by appointment throughout the year. **ADMISSION** £8

Catering for groups by prior arrangement. Groups by appointment throughout the year. Limited for coaches. Accessible. Guided tours by arrangement. Educational and school visits by arrangement. Corporate functions by arrangement.

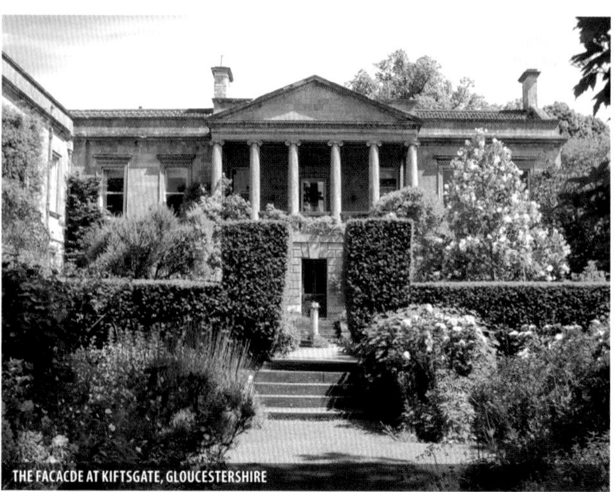

THE FACACDE AT KIFTSGATE, GLOUCESTERSHIRE

# KELMSCOTT MANOR

**www.kelmscottmanor.org.uk**

'The loveliest haunt of ancient peace'. Kelmscott Manor, a Grade I listed Tudor farmhouse adjacent to the River Thames, was William Morris's summer residence from 1871 until his death in 1896. Morris loved Kelmscott Manor, which seemed to him to have 'grown up out of the soil'. Its beautiful gardens with barns, dovecote, meadow and stream provided a constant source of inspiration. The house contains an outstanding collection of the possessions and work of Morris, his family and associates, including furniture, textiles, pictures, carpets and ceramics.

- No flash photography, protruding lenses & tripods or selfie sticks in house.
- Toilets available, including accessible toilet for the disabled
- Changing facilities available in the accessible toilet next to the Tearoom.
- Ample free parking 10 mins walk. Limited for coaches.
- Partial. Good access to the ground floor of the house, gardens, shop and Tearoom for wheelchair users.
- Well-behaved dogs on leads; except in the formal gardens & manor house. Assistant dogs welcome.
- Group tours by arrangement.
- Educational visits by arrangement.
- Freshly prepared delicious homemade food in our licensed Tearoom.
- Shop selling a wide range of items based on William Morris designs.
- Please see the 'What's On' section of the website for events, exhibitions, workshops & lectures etc.

**CONTACT** Owner: Society of Antiquaries of London
Tel: 01367 252486 Email: admin@kelmscottmanor.org.uk

**LOCATION** Kelmscott, Nr Lechlade, Gloucestershire GL7 3HJ (West Oxfordshire) Map Ref: 6:P12 - At South East end of the village, 2 miles due East of Lechlade, off the Lechlade - Faringdon Road.

**OPENING TIMES** House & Garden: Apr - Sept, Weds and Sats, 11am - 5pm (Ticket office opens 10.30am). Last admission to the house, 4pm.
Limited advance bookings on public open days.
House has limited capacity; timed ticket system operates.
Group visits: Apr - Sept, Thurs. Must be booked in advance.

**ADMISSION** Adult £10, Child/Student £5, Family £26.
Garden only: £3.50. Carer accompanying disabled person free.

# KIFTSGATE COURT GARDENS

**www.kiftsgate.co.uk**

Magnificently situated garden on the edge of the Cotswold escarpment with views towards the Malvern Hills. Many unusual shrubs and plants including tree peonies, abutilons, specie and old-fashioned roses.

Winner HHA/Christie's Garden of the Year Award 2003.

**CONTACT** Owner: Mr & Mrs J G Chambers Contact: Mr J G Chambers
Tel: 01386 438777
Email: info@kiftsgate.co.uk

**LOCATION** Chipping Campden, Gloucestershire GL55 6LN Map Ref: 6:09 - 4 miles North East of Chipping Campden. ¼ mile West of Hidcote Garden.

**OPENING TIMES** May, Jun, Jul, Sat-Wed, 12 noon-6pm. Aug, Sat-Wed, 2pm-6pm. Apr & Sep, Sun, Mon & Wed, 2pm-6pm.

**ADMISSION** Adult £ 9, Child £ 3. Groups (20 +) £8.

- Toilets in courtyard, right of car park.
- Limited for coaches.
- Partial. A free map is available.
- No dogs in the garden. Allowed in area next to overflow car park
-  Tea Room serves cream teas, cakes, biscuits and sandwiches.
- Shop next to the plant sales area has garden related gifts.
-  Plants grown in the garden and nursery available to buy.

# OWLPEN MANOR

**www.owlpen.com**

The romantic Tudor manor house stands in a picturesque valley setting with church, Court House and watermill. Stuart terraced gardens with magnificent yew topiary. Unique painted cloths, and family and Arts and Crafts collections. Dining in Cyder Barn dated 1446.

**CONTACT** Owner: Sir Nicholas and Lady Mander. Contact: Hugo Mander
Tel: 01453 860261
E-mail: sales@owlpen.com

**LOCATION** Uley, Nr Dursley, Gloucestershire GL11 5BZ Map 6:M12. - One mile east of Uley village, off the B4066.

**OPENING TIMES** The house will be open by appointment only for groups of 15 people or more. Apr-Oct, Mon-Fri.

**ADMISSION** Group tours £16. Cream Tea £23.50pp incl. tour of the House & Gardens. Or, a two course lunch & coffee for £32pp incl. tour of the House & Gardens.

- Accessible by coach only via Uley Village.
- Restaurant open for cream teas and lunches by appointment.
- At top of drive. Disabled parking next to manor house.
- Usually by owner.
- 9 Self-catering holiday cottages.
- Licensed for 100 people, weddings for up to 150 in garden marquee.
- Working with educational bodies.
- Open all year for weddings and restaurant bookings
- Events.

# SEZINCOTE

**www.sezincote.co.uk**

Exotic oriental water garden by Repton and Daniell.

Large semi-circular orangery.

House by S P Cockerell in Indian style was the inspiration for Brighton Pavilion.

- Please see our website for up-to-date events and special openings.
- Garden open all year apart from Dec.
- For information for disabled visitors email: enquiries@sezincote.co.uk.
- Properties to rent from larger, 6 bed farm houses to 3 bed cottages to quirky 2 bedroom period cottages.
- Obligatory.
- Tea and cake served May to Sep.
- A theatrical and magical summer venue and hosts six weddings a year.
- Civil and religious ceremonies and wedding receptions.

**CONTACT** Contact: Dr E Peake
Tel: 01386 700444 Email: enquiries@sezincote.co.uk

**LOCATION** Moreton-In-Marsh, Gloucestershire GL56 9AW
Map Ref: 6:P10 -2 miles west of Moreton-in-Marsh on the A44 opposite entrance to Batsford Arboretum.

**OPENING TIMES** Garden: Thur, Fri & BH Mons, 2pm-6pm not Dec.
House: As above May - Sep. Teas in Orangery when house open.

**ADMISSION** House: Adult £10 (guided tour).
Garden: Adult £5, Child £1.50 (Under 5s: Free).
Groups: Welcomed weekdays, please contact for details.

# STANWAY HOUSE & WATER GARDEN

**www.stanwayfountain.co.uk**

'As perfect and pretty a Cotswold manor house as anyone is likely to see' (Fodor's Great Britain 1998 guidebook). Stanway's beautiful architecture, furniture, parkland and village are complemented by the restored 18th Century water garden and the magnificent fountain, 300 feet, making it the tallest garden and gravity fountain in the world. The Watermill in Church Stanway, now fully restored as a working flour mill, was recently re-opened by HRH The Prince of Wales. Its massive 24-foot overshot waterwheel, 8th largest waterwheel in England, drives traditional machinery, to produce stoneground Cotswold flour.

- Toilet facilities available.
- Group visits all year round.
- Parking available.
- Telephone for full details of access.
- Dogs are welcome in the grounds of Stanway. Please keep on leads.
- Audio tours available.
- Group visits, coach parties & personal tours can be arranged any time of year.
- School tours of the Water Mill by arrangement.
- Teas, cold drinks and ice cream available.
- Gift shop selling beers.
- Please contact for all corporate enquiries.
- For all upcoming events please see the 'News & Events' section of the website.
- The perfect venue for wedding receptions.
- Film and photographic location.

**CONTACT** Owner: The Earl of Wemyss and March
Contact: Debbie Lewis Tel: 01386 584528 Tours: 07850 585539
Email: office@stanwayhouse.co.uk

**LOCATION** Stanway, Cheltenham, Gloucestershire GL54 5PQ
Map Ref: 6:O10 - North of Winchcombe, just off B4077.

**OPENING TIMES** House & Garden: Jun - Aug: Tue & Thu, 2pm - 5pm.
Private Tours: By arrangement at other times.

**ADMISSION** Please see website for up-to-date admission prices.

GARDEN AT SEZINCOTE ESTATE © NORMANN - FLICKR

South West

## GLASTONBURY ABBEY

**glastonburyabbey.com**

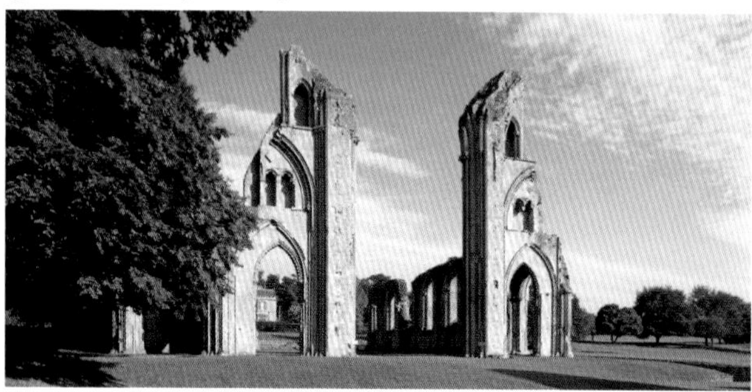

A hidden jewel in the heart of Somerset, Glastonbury Abbey is traditionally associated with the earliest days of Christianity in Britain. It is also the resting place for the legendary King Arthur.

**CONTACT** Owner: Glastonbury Abbey Estate Tel: 01458 832267 Email: info glastonburyabbey.com Twitter: @glastonburyabbe

**LOCATION** Magdalene Street, Glastonbury BA6 9EL Map Ref: 2:N4 - 50 yards from the Market Cross, in centre of Glastonbury.

**OPENING TIMES** Nov-Feb 9am-4pm Mar-May 9am-6pm , Jun-Aug 9am-8pm Sep-Oct 9am-6pm

**ADMISSION** For pricing details visit the website - reduced tickets online up until 6pm the day before you visit.

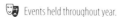

- All year except 25 December.
- Pay and display nearby.
- See the access statement online or contact us prior to your visit.
- Dogs welcome on leads.
- Mar-Oct (groups pre-book Nov-Feb).
- Primary to University, RE, History, workshops & activities 01458 8361103.
- Daily except Christmas Day.
- Glastonbury Abbey Shop is beside the Ticket Office and Main Entrance.
- Events held throughout year.

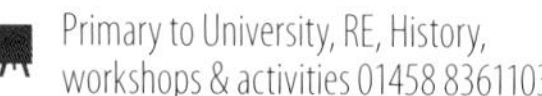

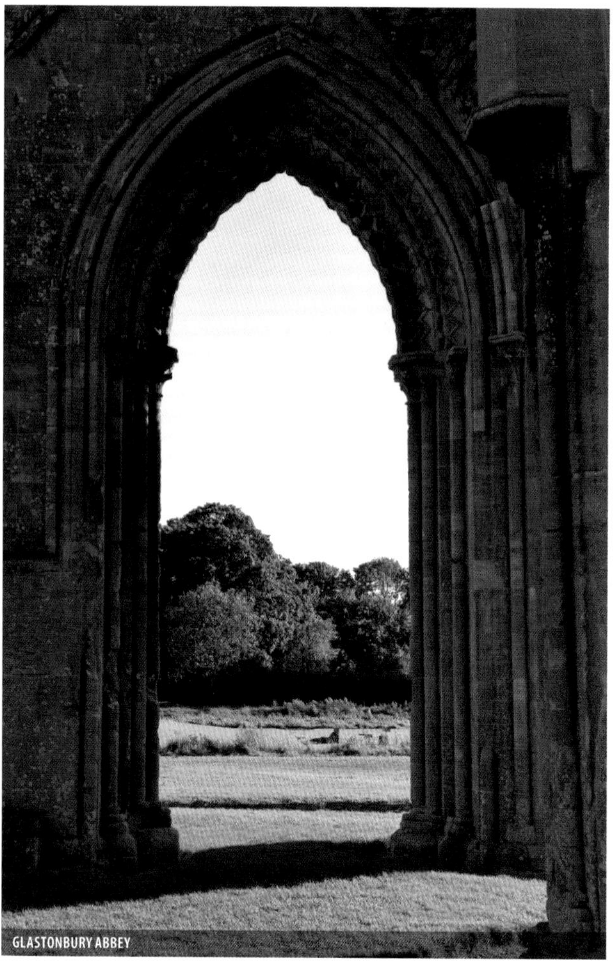

GLASTONBURY ABBEY

## LONGLEAT

**www.longleat.co.uk**

Set within 900 acres of 'Capability' Brown landscaped grounds, Longleat House is widely regarded as one of the best examples of high Elizabethan architecture in Britain and one of the most beautiful stately homes open to the public. Visited by Elizabeth I in 1574, Longleat House was built by Sir John Thynne and substantially completed by 1580. Currently home of the 7th Marquess of Bath, many treasures are included within. The fine collection of paintings range from English portraits dating from 16th century to Dutch landscapes and Italian Old Masters. The ceilings are renowned for their ornate paintings and abundance of gilt made by the firm of John Dibblee Crace in the 1870s and 1880s.

- Guest services / Lost persons.
- Toilet facilities available.
- Baby changing facilities available.
- When the park is closed VIP Safari Park tours are available for a closer view.
- Free parking available.
- Park and attractions made as accessible as possible. See website for details.
- The Bath Arms is a country pub with cosy accommodation located on the Estate.
- Free flow House tours from 11am. Guide House tours subject to availability; private chattels tours on advertised dates.
- For learning opportunities please see the school section of the website.
- The Orangery.
- The Cellar Café.
- Lady Bath's Shop; Emma's Kitchen.
- Book indoor and outdoor events from 45 -500+.
- Please see the 'What's On' section of the website for all seasonal events and exhibitions.

**CONTACT** Owner: Marquess of Bath Tel: 01985 844400 Email: enquiries@longleat.co.uk

**LOCATION** Longleat, Warminster BA12 7NW Map: 2:P4 - Just off the A36 between Bath-Salisbury (A362 Warminster-Frome) 2 hours from London following M3, A303, A36, A362 or M4/J18. A46, A36.

**TRANSPORT ROUTES** Car | Bike

**OPENING TIMES** Feb-Oct. Please see website for more details. Limited House route available during Christmas period; selected dates from Nov-Jan. Please see website for details.

**ADMISSION** Please see website for details: www.longleat.co.uk

# WILTON HOUSE

www.wiltonhouse.com

Wilton House has been the Earl of Pembroke's ancestral home for nearly 500 years. Inigo Jones and John Webb rebuilt the house in the Palladian style after the 1647 fire whilst further alterations were made by James Wyatt from 1801. Recipient of the 2010 HHA/ Sotheby's Restoration Award, the chief architectural features are the 17th Century state apartments (Single and Double Cube rooms) and the 19th Century Cloisters. The House contains one of the finest art collections in Europe and is set in magnificent landscaped parkland featuring the Palladian Bridge.

A large adventure playground provides hours of fun for younger visitors. The Gift Shop offers a varied range of presents and souvenirs and the Palladian Restaurant provides refreshments, lunches and teas.

**CONTACT**

Contact: The Estate Office
Owner: The Earl and Countess of Pembroke
Tel: 01722 746728 General Enquiries: 01722 746700
Email: tourism@wiltonhouse.com

**LOCATION**

Wilton, Salisbury, Wiltshire SP2 0BJ
Map Ref: 3:B4 - Wilton House is situated 3 miles west of Salisbury, just off the A30 and 9 miles from Stonehenge, 37 miles from Bath and 90 miles from London. TRANSPORT ROUTES Car | Bus | Train | Bike

**OPENING TIMES**

House: 19 - 22 Apr inclusive; 5 May - 1 Sep, Suns - Thurs & BH Sats only, 11.30am - 5pm, last admission 4.30pm.

Please check website for up-to-date information.

Grounds: 7 - 22 Apr; 5 May - 5 Sep, Suns - Thurs & BH Sats only, 11am - 5.30pm.

Private groups at other times by arrangement.

**ADMISSION**

House & Ground: Adult £15.50, Child (5 - 15) £8 Conc £13.25, Family £38.50

House & Ground: Adult £15.50, Child (5 - 15) £8 Conc £13.25, Family £38.50

Group Admission:
Adult £13, Child (5 - 15) £6.50, Conc £11

Includes admission to Dining & South Ante Rooms when open.

- No photography in the house. Open 5 days a week during the season. Guide dogs only.
- Toilets and disability WC's available.
- Facilities provided.
- Space for 200 cars and 12 coaches (free coach parking and coach driver meal voucher).
- In the house, grounds, shop & restaurant.
- By arrangement only (15+) Grounds guided tour £8.50.
- National Curriculum KS1/2. Sandford Award Winner 2002 and 2008.
- Licensed.
- Licensed. Group bookings available 20+.
- Gift shop.
- Antiques Fair, Equestrian Event, Country Fair, Vehicle Rallies and Charity Sponsored Walks.
- Film location.

# BOWOOD HOUSE & GARDENS

www.bowood.org

Bowood House & Gardens; home to the Marquis and Marchioness of Lansdowne, surrounded by 2,000 acres of Grade I listed 'Capability' Brown parkland, an award winning Walled Garden and a 30 acre spring Woodland Garden. Visit the Georgian House and discover over 250 years of art and historical memorabilia and the laboratory where Joseph Priestley discovered oxygen gas. There's an adrenalin fuelled children's adventure playground and glorious walks through acres of beautiful grounds.

**CONTACT** Tel: 01249 812102
Email: houseandgardens@bowood.org

**LOCATION** Calne, Wiltshire SN11 0LZ
Map Ref: 3:A2 Follow the brown tourist signs 'Bowood House & Gardens'. The entrance is through the white gates just off Derry Hill. If using a Satnav please use the postcode SN11 9NF.

**OPENING TIMES / ADMISSION**
30 Mar- 3 Nov 2019, 11am-6pm.
See website for up-to-date opening & admission details.

- For information please see website.
- Toilets in House, near the Soft Play Area and in the Treehouse Café.
- Baby changing facilities in Treehouse Café.
- Free ample parking.
- Limited disabled parking spaces near House and WC available.
- Pre-booked tours for a min 15 guests.
- In the heart of the Bowood Estate the hotel is ideal for a range of breaks.
- A haven for children, stimulating their imaginations and educational.
- Treehouse Café has a full range of hot and cold food, sweets and ice cream.
- The Stables Restaurant is also open every day for lunch and afternoon tea.
- The Terrace Gift Shop has souvenirs.

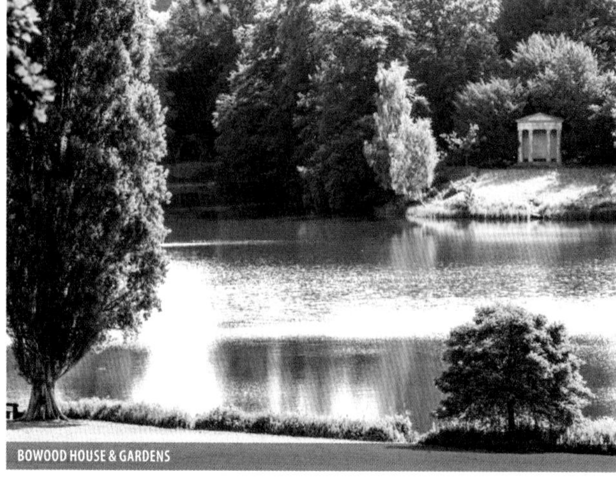

BOWOOD HOUSE & GARDENS

## CORSHAM COURT

corsham-court.co.uk

Historic collection of paintings and furniture. Extensive gardens. Tours by arrangement. Sign-posted from the A4, approximately 4 miles West of Chippenham.

**CONTACT** Owner: Lord Methuen Contact: The Curator Tel: 01249 712214 \ 01249 701610 Email: staterooms@ corsham-court.co.uk LOCATION Corsham, Wiltshire SN13 0BZ Map Ref: 3:A2 **OPENING TIMES** Tue, Wed, Thu, Sat, Sun 20 Mar-30 Sep, 2pm-5.30pm. Weekends only: 1 Oct-19 Mar, 2pm-4.30pm (Closed Dec). **ADMISSION** House & Gardens: Adult £10, Child £5. Gardens only: Adult £5, Child £2.50.

No photography in house. Open all year by arrangement. 120yds from house. Coaches may park in Church Square. Coach parties must book in advance. Platform lift and WC. Dogs on leads welcome in the gardens. Max 45. If requested the owner may meet the group. Morning tours preferred. Available: rate negotiable. A guide will be provided. Guide books, postcards, etc. at the cash desk.

# IFORD MANOR: THE PETO GARDEN

www.ifordmanor.co.uk

Unique Grade I Italian-style garden set on a steep, romantic hillside above the River Frome. Home to the famous Edwardian garden architect Harold Peto from 1899-1933, this Grade I listed garden represents his inspirational 'Tuscan dream', featuring terraces, colonnades, cloisters, casita, statuary, evergreen planting and magnificent rural views. The garden has recently undergone extensive replanting following major restoration of the structures. Winner of 2017 Group Travel 'Little Treasures of Britain' Award.

© PHILIP PIERCE

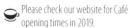

- No professional photography without permission.
- Toilet and disabled WC facilities available.
- On-site parking available for cars. Coaches by appointment only.
- Partial step-free access. Please call in advance for information.
- National Routes 4 and 254 run within 1 mile.
- Dogs welcome on leads.
- Available for groups by appointment.
- Please check our website for Café opening times in 2019.

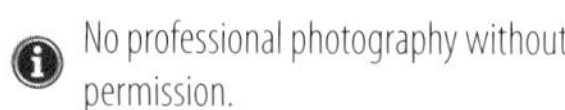

The Razor's Edge (1984)
Robin of Sherwood (1986)
Element of Doubt (1996)
He Knew He Was Right (2004)
Mistresses, s2 e1 (2009)
Gardeners World (2010)
Wild Scene Investigation (2012)
Big Dreams, Small Spaces, s2 e6 (2016)
Manolo: The Boy Who Made Shoes for Lizards (2017).

**CONTACT** Owner/Contact: Mr William Cartwright-Hignett
Tel: 01225 863146 Email: info@ifordmanor.co.uk

**LOCATION** Lower Westwood, Bradford-on-Avon, Wiltshire BA15 2BA Map Ref: 2:P3 - 2 miles SW of Bradford on Avon, signed from B3109. 6 miles S of Bath, signed from A36. Coaches / campervans: Should call in advance for directions. Train: Freshford (& 20 min walk) or Bradford on Avon (& taxi).

**OPENING TIMES** Please see www.ifordmanor.co.uk for details.

**ADMISSIONS** Please see www.ifordmanor.co.uk for details.

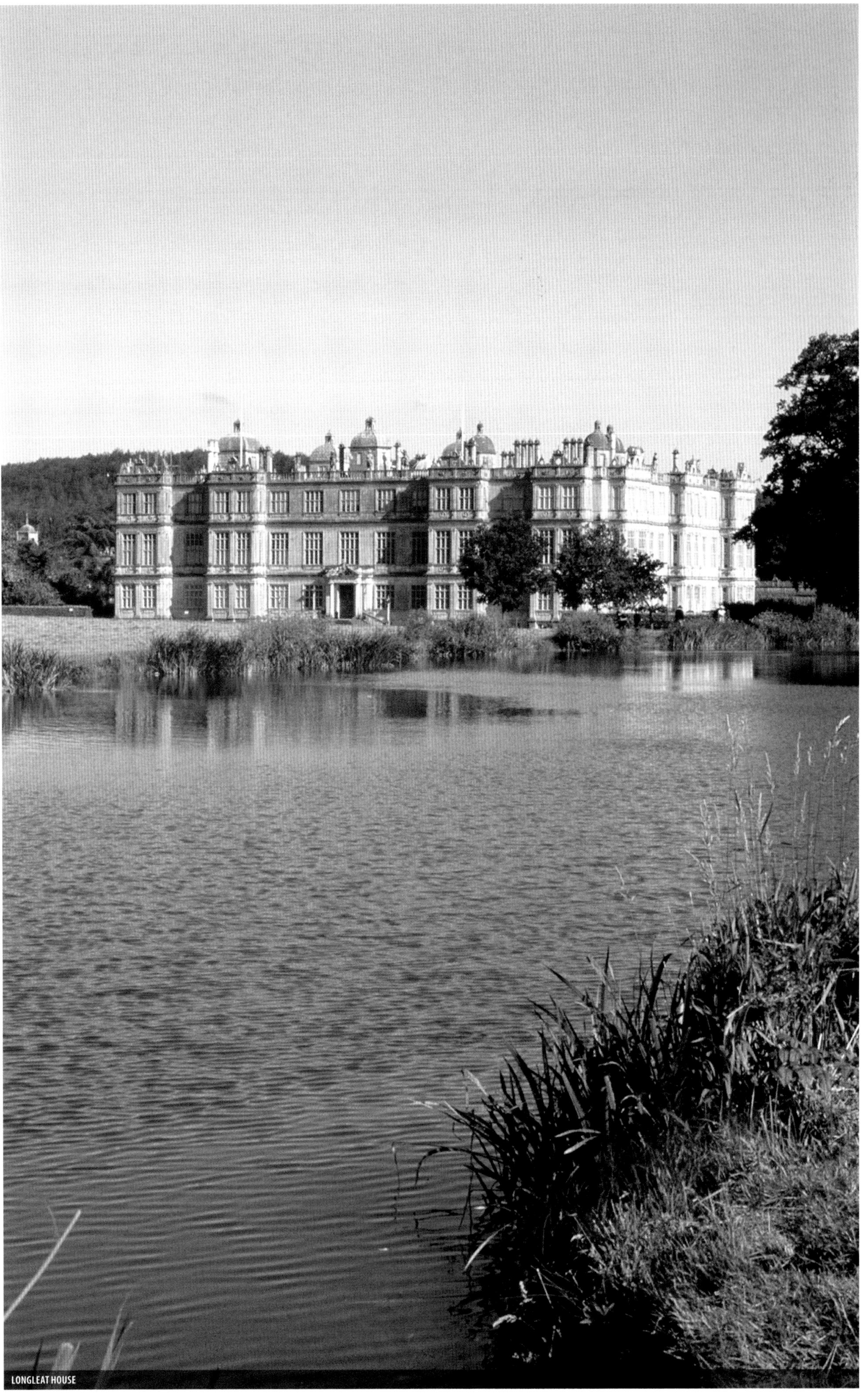

LONGLEAT HOUSE

ANTONY HOUSE & GARDEN
Torpoint, Cornwall PL11 2QA
**Tel:** 01752 812191 **Email:** antony@nationaltrust.org.uk

CAERHAYS CASTLE & GARDEN
Caerhays, Gorran, St Austell, Cornwall PL26 6LY
**Tel:** 01872 5013101 **Email:** enquiries@caerhays.co.uk

ST CATHERINE'S CASTLE
St Catherine's Cove, Fowey, Cornwall PL23 1JH
**Tel:** 0370 333 1181 **Email:** customers@english-heritage.org.uk

CHYSAUSTER ANCIENT VILLAGE
Nr Newmill, Penzance, Cornwall TR20 8XA
**Tel:** 07831 757934 **Email:** customers@english-heritage.org.uk

COTEHELE
Saint Dominick, Saltash, Cornwall PL12 6TA
**Tel:** 01579 351346 **Email:** cothele@nationaltrust.org.uk

LANHYDROCK
Lanhydrock, Bodmin, Cornwall PL30 5AD
**Tel:** 01208 265950 **Email:** lanhydrock@nationaltrust.org.uk

LAUNCESTON CASTLE
Castle Lodge, Launceston, Cornwall PL15 7DR
**Tel:** 01566 772365 **Email:** customers@english-heritage.org.uk

LAWRENCE HOUSE MUSEUM
9 Castle Street, Launceston, Cornwall PL15 8BA
**Tel:** 01566 773277 **Email:** lawrencehousemuseum@yahoo.co.uk

THE LOST GARDENS OF HELIGAN
Pentewan, St Austall, Cornwall PL26 6EN
**Tel:** 01726 845100 **Email:** info@heligan.com

ST MAWES CASTLE
St Mawes, Cornwall TR2 5DE
**Tel:** 01326 270526 **Email:** stmawes.castle@english-heritage.org.uk

MOUNT EDGCUMBE HOUSE & COUNTRY PARK
Cremyll, Torpoint, Cornwall PL10 1HZ
**Tel:** 01752 822236

PENCARROW HOUSE & GARDENS
Washaway, Bodmin, Cornwall PL30 3AG
**Tel:** 01208 841369 **Email:** info@pencarrow.co.uk

PENDENNIS CASTLE
Falmouth, Cornwall TR11 4LP
**Tel:** 01326 316594 **Email:** pendennis.castle@english-heritage.org.uk

PENTILLIE CASTLE & ESTATE
Paynters Cross, St Mellion, Saltash, Cornwall PL12 6QD
**Tel:** 01579 212002 **Email:** contact@pentillie.co.uk

PORT ELIOT HOUSE & GARDENS
St. Germans, Saltash, Cornwall PL12 5ND
**Tel:** 01503 230211 **Email:** info@porteliot.co.uk

RESTORMEL CASTLE
Lostwithiel, Cornwall PL22 0EE
**Tel:** 01208 872687 **Email:** customers@english-heritage.org.uk

TINTAGEL CASTLE
Tintagel, Cornwall PL34 0HE
**Tel:** 01840 770328 **Email:** tintagel.castle@english-heritage.org.uk

TREBAH GARDEN
Mawnan Smith, Nr Falmouth, Cornwall TR11 5JZ
**Tel:** 01326 252200 **Email:** mail@trebah-garden.co.uk

TRELISSICK GARDEN
Feock, Truro, Cornwall TR3 6QL
**Tel:** 01872 862090 **Email:** trelissick@nationaltrust.org.uk

TRERICE
Kestle Mill, Nr Newquay, Cornwall TR8 4PG
**Tel:** 01637 875404 **Email:** trerice@nationaltrust.org.uk

A LA RONDE
Summer Lane, Exmouth, Devon EX8 5BD
**Tel:** 01395 265514 **Email:** alaronde@nationaltrust.org.uk

ARLINGTON COURT
Nr Barnstaple, North Devon EX31 4LP
**Tel:** 01271 850296 **Email:** arlingtoncourt@nationaltrust.org.uk

BERRY POMEROY CASTLE
Totnes, Devon TQ9 6LJ
**Tel:** 01803 866618 **Email:** customers@english-heritage.org.uk

BUCKLAND ABBEY
The National Trust, Yelverton, Devon PL20 6EY
**Tel:** 01822 853607 **Email:** bucklandabbey@nationaltrust.org.uk

CASTLE DROGO
Drewsteignton, Nr Exeter EX6 6PB
**Tel:** 01647 433306 **Email:** castledrogo@nationaltrust.org.uk

CHAMBERCOMBE MANOR
Ilfracombe, Devon EX34 9RJ
**Tel:** 01271 862202 **Email:** chambercombemanor@btconnect.com

CLOVELLY
Nr Bideford, N Devon EX39 5TA
**Tel:** 01237 431781 **Email:** visitorcentre@clovelly.co.uk

COLETON FISHACRE
Brownstone Road, Kingswear, Dartmouth TQ6 0EQ
**Tel:** 01803 842382 **Email:** coletonfishacre@nationaltrust.org.uk

COMPTON CASTLE
Marldon, Paighton TQ3 1TA
**Tel:** 01803 843235 **Email:** compton@nationaltrust.org.uk

DARTMOUTH CASTLE
Castle Road, Dartmouth, Devon TQ6 0JN
**Tel:** 01803 833588 **Email:** dartmouth.castle@english-heritage.org.uk

DOWNES
Crediton, Devon EX17 3PL
**Tel:** 01363 775142 **Email:** info@downes.co.uk

THE GARDEN HOUSE
Buckland Monachorum, Yelverton PL20 7LQ
**Tel:** 01822 854769 **Email:** office@the gardenhouse.org.uk

GREAT FULFORD
Dunsford, Nr. Exeter, Devon EX6 7AJ
**Tel:** 01647 24205 **Email:** francis@greatfulford.co.uk

GREENWAY
Greenway Road, Galmpton, Nr Brixham, Devon TQ5 0ES
**Tel:** 01803 842382 **Email:** greenway@nationaltrust.org.uk

KILLERTON
Broadclyst, Exeter EX5 3LE
**Tel:** 01392 881345 **Email:** killerton@nationaltrust.org.uk

KNIGHTSHAYES
Bolham, Tiverton, Devon EX16 7RQ
**Tel:** 01884 254665 **Email:** knightshayes@nationaltrust.org.uk

POWDERHAM CASTLE
Kenton, Nr Exeter, Devon EX6 8JQ
**Tel:** 01626 890243 **Email:** castle@powderham.co.uk

RHS GARDEN ROSEMOOR
Great Torrington, Devon EX38 8PH
**Tel:** 01805 624067 **Email:** rosemooradmin@rhs.org.uk

SALTRAM
Plympton, Plymouth, Devon PL7 1UH
**Tel:** 01752 333500 **Email:** saltram@nationaltrust.org.uk

SHILSTONE
Modbury, Devon PL21 0TW
**Tel:** 01548 830888 **Email:** events@shilstonedevon.co.uk

TOTNES CASTLE
Castle Street, Totnes, Devon TQ9 5NU
**Tel:** 01803 864406 **Email:** customers@english-heritage.org.uk

UGBROOKE HOUSE & GARDENS
Chudleigh, Devon TQ13 0AD
**Tel:** 01626 852179 **Email:** info@ugbrooke.co.uk

ABBOTSBURY SUBTROPICAL GARDENS
Abbotsbury, Weymouth, Dorset DT3 4LA
**Tel:** 01305 871387 **Email:** info@abbotsbury-tourism.co.uk

ATHELHAMPTON HOUSE & GARDENS
Athelhampton, Dorchester, Dorset DT2 7LG
**Tel:** 01305 848363 **Email:** enquiry@athelhampton.co.uk

**CHURCH OF OUR LADY & ST IGNATIUS**
**North Chideock, Bridport, Dorset DT6 6LF**
A gem of English Catholicism and the Shrine of the Dorset Martyrs built in 1874 in Italian Romanesque style.
**Location:** A35 to Chideock, turn into N Rd & ¼ mile on right.
**Map Ref:** 2:A7.
**Tel:** 01308 488348 **Email:** info@chideockmartyrschurch.org.uk
**Web:** www.chideockmartyrschurch.org.uk
**Open:** All year: 10am-4pm. **Admission:** Donations welcome.

CLAVELL TOWER
Kimmeridge, Nr Wareham, Dorset BH20 5PE
**Tel:** 01628 825925 **Email:** bookings@landmarktrust.org.uk

CORFE CASTLE
Wareham, Dorset BH20 5EZ
**Tel:** 01929 477062 **Email:** corfecastle@nationaltrust.org.uk

EDMONDSHAM HOUSE & GARDENS
Cranborne, Wimborne, Dorset BH21 5RE
**Tel:** 01725 517207 **Email:** edmondsham.estateoffice@homeuser.net

FORDE ABBEY & GARDENS
Forde Abbey, Chard, Somerset TA20 4LU
**Tel:** 01460 221290 **Email:** info@fordeabbey.co.uk

HIGHCLIFFE CASTLE
Highcliffe-On-Sea, Christchurch BH23 4LE
**Tel:** 01425 278807 **Email:** enquiries@highcliffecastle.co.uk

HIGHER MELCOMBE
Melcombe Bingham, Dorchester, Dorset DT2 7PB
**Tel:** 01258 880251 **Email:** mc.woodhouse@hotmail.co.uk

KINGSTON LACY
Wimborne Minster, Dorset BH21 4EA
**Tel:** 01202 883402 **Email:** kingstonlacy@nationaltrust.org.uk

MAPPERTON
Beaminster, Dorset DT8 3NR
**Tel:** 01308 862645 **Email:** office@mapperton.comk

PORTLAND CASTLE
Castletown, Portland, Weymouth, Dorset DT5 1AZ
**Tel:** 01305 820539 **Email:** customers@english-heritage.org.uk

STOCK GAYLARD HOUSE
Nr Sturminster Newton, Dorset DT10 2BG
**Tel:** 01963 23511 **Email:** office@stockgaylard.com

ABLINGTON MANOR
Bibury, Cirencester, Gloucestershire GL7 5NY
**Tel:** 01285 740363 **Email:** prue@ablingtonmanor.com

BATSFORD ARBORETUM
Batsford, Moreton-in-Marsh, Gloucestershire GL56 9QB
**Tel:** 01386 701441 **Email:** arboretum@batsfordfoundation.co.uk

BERKELEY CASTLE
Berkeley, Gloucestershire GL13 9BQ
**Tel:** 01453 810303 **Email:** info@berkeley-castle.com

BOURTON HOUSE GARDEN
Bourton-on-the-Hill, Gloucestershire GL56 9AE
**Tel:** 01386 700754 **Email:** info@bourtonhouse.com

CHAVENAGE HOUSE
Chavenage, Tetbury, Gloucestershire GL8 8XP
**Tel:** 01666 502329 **Email:** info@chavenage.com

CHEDWORTH ROMAN VILLA
Yanworth, Cheltenham, Gloucestershire GL54 3LJ
**Tel:** 01242 890256 **Email:** chedworth@nationaltrust.org.uk

CIRCENCESTER PARK GARDENS

Cirencester, Gloucestershire GL7 2BU
**Tel:** 01285 653135

DYRHAM PARK

Dyrham, Nr Bath, Gloucestershire SN14 8ER
**Tel:** 0117 9372501 **Email:** dyrhampark@nationaltrust.org.uk

## FRAMPTON COURT

**Frampton on Severn, Gloucestershire GL2 7EX**
Built in 1731, still in the Clifford Family and run as a luxury B&B. Superb panelled interior, antique furniture & the 'Frampton Flora' watercolours. **Map Ref:** 6:M12 - 2 miles from M5 J13 via A38 & B4071. **Tel:** B&B 01452 740267 / Tours 01452 740268
**Email:** framptoncourt@framptoncourtestate.co.uk
**Website:** www.framptoncourtestate.co.uk
**Open:** By appointment for groups (10+). Admission: £10

## FRAMPTON MANOR

**Frampton on Severn, Gloucestershire GL2 7EP**
Said to be the birthplace of 'Fair Rosamund' Clifford mistress of Henry II. Walled Garden. **Map Ref:** 6:M12 - 2 miles from M5 J13 via A38 & B4071. **Tel:** 01452 740268 **Email:** themanor@framptoncourtestate.co.uk
**Website:** www.framptoncourtestate.co.uk **Open:** House by appt. for groups 10+. Garden only Mon & Fri 22 Apr-26 Jul, 2.30-4.30pm.
**Admission:** House: £10, Garden: £5, 16th Century Wool Barn: £3.

HARDWICKE COURT

Gloucester, Gloucestershire GL2 4RS
**Tel:** 01452 720212

HIDCOTE MANOR GARDEN

Hidcote Bartrim, Nr Chipping Campden, Gloucestershire GL55 6LR
**Tel:** 01386 438333 **Email:** hidcote@nationaltrust.org.uk

HIGHGROVE GARDENS

The Garden Tours Office, The Barn, Close Farm, Gloucestershire GL8 8PH
**Tel:** 03031 237310 **Email:** customerservices@highgroveshop.com

NEWARK PARK

Ozleworth, Wotton-Under-Edge, Gloucestershire GL12 7PZ
**Tel:** 01453 842644 **Email:** newarkpark@nationaltrust.org.uk

PAINSWICK ROCOCO GARDEN

Painswick, Gloucestershire GL6 6TH
**Tel:** 01452 813204 **Email:** info@rococogarden.org.uk

RODMARTON MANOR

Cirencester, Gloucestershire GL7 6PF
**Tel:** 01285 841442 **Email:** enquiries@rodmarton-manor.co.uk

DR JENNER'S HOUSE & GARDEN

The Chantry, Church Lane, Berkeley, Gloucestershire GL13 9BN
**Tel:** 01453 810631 **Email:** info@edwardjenner.co.uk

MISARDEN PARK GARDEN

Stroud, Gloucestershire GL6 7JA
**Tel:** 01285 821303 **Email:** estate.office@miserdenestate.co.uk

SUDELEY CASTLE & GARDENS

The Cotswolds, Gloucestershire GL54 5JD
**Tel:** 01242 604244 **Email:** enquiries@sudeley.org.uk

SNOWSHILL MANOR

Snowshill, near Broadway, Gloucestershire WR12 7JU
**Tel:** 01386 852410 **Email:** snowshillmanor@nationaltrust.org.uk

## WHITTINGTON COURT

**Cheltenham, Gloucestershire GL54 4HF**
Elizabethan & Jacobean manor house with church.
**Map Ref:** 6:N11 - 4m E of Cheltenham on N side of A40.
**Website:** www.whittingtoncourt.co.uk
**Tel:** 01242 820556 **Email:** lucy@whittingtoncourt.co.uk
**Open:** 20 April to 5 May, 10-26 August 2-5pm.
**Admission:** Adult £5, Child £1, OAP £4.

WOODCHESTER MANSION

Stonehouse, Gloucestershire GL10 3TS
**Tel:** 01453 861541 **Email:** info@woodchestermansion.org.uk

ACTON COURT

Latteridge Road, Iton Acton, Bristol, Gloucestershire BS37 9TL
**Tel:** 01454 228224 **Email:** info@actoncourt.com

THE AMERICAN MUSEUM & GARDENS

Claverton Manor, Bath BA2 7BD
**Tel:** 01225 460503 **Email:** info@americanmuseum.org

ASSEMBLY ROOMS

Bennett Street, Bath BA1 2QH
**Tel:** 01225 477785 **Email:** costume_enquiries@bathnes.gov.uk

COMBE SYDENHAM COUNTRY PARK

Monksilver, Taunton, Somerset TA4 4JG
**Tel:** 01643 702259 **Email:** bcsources@aol.com

BARRINGTON COURT

Barrington, Nr Ilminster, Somerset TA19 0NQ
**Tel:** 01460 241938 **Email:** barringtoncourt@nationaltrust.org.uk

COTHAY MANOR & GARDENS

Greenham, Wellington, Somerset TA21 0JR
**Tel:** 01823 672283 **Email:** cothaymanor@btinternet.com

DODINGTON HALL

Nr Nether Stowey, Bridgwater, Somerset TA5 1LF
**Tel:** 01278 741400

DUNSTER CASTLE

Dunster, Nr Minehead, Somerset TA24 6SL
**Tel:** 01643 821314 **Email:** dunstercastle@nationaltrust.org.uk

FAIRFIELD

Stogursey. Bridgwater, Somerset, TA5 1PU
**Tel:** 01278 732251 / 01278 732617

FARLEIGH HUNGERFORD CASTLE

Farleigh Hungerford, Bath, Somerset BA2 7RS
**Tel:** 01225 754026 **Email:** customers@english-heritage.org.uk

HESTERCOMBE GARDENS

Cheddon Fitzpaine, Taunton, Somerset TA2 8LG
**Tel:** 01823 413923 **Email:** info@hestercombe.com

KENTSFORD

Washford, Watchet, Somerset TA23 0JD
**Tel:** 01984 632309 **Email:** wyndhamest@btconnect.com

MONTACUTE HOUSE

Montacute, Somerset TA15 6XP
**Tel:** 01935 823289 **Email:** montacute@nationaltrust.org.uk

ORCHARD WYNDHAM
Williton, Taunton, Somerset TA4 4HH
**Tel:** 01984 632309 **Email:** wyndhamest@btconnect.com

PRIOR PARK LANDSCAPE GARDEN
Ralph Allen Drive, Bath BA2 5AH
**Tel:** 01225 833422 **Email:** priorpark@nationaltrust.org.uk

ROMAN BATHS
Abbey Church Yard, Bath BA1 1LZ
**Tel:** 01225 477785 **Email:** romanbaths_bookings@bathnes.gov.uk

TYNTESFIELD
Wraxall, North Somerset BS48 1NX
**Tel:** 0844 800 4966 **Email:** tyntesfield@nationaltrust.org.uk

ABBEY HOUSE GARDENS
Malmesbury, Wiltshire SN16 9AS
**Tel:** 01666 827650 **Email:** info@abbeyhousegardens.co.uk

ARUNDELLS
59 Cathedral Close, Salisbury, Wiltshire SP1 2EN
**Tel:** 01722 326546

LACOCK ABBEY
Lacock, Nr Chippenham, Wiltshire SN15 2LG
**Tel:** 01249 730459 **Email:** lacockabbey@nationaltrust.org.uk

THE MERCHANT'S HOUSE
132 High Street, Marlborough, Wiltshire SN8 1HN
**Tel:** 01672 511491 **Email:** admin@merchantshousetrust.co.uk

LYDIARD PARK (SW)
Lydiard Tregoze, Swindon, SN5 3PA
**Tel:** 01793 466 664 **Email:** lydiardpark@swindon.gov.uk

MOMPESSON HOUSE
Cathedral Close, Salisbury, Wiltshire SP1 2EL
**Tel:** 01722 335659 **Email:** mompessonhouse@nationaltrust.org.uk

**NEWHOUSE**
**Redlynch, Salisbury, Wiltshire SP5 2NX**
A brick, Jacobean 'Trinity' House, c1609, with 2 Georgian wings & a basically Georgian interior. **Map Ref:** 3:B5
9m S of Salisbury between A36 & A338. **Tel:** 01725 510055
**Email:** events@newhouseestate.co.uk
**Website:** www.newhouseestate.co.uk **Open:** 1 Mar - 8 Apr & 26 Aug, excluding weekends. **Admission:** Adult £5, Child £3, Conc £5. Groups (15+): Adult £4, Child £3, Conc £4.

NORRINGTON MANOR
Alvediston, Salisbury, Wiltshire SP5 5LL
**Tel:** 01722 780 259

OLD WARDOUR CASTLE
Nr Tisbury, Wiltshire SP3 6RR
**Tel:** 01747 870487 **Email:** customers@english-heritage.org.uk

STONEHENGE
Wiltshire SP4 7DE
**Tel:** 08703 331181 **Email:** customers@english-heritage.org.uk

STOURHEAD
Stourton, Nr Warminster BA12 6QD
**Tel:** 01747 841152 **Email:** stourhead@nationaltrust.org.uk

South West

PRIDEAUX PLACE, CORNWALL

# EAST *of* ENGLAND

BEDFORDSHIRE • CAMBRIDGESHIRE • ESSEX
HERTFORDSHIRE • NORFOLK • SUFFOLK

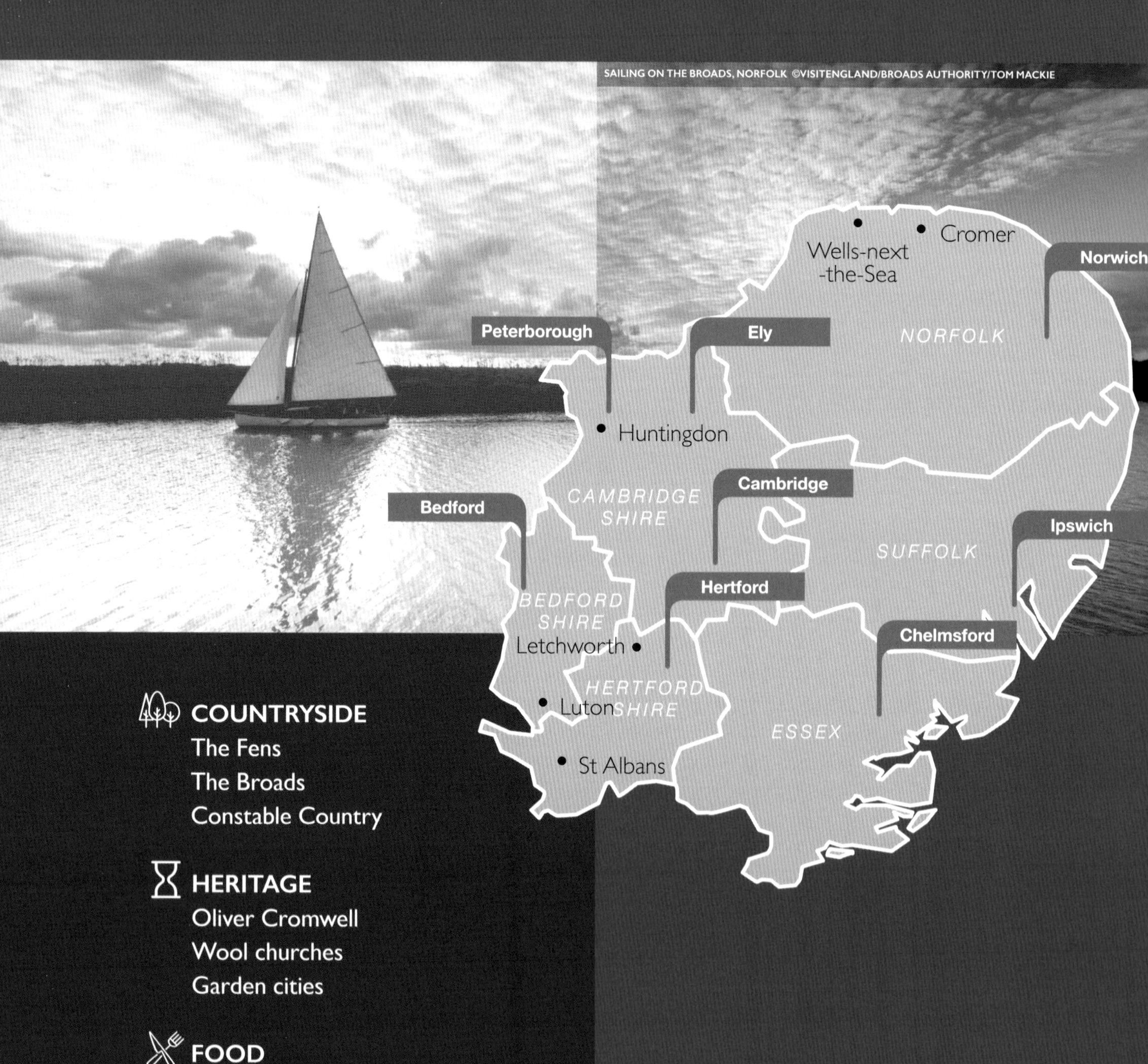


SAILING ON THE BROADS, NORFOLK ©VISITENGLAND/BROADS AUTHORITY/TOM MACKIE

**COUNTRYSIDE**
The Fens
The Broads
Constable Country

**HERITAGE**
Oliver Cromwell
Wool churches
Garden cities

**FOOD**
Cromer crab
Norfolk turkeys
Mustard

# Kimbolton Castle

## Takes your Breath Away

Britain's most spectacular houses of the English Baroque, Castle Howard and Blenheim Palace, are the result of the collaboration of architects Sir John Vanbrugh and Nicholas Hawksmoor. At the heart of a small town in modern Cambridgeshire is another less celebrated example. Kimbolton Castle is the ancestral home of the Dukes of Manchester but since today it is Kimbolton School, few people get a chance to visit it. It's worth the effort for two reasons.

KIMBOLTON CASTLE © DAVE PICKETT

Firstly, this is a house with impact. The long range of the classical gatehouse added by later architect, Robert Adam, hides the impressive bulk of the symmetrical and castellated façade of the mansion to create just the right amount of surprise. The house runs around a central courtyard with a columned portico at the rear surveying a long avenue of Wellingtonias. Inside, Vanbrugh's State Rooms have been restored to their original theatricality. Helmeted and winged figures in swirls of drapery and eddying clouds cover the walls and ceilings of the Staircase, Chapel and Boudoir, brought to life by Italian muralist, Giovanni Antonio Pellegrini. His portrait of the children of the 1st Duke hangs in the White Hall while more forbears of the Dukes of Manchester adorn the gilded walls of the Saloon.

It is a tribute to the power of architecture that Kimbolton is still breath-taking despite seven decades of schoolchildren and the absence of furnishings. You might find yourself listening for an unhappy ghost. Catherine of Aragon, divorced and abandoned first Queen of Henry VIII, lived here for the last two years of her life, dying in 1536. The vestiges of the fortified manor she would have known can just be glimpsed in the Chapel corridor and behind a panel in the Red Room, hidden by Vanbrugh's remodelling. Look out for Kimbolton's rare open days or book a group tour. ■

PELLEGRINI'S MURALS STILL DOMINATE THE STAIRCASE © DAVE PICKETT

# East of England

## Top 3 Venues

© WOBURN WEDDINGS

### Woburn Abbey, Bedfordshire

Woburn is open to host wedding and corporate events all year round. There are three separate venues; The Sculpture Gallery, The Safari Lodge and The Woburn Hotel, all licensed for civil ceremonies as well as being available for corporate events. A dedicated wedding planner will make sure your day is tailored precisely to your needs. The parkland is perfect for hosting team building activities. Rooms can be dressed to your requirements, with fine dining and champagne receptions available. Spend some time in nearby Woburn village to find out more about the history of the estate.

ELTON HALL WEDDING © PETER REDHEAD PHOTOGRAPHY

### Elton Hall, Cambridgeshire

If you are looking for an exclusive venue, Elton Hall holds just five weddings per year, each being given exclusive use of the hall and grounds for their special day. The Orangery or Billiard Room are perfect for intimate ceremonies, for larger parties a marquee can be erected. For corporate events the Dining Room holds up to 50 guests for dinner. The stunning parkland is available for hire for outdoor event hosting and can also be used as a film location or for photoshoots. One of the three libraries at the Hall contains a prayer book which belonged to Henry VIII.

INGATESTONE HALL, ESSEX

### Ingatestone Hall, Essex

Ingatestone has hosted charity balls, open-air theatre and trade exhibitions as well as weddings and corporate events. Events are individually designed to ensure that you hire as much or as little of the estate as is required for your event. Many different rooms are available, the Stone Hall is wood panelled with a stone floor and has a staged area at one end. The Long Gallery walls are lined with 40 Petre family portraits as well memorabilia dating back for centuries. Book a tour to find out more about the many different spaces on offer.

NTS

**The Suffolk Show, Trinity Park, Ipswich, Suffolk** *29th and 30th May 2019*

**Battle Proms Concert, Hatfield House, Hertfordshire** *13th July 2019*

**2000 Guineas at Newmarket, Cambridgeshire** *4th May 2019*

## Top 3 Annual Events

### Willow 10K Race, Hatfield Estate, Hertfordshire

*October*

This annual race has been held for over 10 years. Runners of all abilities take part to raise money to provide Special Days for seriously ill young adults in the UK Runners can choose to do the 10k or 5k routes. For children, there is a 1K junior route and for the smallest participants the Tiny Tots Scampers. All routes take runners around the grounds of Hatfield house, including parts that are not usually open to the public.

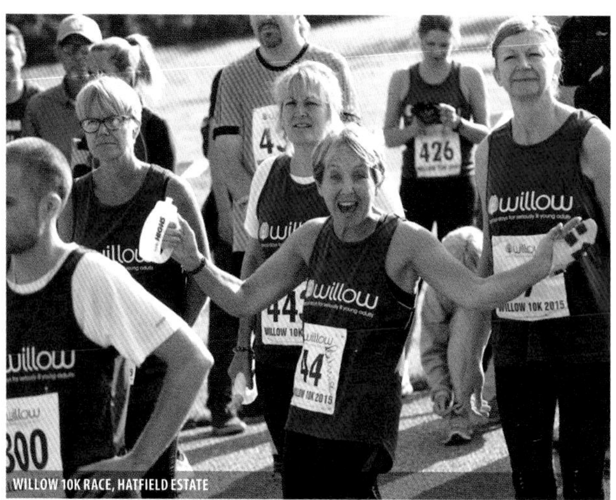

WILLOW 10K RACE, HATFIELD ESTATE

### Retreat Days At Otley Hall, Suffolk

*Various dates throughout the year*

These full-day sessions allow participants time to get away from it all and take time for themselves in the tranquil setting of the grounds of Otley Hall. Retreat days each have a different theme and are run by various leaders who will guide you through the day. Participants do not need to be of any particular faith to benefit from these sessions. A typical day may include group discussion, individual exercises to work on and a period of silence. Find out more and book your place through the Otley Hall website.

RETREAT DAYS AT OTLEY HALL, SUFFOLK

### Christmas at Holkham Hall, Norfolk

*November and December*

Christmas at Holkham is extra special. The estate hosts musical events, specially themed tours of the house and of course, the opportunity to meet Santa! Buy your Christmas decorations, gifts and food and drink in the gift shop. Get involved and make your own decorations; craft activities in previous years have included wreath making and festive flower arranging.

CHRISTMAS AT HOLKHAM HALL

# East of England

## Places to stay and eat

MILSOMS MAISON TALBOOTH

### Milsoms Maison Talbooth

Maison Talbooth is a Victorian house which has been owned by the Milsom family for over 40 years and is now one of the leading hotels of East Anglia. It is situated on the Essex/Suffolk border, ½ mile from the picturesque village of Dedham and overlooking the beautiful Dedham Vale, famous Constable country. The top floor has a Spa with two double treatment rooms and a single treatment room. As well as a tennis court, there is a swimming pool in the grounds, with changing rooms and showers, decked area and a hot tub. Guests can enjoy a cocktail or snack lunch by the pool, relax by a log fire or enjoy a pre or post dinner drink. There is also a beautifully appointed Garden Room for afternoon tea and light lunches.

Serious eating happens at Le Talbooth, the 2 AA rosette restaurant which is only a minute away in the hotel's Range Rover. The 16th century timber framed building was formerly a toll booth. Outside guests can sit under a huge architectural sail on the terrace beside the river Stour.

**Stratford Road, Dedham, Colchester, Essex CO7 6HN**

**01206 322367**

**www.milsomhotels.com/maisontalbooth**
**maison@milsomhotels.com**

### Hintlesham Hall Hotel

*Hotel*

Hintlesham, Ipswich, Suffolk IP8 3NS

01473 652334

www.hintleshamhall.co.uk
reservations@hintleshamhall.com

### Norfolk Mead Hotel

*Hotel*

Church Loke, Coltishall
Norwich, Norfolk NR12 7DN

01603 737531

www.norfolkmead.co.uk
info@norfolkmead.co.uk

### Broom Hall Country Hotel

*Hotel*

Richmond Road, Saham Toney
Watton, Norfolk IP25 7EX

01953 882125

www.broomhallhotel.co.uk
enquiries@broomhallhotel.co.uk

## Hotel Felix

Built in 1852 as a family home by a well-known surgeon at nearby Addenbrooke's Hospital, Hotel Felix is a blend of Victorian architecture and contemporary comfort. It was Cambridge's first independent boutique hotel, just a mile from the city centre, with plenty of free parking and set in three acres of grounds.

Bedrooms and reception rooms are decorated with an eclectic mix of modern artwork. The 52 bedrooms are comfortable and stylish, with king size Hypnos mattresses, finest Egyptian cotton sheets, duck down duvets. Mini bars, laptop safes, WiFi and satellite TV are all available. The bathrooms have underfloor heating, bathrobes and 'White Company' toiletries and suites have remote control TVs at the end of the baths!

Hotel Felix is suitable for a relaxing weekend break, an idyllic Cambridge wedding, a meeting, celebratory dinner or a delicious afternoon tea. The Felix is an oasis of classic indulgence and contemporary style in this historic and buzzing city. The AA 2 Rosette Graffiti Restaurant specialises in modern British cuisine with a Mediterranean twist.

Whitehouse Lane, Huntingdon Road, Cambridge, Cambridgeshire CB3 0LX

01223 277977

www.hotelfelix.co.uk
help@hotelfelix.co.uk

HOTEL FELIX

## The Pier at Harwich

*Hotel*

The Quay, Harwich
Essex CO12 3HH

01255 241212

www.milsomhotels.com/thepier
pier@milsomhotels.com

## Ridgmont Station Vintage Tea Room

*Tea Room*

Ridgmont Station, Station Road
Ridgmont MK43 0XP

01525 287120

www.facebook.com/Ridgmont-Station-Vintage-Tea-Room-and-Heritage-Centre
ridgmonttearoom@gmail.com

## Sophie T's Vintage Teashop

*Tea Room*

183 Main Street, Yaxley
Peterborough PE7 3LD

07768 351227

info@sophiets.co.uk
www.sophiets.co.uk

WOBURN ABBEY WEST FRONT

# WOBURN ABBEY AND GARDENS

www.woburnabbey.co.uk

FOLLY AT WOBURN ABBEY GARDENS

LONG GALLERY ARMADA PAINTING & GUIDE

**Step inside Woburn Abbey to immerse yourself in 500 years of history, explore 28 acres of award-winning gardens and enjoy a drive through the extensive deer park.**

Home of the Duke and Duchess of Bedford, Woburn Abbey was gifted to the family by Henry VIII in his will of 1547. Explore nearly 500 years of one family's history, including the popularisation of afternoon tea, a Royal pardon, political reform and Royal visits.

Discover an art collection including an unrivalled group of 16th and 17th Century portraits, works by Reynolds and Van Dyck and the largest private collection of Canaletto's Venetian views on public display. Many unique pieces fine English and French furniture are on display throughout the house.

The exhibition 'Humphry Repton: Art & Nature for the Duke of Bedford' continues in 2019, including the most elaborate of Repton's Red Books.

The 28 acres of Woburn Abbey Gardens are exceptional. Enjoy elegant horticultural designs, woodland glades, ponds and architectural features; much of which were the inspiration of Humphry Repton. The restoration of Repton's original Pleasure Grounds from 200 years ago continues today.

On 1st September 2019 Woburn Abbey will close its doors to visitors for around 18 months in order to undergo an exciting transformation.

**OWNER**
The Duke and Duchess of Bedford & The Trustees of the Bedford Estates

**CONTACT**
Woburn Abbey
Tel: 01525 290333
Email: admissions@woburn.co.uk

**LOCATION**
Woburn, Bedfordshire MK17 9WA
Map Ref: 7:D10
Signposted from M1 J12/J13 and A4012.
Easy access from A5 via Hockliffe, follow signs to Woburn village.

**OPENING TIMES**
Fri 5 Apr - Sun 1 Sep Gardens: 10am - 6pm
The Abbey: 11am - 5pm

**ADMISSION**
Please call or visit our website for details.
Group rates available.

**SPECIAL EVENTS**
Please visit our website for a full list of our events, guided tours and study days.

Our exhibition - Humphry Repton: Art & Nature for the Duke of Bedford continues in 2019.

Don't miss the Woburn Abbey Garden Show: 22 & 23 June 2018.

Housekeeper's Know-How 22 March.

How to Run a Stately Home - 16 May and 11 July.

Carriage Tours: Available monthly from Apr-Aug, please check our website for details.

Photography is not permitted inside the Abbey & we ask that mobile phones are switched to silent.

Toilet facilities available.

Baby changing facilities available.

Free parking.

Very limited access in the house. Good access in the gardens.

Except assistance dogs.

The Woburn Hotel in the village of Woburn.

By arrangement.

Please telephone for details.

Licensed Tea Room. Freshly prepared, homemade meals, snacks, sweet treats and afternoon tea.

Gift and souvenir shop.

Woburn grown plants available to buy throughout the main season.

Conferences, exhibitions, banqueting, luncheons & dinners. www.sculpturegallerywoburn.co.uk

www.woburnabbey.co.uk/events

Weddings are held in the Sculpture Gallery, visit website or call for more information.

Provides a variety of filming locations.

# ELTON HALL

www.eltonhall.com

Elton Hall is a fascinating mixture of styles and has always been a family house since the late 15th Century. The house contains wonderful furniture, porcelain and magnificent paintings. Artists represented in the collection include Gainsborough, Constable, Reynolds and Old Masters from the early Italian Renaissance. The library is one of the finest in private ownership and contains such treasures as Henry VIII's prayer book. The formal gardens have been restored during the last 30 years and include a Gothic Orangery, a Flower Garden with spectacular fountain, Shrub Garden and Box Walk. Billowing borders surround the lily pond, while topiary, parterres and immaculately kept lawns and paths give structure to the many unusual plants.

**CONTACT**

Owner: Sir William Proby Bt, CBE

Contact: Events Office Tel: 01832 280468

Email: events@eltonhall.com

**LOCATION**

Elton Hall & Gardens, Elton, Cambridgeshire PE8 6SH

Map Ref: 7:E7

Close to A1 in the village of Elton, off A605 Peterborough - Oundle Road.

**OPENING TIMES**

2pm - 5pm, May, last May BH, Sun & Mon. Jun & Jul, Wed, Thu. Aug, Wed, Thu, Sun & BH Mon. Private groups by arrangement daily May - Sep.

Opening days subject to change, please check the website or call before visiting.

**ADMISSION**

Please see website www.eltonhall.com for current house and garden prices. Children under 16 free. Call 01832 280468.

No photography in house.

Lavatories & disabled WC facilities at both Bosworth's Garden Centre and the Hall.

Baby changing facilities available.

Bosworth's Garden Centre adjacent to Elton Hall.

Garden suitable. Ample room with provision for disabled parking.

Obligatory. Except Bank Holidays when there are room guides. Tours approx. 1 hour.

Contact events@eltonhall.com

The Mulberry Café at Bosworth's Garden Centre provides delicious lunches, teas and light refreshments.

Bosworth's Garden Centre

Bosworth's Garden Centre offers plant sales.

For meetings and dinners, Parkland for outdoor activities.

Please see the 'What's On' section of the website for all upcoming events.

The Orangery and the Billiard Room are licensed for wedding ceremonies.

Provides the perfect backdrop for filming or photo-shoots.

# KIMBOLTON CASTLE

## www.kimbolton.cambs.sch.uk/castle

Vanbrugh and Hawksmoor's 18th Century adaptation of 13th Century fortified house. Katherine of Aragon's last residence. Tudor remains still visible. Courtyard by Henry Bell of King's Lynn. Outstanding Pellegrini murals. Gatehouse by Robert Adam. Home of Earls and Dukes of Manchester, 1615-1950. Family portraits in State Rooms. Wooded grounds with fine Wellingtonia avenue. Now owned by Kimbolton School. Children's animal, Tudor and Victorian trails and dressing-up box. Light refreshments available. Group tours by prior arrangement: special rates apply. The Castle can be booked for weddings and other events.

- Toilet facilities are available in Castle.
- 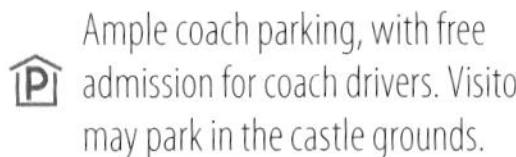 Ample coach parking, with free admission for coach drivers. Visitors may park in the castle grounds.
-  A tour of the interior of the Castle takes approximately 1½ hours and 2 hours with the exterior included.
-  School groups admitted to the Castle free of charge, by special arrangement.
-  Postcards, guidebooks and a limited range of souvenirs on sale to visitors.
-  Highly experienced in hosting a wide variety of formal and informal celebrations and functions.
-  The perfect setting for wedding ceremonies and receptions.

**CONTACT** Owner: Governors of Kimbolton School
Contact: Mrs N Butler Tel: 01480 860505
Email: reception@kimbolton.cambs.sch.uk
Additional Email: ncb@kimbolton.cambs.sch.uk

**LOCATION** Kimbolton, Huntingdon, Cambridgeshire PE28 0EA
Map Ref: 7:E8 - 7 miles North West of St Neots on B645.

**OPENING TIMES**
2019 Dates: 3 Mar at 1pm - 4pm and 3 Nov at 1pm - 4pm.

**ADMISSION** Adult £5, Child £2.50, Over 60s £4
Groups: Tours by arrangement throughout the year, including evenings, subject to Kimbolton School use. Min charge £60.

# THE MANOR, HEMINGFORD GREY

## www.greenknowe.co.uk

One of the oldest continuously inhabited houses in Britain built about 1130. The three walls of The Music Room have seen and heard nearly nine hundred years of family life. The house was made famous as 'Green Knowe' by the author Lucy M. Boston. The internationally known patchwork collection sewn by Lucy Boston is also shown. Surrounded by a moat and on the fourth side by a river the four acre garden, laid out by Lucy Boston, has topiary, old roses, award-winning irises and herbaceous borders.

- No photography in house.
- The garden is open all year and the House is open throughout the year but strictly by appointment.
- Cars: Disabled plus a few spaces if none in High Street. Coaches: Nearby.
- Partial. Access to hall and dining room only. Garden has some gravel areas.
- Obligatory.
- Particularly suitable for children.
-  Cafés in the village.
- The Cock pub in village.
- Cash, cheque or bank transfer payments only.
- Plants sales available.
- Please see homepage for all events and shows.
- Film location.

**CONTACT** Owner/Contact: Diana Boston
Tel: 01480 463134 Email: diana_boston@hotmail.com

**LOCATION** Norman Court, High Street, Hemingford Grey, Cambridgeshire PE28 9BN Map Ref: 7:F8 - A14, 3m SE of Huntingdon. 12m NW of Cambridge. Access via small gate on riverside.

**OPENING TIMES** House: All year to individuals or groups by prior arrangement. Also in May guided tours daily at 2pm (booking advisable). Garden: All year, daily, 11am-5pm (4pm in winter).

**ADMISSION** House & Garden: Adult £8, Concessions £7, Child £3, Family £22. Garden only: Adult £5, Concessions £4.50, Child Free.

## ISLAND HALL

**www.islandhall.com**

An important mid-18th Century mansion of great charm, owned and restored by an award-winning interior designer. This family home has lovely Georgian rooms, with fine period detail, and interesting possessions relating to the owners' ancestors since their first occupation of the house in 1800. A tranquil riverside setting with formal gardens and ornamental island forming part of the grounds in an area of Best Landscape.

**CONTACT** Mr C Vane Percy
Tel: Groups 01480 459676. Individuals via Invitation to View: 01206 573948.
E-mail: enquire@islandhall.com

**LOCATION** Centre of Godmanchester, Post Street next to free car park. 1m S of Huntingdon, 15m NW of Cambridge A14. Map 7:F8.

**OPENING TIMES** Groups by arrangement: All year round.

**ADMISSION** Groups(40+) £9 per person, (30+) £9.50 and parties under 20 a minimum charge £200. Individuals via 'Invitation to View'

See website for more details.

Homemade teas. Tours.

Dogs allowed in grounds on leads.

Open all year.

Accommodation.

Wedding receptions.

## INGATESTONE HALL

**ingatestonehall.com**

16th Century mansion, with 11 acres of grounds (formal garden and wild walk), built by Sir William Petre, Secretary of State to four Tudor monarchs, which has remained in his family ever since. Furniture, portraits and memorabilia accumulated over the centuries - and two Priests' hiding places.

**CONTACT** Owner/Contact: The Lord Petre
Tel: 01277 353010
Email: house@ingatestonehall.co.uk

**LOCATION** Hall Lane, Ingatestone, Essex CM4 9NR Map Ref: 7:H12 Off A12 between Brentwood & Chelmsford. London end of Ingatestone High Street.

**OPEN** 21 Apr - 29 Sept. Wed, Suns & BH 12.00pm - 5.00pm.

**ADMISSION** Adult £7, Child £3, Under 5yrs Free, Conc £6. Groups: 20+ Booked in advance. Adult £6, Child £2, Conc £5.

No photography in house.

Free parking.

Partial. WC's.

Available out of hours by arrangement.

Teas/light lunches in Summer Parlour.

A range of gifts and souvenirs.

Receptions up to 100 inside the House. No limit outside

Weddings up to 80.

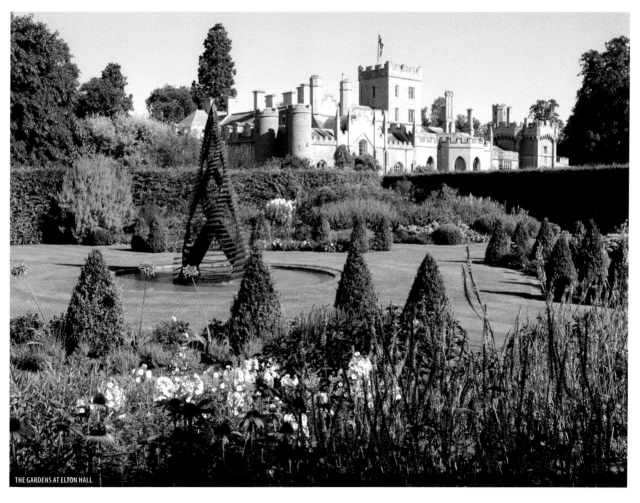

THE GARDENS AT ELTON HALL

## COPPED HALL

**www.coppedhalltrust.org.uk**

Mid-18th Century Palladian mansion under restoration. Situated on ridge overlooking landscaped park. Ancillary buildings including stables and racquets court. Former elaborate gardens being rescued from abandonment. Large 18th Century walled kitchen garden - adjacent to site of 16th Century mansion where 'A Midsummer Night's Dream' was first performed. Ideal film location.

**CONTACT** Owner: The Copped Hall Trust Contact: Alan Cox Tel: 020 7267 1679 Mobile: 07799 473 108 Email: coxalan1@aol.com

**LOCATION** Crown Hill, Epping, Essex CM16 5HS Map Ref: 7:G12 4 miles South West of Epping, North of M25. Satnav postcode for entry is CM16 5HR.

**OPENING TIMES** Ticketed events and special open days. See website for dates. Private tours by appointment.

**ADMISSION** Open Days: £10. Guided Tour Days: £8 Gardens Only: £5

Parking available. Partial access.

Dogs welcome in grounds on leads. No dogs in mansion.

3hr Guided Tours every 3rd Sun of month except Dec. Access 10 - 11am only.

Workshops and study days.

Pudding evening & afternoon tea.

Purchase a variety of goods in the shop appealing to all tastes.

Please see website for events.

COPPED HALL GARDENS

## BENINGTON LORDSHIP GARDENS

**www.beningtonlordship.co.uk**

7 acre garden in timeless parkland setting.

**CONTACT** Susanna Bott Tel: 01438 869668 E-mail: garden@beningtonlordship.co.uk

**LOCATION** Benington Lordship, Benington, Stevenage, Hertfordshire SG2 7BS Map Ref: 7:F11 In village of Benington next to the church. 4m E of Stevenage.

**OPENING TIMES** Snowdrops in Feb, Easter and May BHs, Chilli Festival Aug BH and Groups welcome by appointment. See website for details. **ADMISSION** £5

Toilets. Parking. Cafe/tearoom/refreshments

In the movies (C4 Humans and Summer of Rockets - to be screened BBC 2018/19)

Member of HHA giving free access (except during Chilli Festival)

all to yourself?
See our QUICKGUIDES at the back of this book for a helpful list of properties
PRIVATE HIRE

# HATFIELD HOUSE

www.hatfield-house.co.uk



THE KNOT GARDEN

THE RAINBOW PORTRAIT

## Over 400 years of culture, history and entertainment.

Hatfield House is the home of the 7th Marquess and Marchioness of Salisbury and their family. The Estate has been in the Cecil family for over 400 years. Superb examples of Jacobean craftsmanship can be seen throughout the House.

In 1611, Robert Cecil, 1st Earl of Salisbury built his fine Jacobean House adjoining the site of the Old Palace of Hatfield. The House was splendidly decorated for entertaining the Royal Court, with State Rooms rich in paintings, fine furniture and tapestries.

Superb examples of Jacobean craftsmanship can be seen throughout Hatfield House such as the Grand Staircase with its fine carving and the rare stained glass window in the private chapel. Displayed throughout the House are many historic mementos collected over the centuries by the Cecils', one of England's foremost political families.

The garden at Hatfield House dates from the early 17th Century when Robert Cecil employed John Tradescant the Elder to collect plants for his new home. Tradescant was sent to Europe where he found and brought back trees, bulbs, plants and fruit trees, which had never previously been grown in England.

In the Park, an oak tree marks the place where the young Princess Elizabeth first heard of her accession to the throne. Visitors can enjoy extensive walks in the park, following trails through the woods and along the Broadwater. The Veteran Tree Trail also provides the opportunity to learn more about our ancient oaks.

**OWNER**
The 7th Marquess of Salisbury

CONTACT
Visitors Department Tel: 01707 287010
Email: visitors@hatfield-house.co.uk
Website: www.hatfield-house.co.uk

**LOCATION**
Hatfield House, Hatfield Hertfordshire AL9 5HX
Map Ref: 7:F11

Car: 21 miles north of London, M25 Jct 23, A1(M) Jct 4. Pedestrian Entrance directly opposite Hatfield Railway Station.

Bus: Nearest stop at Hatfield Station, also regular buses from surrounding towns.

Rail: Kings Cross to Hatfield 22mins. Station is opposite entrance to Park. Underground links to main line at Finsbury Park.

**OPENING TIMES**
Hatfield House, Park & Gardens:
Sat 6 Apr - Sun 29 Sept
Hatfield House: Weds-Sun & BH 11am-5pm.
Hatfield Park & Gardens: Tues-Sun 10am-5:30pm

Hatfield Park Farm
Mar - Nov 2019.
Tues-Sun & BH 10am-5pm.

Stable Yard Shops & River Cottage Kitchen & Deli
Open throughout the year Tues-Sun & BH
10am-5pm (please check with individual retailers).

**ADMISSION**
House, Park and West Garden:
Adult £19
Seniors £18
Child £9
Group rates available

East Garden:
Wed only: £4 per person

West Garden and Park only:
Adult £11
Seniors £10
Child £7
Group rates available

No flash photography in house. Tours of Old Palace when building is not in use.

Toilet, disabled toilet and baby changing facilities available.

Free car and coach parking available.

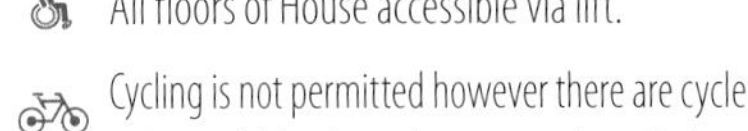
All floors of House accessible via lift.

Cycling is not permitted however there are cycle racks available, if you choose to cycle to the house.

Dogs are permitted in the Park only. Assistance dogs, are allowed in the House and Gardens.

Audio tours of house.

Group tours by arrangement, call 07107 287052.

Living History Schools programme.

Morning coffee, cakes, hot & cold lunches. Tel: 01707 262030.

River Cottage Kitchen & Deli. Tel: 01707 262030.

Newly refurbished Stable Yard home to variety of independent retailers & Hatfield House Gift Shop.

Weddings, Banquets and Conferences venue and catering. Tel 01707 262055.

There are a number of events held throughout the year, please see the website for more details.

Wedding venue available, please contact for further information.

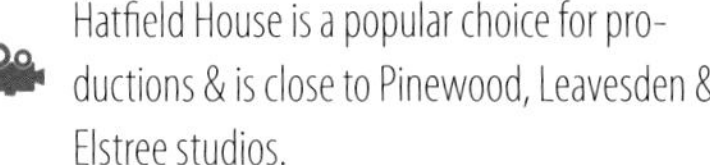
Hatfield House is a popular choice for productions & is close to Pinewood, Leavesden & Elstree studios.

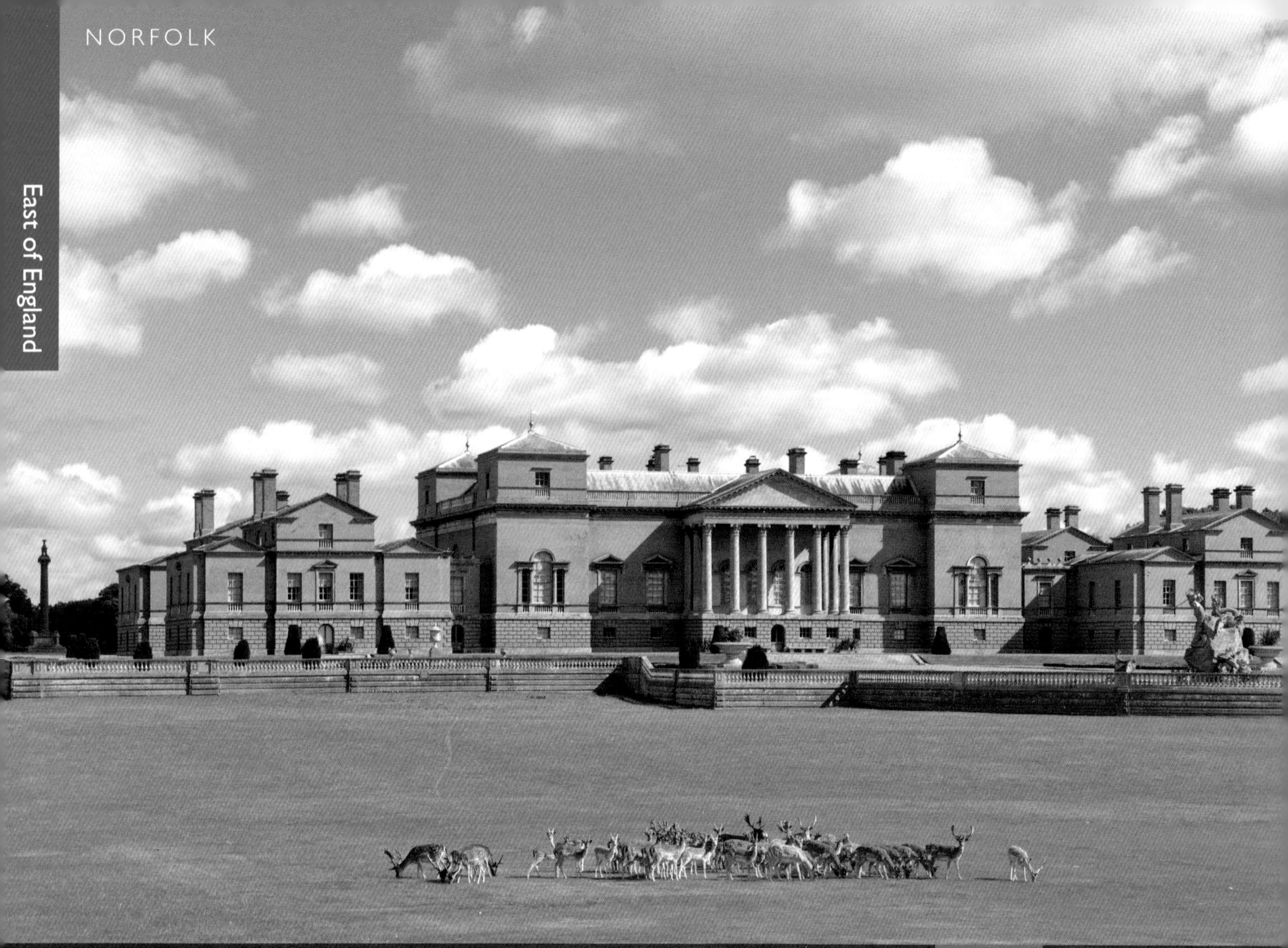

# HOLKHAM HALL

www.holkham.co.uk

WINNER
WONDERFUL PLACES TO STAY
THE VICTORIA INN

THE MARBLE HALL

THE FIELD TO FORK EXPERIENCE

## A breathtaking Palladian house with an outstanding art collection, panoramic landscapes and the best beach in England.

Holkham is described as an exceptional place, rich in history, architecture and wildlife, but probably best defined by its epic landscape. The combination of coast and countryside makes for a spectacular destination for visitors.

The grand 18th century masterpiece, Holkham Hall, has the perfect location, surrounded by rolling parkland. Inside this magnificent family home there are treasures to be discovered in every room with incredible architecture, tapestries, paintings, original furniture and ancient statuary.

Visit the exciting, interactive Field to Fork Experience; all about food and farming on the estate, and with its virtual tractor driving simulator, quick-fire table top game and memorable 'Holkham Year', film. It's a great opportunity to learn about farming without having to put your wellies on!

Holkham has a passion for gardening on the grandest scale with the vast, six acres of walled garden. Step through the ornate Venetian gates and enjoy the tranquil atmosphere, stunning array of flowers, fruit and vegetables and beautiful colours and scents.

Appreciate nature at its best and explore the parkland with designated walks and trails, cycle hire and summer boating. A children's woodland play area is great fun for young adventurers. For shopping and refreshments, the cobbled courtyard houses a spacious gift shop and café, both showcasing the work and produce of local artisans and suppliers.

At the north entrance to the park lies Holkham village with the estate-owned inn, The Victoria, several shops and the entrance to Holkham National Nature Reserve and Beach, with its abundant wildlife, wide horizons and miles of golden sands.

**OWNER**
Trustees of the Holkham Estate
Home of the Earls of Leicester

**CONTACT**
Contact: Marketing Manager Laurane Herrieven
Tel: 01328 710227
Email: enquiries@holkham.co.uk

**LOCATION**
Holkham Estate, Wells-next-the-Sea,
Norfolk, NR23 1AB
Map Ref: 8:14 Car: London 120m, Norwich 35m, King's Lynn 30m. Sat Nav: NR23 1RH. OS Ref: TF885 428
Bus: Coastal bus routes from King's Lynn to North Walsham, Rail: Norwich 35m. King's Lynn 30m.
Air: Norwich Airport 32m.

**OPENING TIMES**
Hall: 1 Apr-31 Oct, 12pm-4pm, Sun, Mon, Thu.
Plus Good Fri & Easter Sat.
NB Chapel, Libraries & Strangers' Wing, open at family's discretion.
Field to Fork, Walled Garden, Woodland Play Area, Courtyard Gift Shop & Café:
1 Apr-31 Oct, 10am-5pm, every day.
Cycle & Boat Hire see website.
For winter opening & admission see website.

**ADMISSION**
Holkham Hall, Field to Fork & Walled Garden
Adult: £16, Child (5-16yrs): £8, Family: £44

Field to Fork & Walled Garden:
Adult £7.50, Child (5-16yrs) £3.75, Family £21

Field to Fork Only:
Adult £5, Child (5-16yrs) £2.50, Family £13.50

NB Family ticket = 2 adults & up to 3 children.
For children's events age = 2 years.

Car parking £3 per day, redeemable in gift shop on £12+ purchases.

Pre-booked groups: 15+ people 20% discount, free parking, organiser ticket free, coach driver entitled to free refreshments.

Private guided tours: 12+ people £22 per person.

- Photography allowed for personal use, no drones.
- Lavatories, including accessible facilities in the courtyard. Lavatories also in the hall & walled garden.
- Baby changing facilities are located in the courtyard.
- Open for events and functions outside main season.
- Accessible lavatories in main courtyard only. Stairclimbing machine in hall offers access for most manually operated wheelchairs. Full accessibility guide on Holkham website.
- Ample. Parking charge.
- Cycle hire centre on site. Check website for details. Sustrans Route No: 1.
- On leads in park. Assistance dogs only in the hall.
- The Victoria Inn, Holkham village.
- Private guided tours by arrangement.
- All year round comprehensive educational programme.
- Courtyard Café. Licensed. Local produce.
- The Victoria Inn, Holkham village. Licensed.
- Courtyard Gift Shop. Local Norfolk produce and items.
- Plant sales in gift shop and walled garden.
- Hall, Lady Elizabeth Wing and grounds.
- Events and functions all year round. Please see full events programme.
- Civil ceremonies and partnerships.

# CASTLE RISING CASTLE

**www.castlerising.co.uk**

Castle Rising Castle is one of the most famous 12th Century castles in England. The stone keep, built in around 1140 AD, is amongst the finest surviving example of its kind anywhere in the country and, together with the massive surrounding earthworks, ensures that Rising is a castle of national importance. In its time Rising has served as a hunting lodge, royal residence, and for a brief time in the 18th Century even housed a mental patient. The most famous period in its history was when it came to the mother of Edward III, Queen Isabella, following her part in the murder of her husband Edward II. The castle passed to the Howard family in 1544 and it remains in their hands today, the current owner being a descendant of William D'Albini II, the Norman baron who raised the castle.

- Picnic area.
- Toilet facilities adjoining the car park.
- Closed 24-26 Dec.
- Large car park.
- Suitable. Disabled access to the shop and grounds only.

- There is an audio guide available to guide you around the Castle.

- School visits welcome. Pre-booking is essential.

- Gift shop.

- Please see the 'Events' section of the website for all upcoming activities.

**CONTACT** Owner: Lord Howard Contact: The Custodian
Tel: 01553 631330 Fax: 01533 631724
Email: thecastle@castlerising.com

**LOCATION** Castle Rising, King's Lynn, Norfolk PE31 6AH
Map Ref: 7:H5 - Located 4m NE of King's Lynn off A149.

**OPENING TIMES** 1 Apr - 1 Nov, daily, 10am - 6pm (closes at dusk if earlier in Oct). 2 Nov - 31 Mar, Wed - Sun, 10am - 4pm.

**ADMISSION** Adult £4.50, Child £3, Concession £3.80, Family (2 adults + 2 children) £14. Groups 11+ (15% discount for groups). Opening times and prices are subject to change.

---

# HOUGHTON HALL & GARDENS

**www.houghtonhall.com**

Houghton Hall is one of the finest examples of Palladian architecture in England. Built in the 1720s for Sir Robert Walpole, Britain's first Prime Minister. Original designs by James Gibbs & Colen Campbell, interior decoration by William Kent. The hall is currently home to the 7th Marquess of Cholmondeley, Walpole's descendant, and his family.

The award-winning 5-acre walled garden is divided into themed areas and includes a double-sided herbaceous border, formal rose parterre, mixed kitchen garden, fountains and statues. Contemporary sculptures by world renowned artists including Jeppe Hein, Stephen Cox, Zhan Wang, Richard Long, Rachel Whiteread, Anya Gallaccio, Phillip King and James Turrell are displayed in the gardens and grounds.

- Toilet facilities available and a disabled WC in the stable block.
- Allocated disabled parking near House.
- Lift to 1st floor State Rooms. For further details see the 'Disabled Access' section of the website.
- 2 hour private guided tour of the House – between 10am - 12noon. Subject to availability.
- Provides opportunities for local schools & educational groups to discover and explore.
- The fully licensed Stables Café offers a range of seasonally inspired hot & cold food, afternoon teas etc.
- The Gift Shop is located in The Stables.
- Please see the website for upcoming events and exhibitions.

**CONTACT** Owner: The Marquess of Cholmondeley
Contact: The Estate Office Tel: 01485 528569 Fax: 01485 528167
Email: info@houghtonhall.com

**LOCATION** Houghton, King's Lynn, Norfolk PE31 6UE
Map Ref: 8:15 13m E of King's Lynn, 10m W of Fakenham, 1½m N of A148.

**OPENING TIMES** See website www.houghtonhall.com

**ADMISSION** See website for prices / booking details.

COMMENDED
BEST
EVENT/EXHIBITION

# RAVENINGHAM GARDENS

**www.raveningham.com**

Superb herbaceous borders, 19th Century walled kitchen garden, Victorian glasshouse, herb garden, rose garden, time garden, contemporary sculptures, Millennium lake, arboretum with newly created stumpery, 14th century church, all in a glorious parkland setting surrounding Raveningham Hall. Tea Room serving homemade cake and refreshments.

- Visitors welcome to browse through The Raveningham Centre offering antiques, rugs, arts, gifts and crafts.
- Toilet facilities available.
- Parking is available.
- Disabled toilet, gardens accessible via gravel paths.
- Well behaved dogs on leads welcome.
- The Raveningham Estate has various properties, both residential and commercial, available to let.
- Tea Room, homemade cakes, quiches & other refreshments.
- Plants from the Garden on sale at the Tearoom.
- Corporate functions available.
- Please see the website for all upcoming Garden Events.

**CONTACT** Owner: Sir Nicholas Bacon Bt OBE DL
Contact: Sonya Roebuck
Tel: 01508 548480 Email: sonya@raveningham.com

**LOCATION** Raveningham, Norwich, Norfolk NR14 6NS
Map Ref: 8:L7 Between Norwich & Lowestoft off A146 then B1136.

**OPENING TIMES**
Snowdrop season: February, Sun - Fri (closed Sats) 11am - 4pm.

NGS opening: Sun 11 Mar

Main season: April to August please see website for details www.raveningham.com

**ADMISSION** Adult £5, Child (under 16yrs) Free, Concessions £4.50.

# MANNINGTON ESTATE

**manningtonestate.co.uk**

Mannington Hall was built around 1460 and bought by the first Lord Walpole in the 18th Century; it is still a family home today. The Heritage Rose Garden includes over 1000 varieties of rose in period settings and was designed in 1980's. Around the hall are colour themed borders and a scented garden. On the South Lawn is a classic temple brought to Mannington in the 19th Century and sensory beds with central rill. There is a woodland walk, wildflower meadow with boardwalk and hide, and a wild garden around ruined Saxon chapel and many varieties of plants and trees.

- £2 car park fee (walkers only).
- Grounds. WC's.
- Dogs welcome in park only.
- Guided tours of the garden and ground floor of the hall by arrangement.
- The Mannington Minnows Nature Club runs in the school holidays (usually Tue & Thu) for 6 + yrs old.
- Marquee within grounds & tearoom can be hired.
- Greedy Goose Tearoom serves refreshments and homemade treats when the garden is open.
- Shop is stocked with souvenirs, crafts, drinks and snacks.
- Purchase plants at the gift shop.
- In 2019 there will be the usual wide variety of events.
- Wing Cottage sleeps up to 5 Ambers Bell Tents, luxury glamping.

**CONTACT** Owner: Lord Walpole Contact: Lady Walpole
Tel: 01263 584175 Email: admin@walpoleestate.co.uk

**LOCATION** Mannington Hall, Norwich NR11 7BB Map Ref: 8:K5

**OPEN** Walks open every day of the year. Events from Apr and Gardens from late May. See website for opening times.
Party visits and tours by arrangement.

**ADMISSION** Please see website.

East of England

## SANDRINGHAM

**www.sandringhamestate.co.uk**

Sandringham House, the Norfolk retreat of Her Majesty The Queen, is set in 60 acres of beautiful gardens. The main ground floor rooms used by The Royal Family, still maintained in the Edwardian style, are open to the public, as well as the fascinating Museum and the charming parish church.

**CONTACT** Owner: H M The Queen Contact: The Public Enterprises Manager Tel: 01485 545408 E-mail: visits@sandringhamestate.co.uk **LOCATION** The Estate Office, Sandringham, Norfolk PE35 6EN Map Ref: 7:H5 8m NE of King's Lynn on B1440 off A148. **OPENING TIMES** 1 Apr – late July & early Aug to 20 Oct. **ADMISSION** House, Museum & Gardens: Adult £17, Child £8.50, Conc. £15. Museum & Gardens: Adult £11.50, Child £5.50, Conc. £10.

No photography in house. Ample. By arrangement, Private evening tours. WCs. Guide dogs only. Plant Centre. Visitor Centre only. Licensed. Licensed. Events please see website.

SANDRINGHAM HOUSE-COURTYARD ENTRANCE - B GILMOUR

## ICKWORTH HOUSE, PARKLAND, WOODLAND & GARDENS

**nationaltrust.org.uk/ickworth**

Unconventional and unforgettable. An Italianate Palace in the heart of Suffolk. The grand Rotunda is full of treasures collected by the Hervey family and sits in 1800 acres of tranquil parkland. Walk around a truly unique Italianate garden. Explore 1930s life in restored Servants Quarters and take part in events throughout the year.

**CONTACT** Owner: National Trust Contact: Business Support Officer Tel: 01284 735270 Email: ickworth@nationaltrust.org.uk

**LOCATION** The Rotunda, Horringer, Bury St Edmunds, Suffolk IP29 5QE Map Ref: 8:I9 - From A14 take J42 towards Westley; on West side of A143. For all other routes head towards Horringer. SatNav - follow signs to Horringer.

**OPENING** House - 1 Jan-3 Mar 11am-3pm, 4 Mar-28 Oct 11am-5pm, 29 Oct-31 Dec 11am-3pm. Tours 11am-12pm & 4pm-5pm. Parkland & Gardens: All year 9am-5.30pm. Shop & Cafe: 1 Jan-3 Mar 10.30am-4pm, 4 Mar-28 Oct 10.30am-5pm, 29 Oct-31 Dec 10.30am-4pm.

**ADMISSION** Please refer to website for ticket prices.

Toilet facilities available.

Baby changing facilities available. Carrying equipment for loan.

Closed Christmas Eve & Christmas Day.

Parking 200m from West Wing Parking for coaches.

Lift in main house. Mobility scooters available. West Wing drop off point.

Assistance dogs only in Italianate gardens. All dogs on leads on the Estate.

5 Holiday cottages available.

Basement audio tour on selected days.

## GAINSBOROUGH'S HOUSE

**www.gainsborough.org**

Gainsborough's House is the childhood home of the artist Thomas Gainsborough, R.A. (1727–1788) and shows the most comprehensive collection of his paintings, drawings and prints on display within a single setting. A varied programme of temporary exhibitions is also shown throughout the year. The historic house dates back to the 16th Century and has an attractive walled garden filled with 18th Century plant species.

**CONTACT** Owner: Gainsborough's House Society Contact: Liz Cooper Tel: 01787 372958 Email: mail@gainsborough.org

**LOCATION** 46 Gainsborough Street, Sudbury, Suffolk CO10 2EU Map Ref: 8:I10 - From Sudbury town centre head down Gainsborough Street towards Weaver's Lane.

**OPEN** All year: Mon-Sat, 10am-5pm; Sun, 11am-5pm. Closed: Good Friday & Christmas to New Year.

**ADMISSION** Please call for price details or see our website.

No photography in the Exhib. Gallery.

Suitable WC's.

By arrangement.

Shop has themes based on heritage of Gainsborough and Georgian period.

A small selection of plants from Gainsborough's Garden for sale.

## OTLEY HALL

**www.otleyhall.co.uk**

The outstanding late medieval house in East Suffolk. Stunning medieval Moated Hall (Grade I) frequently described as 'one of England's loveliest houses'. Noted for its richly carved beams, superb linenfold panelling and 16th Century wall paintings. The unique 10 acre gardens include historically accurate Tudor re-creations and voted among the top 10 gardens to visit in Great Britain.

**CONTACT** Owners: Dr Ian Beaumont & Catherine Bond Contact: Karen Gwynne-Vince Tel: 01473 890264 Email: events@otleyhall.co.uk Facebook: facebook.com/otleyhallsuffolk Twitter: @OtleyHall

**LOCATION** Hall Lane, Otley, Suffolk IP6 9PA Map Ref: 8:K9 7 miles North of Ipswich, off the B1079.

**OPENING TIMES** Gardens & Café: May - Sep, 11am-5pm, every Weds.

**ADMISSION** £3 entrance fee. By appointment only.

No commercial photography.

Grounds open all year round.

Available. Partial.

In grounds only and on a short lead.

By appointment Café.

Private & corporate events available.

Please see website for events.

Wedding ceremonies and receptions.

THE GARDEN AT HOLKHAM HALL

CECIL HIGGINS ART GALLERY
Castle Lane, Bedford MK40 3RP
**Tel:** 01234 718618 **Email:** thehiggins@bedford.gov.uk

HOUGHTON HOUSE
Ampthill, Bedford, Bedfordshire MK45 2EZ
**Tel:** 01223 582700 **Email:** customers@english-heritage.org.uk

THE LUTON HOO WALLED GARDEN
Luton Hoo Estate, Luton, Bedfordshire LU1 3TQ
**Tel:** 01582 879089 **Email:** office@lhwg.org.uk

MOGGERHANGER PARK
Park Road, Moggerhanger, Bedfordshire MK44 3RW
**Tel:** 01767 641007 **Email:** enquiries@moggerhangerpark.com

QUEEN ANNE'S SUMMERHOUSE
Shuttleworth, Old Warden, Bedfordshire SG18 9DU
**Tel:** 01628 825925 **Email:** bookings@landmarktrust.org.uk

SWISS GARDEN
Old Warden Park, Bedfordshire SG18 9EP
**Tel:** 01767 627927 **Email:** enquiries@shuttleworth.org

**TURVEY HOUSE**
**Turvey, Bedfordshire MK43 8EL**
A neo-classical house set in picturesque parkland bordering the River Great Ouse; with a fine collection of 18th & 19th Century antiques. Map Ref: 7:D9 - Between Bedford and Northampton on A428. **Tel:** 01234 881621 **Email:** info@turveyhouse.co.uk **Website:** www.turveyhouse.co.uk **Open:** For opening dates see Turvey House website, dates will be available from 1st July 2019.

WREST PARK
Silsoe, Luton, Bedfordshire MK45 4HS
**Tel:** 01525 860000 **Email:** customers@english-heritage.org.uk

ANGLESEY ABBEY, GARDENS & LODE MILL
Quy Road, Lode, Cambridgeshire CB25 9EJ
**Tel:** 01223 810080 **Email:** angleseyabbey@nationaltrust.org.uk

CAMBRIDGE UNIVERSITY BOTANIC GARDEN
1 Brookside, Cambridge CB2 1JE
**Tel:** 01223 336265 **Email:** enquiries@botanic.cam.ac.uk

DENNY ABBEY
Ely Road, Chittering, Waterbeach, Cambridgeshire CB25 9PQ
**Tel:** 01223 860988 **Email:** info@farmlandmuseum.org.uk

ELY CATHEDRAL
The Chapter House, The College, Ely, Cambridgeshire CB7 4DL
**Tel:** 01353 667735 ext.261

LONGTHORPE TOWER
Thorpe Road, Longthorpe, Cambridgeshire PE1 1HA
**Tel:** 01733 864663 **Email:** customers@english-heritage.org.uk

PECKOVER HOUSE & GARDEN
North Brink, Wisbech, Cambridgeshire PE13 1JR
**Tel:** 01945 583463 **Email:** peckover@nationaltrust.org.uk

WIMPOLE ESTATE
Arrington, Royston, Cambridgeshire SG8 0BW
**Tel:** 01223 206000 **Email:** wimpolehall@nationaltrust.org.uk

AUDLEY END
Audley End House, Audley End, Saffron Walden, Essex CB11 4JF
**Tel:** 01799 522842 **Email:** customers@english-heritage.org.uk

BOURNE MILL
Bourne Road, Colchester, Essex CO2 8RT
**Tel:** 01206 549799 **Email:** bournemill@nationaltrust.org.uk

HEDINGHAM CASTLE
Castle Hedingham, Halstead, Essex, CO9 3DJ
**Tel:** 01787 460261 **Email:** mail@hedinghamcastle.co.uk

HILL HALL
Theydon Mount, Essex CM16 7QQ
**Tel:** 01799 522842 **Email:** customers@english-heritage.org.uk

HYLANDS ESTATE
Hylands Park, London Road, Chelmsford CM2 8WQ
**Tel:** 01245 605500 **Email:** hylands@chelmsford.gov.uk

LAYER MARNEY TOWER
Nr Colchester, Essex CO5 9US
**Tel:** 01206 330784 **Email:** info@layermarneytower.co.uk

THE MUNNINGS ART MUSEUM
Castle House, Castle Hill, Dedham, Essex CO7 6AZ
**Tel:** 01206 322127 **Email:** enquiries@munningsmuseum.org.uk

PAYCOCKE'S HOUSE & GARDEN
25 West Street, Coggeshall, Essex C06 1NS
**Tel:** 01376 561305 **Email:** paycockes@nationaltrust.org.uk

RHS HYDE HALL
Creephedge Lane, Rettendon, Chelmsford, Essex CM3 8ET
**Tel:** 08452 658071 **Email:** hydehall@rhs.org.uk

ASHRIDGE GARDENS
Berkhamsted, Hertfordshire HP4 1NS
**Tel:** 01442 843491 **Email:** reception@ashridge.org.uk

GORHAMBURY
St Albans, Hertfordshire AL3 6AH
**Tel:** 01727 854051 **Email:** office@grimstontrust.co.uk

KNEBWORTH HOUSE
Knebworth Park,Knebworth, Hertfordshire, SG1 2AX
**Tel:** 01438 812661 **Email:** info@knebworthhouse.com

SHAW'S CORNER
Ayot St Lawrence, Welwyn, Hertfordshire AL6 9BX
**Tel:** 01438 829221 **Email:** shawscorner@nationaltrust.org.uk

BACONSTHORPE CASTLE
Hall Lane, Baconsthorpe, Norfolk NR25 9LN
**Tel:** 01223 582700 **Email:** customers@english-heritage.org.uk

BLICKLING ESTATE
Blickling, Norwich, Norfolk NR11 6NF
**Tel:** 01263 738030 **Email:** blickling@nationaltrust.org.uk

CASTLE ACRE PRIORY
Stocks Green, Castle Acre, King's Lynn, Norfolk PE32 2XD
**Tel:** 01760 755394 **Email:** customers@english-heritage.org.uk

East of England

CLIFTON HOUSE
Queen Street, King's Lynn PE30 1HT
**Email:** anna@kingstaithe.com

DRAGON HALL
115-123 King Street, Norwich, Norfolk NR1 1QE
**Tel:** 01603 663922 **Email:** info@dragonhall.org

EUSTON HALL
Thetford, Suffolk IP24 2QP
**Tel:** 01842 766366 **Email:** info@euston-estate.co.uk

FAIRHAVEN WOODLAND & WATER GARDEN
School Road, South Walsham, Norfolk NR13 6DZ
**Tel:** 01603 270449 **Email:** fairhavengarden@btconnect.com

FELBRIGG HALL
Felbrigg, Norwich, Norfolk NR11 8PR
**Tel:** 01263 837444 **Email:** felbrigg@nationaltrust.org.uk

HINDRINGHAM HALL & GARDENS
Blacksmiths Lane, Hindringham, Norfolk NR21 0QA
**Tel:** 01328 878226 **Email:** info@hindringhamhall.org

KIMBERLEY HALL
Wymondham, Norfolk NR18 0RT
**Tel:** 01603 759447 **Email:** events@kimberleyhall.co.uk

NORWICH CASTLE MUSEUM & ART GALLERY
Norwich, Norfolk NR1 3JU
**Tel:** 01603 493625 **Email:** museums@norfolk.gov.uk

OXBURGH HALL
Oxborough, King's Lynn, Norfolk PE33 9PS
**Tel:** 01366 328258 **Email:** oxburghhall@nationaltrust.org.uk

SHERINGHAM PARK
Upper Sheringham, Norfolk NR26 8TL
**Tel:** 01263 820550 **Email:** sheringhampark@nationaltrust.org.uk

WALSINGHAM ABBEY GROUNDS & THE SHIREHALL MUSEUM
Common Place, Walsingham, Norfolk NR22 6BP
**Tel:** 01328 820510 **Email:** museum@walsinghamabbey.com

BELCHAMP HALL
Belchamp Walter, Sudbury, Suffolk CO10 7AT
**Tel:** 01787 881961

BRUISYARD HALL
Bruisyard, Saxmundham, Woodbridge IP17 2EJ
**Tel:** 01728 639000 **Email:** info@bruisyardhall.com

FLATFORD
Bridge Cottage, East Bergholt, Suffolk CO7 6UL
**Tel:** 01206 298260 **Email:** flatfordbridgecottage@nationaltrust.org.uk

FRAMLINGHAM CASTLE
Framlingham, Suffolk IP13 9BP
**Tel:** 01728 724189 **Email:** customers@english-heritage.org.uk

FRESTON TOWER
Nr Ipswich, Suffolk IP9 1AD
**Tel:** 01628 825925 **Email:** bookings@landmarktrust.org.uk

GLEMHAM HALL
Little Glemham, Woodbridge, Suffolk IP13 0BT
**Tel:** 01728 746704 **Email:** events@glemhamhall.co.uk

HAUGHLEY PARK
Stowmarket, Suffolk, IP14 3JY
Tel: 01359 240205 Email: robert@haughleypark.co.uk

HELMINGHAM HALL GARDENS
Helmingham, Stowmarket, Suffolk IP14 6EF
**Tel:** 01473 890799 **Email:** events@helmingham.com

KENTWELL HALL & GARDENS
Long Melford, Suffolk CO10 9BA
**Tel:** 01787 310207 **Email:** info@kentwell.co.uk

LANDGUARD FORT
Felixstowe, Suffolk IP11 3TX
**Tel:** 01394 675900 **Email:** customers@english-heritage.org.uk

LAVENHAM: THE GUILDHALL OF CORPUS CHRISTI
The Market Place, Lavenham, Sudbury CO10 9QZ
**Tel:** 01787 247646 **Email:** lavenhamguildhall@nationaltrust.org.uk

MELFORD HALL
Long Melford, Sudbury, Suffolk CO10 9AA
**Tel:** 01787 379228 **Email:** melford@nationaltrust.org.uk

ORFORD CASTLE
Orford, Woodbridge, Suffolk IP12 2ND
**Tel:** 01394 450472 **Email:** customers@english-heritage.org.uk

THE RED HOUSE - ALDEBURGH
Golf Lane, Aldeburgh, Suffolk IP15 5PZ
**Tel:** 01728 452615 **Email:** enquiries@brittenpears.org

SOMERLEYTON HALL & GARDENS
Somerleyton, Lowestoft, Suffolk NR32 5QQ
**Tel:** 08712 224244 **Email:** info@somerleyton.co.uk

SUTTON HOO
Woodbridge, Suffolk IP12 3DJ
**Tel:** 01394 389700 **Email:** suttonhoo@nationaltrust.org.uk

WYKEN HALL GARDENS
Stanton, Bury St Edmunds, Suffolk IP31 2DW
**Tel:** 01359 250287

HATFIELD HOUSE - HERTFORDSHIRE

# EAST MIDLANDS

DERBYSHIRE • LEICESTERSHIRE & RUTLAND • LINCOLNSHIRE
NORTHAMPTONSHIRE • NOTTINGHAMSHIRE

PATH LEADING THROUGH FOREST, NATIONAL FOREST ©VISITENGLAND/2020 VISION/BEN HALL

### COUNTRYSIDE

Peak District
Robin Hood Country
Rutland Water

### HERITAGE

Elizabethan prodigy houses
English Civil War
Magna Carta at Lincoln Castle

### FOOD

Grantham gingerbread
Melton Mowbray pork pies
Bakewell tart

# Melbourne Hall Gardens

## Strolling down the Allée

Pretty Melbourne Hall is a Queen Anne house with none of the egregious additions of the Victorians. It was a secondary house; the family of the Viscount Melbourne, who owned it, preferring to be nearer to London and government. Now it is home to the Kerr family and open to the public in August. When you arrive, you will find it much as it was left by its builder Thomas Coke, Vice-Chamberlain to Queen Anne and George I, in the 1720s. Remarkably, Thomas would also still feel right at home in the gardens as well, a rare survival of an early 18th century formal garden, created by him between 1704 and 1727.

MELBOURNE HALL FROM THE GREAT BASIN © ANDREA JONES

The essence is a series of interlocking walks punctuated by statuary. From the house, geometric lawns separated by radiating paths lead down to the Great Basin. Beyond, the once trim Yew Walk has matured into an atmospheric tunnel of twisted branches, while beyond are another series of smaller ponds linked by gravel paths. It is a garden for strolling, an activity close to the hearts of Georgian gentlefolk.

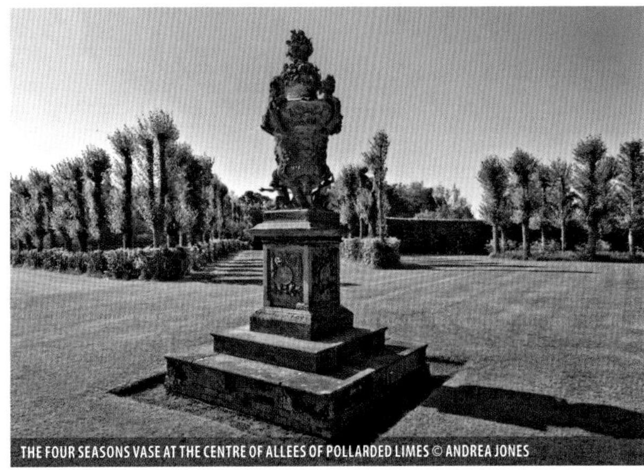
THE FOUR SEASONS VASE AT THE CENTRE OF ALLEES OF POLLARDED LIMES © ANDREA JONES

Many of the statues come from the workshop of John Nost, a Flemish sculptor whose work was in high demand in his lifetime. Look out for lead figures from classical mythology, Andromeda, Perseus and Mercury; charming chubby cupids; a pair of kneeling slaves representing Africa and India, crafted at a time when the infamous slave trade was at its height. Two pieces are outstanding: John Nost's Vase of the Four Seasons and The Birdcage, an ornate arbour made of wrought iron by local blacksmith, Robert Bakewell. A masterpiece of the Golden Age of English Blacksmithing, the Birdcage alone justifies a visit to Melbourne Hall. After thirty years of imaginative planting, the gardens today are as botanically as historically interesting but come here not just for flowers but for trees, vistas and a sense of order. ■

CAREFUL COLOUR THEMING BRINGS LIFE TO THE BORDERS © ANDREA JONES

# East Midlands

## Top 3 Venues

STANFORD HALL, LEICESTERSHIRE

### Stanford Hall, Leicestershire

Stanford Hall is set in 700 acres of Leicestershire countryside and has its own ballroom as well as 15 rooms of private accommodation, making it perfect for those desiring exclusive use. The river Avon runs through the parkland, providing a perfect backdrop for your photographs. The park provides ample space for outdoor pursuits such as clay pigeon shooting and archery. Relax in the Billiards Room or spend some quiet time in the Library. The hall is home to an important collection of Royal Stuart portraits including one of Bonnie Prince Charlie.

LAMPORT HALL, NORTHAMPTONSHIRE

### Lamport Hall, Northamptonshire

Lamport Hall is perfect for the more intimate wedding ceremony with two rooms licensed for civil ceremonies. Weddings take place in the High Room or the Oak Room which provides the bride with a staircase entrance into the room. The Hall, Stables and Grounds are also available for exclusive hire for your chosen event. Lamport Hall is home to the first ever garden gnome, one of several made for keen gardener Sir Charles Isham's rockery in 1874. The last surviving gnome is on display at Lamport; the others were reportedly shot with an air rifle by Sir Isham's daughters!

HOLDENBY HOUSE © WEDDINGVENUES.COM

### Holdenby House, Northamptonshire

Holdenby offers exclusive use and a very personal experience for your special day. The stunning ballroom seats 108 for a wedding breakfast and transforms into a fantastic space for dancing in the evening. The Library offers a quieter area for cutting your cake or relaxing with a drink. For larger parties, a marquee can be erected on the South Lawn. The original house was built in 1583 and was once a Royal Palace, home to James I and then Charles I in the 17th century.

**Goose Fair, Forest Recreation Ground, Nottinghamshire** *October 2019*

**The Lincolnshire Show, Lincolnshire Showground** *19th - 20th June 2019*

**Formula 1® Rolex British Grand Prix, Silverstone, Northamptonshire** *12th - 14th July 2019*

## Top 3 Annual Events

### Althorp Food & Drink Festival, Althorp
*11th and 12th May 2019*

This annual festival attracts exhibitors celebrating food from all over the world as well as the best of British. There are plenty of opportunities to sample and shop at the many stands. Watch cooking displays from well-known chefs and take part in a workshop or masterclass. There are displays and activities designed specifically for children as well as live music and, as you would expect, plenty of refreshments available.

ALTHORP FOOD & DRINK FESTIVAL, ALTHORP

### Land Rover Burghley Horse Trials, Lincolnshire
*5th-8th September 2019*

The event features dressage, cross-country, show-jumping as entrants compete across three days to be crowned champion. HRH Princess Anne won the event in 1971, and her daughter Zara Phillips has also been a competitor. The Burghley Young Event Horse competition takes place at the same time and aims to find high-quality eventing horses of the future. Away from the action there are plenty of shopping opportunities for merchandise, food and drink.

LAND ROVER BURGHLEY HORSE TRIALS, 2014 © CROSSAXLE

### Chatsworth Country Fair, Chatsworth Park,
*30th August -1st September 2019*

Well-loved as a fantastic family day out there is plenty for everyone to see and do. Take part in country sports or crafts or browse the many food and gift stalls. Military vehicles and vintage cars are on display. The main action takes place in the grand ring which in previous years has seen dancing diggers, birds of prey, horse displays and aircraft acrobatics.

CHATSWORTH COUNTRY FAIR

# East Midlands

## Places to stay and eat

WASHINGBOROUGH HALL HOTEL

### Washingborough Hall Hotel

A quintessential Georgian country house dating back to the early 1700s, the Hall is set in three acres of secluded grounds, just over two miles from Lincoln's historic city centre. Privately owned and managed by Edward and Lucy Herring, the Hall is a stylish, relaxed hotel renowned for its friendly atmosphere, great food and personal service. The elegant, yet informal dining room serves a seasonal British menu, using prime Lincolnshire ingredients where possible. A delicious Lincolnshire afternoon tea is available, and all day snacks and bar meals are served in the lounge bar. The hotel is perfect for weddings or special occasions and can cater for receptions for up to 150 people. Three well equipped function rooms can accommodate meetings and private parties. The Hall can also be hired on an exclusive use basis.

Church Hill, Washingborough, Lincoln
Lincolnshire LN4 1BE

01522 790340

www.washingboroughhall.com
enquiries@washingboroughhall.com

### Petwood Hotel

*Hotel*

Stixwould Road, Woodhall Spa,
Lincoln LN10 6QG

01526 352411

www.petwood.co.uk
reception@petwood.co.uk

### The Cavendish Hotel

*Hotel*

Church Lane, Baslow
Derbyshire DE45 1SP

01246 582311

www.cavendish-hotel.net
info@cavendish-hotel.net

### Biggin Hall Hotel

*Restaurant*

Biggin by Hartington, Buxton
Derbyshire SK17 0DH

01298 84451

www.bigginhall.co.uk
enquiries@bigginhall.co.uk

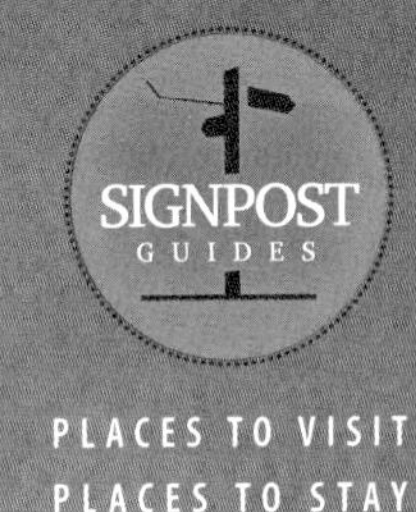




## Langar Hotel

I always love my visits to Langar Hall. Beautifully situated overlooking the Vale of Belvoir - a lovely country house, built in 1837, standing beside an early English church, with glorious views over the gardens and parkland. The hall is the family home of the late Imogen Skirving, who worked tirelessly to build the prestigious reputation of the hall, with her daughter and granddaughter maintaining this tradition. Imogen's father used to entertain famous cricketers of the 1930's, with the Test Match Special team and other esteemed cricketers still staying at the hall. The exceptional team make every effort for their guests' happiness, with their inviting demeanour and dedication. Chef Gary Booth works hard to produce excellent, reasonably priced menus of French and English cuisine; using local produce such as, garden vegetables and herbs, Langar lamb, Stilton, game from the Belvoir Estate, and fish direct from Brixham. A truly lovely spot, with a tranquil and enchanting ambience.

Langar, Nottingham NG13 9HG

01949 860559

www.langarhall.com
info@langarhall.co.uk

LANGAR HOTEL

## The Devonshire Arms

*Restaurant*

Lightwood Lane, Middle Handley
Sheffield S21 5RN

01246 434 800

www.devonshirearmsmiddlehandley.co.uk
hello@devonshirearmsmiddlehandley.co.uk

## Ivy's Vintage Tea Room

*Tea Room*

10 High Street
Lutterworth LE17 4AD

01455 556974

www.ivysvintagetearoom.co.uk
katrina@ivysvintagetearoom.co.uk

## The Tearoom in Cliffe Park

*Tea Room*

Callywhite Lane
Dronfield S18 2XP

07906 549694

vintagerosecatering.com/vintage-rose-tearoom/
vintagerosecatering@gmail.com

East Midlands

# CHATSWORTH

**www.chatsworth.org**

Chatsworth, home of the Duke and Duchess of Devonshire is set in the heart of the Peak District. Explore the historic house for fascinating stories and one of Europe's most significant art collections. In the garden, discover water features, giant sculptures and beautiful flowers set in Britain's most stunning and surprising country estate. Or come face to face with our farm animals in our working farmyard and enjoy adventurous fun in the playground.

Toilet facilities available.

Baby changing facilities available.

Open until 7pm. Online bookings free parking. £4 per vehicle. Blue badge holders free.

Please see access statement on website for details on how we can assist.

Dogs welcome.

Stay at Chatsworth; Holiday Cottages, Luxury Hotels & Beautiful Inns.

Audio guides available - £3 per person.

The house taster tour lasts 45 mins & costs £4 per adult & £2 per child. Buggy & walking tours in Garden.

Enrich your students' curriculum - For all stages of learning.

Offering light bites, hearty meals or indulgent afternoon teas.

The Cavendish restaurant, The Flying Childers restaurant & The Carriage House (self-service.)

Farm Shop, the Orangery shop & the Stables shop.

Team building days; product launches, exhibitions, meetings & conferences.

Award ceremonies & banquets, to christenings & bar mitzvahs.

Wedding packages to create a special day, whatever your style and budget.

35,000-acre Estate in Derbyshire offers a wide range of beautiful locations.

**CONTACT** Owner: Chatsworth House Trust Contact: The Booking Office
Tel: 01264 565300 Email: Info@chatsworth.org

**LOCATION** Bakewell, Derbyshire DE45 1PP Map Ref: 6:P2
Car: From London 3 hrs M1/J29, signposted via Chesterfield. 3m E of Bakewell, off B6012,10m W of Chesterfield. Rail: Chesterfield Station 11m. Bus: Chesterfield - Baslow 9½m.

**OPENING TIMES** Please see www.chatsworth.org for opening times.

**ADMISSION** Visit www.chatsworth.org for all ticket options.

# RENISHAW HALL & GARDENS

**www.renishaw-hall.co.uk**

Renishaw Hall and Gardens have been home to the Sitwell family for over 400 years. Its present owner, Alexandra Hayward, welcomes you. Renishaw Hall is set in 8 acres of Italianate gardens which were designed in the 19th century by Sir George Sitwell Bt, and feature statues, yew hedges, beautiful borders and ornamental ponds. Mature woodlands and lakes offer wonderful walks. The Hall offers an intriguing insight into the Sitwell family's history, with a fascinating collection of paintings including work by John Piper. The Hall and Gardens are open for group and public tours, see website for details.

Toilet facilities inlcuding disabled WC's available during garden opening.

Baby changing facilities available.

Parking £1 per car for the day.

Partial. See the full access statement on the website for further details.

Dogs welcome on leads.

Pre-booking advisable. Hall, Garden & Vineyard tours throughout the year. Private & coach tours, by appointment.

Educational visits by arrangement.

Licensed café open during garden opening times in the stables.

Shops situated in the stables.

Plant sales by Handley Rose Nursery available at the Visitor Centre.

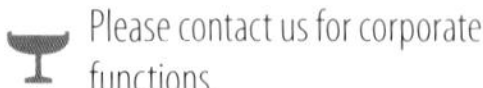
Please contact us for corporate functions.

Please see the 'What's On' section of the website for all upcoming events.

**CONTACT** The Hall & Visitor Manager - Rachael Gorman
Tel: 01246 432310 Email: enquiries@renishaw-hall.co.uk

**LOCATION** Renishaw, Nr Sheffield, Derbyshire S21 3WB Map Ref: 7:A2 - On A6135, 3 miles from M1/J30, located between Sheffield and Chesterfield.

**OPENING TIMES** 27 Mar - 29 Sep. Gardens open Wed - Sun & BH Mons, 10.30am - 4.30pm. Hall open to public on Fridays throughout the season 1pm/2.30pm & weekends in Aug. For visits in June please contact the office before your visit.

**ADMISSION** HHA /RHS members: Free entry to Gardens.
Guided Hall Tours £6.50. Discounts for coach/group bookings over 20 people. Gardens only: Adults £7, Conc £6.50, Child £3, under 5's free. Family (1+3) £12.75, Family (2+3) £18.75. Non-member Hall & Gardens: Adults £13.50, Conc £12.50.

# HADDON HALL

www.haddonhall.co.uk

A visit to Haddon Hall is unlike any other. Stepping through its gates will transport you back in time to an age of medieval splendour. Left untouched for centuries. Rich tapestries adorn panelled walls, ancient furniture shows the marks of past lives, exquisite frescoes, carved paneling, graffiti on glass and stone tell the story of this extraordinary nine hundred year old home. This is a place of atmosphere and beauty.

Home to Lord and Lady Edward Manners, Haddon Hall is one of England's most elegant and timeless stately homes and a magnificent example of a fortified manor house. Enjoying fine Tudor and Elizabethan architecture, the Hall allows visitors the opportunity to immerse themselves in centuries of history, art and craftsmanship, and to also explore the Hall's magnificent walled Tudor gardens.

The gardens are reknowned for their roses, structure and views and were recently redesigned by Arne Maynard, the Chelsea award winning gardener.

Haddon has also become the choice location for many film-makers, playing host to no less than three versions of 'Jane Eyre', became Prince Humperdinck's Castle in the cult movie 'The Princess Bride' and was also used in 'Pride & Prejudice', and latterly the BBC series 'Gunpowder'.

**CONTACT**

Contact: Isabelle Stuart Owner: Lord Edward Manners
Tel: 01629 810912 Email: isabelle@haddonhall.co.uk

**LOCATION**

Haddon Hall, Bakewell, Derbyshire DE45 1LA
Map Ref: 3:P2 - Located on the A6 between Bakewell and Rowsley in the Peak District National Park.

TRANSPORT ROUTES Car | Bus | Train | Bike

**OPENING TIMES**

Apr 12 to Oct 31 10.30 - 17.00
Dec 1 to 23 10.30 - 16.00

**ADMISSION**

Adult From £16
Children under 16 admitted free

Included in the Admission Price are free Guided Tours, Estate Walks and Musical Events throughout the season. Please check our website for specific dates.
www.haddonhall.co.uk

- Please see our website www.haddonhall.co.uk
- Accessible toilets available on the ground floor of the Stable Block
- Available within the Lower Courtyard Toilet Block
- Please check website for full details.
- Parking charges apply
- Speak with Car Park Attendant for guidance on Disabled Parking or phone the Estate Office. A Buggy Service is available from the Gatehouse Entrance to the Hall
- No dogs allowed in the Hall, Gardens or Estate grounds.
- Group welcome by appointment. Call 01629 810 912.
- Primary, Secondary and University Student Groups welcome by appointment
- Haddon Restaurant in Stable Block
- Gift Shop by the main entrance inc. plant sales.
- Available for Private and Corporate Events

- The Peacock at Rowsley, 01629 733518 reception@thepeacockatrowsley.com

- Please see our website for details or telephone The Estate Office on 01629 812 855

- Available for Civil Ceremonies. Please contact our Events Co-ordinator, Julie Mellor

- The Princess Bride, Jane Eyre, The Other Boleyn Girl, The Hollow Crown, Gunpowder, Gardeners' World, The Sweet Makers, House ofCards, Death Comes to Pemberley

## MELBOURNE HALL & GARDENS

www.melbournehall.com

This beautiful house of history, in its picturesque poolside setting, was once the home of Victorian Prime Minister William Lamb. The fine gardens, in the French formal style, contain Robert Bakewell's intricate wrought iron arbour and a fascinating yew tunnel. Upstairs rooms available to view by appointment.

**CONTACT** Owner: Lord & Lady Ralph Kerr
Contact: Melbourne Hall Estate Office
Tel: 01332 862502
Email: melbhall@globalnet.co.uk

**LOCATION** Melbourne, Derbyshire DE73 8EN Map Ref: 7:A5 - 8m South of Derby. From London, exit M1/J24.

**OPENING TIMES** Hall open August only, everyday (except for the first 3 Mondays) from 2pm-5pm. Last admission 4.15 Gardens open 1st Apr - 30th Sept on Weds, Sat and Sun, 1.30-5.30 except in August when the gardens are open every afternoon (except for the first 3 Mondays).

**ADMISSION** www.melbournehall.com or call 01332 862502

- No photography in house.
- Toilets available in the Visitors Centre.
- Church Square/Castle Square. No coaches
- Partial. WC's.
- Around Melbourne Pool on a lead. Assistance dogs in the hall & gardens.
- Obligatory in house Tue-Thurs.
- Melbourne Hall Tea Room.
- Hospice shop, gift shop, wine & more

HADDON CHAPEL - CANDLE LIT

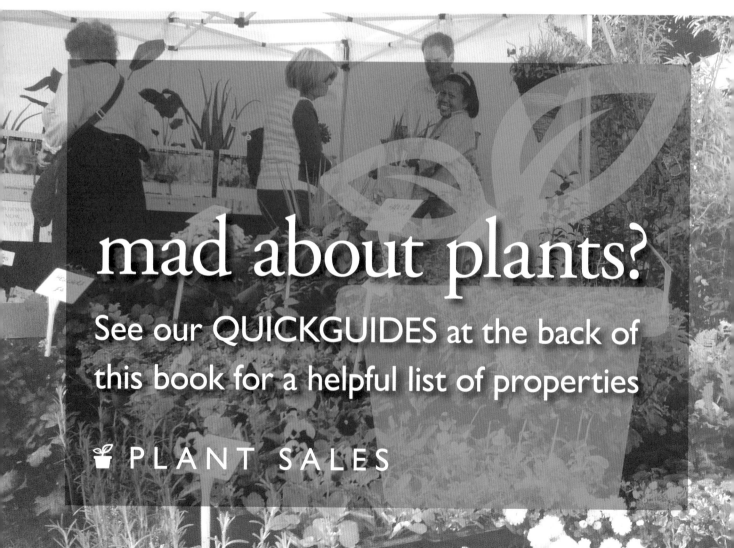

# STANFORD HALL

**www.stanfordhall.co.uk**

Stanford has been the home of the Cave family, ancestors of the present owner since 1430. In the 1690s, Sir Roger Cave commissioned the Smiths of Warwick to pull down the old Manor House and build the present Hall. Throughout the house are portraits of the family and examples of furniture and objects which they collected over the centuries. There is also a collection of Royal Stuart portraits. The Hall and Stables are set in an attractive Park on the banks of Shakespeare's Avon. There is a walled Rose Garden and an early ha-ha.

**CONTACT**
Owner: Mr & Mrs N Fothergill
Contact: Nick Fothergill
Tel: 01788 860250
Email: enquiries@stanfordhall.co.uk

**LOCATION**
Lutterworth, Leicestershire LE17 6DH
Map Ref: 7:B7 - M1/J18 6m. M1/J20, 6m.
M6 exit/access at J1, 4m. Historic House signs.

**OPENING TIMES**
Special 3 week Easter opening: From Mon 8 Apr - Sun 28 Apr 2019. Please note we are closed Easter Sat 20th Apr. Bank holiday Monday's only.
The House is also open in conjunction with park events, please see website or call for details.

Pre-booked groups (20+)
Mon-Fri by appointment only.

**ADMISSION**
House & Grounds:
Adult £8
Child (5-15 yrs) £2.50.

Private group tours (20+):
Adult £8
Child £2.50.

Special admission prices will apply on event days

- Parkland, helicopter landing area & lecture room.
- Toilet facilities available.
- 1,000 cars and 6-8 coaches. Coach parking on gravel in front of house.
- Partial. WC's.
- Dogs on leads only.
- Accommodation available for Group bookings only. Caravan Site 01788 860387.
- Tour time: ¾ hour in groups of approximately 25 people.
- Educational visits available.
- Stables Tea Room.
- On site Gift shop selling Antiques, Confectionery and Stanford Hall memorabilia.
- Corporate days including lunches & dinners, small conferences & clay pigeon shoots etc.
- For all upcoming events please see 'Public Events' on the website.
- Offering civil ceremonies and wedding receptions.
- Filming opportunities available.

# BURGHLEY HOUSE

www.burghley.co.uk

## Burghley House, home of the Cecil family for over 400 years is one of England's Greatest Elizabethan Houses.

Burghley was built between 1555 and 1587 by William Cecil, later Lord Burghley, principal adviser and Lord High Treasurer to Queen Elizabeth I. During the 17th and 18th Centuries, the House was transformed by John 5th Earl of Exeter and Brownlow, the 9th Earl; travelling to the cultural centres of Europe and employing many of the foremost craftsmen of their day.

Burghley contains one of the largest private collections of Italian art, unique examples of Chinese and Japanese porcelain and superb items of 18th Century furniture. Principal artists and craftsmen of the period are to be found at Burghley: Antonio Verrio, Grinling Gibbons and Louis Laguerre all made major contributions to the beautiful interiors.

### Park and Gardens

The house is set in a 300-acre deer park landscaped by 'Capability' Brown and is one of the finest examples of his work. A lake was created by him and delightful avenues of mature trees feature largely in his design. Brown also carried out alterations to the architecture of the House and added a summerhouse in the South Gardens. The park is home to a large herd of Fallow deer, established in the 16th Century. The Garden of Surprises is a modern oasis of flowing water and fountains, statues, and obelisks. The contemporary Sculpture Garden was reclaimed from 'Capability' Brown's lost lower gardens in 1994 and is dedicated to exhibiting innovative sculptures. The private gardens around the house are open from mid-March to mid-April for the display of spring bulbs.

**OWNER**
Burghley House Preservation Trust Ltd

**CONTACT**
Contact: House Manager
Tel: 01780 752451
Email: burghley@burghley.co.uk

**LOCATION**
Stamford, Lincolnshire PE9 3JY
Map Ref: 7:E7
Burghley House is 1m SE of Stamford.
From London, A1 2hrs. Visitors entrance is on B1443.

Rail: London - Peterborough 1hr (East Coast mainline). Stamford Station 12mins, regular service from Peterborough.

Taxi: Direct line 01780 481481

**OPENING TIMES**
House & Gardens: 16 Mar - 3 Nov (closed 5 - 8 Sept). Open Daily, (House closed on Fridays) 11am - 5pm (Last admission 4.30pm).

**ADMISSION**
Please see our website for all details on admission prices and the ticket options available.

**REGULAR EVENTS**
Please see 'The Burghley Events Diary' on the 'What's on' page of the website for all upcoming special events.

- Photography is now permitted within the House and Gardens, for personal use only.
- Toilet facilities available.
- Baby changing facilities available.
- Ample. Free refreshments for coach drivers.
- Disabled parking is available close to the house entrance and there are disabled toilet facilities.
- The Bull & Swan at Burghley and the William Cecil Hotel are places to stay near Burghley.
- By arrangement.
- Welcome. Guide provided.
- Licensed. The Garden Café is open daily from 11am-5pm.
- The Orangery Restaurant is open daily from 11am -5pm. Closes occasionally for private events.
- Courtyard shop is open daily from 11am-5pm.
- The Garden Shop is open daily from 11am-5pm.
- Ideally situated for corporate events and functions.
- Suitable for a variety of events, large park, golf course, helicopter landing area, cricket pitch.
- Civil wedding licence.

## AUBOURN HALL
**aubournhall.co.uk**

The garden and lawns surround this mellow brick manor house dating from the early 17th Century and still lived in by the Nevile family. In recent years, the Rose Garden and Prairie gardens have become fully established giving a new emphasis to the shape of the gardens which continue to delight with their sweeping lawns, ponds and woodland walk.

**CONTACT**
Owner: Mr & Mrs Christopher Nevile
Contact: Paula Dawson, Estate Office
Tel: 01522 788224
Fax: 01522 788199
Email: estate.office@aubournhall.co.uk

**LOCATION** Lincoln LN5 9DZ
Map Ref: 7:D3 - 6m SW of Lincoln.
2m SE of A46.

**OPENING TIMES** Garden open for events. Groups and Garden visits from May-Sep. Contact or go to the website for details www.aubournhall.co.uk.

**ADMISSION** Adult £5.50, Child Free.

 National Gardens Scheme - gardens open for charity.

 Limited for coaches.

 Partial. WC's.

 Guide dogs only.

 By arrangement.

 Homemade refreshments available.

 Available as a wedding reception venue. Please contact to find out more.

## FULBECK MANOR

Fulbeck Manor was built in c1580s. The house stands 3 storeys high including garrets, with a 5 bay front. The interiors feature portraits of the Fane family, who have lived in Fulbeck for over 400 years. The most impressive feature is a 17th Century staircase with spiral balusters.

**CONTACT** Owner/Contact:
Mr Julian Francis Fane
Tel: 01400 272231
E-mail: jfane22@outlook.com

**LOCATION** Fulbeck, Grantham, Lincolnshire NG32 3JN Map Ref: 7:D3
11 miles North of Grantham. 15 miles South of Lincoln on A607. Brown signs to Craft Centre, Tearooms and Stables

**OPENING TIMES**
By written appointment.

**ADMISSION** Adult £8,
Groups (10+) £7

 No photography.

Open all year by written appointment.

Ample for cars. Limited for coaches.

 Partial. WC's.

Obligatory. Tours by owner 1¼ hrs.

Tea Rooms at Craft Centre, 100m

# LINCOLN CASTLE
**www.lincolncastle.com**

Discover Lincoln Castle, home to one of the four surviving Magna Carta's; the attraction has undergone a £22m refurbishment. Bringing 1,000 years of history to life – right where it happened.

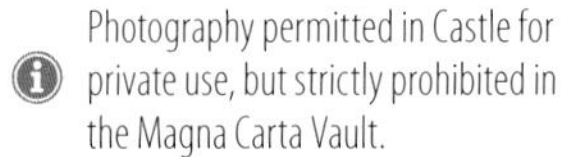 Photography permitted in Castle for private use, but strictly prohibited in the Magna Carta Vault.

 Wheelchair accessible toilets are located on the ground floor of the prison or at the East Gate entrance.

 Baby changing facilities available.

Closed 24 - 26 Dec & 31 Dec - 1 Jan.

Public car parking outside the Castle grounds.

Partial. Please see the access statement on the website for full details.

Audio tour included in admission price. Available in German and French.

Guided Tours available throughout the day.

 Please contact us for education visits. The programme is designed to bring history to life.

Set within the prison and licensed. Offering a range of coffees, teas, sandwiches, snacks & cakes.

Set within the prison with a range to suit all pockets.

Tailor made packages. A unique place to hold events; the perfect setting for you to entertain.

Events through the year. Some events will have separate admission prices.

Wedding packages available.

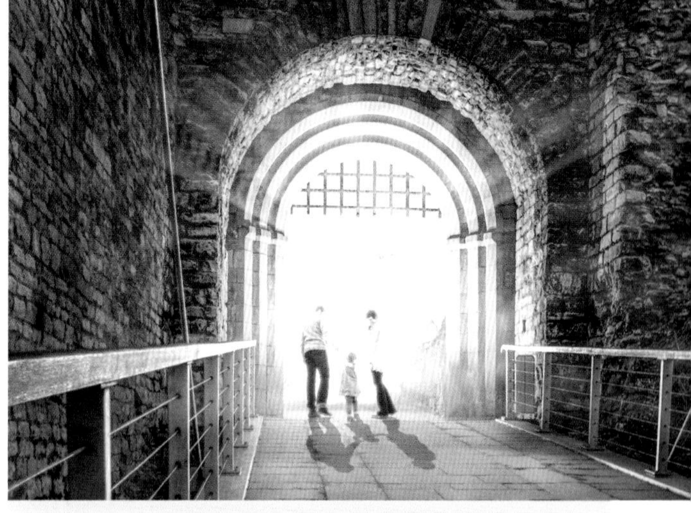

**CONTACT** Owner: Lincolnshire County Council Tel: 01522 554559
Email: lincoln_castle@lincolnshire.gov.uk

**LOCATION** Castle Hill, Lincoln LN1 3AA
Map Ref: 7:D2 Set next to Lincoln Cathedral in the Historic Quarter of the city. Follow signs from A1 Newark or A15 North and South.

**TYPICALLY OPEN** Apr - Sep 10am - 5pm (grounds close at 5:30pm)
Oct - Mar 10am - 4pm (grounds close at 4.30pm)

**ADMISSION** Adult £13.50 (10% discount with online purchase. Day Ticket only) Child 5 & over £7.20 (Under 5's free), Concessions £11, Family £34.20, Groups +16. Walk, Prison & Vault included. Entry to Castle grounds, shop & café are free. Please note, prices may change in April 2019.

# HADDONSTONE SHOW GARDENS

**www.haddonstone.com**

The Haddonstone Show Gardens are set within beautiful walled manor gardens in the idyllic village of East Haddon, amongst the rolling countryside of Northamptonshire. These quintessential English gardens display a vast array of plants, as well as a wide variety of Haddonstone ornamental stonework including garden planters, fountains, statues and furniture. The gardens also feature architectural stonework including an orangery, balustrading and columns, and an attractive outdoor pool. Gastropub in the village.

- No photography without permission.
- Accepts Euros.
- Open all year except weekends, bank holidays and Christmas.
- Limited.
- Almost all areas of garden accessible.
- Groups by arrangement.
- Haddonstone designs can be ordered for worldwide delivery.
- Please see website for upcoming events.

**CONTACT**: Owner: Haddonstone Ltd
Tel: 01604 770711 Email: info@haddonstone.co.uk

**LOCATION:** The Forge House, Church Lane, East Haddon, Northampton NN6 8DB Map Ref: 7:B8 7m north-west of Northampton off the A428. Located in East Haddon village, opposite primary school. Signposted.

**OPENING TIMES:** Mon - Fri, 9am - 5.00pm.
Closed weekends, bank holidays and the Christmas period.
Visit the Haddonstone website for details of the National Garden Scheme weekend and the Saturday Summer Show Garden openings.

**ADMISSION:** Free except donations for the National Garden Scheme weekend. Groups by appointment only. No coach parties.

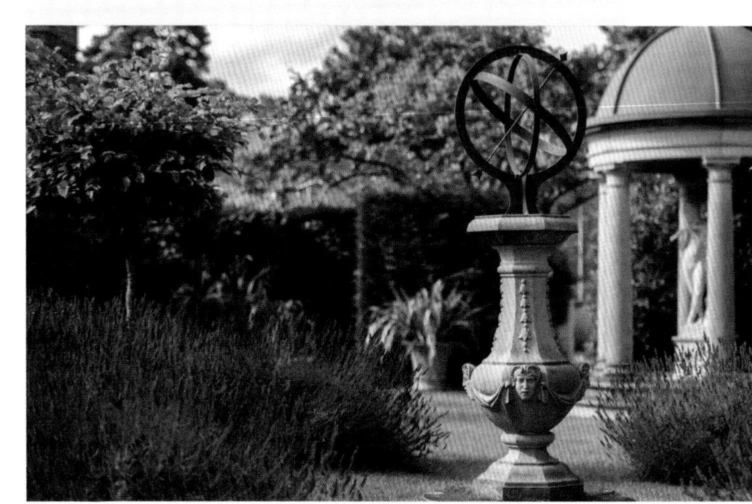

# ALTHORP

**www.spencerofalthorp.com**

Althorp House was built in 1508, by the Spencers, for the Spencers, and that is how it has remained for over 500 years. Today, Althorp contains one of the finest private collections of art, furniture and ceramics in the world, including numerous paintings by Rubens, Reynolds, Lely, Gainsborough and Van Dyck. Visitors can enjoy the House in the company of Althorp's expert tour guides, discovering the fascinating history of one of England's most beautiful, private, historic houses. Wander around the Gardens, the current Exhibitions and visit the Café and Gift Shop in the Stables.

- No indoor photography with still or video cameras.
- Toilet facilities available.
- Baby changing facilities available.
- Free parking with a 5/10 minute walk to the house. Disabled parking.
- House and estate accessible to wheelchairs, except the first floor.
- The house is available for overnight private hire.
- Althorp interior is available to view with our expert tour guides, from the front of the house.
- The Stables Café serves a selection of drinks, cakes, sandwiches and snacks.
- Catering for private hire.
- Gift shop offers bespoke goods, exclusively designed for Althorp.
- Offering lunch parties, corporate functions and activity days etc, email admin@althorp.com
- Please see website for all upcoming events and exhibitions.
- Civil ceremonies and receptions, exclusive hire of house day & night.
- Featuring in photographic & film shoots: Tatler, Harper's Bazaar, Ralph Lauren and Vanity Fair.

**CONTACT** Owner: The Rt Hon The 9th Earl Spencer Contact: Althorp
Tel: 01604 770107 Email: mail@althorp.com

**LOCATION** Northampton NN7 4HQ Map Ref: 7:C9 - From the M1, 7m from J16 and 10m from J18. Situated on A428 Northampton - Rugby.
Rail: 5m from Northampton station and 14m from Rugby station.
Sat Nav Postcode: NN7 4HQ.

**OPENING TIMES** Please visit website for current opening dates & times.

**ADMISSION** Prices on application for adults, concessions and young children. HHA members are free entry. Please call 01604 770107 or email groups@althorp.com to pre-book coach parties and group visits.

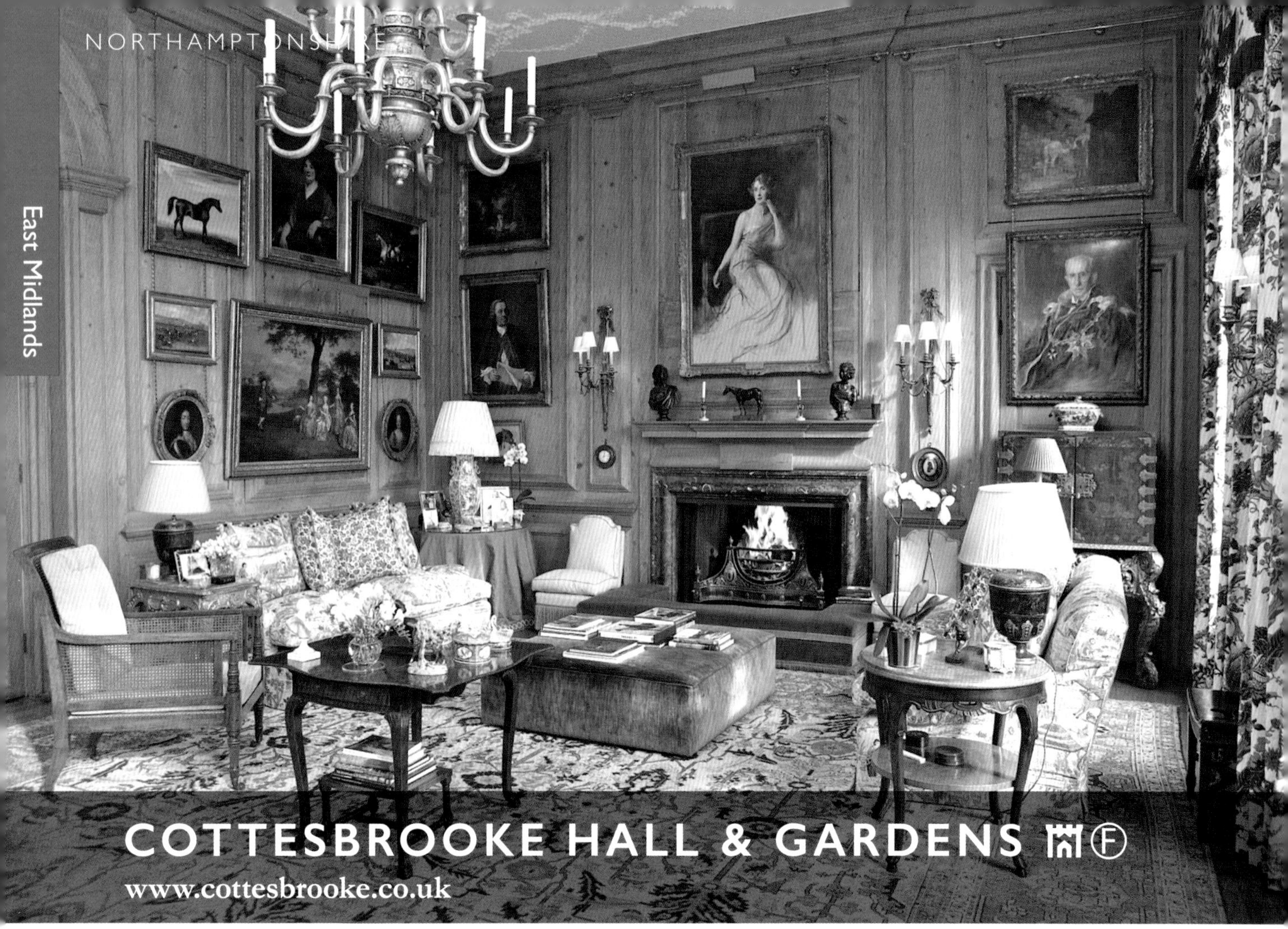

# COTTESBROOKE HALL & GARDENS

www.cottesbrooke.co.uk

Dating from 1702 the Hall's beauty is matched by the magnificence of the gardens and the excellence of the picture, furniture and porcelain collections.

The Woolavington collection of sporting pictures is possibly the finest of its type in Europe and includes paintings by Stubbs, Ben Marshall and artists renowned for works of this genre. Portraits, bronzes, 18th Century English and French furniture and fine porcelain are among the treasures.

The formal gardens are continually being updated and developed by influential designers. The Wild Gardens, a short walk across the Park, are planted along the course of a stream.

**CONTACT**

Owner: Mr & Mrs A R Macdonald-Buchanan
Contact: The Administrator
Tel: 01604 505808
Email: welcome@cottesbrooke.co.uk

**LOCATION**

Cottesbrooke, Northamptonshire NN6 8PF
Map Ref: 7:B8

10m N of Northampton near Creaton on A5199 (formerly A50). Signed from Junction 1 on the A14.

**OPENING TIMES**

May-end of Sep. May & Jun: Wed & Thu, 2pm-5.30pm.
Jul-Sep: Thu, 2pm-5.30pm.
Open BH Mons (May-Sep), 2pm-5.30pm.
The first open day is Wed 1st May 2019.

**ADMISSION**

House & Gardens:
Adult £10, Child £5, Conc £9.
Gardens only:
Adult £7, Child £4, Conc £6.50.
Group & private bookings by arrangement.

No large bags or photography in house. Filming and outside events.

Toilet and disabled WC facilities available.

Baby changing facilities available.

Car and coach parking is included in the admission fee.

Partial. Please contact prior to visit for full access details.

Hall guided tours obligatory. Approx. 45 minutes and max of 18 people per tour.

Educational visits by prior arrangement.

Homemade cakes & drinks available in The Old Laundry between 2:30pm & 5pm on open days.

For intimate and exclusive events. Contact the Estate Office on 01604 505717 for prices & availability.

Special events.

## HOLDENBY HOUSE

www.holdenby.com

Once the largest private house in England and subsequently the palace of James I and prison of Charles I, Holdenby has appeared in the BBC's acclaimed adaptation of 'Great Expectations'. Sitting on a hill overlooking thousands of acres of rolling countryside.

**CONTACT** Owner: James Lowther
Contact: Commercial Manager
Tel: 01604 770074
Email: office@holdenby.com

**LOCATION** Northampton NN6 8DJ
Map Ref: 7:B8 M1/J15a. 7m NW of Northampton off A428 & A5199.

**OPENING TIMES** Gardens: Apr-Sep. See website for details.

**ADMISSION** Adult £5, Child £3.50, Concessions £4.50, Family (2+2) £15. Prices will vary on special event days. Please see our website for details.

- Children's play area. No photography in the house.
- Limited for coaches.
- Accessible. Contact for further details.
- Dogs welcome in the gardens on leads.
- Private guided tours, by arrangement.
- Facilities for educational visits.
- Refreshments available on Sun garden openings May-Aug.
- Gift shop.

## LAMPORT HALL & GARDENS

www.lamporthall.co.uk

Home of the Isham family from 1560-1976, an architectural gem housing the fine collection of furniture and paintings accumulated by the family, including many from the Grand Tour. The gardens are famous as the home of the world's oldest garden gnome.

**CONTACT** Owner: Lamport Hall Preservation Trust
Contact: Executive Director
Tel: 01604 686272 Fax: 01604 686224
Email: house@lamporthall.co.uk

**LOCATION** Northamptonshire NN6 9HD
Map Ref: 7:C8 - Entrance on A508. Midway between Northampton and Market Harborough, 3m S of A14 J2.

**OPENING TIMES** Apr-Oct, every Wed & Thurs (house by guided tour, gardens free-flow). Also open most BH Sun/Mon. Private tours available. Please check website for opening times and prices.

**ADMISSION** House & Garden: Adult £9, Senior £8.50, Groups £8.50.
Garden Only: Adult £6, Senior £5.50, Groups £5.50. Min charges apply.

- No photography in house.
- Lavatory facilities available.
- Open all year for pre-arranged groups.
- Free in stable yard. Limited for coaches.
- Partial see website Disabled lavatory block at the front of the Hall.
- Guide dogs only in the Hall, but all dogs welcome on leads in the gardens.
- 1.45pm & 2.30pm. approx 75 mins.

## DEENE PARK

www.deenepark.com

Home of the Brudenell family since 1514 and seat of the Earls of Cardigan until 1868, this C16th house incorporates a medieval manor with important Georgian additions.

The tranquil gardens include long borders, old fashioned roses, lakes, pleasure walks and a parterre. As well as flora there is also a diversity of bird life.

**CONTACT** Owner: Mr & Mrs Robert Brudenell Contact: House Administrator Tel: 01780 450278 Email: admin@deenepark.com **LOCATION** Deene Rd, Corby NN17 3EW Map Ref: 7:D7 6m NE of Corby off A43, NN17 3EG **OPENING TIMES** Please see website for 2019 opening dates and times. Private Tours: By arrangement only.
**ADMISSION** Please see our website.

Parking available · Plant Sales · Café/Tearoom · Shop · Weddings · Special Events.

DEENE PARK

## PAPPLEWICK HALL

www.papplewickhall.co.uk

A beautiful classic Georgian house, built of Mansfield stone, set in parkland, with woodland garden laid out in the 18th Century. The house is notable for its very fine plasterwork, and elegant staircase. Grade I listed.

**CONTACT** Owner/Contact:
Mr & Mrs J R Godwin-Austen
Tel: 0115 9632623
Email: mail@papplewickhall.co.uk

**LOCATION** Papplewick, Nottinghamshire NG15 8FE Map Ref: 7:B4 Halfway between Nottingham & Mansfield, 3m E of M1/J27. The Hall is 1/2 mile north of Papplewick village, off Blidworth Waye (B683).

**OPENING TIMES** 1, 3 & 5 Wed in each month 2pm-5pm, & by appointment.

**ADMISSION** Adult £5, Groups (10+) £4

- No photography.
- Open all year by appointment.
- Limited for coaches. Free parking for cars.
- Obligatory.
- Garden: NGS open day 26 May, 2-5pm (Adult £4 & Child Free) The Village Fête on 15 Jun, 2-5pm.

BOLSOVER CASTLE
Castle Street, Bolsover, Derbyshire S44 6PR
**Tel:** 01246 822844 **Email:** customers@english-heritage.org.uk

CALKE ABBEY
Ticknall, Derbyshire DE73 7LE
**Tel:** 01332 863822 **Email:** calkeabbey@nationaltrust.org.uk

**CATTON HALL**
**Catton, Walton-On-Trent, South Derbyshire DE12 8LN**
Catton, built in 1745, has been in the hands of the same family since 1405 and is still lived in by the Neilsons as their private home. Acres of flat and undulating parkland ideal for public and sporting events. **Location:** 1 mile from A38 at Alrewas, between Birmingham and Derby **Map Ref:** 6:P5.
**Tel:** 01283 716311 **Email:** estateoffice@catton-hall.com
**Web:** www.catton-hall.com **Open:** Prebooked groups all year round.

ELVASTON CASTLE & COUNTRY PARK
Borrowash Road, Elvaston, Derby, Derbyshire DE72 3EP
**Tel:** 01629 533870 **Email:** countrysideservice@derbyshire.gov.uk

EYAM HALL
Eyam, Hope Valley, Derbyshire S32 5QW
**Tel:** 01433 631976 **Email:** nicolawright@eyamhall.co.uk

HARDWICK ESTATE
Doe Lea, Chesterfield, Derbyshire S44 5QJ
**Tel:** 01246 850430 **Email:** hardwickhall@nationaltrust.org.uk

HARDWICK OLD HALL
Doe Lea, Nr Chesterfield, Derbyshire S44 5QJ
**Tel:** 01246 850431 **Email:** customers@english-heritage.org.uk

HOPTON HALL
Hopton, Wirksworth, Matlock, Derbyshire DE4 4DF
**Tel:** 01629 540923 **Email:** bookings@hoptonhall.co.uk

KEDLESTON HALL
Derbyshire DE22 5JH
**Tel:** 01332 842191 **Email:** kedlestonhall@nationaltrust.org.uk

OGSTON HALL & GARDENS
Ogston New Road, Brackenfield, Derbyshire DE55 6AP
**Tel:** 01773 520970 / 07796 130677

THE PAVILION GARDENS
St John's Road, Buxton, Derbyshire SK17 6XN
**Tel:** 01298 23114 **Email:** terry.crawford@highpeak.gov.uk

PEVERIL CASTLE
Market Place, Castleton, Hope Valley S33 8WQ
**Tel:** 01433 620613 **Email:** customers@english-heritage.org.uk

SUDBURY HALL & MUSEUM OF CHILDHOOD
Ashbourne, Derbyshire DE6 5HT
**Tel:** 01283 585337 **Email:** sudburyhall@nationaltrust.org.uk

SUTTON SCARSDALE HALL
Hall Drive, Sutton Scarsdale, Chesterfield, Derbyshire S44 5UR
**Tel:** 01246 822844 **Email:** bolsover.castle@english-heritage.org.uk

TISSINGTON HALL
Ashbourne, Derbyshire DE6 1RA
**Tel:** 01335 352200 **Email:** events@tissingtonhall.co.uk

WELBECK ABBEY
Welbeck, Worksop, Nottinghamshire S80 3LL
**Tel:** 01909 501700 **Email:** info@harleygallery.co.uk

WINGFIELD MANOR
South Wingfield, Derbyshire DE55 7NH
**Tel:** 0870 333 1181 **Email:** customers@english-heritage.org.uk

THE 1620 HOUSE & GARDEN
Manor Road, Coalville, Leicestershire LE67 2FW
**Tel:** 01455 290429 **Email:** dlhmanorhouse@leics.gov.uk

ASHBY DE LA ZOUCH CASTLE
South Street, Ashby De La Zouch LE65 1BR
**Tel:** 01530 413343 **Email:** customers@english-heritage.org.uk

BELVOIR CASTLE
Belvoir, Grantham, Leicestershire NG32 1PE
**Tel:** 01476 871001

KIRBY MUXLOE CASTLE
Kirby Muxloe, Leicestershire LE9 2DH
**Tel:** 01162 386886 **Email:** customers@english-heritage.org.uk

LYDDINGTON BEDE HOUSE
Blue Coat Lane, Lyddington, Leicester LE15 9LZ
**Tel:** 0157 282 2438 **Email:** customers@english-heritage.org.uk

OAKHAM CASTLE
Castle Lane (Off Market Place), Oakham, Rutland LE15 6DF
**Tel:** 01572 758440

STAUNTON HAROLD HALL
Staunton Harold, Ashby de la Zouch, Leicestershire LE65 1RT
**Tel:** 01332 862599 **Email:** rowan@stauntonharoldhall.co.uk

STONEYWELL
Ulverscroft, Markfield, Leicestershire LE67 9QE
**Tel:** 01530 248040 **Email:** emily.wolfe@nationaltrust.org.uk

WHATTON HOUSE & GARDENS ◇
Loughborough, Leicestershire LE12 5BG
**Tel:** 01509 842268 **Email:** enquiries@whattonhouseandgardens.co.uk

ARABELLA AUFRERE TEMPLE
Brocklesby Park, Grimsby, Lincolnshire DN41 8PN
**Tel:** 01469 560214 **Email:** office@brocklesby.co.uk

AYSCOUGHFEE HALL MUSEUM & GARDENS
Churchgate, Spalding, Lincolnshire PE11 2RA
**Tel:** 01775 764555 **Email:** museum@sholland.gov.uk

BELTON HOUSE
Grantham, Lincolnshire NG32 2LS
**Tel:** 01476 566116 **Email:** belton@nationaltrust.org.uk

BOLINGBROKE CASTLE
Moat Lane, Old Bolingbroke, Spilsby, Lincolnshire PE23 4HH
**Tel:** 01529 461499 **Email:** customers@english-heritage.org.uk

BROCKLESBY MAUSOLEUM
Brocklesby Park, Grimsby, Lincolnshire DN41 8PN
**Tel:** 01469 560214 **Email:** office@brocklesby.co.uk

DODDINGTON HALL & GARDENS
Doddington, Lincolnshire, LN6 4RU
**Tel:** 01522 694308 **Email:** info@doddingtonhall.com

EASTON WALLED GARDENS
Easton, Grantham, Lincolnshire NG33 5AP
**Tel:** 01476 530063 **Email:** info@eastonwalledgardens.co.uk

ELLYS MANOR HOUSE
Great Ponton, Nr Grantham, Lincolnshire NG33 5DP
**Tel:** 01476 530023 **Email:** ellysmanor@btinternet.com

ELSHAM HALL GARDENS & COUNTRY PARK
Elsham Hall, Brigg, Lincolnshire DN20 0QZ
**Tel:** 01652 688698 **Email:** enquiries@elshamhall.co.uk

GAINSBOROUGH OLD HALL
Parnell Street, Gainsborough, Lincolnshire DN21 2NB
**Tel:** 01427 677348 **Email:** gainsborougholdhall@lincolnshire.gov.uk

GRIMSTHORPE CASTLE, PARK & GARDENS
Estate Office, Grimsthorpe, Bourne PE10 0LY
**Tel:** 01778 591205 **Email:** ray@grimsthorpe.co.uk

GUNBY HALL
Spilsby, Lincolnshire PE23 5SL
**Tel:** 01754 890102 **Email:** gunbyhall@nationaltrust.org.uk

## LEADENHAM HOUSE

**Lincolnshire, LN5 0PU**
Late 18th Century house in park setting. **Map Ref:** 7:D3 Entrance on A17 Leadenham bypass (between Newark and Sleaford). **Tel:** 07810 825697 **Email:** williamreeve@leadenhamestate.com **Open:** 1-5, 8-12, 15-19, 22-26, 29-30 Apr; 1-3 May; Spring & Aug Bank Holidays. **Admission:** £5. Please ring door bell. Groups by prior arrangement only.

LINCOLN MEDIEVAL BISHOPS' PALACE
Minster Yard, Lincoln, Lincolnshire LN2 1PU
**Tel:** 01522 527468 **Email:** customers@english-heritage.org.uk

MARSTON HALL
Marston, Grantham NG32 2HQ
**Tel:** 07812 356237 **Email:** johnthorold@aol.com

NORMANBY HALL COUNTRY PARK
Normanby, Scunthorpe DN15 9HU
**Tel:** 01724 720588 **Email:** normanby.hall@northlincs.gov.uk

SCAWBY HALL
Vicarage Lane, Scawby, Brigg, Lincolnshire DN20 9LX
**Tel:** 01652 654272 **Email:** info@scawbyhall.com

SCRIVELSBY WALLED GARDEN
The New Midge Barns, Hatton, Lincs LN8 5QL
**Tel:** 07435 009876 **Email:** info@keymarque.co.uk

TATTERSHALL CASTLE
Sleaford Road, Tattershall, Lincolnshire LN4 4LR
**Tel:** 01526 342543 **Email:** tattershallcastle@nationaltrust.org.uk

WOOLSTHORPE MANOR
Water Lane, Woolsthorpe by Colsterworth NG33 5PD
**Tel:** 01476 862823 **Email:** woolsthorpemanor@nationaltrust.org.uk

78 DERNGATE: THE CHARLES RENNIE MACKINTOSH HOUSE & GALLERIES
82 Derngate, Northampton, UK, NN1 1UH
**Tel:** 01604 603407 **Email:** info@78derngate.org.uk

APETHORPE PALACE
Hunting Way, Apethorpe, Peterborough, Northamptonshire PE8 5AQ
**Tel:** 0370 333 1181 **Email:** customers@english-heritage.org.uk

BOUGHTON HOUSE
Kettering, Northamptonshire NN14 1BJ
**Tel:** 01536 515731 **Email:** blht@boughtonhouse.co.uk

CANONS ASHBY
Daventry, Bolsover, Northamptonshire NN11 3SD
**Tel:** 01327 861900 **Email:** canonsashby@nationaltrust.org.uk

COTON MANOR GARDEN
Nr Guilsborough, Northamptonshire NN6 8RQ
**Tel:** 01604 740219 **Email:** pasleytyler@cotonmanor.co.uk

DELAPRE ABBEY
Abbey Cottage, Delapré Abbey, London Road, Northampton NN4 8AW
**Tel:** 01604 760817 **Email:** info@delapreabbey.org

KELMARSH HALL & GARDENS
Kelmarsh, Northampton NN6 9LY
**Tel:** 01604 686543 **Email:** enquiries@kelmarsh.com

KIRBY HALL
Deene, Corby, Northamptonshire NN17 5EN
**Tel:** 01536 203230 **Email:** customers@english-heritage.org.uk

LYVEDEN
Nr Oundle, Northamptonshire PE8 5AT
**Tel:** 01832 205158 **Email:** lyveden@nationaltrust.org.uk

ROCKINGHAM CASTLE
Rockingham, Market Harborough, Leicestershire LE16 8TH
**Tel:** 01536 770240 **Email:** estateoffice@rockinghamcastle.com

RUSHTON TRIANGULAR LODGE
Rushton, Kettering, Northamptonshire NN14 1RP
**Tel:** 01536 710761

SOUTHWICK HALL
Southwick, Nr Oundle, Peterborough, Northamptonshire PE8 5BL
**Tel:** 01832 274064 **Email:** southwickhall@hotmail.co.uk

STOKE PARK PAVILIONS
Stoke Bruerne, Towcester, Northamptonshire NN12 7RZ
**Tel:** 07768 230325

WESTON HALL
Towcester, Northamptonshire NN12 8PU
**Tel:** 07710 523879 **Email:** george@crossovercapital.co.uk

## WAKEFIELD LODGE

**Potterspury, Northamptonshire NN12 7QX**
Georgian hunting lodge with deer park.
**Location:** 4m S of Towcester on A5. Take signs to farm shop for directions. **Map Ref:** 7:C10 **Tel:** 01327 811395
**Open:** House 16 Apr - 31 May: Mon-Fri (closed BHs), 12 noon-4pm. Appointments by telephone.
Access walk open May & June. **Admission:** £10

### CARLTON HALL
Carlton-On-Trent, Nottingham, Nottinghamshire NG23 6LP
**Tel:** 07775 785344 **Email:** carltonhallnotts@gmail.com

### CLUMBER PARK
Worksop, Nottinghamshire S80 3AZ
**Tel:** 01909 544917 **Email:** clumberpark@nationaltrust.org.uk

### DH LAWRENCE BIRTHPLACE
8a Victoria Street, Eastwood, Nottinghamshire NG16 3AW
**Tel:** 01159 173824 **Email:** dhlawrence@liberty-leisure.org.uk

### HODSOCK PRIORY GARDENS
Blyth, Nr Worksop S81 0TY
**Tel:** 01909 591204

### HOLME PIERREPONT HALL
Holme Pierrepont, Nr Nottingham NG12 2LD
**Tel:** 0115 933 2371 **Email:** rplb@holmepierreponthall.com

### KELHAM HALL
Newark, Nottinghamshire NG23 5QX
**Tel:** 01636 650000 **Email:** info@kelham-hall.com

### MR STRAW'S HOUSE
5-7 Blyth Grove, Worksop S81 0JG
**Tel:** 01909 482380 **Email:** mrstrawshouse@nationaltrust.org.uk

### NEWSTEAD ABBEY
Ravenshead, Nottingham, Nottinghamshire NG15 8GE
**Tel:** 01623 455900 **Email:** sallyl@newsteadabbey.org.uk

### NOTTINGHAM CASTLE & ART GALLERY
Lenton Road, Nottingham NG1 6EZ
**Tel:** 0115 876 1400 **Email:** nottingham.castle@nottinghamcity.gov.uk

### RUFFORD ABBEY
Rufford Abbey Country Park, Ollerton, Nottinghamshire NG22 9DF
**Tel:** 01623 821338 **Email:** customers@english-heritage.org.uk

### THRUMPTON HALL
Nottingham, Nottinghamshire NG11 0AX
**Tel:** 07796 956556 **Email:** enquiries@thrumptonhall.com

### WOLLATON HALL & PARK
Wollaton Park, Nottingham NG8 2AE
**Tel:** 0115 915 3900 **Email:** maria.narducci@nottinghamcity.gov.uk

'CAPABILITY' BROWN PORTRAIT AT BURGHLEY HOUSE

# HEART *of* ENGLAND

HEREFORDSHIRE • SHROPSHIRE • STAFFORDSHIRE
WARWICKSHIRE • WEST MIDLANDS • WORCESTERSHIRE

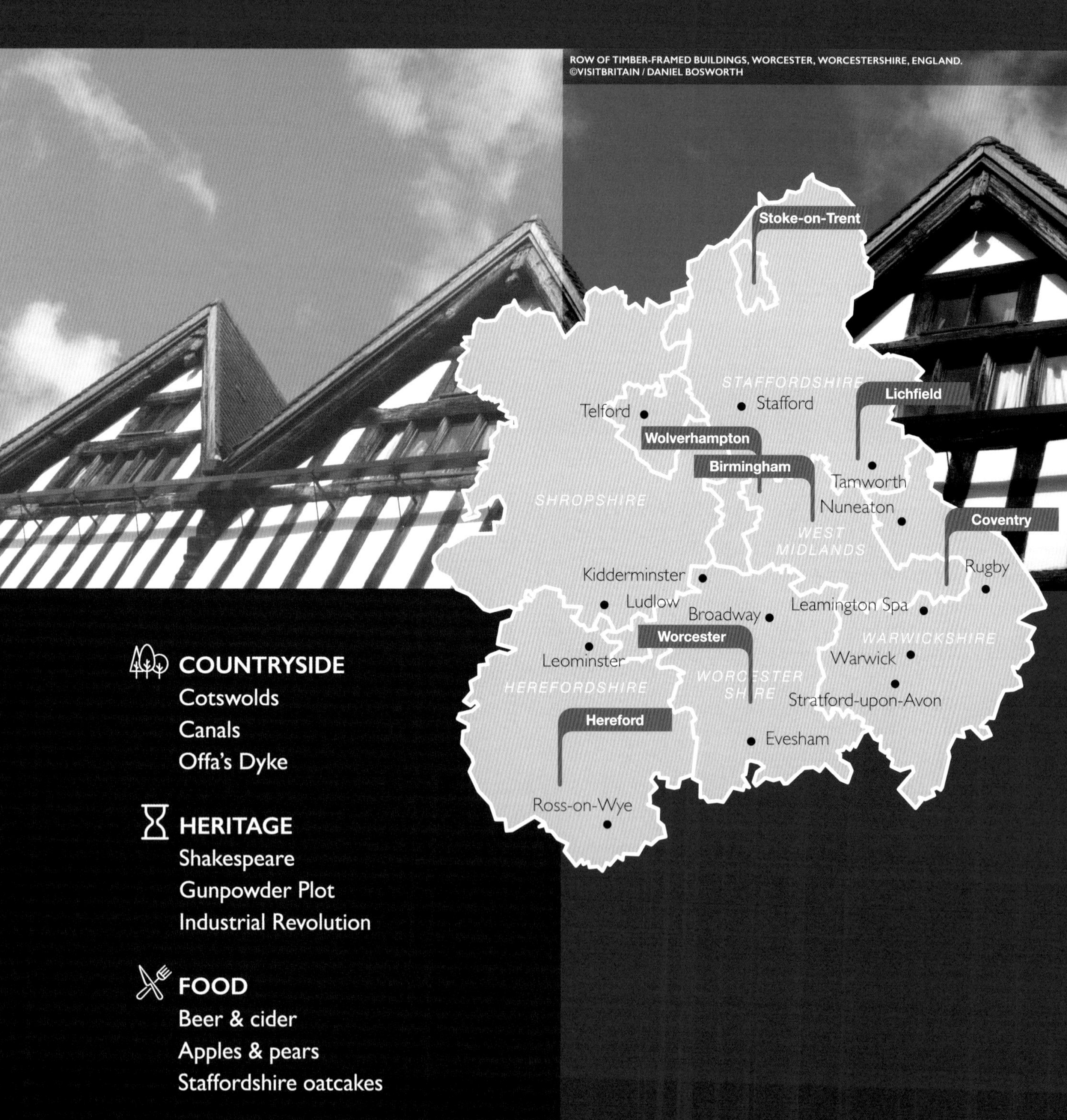


ROW OF TIMBER-FRAMED BUILDINGS, WORCESTER, WORCESTERSHIRE, ENGLAND.


**COUNTRYSIDE**
Cotswolds
Canals
Offa's Dyke

**HERITAGE**
Shakespeare
Gunpowder Plot
Industrial Revolution

**FOOD**
Beer & cider
Apples & pears
Staffordshire oatcakes

# The Treehouse at Pitchford Hall

## Perch in a tree

Imagine a perfect medieval house, all black and white timbering and pointed gables. Now shrink it down until it is child-sized and balance it precariously in the spreading branches of a grand old tree. What a delicious idea!

TAKE IN THE VIEW FROM A TREETOP HIDEAWAY

Amazingly, such a house actually exists; not the fantasy of a modern-day Lego fanatic but a timber-framed treehouse built by the Ottley family of Pitchford Hall. This is probably the oldest treehouse in the world, first mentioned in 1692. About 50 years later, it seems to have been given a facelift by Thomas Farnolls Pritchard, who may have added the gothic arched windows.

Pritchard would have been working here around 1760, between designing the rococo Drawing Room at Tatton Park in 1758 and the world's first cast iron structure at Ironbridge in 1779. The treehouse he 'improved' is a charming timbered building whose appearance echoes the timbering of the main house which was built with a fortune made in the wool trade around 1560.
The treehouse is perched halfway up an ancient lime tree and has views in all directions over the parkland. After 350 years, it needs a bit of extra support from metal legs but is still a perfect retreat. Pitchford Hall itself is back in the hands of a descendant of its original family since Rowena Colthurst and her husband, James Nason, vowed to rescue it from a period of dereliction. Their first task has been to restore a main wing of the house and several cottages for holiday lets so the treehouse is now something many of us can enjoy.

PITCHFORD HALL IN ALL ITS TIMBERED SPLENDOUR

In the past, a 13-year-old future Queen Victoria watched a fox hunt race by from its windows and the future George VI came here the year before the abdication crisis made him King. Its charm is hard to resist. ■

AFTER 350 YEARS THE TREEHOUSE IS ALMOST PART OF THE TREE ITSELF.

# Heart of England

## Top 3 Venues

LUDLOW CASTLE

### Ludlow Castle, Shropshire

The castle can accommodate wedding parties from 6 to 350 and have event planners on hand to help you design your day to your specific requirements. Hire can include the use of the three self-catering apartments in Castle House, which can also be hired for other types of event. The castle itself dates back to the 11th century and was once a Norman fortress and Royal residence. The Council of the Marches of Wales formed by Edward IV had their headquarters here in the 15th century and would house lawyers, judges and royal messengers.

ARBURY HALL

### Arbury Hall, Warwickshire

The dining room at Arbury boasts a spectacular fan-vaulted ceiling and gothic chimney piece and is a popular choice for small parties. Arbury is not licensed for wedding ceremonies but reception parties can be held in the marquee set in the parkland with the hall providing a stunning backdrop and photo opportunity. Mary Ann Evans, who rose to prominence in the Victorian era as a novelist writing under the pseudonym George Eliot, was born on the Arbury estate at South Farm in 1819.

CHILLINGTON HALL © STUART JAMES PHOTOGRAPHY

### Chillington Hall, Staffordshire

Hire Chillington Hall for your birthday, engagement or other special occasions. The Grand Saloon is available to seat up to 80 people for dinner. The Saloon features a Broadwood Grand Piano and is available for use should you choose to hire a pianist. Chillington does not hold a civil licence, however receptions can be held in the Hall after your service at one of the nearby venues. Chillington Hall can provide a room for the bride to get ready before and after the ceremony, and numerous spectacular photo opportunities are available throughout the house and grounds.

NTS

**Crufts, Birmingham NEC, West Midlands** *7th - 10th March 2019*

**Birmingham Literature Festival, Various Venues** *October 2019*

**Horse of the Year Show, Birmingham NEC & Genting Arena** *October 2019*

## Top 3 Annual Events

### Ludlow Spring Festival, Ludlow Castle, Shropshire *11th and 12th May 2019*

Pop into the "Festival Pub" where you can meet local brewers and choose from dozens of real ales to sample, as well as browsing stalls showcasing locally produced food and drink. There is live music in the evening to keep you entertained. The 35th Marches Transport Festival takes place at the same time showcasing over 150 classic and vintage cars in the castle grounds. There are plenty of activities for children as well as talks and demonstrations.

LUDLOW SPRING FESTIVAL - SHROPSHIRE LIVE

### Shakespeare's Birthday/Stratford-Upon-Avon Literary Festival, Warwickshire *April 2019*

Shakespeare's birthday falls on April 23rd, and every year on the weekend closest to this date Stratford celebrates with parades, pageantry and music. Visit Shakespeare's family homes. Shakespeare's Birthplace Trust holds an Annual Birthday Lecture with a special guest speaker. The birthday celebrations are usually closely followed by the Stratford-Upon-Avon Literary Festival taking place across a week and including discussions and debates, guest speakers and interviews with TV, radio and literary stars.

STRATFORD SHAKESPEARE'S BIRTHDAY CELEBRATIONS - CALENDAR CUSTOMS

### Fireworks at Birmingham Botanical Gardens, West Midlands *5th November 2019*

Fireworks are held on the main lawn every year at Birmingham Botanical Gardens, watched by spectators from the terrace. The spectacular display is set to music. Get your tickets in advance for this popular family event. The gardens first opened in 1832 and the Tropical and Subtropical glasshouses here have always been popular attractions as they house species that are not commonly found in many areas of the UK. In 1995 an aviary was constructed which houses extensive collections of birds from different geographical regions.

BIRMINGHAM BOTANICAL GARDENS

# Heart of England

## Places to stay and eat

CASTLE HOUSE

### Castle House

Castle House is an elegant Grade II listed Georgian villa just yards from the historic cathedral, in the city of Hereford. The hotel has 24 individually designed luxury rooms and suites, eight of which are a few steps away in a separate townhouse, Number 25. All the rooms and suites are exceptionally comfortable, fresh and original without being minimalist. In the main hotel, the décor is bold, with tapestries, paintings and filled with fresh flowers while the rooms in Number 25 have a more contemporary design. Bathrooms are all en-suite and decorated with marble and wood. Hereford is steeped in history, having been the old capital of Mercia. The cathedral's famous Mappa Mundi, Chained Library and signed Magna Carta are within walking distance, as are the main shops and new shopping complex. Ideal also for small intimate wedding parties. The hotel is also available for exclusive use.

**Castle Street, Hereford, Herefordshire HR1 2NW**

**01432 356321**

**www.castlehse.co.uk**
**info@castlehse.co.uk**

### The High Field Town House
*Hotel*

23 Highfield Road, Edgbaston
Birmingham B15 3DP

0121 647 6466

www.highfieldtownhouse.co.uk
bookings@highfieldtownhouse.co.uk

### The Townhouse
*Inn*

16 Church Street
Stratford-Upon-Avon CV37 6HB

01789 262222

www.stratfordtownhouse.co.uk
book@stratfordtownhouse.co.uk

### Lamb's Restaurant
*Restaurant*

12 Sheep Street
Stratford-Upon-Avon CV37 6EF

01789 292554

www.lambsrestaurant.co.uk
eat@lambsrestaurant.co.uk

## Soulton Hall

Sixteen generations of the Ashton Family have cherished this ancient Shropshire Manor steeped in history dating back to Henry the Eighth. Set in 500 acres of private country estate and woodland, John and Ann Ashton and son Tim treat guests like members of the family. Drinks are taken in the cosy drawing room, whilst making a choice from the 4 course menu, served in the elegant candle-lit dining room. The 18th century Soulton Court (across the lawn) a wonderful setting for weddings and conferences, further ground floor accommodation being available in the Carriage House and Cedar House.
The walled gardens and extensive grounds offer a peaceful and relaxing spot to unwind. It is also a working farm and an excellent base from which to explore the beauty of the Shires and Welsh Marches, as well as the Ironbridge Gorge and the cities of Shrewsbury and Chester. The Welsh hills and border castles are also within easy reach. Soulton is one of the best kept secrets of Shropshire.

Soulton Road, Wem, Shropshire SY4 5RS

01939 232786

www.soultonhall.co.uk
enquiries@soultonhall.co.uk

SOULTON HALL

## The Lion at Leintwardine

*Restaurant*

Leintwardine, Craven Arms
Shropshire SY7 0JZ

01547 540 203

www.thelionleintwardine.co.uk
enquiries@thelionleintwardine.co.uk

## Hathaway Tea Rooms

*Tea Room*

19 High Street
Stratford-Upon-Avon CV37 6AU

01789 264022

www.hathawaytearooms.com
Rick.Allen@HathawayTeaRooms.com

## Contance Wallis Tea Rooms

*Tea Room*

91 Hewell Road
Barnt Green B45 8NL

0121 679 6917

www.constancewallace.co.uk
info@constancewallace.co.uk

## OLD SUFTON

A 16th Century manor house which was altered and remodelled in the 18th and 19th Centuries and again in this Century. The original home of the Hereford family (see Sufton Court) who have held the manor since the 12th Century.

**CONTACT**
Owner: Trustees of Sufton Heritage Trust
Contact: Mr & Mrs J N Hereford
Tel: 01432 870268 / 01432 850328
Email: james@sufton.co.uk

**LOCATION** Mordiford, Hereford HR1 4EJ
Map Ref: 6:L10 Mordiford, off B4224 Mordiford - Dormington Road.

**OPENING TIMES** By appointment to: james@sufton.co.uk

Open all year by appointment.

Parking is available.

Partial.

Obligatory.

Small groups. No special facilities.

## SUFTON COURT

Sufton Court is a small Palladian mansion house. Built in 1788 by James Wyatt for James Hereford. The park was laid out by Humphry Repton whose *'red book'* still survives. The house stands above the rivers Wye and Lugg giving impressive views towards the mountains of Wales.

**CONTACT** Owner: J N Hereford
Contact: Mr & Mrs J N Hereford
Tel: 01432 870268 / 01432 850328
Email: james@sufton.co.uk

**LOCATION** Mordiford, Hereford HR1 4LUMap Ref: 6:L10 Mordiford, off B4224 Mordiford - Dormington Road.

**OPENING TIMES** 14 - 27 May & 13 - 26 Aug. 2pm-5pm.
Guided tours: 2pm, 3pm & 4pm.

**ADMISSION** Adult £5, Child 50p.

Only small coaches.

In grounds, on leads.

Obligatory.

Accessible.

Small groups. No special facilities.

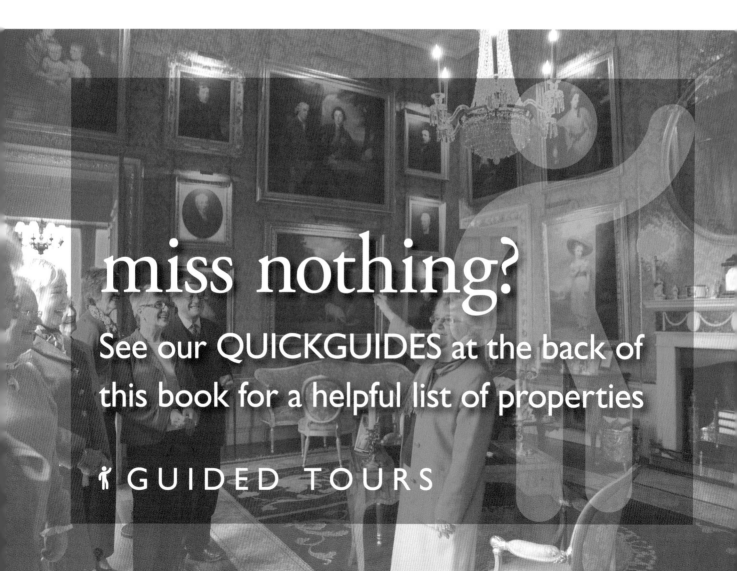

# LUDLOW CASTLE

**www.ludlowcastle.com**

Ludlow Castle started out as a Norman Fortress, became a Fortified Palace where it was visited regularly by royalty and was home briefly to Prince Arthur & Catherine of Aragon. It played a huge part in Shropshire's history when it became an Admin Centre for the Council of the Marches. During the Civil War it was a Royalist stronghold and when the town and castle were besieged by a strong parliamentary force it was quickly abandoned becoming the tourist attraction it is today.

Inside the curtain walls is the 19th Century Castle House. There are 2 independent shops and Castle Kitchen and at the north end are the beautifully restored function rooms and 3 apartments. We host many weddings with packages to suit any size from a Library wedding for 6 people to a marquee wedding for 250 where you take over the whole of Castle House North wing. Imagine the grounds and the Castle as the backdrop for your photos.

The apartments are available for a minimum of three night stays. They each sleep four, are beautifully appointed with all mod cons, a private car parking space each and views of the Castle from many of the windows. Sir Henry Sidney Apartment welcomes dogs.

As a modern day business it is home to the Ludlow Food Festivals and Ludlow Christmas Medieval Fayre and we put on several smaller events during the Bank Holidays. There are several guides to chose from to help you with the history and the buildings including tours that can be arranged with our tour guide and regular weekend archaeological tours with our resident archaeologist Leon Bracelin whose enthusiasm will rub off on you.

**CONTACT**

Owner: The Earl of Powis

Contact: Sonja Belchere (The Custodian)

Tel: 01584 874465

Email: info@ludlowcastle.com

Facebook: Ludlow Castle Twitter:@LudlowCastle1

**LOCATION**

Castle Square, Ludlow, Shropshire SY8 1AY

Map Ref: 6:L8 Ludlow is situated on the A49.

From Birmingham, head west on the A456 through Kidderminster. Continue on the A456 through Tenbury Wells. Turn right onto the A49 & follow signs for Ludlow. From the M5 leave at Junction 3 & continue on the A456 through Kidderminster. Continue on the A456 through Tenbury Wells. Turn right onto the A49 & follow signs for Ludlow.

**OPENING TIMES**

Jan - Feb - Weekends only.

All week, Oct - Mar 10am - 4pm.

Apr - Sep 10am - 5pm.

**ADMISSION**

Visit the website for up-to-date admission charges.

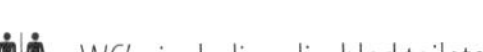

WC's, including disabled toilets.

Baby changing facilities available.

The Castle is closed for events set ups. Always check website before visiting for closures.

The grounds are accessible but uneven in places. We provide WC's.

Welcome throughout Castle, Tea Room & the Sir Henry Sidney Apartment.

Three 4-5* self-catering apartments.

£3 each.

By arrangement.

By arrangement.

Traditional Tea Rooms with waiting staff. Licensed.

2 Independent Shops, Castle Gift Shop and Castle Gallery

Please see website for special events.

Available for Civil Ceremonies, receptions, parties and other functions

## HODNET HALL GARDENS

www.hodnethallgardens.org

Over 60 acres of brilliant coloured flowers, magnificent forest trees, sweeping lawns and a chain of ornamental pools which run tranquilly along the cultivated garden valley to provide a natural habitat for waterfowl and other wildlife. No matter what the season, visitors will always find something fresh and interesting to ensure an enjoyable outing.

**CONTACT** Owner: Sir Algernon and the Hon Lady-Percy
Contact: Secretary
Tel: 01630 685786 Fax: 01630 685853
Email: secretary@hodnethall.com

**LOCATION** Hodnet, Market Drayton Shropshire TF9 3NN Map Ref: 6:L5 - 12 miles North East of Shrewsbury on A53; M6/J15, M54/J3.

**OPENING TIMES** Open Every Sunday and Bank Holiday from Sunday 31 Mar - Sun 29 September.
Wednesdays: 15 May, 12 Jun, 17 Jul.

**ADMISSION** Adult £7.50, Child £1

 Facebook: /hodnethall
Instagram: /Hodnethallgardens

 Parking available.

 Partial. WC's.

Dogs welcome on leads.

Light lunches and afternoon teas during garden open days.

Garden restaurant.

See Facebook page for upcoming special days and events.

## LONGNER HALL

Designed by John Nash in 1803, Longner Hall is a Tudor Gothic style house set in a park landscaped by Humphry Repton. The home of one family for over 700 years. Longner's principal rooms are adorned with plaster fan vaulting and stained glass.

**CONTACT** Richard Burton at Jackson Property
Tel: 01743709249
Email: info@longner.co.uk

**LOCATION** Uffington, Shrewsbury, Shropshire SY4 4TG
Map Ref: 6:L6
4 miles SE of Shrewsbury on Uffington road, ¼ mile off B4380, Atcham.

**OPENING TIMES** Tours at 2pm & 3.30pm on weekdays from Mon 27 May - Frid 28 Jun. Bank holiday Mon 22 Apr, Mon 6 May, Mon 26 Aug.

**ADMISSION** Adult £5, Child/OAP £3.

 No photography in house.

Limited for coaches.

Partial.

Guide dogs only.

Obligatory.

By arrangement.

## WHITMORE HALL

www.hha.org.uk

Whitmore Hall is a Grade I listed building, designated as a house of outstanding architectural and historical interest. Parts of the hall date back to a much earlier period and for 900 years has been the seat of the Cavenagh-Mainwarings, who are direct descendants of the original Norman owners. The hall has beautifully proportioned light rooms and is in excellent order. There are good family portraits to be seen with a continuous line dating from 1624 to the present day. The park encompasses a lime avenue leading from the hall to the parish church, an early Victorian summer house which was refurbished in 2017 and an outstanding, rare Elizabethan stable block. Garden, lake, lily pool, and bluebell wood in season.

 Ample parking available.

 Ground floor and grounds.

Tea and biscuits can be arranged for small booked groups, May-Aug, on days open to the public.

Please contact us for information on Weddings at Whitmore.

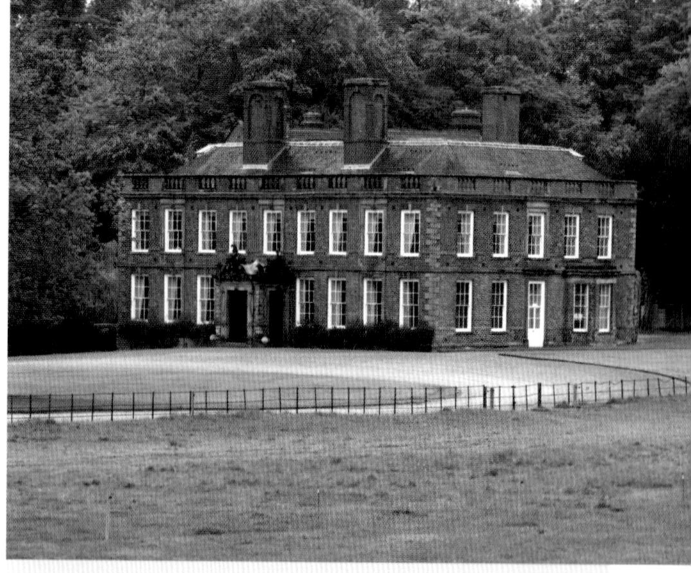

**CONTACT** Contact: Mrs Adrienne Chafe
Tel: 01782 680 478 Email: whitmore.hall@yahoo.com

**LOCATION** Whitmore, Newcastle-Under-Lyme, Staffordshire ST5 5HW
Map Ref: 6:M4 On A53 Newcastle-Market Drayton Road, 3m from M6/J15.

**OPENING TIMES** 1 May - 31 Aug: Tues and Weds, open 2pm - 4.30pm with guided tours at 2.15pm, 3pm and 3.45pm.

**ADMISSION** Adult £5, Child 50p.

# ARBURY HALL

www.arburyestate.co.uk

Arbury Hall, original Elizabethan mansion house, Gothicised in the 18th Century surrounded by stunning gardens and parkland.

Arbury Hall has been the seat of the Newdegate family for over 450 years and is the ancestral home of Viscount Daventry. This Tudor/Elizabethan House was Gothicised by Sir Roger Newdegate in the 18th Century and is regarded as the 'Gothic Gem' of the Midlands. The principal rooms, with their soaring fan vaulted ceilings and plunging pendants and filigree tracery, stand as a most breathtaking and complete example of early Gothic Revival architecture and provide a unique and fascinating venue for corporate entertaining, product launches, fashion shoots and activity days. Exclusive use of this historic Hall, its gardens and parkland is offered to clients. The Hall stands in the middle of beautiful parkland with landscaped gardens of rolling lawns, lakes and winding wooded walks. Spring flowers are profuse and in June rhododendrons, azaleas and giant wisteria provide a beautiful environment for the visitor. George Eliot, the novelist, was born on the estate and Arbury Hall and Sir Roger Newdegate were immortalised in her book 'Scenes of Clerical Life'.

**CONTACT**

Owner: The Viscount Daventry
Contact: Events Secretary
Tel: 01676 540529 Email: info@arburyestate.co.uk

**LOCATION**

Arbury Hall, Nuneaton, Warwickshire CV10 7PT (for SATNAV use CV10 7NF)
Map Ref: 6:P7 - London, M1, M6/J3 (A444 to Nuneaton), 2m SW of Nuneaton. 1m W of A444. Nuneaton 5 mins. Birmingham City Centre 20 mins. London 2 hrs, Coventry 20 mins.

**OPENING TIMES**

Hall & Gardens: Bank Holiday weekends (Suns & Mons) from Easter - Aug Bank Holiday from 1pm - 6pm. Last guided tour of the hall 4.30pm.
Groups: 25+ weekdays by prior arrangement from Apr - end Sep.

**ADMISSION**

Hall & Gardens:
Adult £8.50, Child (up to 14yrs) £4.50, Family (2+2) £20.

Garden only:
Adult £5.50, Child (up to 14yrs) £4.

No cameras or video recorders indoors.

Baby changing facilities available.

200 cars & 3 coaches 250 yds from house. Follow signs. Approach map available for coach drivers.

Partial, WCs.

Dogs on leads in garden. Guide dogs only in house.

Obligatory. Tour time: 50mins.

Stables Tea Rooms (on first floor) open from 1pm.

Small selection of souvenir gifts.

Exclusive lunches and dinners for corporate parties in dining room, max. 50, buffets 80.

Available to host a wide variety of outside events throughout the spring & summer season.

A marquee in the historic parkland with the Hall as a backdrop is available for Wedding receptions.

As a film location, Arbury presents a variety of atmospheric settings for period and contemporary dramas.

# SHAKESPEARE'S FAMILY HOMES

www.shakespeare.org.uk

**Shakespeare's Birthplace** - *Where it all began*
The perfect starting point for exploring Shakespeare's works, family, life and times. Explore Shakespeare's childhood world and hear tales of his life from our costumed guides.

Discover Shakespeare's influence through the centuries and see actors bring his works to life with speech and song.

**Mary Arden's Farm** - *Take a step back in time*
Experience the sights, sounds, smells and tastes of the countryside as Shakespeare would have known on his mother, Mary Arden's, farm.

From falconry, feeding the goats and goose-herding to craft demonstrations, archery, and letting off steam in the adventure playground, every season brings something new.

**Anne Hathaway's Cottage** - *Wander where new love bloomed*
Savour the rural beauty where Shakespeare's future wife grew up and lived for many years, and where their romance bloomed.

Retreat into nine acres of gardens and woodland, and get closer to the Hathaway family and prepare to be captivated by stories handed down from generation to generation

**Shakespeare's New Place** - *Explore the house that isn't there*
Explore the site of Shakespeare's family home where he lived for 19 years in the height of his creative powers, and uncover the fascinating story of why the house that is no longer there.

Discover beautiful gardens and specially-commissioned artworks inspired by Shakespeare's work, life and times.

**Hall's Croft** - *Meet the next generation*
Admire stunning period interiors in the house built for the next generation: Shakespeare's daughter Susanna and her husband, physician John Hall.

Enjoy tales from our guides of extraordinary guests and residents from the house's history. Relax in the tranquil, fragrant walled garden.

**CONTACT** Owner/Contact: The Shakespeare Birthplace Trust General Enquiries Tel: 01789 204016 Group Visits Tel: 01789 201806 Email: info@shakespeare.org.uk groups@shakespeare.org.uk

**LOCATION** Henley Street, Stratford-upon-Avon CV37 6QW Map Ref: 6:P9 Car: 2 hrs from London. 45 mins from Birmingham. 4m from M40/J15 & well signed from all approaches. (Free coach terminal for groups drop off & pick up at Birthplace. Max stay 15 mins). Rail: Service from London (Marylebone).

**OPENING TIMES** Daily throughout the year except Christmas Day & Boxing Day (Shakespeare's Birthplace is open on Boxing Day). Mary Arden's Farm closes for Winter from Nov-Mar. Opening times vary throughout the year. Please see website for up-to-date information.

**ADMISSION** Visit the website for full details on ticket prices. You can enjoy 12 months' free admission with every ticket to Shakespeare's family homes. Tickets are valid for a year with unlimited entry. Pay for a day and take the whole year to explore!

City Sightseeing bus tour connecting town houses with Anne Hathaway's Cottage & Mary Arden's Farm.

Toilet facilities available.

Baby changing facilities available.

Please check for full details.

Parking at Mary Arden's Farm. Pay & display parking at Anne Hathaway's Cottage.

Partial. WC's.

By special arrangement.

Available for all houses. Please call 01789 201806.

Mary Arden's Farm, Anne Hathaway's Cottage, Hall's Croft.

Gifts available.

Corporate functions available, telephone for details.

Please check website for details.

## BIRMINGHAM BOTANICAL GARDENS

**birminghambotanicalgardens.org.uk**

15 acres of beautiful historic landscaped gardens with 7000 shrubs, plants and trees. Four glasshouses, Roses and Alpines, Woodland and Rhododendron Walks, Rock Pool, Herbaceous Borders, Japanese Garden. Children's playground, aviaries, gallery, and bandstand.

**CONTACT** Owner: Birmingham Botanical & Horticultural Society Contact: Kim Hill Tel: 0121 454 1860 Email: Kim@birmingham botanicalgardens.org.uk **LOCATION** Westbourne Rd, Edgbaston, Birmingham B15 3TR Map Ref: 6:O7 - 2m West of city centre. Follow signs to Edgbaston then brown tourist signs. **OPENING TIMES** Daily: 10am-dusk. Closed Christmas Day & Boxing Day. Refer to website for details. **ADMISSION** Adult £7.50, Family £22, Groups/Conc £5.25, Child U5 Free.

Free. Register on arrival for free parking. Excellent wheelchair access throughout Gardens & Glasshouses. On application. Pre-book for schools. Pavilion Tea Room. Gift shop. Plants from the gift shop. An ideal venue for all kinds of events. Please visit the 'What's on' section for all family activities and events.

## CHILLINGTON HALL

**chillingtonhall.co.uk**

Home of the Giffards since 1178, the present house dates from the 18th Century, firstly by the architect Francis Smith of Warwick in 1724 and completed by John Soane in 1786. Parkland laid out by 'Capability' Brown in the 1760s with additional work by James Paine. Chillington was the winner of the HHA/Sotheby's Restoration Award 2009 for work done on Soane's magnificent Saloon.

**CONTACT** Owner: Mr & Mrs J W Giffard Contact: Estate Office Tel: 01902 850236 Email: office@chillingtonhall.co.uk **LOCATION** Codsall Wood, Wolverhampton, Staffordshire WV8 1RE Map Ref: 6:N6 - 2 miles South of Brewood off A449. 4 miles North West of M54/J2. **OPENING TIMES** 21st-25th April, 5th & 6th May, 26th-30th May, 22nd-25th July, 29th July-1st Aug, 5th-8th Aug, 12th-15th Aug Private groups at other times by prior arrangement. **ADMISSION** Adult £8, Child £4. Grounds only: Half price.

Available for Weddings, Corporate Events, Filming, Hire of the Park and Private Parties. Parking available. WC's and car parking. In grounds. Guided tours will give you an in-depth history of this family house and its ancestors, and its contents.

BIRMINGHAM BOTANICAL GARDENS

# CROOME

**www.nationaltrust.org.uk/croome**

There's more than meets the eye at Croome. A secret wartime airbase, now a visitor centre and museum, was once a hub of activity for thousands of people. Outside is the grandest of English landscapes, 'Capability' Brown's masterful first commission, with commanding views over the Malverns. The parkland was nearly lost but is now great for walks and adventures with a surprise around every corner. At the heart of the park lies Croome Court, once home to the Earl's of Coventry. The 6th Earl was an 18th century trend setter, and today Croome follows his lead using artists and craftspeople to tell the story of its eclectic past in inventive ways.

Toilets.

Baby changing.

Open all year.

Parking available.

Suitable for disabled people.

Dogs welcome.

Guided tours.

Educational/School visits.

Café/Tea Room/Refreshments.

Restaurant.

Shop.

Special Events.

Plant Sales.

© TRACEY BLACKWELL

**CONTACT** Owner: National Trust Tel: 01905 371006
Email: croome@nationaltrust.org.uk/croome

**LOCATION** Near High Green, Worcestershire WR8 9DW
Map Ref: 6:N9 - Approx 10 miles south of Worcester. Leave M5 at J7 and follow B4084 towards Pershore. Alternatively access from A38.
Follow brown signs.

**OPENING TIMES** See www.nationaltrust.org.uk/croome for full details
Park, House, Museum, Restaurant & Shop open all year except 24/25 Dec.

**ADMISSION** See www.nationaltrust.org.uk/croome for admission prices

Heart of England

THE PANORAMA TOWER AT CROOME COURT - TATE

# THE TUDOR HOUSE MUSEUM

Upton-Upon-Severn

**tudorhousemuseum.org**

Exhibits of Upton past and present, local pottery and "Staffordshire Blue".

**CONTACT**
Owner: Tudor House Museum Trust
Contact: The Trustees
Tel: 01684 438820
Email: lavendertudor@talktalk.net

**LOCATION** 16 Church Street, Upton-upon-Severn, Worcestershire WR8 0HT Map Ref: 6:N10
Centre of Upton-upon-Severn, 7m SE of Malvern by B4211.

**OPENING TIMES**
Apr-Oct Sat 10.30am - 4.30pm. Tue-Sun and BH afternoons. 1.30pm - 4.30pm. Nov-Mar Suns 2pm - 4pm.

**ADMISSIONS** Adult £3, Concs £2, Child Free (when accompanied by an adult).

Toilet facilities available.
Garden and ground floor only.
Dogs welcome.
Guided tours available if pre-booked.
Educational and school visits are available if pre-booked.

## LITTLE MALVERN COURT Ⓕ

**littlemalverncourt.co.uk**

Prior's Hall, associated rooms and cells, c1489. Former Benedictine Monastery. Oak-framed roof, five bays. Library, collection of religious vestments and relics. Embroideries and paintings. Gardens: 10 acres of former monastic grounds with spring bulbs, blossom, old fashioned roses and shrubs. Access to Hall only by flight of steps.

**CONTACT** Owner: Trustees of the late T M Berington Contact: Mrs T M Berington Tel: 01684 892988 Email: littlemalverncourt@hotmail.com **LOCATION** Nr Malvern, Worcestershire, WR14 4JN Map Ref: 6:M9 3m S of Great Malvern on Upton-on-Severn Rd (A4104). **OPENING TIMES** 24 Apr until 25 Jul, Wed and Thurs afternoons, 2.15pm - 5.00pm. **ADMISSION** House & Garden: Adult £10, Child £3. Garden only: Adult £8, Child £2. (cash only) Groups by prior arrangement.

Toilet facility on site upstairs. Parking across the road - signposted. Partial. Garden on a slope and access to the Prior's Hall is also up steps. Guided tours of house only. Tea, coffee, cake in Courtyard Tea Room 2.30pm-5pm. See our website.

## HARVINGTON HALL Ⓕ

**harvingtonhall.com**

Tucked away in a peaceful corner of Worcestershire, Harvington Hall is a remarkable moated manor house with the largest surviving series of priest hides in the country and a rare collection of original Elizabethan wall paintings. The Hall is surrounded by beautiful walled gardens in a peaceful moatside setting. The Moatside Tea Room offers superb homemade cakes, scones and light lunches, and the Hall's gift shop offers a selection of Fairtrade and unusual gifts.

**CONTACT** Contact: Hall Manager Tel: 01562 777846 Email: harvingtonhall@btconnect.com
**LOCATION** Harvington, Kidderminster, Worcestershire DY10 4LR Map Ref: 6:N8
On minor road, ½m NE of A450/A448 crossroads at Mustow Green. 3m SE of Kidderminster.
**OPENING TIMES** Mar-Oct, Wed-Sun, from 11.30am (closing times vary) **ADMISSION** Adult £10, Child (5-15) £6, Senior £9, Family (2+3) £26. Garden & Malt House Visitor Centre: £3.50.

Limited for coaches. Partial. WC's. Pre-booked groups and schools also available. Tea Room for light lunches. See website. Available for wedding receptions up to 50.

## MADRESFIELD COURT

**www.madresfieldestate.co.uk**

Moated family home with mainly Victorian architecture and fine collection of furniture and art. Extensive gardens and arboretum.

**CONTACT** Natalie Cull Tel: 01684 573614
E-mail: tours@madresfieldestate.co.uk
**LOCATION** Madresfield, Malvern WR13 5AJ
Map 6:M9. 6m SW of Worcester. 1½ m SE of A449. 2m NE of Malvern.
**OPENING TIMES** Guided tours of about 1.5 hours on specified dates and times between Apr and Sep. Numbers are restricted and prior booking is essential to avoid disappointment. We have no refreshment facilities.
**ADMISSION** £15 if booked online or £17 if paying on the day. Advance booking essential. No concessions and no Under 16s.

Guide books. WCs. Obligatory.

MADRESFIELD COURT TREES - MACNABBS FLICKR

BERRINGTON HALL
Nr Leominster, Herefordshire HR6 0DW
**Tel:** 01568 615721 **Email:** berrington@nationaltrust.org.uk

BROCKHAMPTON ESTATE
Bringsty, Nr Bromyard WR6 5TB
**Tel:** 01885 488099 **Email:** brockhampton@nationaltrust.org.uk

CROFT CASTLE
Aymestrey, Nr Leominster, Herefordshire HR9 9PW
**Tel:** 01568 780246 **Email:** croftcastle@nationaltrust.org.uk

EASTNOR CASTLE
Nr Ledbury, Herefordshire HR8 1RL
**Tel:** 01531 633160 **Email:** enquiries@eastnorcastle.com

GOODRICH CASTLE
Ross-On-Wye, Herefordshire HR9 6HY
**Tel:** 01600 890538 **Email:** customers@english-heritage.org.uk

HERGEST CROFT GARDENS
Kington, Herefordshire HR5 3EG
**Tel:** 01544 230160 **Email:** gardens@hergest.co.uk

KINNERSLEY CASTLE
Kinnersley, Herefordshire HR3 6QF
**Tel:** 01544 327407 **Email:** katherina@kinnersley.com

## LANGSTONE COURT

**Llangarron, Ross on Wye, Herefordshire HR9 6NR**
Mostly late 17th Century house with older parts. Interesting staircases, panelling and ceilings. **Map Ref:** 6:L11- Ross on Wye 5m, Llangarron 1m. **Tel:** 01989 770254 **Email:** richard.jones@langstone-court.org.uk **Website:** www.langstone-court.org.uk **Open:** 1st 3 Tue May-Sep, 4th Tue Jul-Aug, 2nd w/e Jun & Sep, last w/e Jul & Aug, May & Aug BHs. **Admission:** Free

THE LASKETT GARDEN
Laskett Lane, Much Birch, Herefordshire HR2 8HZ
**Tel:** 07989 338217 **Email:** info@thelaskettgardens.co.uk

ACTON BURNELL CASTLE
Acton Burnell, Shrewsbury, Shropshire SY5 7PF
**Tel:** 0121 625 6832 **Email:** andrea.fox@english-heritage.org.uk

ATTINGHAM PARK
Atcham, Shrewsbury, Shropshire SY4 4TP
**Tel:** 01743 708170/162 **Email:** attingham@nationaltrust.org.uk

BENTHALL HALL
Broseley, Shropshire TF12 5RX
**Tel:** 01746 780838 **Email:** wendy.barton@nationaltrust.org.uk

COUND HALL
Cound, Shropshire SY5 6AH
**Tel:** 01743 761721

DUDMASTON ESTATE
Quatt, Bridgnorth, Shropshire WV15 6QN
**Tel:** 01746 780866 **Email:** dudmaston@nationaltrust.org.uk

HAWKSTONE HALL & GARDENS
Marchamley, Shrewsbury, Shropshire SY4 5LG
**Tel:** 01630 685242 **Email:** hawkhall@aol.com

MAWLEY HALL
Cleobury Mortimer DY14 8PN
**Tel:** 0208 298 0429 **Email:** rsharp@mawley.com

MUCH WENLOCK PRIORY
Much Wenlock, Shropshire TF13 6HS
**Tel:** 01952 727466 **Email:** customers@english-heritage.org.uk

SOULTON HALL
Soulton, Nr. Wem, Shrewsbury, Shropshire SY4 5RS
**Tel:** 01939 232786 **Email:** enquiries@soultonhall.co.uk

STOKESAY CASTLE
Nr Craven Arms, Shropshire SY7 9AH
**Tel:** 01588 672544 **Email:** customers@english-heritage.org.uk

STOKESAY COURT
Onibury, Near Craven Arms, Shropshire, SY7 9BD
**Tel:** 01584 856238 **Email:** info@stokesaycourt.com

UPTON CRESSETT HALL & GATEHOUSE
Bridgnorth, Shropshire WV16 6UH
**Tel:** 01746 714616 **Email:** laura@uptoncressett.co.uk

## PITCHFORD HALL & TREE HOUSE

**Condover, Shrewsbury, Shropshire SY5 7DN**
In the grounds of Britain's finest half-timbered house; Pitchford Hall. Perched in a lime tree is the world's oldest treehouse; standing since the late 1600s. **Map Ref: 6:K6** - Sat Nav Postcode: SY5 7DN **Website:** www.pitchfordestate.com **Open:** Please book 90 minute guided tours in advance through www.InvitationtoView.co.uk **Admission:** £20

WALCOT HALL
Lydbury North, Shropshire SY7 8AZ
**Tel:** 01588 680570 **Email:** enquiries@walcothall.com

WENLOCK PRIORY
5 Sheinton Street, Much Wenlock, Shropshire TF13 6HS
**Tel:** 01952 727466 **Email:** customers@english-heritage.org.uk

BIDDULPH GRANGE GARDEN
Grange Road, Biddulph, Staffordshire ST8 7SD
**Tel:** 01782 517999 **Email:** biddulphgrange@nationaltrust.org.uk

BOSCOBEL HOUSE & THE ROYAL OAK
Bishop's Wood, Brewood, Staffordshire ST19 9AR
**Tel:** 01902 850244 **Email:** customers@english-heritage.org.uk

CASTERNE HALL
Ilam, Nr Ashbourne, Derbyshire DE6 2BA
**Tel:** 01335 310489 **Email:** mail@casterne.co.uk

ERASMUS DARWIN HOUSE
Beacon Street, Lichfield, Staffordshire WS13 7AD
**Tel:** 01543 306260 **Email:** enquiries@erasmusdarwin.org

## THE HEATH HOUSE

**Tean, Stoke-On-Trent, Staffordshire ST10 4HA**
Set in rolling parkland with fine formal gardens, Heath House is an early Victorian mansion built 1836-1840 in the Tudor style. **Map Ref:** 6:O4 **Tel:** 01538 722212 **Email:** info@theheathhouse.co.uk **Website:** www.theheathhouse.co.uk **Open:** 2-6pm. Last entries 4.30pm. Dates are subject to change due to refurbishment please phone in advance to confirm. **Admission:** £6.50pp. No concessions.

MOSELEY OLD HALL
Moseley Old Hall Lane, Wolverhampton WV10 7HY
**Tel:** 01902 782808 **Email:** moseleyoldhall@nationaltrust.org.uk

SANDON HALL
Sandon, Staffordshire ST18 OBZ
**Tel:** 01889 508004 **Email:** info@sandonhall.co.uk

SHUGBOROUGH ESTATE
Milford, Stafford, Staffordshire ST17 0XB
**Tel:** 08454 598900 **Email:** shugborough@nationaltrust.org.uk

SINAI PARK HOUSE
Shobnall Road, Burton upon Trent, Staffordshire DE13 0QJ
**Tel:** 01889 598600 **Email:** kate@brookesandco.net

THE TRENTHAM ESTATE
Stone Road, Trentham, Staffordshire ST4 8AX
**Tel:** 01782 646646 **Email:** enquiry@trentham.co.uk

ASTLEY CASTLE
Nuneaton, Warwickshire CV10 7QS
**Tel:** 01628 825925 **Email:** bookings@landmarktrust.org.uk

BAGOTS CASTLE
Church Road, Baginton CV8 3AR
**Tel:** 07786 438711 **Email:** delia@bagotscastle.org.uk

CHARLECOTE PARK
Wellesbourne, Warwick, Warwickshire CV35 9ER
**Tel:** 01789 470277 **Email:** charlecotepark@nationaltrust.org.uk

COMPTON VERNEY ART GALLERY & PARK
Warwickshire CV35 9HZ
**Tel:** 01926 645500 **Email:** info@comptonverney.org.uk

COUGHTON COURT
Alcester, Warwickshire B49 5JA
**Tel:** 01789 400777 **Email:** office@throckmortons.co.uk

FARNBOROUGH HALL
Banbury OX17 1DU
**Tel:** 01295 690002 **Email:** farnboroughhall@nationaltrust.org.uk

HILL CLOSE GARDENS TRUST
Bread and Meat Close, Warwick, Warwickshire CV34 6HF
**Tel:** 01926 493339 **Email:** centremanager@hcgt.org.uk

HONINGTON HALL
Shipston-On-Stour, Warwickshire CV36 5AA
**Tel:** 01608 661434 **Email:** bhew@honingtonhall.plus.com

KENILWORTH CASTLE & GARDEN
Kenilworth, Warwickshire CV8 1NE
**Tel:** 01926 852078 **Email:** customers@english-heritage.org.uk

LORD LEYCESTER HOSPITAL
High Street, Warwick CV34 4BH
**Tel:** 01926 491422

PACKWOOD HOUSE
Packwood Lane, Lapworth, Warwickshire B94 6AT
**Tel:** 01564 783294 **Email:** packwood@nationaltrust.org.uk

## STONELEIGH ABBEY

**Kenilworth, Warwickshire CV8 2LF**
A fine Grade I listed English Mansion House, was converted at the Dissolution into a comfortable family home.
**Tel:** 01926 858535 **Email:** enquire@stoneleighabbey.org
**Map Ref:** 6:P8 **Website:** www.stoneleighabbey.org
**Open:** Sun - Thur 11am - 5pm
**Admission:** Adult £5, Child (4-16) £1, Under 4 yrs Free.

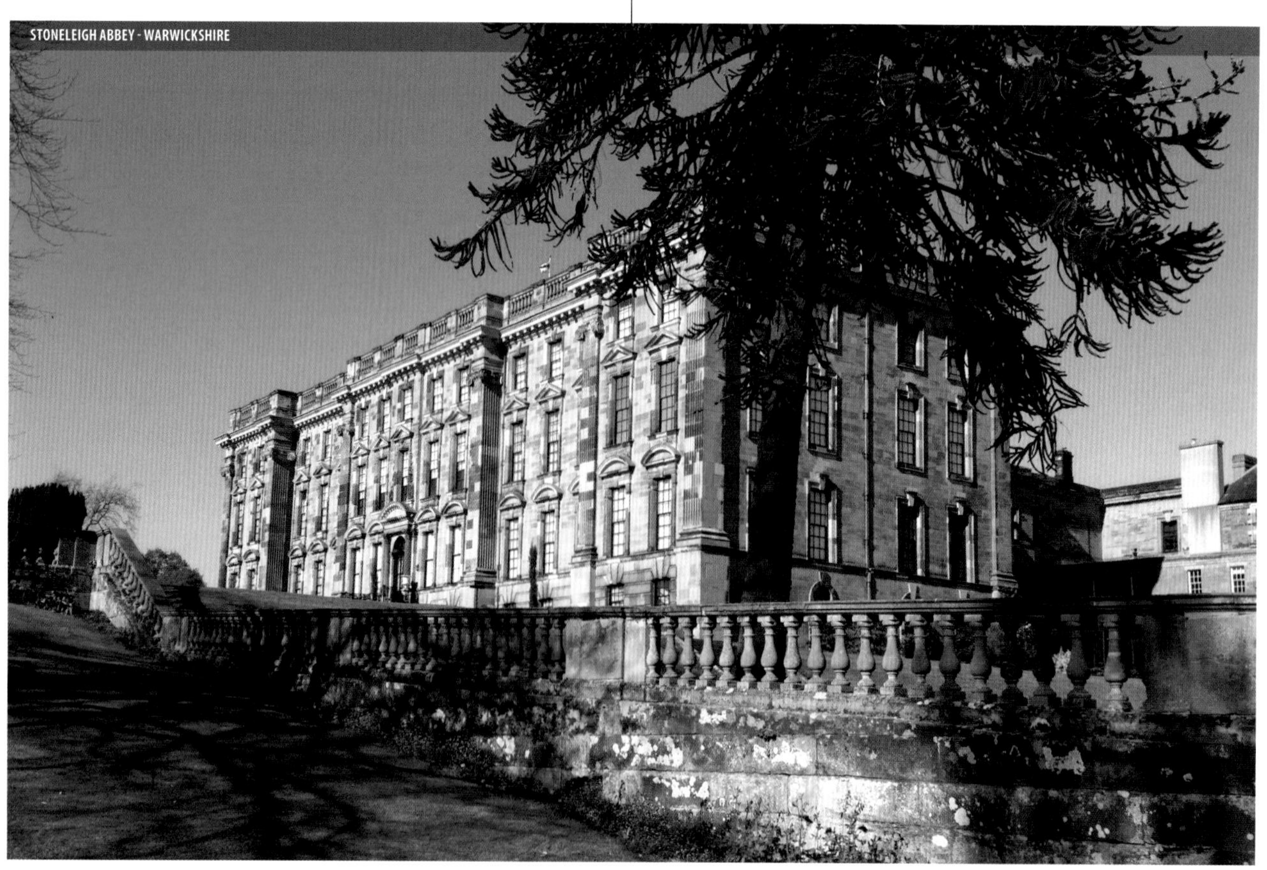
STONELEIGH ABBEY - WARWICKSHIRE

UPTON HOUSE & GARDENS
Upton, Near Banbury, Warwickshire OX15 6HT
**Tel:** 01295 670266 **Email:** uptonhouse@nationaltrust.org.uk

WARWICK CASTLE
Warwick CV34 4QU
**Tel:** 01926 495421 **Email:** customer.information@warwick-castle.com

BACK TO BACKS
55-63 Hurst Street, Birmingham, West Midlands B5 4TE
**Email:** backtobacks@nationaltrust.org.uk

BIRMINGHAM MUSEUMS
Chamberlain Square, Birmingham, B3 3DH
**Tel:** 0121 348 8000 **Email:** bmag.enquiries@birminghammuseums.org.uk

BADDESLEY CLINTON
Rising Lane, Baddesley Clinton, Warwickshire B93 0DQ
**Tel:** 01564 783294 **Email:** baddesleyclinton@nationaltrust.org.uk

CASTLE BROMWICH HALL GARDENS TRUST
Chester Road, Castle Bromwich, Birmingham B36 9BT
**Tel:** 0121 749 4100 **Email:** admin@cbhgt.org.uk

HAGLEY HALL
Hall Lane, Hagley, Nr. Stourbridge, Worcestershire DY9 9LG
**Tel:** 01562 882408 **Email:** info@hagleyhall.com

KINVER EDGE & THE ROCK HOUSES
Compton Road, Kinver, Nr Stourbridge, Staffordshire DY7 6DL
**Tel:** 01384 872553 **Email:** kinveredge@nationaltrust.org.uk

WIGHTWICK MANOR & GARDENS
Wightwick Bank, Wolverhampton, West Midlands WV6 8EE
**Tel:** 01902 761400 **Email:** wightwickmanor@nationaltrust.org.uk

WINTERBOURNE HOUSE & GARDEN
58 Edgbaston Park Road, Birmingham B15 2RT
**Tel:** 0121 414 3003 **Email:** enquiries@winterbourne.org.uk

BEWDLEY MUSEUM
12 Load Street, Bewdley, Worcestershire DY12 2AE
**Tel:** 0845 603 5699 **Email:** Alison.bakr@wyreforestdc.gov.uk

BROADWAY TOWER
Middle Hill, Broadway, Worcestershire WR12 7LB
**Tel:** 01386 852390

HANBURY HALL
Droitwich, Worcestershire WR9 7EA
**Tel:** 01527 821214 **Email:** hanburyhall@nationaltrust.org.uk

WESTON PARK
Weston-under-Lizard, Shifnal, TF11 8LE
**Tel:** 01952 852100 **Email:** enquiries@weston-park.com

SPETCHLEY PARK GARDENS
Spetchley Park, Worcester WR5 1RS
**Tel:** 01453 810303 **Email:** hb@spetchleygardens.co.uk

WITLEY COURT & GARDENS
Great Witley, Worcestershire WR6 6JT
**Tel:** 01299 896636 **Email:** customers@english-heritage.org.uk

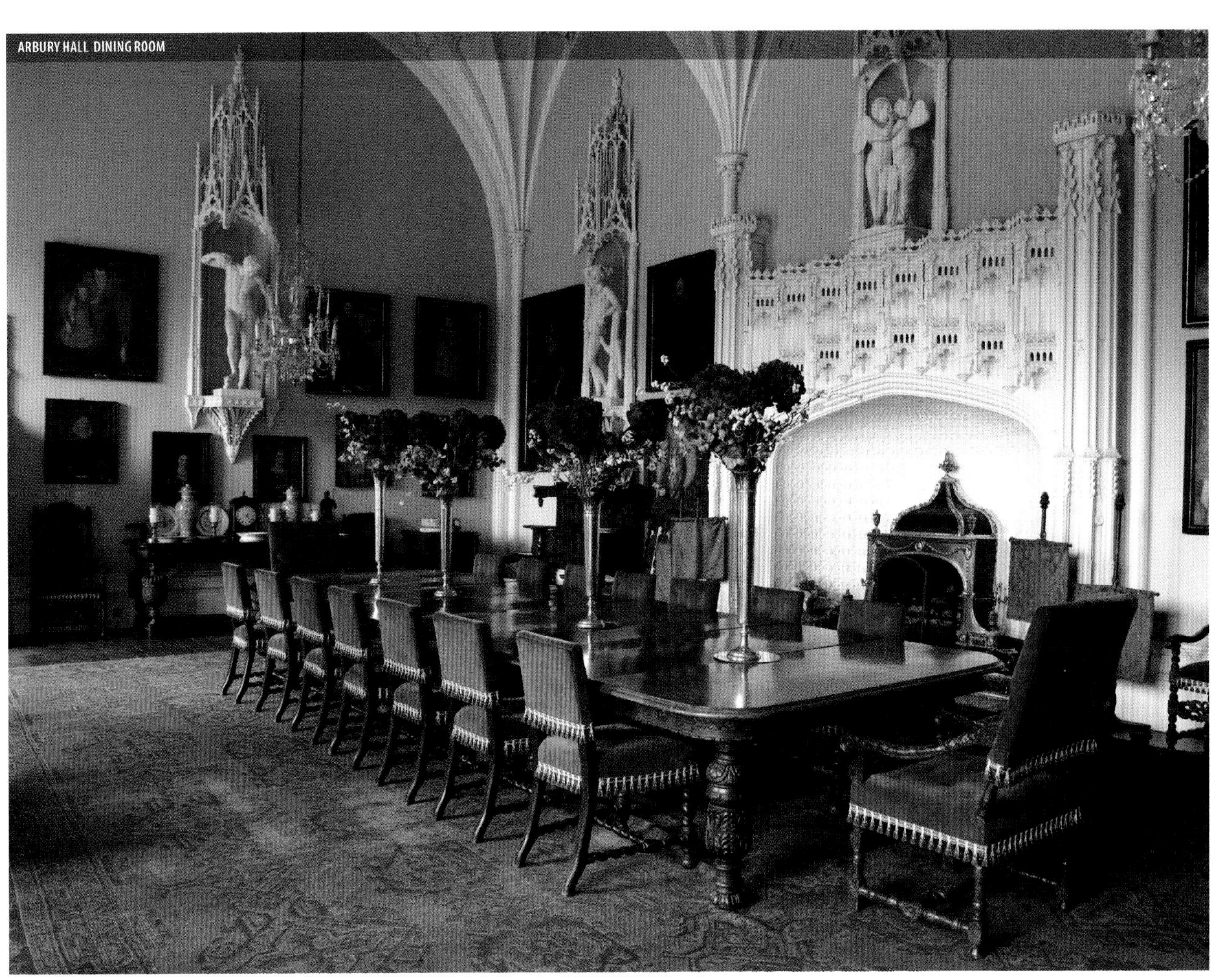
ARBURY HALL DINING ROOM

# YORKSHIRE

EAST YORKSHIRE • NORTH YORKSHIRE
SOUTH YORKSHIRE • WEST YORKSHIRE

PEOPLE WALKING ALONG THE BEACH NEAR ROBIN HOOD'S BAY, ©CRAIG FAST

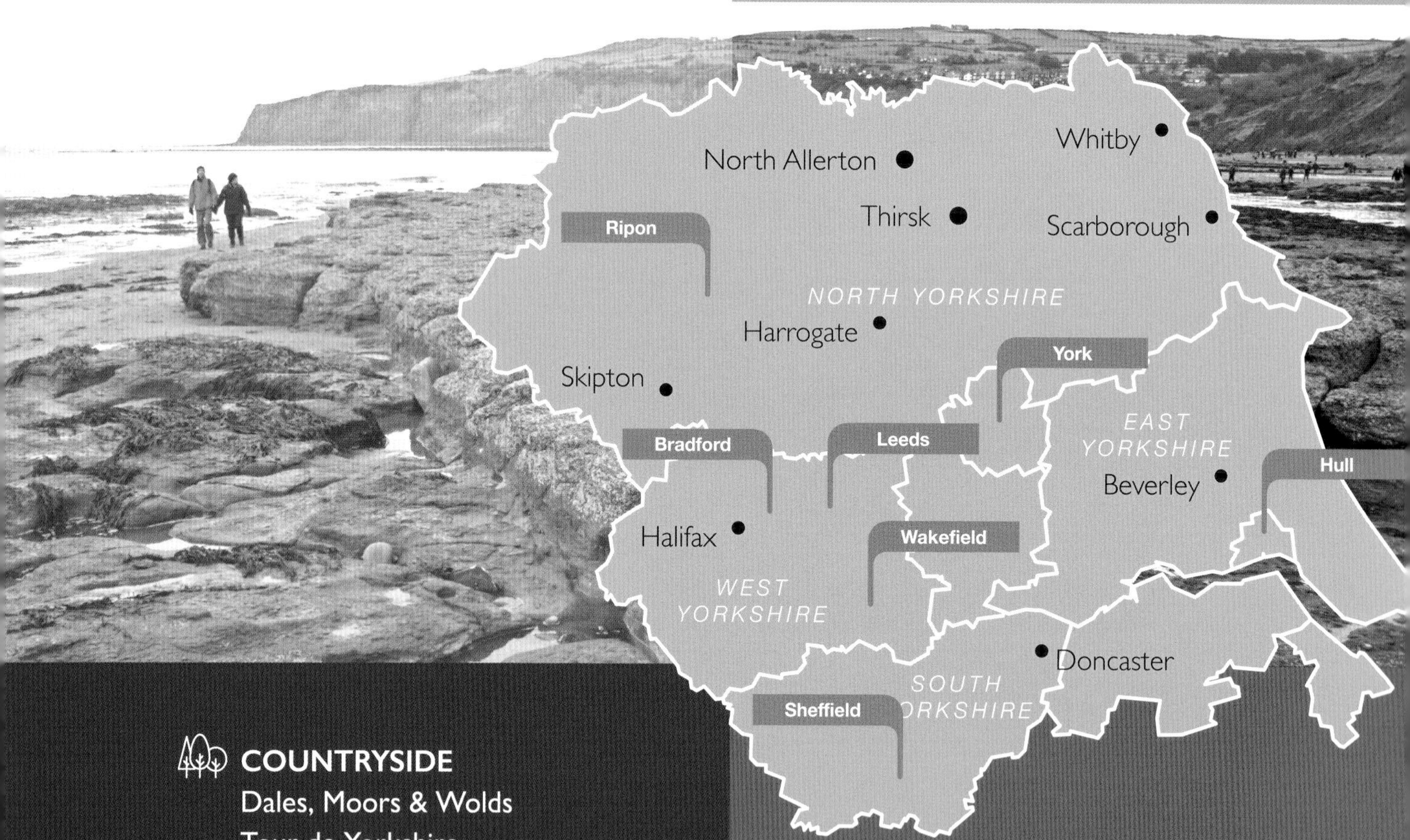

**COUNTRYSIDE**
Dales, Moors & Wolds
Tour de Yorkshire
Herriot Country

**HERITAGE**
Wars of the Roses
Thomas Chippendale
Abolition of slavery

**FOOD**
Yorkshire parkin
Pontefract cakes
Yorkshire pudding

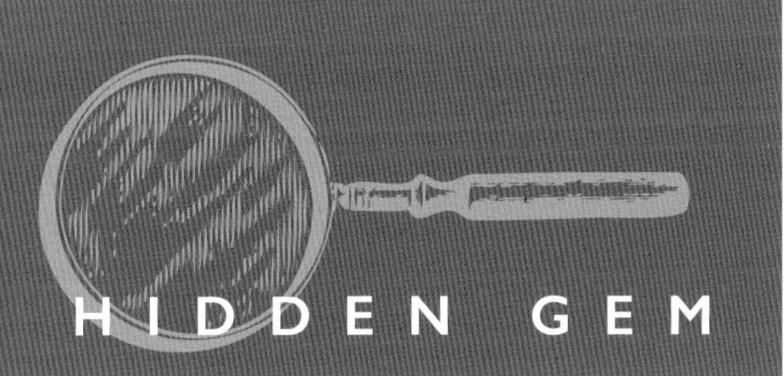


# Wassand Hall

## Butterfly Haven

Land protected by the estates of country houses can prove an extraordinary refuge for wildlife. Wassand Hall, tucked away on the far East coast of Yorkshire, provides a perfect model.

THE REGENCY HOUSE AT THE HEART OF THE WASSAND ESTATE

The estate has belonged to the Constable family since 1520 and in 1530, Dame Joan Constable purchased Hornsea Mere, Yorkshire's largest freshwater lake. Its 2km expanse is an important stop for migrating birds including swallows returning from Southern Africa and ospreys en route between Scotland and The Gambia. The shallow lake, a legacy from the Ice Age, holds fish that support populations of otters, herons and rare bitterns. You might be lucky enough to spot marsh harriers circling the reed beds. The Mere forms a feature in the landscaped parkland that makes a setting for the elegant Regency house at the heart of the estate. Between the two, the Constable family have established walks, not only around the Mere to the Bird Hide, but through the woods and gardens. Here you may see grass snakes lurking in the leaf litter, woodpeckers, warblers and butterflies, perhaps brimstones and speckled woods. There is a bug hotel for overwintering lacewings, ladybirds and bees.

LOOKING INTO THE PARKLAND AT WASSAND HALL

This conservation approach is the vision of the late Lady Strickland Constable, who set up a trust to maintain the estate for the protection of wildlife. The gardens were restored in 1997, providing a varied range of planting around two walled gardens. Keen gardeners will enjoy rare alpines, a cacti and succulent house in the Victorian glasshouses, specimen trees in the Arboretum while the Wetlands and Stumpery take advantage of the natural terrain.

On days when the house is open, enjoy the cool Regency interiors designed by Thomas Cundy (better known as the architect of Belgravia) for Rev Charles Constable in 1813. There is plenty of interest among the collections of paintings, silver and furniture. You will find that butterflies populate the porcelain as well. ■

SYMMETRY IN THE WALLED GARDEN, WASSAND HALL

# Yorkshire & the Humber

## Top 3 Venues

WEDDING PARTY PHOTOGRAPH BY CONSERVATORY - BROUGHTON HALL ESTATE

### Broughton Hall Estate, North Yorkshire

The backdrop of the Yorkshire Dales provides a breath-taking backdrop to your wedding photographs on this stunning estate available for exclusive hire. The estate has three venues; Utopia, Eden and The Hall which can be hired individually or combined to suit your needs. Avalon is the estates health and wellbeing centre where retreats and wellbeing days can be organised. The estate is part of Brontë country and is surrounded by the sweeping landscapes immortalised in Emily Brontë's novel Wuthering Heights.

WEDDING AT SKIPTON CASTLE

### Skipton Castle, North Yorkshire

There are several meeting spaces available for hire including boardroom, theatre and banqueting rooms for small to medium gatherings. Hold your wedding ceremony in the Banqueting Hall or The Granary before heading off to your chosen reception venue. In 1536 Eleanor Brandon, niece of Henry VIII married Henry Clifford in the castle's long gallery with specially constructed Octagon Tower. The Chapel at Skipton saw numerous high profile weddings before being converted to a stable in the 17th century. The Castle is situated above the pretty market town of Skipton.

NEWBURGH PRIORY WEDDING – JOE DODSWORTH PHOTOGRAPHY

### Newburgh Priory, North Yorkshire

Civil ceremonies can take place in one of the three Georgian staterooms available. Originally built as a monastery in 1145, Newburgh Priory is set in an Area of Outstanding Natural Beauty with amazing views across the parkland and lake toward the Hambleton Hills and White Horse. Small wedding receptions can be held inside the house, with marquees available on the lawns for larger parties. The family-run team at Newburgh offers the personal touch to make your day perfect, including assisting with local accommodation for your party.

NTS

**Yorkshire Day** *1st August 2019*

**Tour De Yorkshire Cycling Race 2nd** *5th May 2019*

**Leeds Festival, Bramham Park, Leeds** *23rd - 25th August 2019*

## Top 3 Annual Events

### Countryfile Live, Castle Howard, North Yorkshire *15th-18th August 2019*

For the first time in 2019 Countryfile's annual live event will be held at a venue in the North of England. Browse stands from over 400 exhibitors, hear from your favourite presenters and meet the animals on Adam's Farm. The event is dog-friendly and camping is available onsite. See cooking displays, listen to live music and pop into the pub. There are also plenty of activities on offer for children of all ages.

COUNTRYFILE © YORK PRESS

### Flower Power Plant Fairs, Newburgh Priory, North Yorkshire *April 14th 2019*

A chance to access well-known, knowledgeable local nurseries that can source rare and unusual species of plant. Some of the species are no longer easily available so this can be a rare opportunity to purchase as well as gain expert information. The fairs have been held at Newburgh for over 10 years, often with an additional date later in the year. Entry includes access to the house as well as 40 acres of parkland to explore.

NEWBURGH PRIORY - FLOWER POWER FAIRS

### VW Festival, Harewood House & Gardens, West Yorkshire *9th-11th August 2019*

The largest family-friendly show in the UK for VW enthusiasts. Buy a raffle ticket to be in with a chance of winning your very own VW Beetle. 250 vehicles are pre-selected to take part in the Show & Shine Parade. As well as the cars on show visitors can listen to live music and have a go at Scalextric racing. Children's entertainment is provided in a special marquee, and they also have access to the Harewood adventure playground. The event is dog-friendly.

VW FESTIVAL - HAREWOOD HOUSE

# Yorkshire & the Humber

## Places to stay and eat

THE CONISTON HOTEL AND COUNTRY ESTATE

### The Coniston Hotel and Country Estate

Nestled in the heart of the Yorkshire Dales, the hotel forms part of the stunning 1400 acre Estate. A host of country activities and pursuits await - home to the luxurious Coniston Spa, a CPSA Premier Plus shooting ground, Falconry Centre, Coniston 4x4 Off Roading Experience, Fly Fishing and Clay Pigeon shooting there is something for all to enjoy. Free WiFi makes it an ideal place to meet for a business get-together or indeed to join up with friends and family. Function suites are available for up to 120, offering the perfect space for your special event or occasion. The Huntsman's Lodge and Terrace is the perfect place to unwind, with stunning panoramic views of the Yorkshire Dales. Items such as morning coffee, lunch and afternoon tea are on the all-day menu. Alternatively, guests can enjoy a meal in the award-winning Macleod's Restaurant. This serves a traditional array of home cooked foods from local produce or indeed from the estate itself.

Coniston Cold, Skipton, North Yorkshire BD23 4EA

01756 748080

www.theconistonhotel.com
reservations@theconistonhotel.com

### Lastingham Grange
*Hotel*

High Street, Lastingham
Nr Kirbymoorside YO62 6TH

01751 417345

www.lastinghamgrange.com
reservations@lastinghamgrange.com

### Swinton Park Country Club and Spa
*Hotel*

Swinton Park, Masham
Ripon HG4 4JH

01765 680900

www.swintonestate.com
reservations@swintonestate.com

### The Traddock
*Restaurant/Hotel*

Austwick, nr Settle
North Yorkshire LA2 8BY

015242 51224

www.thetraddock.co.uk
info@thetraddock.co.uk

## The Feversham Arms, Helmsley

This secluded luxury retreat lies in the heart of Helmsley in North Yorkshire. Surrounded by countryside, the award-winning hotel and spa is hidden away so you can relax, unwind and indulge. Cosy yet contemporary and with artwork to rival a gallery. Outdoors the hotel boasts a unique Mediterranean terrace and outdoor pool while indoors open fires and snugs make our guests feel welcome all year round. Guests are welcomed from all over the world who have simply come to get away from it all or to sample the famous Yorkshire hospitality.

High Street, Helmsley, North Yorkshire YO62 5AG

01439 770766

www.fevershamarmshotel.com
stay@fevershamarmshotel.com

THE FEVERSHAM ARMS

## The General Tartleton Inn

*Inn*

Boroughbridge Road, Ferrensby
Knaresborough HG5 0PZ

01423 340284

www.generaltarleton.co.uk
gti@generaltarleton.co.uk

## Just Grand! Vintage Tearoom

*Tea Room*

Ground Floor
8-9 Grand Arcade
Leeds LS1 6PG

0113 243 1306

www.just-grand.co.uk
hello@just-grand.co.uk

## Dulcie Butterfly

*Tea Room*

148 Boston Spa High Street
Leeds LS23 6BW

01937 845200

www.dulciebutterflyuk.com
dulciebutterfly@hotmail.com

# WASSAND HALL

**www.wassand.co.uk**

Fine Regency house by Thomas Cundy the elder. Beautifully restored Walled Gardens, woodland walks, Parks and vistas over Hornsea Mere, part of the Estate since 1530. The Estate has been in the family since 1530 to the present day. Rupert Russell being the great nephew of the late Lady Strickland-Constable.

The House contains a fine collection of 18th/19th Century paintings, English and Continental silver, furniture and a very fine collection of Meissen porcelain. Wassand is very much a family home and retains a very friendly atmosphere. Homemade afternoon teas are served in the conservatory on open days.

**CONTACT**

Owner: Trustees of Wassand Will Trust
Contact: Shirley Power - 01964 537474
Office Tel: 01965 537047 / 01672 564352
Email: rupert@reorussell.co.uk

**LOCATION**

Seaton, Hull, East Yorkshire HU11 5RJ
Map Ref: 11:F9 - On the B1244 Seaton-Hornsea Road.
Approximately 2 miles from Hornsea.

**OPENING TIMES (2019)**

May: Fri 24, Sat 25, Sun 26, Mon 27 - Vintage Cars.
Jun: Wed 12, Thu 13, Fri 14, Sat 15, Sun 16, Thu 27, Fri 28, Sat 29, Sun 30.
July: Mon 1, Wed 10, Thu 11, Fri 12, Sat 13, Sun 14 - concert hall closed, Wed 31.
Aug: Thu 1, Fri 2, Sat 3 - Hall & Garden Closed Sun 4, Mon 5, Fri 23, Sat 24, Sun 25, Mon 26.

**ADMISSION**

Hall & Gardens: Adult £6.50, OAP £6, Child (11 - 15yrs) £3.50, Child (Under 10) Free.

Hall or Garden Only:
Adult £4.50, OAP £4, Child (11-15yrs) £2, Child (Under 10) Free.

Group Bookings - Guided Tours, Bird Hide inclusive ticket contact Shirley Power 01964 537474.

Toilets (including disabled).

Baby changing facilities available.

Ample parking for cars, free. Limited space for coaches.

Limited. Wheelchair access to ground floor of hall. Disabled parking close to the Walled Garden.

Dogs welcome in grounds, on leads.

By arrangement.

Ideal place for outdoor school visits. National Curriculum can be met through fun & challenging activities.

Refreshments available for ticket holders.

See open days and events on the website for all up to date events. Vintage Car Rally.

# CASTLE HOWARD

**www.castlehoward.co.uk**

Discover the rich and varied history, dramatic interiors and sweeping parklands of this magnificent house, home to the Howard Family for over 300 years.

Free flowing tours of the house allow you to explore the architectural wonders and world-renowned collections at your leisure, with friendly and knowledgeable guides throughout.

Spend a day exploring the beautiful gardens; with meandering woodland paths, lakeside terraces and sweeping vistas dotted with temples, statues and follies.

Enjoy a changing programme of exhibitions and events, plus free outdoor tours, illustrated children's trail, adventure playground and summer boat trips on the Great Lake (weather permitting). Treat yourself at a range of cafés and shops, including garden centre and farm shop.

- Gardens, shops and cafés open all year.
- Free parking.
- Disabled Access.
- Dogs on leads welcome (only assistance dogs are allowed in the House).
- Camping and caravanning.
- Guides in each room.
- Groups Welcome.
- Garden Centre & Farm Shop.
- Available for private events & weddings.
- Full programme for all the family.

**OWNER** Castle Howard Estate Ltd

**CONTACT** Visitor Services Tel: 01653 648333
Email: house@castlehoward.co.uk

**LOCATION** Castle Howard, York, North Yorkshire YO60 7DA

**OPENING TIMES** Visit www.castlehoward.co.uk for details of opening times. Grounds Open all year except Christmas Day.

**ADMISSION** Visit www.castlehoward.co.uk for admission prices.

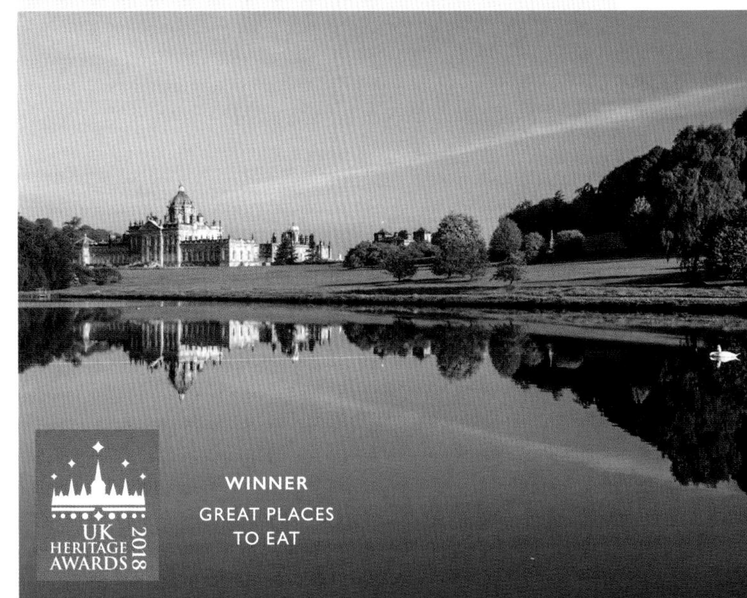

UK HERITAGE AWARDS 2018
WINNER
GREAT PLACES
TO EAT


# FAIRFAX HOUSE

**www.fairfaxhouse.co.uk**

Come and unlock the splendour within one of the finest Georgian townhouses in England. A classical architectural masterpiece with superb period interiors, incomparable stucco ceilings and the outstanding Noel Terry collection of furniture, Fairfax House transports you to the grandeur of 18th Century city living. Don't miss a programme of special events and exhibitions.

- No photography or video filming is permitted within the house without special permission.
- Open all year. Closed 24-26 Dec and Jan.
- Parking in adjacent Clifford's Tower car park nearby.
- The 1st floor is accessible via a staircase therefore limited. Contact to discuss your requirements.
- Audio guides in French, German, Italian, Spanish, Polish, Japanese & Chinese
- A range of group tours bring this superb townhouse to life, exploring its fascinating history.
- Engaging learning opportunities available to all levels of education.
- Gift shop.
- Stunning venue for private dining & drinks receptions.
- Please see the 'What's On' section of the website for all the dates you need to keep free in your diary.

**CONTACT** Owner: York Civic Trust Contact: Hannah Phillip, Director
Tel: 01904 655543 Email: info@fairfaxhouse.co.uk

**LOCATION** Castlegate, York, North Yorkshire YO1 9RN
Map Ref: 11:B9 - Centrally located behind Fenwicks, close to Clifford's Tower & Jorvik Centre. Park & Ride 2 mins away.

**OPENING TIMES** 10 Feb - 31 Dec (closed 24-26 Dec). Tue-Sat & BHs: 10am-5pm. Sun: 11am - 4pm. Mon: Guided tours at 11am and 2pm.

**ADMISSION** Adult £7.50, Conc £6, Child (6-16) £3 (Under 6 Free), Family (2+3) £17.50. Daytime & exclusive access evening group tours available, plus catering package options.

# MARKENFIELD HALL

www.markenfield.com

From the first glimpse of the Hall from between the farm buildings, to the moment the Mediaeval Courtyard opens up as visitors pass beneath the Tudor Gatehouse, Markenfield never fails to astound.

The earliest part of the house was built circa 1230, with its Undercroft consisting of the three surviving vaulted ground floor rooms on the east side of the house.

This earlier house was enlarged by Canon John de Markenfield, who received the Licence to Crenellate the Hall on 28 February 1310 resulting in the distinctive outline that you see to this day. The house was bought - and essentially saved - in 1761 by Fletcher Norton, the first Lord Grantley of Markenfield (a title still held by the family).

**CONTACT**

Owner: Mr Ian & Lady Deirdre Curteis
Contact: The Administrator Sarah Robson
Tel: 01765 692303
Fax: 01765 607195
Email: info@markenfield.com

**LOCATION**

Nr Ripon, North Yorkshire HG4 3AD

Map Ref: 10:P8 Car: Access from West side of A61. 2½ miles South of the Ripon bypass. Entrance off the A61. Bus: Stop 100m from end of drive & drive a mile long.

**OPENING TIMES**

Sun 5 May to Sun 19 May and Sun 16 Jun to Sun 30 Jun, 2pm-5pm each day.
Last entry 4:30pm. Group bookings can be accepted all year round by appointment.

**ADMISSION**

Adult £6
Child £3
Concessions £5

Booked Groups: From £8 per person for a guided tour (min charge £120).

- For more information please visit the website or contact the hall.
- Parking during open days is in the one acre paddock.
- Wheelchair access to ground floor only.
- Dogs welcome in grounds only.
- Offering tea & cake for groups at a cost of £12 pp (including the tour).
- Small gift shop.
- Tours last approx 1½ hrs, followed by time to wander around. 2 hours in all.
- Educational visits by arrangement.
- Plant sales available.
- Corporate functions are available, please contact for further details.
- For all upcoming events please see the 'Events' section of the website.
- Provides a wonderfully intimate venue for a wedding.

# KIPLIN HALL AND GARDENS

**www.kiplinhall.co.uk**

This award-winning house & garden was the Jacobean country seat of founder of Maryland, George Calvert. 'Gothic' wing added in 1820s & redesigned in 1887 by W.E. Nesfield. This intriguing property is now furnished as a comfortable Victorian home with an eclectic mix of previous owners' furniture & personalia, plus enough original 16th-19th century paintings to fill a small gallery. Special Exhibition - 'The Creative Life of Bridget Talbot'. Attractive gardens, productive walled garden, woodland/lakeside walks & small garden museum. Tea room serving homemade scones, cakes & lunches. Family fun - activity room, play ship, garden games, dipping pond, croquet, natural play-area, table tennis & more!

Special Events, incl. Christmas.

Parking.

Wheelchair access to ground floor & gardens. Accessible W.C.

In gardens only. Assistance dogs are welcome in Hall.

Pre-booked for groups.

Education

Homemade cakes, scones & lunches. Local produce & fruit and veg from Walled Garden used in season.

Please telephone to discuss.

Small, but well-stocked.

Fruit/Veg & Plants from Walled Garden in season.

Please see our website.

**CONTACT** Owner: Kiplin Hall CIO General Manager
Tel: 01748 818178 Email: info@kiplinhall.co.uk

**LOCATION** nr Scorton, Richmond, N Yorkshire DL10 6AT Map 11:A7. Midway between Richmond & Northallerton, 5 miles east of A1(M), on B6271 Scorton - Northallerton road.

**OPENING TIMES** **Gardens and Tearoom:** Sat, Sun, Mon, Tue & Wed from 2 Feb - 30 Oct, 10am - 5pm (4pm Feb & Mar). Also Good Fri.
**Hall:** Sat, Sun, Mon, Tue & Wed from 30 Mar - 30 Oct, also Good Fri 11am - 5pm. Christmas opening – see website for dates and information.

**ADMISSION** **Hall/Gardens/Grounds:** With Gift Aid/Without G/A - Adult £10.50/9.50, Conc. £9.50/8.50, Child £5.50/5, Family (2+2) £28/26.
**Gardens/Grounds only:** Adult £6.80/6.20, Conc. £5.80/5.30, Child £3.80/3.50, Family (2+2) £21/19.

# NEWBURGH PRIORY

**www.newburghpriory.co.uk**

Home to the Earls of Fauconberg and the Wombwell family the house was built in 1145 and contains the tomb of Oliver Cromwell together with the family collection of art and furniture. The beautiful grounds contain a lake, water garden, walled garden, amazing topiary yews and woodland walks set against the backdrop of the White Horse.

**CONTACT** Owner: Stephen Wombwell
Tel: 01347 868372
Email: estateoffice@newburghpriory.co.uk

**LOCATION** Coxwold, York, North Yorkshire YO61 4AS Map 11:B8. OS Ref SE541 764. 4m E of A19, 18m N of York, ½ m E of Coxwold..

**OPENING TIMES** Wed & Sun from 3 Apr - 30 Jun, B H Mon 27 May & 26 Aug. Gardens 2-6pm, House 2.30 – 4.45pm

**ADMISSION** House & Gardens: Adult £8.00, Child £2.00. Gardens only: Adult £4.00, Child Free. Special tours of private apartments Wed 3, 10, 17, 24 April & 1 May, £5pp

No photography in house.

Available for corporate hospitality.

Obligatory. See website for tour times.

Partial.

Parking for cars & coaches.

Civil weddings & Wedding receptions throughout the year.

## BURTON CONSTABLE HALL & GROUNDS

**burtonconstable.com**

There's so much to discover inside and out at this fascinating stately home. Visit the Hall's many grand rooms crammed with fine and decorative art, furniture and country house paraphernalia, explore the 'Capability Brown' parkland and visit the historic stables. Burton Constable has had its share of what would probably have been called 'difficult' independent women over the centuries and in 2019 the spotlight in the hall will fall on their fascinating and sometimes surprising stories.

**CONTACT** Owner: Burton Constable Foundation Contact: Mrs Helen Dewson Tel: 01964 562400 Email: enquiries@burtonconstable.com **LOCATION** Skirlaugh, Hull, East Yorks HU11 4LN Map Ref: 11:E10 Beverley 14 miles, Hull 10 miles. Signed from Skirlaugh. **OPENING TIMES / ADMISSION** Please visit our website for opening times and prices.

Ample free parking. Mostly accessible. On leads in grounds. Guide dogs only in hall. Stables Tea Room. Small gift shop.

## SUTTON PARK

**www.statelyhome.co.uk**

The Yorkshire home of Sir Reginald and Lady Sheffield. Early Georgian architecture. Magnificent plasterwork by Cortese. Rich collection of 18th century furniture. Award-winning gardens attract enthusiasts from home and abroad. Tranquil Caravan and Camping Club Site also available for Rallies. Woodland Walk. Tearooms.

**CONTACT** Administrator Tel: 01347 810249 E-mail: suttonpark@statelyhome.co.uk **LOCATION** Sutton-On-The-Forest, N. Yorkshire YO61 1DP Map 11:B9. 8 miles N of York on B1363 York-Helmsley Road follow brown signs. **OPENING TIMES** Private parties all year by appointment (min. charge for 15). For House and gardens opening dates, tour times & admission prices please see website.

No photography. Shop. Limited for coaches. Partial. WC's. Woodland Walk only. Obligatory. Tearooms. Events, please visit our website.

# BROUGHTON HALL ESTATE

**www.broughtonhall.co.uk**

Broughton Hall on the edge of the stunning Yorkshire Dales National Park is available for private hire. With seventeen en-suite bedrooms, Broughton provides the ultimate destination for reunions, house parties, corporate events and filming.

Avalon, our state of the art, pioneering wellbeing and retreat centre, is now open and available for hire.

Guests can also exclusively hire Utopia, a contemporary space designed by Sir Michael Hopkins and set in the Dan Pearson designed Walled Garden and Eden, our party house - both perfect for Weddings and Events.

In addition, there are six holiday cottages on the 3000 acre Estate.

- Ample car parking available.
- Accessible for Disabled.
- Cycle routes on site.
- Dogs welcome.
- 17 luxury bedrooms with stunning en-suite bathrooms. Six holiday cottages on The Estate
- By arrangement.
- Must be pre-booked.

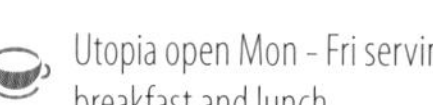

- Utopia open Mon - Fri serving breakfast and lunch
- Lunch and dinner - Licensed.
- The Hall, Avalon, Eden and Utopia available for retreats, corporate events, weddings and parties. Meeting rooms available at Utopia.

- Wellbeing days available at Avalon. www.avalonwellbeing.com
- Chapel on site for Catholic services.

**CONTACT** Owner: Tempest Family Contact: The Estate Office Tel: 01756 799608 Email: info@broughtonhall.co.uk

**LOCATION** Skipton, Yorkshire BD23 3AE Map Ref: 10:N9 On A59, 2 miles West of Skipton.

**OPENING TIMES** Utopia, set in the Dan Pearson designed Walled Garden at Broughton is open for breakfast and lunch, Mon - Fri.

Viewings of other properties are by prior arrangement only.

**ADMISSION** Please contact for prices.

# HOVINGHAM HALL

**www.hovingham.co.uk**

Attractive Palladian family home, designed and built by Thomas Worsley. The childhood home of Katharine Worsley, Duchess of Kent. It is entered through a huge riding school and has beautiful rooms with collections of pictures and furniture. The house has attractive gardens with magnificent Yew hedges and cricket ground.

**CONTACT** Owner: Sir William Worsley Tel: 01653 628771 Email: office@hovingham.co.uk

**LOCATION** Hovingham, York, North Yorkshire YO62 4LU Map Ref: 11:C8 18 miles North of York on Malton/Helmsley Road (B1257)

**OPENING TIMES** Please see the information on our website www.hovingham.co.uk

**ADMISSION** Adult £10.50, Child £5, Concs £10, Family (2+3) £27 Garden Only: £5

- No photography in the Hall.
- Limited. None for coaches.
- Partial ground floor only.
- Obligatory. Last tour at 3.30pm.
- Tea Room open daily 12.30-16.30 June.
- Magnificent reception rooms are special setting for entertaining.

# NEWBY HALL & GARDENS

**www.newbyhall.com**

Designed under the guidance of Sir Christopher Wren, this graceful country house, home to the Compton family, epitomises the Georgian 'Age of Elegance'. Its beautifully restored interior presents Robert Adam at his best with rare Gobelins tapestries and one of the UK's largest private collections of classical statuary.

**CONTACT** Owner: Mr Richard Compton Contact: Visitor Services Tel: 01423 322583 opt 3 Email: info@newbyhall.com

**LOCATION** Ripon, N Yorkshire HG4 5AE Map Ref: 11:A8 - Midway between London & Edinburgh. 40 mins from York, 30 mins from Harrogate.

**OPENING TIMES** 2 Apr - 29 Sept. Apr-Jun & Sept Closed Mon (except BH)

**ADMISSION** See website for 2019 prices.

- *Areas of House closed to public at times, please check website for details.
- Ample. Hard standing for coaches.
- Obligatory. See website for tour times.
- Suitable. WC's. Parking. Wheelchairs available - booking essential.
- Wedding receptions, special functions. Licensed for civil ceremonies.

## SKIPTON CASTLE

www.skiptoncastle.co.uk

For over 900 years Skipton Castle has stood firm through wars and sieges at the gateway to the Yorkshire Dales. Once home to the famous Clifford Lords, it is one of the best preserved and most complete medieval castles in England. Fully roofed, it is a fascinating and delightful place to explore in any season - from the atmospheric Dungeon to the great Watch Tower, from the Chapel to the beautiful Conduit Court.

**CONTACT** Janet Simmonds
Tel: 01756 792442
Email: info@skiptoncastle.co.uk

**LOCATION** Skipton, North Yorkshire BD23 1AW Map Ref: 10:09 - In the centre of Skipton, at the North end of the High St.

**OPENING TIMES** All year Mon-Sat 10am-5pm Sun 11am-5pm (Oct-Mar 4pm).Closed 23-25 Dec.

**ADMISSION** Adult £8.50, Child £5.30, Conc £7.40, Family £27.20.

By arrangement.

Tour guides, educational rooms and teachers packs available.

Licensed. Open all year.

 Books, cards, gifts. Online shop.

 Historical Re-enactments. Plays. Art Exhibitions. Please visit the website.

 Civil wedding licence. Max 80 guests.

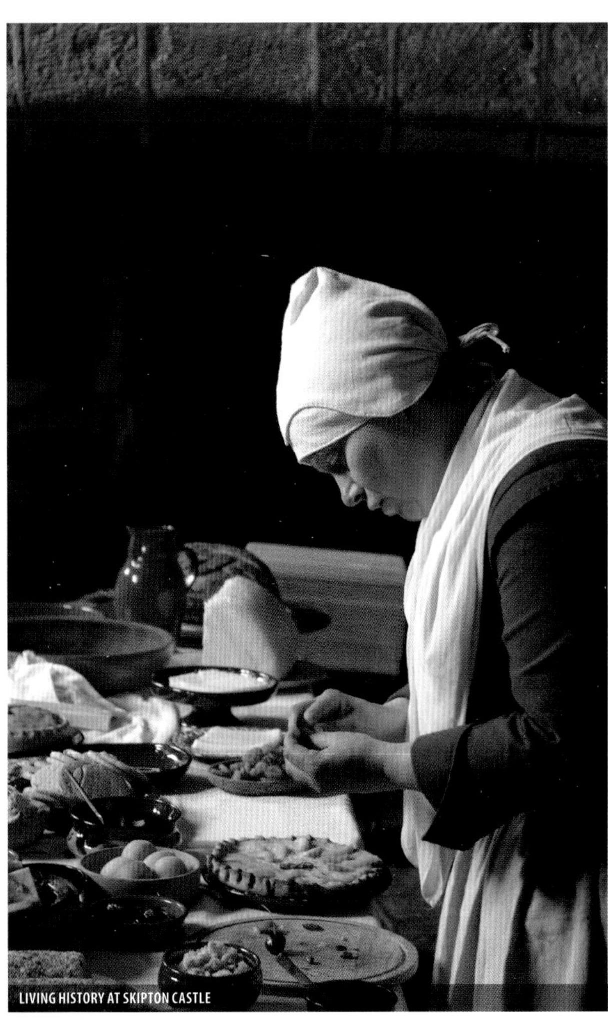

LIVING HISTORY AT SKIPTON CASTLE

BURTON AGNES HALL & GARDENS
Driffield, East Yorkshire YO25 4NB
**Tel:**01262 490324 **Email:** office@burtonagnes.com

SEWERBY HALL & GARDENS
Church Lane, Sewerby, Bridlington YO15 1EA
**Tel:** 01262 673769 **Email:** sewerby.hall@eastriding.gov.uk

SLEDMERE HOUSE
Sledmere, Driffield, East Yorkshire YO25 3XG
**Tel:** 01377 236637 **Email:** info@sledmerehouse.com

ALLERTON PARK
Knaresborough, North Yorkshire HG5 0SE
**Tel:** 01423 330927

**ASKE HALL**
**Richmond, North Yorkshire DL10 5HJ**
A predominantly Georgian collection of paintings, furniture and porcelain in house. **Map Ref:** 10:P6 - 4m SW of A1 at Scotch Corner, 2m from the A66, B6274. **Tel:** 01748 822000
**Email:** office@aske.co.uk **Website:** www.aske.co.uk
**Open:** Wed 18 & Thur 19 Sep. Tours at 10.00, 11.00 & 12.00
Booking advisable. **Admission:** Free.

BARLEY HALL
2 Coffee Yard, Off Stonegate, York YO1 8AR
**Tel:** 01904 610275 **Email:** dscott@yorkat.co.uk

BENINGBROUGH HALL & GARDENS
Beningbrough, North Yorkshire YO30 1DD
**Tel:** 01904 472027 **Email:** beningbrough@nationaltrust.org.uk

BOLTON ABBEY
Skipton, North Yorkshire BD23 6EX
**Tel:** 01756 718009 **Email:** tourism@boltonabbey.com

BOLTON CASTLE
Nr Leyburn, North Yorkshire DL8 4ET
**Tel:** 01969 623981 **Email:** info@boltoncastle.co.uk

BROCKFIELD HALL
Warthill, York YO19 5XJ
**Tel:** 01904 489362 **Email:** simon@brockfieldhall.co.uk

CLIFFORD'S TOWER
Tower Street, York YO1 9SA
**Tel:** 01904 646940 **Email:** customers@english-heritage.org.uk

CONSTABLE BURTON HALL GARDENS
Leyburn, North Yorkshire YO62 5EB
**Tel:** 01677 450428 **Email:** gardens@constableburton.com

DUNCOMBE PARK
Helmsley, North Yorkshire YO25 4NB
**Tel:** 01439 770213 **Email:** info@duncombepark.com

THE FORBIDDEN CORNER LTD
Tupgill Park Estate, Coverham, Nr Middleham, North Yorkshire DL8 4TJ
**Tel:** 01969 640638 **Email:** forbiddencorner@gmail.com

FOUNTAINS ABBEY & STUDLEY ROYAL
Ripon, North Yorkshire HG4 3DY
**Tel:** 01765 608888 **Email:** fountainsabbey@nationaltrust.org.uk

THE GEORGIAN THEATRE ROYAL
Victoria Road, Richmond, North Yorkshire DL10 4DW
**Tel:** 01748 823710 **Email:** admin@georgiantheatreroyal.co.uk

HELMSLEY CASTLE
Castlegate, Helmsley, York YO62 5AB
**Tel:** 01904 601946 **Email:** www.english-heritage.org.uk

HELMSLEY WALLED GARDEN
Cleveland Way, Helmsley, North Yorkshire YO62 5AH
**Tel:** 01439 771427 **Email:** info@helmsleywalledgarden.org.uk

JERVAULX ABBEY
Ripon, North Yorkshire HG4 4PH
**Tel:** 01677 460226

MERCHANT ADVENTURERS' HALL
Fossgate, York YO1 9XD
**Tel:** 01904 654818 **Email:** enquiries@theyorkcompany.co.uk

MIDDLEHAM CASTLE
Castle Hill, Middleham, Leyburn, North Yorkshire DL8 4QR
**Tel:** 01969 623899

NORTON CONYERS
Wath, Nr Ripon, North Yorkshire HG4 5EQ
**Tel:** 01765 640333 **Email:** info@nortonconyers.org.uk

NUNNINGTON HALL
Nunnington, North Yorkshire YO62 5UY
**Tel:** 01439 748283 **Email:** nunningtonhall@nationaltrust.org.uk

ORMESBY HALL
Ladgate Lane, Ormesby, Middlesbrough TS7 9AS
**Tel:** 01642 324188 **Email:** ormesbyhall@nationaltrust.org.uk

PARCEVALL HALL GARDENS
Skyreholme, Nr Appletreewick, North Yorkshire BD23 6DE
**Tel:** 01756 720311 **Email:** parcevallhall@btconnect.com

PLUMPTON ROCKS
Wetherby Road, Harrogate, North Yorkshire, HG5 8NA
**Tel:** 01289 382 322 **Email:** info@plumptonrocks.com

RHS GARDEN HARLOW CARR
Crag Lane, Harrogate, North Yorkshire HG3 1QB
**Tel:** 01423 565418 **Email:** harlowcarr@rhs.org.uk

RICHMOND CASTLE
Richmond, North Yorkshire DL10 4QW
**Tel:** 01748 822493 **Email:** caroline.topps@english-heritage.org.uk

RIEVAULX TERRACE & TEMPLES
The National Trust, Rievaulx, North Yorkshire YO62 5LJ
**Tel:** 01723 870423 **Email:** nunningtonhall@nationaltrust.org.uk

RIPLEY CASTLE
Ripley, Harrogate, North Yorkshire HG3 3AY
**Tel:** 01423 770152 **Email:** enquiries@ripleycastle.co.uk

RIPON CATHEDRAL
Ripon, North Yorkshire HG4 1QR
**Tel:** 01765 602072

SCAMPSTON WALLED GARDEN
Scampston Hall, Malton, North Yorkshire YO17 8NG
**Tel:** 01944 759111 **Email:** info@scampston.co.uk

SCARBOROUGH CASTLE
Castle Road, Scarborough, North Yorkshire YO11 1HY
**Tel:** 01723 383636 **Email:** scarborough.castle@english-heritage.org.uk

SHANDY HALL
Coxwold, Thirsk, North Yorkshire YO61 4AD
**Tel:** 01347 868465 **Email:** shandyhall@dial.pipex.com

SION HILL HALL
Kirby Wiske, Thirsk, North Yorkshire YO7 4EU
**Tel:** 01845 587206 **Email:** sionhill@btconnect.com

STOCKELD PARK
Off the A661, Wetherby, North Yorkshire LS22 4AN
**Tel:** 01937 586101 **Email:** office@stockeldpark.co.uk

THORP PERROW ARBORETUM
Bedale, North Yorkshire DL8 2PR
**Tel:** 01677 425323 **Email:** enquiries@thorpperrow.com

TREASURER'S HOUSE
Minster Yard, York, North Yorkshire YO1 7JL
**Tel:** 01904 624247

WHITBY ABBEY
Whitby, North Yorkshire YO22 4JT
**Tel:** 01947 603568 **Email:** customers@english-heritage.org.uk

YORK GATE GARDEN
**Tel:** 01132 678240 **Email:** yorkgate@perennial.org.uk

BRODSWORTH HALL & GARDENS
Brodsworth, Nr Doncaster, Yorkshire DN5 7XJ
**Tel:** 01302 722598 **Email:** customers@english-heritage.org.uk

CANNON HALL MUSEUM, PARK & GARDENS
Cawthorne, Barnsley, South Yorkshire S75 4AT
**Tel:** 01226 790270 **Email:** cannonhall@barnsley.gov.uk

CONISBROUGH CASTLE
Castle Hill, Conisbrough, Doncaster DN12 3BU
**Tel:** 01709 863329 **Email:** enquiries@english-heritage.org.uk

CUSWORTH HALL, MUSEUM & PARK
Cusworth Lane, Doncaster DN5 7TU
**Tel:** 01302 782342 **Email:** museum@doncaster.gov.uk

HAREWOOD HOUSE & GARDENS
Harewood, Leeds, West Yorkshire, LS17 9LG
**Tel:** 0 113 218 1010 **Email:** info@harewood.org

LOTHERTON HALL
Off Collier Lane, Aberford, Leeds, LS25 3EB
**Tel:** 0113 378 2959 **Email:** lotherton.hall@leeds.gov.uk

TEMPLE NEWSAN
Temple Newsam Road, Selby Road, Leeds, LS15 0AE
**Tel:** 0113 336 7461 **Email:** temple.newsam@leeds.gov.uk

WENTWORTH CASTLE GARDENS
Lowe Lane, Stainborough, Barnsley S75 3ET
**Tel:** 01226 776040 **Email:** heritagetrust@wentworthcastle.org

WENTWORTH WOODHOUSE
The Mansion, Wentworth, Rotherham S62 7TQ
**Tel:** 01226 351161 **Email:** tours@wentworthwoodhouse.co.uk

BRAMHAM PARK
The Estate Office, Bramham Park, Bramham LS23 6ND
**Tel:** 01937 846000 **Email:** enquiries@bramhampark.co.uk

BRONTE PARSONAGE MUSEUM
Church Street, Haworth BD22 8DR
**Tel:** 01535 642323 **Email:** lauren.livesey@bronte.org.uk

CLIFFE CASTLE MUSEUM
Spring Gardens Lane, Keighley BD20 6LH
**Tel:** 01535 618241 **Email:** daru.rooke@bradford.gov.uk

EAST RIDDLESDEN HALL
Bradford Road, Riddlesden, Keighley, West Yorkshire BD20 5EL
**Tel:** 01535 607075 **Email:** eastriddlesden@nationaltrust.org.uk

## LEDSTON HALL

**Hall Lane, Ledston, Castleford, West Yorkshire WF10 2BB**
17th Century mansion with some earlier work, lawned grounc
**Location:** 2m N of Castleford, off A656. **Map Ref:** 11:A11
**Tel:** 01423 707838 **Email:** victoria.walton@carterjonas.co.uk
**Website:** www.whelerfoundation.co.uk
**Open:** Exterior only: May-Aug: Mon-Fri, 9am-4pm.
Other days by appointment. **Admission:** Free.

NOSTELL PRIORY & PARKLAND
Doncaster Road, Wakefield, West Yorkshire WF4 1QE
**Tel:** 01924 863892 **Email:** nostellpriory@nationaltrust.org.uk

OAKWELL HALL & RED HOUSE
Nutter Lane, Birstall WF17 9LG / Oxford Road, Gomersal BD19 4JP
**Email:** oakwell.hall@kirklees.gov.uk / red.house@kirklees.gov.uk

PONTEFRACT CASTLE
Castle Chain, Pontefract, West Yorkshire WF8 1QH
**Tel:** 01977 723 440 **Email:** castles@wakefield.gov.uk

SHIBDEN HALL
Lister's Road, Halifax, West Yorkshire HX3 6XG
**Tel:** 01422 352246 **Email:** shibden.hall@calderdale.gov.uk

# NORTH WEST

CHESHIRE • CUMBRIA • LANCASHIRE
MANCHESTER • MERSEYSIDE

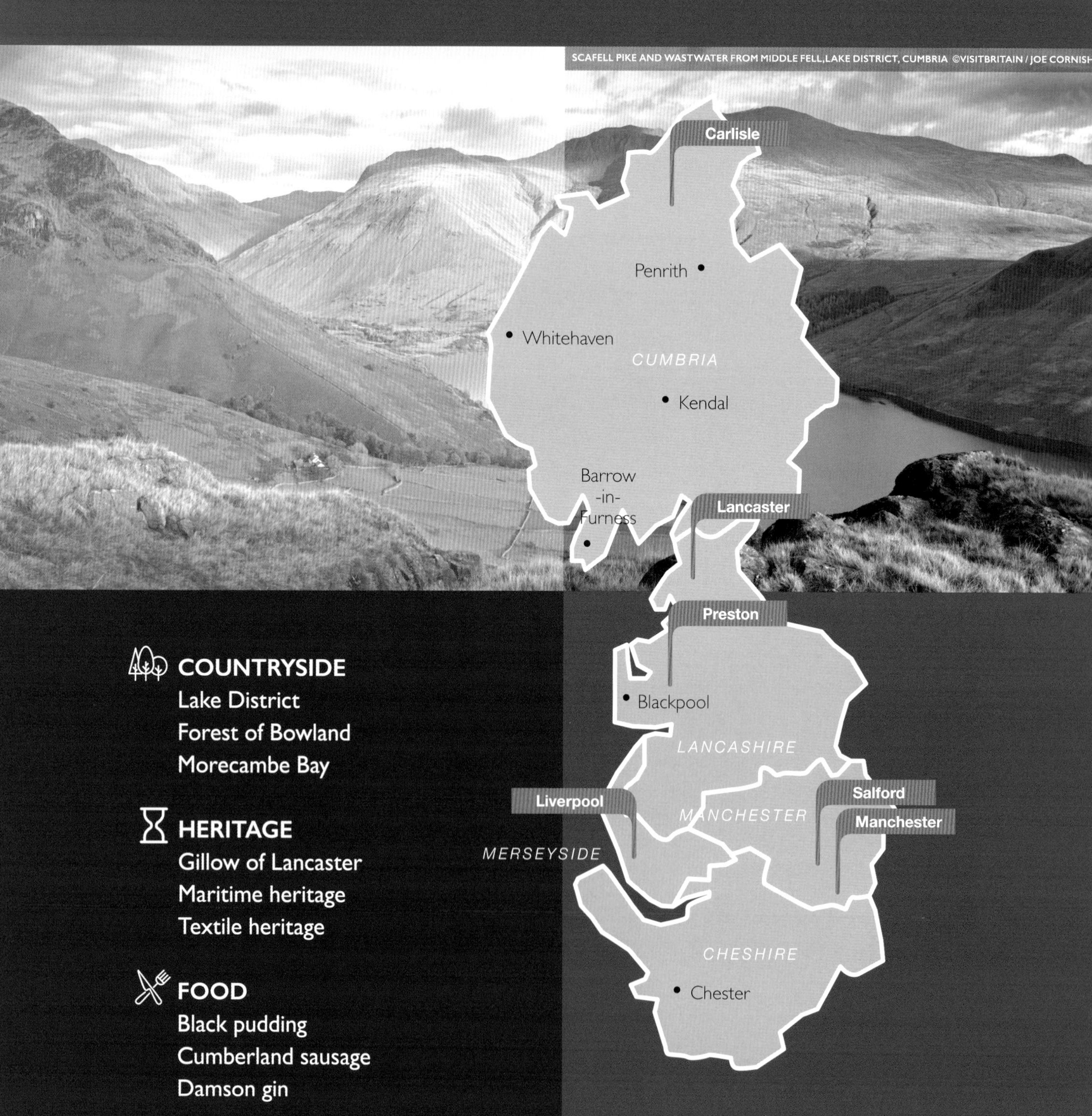


SCAFELL PIKE AND WASTWATER FROM MIDDLE FELL, LAKE DISTRICT, CUMBRIA ©VISITBRITAIN / JOE CORNISH

**COUNTRYSIDE**
Lake District
Forest of Bowland
Morecambe Bay

**HERITAGE**
Gillow of Lancaster
Maritime heritage
Textile heritage

**FOOD**
Black pudding
Cumberland sausage
Damson gin

# Kirklinton Hall

## Ruin in time

Ruins were once highly prized for the melancholy contemplation of the fleeting nature of time. The ruined house at Kirklinton Hall engenders precisely the opposite atmosphere. There is no gothic gloom here, rather the shell of a graceful house into which new life is being breathed.

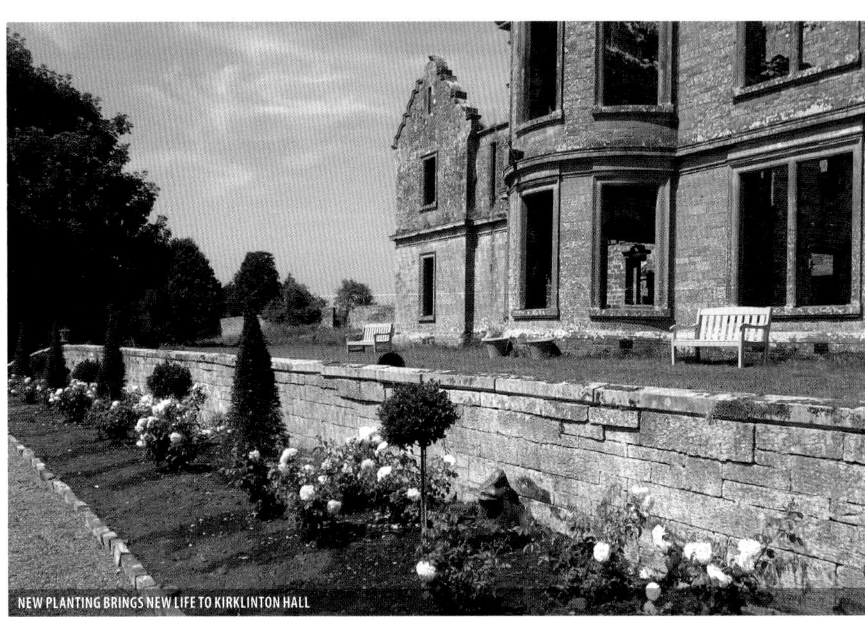
NEW PLANTING BRINGS NEW LIFE TO KIRKLINTON HALL

The setting is gorgeous, a secluded and tranquil curve of the River Lyne, a few miles North East of Carlisle, with walks through sun-dappled woodland to a viewpoint over an ancient river, cliff marked with an enigmatic carved face. In the restored gardens, rose terraces step down to the gurgling stream and paths lead along the Victorian hot wall where profusions of flowers and fruit give way to nut trees and quinces. Children are encouraged to play games or talk to the resident pigs and among many events, the Picnic Cinema has put the house on the map. Weddings are a regular feature of Saturdays, bringing a sense of promise to the spacious wing added to the Stuart house in 1875. The centrepiece is still the 17th century façade with stepped gables. Empty and roofless, the house has fine proportions and its potential for restoration promises a new history.

KIRKLINTON HALL, STILL ELEGANT ABOVE THE TERRACE

Meanwhile, this is a place where you can feel the calm that followed two centuries of cross-border violence, allowing the gentry to stop building fortified tower houses and opt instead for the new fashions of baroque architecture. It is no accident that the gardens feature fruit and vegetables as Kirklinton is a centre of the Slow Food movement, celebrating local artisan producers. The teas served on the Terrace in summer and by the log burner on chillier days are popular, or if you fancy having the grounds to yourself, rent the Kirklinton yurt through Air BnB. Either way, you'll feel that time is only on pause at Kirklinton and the future is bright. ■

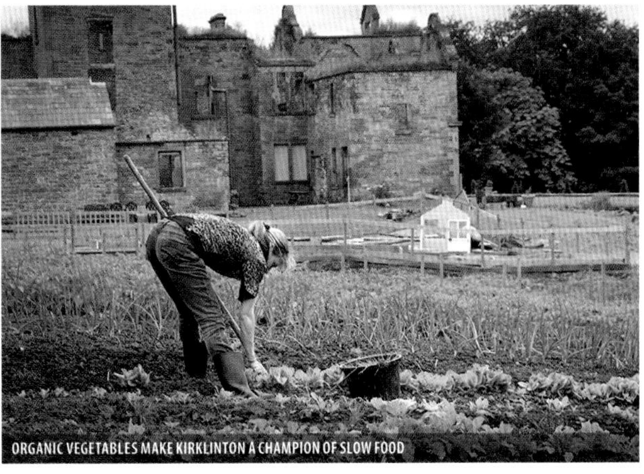
ORGANIC VEGETABLES MAKE KIRKLINTON A CHAMPION OF SLOW FOOD

# North West

## Top 3 Venues

ADLINGTON HALL & GARDENS

### Adlington Hall & Gardens, Cheshire

Set in the heart of the stunning Cheshire countryside Adlington Hall can host your wedding in The Great Hall or The Hunting Lodge and can also offer a great selection of outdoor spaces including the Walled Courtyard and the English Rosegarden. Adlington can also set up spaces to host conferences, meetings and theatre-style presentations for up to 200 people. In the Great Hall a unique 17th century organ overlooks guests and The Hunting Lodge offers an entrance via a beautiful sweeping staircase.

CAPESTHORNE HALL

### Capesthorne Hall, Cheshire

The amount of space here makes Capesthorne an ideal space for larger weddings. Indoor ceremonies are held in the Drawing Room, complete with Italian chandeliers, and for outdoor ceremonies the lakeside gazebo is a popular choice. Host your Wedding Breakfast in the Queen Anne Room with its breath-taking fireplace and marble and fine porcelain collections on display. The larger Lakeside Wing offers guests stunning views over the lake and surrounding parkland. Exhibitions, seminars, parties and meetings also catered for.

LEIGHTON HALL CIVIL PARTNERSHIP VENUE - LEIGHTON HALL

### Leighton Hall, Lancashire

Brides can really make an entrance at Leighton Hall with a red carpet into the magnificent entrance hall, or even arrival by helicopter! The turrets, towers and beautiful 19th century Walled Garden provide stunning photo opportunities. Leighton Hall can also take care of your stag or hen party with activities such as archery and clay pigeon shooting easily arranged as well as afternoon tea. Exclusive hire is available to really make your experience special. The Hall dates back to 1246 and the owner today is a descendant of the first recorded owner.

**Great Manchester Half Marathon and 10K Run, Manchester** *19th May 2019*

**Manchester Pride, Manchester** *August Bank Holiday Weekend*

**Southport Flower Park, Victoria Park, Southport** *15th - 18th August 2019*

## Top 3 Annual Events

### Rode Hall Farmer's Market, Cheshire
*First Saturday of Each Month (except January)*

Browse over 70 stalls from specialist producers (most who grow what they sell). This popular monthly event takes place in the picturesque grounds of Rode Hall. You can walk around the gardens and visit the Tea Rooms or listen to live music. Craft activities are available for children. Each month a seasonal recipe is published on the website and all the ingredients can be purchased at the market.

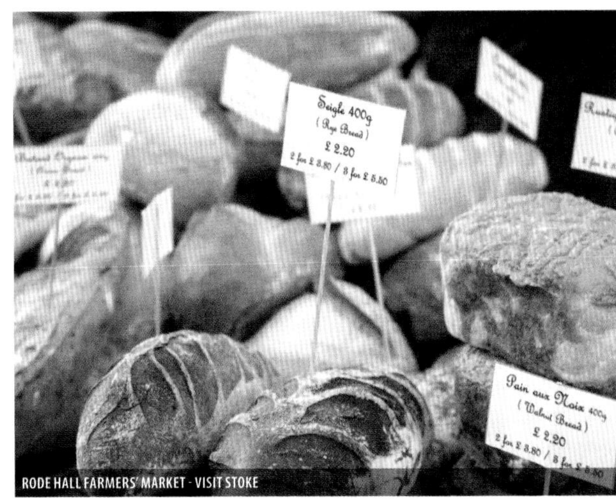

RODE HALL FARMERS' MARKET - VISIT STOKE

### The Marmalade Festival & Awards, Dalemain Mansion, Cumbria *16th & 17th March 2019*

Founded in 2005 by current Dalemain Mansion owner Jane Hassell-McCosh, the Marmalade Awards receive entries from all over the world, all competing to be crowned as champion in their chosen category. There are categories for Homemade, Small & Artisan and Hotel/B&B producers. The festival includes demonstrations, talks and exhibitions to inspire you. During the festival, the town of Penrith goes orange with family-friendly activities taking place in support of the festival.

THE MARMALADE FESTIVAL & AWARDS - DALEMAIN MANSION

### Hoghton Tower Ghost Tours, Preston
*from October-January*

Hoghton Tower is said to be the third most-haunted house in Britain. See for yourself by taking part in one of Hoghton's ghost tours. You will be lead through the tower, including underground passages by silent torchbearers. You might meet the black dog in the Well House, or one of the tower's other ghostly spectres. Learn all about the Towers' previous residents. Wrap up warm and wear practical shoes as there are uneven steps and stairs and narrow passages. Tours include a 2 course meal.

HOGHTON TOWER GHOST TOURS

# North West

## Places to stay and eat

GILPIN HOTEL & LAKE HOUSE

### Gilpin Hotel & Lake House

At the heart of Gilpin are a passionate family and team, dedicated to creating lasting memories for their guests, who return time and time again for celebrations and escapes. Warmth and friendliness are balanced with extraordinary service, exquisite décor and stunning culinary experiences at these 2 luxurious country houses spanning 2 estates in the beautiful Lake District. All the bedrooms have lovely Lakeland views, most leading onto the gardens; 6 with their own cedarwood hot tubs and 5 with their own treatment area, steam room, stone bath, sauna and hydrotherapy hot tub. Just a mile away, 6 rooms enjoy exclusive access to 100 acres of grounds, private lake, boat house, pool, hot-tubs and spa.

Dine at either the Michelin starred HRiSHi, where Hrishikesh Desai combines great Lake District produce and classic methods to deliver unbelievable textures and flavours (modern British cuisine with a twist), or at the laid-back Gilpin Spice, with its open kitchen serving tapas-style pan-Asian dishes.

**Crook Road, Windermere, Cumbria LA23 3NE**

**015394 88818**

**www.thegilpin.co.uk**
**hotel@thegilpin.co.uk**

### Lovelady Shield Country House Hotel
*Hotel*

Nenthead Road, Alston
Cumbria CA9 3LF

01434 381203

www.lovelady.co.uk
enquiries@lovelady.co.uk

### Stanley House Hotel & Spa
*Hotel*

Further Lane
Mellor BB2 7NP

01254 769200

www.stanleyhouse.co.uk
info@stanleyhouse.co.uk

### Sutton Hall
*Restaurant*

Bullocks Lane
Macclesfield SK11 0HE

01260 253211

www.suttonhall.co.uk
sutton.hall@brunningandprice.co.uk

## Aynsome Manor Hotel

The age of elegance is not past; it still lives on at this lovely old manor house where 2 generations of the Varley family have created a special atmosphere of warmth and comfort. Once the distinguished residence of the descendants of William Marshall, the Earl of Pembroke, founder of the historic 12th century Cartmel Priory, Aynsome still echoes with the character and traditions of that bygone era. The candle lit dining room creates an ideal setting for a relaxed meal where guests can enjoy the imaginative and carefully chosen table d'hôte menu, changed daily using fresh local produce. Service will be attentive, without being obtrusive. Good food is extremely important at Aynsome and constant attention ensures commendable ratings in the independent guide books. Local produce, imaginative menus and professional expertise will enable you to approach each meal with anticipation. Chris, Andrea and their dedicated team will ensure a warm welcome to both Aynsome Manor Hotel and Cartmel. *'A vibrant village in every season with an ancient medieval heart'.*

**Cartmel, Grange-over-Sands, Cumbria LA11 6HH**

**015395 36653**

**www.aynsomemanorhotel.co.uk**
**aynsomemanor@btconnect.com**

AYNSOME MANOR HOTEL

### Freemasons Knutsford
*Restaurant*

Silk Mill Street
Knutsford WA16 6DF

01565 632368

www.freemasons-knutsford.co.uk
info@freemasons-knutsford.co.uk

### Miss Marmalades
*Tea Room*

31 Pepper Street
Nantwich CW5 5AB

01270 627835

www.facebook.com/missmarmalades

### The Hoghton Tower
*Tea Room*

Vaio Tea Room
Hoghton PR5 0SH

01254 852986

www.hoghtontower.co.uk
mail@hoghtontower.co.uk

# ADLINGTON HALL & GARDENS

www.adlingtonhall.com

Adlington Hall, home of the Leghs from 1315 was built on the site of a Hunting Lodge in the Forest of Macclesfield in 1040. Two oaks, part of the original building, remain rooted in the ground supporting the east end of the Great Hall. Between the trees in the Great Hall stands an organ built by 'Father' Bernard Smith. Played on by Handel. The Gardens, laid out over many centuries, include a Lime walk planted in 1688 and a Regency rockery surrounding the Shell Cottage. The Wilderness area includes a Rococo styled landscape garden containing the chinoserie T'Ing House, a Pagoda bridge and the classical Temple to Diana. The 60 acres of gardens also include the stunning Rose Garden and Yew Tree Maze.

**CONTACT**

Contact: Philippa Reed
Tel: 01625 827595
Email: enquiries@adlingtonhall.com

**LOCATION**

Mill Lane, Adlington, Macclesfield,
Cheshire SK10 4LF Map Ref: 6:N2
5 miles North of Macclesfield, A523,13 miles South of Manchester. London 178m.

**OPENING TIMES (2019)**

May: 5, 12 & 19.
Jun: 2, 9, 16, 23 & 30.
Jul: 7, 14, 21 & 28.
Aug: 4, 11, 18 & 25.
Sep: 1, 8, 15, 22 & 29.

(Please always check website before travelling).

**ADMISSION**

Adult £10
Student:£5
Child £5
Private Tours available for groups of 20 or more.

Garden only
Adult £6
Student/Child Free.

- The highlight of any visit to the house is The Great Hall.
- WC's. Accessible toilets in both the Hall and The Hunting Lodge.
- Baby facilities available.
- Open Days on Sundays May-Sep.
- There is ample free car parking in the grounds so there will be no problems reaching the hall.
- Lift in the Hunting Lodge. Wheelchair access is limited, contact for more information
-  Well behaved dogs allowed in the grounds on leads.
-  Groups of 20 or more by arrangement any time.
-  By arrangement.
-  Tearoom open on Hall open days. Offering hot and cold drinks, homemade cakes & scones.
- Plant Hunters Fair.
- Corporate hospitality available - please call or check website for more detail.
- Please see the 'What's on' section of the website for special events.
- Beautiful venue for weddings and celebrations.

# CAPESTHORNE HALL

www.capesthorne.com

Capesthorne Hall, built between 1719 and 1732 and set in 100 acres of picturesque Cheshire parkland, has been touched by nearly 1,000 years of history. The Hall has a fascinating collection of fine art, marble sculptures, furniture and tapestries. In the grounds enjoy the family Chapel, the 18th Century Italian Milanese gates, the beautiful lakeside gardens and woodland walks.

The Hall and grounds can also be hired for Civil Wedding ceremonies and receptions, corporate events and family celebrations.

## CONTACT

Owner: Sir William and Lady Bromley-Davenport
Contact: Christine Mountney
Tel: 01625 861221 Email: info@capesthorne.com

## LOCATION

Siddington, Macclesfield, Cheshire SK11 9JY
Map Ref: 6:N2 OS Ref: SJ840 727
West of Macclesfield. 30 minutes South of Manchester on A34. Near M6, M60 and M62.

## OPENING TIMES

Mar-Oct Suns/Mons & Bank Holidays.
Hall: 1.30pm-4pm. Last admission 3.30pm.
Gardens & Chapel: 12 noon-5pm.
Groups: Welcome by appointment with discounts.

## ADMISSION

Suns & BHs - Hall, Gardens & Chapel:
Adult £10, Child (5-16 yrs) £5,
Senior £9, Family £27.50.
Suns - Gardens & Chapel only:
Adult £7, Child (5-16 yrs) £3, Senior £6.
Mons Only - Park, Gardens & Chapel: £12 per car,
Hall Entrance: £3 per person, Group discounts available.

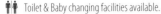

 Toilet & Baby changing facilities available.

 100 cars/20 coaches on hard-standing & unlimited in park.

 Partial. WC's and designated parking bays are available.

 Dogs allowed in certain areas of the grounds.

 Caravan Park 4* AA Rated, open Mar-Oct inclusive.

 Guided tours available for pre-booked parties (not Suns).

 Pre-booked educational visits available.

 The Butler's Pantry offers light refreshments including afternoon teas. Open 12 noon until 4:30pm.

 Available for corporate functions. Catering can be provided for groups (full menus on request).

 Available for festivals, activity days and garden parties.

 Licensed for civil weddings.

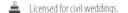

 Provides a variety of film locations and creates the perfect backdrop for any shoot.

## TABLEY HOUSE

**www.tableyhouse.co.uk**

The finest Palladian House in the North West, Tabley a Grade I listing contains one of the first collections of English paintings, including works of art by Turner and Reynolds. Furniture by Chippendale, Bullock and Gillow and fascinating family memorabilia adorn the rooms. Interesting Tea Room and 17th Century Chapel adjoin.

**CONTACT** Owner: The University of Manchester Contact: The Collection Manager Tel: 01565 750151 Email: tableyhouse@btconnect.com

**LOCATION** Tabley Lane, Knutsford, Cheshire WA16 0HB Map Ref: 6:M2 M6/J19, A556 S on to A5033. 2 miles West of Knutsford

**OPENING TIMES** House: Apr-end Oct, Thu-Sun & Bank Holidays, 1pm-5pm. Last admission at 4.30pm. Tea Room: From 12pm-5pm.

**ADMISSION** Adult £5, Child/Student £1.50. Groups by arrangement.

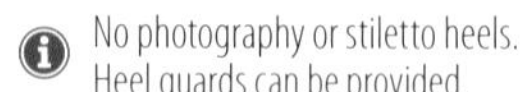

No photography or stiletto heels. Heel guards can be provided.

Parking is free follow burgundy signs.

Call office prior to arrival.

By arrangement, outside normal opening hours, guides provided free.

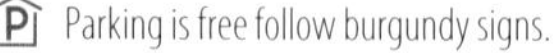

Suitable for post 16 students.

Serving light lunches, afternoon teas.

## PEOVER HALL & GARDENS

**www.peoverhall.com**

A Grade 2* listed Elizabethan family house dating from 1585. Situated within some 500 acres of landscaped 18th Century parkland with formal gardens designed between 1890-1900 that include a series of 'garden rooms' filled with clipped box, lily ponds, Romanesque loggia, warm brick walls, unusual doors, secret passageways, beautiful topiary work and walled gardens. The grounds of the Hall house working stables, estate cottages and the parish church of St Laurence which, contains 2 Mainwaring Chapels. The architectural jewel Grade I listed Carolean stables built in 1654, with richly carved stalls and original Tuscan columns and strap work.

**CONTACT** Owner: Mr R Brooks Contact: The House Manager Tel: 07553153383 Email: bookings@peoverhall.com

**LOCATION** Over Peover, Knutsford WA16 9HW Map Ref: 6:M2 - 4 miles S of Knutsford off A50 at Whipping Stocks Inn.

**OPENING TIMES** May-Aug, Tue & Thu afternoons. Stables & Gardens: 2-5pm. Church: 2pm-4pm.

**ADMISSION** Please see website for updated admission prices.

Hall tours at 14.30 and 15.30, other days and times by arrangement.

Teas and cakes.

## RODE HALL

**www.rodehall.co.uk**

Rode Hall is a fine early 18th Century country house with a beautiful collection of English porcelain, set in a Repton landscape. Home to the Wilbraham family since 1669, the extensive gardens include a woodland garden, formal rose garden designed by Nesfield in 1860 and a stunning two acre walled kitchen garden which provides produce for the monthly farmers' market and delightful Tea Rooms.

**CONTACT** Owner/Contact: Randle Baker Wilbraham Tel: 01270 873237 Email: enquiries@rodehall.co.uk

**LOCATION** Church Lane, Scholar Green, Cheshire ST7 3QP Map Ref: 6:M3 - 5m SW of Congleton between the A34 & A50. Kidsgrove railway station 2 miles North West of Kidsgrove.

**OPENING TIMES** 3 April-25 Sep Weds & BH Mons. Gardens: 11am-5pm, House: 12pm-4pm. Snowdrop Walks: 2 Feb-3 Mar. Bluebell Walks: 27 Apr-8 May.

**ADMISSION** House & Garden: Adult £8, Concessions £7, Child £2. Gardens: Adult £5, Child £2.

Special packages: entrance with lunch or afternoon tea can be booked.

Group bookings by appointment.

Well behaved dogs on leads are most welcome.

Plants and seasonal produce for sale.

Lunches, cream teas, homemade cakes & refreshments.

Farmers' Market on first Sat of every month (excl. Jan).

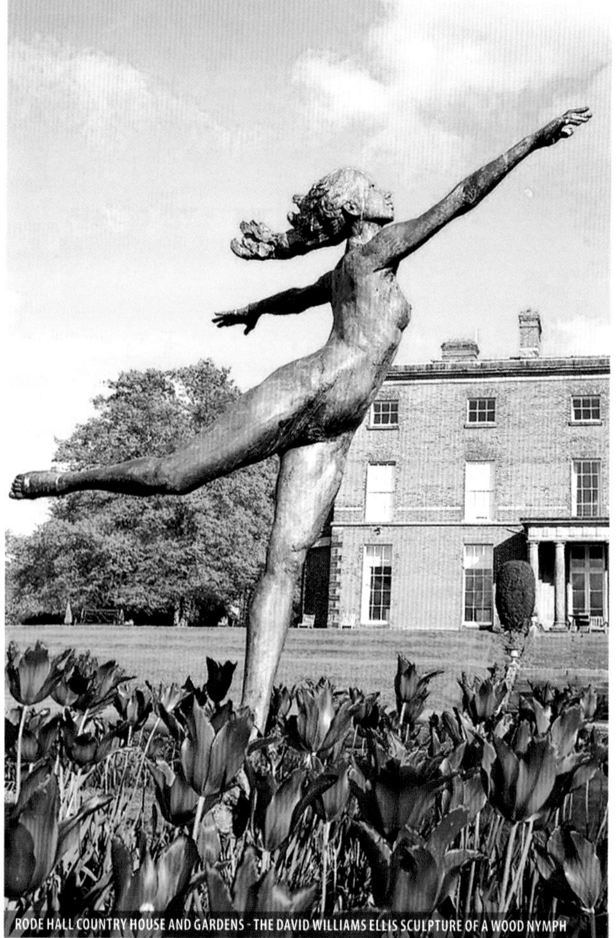

RODE HALL COUNTRY HOUSE AND GARDENS - THE DAVID WILLIAMS ELLIS SCULPTURE OF A WOOD NYMPH

# ASKHAM HALL Ⓕ

**www.askhamhall.co.uk**

Meander through the beautiful gardens, visit the animals and enjoy lunch in the Kitchen Garden Café.

Askham Hall is Grade I listed, dating back to the late 1200s. It has recently been transformed from a stately family home into a stylish retreat also with a restaurant, 18 bedrooms and a wedding barn.

- Askham Spa & Pool is open Apr-Oct.
- A large ground floor toilet with separate area for a wheelchair is provided for public & disabled use.
- Free parking in courtyard and drop off points directly outside hotel.
- Accessible. See the access statement on our website for further details.
- Permitted in café and events barn but not gardens.
- Beautiful rooms to choose from. Individual bookings can be made five months in advance or less.
- Groups by arrangement.
- By arrangement.
- Enjoy something delicious in our Kitchen Garden Café. Free to enter.
- The Askham restaurant is open to both residents and non residents.
- Exclusive & personalised gift vouchers now available to buy securely online.
- Please contact for corporate events and functions.
- Please visit the 'News' section of our website for upcoming events.
- 2 stunning churches within ½ mile & approved venue for civil ceremonies. Perfect for weddings.

**CONTACT** Owner: Charles Lowther Contact: Marie-Louisa Raeburn
Tel: 01931 712350 Email: enquiries@askhamhall.co.uk

**LOCATION** Askham, Penrith, Cumbria CA10 2PF
Map Ref: 10:L5 Askham Hall in Cumbria is situated in a quiet and picturesque village within easy access (about 10 mins' drive) from Penrith and junction 40 of the M6. Follow the brown tourist signs.

**OPENING TIMES** Gardens & café: Every day except Sat. 10am - 5pm in high season, reduced hours and times in low season. Restaurant & accommodation: Tue - Sat for dinner and overnight stays.

**ADMISSION** Gardens & Animals: Adult £4 Child Free.

# DALEMAIN MANSION & HISTORIC GARDENS

**www.dalemain.com**

Home of the Hasell family since 1679, Dalemain boasts a fine mixture of Mediaeval, Tudor and early Georgian architecture. The Award winning historic gardens cover 5 acres of richly planted borders with intriguing and unusual flower combinations. Highlights are the Rose Walk with over 100 old-fashioned roses, ancient apple trees and Tudor Knot Garden. The famous blue Himalayan Poppies bloom in early Summer in the wild garden, and the International Marmalade Awards and Festival take place every March.

- No photography in house.
- Baby changing facilities available.
- 50 yards. Free parking.
- Partial. WC's.
- 1hr tours. Japanese and French translations. Garden tours available. Guided tour details on website.
- Please contact for more information on educational visits.

- Medieval Hall Tea Room - licensed.

- Gift shop with antiques and a selection of the world's best marmalades.
- Plant sales.
- Please contact for more information on corporate events.
- Phone for event enquiries.
- Dalemain offers the film-maker a wide variety of versatile locations. (Jane Eyre, Songs of Praise etc.)

**CONTACT** Owner: Robert Hasell-McCosh Esq
Contact: Florence Lindeman - Marketing
Tel: 017684 86450 Fax: 017684 86223 Email: marketing@dalemain.com

**LOCATION** Dalemain Estates, Penrith, Cumbria CA11 0HB
Map Ref: 10:L5 - On A592 1m S of A66. 4m SW of Penrith. London, M1, M6/J40. Edinburgh, A73, M74, M6/J40.

**OPENING TIMES** 7 April - 27 Oct, Sun - Thu. House: 10.30am - 3.30pm. Gardens, Tearoom & Gift Shop: 10am - 4.30pm (3pm in Oct).
Special Garden openings: 10am - 4.30pm on Fridays in Jun, Jul & Aug. See website for further details.

**ADMISSION** House & Gardens or Gardens Only. Please see website for details. Group Prices on application. Groups:12+ please book.

# KIRKLINTON HALL & GARDENS

www.kirklintonhall.co.uk

Adjacent to the 12th Century de Boyville stronghold, Kirklinton Hall is said to have been built from its stone. Begun in the 1670's, extended in the 1870's and ruined in the 1970's, the Hall has been a Restoration Great House, an RAF base, a school, a gangsters' gambling den and worse. Walk in the footsteps of Norman Knights, Cavalier Commanders, Victorian Plutocrats and the Kray twins. Now, Kirklinton Hall and its Gardens are being restored by the Boyle family to its former glory, a painstaking and fascinating process.

- Faerie Glen & Dragon's Lair.
- Toilet/disabled facilities available.
- Free car parking.
- Accessible for wheelchairs in the Hall, Shop, Toilet & Terrace except most of the woodlands walks.
- Route 10 on Sustrans heads past the hall.
- Dogs welcome as long as kept on a lead and you clean up after them.
- Glamping, including our yurt. To book: info@kirklintonhall.co.uk
- By arrangement for groups.
- Contact property.
- Tea, coffee, cakes & scones, ice cream, soft & alcoholic drinks. Also, we do pick your own/picked to order fruit and veg, whatever is in season. Call or email ahead to check what is available
- Gifts, treats, postcards, jams & chutneys.
- Homegrown fruit, veg & plants, David Austin roses.
- Please see the 'Events' section of the website for all upcoming events.
- Contact for information on special celebrations. Exclusive use, flexible space & truly unique.

**CONTACT** Owner: Mr & Mrs Christopher Boyle
Contact: Lisa Cullen
Tel: 01228 231045 Email: info@kirklintonhall.co.uk
Facebook: Kirklinton Hall Twitter: @kirklintonhall

**LOCATION** Kirklinton, Carlisle CA6 6BB Map Ref: 10:K3
6 miles North East of M6 junction 44, follow A7 towards Longtown. Kirklinton 5 miles. Then follow brown signs.

**OPENING TIMES** 21 Apr - 30 Sept , 12pm - 5pm Weekdays and Suns. Sats for public or private events. Available for weddings and receptions.

**ADMISSION** Adult £4, Child (Under 16yrs) £1
Season Tickets: Single £10 & Family £22
Free to Historic Houses and MyCumbria Card Holders.

# HOLKER HALL & GARDENS

www.holker.co.uk

Holker is the family home of the Cavendish family near the Lake District. Steeped in history, this magnificent Victorian Mansion of neo-Elizabethan Gothic style was largely re-built in the 1870's following a fire, but origins date back to the 1600's. The glorious gardens, café, brasserie, food hall and gift shop complete the visitor experience.

**CONTACT** Owner: Cavendish Family
Contact: Jillian Rouse Tel: 015395 58328
Fax: 015395 58378 Email: info@holker.co.uk

**LOCATION** Cark-In-Cartmel, Grange-Over-Sands, Cumbria LA11 7PL Map Ref: 10:K8 - From Motorway M6/J36, Signed Barrow A590.

**OPENING** Mar to Oct, Wed to Sun and Bank Holiday Monday, please see our website for full details.

**ADMISSION** House & Garden ticket £13, please see our website for further details.

- No photography in house.
- Disabled toilets in The Courtyard Café complex and are signposted.
- Baby changing facilities and milk warming at The Courtyard Café.
- Parking available.
- 2 wheelchairs can be borrowed. Please request further information.
- Dogs on leads are allowed in the Parkland. Access all for Service Dogs.
- Tours by arrangement. Tailor made for disabled visitors.

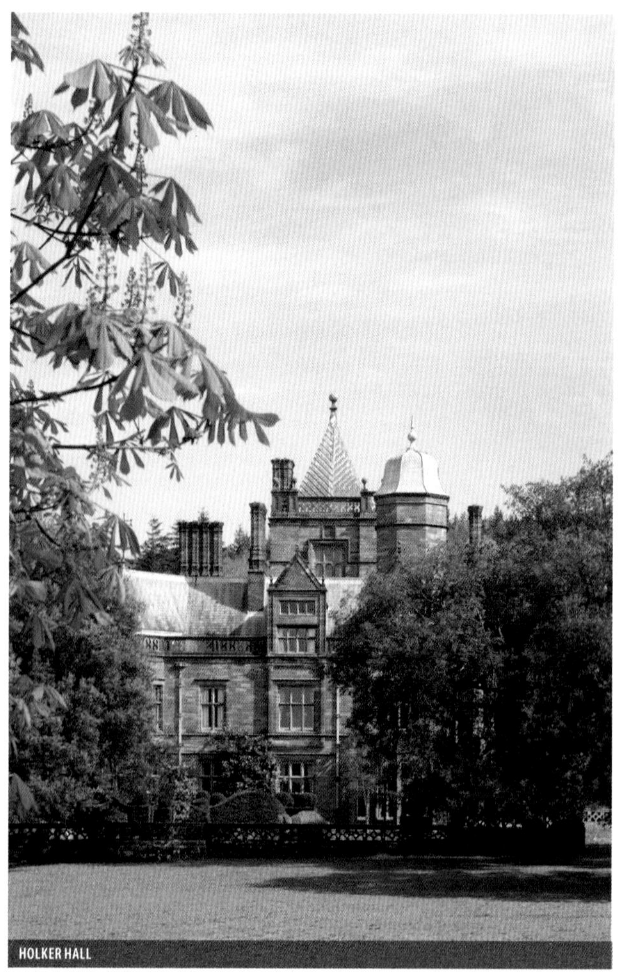

HOLKER HALL

# LEIGHTON HALL

**www.leightonhall.co.uk**

Leighton Hall's setting can only be described as spectacular; the Hall is nestled in a lush parkland with the Lake District as its backdrop. This romantic Gothic house is the lived-in home of the famous Gillow furniture making family, with some unique pieces on display. Visits include: entertaining house tours with no roped off areas, birds of prey displays, charming tea rooms, children's play area, beautiful gardens with a woodland walk and maze to explore.

- No photography in the hall.
- Toilet facilities available.
- Baby changing facilities available.
- Free and ample parking - with disabled parking located closer to the Hall.
- Partial. WC's. Regrettably the halls first floor inaccessible for wheelchair users.
- Only Assistance dogs allowed in the Hall & grounds.
- Enthusiastic guides, bring Leighton's history to life.Informal and relaxed tours.
- Playground, Woodland Walk, Garden & Maze
- 3 themed packages available for Key Stage 1 & 2. Child friendly guides.
- Enjoy a relaxing cuppa, sandwich, home made cakes or scones, located in the Old Kitchens.
- Gift shop with a range of charming reasonably priced items.
- Plants for sale, located by the gift shop.
- Functions for corporate events i.e. brand awareness / product launches.
- Please see the 'Special Events' section of the website for all upcoming events.
- The House & Gardens are exclusive for your wedding.

**CONTACT** Owner: Mr & Mrs R Reynolds
Contact: Mrs Lucy Arthurs / Mrs Suzie Reynolds
Tel: 01524 734474 Fax: 01524 720357 Email: info@leightonhall.co.uk
Facebook: LeightonHallLancashire Twitter: @Leighton_Hall
Instagram: leightonhalllancashire

**LOCATION** Carnforth, Lancashire LA5 9ST Map Ref: 10:L8
Located 10 minutes drive from the M6, junction 35. Follow brown tourism signs North along the A6, travel through the village of Yealand Conyers, turn right up Peter Lane until you arrive at the main entrance.
Do not follow Satnav.

**OPENING TIMES** May - Sept, Tue - Fri (also BH Sun and Mon, Suns in Aug) 2pm - 5pm. Pre-booked groups and coach parties (25+) all year by arrangement. Group rates.

**ADMISSION** Adult £9.50, OAP / Student £8.50, Child £5.50, Family £30.00, Grounds Only £5.50, Accompanying Carer £5.50

CHOOSE LEIGHTON HALL AS YOUR WEDDING VENUE - THE HOUSE AND GARDENS ARE YOURS EXCLUSIVELY FOR THE DAY

## BROWSHOLME HALL

**browsholme.com**

Browsholme Hall has been the ancestral home of the Parkers, Bowbearers of the Forest of Bowland since the time Tudor times. Today it is still the family's home and Robert and Amanda Parker invite visitors to enjoy its magnificent architecture, fabulous interiors, antique furnishings and lovely gardens set in the beautiful landscape of the Forest of Bowland. Superb oak chests, Gillow furniture, portraits, porcelain, Civil War arms and many unique relics.

**CONTACT** Owner: Robert & Amanda Parker Contact: Catherine Turner Tel: 01254 827160 Email: info@browsholme.com **LOCATION** Clitheroe, Lancashire BB7 3DE Map Ref:10:M10 5m NW of Clitheroe off B6243. What3Words: rumble.crunchy.roost **OPENING TIMES** Gardens & Tea Room: 11.30am-4pm. Hall Tours: from 12pm. May-end Sep, every Wed. See website for Bank Holiday and Christmas openings. **ADMISSION** See website for full details.

Booked parties & groups welcome. Car park situated by the Tithe Barn 300m from the Hall. Accessible. WC. There is a drop-off and pick up point for the disabled at front of Hall. The Tithe Barn Café and Bar for light meals. See our website. Giving the bride and groom as much choice and assistance as possible in planning their wedding.

BROWSHOLME HALL

## HOGHTON TOWER

**www.hoghtontower.co.uk**

A Tudor fortified Manor House, the ancestral home of the de Hoghton family. Join a tour of the staterooms to learn about the history of the house. Stroll through the stunning walled gardens. Browse the gift shop and finish with an afternoon tea in our Vaio Tea Room. Self-catering accommodation is available in your very own tower. Private and school tours welcome by pre-booking. Wedding Venue.

**CONTACT** Owner: Hoghton Tower Preservation Trust Booking Enquiries: Kasia Palinska Marketing Enquiries: Brandon Taylor Business/Corporate Enquiries: Lisa Higson Tel: 01254 852986 Email: mail@hoghtontower.co.uk **LOCATION** Hoghton, nr Preston, Lancashire PR5 0SH Map Ref: 10:L11 M65/J3. Midway between Preston & Blackburn on A675. **OPEN** May-Sep (Sun-Thu), BHs (except Christmas & New Year) and every 3rd Sun of the Month. Mon-Thu 11am-5pm, Sun 10am-5pm (First Tour 11:30am, last tour 3:30pm). Tea Room Mon-Thu 11am-5pm, Sun 10am-5pm. Group visits by appointment all year round. Please see our website for variations. **ADMISSION** Please check website.

Toilets in house, disabled toilets in the outer courtyard. For 134 cars, book for coaches.

## MEOLS HALL

**www.meolshall.com**

17th Century house with subsequent additions. Interesting collection of pictures and furniture. Tithe Barn available for wedding ceremonies and receptions all year.

**CONTACT** Owner: The Hesketh Family Contact: Pamela Whelan Tel: 01704 228326 Email: events@meolshall.com **LOCATION** Churchtown, Southport, Merseyside PR9 7LZ Map Ref: 10:K11 - 3m NE of Southport town centre in Churchtown. SE of A565. **OPENING TIMES** May BH Mon: 7 & 28 May, 20 Aug-14 Sep, 1.30-5.30pm **ADMISSION** Adult £4, Child £1. Groups welcome. Afternoon Tea is only available for bookings of 25+.

Parking available. Accessible. Assistance dogs only. One month of the year visitors to Meols Hall have the unique opportunity to visit the house. See the website for all upcoming events. Wedding ceremonies/receptions in the Tithe Barn. Hosting challenging outdoor activities, product launches, staff motivation & incentive schemes.

in the movies?

See our QUICKGUIDES at the back of this book for a helpful list of properties

IN THE MOVIES

ARLEY HALL & GARDENS
Northwich, Cheshire CW9 6NA
**Tel:** 01565 777353 **Email:** helen.begent@arleyhallandgardens.com

BEESTON CASTLE
Chapel Lane, Beeston, Tarporley, Cheshire CW6 9TX
**Tel:** 01829 260464

CHOLMONDELEY CASTLE GARDEN
Malpas, Cheshire, SY14 8AH
**Tel:** 01829 720383 **Email:** dilys@cholmondeleycastle.co.uk

COMBERMERE ABBEY
Whitchurch, Shropshire SY13 4AJ
**Tel:** 01948 662880 **Email:** estate@combermereabbey.co.uk

DORFOLD HALL
Acton, Nr Nantwich, Cheshire CW5 8LD
**Tel:** 01270 625245 **Email:** info@dorfold.com

DUNHAM MASSEY
Altrincham, Cheshire WA14 4SJ
**Tel:** 0161 941 1025 **Email:** dunhammassey@nationaltrust.org.uk

GAWSWORTH HALL
Church Lane, Gawsworth, Cheshire, SK11 9RN
**Tel:** 01260 223456 **Email:** gawsworthhall@btinternet.com

LITTLE MORETON HALL
Congleton, Cheshire CW12 4SD
**Tel:** 01260 272018 **Email:** littlemoretonhall@nationaltrust.org.uk

LYME
Disley, Stockport, Cheshire SK12 2NX
**Tel:** 01663 762023 **Email:** lyme@nationaltrust.org.uk

NESS BOTANIC GARDENS
Neston Road, Ness, Cheshire CH64 4AY
**Tel:** 0845 030 4063 **Email:** nessgdns@liv.ac.uk

TATTON PARK
Knutsford, Cheshire WA16 6QN
**Tel:** 01625 374400/01625 374435 **Email:** tatton@cheshireeast.gov.uk

ABBOT HALL ART GALLERY
Abbot Hall, Kendal, Cumbria LA9 5AL
**Tel:** 01539 722464 **Email:** info@abbothall.org.uk

ALLAN BANK
Grasmere, Cumbria LA22 9QZ
**Tel:** 015394 35143 **Email:** allanbank@nationaltrust.org.uk

BLACKWELL, THE ARTS & CRAFTS HOUSE
Bowness-on-Windermere, Cumbria LA23 3JT
**Tel:** 015394 46139 **Email:** info@blackwell.org.uk

BRANTWOOD
Coniston, Cumbria LA21 8AD
**Tel:** 01539 441396 **Email:** enquiries@brantwood.org.uk

BROUGHAM CASTLE
Penrith, Penrith CA10 2AA
**Tel:** 01768 862488 **Email:** customers@english-heritage.org.uk

CARLISLE CASTLE
Carlisle, Cumbria CA3 8UR
**Tel:** 01228 591922 **Email:** customers@english-heritage.org.uk

CARLISLE CATHEDRAL
Carlisle, Cumbria CA3 8TZ
**Tel:** 01228 548151

DOVE COTTAGE & WORDSWORTH MUSEUM
Grasmere, Cumbria LA22 9SH
**Tel:** 01539 435544 **Email:** enquiries@wordsworth.org.uk

HALECAT GARDEN NURSERY & GARDENS
Witherslack, Grange-over-Sands, Cumbria LA11 6RT
**Tel:** 015395 520963 **Email:** matthewbardgett@hotmail.com

**LEVENS HALL**

**Kendal, Cumbria LA8 0PD**
Elizabethan mansion built around a 13th Century pele tower, with world's oldest and largest topiary gardens. **Map Ref:** 10:L7. 5 miles South of Kendal on the A6. Exit M6/J36.
**Tel:** 015395 60321 **Email:** houseopening@levenshall.co.uk
**Web:** www.levenshall.co.uk **Open:** Please see website for full details. **Admission:** Please see website for full details.

ADLINGTON HALL - DINING ROOM

HILL TOP
Near Sawrey, Hawkshead, Ambleside, Cumbria LA22 0LF
**Tel:** 01539 436269 **Email:** hilltop@nationaltrust.org.uk

HOLEHIRD GARDENS
Patterdale Road, Windermere, Cumbria LA23 1NP
**Tel:** 01539 446008 **Email:** maggie.mees@btinternet.com

HUTTON-IN-THE-FOREST
Penrith, Cumbria CA11 9TH
**Tel:** 01768 484449 **Email:** info@hutton-in-the-forest.co.uk

LANERCOST PRIORY
Lanercost, Brampton, Cumbria CA8 2HQ
**Tel:** 01697 73030 **Email:** customers@english-heritage.org.uk

LOWTHER CASTLE & GARDENS TRUST
Penrith, Cumbria CA10 2HG
**Tel:** 01931 712192

MIREHOUSE
Keswick, Cumbria CA12 4QE
**Tel:** 0117687 72287 **Email:** info@mirehouse.com

MUNCASTER CASTLE GARDENS
Muncaster Castle, Ravenglass, Cumbria CA18 1RQ
**Tel:** 01229 717614 **Email:** info@muncaster.co.uk

NAWORTH CASTLE
Brampton, Cumbria CA8 2HF
**Tel:** 016977 3229 **Email:** office@naworth.co.uk

RYDAL MOUNT & GARDENS
Rydal, Cumbria LA22 9LU
**Tel:** 01539 433002 **Email:** info@rydalmount.co.uk

SIZERGH CASTLE & GARDEN
Sizergh, Kendal, Cumbria LA8 8AE
**Tel:** 0115395 60951 **Email:** sizergh@nationaltrust.org.uk

SWARTHMOOR HALL
Swarthmoor Hall Lane, Ulverston, Cumbria LA12 0JQ
**Tel:** 01229 583204 **Email:** info@swarthmoorhall.co.uk

TOWNEND
Troutbeck, Windermere, Cumbria LA23 1LB
**Tel:** 015394 32628 **Email:** townend@nationaltrust.org.uk

TULLIE HOUSE MUSEUM & ART GALLERY
Castle Street, Carlisle, Cumbria CA3 8TP
**Tel:** 01228 618718 **Email:** enquiries@tulliehouse.org

WINDERWATH GARDENS
Winderwath, Temple Sowerby, Penrith, Cumbria CA10 2AG
**Tel:** 01768 88250

WORDSWORTH HOUSE & GARDEN
Main Street, Cockermouth, Cumbria CA13 9RX
**Tel:** 01900 820884 **Email:** wordsworthhouse@nationaltrust.org.uk

WRAY CASTLE
Low Wray, Ambleside, Cumbria LA22 0JA
**Tel:** 015394 33250 **Email:** wraycastle@nationaltrust.org.uk

ASTLEY HALL MUSEUM & ART GALLERY
Astley Park, Off Hallgate, Chorley PR7 1XA
**Tel:** 01257 515151 **Email:** astley.hall@chorley.gov.uk

THE BEATLES CHILDHOOD HOMES
Woolton and Allerton, Liverpool L18 9TN
**Tel:** 0151 427 7231 **Email:** thebeatleshomes@nationaltrust.org.uk

GAWTHORPE HALL
Padiham, Nr Burnley, Lancashire BB12 8UA
**Tel:** 01282 771004 **Email:** gawthorpehall@nationaltrust.org.uk

LANCASTER CASTLE
Shire Hall, Castle Parade, Lancaster, Lancashire LA1 1YJ
**Tel:** 01524 64998 **Email:** lancastercastle@lancashire.gov.uk

LYTHAM HALL
Ballam Road, Lytham FY8 4JX
**Tel:** 01253 736652 **Email:** lytham.hall@htnw.co.uk

ORDSALL HALL
322 Ordsall Lane, Ordsall, Salford M5 3AN
**Tel:** 0161 872 0251 **Email:** ordsall.hall@scll.co.uk

RUFFORD OLD HALL
Rufford, Nr Ormskirk, Lancashire L40 1SG
**Tel:** 01704 821254 **Email:** ruffordoldhall@nationaltrust.org.uk

SAMLESBURY HALL
Preston New Road, Samlesbury, Preston PR5 0UP
**Tel:** 01254 812010 **Email:** info@samlesburyhall.co.uk

SMITHILLS HALL
Smithills Dean Road, Bolton BL7 7NP
**Tel:** 01204 332377 **Email:** historichalls@bolton.gov.uk

TOWNELEY HALL ART GALLERY & MUSEUMS
Burnley BB11 3RQ
**Tel:** 01282 447130

ELIZABETH GASKELL'S HOUSE
84 Plymouth Grove, Manchester M13 9LW
**Tel:** 0161 273 2215

HEATON HALL
Heaton Park, Prestwich, Manchester M25 9WL
**Tel:** 0161 235 8815

## MANCHESTER CATHEDRAL

**Victoria Street, Manchester M3 1SX**
Manchester Cathedral Grade I listed masterpiece.
**Map Ref:** 6:N1 **Tel:** 0161 833 2220 **Fax:** 0161 839 6218
**Email:** office@manchestercathedral.org
**Website:** www.manchestercathedral.org
**Open:** Every day. Times vary, please check website for up-to-date information. **Admission:** Donations welcome.

SPEKE HALL GARDEN & ESTATE
The Walk, Speke, Liverpool L24 1XD
**Tel:** 0151 427 7231

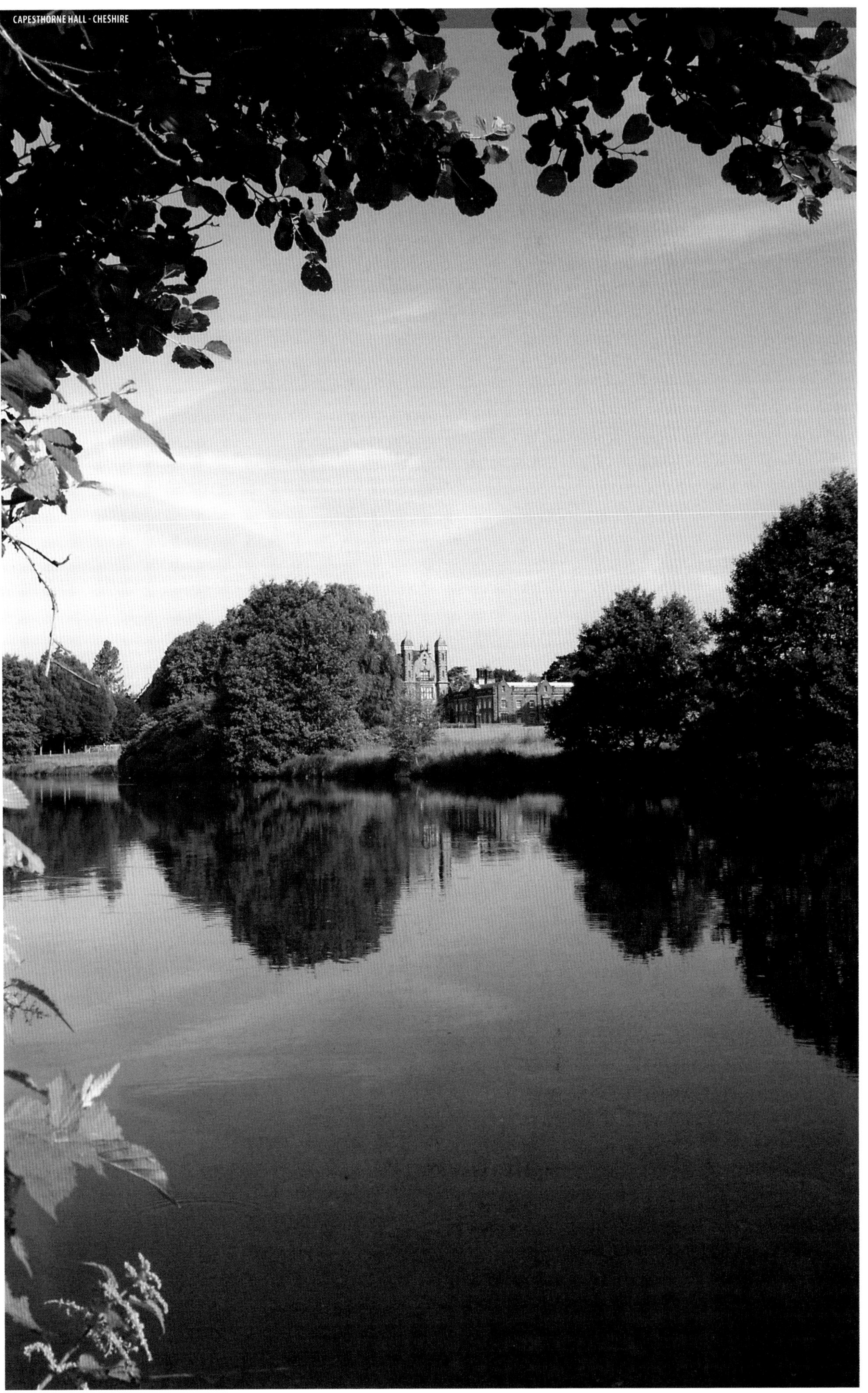
CAPESTHORNE HALL · CHESHIRE

# NORTH EAST

COUNTY DURHAM • NORTHUMBERLAND
TYNE & WEAR

VIEW OVER ROOFTOPS OF THE TYNE BRIDGE, ©VISITBRITAIN / PAWEL LIBERA

**COUNTRYSIDE**
Heather moorlands
Sandy beaches
Dark skies

**HERITAGE**
Hadrian's Wall
Border castles
Mining & railway heritage

**FOOD**
Pease pudding
Craster kippers
Singing Hinnies

# The Chapel, Auckland Castle

## Power to the Prince-Bishops

It is hard to imagine today just how much power the Prince-Bishops of Durham once wielded in the North of England. The purpose of the Auckland Project, launched in 2012, is to put Auckland Castle and the town around it back on the cultural map. The castle, which reopens in 2019, has many treasures but hides a hidden gem at its heart; a room which manages to link together the complex history of the castle while retaining its own distinct identity.

GENERATIONS OF POWERFUL BISHOPS RECORDED IN ST PETER'S CHAPEL

Auckland Castle still houses the private chapel of today's Bishop of Durham, the Right Reverend Paul Butler, but this room is also the largest private chapel in Europe. The chapel of St Peter is a distinct amalgam of styles, mixing Early English gothic with Jacobean baroque encased in an exterior with 18th century gothic flourishes. Around 1661, Bishop John Cosin reused the early English gothic Great Hall of the medieval castle, which had been destroyed in the Civil War, for a new chapel. He commissioned an extravagant decoration of carved woodwork, mixing gothic trefoils and religious symbolism with chubby cherubs and swags of fruit and flowers while putting his heraldic signature firmly on a spectacular painted ceiling. His monument in local Frosterley Marble bears comparison with the full-scale figure of his successor, the art collector Bishop Trevor, immortalised in marble by sculptor, Joseph Nollekens. The Prince-Bishops became mere Bishops in 1836 when Bishop van Mildert had his power curtailed but he changed the architectural balance of the chapel by raising the side aisles. In the 19th century, the scholarly Bishop Lightfoot added a finely carved altarpiece featuring local saints, St Cuthbert and St Hild. Lines of armorial shields along the walls of the side aisles, are a reminder of centuries of power in this palace of the North, part country house, part castle with a unique chapel at its heart. ■

GOTHIC PINNACLES GIVE AUCKLAND CASTLE CHAPEL A DISTINCTIVE SKYLINE

BRIGHT COLOURS ON THE ARMORIALS IN BISHOP COSIN'S CEILING

# North East

## Top 3 Venues

ALNWICK CASTLE

### Alnwick Castle, Northumberland

Alnwick has three different wedding venues available including for those choosing to marry in Winter. The Guest Hall, Hulne Abbey and Friar's Well all have their own unique charm and all offer an equally stunning setting for your big day. Friar's Well also has eight guest bedrooms and an indoor heated swimming pool. Menus can be prepared by the Head Chef to meet your own requirements. You can even treat your guests to a broomstick flying lesson in the same place that Harry Potter learned to fly!

KINGS HALL AT BAMBURGH CASTLE - BRIDE AND GROOM WEDDING PHOTOGRAPHY

### Bamburgh Castle, Northumberland

Bamburgh Castle is set on the edge of a stunning stretch of Northumberland coastline to provide you with endless photo opportunities. Hold your ceremony in The King's Hall with its stained-glass windows and teak-panelled walls or, for more intimate gatherings, The Keep is perfect. The Battery Terrace offers views out towards Holy Island and the Farne Islands. Bamburgh Castle was the first castle to be defeated by gunpowder in the Yorkists' Wars of the Roses victory in 1464 which ended the Lancastrian campaign in Northumberland.

DURHAM CATHEDRAL – TOM BRADLEY

### Durham Cathedral, County Durham

There are various spaces in the Cathedral that can host conferences, concerts, meetings and other special events. Catering is available to suit your requirements from buffets to fine dining. Treat your guests to a tour of the Cathedral as part of your event and discover its fascinating history as a place of worship for over 900 years and current seat of the Bishop of Durham. Weddings, baptisms and funerals only take place at the Cathedral on rare occasions, these being reserved for members of the Cathedral congregation.

**The Great North Run, Newcastle-Upon Tyne** *8th September 2019*

**Sunderland Air Show, Roker & Seaburn Seafront** *26th - 28th July 2019*

**Bishop Auckland Food Festival, County Durham** *13th & 14th April 2019*

## Top 3 Annual Events

### Chillingham Castle Ghost Tours, Northumberland *all year*

Many prisoners of war were brought to Chillingham, tortured and killed during the conflict between England and Scotland during the Scottish War of Independence in the 13th century. Due to this, there is a considerable level of reported paranormal activity here and Chillingham's ghost tours are legendary. You might see the ghost of the Blue Boy, or smell the scent of Lady Mary Berkeley's rose pomander. Walk through the Chapel or the Torture Chamber after dark if you dare!

CHILLINGHAM CASTLE

### Christmas at the Alnwick Garden, Alnwick, Northumberland *November & December*

The run-up to Christmas at the Alnwick Garden usually starts with the Green Lantern Parade, a procession of sound and light led by Father Christmas from the Alnwick Garden into Alnwick town. On weekends from mid-November to Christmas there is a Christmas Market in the garden, where you can shop for gifts, take the winter trail and take part in craft activities and ice skating. If you want to visit Santa, make sure you book early.

FESTIVE FUN AT THE ALNWICK GARDEN CHRISTMAS MARKET © VISIT ENGLAND

### Durham Christmas Festival, County Durham *Late November/Early December*

Usually taking place over the first weekend of December this three-day festival makes the most of everything the city of Durham has to offer. There are carol services in the Cathedral, Christmas gift, food and drink markets and Santa's grotto. Music and entertainment is held across the city at various locations. Reserve your lantern to take part in the Children's Lantern Procession through the city's cobbled streets from the Market Place to the Cathedral.

FESTIVE MARKETS DURHAM - DURHAM MAGAZINE

# North East

## Places to stay and eat

WAREN HOUSE

### Waren House Hotel

Set in six acres of gardens and woodland, Waren House is a peaceful and tranquil centre from which to visit one of this country's most naturally beautiful and historic areas, largely unspoiled by tourism and commercialism. The castles of Bamburgh, Dunstanburgh, Alnwick and Warkworth are all easily accessible. The holy Island of Lindisfarne is nearby. There is a wealth of birdlife along miles of magnificent coastline, particularly at Budle Bay and the Farne Islands. After a day's sightseeing, you can return to the quiet luxury of Waren House where owners Peter and Anita Laverack and their staff, led by manager Lynne, will pamper you. As you enjoy the hospitality, reflect on your good fortune at having stopped here, rather than speeding by on the A1 without discovering the splendours of this historic region and of Waren House in particular.

**Waren Mill, Bamburgh, Northumberland NE70 7EE**

**01668 214581**

**www.warenhousehotel.co.uk**
**enquiries@warenhousehotel.co.uk**

### The Coach House
*B&B*

Crookham
Cornhill-on-Tweed TD12 4TD

01890 820293

www.coachhousecrookham.com
stay@coachhousecrookham.com

### Lumley Castle
*Hotel*

Chester le Street
Country Durham DH3 4NX

0191 389 1111

www.lumleycastle.com
hello@lumleycastle.com

### The Bridgewater Arms
*Restaurant*

Winston
Teesdale DL2 3RN

01325 730302

www.thebridgewaterarms.com
bridgewater88restaurantltd@
btinternet.com

## The Cookie Jar

The Cookie Jar a cosy retreat in the heart of Alnwick. Formerly the Convent of Mercy, this historical building has been tastefully renovated into 11 luxurious rooms and suites, and offers all the home comforts you could need with an added little bit of unexpected cookie-ness. We're all about the comforts - So we've made sure we offer all the important features that make all the difference to your stay with us. We offer safe storage for your guns and the Snug is perfect for your after-pursuit tipple. Our outdoor terrace makes for a delightful al fresco afternoon tea and sunset beverage. We also offer kennels to keep your canines cosy for the duration. The Cookie Jar has 11 individual bedrooms ranging in size and character from intimate and cosy to large and spacious. Each has its own unique character and are named taking inspiration from the local area and the places that the Cook family hold close to their hearts. Designed with absolute comfort in mind, you'll find tactile furnishings, both classic and modern details, special features including exquisite artwork from local artists on the walls, and all the little luxuries you could want for a cosy retreat to make you feel right at home.

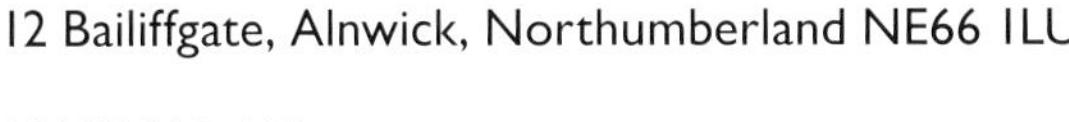

12 Bailiffgate, Alnwick, Northumberland NE66 1LU

01665 510 465

www.cookiejaralnwick.com
hello@cookiejaralnwick.com

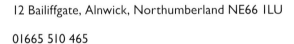

HE COOKIE JAR, ALNWICK - THE TIMES

### The Percy Arms
*Restaurant*

Main Road, Chatton
Alnwick NE66 5PS

01668 215244

www.percyarmschatton.co.uk
percyarmschatton@gmail.com

### Number 8 The Bank
*Tea Room*

8 The Bank, Barnard Castle
DL12 8PQ

01833 631277

www.facebook.com/
TheAmenContinentalCafe

### Earl Grey Tea House
*Tea Room*

The Earl Grey Teahouse
Howick Hall, Alnwick NE66 3LB

01665 572232

www.theearlgreyteahouse.com
peepopepper@btinternet.com

# RABY CASTLE

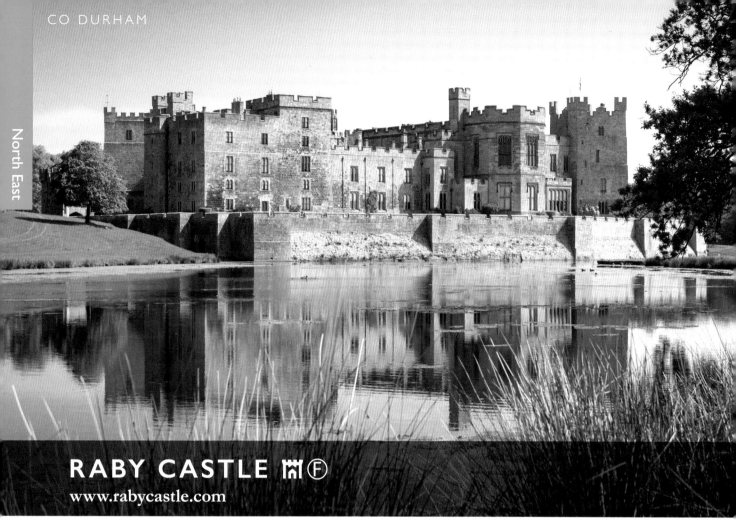

www.rabycastle.com

Raby Castle is surrounded by a large deer park, with two lakes and a beautiful walled garden with formal lawns, yew hedges and an ornamental pond. It was built by the mighty Nevill family in the 14th Century, and has been home to Lord Barnard's family since 1626. Highlights include the vast Barons' Hall, where it is reputed 700 knights gathered to plot the doomed 'Rising of the North' rebellion, and the stunning Octagon Drawing Room. With Meissen porcelain, fine furniture and paintings by Munnings, Reynolds, Van Dyck, Batoni, Teniers, Amigoni and Vernet. Also in the grounds is the 18th Century Stable block with impressive horse-drawn carriage collection, and a delightfully converted Gift Shop and Tea Rooms, and woodland play area.

**CONTACT**

Owner: Lord & Lady Barnard
Contact: Castle Admin Office
Tel: 01833 660202
Email: admin@rabycastle.com

**LOCATION**

Staindrop, Darlington, Co. Durham DL2 3AH
Map Ref: 10:05
On A688, 1 mile North of Staindrop. 8 miles North East of Barnard Castle, 12 miles West North West of Darlington.

**OPENING TIMES (2018)**

Open to the public March-Oct and year round for pre-booked groups.

**ADMISSION**

Please check website for admission prices.
Free entry to Tearooms and Gift Shop open year round.

- Photography for personal use is permitted inside. Colour guidebook on sale.
- Toilet facilities located in the coach yard, also accessible toilets available.
- Baby changing facilities located in the accessible toilets.
- Ample car parking mainly on grass and coach parking on hard standing & designated access parking.
- Limited disabled access to castle interior. Free wheelchair loan.
- Well behaved dogs on leads, not allowed inside buildings or walled gardens unless assistance dogs.
- Guided tours take place at various times each day
- For school visits please call for further information.
- Tearooms in coach yard serving homemade scones, cakes, lunches, hot & cold drinks & ice cream.
- Gift shop on site in coach yard.
- Regular events programme throughout the year.
- Victoria (ITV, Series 1, 2016), Elizabeth (1998).

THE OCTAGON DRAWING ROOM INSIDE RABY CASTLE

# ALNWICK CASTLE

www.alnwickcastle.com

UK HERITAGE AWARDS 2018

WINNER
FAMILY DAY OUT

DINING ROOM, ALNWICK CASTLE

GRAND STAIRCASE

**Home to the Duke of Northumberland's family, the Percy's, for over 700 years; Alnwick Castle offers history on a grand scale.**

Alnwick Castle's remarkable history is brimming with drama, intrigue, and extraordinary people; from a gunpowder plotter and visionary collectors, to decadent hosts and medieval England's most celebrated knight: Harry Hotspur.

Combining magnificent medieval architecture with sumptuous Italianate State Rooms, Alnwick Castle is one of the UK's most significant heritage destinations. In recent years it has also taken starring roles in a number of film and television productions, featuring as a location for ITV's Downton Abbey and as Hogwarts School of Witchcraft and Wizardry in the Harry Potter films. With a history beginning in the Norman Age, Alnwick Castle was originally built as a border defence, before eventually being transformed from a fortification into a family home for the first Duke and Duchess of Northumberland in the 1760s. The castle's State Rooms were later recreated by the 4th Duke in the lavish Italian Renaissance style that we see today, now boasting one of the country's finest private collections of art and furniture.

This remarkable collection includes works by Canaletto, Titian, Van Dyck, Turner, and Dobson; an extensive gallery of Meissen, Chelsea, and Paris porcelain; and the priceless Cucci cabinets, originally created for Louis XIV of France. Alnwick Castle aims to create a vibrant and engaging heritage experience for families, with opportunities aplenty for children to get hands-on with history in the Artisans Courtyard, with dressing up, swordplay, medieval crafts and games.

**OWNER**
His Grace The Duke of Northumberland

**CONTACT**
Tel: 01665 511100
Group bookings: 01665 511184
Media & Filming: 01665 511794
Corporate: 01665 511086
Email: info@alnwickcastle.com

**LOCATION**
Alnwick, Northumberland NE66 1NQ
Map Ref: 14:M11
Well signposted less than a mile off A1; 35 miles north of Newcastle and 80 miles south of Edinburgh.

**TRANSPORT ROUTES**
Car | Bus | Train | Aeroplane | Ferry

**OPENING TIMES**
House: 29 Mar-27 Oct, 10am-5.30pm (last admission 3.45pm).

State Rooms: 10.30am-4.30pm (last admission 4pm, Chapel closes at 2.30pm).

Check website for up-to-date opening dates & times.

**ADMISSION**
Adult £16
Concession £13
Child £8.50
Family £44

Group Discount: 14+

Prices are subject to change, please check the website.

Additional: Tickets can be validated for unlimited free visits for 12 months, at no extra cost. (See website for T&Cs).

**REGULAR EVENTS**
Daily: Guided tours of the State Rooms & grounds. craft activities, and broomstick training.

Seasonal: Knights tournaments, falconry displays, jester performances, and visits from skilled artisans.

- Photography not permitted in the state rooms.
- Toilet facilities available.
- Baby changing facilities available.
- Coach parking also available.
- Accessible WC's. Free wheelchair/mobility scooter hire. Limited access in areas.
- Free daily tours of the state rooms and grounds.
- Workshops, activities and discounted admission available. Call 01665 511184.
- Courtyard Café. Licensed.
- Courtyard Café and Stables Fryery
- Gift shop open daily.
- Guest Hall - capacity 300 & Hulne Abbey - capacity 500. Team-building, banqueting, dinner & dances.
- See website for details.
- Wedding ceremonies / receptions. Call 01665 511086.

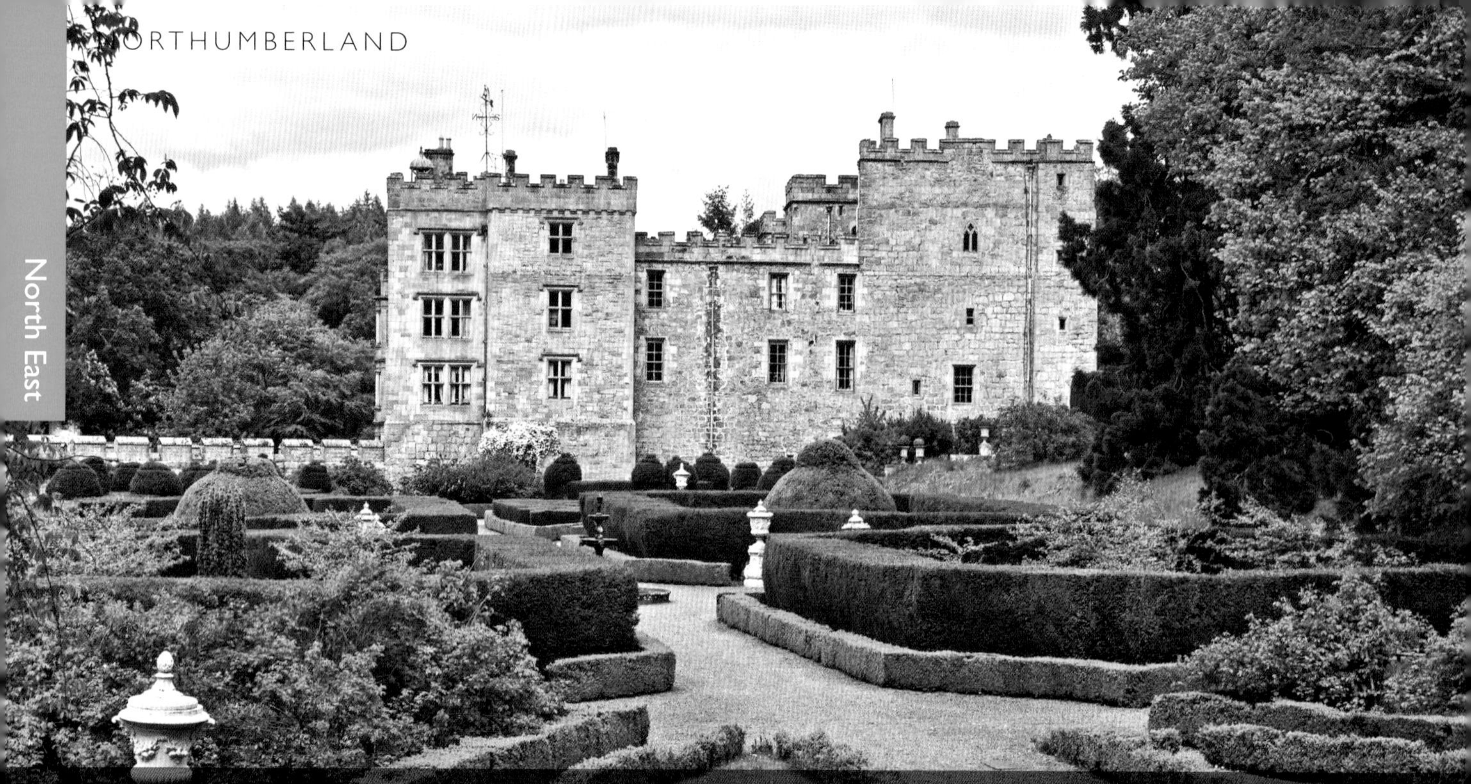

# CHILLINGHAM CASTLE

www.chillingham-castle.com

This remarkable and very private castle has been continuously owned by just one family line since the 1200's. A visit from Edward I in 1298 was followed by many other Royal visits right down through this century. See Chillingham's alarming dungeons as well as active restoration in the Great Halls and State Rooms which are gradually brought back to life with tapestries, arms and armour. We even have a very real torture chamber.

The 1100s stronghold became a fortified castle in 1344, see the original Royal Licence to Crenellate on view. Wrapped in the nation's history Chillingham also occupied a strategic position during Northumberland's bloody border feuds being a resting place to many royal visitors. Tudor days saw additions but the underlying medievalism remains. 18th and 19th Centuries saw decorative extravagances including 'Capability' Brown lakes and grounds with gardens laid out by Sir Jeffrey Wyatville, fresh from his triumphs at Windsor Castle.

Prehistoric Wild Cattle roam the park beyond more rare than mountain gorilla (a separate tour) and never miss the family tomb in the church.

## Gardens

With romantic grounds, the castle commands breathtaking views of the surrounding countryside. As you walk to the lake you will see, according to season, drifts of snowdrops, daffodils or bluebells and an astonishing display of rhododendrons. This emphasises the restrained formality of the Elizabethan topiary garden, with its intricately clipped hedges of box and yew. Lawns, the formal gardens and woodland walks are all fully open to the public.

**CONTACT**

Owner: Sir Humphry Wakefield Bt
Contact: The Administrator Tel: 01668 215359
Email: enquiries@chillingham-castle.com

**LOCATION**

Northumberland NE66 5NJ
Map Ref: 14:L11 45 miles North of Newcastle between A697 & A1. 2 miles South of B6348 at Chatton. 6 miles South East of Wooler.
Rail: Alnmouth or Berwick.

**OPENING TIMES**

6 Apr - the 3 Nov, 12 noon – 5pm.
Groups & Coach Tours any time by appointment.
All function activities available.

**ADMISSION**

Adults £10.50,
Concessions £9.50,
Children £6.50
Family £26.00 (2 adults & up to 3 children under 15).

 Sir Humphry has produced a room by room guide which can be purchased on arrival for £2.50.

 Toilet facilities available.

Avoid Lilburn route, coach parties welcome by prior arrangement. Limited for coaches.

Self-catering apartments to hire all year round.

 Private guided castle tours, call for details.

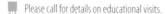

Please call for details on educational visits.

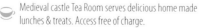

 Medieval castle Tea Room serves delicious home made lunches & treats. Access free of charge.

 Gift shop.

 Corporate entertainment, lunches, drinks & dinners.

 Please see the 'Events' page on the website for all upcoming tours and events.

 Wedding ceremonies and receptions.

'Elizabeth' staged many historic scenes here.
'The Making of Harry Potter' was based here.

## BAMBURGH CASTLE Ⓕ

**www.bamburghcastle.com**

These formidable stone walls have witnessed dark tales of royal rebellion, bloody battles, spellbinding legends and millionaire benefactors. With 14 public rooms and over 3000 artefacts, including arms and armour, porcelain, furniture and artwork.

**CONTACT** Owner: F Watson-Armstrong Contact: Katie Davidson Tel: 01668 214208 E-mail: administrator@bamburghcastle.com

**LOCATION** Bamburgh, Northumberland NE69 7DF Map 14:M10. 42m N of Newcastle-upon-Tyne. 20m S of Berwick-upon-Tweed. 6m E of Belford by B1342 from A1 at Belford.

**OPENING TIMES** 9 Feb - 3 Nov 2019, Daily, 10am - 5pm. Last admission 4pm. 4 Nov 2019 - 7 Feb 2020, Weekends only, 11am-4.30pm. Last admission 3.30pm.

**ADMISSION** Adult £11.25, Child (5-16 yrs) £5.50, Family (2 + 3) £28.

For groups please contact administrator@bamburghcastle.com

No flash photography in State Rooms.

100 cars, coaches park on drive.

WCs.

Guide dogs only.

Arranged any time, out of hours £150.

Welcome. Guide provided if requested.

Licensed.

Gift shop.

## PRESTON TOWER Ⓕ

**www.prestontower.co.uk**

Built by Sir Robert Harbottle in 1392.

**CONTACT** G J Baker Cresswell Tel: 01665 589227 / 07966 150216 Email: gilfrid.bakercresswell@btinternet.com

**LOCATION** Chathill, Northumberland NE67 5DH Follow Historic Property signs on A1 7m N of Alnwick. Map Ref: 14:M11

**OPEN** All year daily, 10am-6pm, or dusk, whichever is earlier.

**ADMISSION** Adult £2, Child 50p, Concessions £1.50. Groups £1.50.

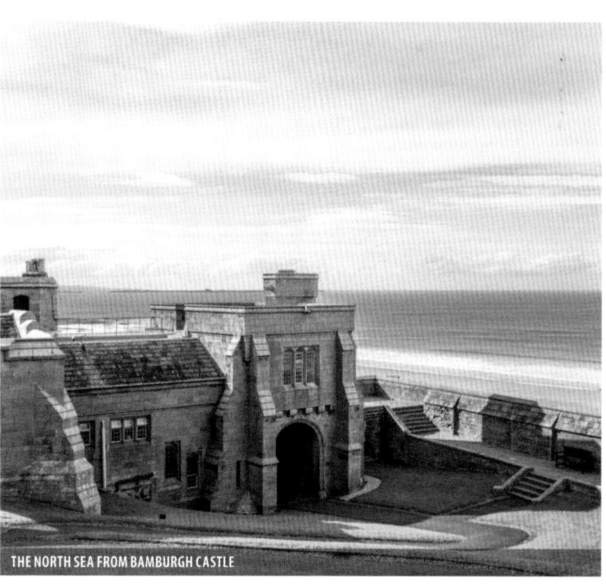

THE NORTH SEA FROM BAMBURGH CASTLE

THE AUCKLAND PROJECT
Auckland Castle, Market Place, Bishop Auckland, DL14 7NR
**Tel:** 01388 743 750 **Email:** enquiries@aucklandproject.org

BARNARD CASTLE
Nr Galgate, Barnard Castle, Durham DL12 8PR
**Tel:** 01833 638212 **Email:** barnard.castle@english-heritage.org.uk

BEAMISH, THE LIVING MUSEUM
Beamish Museum, Beamish, County Durham DH9 0RG
**Tel:** 0191 370 4000 **Email:** museum@beamish.org.uk

BOWES CASTLE
Bowes, Barnard Castle, County Durham DL12 9HP
**Tel:** 01912 691215 **Email:** grace.dunne@english-heritage.org.uk

THE BOWES MUSEUM
Barnard Castle, County Durham DL12 8NP
**Tel:** 01833 690606 **Email:** info@thebowesmuseum.org.uk

CROOK HALL & GARDENS
Sidegate, Durham DH1 5SZ
**Tel:** 0191 3848028

DURHAM CASTLE
Palace Green, Durham DH1 3RW
**Tel:** 0191 3343800

DURHAM CATHEDRAL
The College, Durham, DH1 3EH
**Tel:** 0191 338 7178 **Email:** enquiries@durhamcathedral.co.uk

ROKEBY PARK
Barnard Castle, County Durham DL12 9RZ
**Tel:** 01609 748612 **Email:** admin@rokebypark.com

THE ALNWICK GARDEN
Denwick Lane, Alnwick, Northumberland NE66 1YU
**Tel:** 01665 511350 **Email:** info@alnwickgarden.com

AYDON CASTLE
Corbridge, Northumberland NE45 5PJ
**Tel:** 01434 632450 **Email:** customers@english-heritage.org.uk

BELSAY HALL, CASTLE & GARDENS
Belsay, Nr Morpeth, Northumberland NE20 0DX
**Tel:** 01661 881636

BRINKBURN PRIORY
Long Framlington, Morpeth, Northumberland NE65 8AR
**Tel:** 01665 570628 **Email:** customers@english-heritage.org.uk

CHERRYBURN
Station Bank, Mickley, Stocksfield, Northumberland NE43 7DD
**Tel:** 01661 843276 **Email:** cherryburn@nationaltrust.org.uk

CHESTERS ROMAN FORT
Chollerford, Hexham, Northumberland NE46 4EU
**Tel:** 01434 681379 **Email:** customers@english-heritage.org.uk

CHIPCHASE CASTLE
Wark, Hexham, Northumberland NE48 3NT
**Tel:** 01434 230203 **Email:** info@chipchasecastle.com

CORBRIDGE ROMAN TOWN
Corchester Lane, Corbridge, Northumberland NE45 5NT
**Tel:** 01434 632349 **Email:** customers@english-heritage.org.uk

CRAGSIDE
Rothbury, Morpeth, Northumberland NE65 7PX
**Tel:** 01669 620333 **Email:** cragside@nationaltrust.org.uk

ALNWICK CASTLE - SUMMER 2018

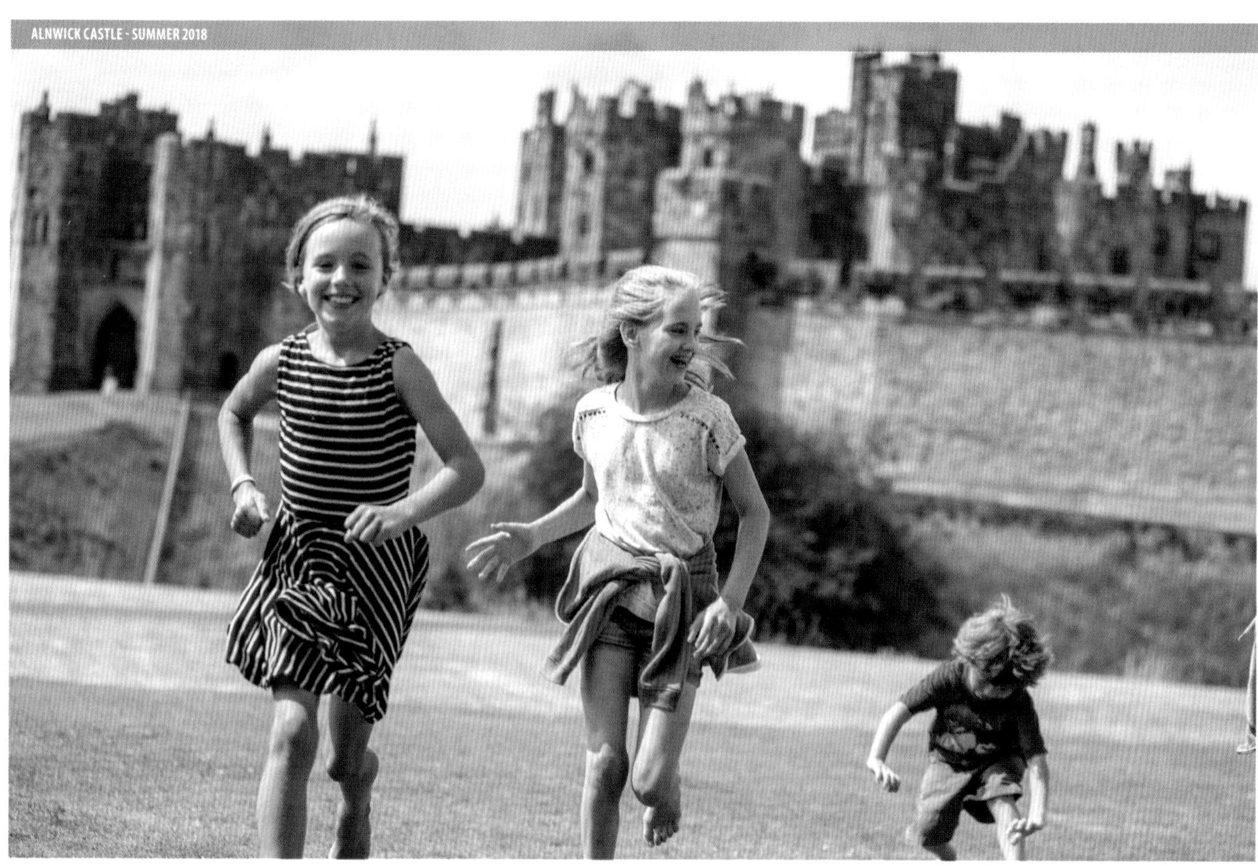

DUNSTANBURGH CASTLE
Dunstanburgh Road, Craster, Northumberland NE66 3TT
**Tel:** 01665 576231

EDLINGHAM CASTLE
Edlingham, Alnwick NE66 2BW
**Tel:** 0191 269 1200

ETAL CASTLE
Cornhill-On-Tweed, Northumberland TD12 4TN
**Tel:** 01890 820332 **Email:** customers@english-heritage.org.uk

GEORGE STEPHENSON'S BIRTHPLACE
Wylam, Northumberland NE41 8BP
**Tel:** 01661 853457 **Email:** georgestephensons@nationaltrust.org.uk

HERTERTON HOUSE GARDENS
Hartington, Cambo, Morpeth, Northumberland NE61 4BN
**Tel:** 01670 774278

HOUSESTEADS ROMAN FORT
Haydon Bridge, Hexham, Northumberland NE47 6NN
**Tel:** 01434 344363 **Email:** customers@english-heritage.org.uk

HOWICK HALL GARDENS & ARBORETUM
Alnwick, Northumberland NE66 3LB
**Tel:** 01665 577285 **Email:** estateoffice@howickuk.com

LADY WATERFORD HALL & GALLERY
Ford Village, Berwick-upon-Tweed, TD15 2QG
**Tel:** 07971 326177 **Email:** ladywaterfordhall@gmail.com

LINDISFARNE CASTLE
Holy Island, Berwick-Upon-Tweed, Northumberland TD15 2SH
**Tel:** 01289 389244 **Email:** lindisfarne@nationaltrust.org.uk

LINDISFARNE PRIORY
Holy Island, Berwick-Upon-Tweed, Northumberland TD15 2RX
**Tel:** 01289 389200 **Email:** lindisfarne.priory@english-heritage.org.uk

MELDON PARK KITCHEN GARDEN
Morpeth, Northumberland NE61 3SW
**Tel:** 01670 772341 **Email:** michelle@flyingfox.co.uk/james@flying-fox.co.uk

NORHAM CASTLE
Norham, Northumberland TD15 2JY
**Tel:** 01289 304493 **Email:** customers@english-heritage.org.uk

PRUDHOE CASTLE
Prudhoe, Northumberland NE42 6NA
**Tel:** 01661 833459 **Email:** customers@english-heritage.org.uk

SEATON DELAVAL HALL
The Avenue, Seaton Sluice, Northumberland NE26 4QR
**Tel:** 0191 237 9100 **Email:** seatondelavalhall@nationaltrust.org.uk

WALLINGTON
Cambo, Morpeth, Northumberland NE61 4AR
**Tel:** 01670 773600 **Email:** wallington@nationaltrust.org.uk

WARKWORTH CASTLE
Warkworth, Alnwick, Northumberland NE65 0UJ
**Tel:** 01665 711423 **Email:** warkworth.castle@english-heritage.org.uk

**WHALTON MANOR GARDENS**
**Whalton, Morpeth, Northumberland NE61 3UT**
The three-acre garden is bursting with inspirational planting, influenced by Gertrude Jekyll, and magnificent architectural structures designed by Sir Edwin Lutyens.
**Tel:** 01670 775205 **Email:** gardens@whaltonmanor.co.uk
**Map Ref:** 10:O2 **Website:** www.whaltonmanor.co.uk
**Open:** By appointment only. Available for Group Visits

BESSIE SURTEES HOUSE
41-44 Sandhill, Newcastle, Tyne & Wear NE1 3JF
**Tel:** 0191 269 1200 **Email:** customers@english-heritage.org.uk

GIBSIDE
Nr Rowlands Gill, Burnopfield, Newcastle upon Tyne NE16 6BG
**Tel:** 01207 541820 **Email:** gibside@nationaltrust.org.uk

HYLTON CASTLE
Castle Garth, Sunderland, Tyne and Wear SR5 3PB
**Tel:** 01912 611585

NEWCASTLE CASTLE
Nr Galgate, Newcastle, Tyne & Wear NE1 1RQ
**Tel:** 0191 230 6300 **Email:** info@newcastlecastle.co.uk

SOUTER LIGHTHOUSE
Coast Road, Whitburn, Sunderland, Tyne & Wear SR6 7NH
**Tel:** 0191 529 3161 **Email:** souter@nationaltrust.org.uk

TYNEMOUTH CASTLE & PRIORY
Tynemouth, Tyne & Wear NE30 4BZ
**Tel:** 01912 691215 **Email:** customers@english-heritage.org.uk

WASHINGTON OLD HALL
The Avenue, Washington Village, Tyne & Wear NE38 7LE
**Tel:** 0191 416 6879 **Email:** washington.oldhall@nationaltrust.org.uk

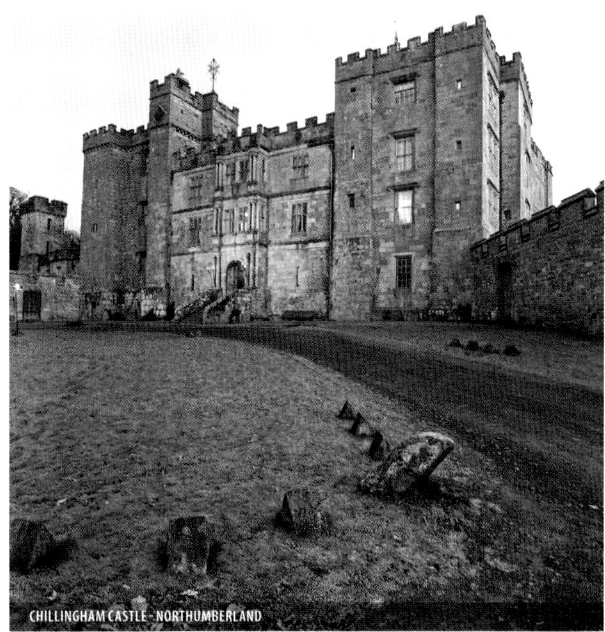
CHILLINGHAM CASTLE - NORTHUMBERLAND

# SCOTLAND

BORDERS • SOUTH WEST SCOTLAND • EDINBURGH
GREATER GLASGOW • TAYSIDE • WEST HIGHLANDS & ISLANDS
GRAMPIAN HIGHLANDS • HIGHLANDS & SKYE

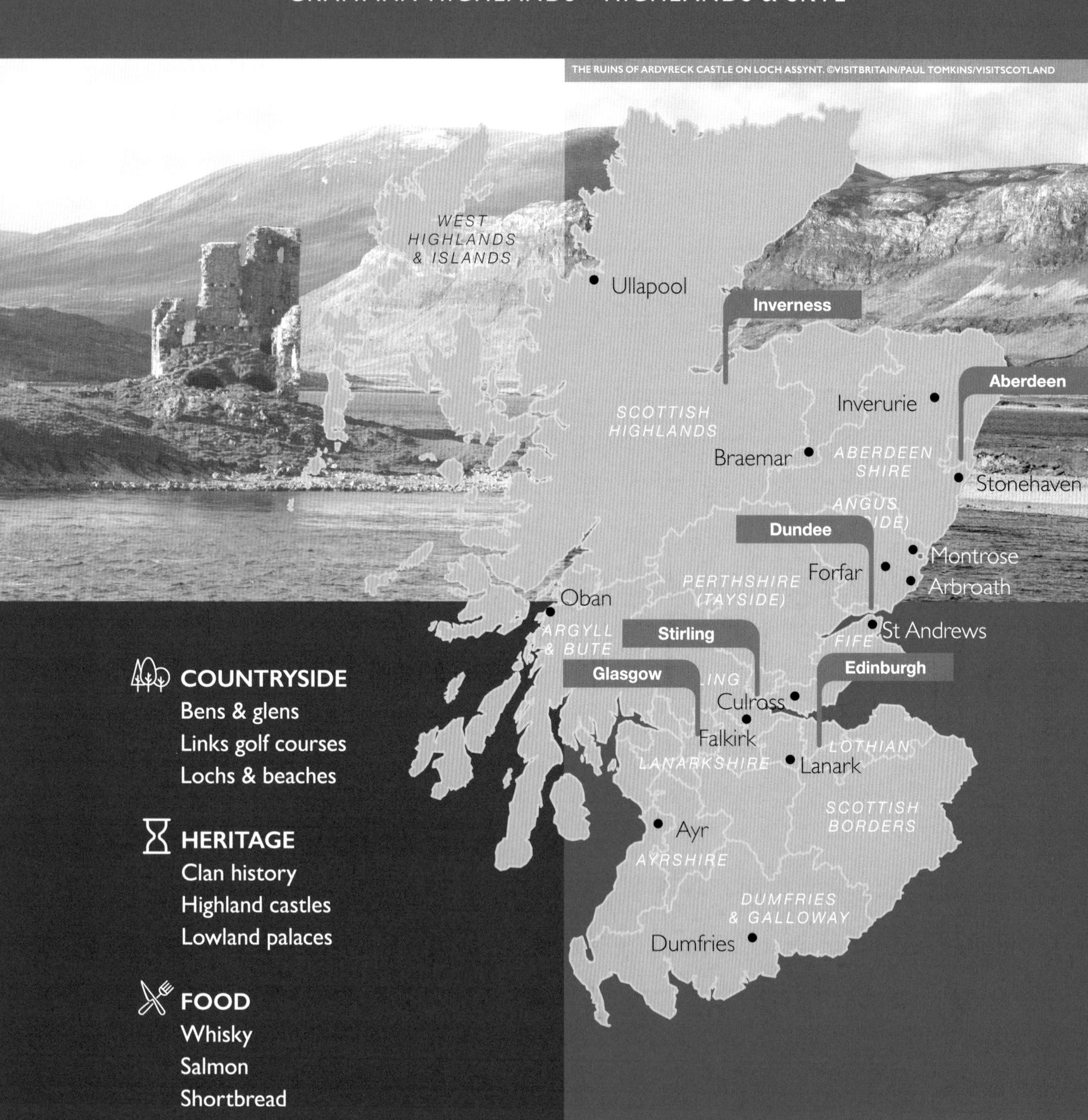


THE RUINS OF ARDVRECK CASTLE ON LOCH ASSYNT. ©VISITBRITAIN/PAUL TOMKINS/VISITSCOTLAND

**COUNTRYSIDE**
Bens & glens
Links golf courses
Lochs & beaches

**HERITAGE**
Clan history
Highland castles
Lowland palaces

**FOOD**
Whisky
Salmon
Shortbread

# Gosford House

## Gosford and Golf

The very first time a player of golf is actually named was when King James V was on the links at Gosford House in the 1530s. Today, he'd recognise the game played at nearby Craigielaw Golf Club but in the 1790s, the old house was replaced by a lowland palace, one of the last houses commissioned from the great Scottish neo-classical architect, Robert Adam. This was the home of the 7th Earl of Wemyss but the Earl's heir was not enamoured of Adam's designs and demolished the flanking pavilions.

VICTORIAN BAROQUE ON A CLASSICAL BASE AT GOSFORD HOUSE

Today the house owes most to William Young who was at work here in 1891. Young was a lover of the Baroque and rebuilt the pavilions in more decorated style. His masterpiece, and the finest interior at Gosford, is the Marble Hall; two storeys of Italianate splendour in marble and pink alabaster that delivers a real wow factor. The bravura central dome is held up by the skill of Scottish engineer Sir William Arrol, fresh from the triumph of his Tay and Forth Bridges. A double staircase leads to a picture gallery showing works by Botticelli, Murillo and Rubens collected by fine art connoisseur, the 10th Earl. Though the house is only open sporadically, a ticket from the Bothy Farm Shop gives you access to the pleasure grounds - pick up some wild boar sausages while you are there. The landscape was designed as a setting for the house around 1800 by James Ramsay.

DEFINITELY A WOW FACTOR IN THE MARBLE HALL

Walks link a wild variety of garden buildings including a shell-decorated rustic Curling House, still in regular use. Fans of the Outlander stories will feel like time travellers as Gosford features in two series of the TV drama.
If, like James V, you've come for a golfing holiday, you are spoilt for choice with courses at Craigielaw, Gullane and Muirfield. ■

# Scotland

## Top 3 Venues

CRAIGSTON CASTLE, ABERDEENSHIRE

### Craigston Castle, Aberdeenshire

Weddings and receptions are catered for on an exclusive use basis. Ceremonies take place in the drawing room with space in front of the house for a marquee. The team at Craigston are in touch with a host of local suppliers to help make your day perfect. Meetings and dinners can also be held here as well as gourmet dinners for small groups. Six bedrooms are available each containing an original four-poster bed and period furnishings. The Urquhart family can be traced back to Adam Urquhart, who was the Sheriff of Cromarty in 1357.

ADAM BALLROOM - WEDDING BREAKFAST - HOPETOUN HOUSE

### Hopetoun House, Edinburgh

Hopetoun offers a vast array of outdoor pursuits including orienteering, treasure hunts and even a mini Highland Games! There are rooms to host large-scale conferences and small private dinners. Weddings here are a personal affair and the number of weddings held per year is limited to ensure you get the right amount of support from the team for your big day. The Hope family have lived in the house since the late 17th century, and the current Lord Hopetoun still lives in the house with his family today.

FLOORS CASTLE

### Floors Castle, Borders

The Head Gardener's House is a luxurious self-catering cottage and is available for two nights as part of the wedding packages at Floors Castle providing some peace and tranquillity for the bride and groom on their first days of married life. The Castle Wedding Package affords you exclusive hire and the freedom to create the experience of your dreams. Built for the 1st Duke of Roxburghe in 1721, and still in the Roxburghe family today, the current Duke and Duchess are dedicated to preserving and maintaining the castle and its treasures for future generations to enjoy.

**Edinburgh Festival Fringe, Edinburgh** *2nd - 26th August 2019*

**Burns Night Celebrations, Scotland** *25th January 2019*

**Royal Edinburgh Military Tattoo, Edinburgh Castle** *2nd - 24th August 2019*

# Top 3 Annual Events

### Snowdrop Open Days, Dunvegan Castle, Isle of Skye

The appearance of snowdrops usually signals that winter is coming to an end. To allow the Dunvegan snowdrops to be enjoyed by all there are several garden open days during February where visitors can also take a tour of the grounds with the Head Gardener. There has been a large amount of landscaping and planting at Dunvegan within the last 30 years to restore the gardens to their former glory and there is much to see and enjoy besides the snowdrops.

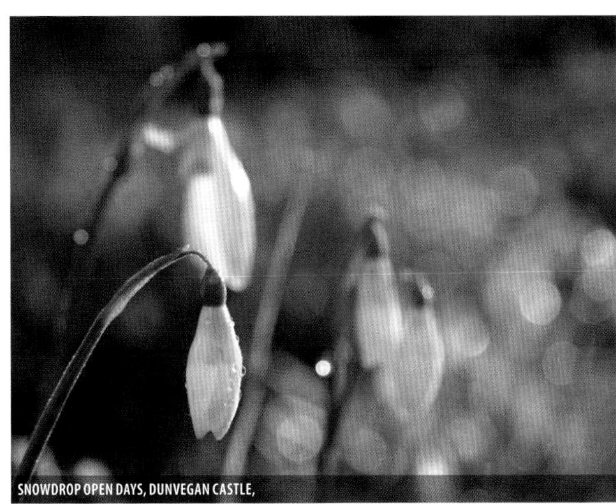

SNOWDROP OPEN DAYS, DUNVEGAN CASTLE,

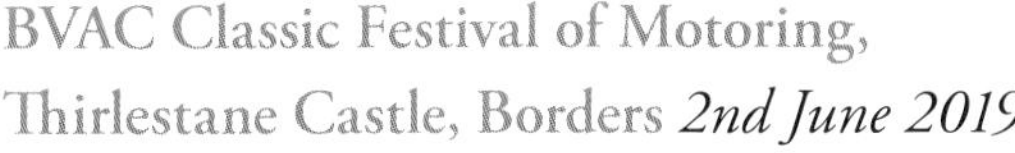

### BVAC Classic Festival of Motoring, Thirlestane Castle, Borders *2nd June 2019*

One of the most prestigious classic car events in the UK and listed in the Sunday Times Top 10 car festivals in the UK. The festival supports Sporting Bears Dream Rides, classic car owners who offer you the chance to ride in a car of your dreams in return for a donation to a children's charity. There are over 1000 vintage cars on display as well as live music, entertainment, shopping and the Food Village.

BVAC CLASSIC - FESTIVAL OF MOTORING - THIRLESTANE CASTLE

### A Victorian Christmas, Delgatie Castle, Aberdeenshire *November/December*

Taking place over two weekends in late November/ early December the Victorian Christmas experience has been a hugely popular attraction for many years. See the castle decorated as it would have been in the Victorian era complete with staff in period costume. Children will be able to visit Santa, who will have a gift for them. The award-winning Laird's Kitchen offers fantastic home baking if you fancy a bite to eat after you have looked around the castle.

ITS BEGINNING TO LOOK A LOT LIKE CHRISTMAS AT DELGATIE CASTLE - TREND ABERDEEN

# Scotland

## Places to stay and eat

VIEWFIELD HOUSE

### Viewfield House

Viewfield House has been the home of the Macdonald family for over 200 years. Iona, and her husband Jasper Buxton, recently took the reins from Iona's father Hugh. Iona is the third generation in charge since Viewfield first opened its doors to guests in 1954. The house is full of character and charm, with a comfortable and relaxed atmosphere, and has retained many of its Victorian features. It stands in extensive wooded grounds on the outskirts of Portree, overlooking Portree Bay and within easy walking distance of the town centre. There is plenty to do on Skye: boat trips, fishing, sailing (half day trips can be arranged on Viewfield's own yacht), walking in the Cuillin hills, pony trekking and golf. Visit the otter haven at Kylerhea or visit Dunvegan Castle, home to the MacLeod clan since time immemorial. Iona and Jasper can offer dinner, by prior arrangement, or can recommend several eateries in and around Portree.

Portree, Isle of Skye, Scotland IV51 9EU

01478 612217

www.viewfieldhouse.com
info@viewfieldhouse.com

### Coul House Hotel
*Hotel*

Contin, by Strathpeffer
Ross-shire IV14 9ES

01997 421487

www.coulhousehotel.com
stay@coulhouse.com

### New Lanark Mill Hotel
*Hotel*

New Lanark Mills
South Lanarkshire ML11 9DB

01555 667 200

www.newlanarkhotel.co.uk
hotel@newlanark.org

### Roman Camp Country House & Restaurant
*Restaurant*

High Street, Callander
Perthshire FK17 8BG

01877 330003

www.romancamphotel.co.uk
mail@romancamphotel.co.uk

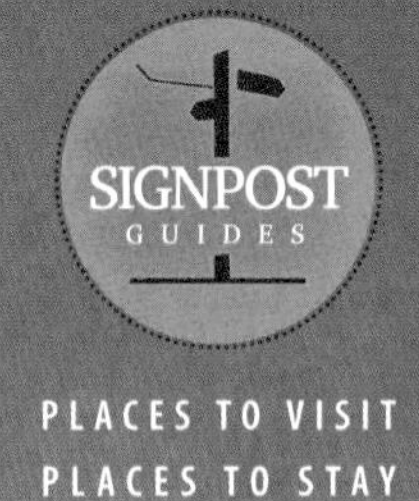




## Blackaddie Country House Hotel

A superb small restaurant with rooms set in its own gardens on the banks of the river Nith, one of Scotland's great yet little known salmon rivers and with extensive views across Scotland's Southern Upland Way. Seven beautiful bedrooms and suites, many of which overlook the gardens or the river. There are also 2 self-contained cottages in the grounds, each with fully fitted kitchen for those who wish to be independent, but who would when the hotel boasts food to rival the best anywhere? Far and away above what one would expect in a small tucked away country house hotel. Chef/Proprietor Ian McAndrew has held a Michelin Star for many years in previous restaurants and his menus use fresh local produce with all dishes prepared on the premises. Now offering 2 menus; a 5 course fine dining menu and a gourmet tasting menu, both changing daily. Dumfries House and Drumlanrig Castle are within a short drive with Caerlaverock and Threave Castle also nearby.

Blackaddie Road, Sanquhar
Dumfries and Galloway DG4 6JJ

01659 50270

www.blackaddiehotel.co.uk
ian@blackaddiehotel.co.uk

BLACKADDIE COUNTRY HOUSE HOTEL

## Hickety Pickety
*Restaurant*

Muirfoot Farm
Lanark ML11 8NZ

01555 871486

www.houseofherby.com

## Single Track
*Tea Shop*

Kendram, Kilmaluag
Isle of Skye IV51 9UL

www.facebook.com/SingleTrackSkye
info@single-track.co.uk

## The Little Bakery
*Tea Shop*

6-7 High Street, South Queensferry
Edinburgh EH30 9PP

0131 319 3322

hello@littlebakery.co.uk

# MELLERSTAIN HOUSE & GARDENS

**www.mellerstain.com**

One of Scotland's finest stately homes, this outstanding Georgian mansion house is a unique example of Adam design, begun in 1725 by Scottish architect William Adam and completed in 1778 by his more famous son, Robert. Some say this is one of Robert Adam's finest works, complemented by the fine art, period furniture, china and embroidery collections. Its idyllic location does not disappoint, with acres of parkland, gardens, lakeside walks, playground, coffee shop and holiday cottages.

- Outdoor shoes/boots recommended for the grounds & gardens.
- Accessible WC facility in courtyard.
- Free on site parking. Accessible parking and drop-off point at main reception.
- Partially suitable for visitors with limited mobility.
- Dog friendly in grounds and gardens on leads. Guide dogs only in the house.
- Self-catering holiday cottages, The Clock House, Courtyard Cottage, West Lodge.
- Groups and guided tours welcome by prior arrangement.
- Educational and school visits by arrangement.
- Free entry to coffee shop/ ticket entry to House and Gardens.
- For corporate functions please contact.
- See the 'What's On' page on the website for all upcoming events at Mellerstain House.

**CONTACT** Owner: The Mellerstain Trust Contact: The Trust Office
Tel: 01573 410225 Email: enquiries@mellerstain.com

**LOCATION** Mellerstain, Gordon, Berwickshire TD3 6LG
Map Ref: 14:J10 From Edinburgh A68 to Earlston, turn left 5 miles, signed.

**OPENING TIME** Easter weekend (4 days) to Sept.
See website for opening days. House: 12pm - 5pm. Last ticket 4.15pm.
Coffee shop & gardens: 11am - 5pm.

**ADMISSION** Please see our website or call us.

# THIRLESTANE CASTLE

**www.thirlestanecastle.co.uk**

Thirlestane Castle nestles in the hills of the Scottish Borders just 35 minutes from Edinburgh. Built in 1590, it was originally a great stone keep but over the years became a grand ducal palace and then a country mansion. It is the ancient seat of the Earls and Duke of Lauderdale, and the Maitland family still live there. Explore and discover exquisite 17th Century plasterwork ceilings, fine furnishings, pictures, and historic toys. Facilities include free parking, a woodland walk, gift shop and Tea Room.

- Public toilets located on both the lower ground floor and the ground floor.
- Baby changing facilities available in both male and female toilets.
- Ample free parking for cars and coaches.
- Restricted access, no lift for first floor.
- Well-behaved dogs on leads are welcome in the castle grounds.
- Self-catering apartments available within the castle.
- Groups welcome. Guided tours are available by arrangement.
- Enjoy delicious cakes or light lunch with tea and coffee in the cosy Tea Room.
- Gift shop selling a range of Thirlestane Castle souvenirs and gifts.
- Beautiful events venue for private dining, corporate and large outdoor events.
- Calendar of special events throughout the opening season. See website
- Thirlestane Castle is a fairytale setting for weddings.

**CONTACT** Owner: Thirlestane Castle Trust
Contact: Rhona Jamieson Tel: 01578 722430
Email: enquiries@thirlestanecastle.co.uk

**LOCATION** Lauder, Scottish Borders TD2 6RU
Map Ref: 14:I9 - Signposted just off the A68 at Lauder.

**OPENING TIMES** 28 Apr - 3 Oct 2019. Sun - Thurs, 10am - 4pm.
For up-to-date opening times please visit website.

**ADMISSION** Castle & Grounds: Adult £9.50, Child £5,
Concessions £8.50, Family (2+3) £25,
Groups of 15+ £8 (includes guided tour).
Grounds Only: Adult £4, Child £2.

## FLOORS CASTLE

www.floorscastle.com

An architectural masterpiece overlooking the River Tweed and Cheviot Hills. Home to the 10th Duke of Roxburghe, Floors Castle showcases spectacular state rooms with outstanding collections of paintings, tapestries, ceramics and furniture. Explore the picturesque Victorian walled gardens, extensive grounds, walks and cycle trails. Enjoy seasonal castle kitchen-made food at one of our cafés, serving morning coffee, delicious lunch or afternoon tea.

**CONTACT** Owner: His Grace the Duke of Roxburghe Contact: Candy Rafferty/Laura Finkle Tel: 01573 223333 Email: enquiries@floorscastle.com

**LOCATION** Floors Castle,Roxburghe Estates, Kelso TD5 7SF Map Ref: 14:J10 OS Ref: NT11 374 From S A68, A698. From N A68.

**OPENING** Castle & Grounds 1 May-30 Sep & Wknds in Oct 10.30am-5pm. Gardens & Terrace Café open all year round. 10.30am-5pm, Apr-Oct.10.30am-4pm Nov- Mar.

**ADMISSION** Castle, Gardens & Grounds: Adult £11.50, Conc £10.50, Child (5-15) £6, Family £29 (2+3).
Gardens & Grounds: Adult £6.50, Conc £5.50, Child (5-15) £3, Family £16.

Free for cars, coaches and Disabled.

Dog friendly grounds.

Experienced guides throughout Castle.

2 Cafés, serving food from Castle kitchen.

Two delightful gift shops.

Activities, corporate events, weddings.

## DALMENY HOUSE

www.roseberyestates.co.uk

Dalmeny House, the family home of the Earls of Rosebery for over 300 years. Boasting superb collections of porcelain and tapestries, fine paintings by Gainsborough, Raeburn, Reynolds and Lawrence, together with exquisite 18th Century French furniture and a superb Napoleonic collection.

**CONTACT** Owner: The Earl of Rosebery Contact: Head of Events Tel: 0131 331 1888 Email: events@roseberyestates.co.uk **LOCATION** South Queensferry, Edinburgh EH30 9TQ Map Ref:13:G8 From Edinburgh A90, B924, 7 miles North, A90 ½m. On South shore of Firth of Forth. **OPENING TIMES** Jun & Jul Sun-Wed 2pm-5pm. Entry is by guided tour only & tours are 2.15pm & 3.30pm. **ADMISSION** Adult £10, Child (under 14yrs) Free, 14-16yrs £6.50, Concessions £9, Groups: (20+) £9.

60 cars, 3 coaches. WCs. Dogs on leads in grounds only. Obligatory. Café.

## HOPETOUN HOUSE

hopetoun.co.uk

As you approach Hopetoun House the impressive panoramic view of the main façade is breathtakingly revealed. Designed by William Bruce and then altered and extended by William Adam, Hopetoun House is one of the finest examples of 18th Century architecture in Britain.

**CONTACT** Owner: Hopetoun House Preservation Trust Contact: Reception Tel: 0131 331 2451 Email: enquiries@hopetoun.co.uk **LOCATION** South Queensferry, EH30 9SL Map Ref: 13:F7 Exit A90 at A904, Follow Brown Signs. **OPENING TIMES** Daily from Apr-Sep; 10.30am 4.30pm. Last adm. 4pm. **ADMISSION** House & Grounds: Adult £10.50, Child (5-16yrs) £5.50, Conc/Student £9, Family (2+2) £28. Grounds only: Adult £4.75, Child (5-16yrs) £2.95, Conc/Student £4.25, Family (2+2): £14.

Cars & coaches welcome. Lift to 1st floor, Virtual access to upper floors. WC's. Dogs welcome on leads in grounds. Daily tour at 2pm. Groups (20+) welcome out of season by appointment. Stables Kitchen for traditional afternoon teas in stunning surroundings. Private functions, banquets & gala evenings, meetings, conferences, exhibitions & outdoor activities. See www.hopetoun.co.uk for events. Wedding ceremonies.

## GOSFORD HOUSE

www.gosfordhouse.co.uk

1791 the 7th Earl of Wemyss, aided by Robert Adam, built one of the grandest houses in Scotland, with a 'paradise' of lakes and pleasure grounds. New wings, including the celebrated Marble Hall were added in 1891 by William Young. The house has a fine collection of paintings and furniture.

NO photographs are allowed to be taken inside the house. NO bags are allowed into the house.

Toilet facilities available.

Limited for coaches.

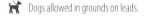

The house has very limited disabled access and part of the tour requires climbing stairs.

Dogs allowed in grounds on leads.

Book in advance for groups of 8+. Each tour of the house lasts approximately 1 hour.

Providing the back drop you need for your event; such as black tie grandeur or party informality.

Hosting a variety of large scale group activity days for groups.

Gosford House is available for a limited number of wedding receptions each year.

Played host to several major feature films, TV series and top brand fashion shoots etc.

**CONTACT** Owner/Contact: The Earl of Wemyss Tel: 01875 870201 Email: info@gosfordhouse.co.uk

**LOCATION** Longniddry, East Lothian EH32 0PX Map Ref: 14:I7 - Off A198 2 miles North East of Longniddry.

**OPENING TIMES** Please check our website for most up-to-date opening times/days.

**ADMISSION** Adult £8 O.A.P/Students £5 Child (under 16) Free

## TRAQUAIR HOUSE

**www.traquair.co.uk**

Dating back to 1107, Traquair was originally a hunting lodge for the kings and queens of Scotland. Later a refuge for Catholic priests in times of terror the Stuarts of Traquair supported Mary Queen of Scots and the Jacobite cause. Today, Traquair is a unique piece of living history.

**CONTACT** Traquair House Office
Tel: 01896 830323
E-mail: enquiries@traquair.co.uk

**LOCATION** Innerleithen, Peeblesshire EH44 6PW Map 13:H10. On B709 near junction with A72. Edinburgh 1hr, Glasgow 1½ hrs, Carlisle 1½ hrs.

**OPENING TIMES** 1 Apr - 31 Oc
Weekends only in Nov.
Apr-Jun 11am-5pm. Jul & Aug 10am-5pm
Sep 11am-5pm. Oct 11am-4pm
Nov 11m-3pm

**ADMISSION** House & Grounds: Adult £9, Child £4.50, Senior £8, Family £25 (2+3). Grounds: Adult £4.50, Conc £3.50
Groups (20+): Adult £8, Child £4, Senior £7. Guide Book £4.95.

- Coaches; please book.
- Ground floor access, toilet behind restaurant.
- Brewery & Gift Shops.
- In grounds only, on leads.
- Licensed.
- Traquair App and tablet hire.
- 3 double en suite bedrooms.

## BALCARRES

16th Century tower house with 19th Century additions by Burn and Bryce.

Woodland and terraced gardens.

**CONTACT** Owner: Balcarres Heritage Trust Contact: Lord Balniel
Tel: 01333 340206

**LOCATION** Colinsburgh, Fife KY9 1HN
Map Ref:14:I6
½ mile North of Colinsburgh.

**OPENING TIMES** Woodland & Gardens: 1 Mar-30 Sep, 2pm-5pm.
The house is not open except by written appointment and on 1-30 Apr, excluding Sun.

**ADMISSION** House: £8 Garden: £8
House & Garden: £15

- Partial access.
- Dogs welcome on leads only.
- Guided tours by arrangement.

# NEW LANARK MILLS

## WORLD HERITAGE SITE

**www.newlanark.org**

New Lanark Mills World Heritage Site is a unique 18th century mill village sitting alongside the picturesque River Clyde, less than one hour from Glasgow and Edinburgh. Visitors can discover Scotland's hidden past and see how villagers lived, learned and worked with recreated millworkers' houses, historic working machinery and the 'Annie McLeod Experience', a 'dark ride' that tells the story of a child millworker. The Mill Shop offers an extensive range of contemporary gifts, souvenirs, Scottish produce and the New Lanark Wool & Textiles range. There's the 4-star, 38-bedroom New Lanark Mill Hotel and the nearby 'Falls of Clyde' waterfalls.

- Toilet facilities available.
- Baby changing facilities available.
- Closed 25 Dec and 1 Jan.
- Cars & coaches. 5 min walk. The main Visitor Centre car park and spaces in the village are limited.
- Suitable. WC. Please see the mobility needs information guide.
- Hotel, self-catering & hostel.
- Book guided tours in advance.
- Contact for information on education and school visits.
- 
- 
- The New Lanark Mill Shop offers a superb range of contemporary gifts, books & Scottish produce.
- 
- Please see the 'What's On' section of the website for a list of events and exhibitions.
- 
- 

**CONTACT** Owner: New Lanark Trust Contact: Trust Office
Tel: 01555 661345 Email: trust@newlanark.org

**LOCATION** New Lanark Mills, Lanark, South Lanarkshire ML11 9DB
Map Ref: 13:E9 - Sat Nav code ML11 9BY. Nearest train station is Lanark. Glasgow > Lanark Bus from Buchanan Bus Station.

**OPENING TIMES** 10am - 5pm Apr - Oct, 10am - 4pm Nov-Mar. Shops/catering open until 5pm daily. Closed 25 Dec and 1 Jan.

**ADMISSION** Visitor Centre: Adult £13.95, Concs (Senior/Student) £11.50, Child £9.95, Family (2+2/3) £43.95, Groups 1 free/15 booked.

## CORTACHY ESTATE

www.airlieestates.com

Countryside walks including access through woodlands to Airlie Monument on Tulloch Hill with spectacular views of the Angus Glens and Vale of Strathmore. Footpaths are waymarked and colour coded.

**CONTACT** Owner: Trustees of Airlie Estates Contact: Estate Office
Tel: 01575 570108
Fax: 01575 540400
Email: office@airlieestates.com

**LOCATION** Cortachy, Kirriemuir, Angus DD8 4LX Map Ref:13:H3
Off the B955 Glens Road from Kirriemuir.

**OPENING TIMES** Walks all year.
Gardens: 3 - 27 May 2019.
Last admission 3.30pm.

Please see estate website for admission prices and opening alterations

- The estate network of walks are open all year round.
- Limited.
- Unsuitable.
- Dogs on leads only.
- Please contact for corporate events.
- Please see the 'Events' section of the website.
- Weddings and Celebrations can be held either in a marquee or inside Downiepark House.

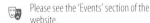

## CASTLE KENNEDY GARDENS

www.castlekennedygardens.com

Glorious 75 acre gardens situated on an isthmus between two natural lochs, with ruined Castle Kennedy at one end overlooking a beautiful herbaceous walled garden and Lochinch Castle at the other.

**CONTACT** Owner: The Earl and Countess of Stair Contact: Stair Estates
Tel: 01776 702024 / 01581 400225
Email: info@castlekennedygardens.com

**LOCATION** Stranraer, Dumfries and Galloway DG9 8SJ Map Ref: 9:D3 - 3m E of Stranraer on A75.

**OPENING TIMES** Gardens & Tea Room:
29 Mar-31 Oct, daily 10am-5pm.
Feb & Mar, weekends only.

**ADMISSION** Adult £5.50, Child £2, Conc £4.50, Family (2+2) £12.
Groups of 20 or more 10% discount.

- For information please visit website.
- Toilet & disabled WC facilities.
- Car and bus parking available adjacent to the entrance to the Gardens.
- A free wheelchair is available. Please contact prior to visit for further details.
- Welcoming responsible dog owners and all friendly dogs on leads.
- Luxury self-catering accommodation on Lochinch Castle Heritage Estate.
- Castle Kennedy Gardens Group Tour.
- Working with educational bodies.
- Coffee, light lunch, at the Tea Room.
- Gift Shop sells original gifts.
- Plant Centre has a selection of plants.

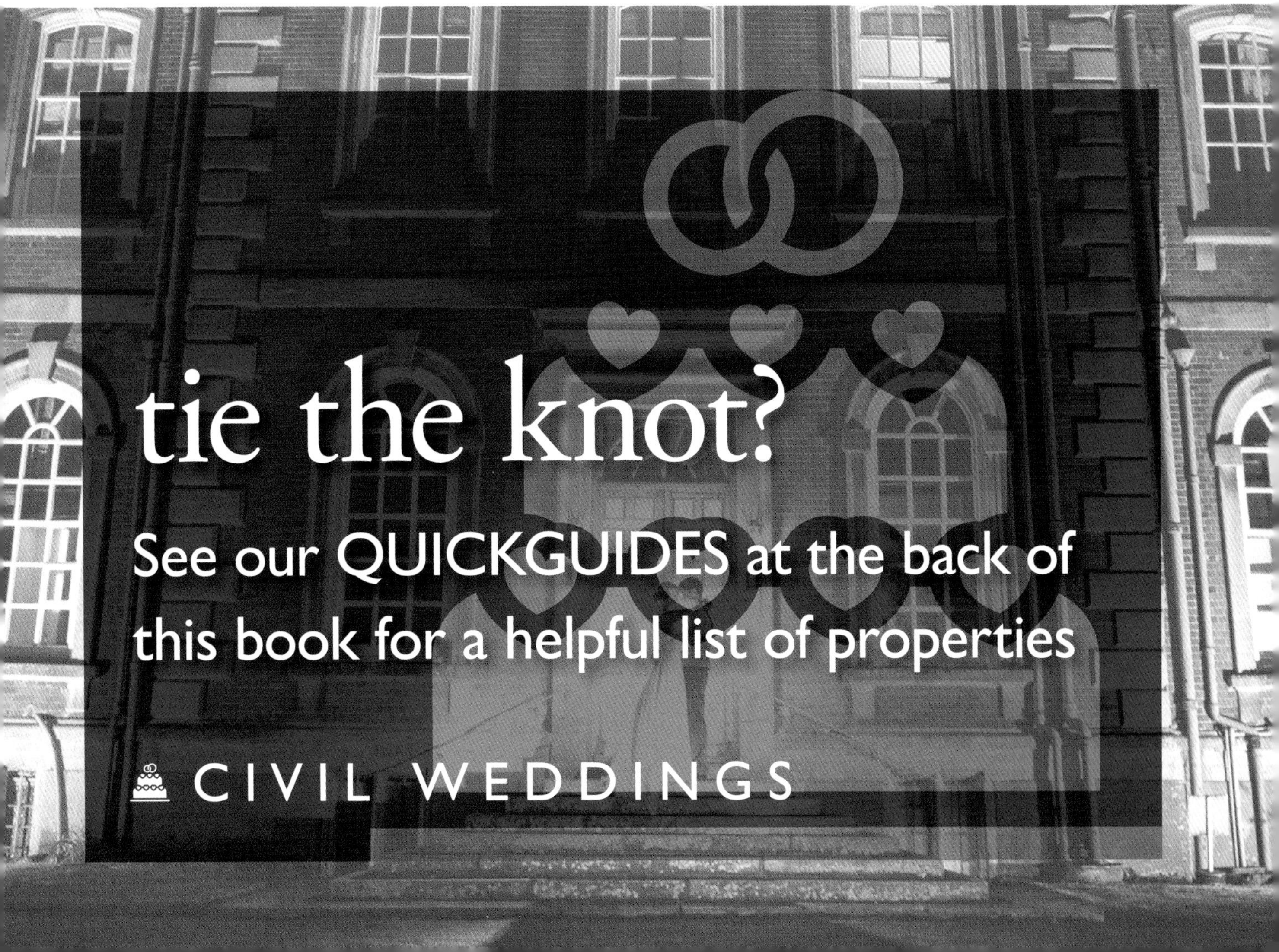

# tie the knot?

**See our QUICKGUIDES at the back of this book for a helpful list of properties**

CIVIL WEDDINGS

# DELGATIE CASTLE

**www.delgatiecastle.com**

Dating from 1030 the castle is steeped in Scottish history but still gives the feel of a lived in home. It has some of the finest painted ceilings in Scotland. Mary Queen of Scots stayed here for 3 days after the Battle of Corrichie.

Our pretty tearoom has a *'Taste Our Best Award'* from Visit Scotland and also *'Scottish Home Baking Award'* winner.

- No photography.
- Toilet facilities available.
- Open all year.
- Parking available.
- WC's.
- Two self-catering apartments in Castle.
- By arrangement.
- Educational and school visits by arrangement.
-  The Laird's kitchen is open from 10am-5pm serving hot drinks, cakes, lunches & afternoon teas.
- Restaurant.
- Gift shop.
- The 'Yester' room or 'Ballroom' are perfect for business meetings, parties, anniversaries etc.
- Special events.
- For a once in a lifetime experience Delgatie Castle is the perfect wedding venue.

**CONTACT** Owner: Delgatie Castle Trust Contact: Mrs Joan Johnson Tel: 01888 563479 Email: joan@delgatiecastle.com

**LOCATION** Turriff, Aberdeenshire AB53 5TD Map Ref: 17:D9 - Off A947 Aberdeen to Banff Road.

**OPENING TIMES** Daily 15 Jan - 20 Dec, 1 Apr - 30 Sep, 10am - 5pm. 1 Oct - 31 Mar, 10am - 4pm.

**ADMISSION** Adult £8, Child/Con £5, Family £21 (2 Adults & 2 Children), Groups (10+) £5.

# CRIMONMOGATE

**www.cmg-events.co.uk**

Situated in Aberdeenshire, Crimonmogate is a Grade A listed mansion house and one of the most easterly stately homes in Scotland. It is now owned by William and Candida, Viscount and Viscountess Petersham. Pronounced 'Crimmon-moggat'. This exclusive country house stands within beautiful, seasonal parkland and offers one of Aberdeenshire's most outstanding and unusual venues for corporate events, parties, dinners and weddings.

**CONTACT** Owner/Contact: Viscount Petersham Tel: 01346 532401 Email: info@cmg-events.co.uk

**LOCATION** Lonmay, Fraserburgh, Aberdeenshire AB43 8SE Map Ref:17:F8

**OPENING TIMES** Please refer to the website for visiting dates.

**ADMISSION** Adult £7, Conc £6, Child £5. Max of 12 at any one time, guided tours only.

- Parking available.
- Principal rooms only in tour.
- Weddings & special events: max 60 in hall & up to 200 in marquee.
-  Please see website for all upcoming events.
- 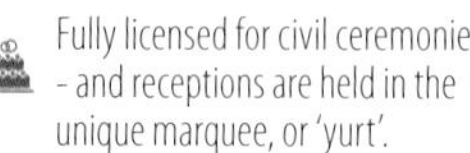 Fully licensed for civil ceremonies - and receptions are held in the unique marquee, or 'yurt'.

DELGATIE CASTLE

# CRAIGSTON CASTLE

**www.craigston-castle.co.uk**

The beautiful sculpted balcony, unique in Scottish architecture, depicts a piper, two grinning knights and David and Goliath. Carved oak panels of Scottish kings' biblical heroes, originally from the family seat at Cromarty Castle were mounted in doors and shutters in the early17th Century.

**CONTACT** Owner: William Pratesi Urquhart Contact: Elisabetta Calvi Tel: 01888551707 Email: info@craigston.co.uk **LOCATION** Turriff, Aberdeenshire AB53 5PX Map Ref: 17:D8 - On B9105, 4.5 miles North East of Turriff. **OPENING TIMES** 3-17, 20-26 May, 21-22, 28-29 Sept. Plus throughout the year by appointment. **ADMISSION** Adult £6, Child £2 , Concession £4. Groups Adult £5, Child/School £2.

Please contact for details. Parking available. Very limited wheelchair access. Dogs welcome in the castle grounds. Your choice of room, with period furniture. Craigston is available for exclusive self catering lets. Guided tours are obligatory. Courses held at specific times of year. Bespoke events can be organised. Please see our website.

DUNVEGAN CASTLE

# DUNVEGAN CASTLE & GARDENS

www.dunvegancastle.com

DUNVEGAN CASTLE ©MACLEOD ESTATE

DUNVEGAN CASTLE GARDENS ©MACLEOD ESTATE

BOAT TRIPS TO SEAL COLONY ©MACLEOD ESTATE

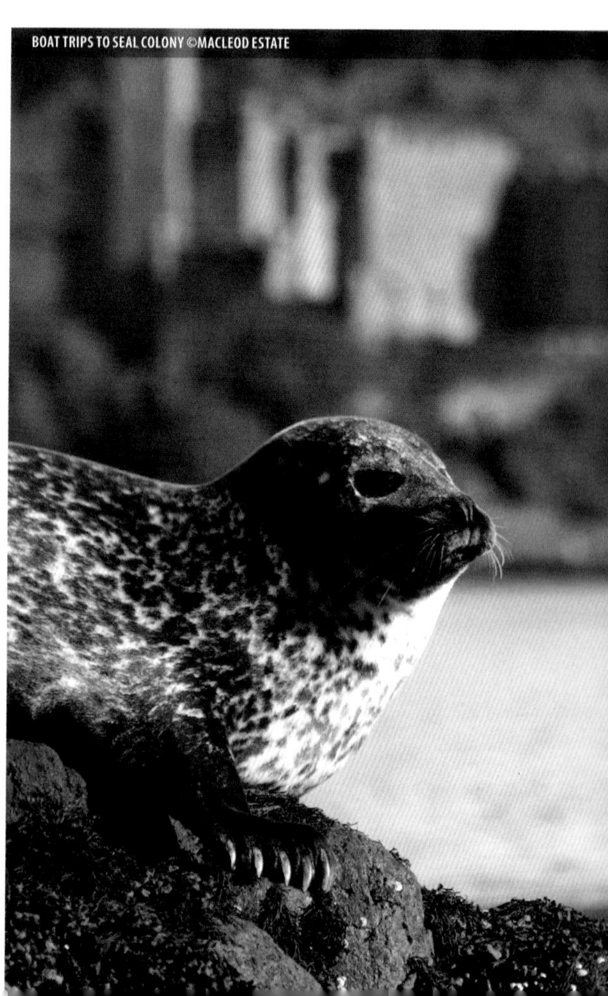

## Experience living history at Dunvegan Castle, the ancestral home of the Chiefs of Clan MacLeod for 800 years.

Any visit to the Isle of Skye is incomplete without savouring the wealth of history on offer at Dunvegan Castle & Gardens, the ancestral home of the Chiefs of Clan MacLeod for 800 years. Originally designed to keep people out, it was first opened to visitors in 1933 and is one of Skye's most famous landmarks.

On display are many fine oil paintings and Clan treasures, the most famous of which is the Fairy Flag. Legend has it that this sacred Banner has miraculous powers and when unfurled in battle, the Clan MacLeod will defeat their enemies. Another of the castle's great treasures is the Dunvegan Cup, a unique 'mazer' dating back to the Middle Ages.

It was gifted by the O'Neils of Ulster as a token of thanks to one of the Clan's most celebrated Chiefs, Sir Rory Mor, for his support of their cause against the marauding forces of Queen Elizabeth I of England in 1596.

Today visitors can enjoy tours of an extraordinary castle and Highland estate steeped in history and clan legend, delight in the beauty of its formal gardens, take a boat trip onto Loch Dunvegan to see the seal colony, enjoy an appetising meal at the MacLeods Table Café or browse in one of its four shops offering a wide choice to suit everyone.

Over time, we have given a warm Highland welcome to visitors including Sir Walter Scott, Dr Johnson and Queen Elizabeth II and we look forward to welcoming you.

**OWNER**
Hugh Macleod of Macleod

**CONTACT**
Contact: Lynne Leslie
Tel: 01470 521206
Email: info@dunvegancastle.com

**LOCATION**
Dunvegan Castle, Dunvegan, Isle of Skye, Scotland IV55 8WF
Map Ref: 15:F9
1 mile North of village. North West corner of Skye.
Kyle of Lochalsh to Dunvegan via Skye Bridge.
Rail: Inverness to Kyle of Lochalsh.
Ferry: Mallaig to Armadale.

**OPENING TIMES**
1 Apr-15 Oct Daily 10am-5.30pm.
Last admission 5pm. Closed 6 Oct-31 Mar.
Castle and Gardens closed Christmas & New Year.

**ADMISSION**
Castle & Gardens
Adult: £14, Child (5-15yrs): £9,
Senior/Student/Group (min 10 adults): £11,
Family Ticket (2 Adults, 4 Children): £34.

Gardens only:
Adult £12, Child (5-15yrs) £7,
Senior/Student/ Group £9.

Sealboat trips:
(prices valid with a castle or garden ticket)
Adult £8, Child £6.
Senior/Students/Groups £7
Infants under 3yrs free.

Loch Cruises & Fishing Trips:
Adult £45, Child (5-15yrs) £35.

- Boat trips to seal colony, fishing trips & loch cruises. Weather dependent. No photography in castle.
- Toilet facilities available.
- Baby changing facilities available.
- 120 cars & 10 coaches. Coaches please book if possible.
- Partial. WC's. Laptop tour of Castle available.
- Dogs on leads in gardens only.
- 5 self-catering holiday cottages sleeping up to 6
- By appointment. Self-guided.
- Welcome by arrangement. Guide available on request.
- MacLeod Table Café (seats 76).
- Gift shops sell a wide range of quality items, Harris Tweed products, knitwear, jewellery and small gifts.
- Offering an award-winning highland hospitality for every occasion.
- For events and exhibitions please see the 'What's on' section of the website.
- Perfect wedding venue in glorious surroundings, a warm highland welcome and rich in history.
- A unique location for film, TV or advertising. Check website for details.

ABBOTSFORD, HOME OF SIR WALTER SCOTT
The Abbotsford Trust, Abbotsford, Melrose, Roxburghshire TD6 9BQ
**Tel:** 01896 752043 **Email:** enquiries@scottsabbotsford.co.uk

BEMERSYDE GARDENS
Melrose, Roxburghshire TD6 9DP
**Tel:** 01968 678465

BOWHILL HOUSE & COUNTRY ESTATE
Bowhill, Selkirk TD7 5ET
**Tel:** 01750 22204

BUGHTRIG GARDEN
Bughtrig, Coldstream TD12 4JP
**Tel:** 01890 840777 **Email:** ramsay@bughtrig.co.uk

DUNS CASTLE
Duns, Berwickshire TD11 3NW
**Tel:** 01361 883211

FERNIEHIRST CASTLE
Jedburgh, Roxburghshire, Scottish Borders TD8 6NX
**Tel:** 01450 870051 **Email:** curator@clankerr.co.uk

HERMITAGE CASTLE
Scottish Borders TD9 0LU
**Tel:** 01387 376222

HIRSEL ESTATE
Coldstream TD12 4LP
**Tel:** 01555 851536 **Email:** joy.hitchcock@daestates.co.uk

MANDERSTON
Duns, Berwickshire TD11 3PP
**Tel:** 01361 883450 **Email:** palmer@manderston.co.uk

**MERTOUN GARDENS**

**St. Boswells, Melrose, Roxburghshire TD6 0EA**
26 acres of beautiful grounds. Walled garden and well preserved circular dovecot. **Map Ref:** 14:J10 **Tel:** 01835 823236
**Email:** estateoffice@mertoun.com
**Website:** www.mertoungardens.co.uk
**Open:** Apr-Sep, Fri-Mon 2-6pm. Last Admission 5.30pm.
**Admission:** Adult £5, Child Free.

PAXTON HOUSE, GALLERY & COUNTRY PARK
Berwick-Upon-Tweed TD15 1SZ
**Tel:** 01289 386291 **Email:** info@paxtonhouse.com

SMAILHOLM TOWER
Smailholm, Kelso TD5 7PG
**Tel:** 01573 460365

ARDWELL GARDENS
Ardwell House, Ardwell, Stranraer, Wigtownshire DG9 9LY
**Tel:** 01776 860227 **Email:** info@ardwellestate.co.uk

AUCHINLECK
Ochiltree, Ayrshire KA18 2LR
**Tel:** 01896 752043 **Email:** bookings@landmarktrust.org.uk

BLAIRQUHAN CASTLE
Maybole, Ayrshire KA19 7LZ
**Tel:** 01655 770239

BRODICK CASTLE
Isle Of Arran KA27 8HY
**Tel:** 0131 243 9300

CAERLAVEROCK CASTLE
Glencaple, Dumfries DG1 4RU
**Tel:** 01387 770244

CRAIGDARROCH HOUSE
Moniaive, Dumfriesshire DG3 4JB
**Tel:** 01848 200202

CULZEAN CASTLE & COUNTRY PARK
Maybole, Ayrshire KA19 8LE
**Tel:** 0844 493 2149 **Email:** culzean@nts.org.uk

DRUMLANRIG CASTLE
Thornhill, Dumfriesshire DG3 4AQ
**Tel:** 01848 331555 **Email:** info@drumlanrigcastle.co.uk

DUMFRIES HOUSE
Cumnock, East Ayrshire KA18 2NJ
**Tel:** 01290 421742/01290 427975 **Email:** DHtours@dumfries-house.org.uk

GLENMALLOCH LODGE
Newton Stewart, Dumfries And Galloway DG8 6AG
**Tel:** 01628 825925 **Email:** bookings@landmarktrust.org.uk

KELBURN CASTLE & COUNTRY CENTRE
Fairlie, By Largs, Ayrshire KA29 0BE
**Tel:** 01475 568685/568595 **Email:** admin@kelburncountrycentre.com

RAMMERSCALES
Lockerbie, Dumfriesshire DG11 1LD
**Tel:** 01387 810229 **Email:** malcolm@rammerscales.co.uk

SORN CASTLE
Sorn, Mauchline, Ayrshire KA5 6HR
**Tel:** 01290 551476 **Email:** info@sorncastle.com

**AMISFIELD MAINS**

**Nr Haddington, East Lothian EH41 3SA**
Georgian farmhouse with gothic barn and cottage.
**Location:** Between Haddington and East Linton on A199.
**Map Ref:** 14:I8 Tel: 01875 870201 Fax: 01875 870620
**Open:** Exterior only: By appointment, Wemyss and March Estates Office, Longniddry, East Lothian EH32 0PY.
**Admission:** Please contact for details.

**ARNISTON HOUSE**

**Gorebridge, Midlothian EH23 4RY**
Magnificent country setting, purchased 1571, beloved by Sir Walter Scott, William Adam Mansion commissioned 1726.
**Map Ref:** 13:H9 - 1 mile from A7 at Gorebridge.
**Tel:** 01875 830515 **Email:** info@arniston-house.co.uk
**Website:** www.arnistonhouse.com **Open:** May & Jun: Tue & Wed; Jul-15 Sep: Tue, Wed & Sun, guided tours at 2pm & 3.30pm. Pre-arranged groups. **Admission:** Adult: £7, Child: £3.

## BEANSTON

**Nr Haddington, East Lothian EH41 3SB**
Georgian farmhouse with Georgian orangery.
**Map Ref:** 14:I8 - Between Haddington and East Linton on A199
**Tel:** 01875 870201
**Open:** Exterior only: By appointment, Wemyss and March Estates Office, Longniddry, East Lothian EH32 0PY.
**Admission:** Please contact for details.

BLACKNESS CASTLE
Blackness, Linlithgow EH49 7NH
**Tel:** 01506 834807

DIRLETON CASTLE
North Berwick EH39 5ER
**Tel:** 01620 850 330

EDINBURGH CASTLE
Castle Hill, Edinburgh EH1 2NG
**Tel:** 0131 225 9846 **Email:** hs.explorer@scotland.gsi.gov.uk

GLADSTONE'S LAND
477B Lawnmarket, Royal Mile EH1 2NT
**Tel:** 0131 226 5856

## HARELAW FARMHOUSE

**Nr Longniddry, East Lothian EH32 0PH**
Early 19th Century 2-storey farmhouse built as an integral part of the steading. Dovecote over entrance arch. Location: Between Longniddry and Drem on B1377. **Map Ref:** 14:I8 **Tel:** 01875 870201
**Open:** Exteriors only: By appointment, Wemyss and March Estates Office, Longniddry, East Lothian EH32 0PY.
**Admission:** Please contact for details.

HOUSE OF THE BINNS
Linlithgow, West Lothian EH49 7NA
**Tel:** 0844 493 2127 **Email:** information@nts.org.uk

INVERESK LODGE GARDEN
24 Inveresk Village, Musselburgh EH21 7TE
**Tel:** 0131 6651855 **Email:** inveresk@nts.org.uk

LENNOXLOVE HOUSE
Haddington, East Lothian EH41 4NZ
**Tel:** 01620 828614 **Email:** ken-buchanan@lennoxlove.com

LINLITHGOW PALACE
Linlithgow, West Lothian EH49 7AL
**Tel:** 01506 842896 **Email:** hs.explorer@scotland.gsi.gov.uk

NEWLISTON
Kirkliston, West Lothian EH29 9EB
**Tel:** 0131 333 3231

PALACE OF HOLYROODHOUSE
Edinburgh EH8 8DX
**Tel:** +44 (0)131 556 5100 **Email:** bookinginfo@royalcollection.org.uk

## RED ROW

**Aberlady, East Lothian EH32 0DE**
Terraced Cottages.
**Location:** Main Street, Aberlady, East Lothian. Map Ref: 14:I7
**Tel:** 01875 870201 **Fax:** 01875 870620
**Open:** Exterior only. By appointment, Wemyss and March Estates Office, Longniddry, East Lothian EH32 0PY.
**Admission:** Please contact for details.

ROSSLYN CHAPEL
Chapel Loan, Roslin, Midlothian EH25 9PU
**Tel:** 0131 440 2159 **Email:** mail@rosslynchapel.com

## COREHOUSE

**Lanark ML11 9TQ**
Grade A Tudor style house designed by Sir Edward Blore and built in 1820s **Map Ref:** 13:E9, located on South bank of Clyde above Kirkfieldbank. At West Lodge, drive to bottom of hill.
**Tel:** 01555 663126 **Email:** dcranstouncorehouse@gmail.com
**Open:** 4-29 May & 3-7 Aug, Sat - Wed, Tours wkdays 1&2pm, wknds 2&3pm **Admission:** Adults £7, Conc. £4. Groups by arrangement.

GLASGOW CATHEDRAL
Castle Street, Glasgow G4 0QZ
**Tel:** 0141 552 6891

THE HILL HOUSE
Upper Colquhoun Street, Helensburgh G84 9AJ
**Tel:** 0844 493 2208 **Email:** thehillhouse@nts.org.uk

POLLOK HOUSE
2060 Pollokshaws Road, Glasgow G43 1AT
**Tel:** 0844 493 2202 **Email:** information@nts.org.uk

ABERDOUR CASTLE
Aberdour KY3 0SL
**Tel:** 01383 860519

ARBROATH ABBEY
Arbroath, Abbotsford, Tayside DD11 1EG
**Tel:** 01241 878756

ARBUTHNOTT HOUSE & GARDEN
Arbuthnott, Laurencekirk AB30 1PA
**Tel:** 01561 361226

BLAIR CASTLE & GARDENS
Blair Atholl, Pitlochry, Perthshire PH18 5TL
**Tel:** 01796 481207 **Email:** bookings@blair-castle.co.uk

BRANKLYN GARDEN
116 Dundee Road, Perth PH2 7BB
**Tel:** 0844 493 2193 **Email:** information@nts.org.uk

BRECHIN CASTLE
Brechin, Angus DD9 6SG
**Tel:** 01356 624566 **Email:** enquiries@dalhousieestates.co.uk

CAMBO GARDENS
Cambo Estate, Kingsbarns, St. Andrews, Fife KY16 8QD
**Tel:** 01333 450054 **Email:** cambo@camboestate.com

## CHARLETON HOUSE

**Colinsburgh, Leven, Fife KY9 1HG**
**Map Ref:** 14:I6 - Off A917
1 mile North West of Colinsburgh. 3 miles North West of Elie.
**Tel:** 01333 340249 / 00467 35463865
**Open:** 31 Aug to 29 Sept 2019, 12 noon-3pm.
Guided tours obligatory, admission every ½hr.
**Admission:** £12.

CLUNY HOUSE
Aberfeldy PH15 2JT
**Email:** wmattingley@btinternet.com

DUNNINALD, CASTLE & GARDENS
Montrose, Angus TD6 9BQ
**Tel:** 01674 672031 **Email:** visitorinformation@dunninald.com

DRUMMOND GARDENS
Muthill, Crieff, Perthshire, PH7 4HZ
**Tel:** 01764 681433 **Email:** info@drummondcastlegardens.co.uk

EDZELL CASTLE
Perthshire DD9 7UE
**Tel:** 01356 648 631

FALKLAND PALACE & GARDEN
Falkland, Fife KY15 7BU
**Tel:** 0844 493 2186 **Email:** information@nts.org.uk

GLAMIS CASTLE & GARDENS
Glamis, Forfar, Angus DD8 1RJ
**Tel:** 01307 840393 **Email:** enquiries@glamis-castle.co.uk

GLENEAGLES
Auchterarder, Perthshire PH3 1PJ
**Tel:** 01764 682388 **Email:** jmhaldane@gleneagles.org

HILL OF TARVIT MANSION HOUSE
Cupar, Fife KY15 5PB
**Tel:** 0844 493 2185 **Email:** hilloftarvit@nts.org.uk

HOUSE OF DUN
Montrose, Angus DD10 9LQ
**Tel:** 0844 493 2144 **Email:** houseofdun@nts.org.uk

HOUSE OF PITMUIES GARDENS
Guthrie, By Forfar, Angus DD8 2SN
**Tel:** 01241 828245

HUNTINGTOWER CASTLE
Perth PH1 3JL
**Tel:** 01738 627 231

KELLIE CASTLE & GARDEN
Pittenweem, Fife KY10 2RF
**Tel:** 0844 493 2184 **Email:** information@nts.org.uk

## MONZIE CASTLE

**Crieff, Perthshire PH7 4HD**
Built in 1791. Destroyed by fire in 1908 and rebuilt and furnished by Sir Robert Lorimer. Map Ref: 13:E5 - 2 miles North East of Crieff. **Tel:** 01764 653110 **Open:** May 18 - June 16, daily, 2-4.30pm. By appointment at other times. **Admission:** Adult £7, Child £1. Group rates available, contact property for details.

SCONE PALACE & GROUNDS
Perth PH2 6BD
**Tel:** 01738 552300 **Email:** visits@scone-palace.co.uk

ST ANDREW'S CASTLE
St Andrews, Fife KY16 9AR
**Tel:** 01334 477196

STRATHTYRUM HOUSE & GARDENS
St Andrews, Fife, KY16 9SF
**Tel:** 01334 473600 **Email:** info@strathtyrum.co.uk

## TULLIBOLE CASTLE

**Crook Of Devon, Kinross KY13 0QN**
Scottish tower house c1608 with ornamental fishponds, a roofless lectarn doocot, 9th Century graveyard. **Map Ref:** 13:F6 - B9097 1m E of Crook of Devon. **Tel:** 01577 840236
**Email:** info@tullibole.co.uk **Website:** www.tullibole.co.uk
**Open:** Last week in Aug-30 Sep: Tue-Sun, 1pm-4pm. **Admission:** Adult: £5.50, Child/Conc: £3.50. Free for Doors Open weekend.

ARDCHATTAN PRIORY GARDENS
Connel, Argyll PA37 1RQ
**Tel:** 01796 481355

ARDENCRAIG GARDENS
Ardencraig, Rothesay, Isle Of Bute, West Highlands PA20 9ZE
**Tel:** 01700 504644 **Email:** enquires@argyll-bute.gov.uk

ARDKINGLAS HOUSE & WOODLAND GARDEN
Estate Office, The Square, Cairndow, Argyll PA26 8BH
**Tel:** 01499 600261 **Email:** info@ardkinglas.com

ARDTORNISH ESTATE & GARDENS
Morvern, Nr. Oban, Argyll & Bute PA80 5UZ
**Tel:** 01967 421288 **Email:** stay@ardtornish.co.uk

ARDUAINE GARDEN
Arduaine, Oban PA34 4XQ
**Tel:** 0844 493 2216 **Email:** information@nts.org.uk

ATTADALE GARDENS
Attadale Gardens, Strathcarron, Wester Ross IV54 8YX
**Tel:** 01520 722217 **Email:** houseofkeil@hotmail.com

CASTLE STALKER
Portnacroish, Appin, Argyll PA38 4BL
**Tel:** 01631 730354 **Email:** enquiries@scottsabbotsford.co.uk

CRARAE GARDEN
Inveraray, Argyll, Bute & Loch Lomond PA32 8YA
**Tel:** 0844 493 2210 **Email:** CraraeGarden@nts.org.uk

DOUNE CASTLE
Doune FK16 6EA
**Tel:** 01786 841742

DUART CASTLE
Isle Of Mull, Argyll PA64 6AP
**Tel:** 01680 812309 **Email:** guide@duartcastle.com

INVERARAY CASTLE & GARDENS
Inveraray Castle, Inveraray, Argyll PA32 8XE
**Tel:** 01499 302203 **Email:** enquiries@inveraray-castle.com

KISIMUL CASTLE
Castlebay, Isle of Barra HS9 5UZ
**Tel:** 01871 810313

MOUNT STUART
Isle Of Bute PA20 9LR
**Tel:** 01700 503877 **Email:** contactus@mountstuart.com

STIRLING CASTLE
Stirling FK8 1EJ
**Tel:** 01786 450000 **Email:** hs.explorer@scotland.gsi.gov.uk

BALFLUIG CASTLE
Alford, Aberdeenshire AB33 8EJ
**Tel:** 020 7624 3200

CASTLE FRASER & GARDEN
Sauchen, Inverurie AB51 7LD
**Tel:** 0131 243 9300

CRAIG CASTLE
Rhynie, Huntly, Aberdeenshire AB54 4LP
**Tel:** 01464 861705

CRATHES CASTLE, GARDEN & ESTATE
Banchory, Aberdeenshire AB31 3QJ
**Tel:** 0844 493 2166 **Email:** crathes@nts.org.uk

DRUM CASTLE & GARDEN
Drumoak, Melrose, By Keith, Banffshire AB55 5JE
**Tel:** 01542 810332

DRUMMUIR CASTLE
Drummuir, Abbotsford, Melrose, Roxburghshire TD6 9BQ
**Tel:** 01542 810332

DUFF HOUSE
Banff AB45 3SX
**Tel:** 01261 818181 **Email:** hs.explorer@scotland.gsi.gov.uk

DUNOTTAR CASTLE
Stonehaven, Aberdeenshire AB39 2TL
**Tel:** 01569 762173 **Email:** dunnottarcastle@btconnect.com

FORT GEORGE
Grampian Highlands IV2 7TD
**Tel:** 01667 460232

FYVIE CASTLE & GARDEN
Turriff, Aberdeenshire AB53 8JS
**Tel:** 0844 493 2182 **Email:** information@nts.org.uk

GORDON CASTLE
Estate Office, Fochabers, Morayshire IV32 7PQ
**Tel:** 01343 820244

HADDO HOUSE
Tarves, Ellon, Aberdeenshire AB41 0ER
**Tel:** 0844 493 2179 **Email:** information@nts.org.uk

HUNTLY CASTLE
Huntly, North and Grampian AB54 4SH
**Tel:** 01466 793191

KILDRUMMY CASTLE
Alford, Aberdeenshire AB33 8RA
**Tel:** 01975 571331

LICKLEYHEAD CASTLE
Auchleven, Insch, Aberdeenshire AB52 6PN
**Tel:** 07495756122

PITMEDDEN GARDEN
Pitmedden Garden, Ellon, Aberdeenshire AB41 7PD
**Tel:** 01651 842352 **Email:** information@nts.org.uk

SPYNIE PALACE
Spynie Palace, Elgin IV30 5QG
**Tel:** 01343 546358

DAVID WELCH WINTER GARDENS
Duthie Park, Polmuir Road, Aberdeen AB11 7TH
**Tel:** 01224 585310 **Email:** wintergardens@aberdeencity.gov.uk

ARMADALE CASTLE & GARDENS
Aramadale, Sleat, Isle of Skye IV45 8RS
**Tel:** 01471 844305 **Email:** jan@armadalecastle.com

BALLINDALLOCH CASTLE
Ballindalloch, Banffshire AB37 9AX
**Tel:** 01807 500205 **Email:** enquiries@ballindallochcastle.co.uk

CASTLE & GARDENS OF MEY
Mey, Thurso, Caithness KW14 8XH
**Tel:** 01847 851473 **Email:** enquiries@castleofmey.org.uk

CAWDOR CASTLE & GARDENS
Cawdor Castle, Nairn IV12 5RD
**Tel:** 01667 404401 **Email:** info@cawdorcastle.com

THE DOUNE OF ROTHIEMURCHUS
By Aviemore PH22 1QP
**Tel:** 01479 812345 **Email:** info@rothie.net

DUNROBIN CASTLE & GARDENS
Golspie, Sutherland KW10 6SF
**Tel:** 01408 634081 **Email:** info@dunrobincastle.co.uk

EILEAN DONAN CASTLE
Dornie, Kyle Of Lochalsh, Wester Ross IV40 8DX
**Tel:** 01599 555202 **Email:** eileandonan@btconnect.com

INVEREWE GARDEN
Poolewe IV22 2LG
**Tel:** 01445 712952 **Email:** 01445 712952

SKAILL HOUSE
Breckness Estate, Sandwick, Orkney KW16 3LR
**Tel:** 01856 841501 **Email:** info@skaillhouse.co.uk

URQUHART CASTLE
Drumnadrochit, Loch Ness, Inverness-shire IV63 6XJ
**Tel:** 01456 450551

THE LIBRARY - DUNVEGAN CASTLE

# WALES

SOUTH WALES • MID WALES • NORTH WALES

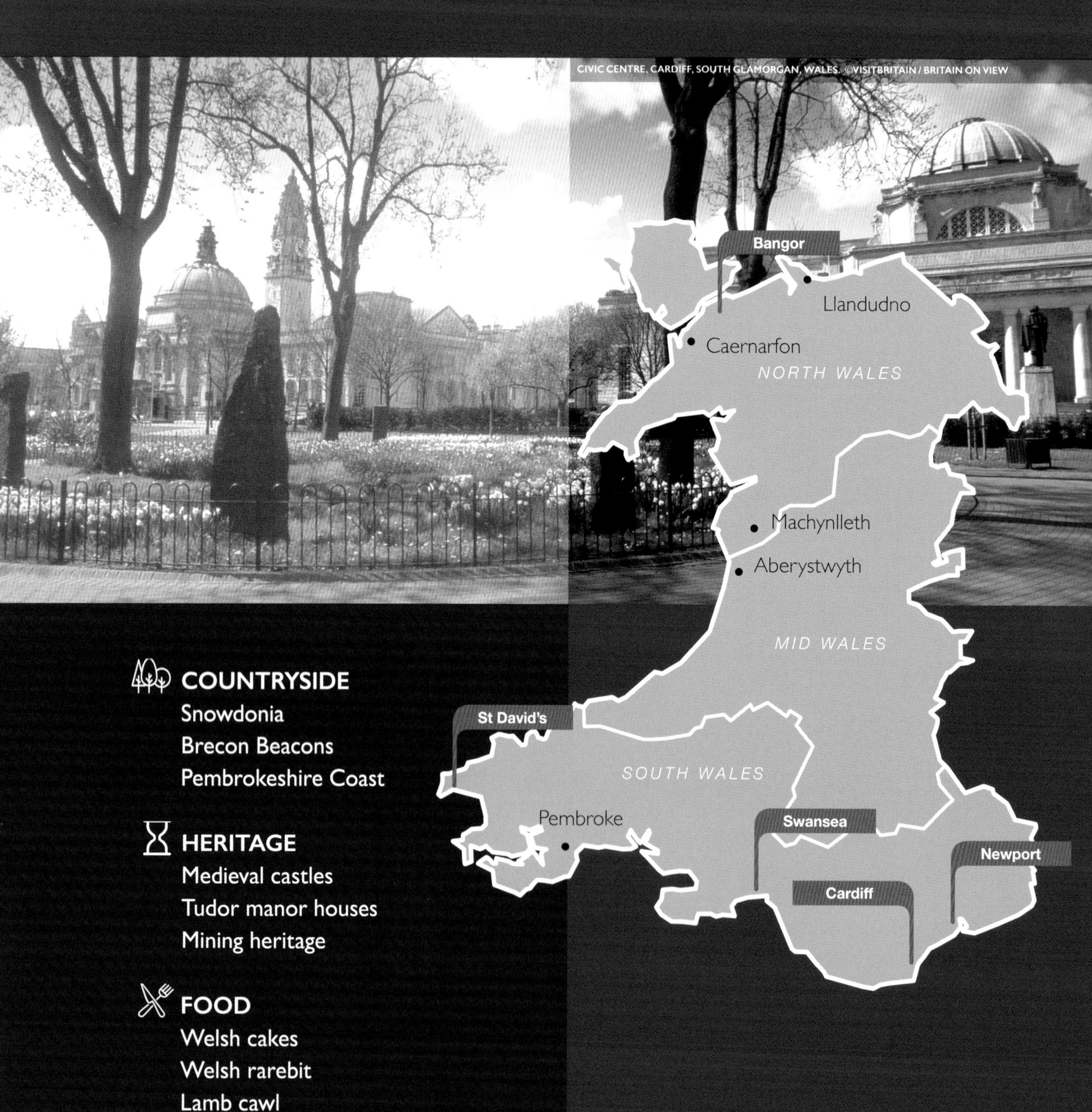


**COUNTRYSIDE**
Snowdonia
Brecon Beacons
Pembrokeshire Coast

**HERITAGE**
Medieval castles
Tudor manor houses
Mining heritage

**FOOD**
Welsh cakes
Welsh rarebit
Lamb cawl

# The Judge's Lodging

## The comfort of judges

Until 1972, law and order in Britain relied on a series of regional assise courts presided over by travelling judges. The judge arriving in the Welsh border town of Presteigne any time after 1829, found himself accommodated in a handsome set of comfortable lodgings, part of the new Court and Shire Hall. Visitors to the Judge's Lodgings in Presteigne today find an award-winning attraction that is less of a museum and more of a working Victorian household. In 1855, these were 'the most commodious and elegant apartments for a judge in all England and Wales' and the judge's private apartments and public rooms upstairs still contrast vividly with the servants' quarters and cells below.

DOWNSTAIRS AT THE JUDGE'S LODGING, THE SERVANTS' HALL RETAINS ITS VICTORIAN INTERIOR

The stories of the house are brought out by audio projections and the rooms have been restored with furnishings and objects from their Victorian heyday, many retrieved from the attics.

Judges were expected to entertain and the candlelit dining room was very much a public room, now readied for a dinner party and hung with portraits of local personalities. Downstairs, the well equipped Victorian kitchen, lit with gas lamps, is sometimes used for recreations of Victorian meals and specialities. At the centre of the building is the Courtroom, one of the least changed Victorian courts in the country. The real life of the Courtroom is conveyed by a dramatisation of the actual trial of one William Morgan, convicted of stealing ducks from nearby Llanshay Farm, which was conducted here in the 1860s while Morgan himself was held in the cells. A visit to this remarkable building will bring home the pleasures and pains of day-to-day life as you eavesdrop on the Victorian household as well as giving context to the administration of justice 150 years ago. ■

STAND AND BE JUDGED IN THE VICTORIAN COURTROOM AT THE JUDGE'S LODGING, PRESTEIGNE

THE JUDGE'S LODGING, PRESTEIGNE

# Wales

## Top 3 Venues

WEDDING MARQUEE DECOR FOR ALL SEASONS - ISCOYD PARK

### Iscoyd Park, Shropshire, North Wales

You can rest assured that any occasion planned by Iscoyd Park's events team will be designed with just you in mind as the house is available on an exclusive hire only basis. The permanent glass-fronted hard-floored marquee even has heating so you don't need to worry about the weather. Your guests can be accommodated in the 14 individually designed guest bedrooms and four further bedrooms in Wolvesacre Cottage at the edge of the estate. If your party is larger, local accommodation can be recommended. Iscoyd is on the Wales/Shropshire/Cheshire borders.

MANSION AND CLOISTER GARDEN AT ABERGLASNEY

### Aberglasney Gardens, Carmarthenshire, South Wales

Dating from the 16th century this grade II listed mansion and surrounding gardens had suffered a period of neglect before being rescued by the Aberglasney Restoration Trust in 1995 and restored to its former glory. Once home to Poets and Bishops the gardens can provide the perfect romantic backdrop to your special day. Small conferences can be held in the house, at the centre of which is the Ninfarium, a sub-tropical indoor garden. Two 5* star holiday cottages are situated within the grounds and offer the perfect opportunity to get away from it all for a while.

LLANDAFF CATHEDRAL

### Llandaff Cathedral, Cardiff, South Wales

Built in around 1120 the Cathedral has undergone several restorations since that time. On January 2nd 1941 Cardiff suffered its heaviest air raid of World War II. A German landmine exploded outside the South Aisle causing devastation that was unable to be fully rectified until the 1950s. Today the Cathedral is the Seat of the Bishop of Llandaff. This is a fantastic venue for couples opting for a traditional Christian ceremony. The City of Llandaff itself is also popular with Doctor Who fans as some of the recent series were filmed there.

NTS

**RHS Flower Show Cardiff, Bute Park, Cardiff** *12th-14th April 2019*

**Royal Welsh Agricultural Show, Llanelwedd** *22nd-25th July 2019*

**Green Man Festival, Brecon Beacons, Mid Wales** *5th-18th August 2019*

## Top 3 Annual Events

### Abergavenny Food Festival, South Wales
*21st & 22nd September 2019*

Chose from food and drink markets, chef demonstrations, cookery classes, talks, tasting and much more at this family-friendly event which offers free entry for children. Visit the Farmyard to see the livestock and find out more about farming today. The festival is home to the Young Chef of the Year Finals where the stars of the future are discovered. Fringe activities also take place in the wider community during and after the festival.

ABERGAVENNY FOOD FESTIVAL - ABERGAVENNY NOW

### Hay Literary Festival, Hay-On-Wye, Mid Wales *23rd May – 2nd June 2019*

This annual festival takes place in a tented village in Hay-On-Wye and features writers, academics, performers and artists that have been invited by the organisers to take part by speaking or exhibiting. Take part in a writers' workshop or a wine tasting session. Entry to the festival itself is free of charge and visitors pay just for the events they wish to attend. Parts of the festival are dedicated to families and children ensuring there is something for everyone to enjoy.

HAY FESTIVAL - BRITISH COUNCIL LITERATURE

### Wales Rally GB, Mid/North Wales (See website for 2019 Routes) *October 2019*

This world class 3-day event is part of the FIA World Rally Championship calendar. Spectators can watch the teams prepare for the race in the Rally Village which also hosts driver interviews, exhibitions, entertainment and refreshments. A great opportunity to spend some time admiring scenic Snowdonia as well as parts of the Welsh coastline, dense forests and pretty seaside towns. Spectators can expect to see up to two hundred cars competing on each race day.

WALES RALLY GB - WHEELS WITHIN WALES

# Wales

## Places to stay and eat

TRE-YSGAWEN HALL COUNTRY HOUSE HOTEL & SPA

### Tre-Ysgawen Hall Country House Hotel & Spa

Reached along a private wooded drive, Tre-Ysgawen is set in 11 acres of landscaped gardens and woodland a short drive inland from the breathtaking East coast of Anglesey. The house has been sympathetically and luxuriously refurbished and extended to become one of the leading country house hotels in North Wales.
Tre-Ysgawen Spa, built and equipped to the highest standards, was converted from the Victorian stables and retains many original features including the Clock Tower. Facilities include a 16m level-deck pool, salt inhalation room, ice fountain, experience shower, herbal sauna, whirlpool, beauty/therapy suite, and airconditioned gymnasium. Ideally placed for exploring Anglesey and North Wales.

Capel Coch, Llangefni, Isle of Anglesey LL77 7UR

01248 750750

www.treysgawen-hall.co.uk
enquiries@treysgawen-hall.co.uk

### Wolfscastle Country Hotel

*Hotel*

Wolfscastle, Haverfordwest
Pembrokeshire SA62 5LZ

01437 741225

www.thewolfscastle.com
enquiries@thewolfscastle.com

### Glen-Yr-Afon House

*Hotel*

Pontypool Road, Usk
Monmouthshire NP15 1SY

01291 672302

www.glen-yr-afon.co.uk
enquiries@glen-yr-afon.co.uk

### Y Tallbot

*Restaurant*

The Square, Tregaron
Ceredigion SY25 6JL

01974 298208

www.ytalbot.com
info@ytalbot.com

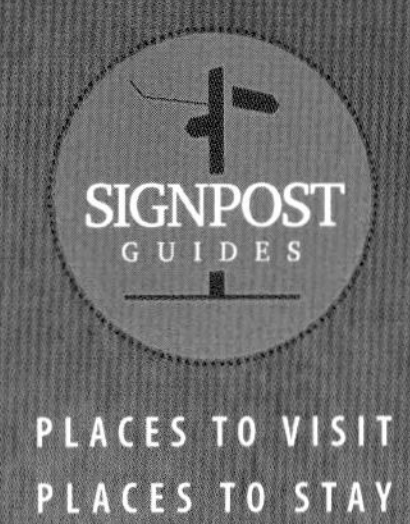




## Nanteos Mansion

Nanteos Mansion is a perfect blend of old and new, laid out across this historic Grade I listed Georgian mansion, its adjoining former bakery and Palladian carriage house. The mansion is unveiled at the end of a mile-long drive, with a small lake, walled garden and 40 acres of ancient woodland. Views take in nearby hills, four pillars stand sentinel at the front door, sofas by log fires await in the hall. The house dates back to 1731 but has medieval foundations. It is most famous for the Nanteos Cup - The Holy Grail - which, legend says, was borne here by the monks of Glastonbury Abbey during the Dissolution of the Monasteries. A magnificent renovation has brought the house back to vibrant life. Downstairs there's a morning room, sitting room bar and the elegant Nightingale Restaurant where you can sample chef/patron Nigel Jones' delicious cuisine. Upstairs the suites are grand and gracious, some panelled, others with fine wallpaper. The luxury rooms burst with colour and original art.

NANTEOS MANSION

Rhydyfelin, Aberystwyth, Ceredigion SY23 4LU

01970 600522

www.nanteos.com
info@nanteos.com

## The Hand at Llanarom

*Restaurant*

Llanarmon Dyffryn Ceiriog
Ceiriog Valley, Llangollen
Denbighshire LL20 7LD

01691 600666

www.thehandhotel.co.uk
reception@thehandhotel.co.uk

## Sophie Bach Tea & Coffee Room

*Tea Shop*

13 Cambrian Place
Aberystwyth SY23 1NT

07432 252671

www.facebook.com/sophiebachcafe/

## The Polkadot Teapot

*Tea Shop*

Swan Street
Llantrisant CF72 8EB

07730 776534

www.facebook.com
thepolkadotteapot/

Wales

## ABERGLASNEY GARDENS

**www.aberglasney.org**

Aberglasney was made famous by the BBC television series 'A Garden Lost in Time', which followed its restoration. Today it is quite simply one of Wales' finest gardens. A renowned plantsman's paradise with a unique Elizabethan cloister garden at its heart.

**CONTACT** Owner: Aberglasney Restoration Trust (Private Charitable Trust) Contact: Booking Department Tel: 01558 668998 Email: info@aberglasney.org

**LOCATION** Llangathen, Carmarthenshire, Wales SA32 8QH Map Ref: 5:F10 Aberglasney is 12 miles E of Carmarthen & 4 miles W of Llandeilo on A40 at Broad Oak.

**OPENING TIMES** All year: daily (except Christmas day). Apr-Oct: 10am-6pm, last entry 5pm. Nov-Mar: 10.30am-4pm, last entry 3pm.

**ADMISSION** Adult/Concessions £8.50 Children (16 years & under) FREE Groups 10+ Adult £7.25, By arrangement.

- More than 10 acres of historic gardens including walled gardens and woodland.
- Idyllically located Tearooms overlooking the Pool Garden.
- Discounted group admission.
- Shop and plant sales area.
- Exhibitions/events all year, see website.
- Two 5* self-catering cottages on site.
- Regular horticultural workshops.
- Mansion House and Garden weddings and receptions. Contact for information.

## LLANDAFF CATHEDRAL

**www.llandaffcathedral.org.uk**

A holy place of peace and tranquillity, art, architecture and music with a very warm welcome. Over 1500 yrs of history, standing on one of the oldest Christian sites in Britain. Works include Epstein, Piper, Pace, Rossetti, William Morris, Goscombe John, Frank Roper and Burne Jones. Services daily, some sung by the Cathedral Choir.

**CONTACT** Owner: Representative body of the Church In Wales Cathedral Office Tel: 02920 564554 E-mail: office@llandaffcathedral.org.uk

**LOCATION** Llandaff Cathedral Green, Cardiff CF5 2LA, drive West and cross River Taff; turn right into Cathedral Road (A4119) and follow signs to Llandaff. Map 2:L2.

**OPENING TIMES** Every week day 9am-6pm; Sun 7.30am-4.30pm.

**ADMISSION** Free. Donations gratefully received.

Nearby. Access. Shop. By arrangement. Guide dogs only. Events. Open all year round.

LLANDAFF CATHEDRAL

## LLANCAIACH FAWR MANOR

**www.llancaiachfawr.co.uk**

This superbly restored gentry manor house is no ordinary heritage attraction. History here is tangible. The costumed servants of the house are living and working in 1645 and allow you to share and engage in their world. Fires crackle, candles flicker and the sounds and smells of domestic life make your visit a memorable experience of the past. Meet ordinary people living in extraordinary times.

- No photography indoors.
- Lavatory facilities available.
- Baby changing facilities available.
- Closed 24 Dec - 1 Jan inclusive.
- 90 free spaces. Disabled spaces close to visitor centre entrance.
- Accessible WC's. Lift for access to upper floors.
- Dogs in grounds only. Not in walled gardens.
- Costumed 17th Century servants lead tours. Approx 1.5 hours.
- Tours, activities, trails & workshops.
- Licensed. 10am - 4pm. Hot & cold drinks, sandwiches cakes & snacks. Hot food served 12pm - 2pm.
- Licensed. Sun lunches and private functions.
- Boutique gift shop.
- Plant sales available.
- Provides a distinctive environment for any conference, business meeting, banquet or dinner party.
- Please see the 'Events' section of the website for all upcoming events.
- Ideal location for your wedding; overlooking the peaceful surroundings of the Rhymney Valley.

**CONTACT** Owner: Caerphilly County Borough Council Contact: Reception Tel: 01443 412248 Email: llancaiachfawr@caerphilly.gov.uk

**LOCATION** Gelligaer Road, Nelson, Treharris, Caerphilly County Borough CF46 6ER Map Ref: 2:M1 South side of B4254, 1 mile North of A472 at Nelson.

**TYPICALLY OPEN** 10am - 5pm Tue - Sun and BH Mons all year round. Last entry to the Manor 4pm. Closed 24 Dec - 1 Jan inclusive.

**ADMISSION** Adult £8.50, Conc £6.95, Child £6.95, Family (2+3) £25

COMMENDED
GREAT PLACES TO EAT

# ISCOYD PARK

**www.iscoydpark.com**

A red brick Georgian House in an idyllic 18th Century parkland setting situated on the Welsh/Shropshire border. Still a family home, Iscoyd has undergone a complete restoration over the last nine years whilst building a reputation as an award-winning wedding venue. We have 14 double bedrooms with plans to increase this number over the next few years. From September 2017 we bought all catering 'in-house' under the direction of our Michelin trained Head Chef. While continuing to focus on weddings, we will also be open for company retreats, private parties and photography/film shoots as well as hosting 'in-house' ticketed events such as pop-up restaurants, residential events and cooking classes. The house is only let on an exclusive basis meaning there is never more than one event occurring at any time.

- Open all year.
- Limited for coaches.
- WC's.
- Rooms in the Stable Rooms & the Laundry Cottage are let on a B&B basis.
- Obligatory.
- By arrangement.
- Licensed.
- Private dinners and weddings a speciality.
- Please see website for special events.
- Licensed.

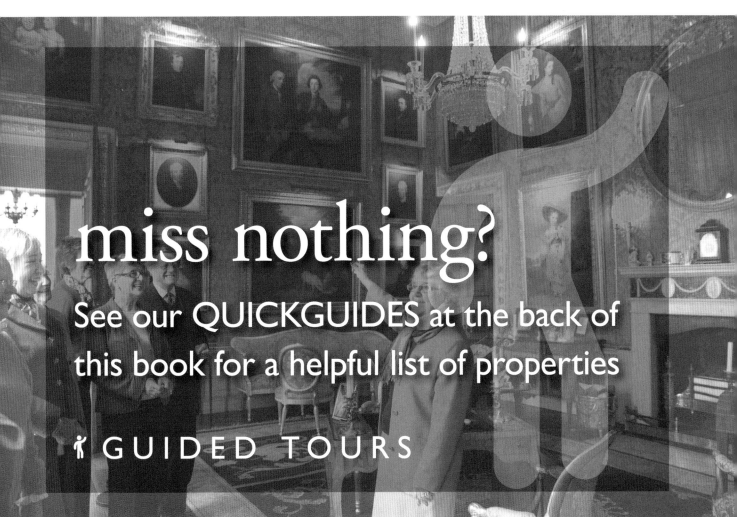

**CONTACT**

Contact/Owner: Philip L Godsal
Tel: 01948 780785
E-mail: info@iscoydpark.com

**LOCATION**

Nr Whitchurch, Shropshire SY13 3AT
Map Ref: 6:L4 - 2 miles West of Whitchurch off A525.

**OPENING TIMES**

House visits by written appointment.

## COCHWILLAN OLD HALL

A fine example of medieval architecture with the present house dating from 1450. It is thought to have been built by William Gryffydd who fought for Henry VII at Bosworth. Once owned in the 17th Century by John Williams who became Archbishop of York. The house was restored from a barn in 1971.

**CONTACT** Owner: RCH Douglas Pennant
Contact: Mark & Christopher Chenery
Tel: 01248 355139
Email: risboro@hotmail.co.uk

**LOCATION** Halfway Bridge, Bangor, Gwynedd LL57 3AZ

Map Ref: 5:G2 - 3 ½ miles South East of Bangor. 1 mile South East of Talybont off A55.

**OPENING TIMES** By appointment.

**ADMISSION** Please email or telephone for details.

For all enquiries please contact.
Parking available on site.
Accompanied tours available.
For all enquiries please contact.

## WERN ISAF

This Arts and Crafts house was built in 1900 by the architect H L North as his family home and contains much of the original furniture and William Morris fabrics.

Situated in a woodland garden with extensive views over the Menai Straits and Conwy Bay.

**CONTACT** Owner/Contact:
Mrs P J Phillips
Tel: 01248 680437

**OPENING TIMES** 2 - 30 May (Not Wed)
10:30am - 2:30pm

**LOCATION** Penmaen Park, Llanfairfechan, Conwy LL33 0RN
Map Ref: 5:G2 Off A55 midway between Bangor and Conwy.

**ADMISSION** Free.

For all further enquiries please contact.
Guided tours available.
Parking available on site.

## HARTSHEATH

A rock-faced stone Neo-Classical house substantially remodelled in the early 19th Century around an earlier 18th Century house.

Situated in a fine 19th Century landscaped park.

**CONTACT**
Owner: Dr M.C. Jones-Mortimer Will Trust
Contact: Dr Miranda Dechazal
Tel: 01352 770204

**LOCATION** Pontblyddyn, Mold, Flintshire CH7 4HP Map Ref: 6:J3 Access from A5104, 3.5 miles South East of Mold between Pontblyddyn and Penyffordd.

**OPENING TIMES** 2pm-5pm
May: 1, 2, 4, 5, 6, 8*,25, 26, 27
Jun: 8, 12*
July: 3*, 13*
Aug: 21*, 24, 25, 26
Sep: 7, 11, 12, 13, 14, 16*, 17, 18
(* Invitation to View days)

**ADMISSION** £6

For further enquiries please contact.
Guided tours available.
Parking available on site.

## Y FFERM

A late 16th Century small manorial house which underwent major alteration in the 17th Century.

**CONTACT**
Owner: Dr M.C. Jones-Mortimer Will Trust Contact: Dr Miranda Dechazal
Tel: 01352 770204

**LOCATION** Pontblyddyn, Mold, Flintshire CH7 4HN Map Ref: 6:J3 - Access from A541 in Pontblyddyn, 3½ miles South East of Mold.

**OPENING TIMES** 2pm-5pm
May: 1, 2, 4, 5, 6, 8*,25, 26, 27
Jun: 8, 12*
July: 3*, 13*
Aug: 21*, 24, 25, 26
Sep: 7, 11, 12, 13, 14, 16*, 17, 18
(* Invitation to View days)

**ADMISSION** £6

For all further enquiries please contact.
Guided tours available.
Parking available on site.

ABERDEUNANT
Taliaris, Llandeilo, Carmarthenshire SA19 6DL
**Tel:** 01588 650177 **Email:** aberdeunant@nationaltrust.org.uk

CAERPHILLY CASTLE
Caerphilly CF83 1JD
**Tel:** 029 2088 3143

CARDIFF CASTLE
Castle Street, Cardiff CF10 3RB
**Tel:** 029 2087 8100

CARDIGAN CASTLE
Green Street, Cardigan, Ceredigion SA43 1JA
**Tel:** 01239 615131 **Email:** cadwganbpt@btconnect.com

CARREG CENNEN CASTLE
Tir y Castell Farm, Llandeilo, Carmarthenshire SA19 6UA
**Tel:** 01558 822291

CASTELL COCH
Tongwynlais, Cardiff CF15 7JS
**Tel:** 029 2081 0101

CHEPSTOW CASTLE
Chepstow, Monmouthshire NP16 5EY
**Tel:** 01291 624065

CILGERRAN CASTLE
Cardigan, Pembrokeshire SA43 2SF
**Tel:** 01239 621339 **Email:** cilgerrancastle@nationaltrust.org.uk

**CORNWALL HOUSE**

**58 Monnow Street, Monmouth NP25 3EN**
Town house, Georgian street façade, walled garden.
**Location:** Half way down main shopping street, set back from street behind brown railings. Please use centre door. **Map Ref:** 6:L11
**Tel:** 01600 712031 **Email:** jane2harvey@tiscali.co.uk
**Open:** 2-5pm on Fridays in Jul & Aug and on 18 -22 Apr, 27 & 28 Apr, 4-6 May, 25-27 May, 24-26 Aug. **Adm:** Adult £4, Conc. £2.

**CRESSELLY**

**Kilgetty, Pembrokeshire SA68 0SP**
Home of the Allen family for 250 years. The house is of 1770 with matching wings of 1869 and contains good plasterwork and fittings of both periods. **Email:** hha@cresselly.com
**Map Ref:** 5:C12 **Website:** www.cresselly.com
**Open:** 7 May - 21 May (excluding 14 May), 15 Aug -29 Aug (excl 21st Aug), Tours 10am and 1pm. Mon 26 Aug - Tours 1pm, 2pm and 3pm. **Admission:** Adult £4.00, no children under 12.

ST DAVIDS BISHOP'S PALACE
St Davids, Pembrokeshire SA62 6PE
**Tel:** 01437 720517

DINEFWR
Llandeilo, Carmarthenshire SA19 6RT
**Tel:** 01443 336000 **Email:** cadw@wales.gsi.gov.uk

DYFFRYN GARDENS
St Nicholas, Vale of Glamorgan CF5 6SU
**Tel:** 02920 593328 **Email:** dyffryn@nationaltrust.org.uk

DYLAN THOMAS BIRTHPLACE
5 Cwmdonkin Drive, Uplands, Swansea, SA3 5AR
**Tel:** 01792 472 555 **Email:** info@dylanthomasbirthplace.com

FONMON CASTLE
Fonmon, Barry, Vale of Glamorgan, Wales, CF62 3ZN.
**Tel:** 01446 710206 **Email:** fonmon_castle@msn.com

ST FAGANS: NATIONAL HISTORY MUSEUM
Cardiff CF5 6XB
**Tel:** 029 2057 3500

GROSMONT CASTLE
Nr Abergavenny, Monmouthshire NP7 8EQ
**Tel:** 01443 336000 **Email:** cadw@wales.gsi.gov.uk

KIDWELLY CASTLE
Kidwelly, Carmarthenshire SA17 5BQ
**Tel:** 01554 890104

THE KYMIN
The Round House, The Kymin, Monmouth NP25 3SF
**Tel:** 01600 719241 **Email:** kymin@nationaltrust.org.uk

LAUGHARNE CASTLE
King Street, Laugharne, Carmarthenshire SA33 4SA
**Tel:** 01994 427906

LLANVIHANGEL COURT
Nr Abergavenny, Monmouthshire NP7 8DH
**Tel:** 01873 890217 **Email:** jclarejohnson@googlemail.com

MARGAM COUNTRY PARK & CASTLE
Margam, Port Talbot, West Glamorgan SA13 2TJ
**Tel:** 01639 881635 **Email:** margampark@npt.gov.uk

MONMOUTH CASTLE
Castle Hill, Monmouth NP25 3BS
**Tel:** 01443 336000 **Email:** cadw@wales.gsi.gov.uk

NATIONAL BOTANIC GARDEN OF WALES
Llanarthne, Carmarthenshire SA32 8HG
**Tel:** 01558 667149 **Email:** info@gardenofwales.org.uk

OGMORE CASTLE & STEPPING STONES
Ogmore, St Brides Major, Vale Of Glamorgan CF32 0QP
**Tel:** 01443 336000 **Email:** cadw@wales.gsi.gov.uk

OXWICH CASTLE
Oxwich, Swansea SA3 1NG
**Tel:** 01792 390359

PEMBROKE CASTLE
Pembroke SA71 4LA
**Tel:** 01646 681510 **Email:** info@pembrokecastle.co.uk

PICTON CASTLE & WOODLAND GARDENS
Taliaris, Nr Haverfordwest, Pembrokeshire SA62 4AS
**Tel:** 01437 751326 **Email:** info@pictoncastle.co.uk

RAGLAN CASTLE
Raglan, Monmouthshire NP15 2BT
**Tel:** 01291 690228

SKENFRITH CASTLE
Skenfrith, Nr Abergavenny, Monmouthshire NP7 8UH
**Tel:** 01443 336000 **Email:** cadw@wales.gsi.gov.uk

STRADEY CASTLE
Llanelli, Carmarthenshire SA15 4PL
**Tel:** 01554 774626 **Email:** info@stradeycastle.com

TINTERN ABBEY
Tintern NP16 6SE
**Tel:** 01291 689251 **Email:** TinternAbbey@wales.gsi.gov.uk

TREBINSHWN
Llangasty, Nr Brecon, Powys LD3 7PX
**Tel:** 01874 730653 **Fax:** 01874 730843

TREDEGAR HOUSE & PARK
Newport, South Wales NP10 8YW
**Tel:** 01633 815880 **Email:** tredegar@nationaltrust.org.uk

**TREOWEN**

**Wonastow, Monmouth, NP25 4DL**
The most important early 17th Century gentry house in the county. Particularly fine open well staircase. **Location:** Map 6:K11. OS Ref SO 461 111. 3 m WSW of Monmouth. **Tel** 07530 357390 **Website:** www.treowen.co.uk **Open:** 24 May- 30 Aug Fri 10am-4pm. Also Sat & Sun 23-24 & 30-31 Mar, 6-7 Apr and 11-12 & 18-19 May 2-5pm **Admission:** £6.00. Free to HH Members on Fridays only

TRETOWER COURT & CASTLE
Taliaris, Llandeilo, Carmarthenshire SA19 6DL
**Tel:** 01588 650177 **Email:** aberdeunant@nationaltrust.org.uk

TUDOR MERCHANT'S HOUSE
Quay Hill, Tenby, Pembrokeshire SA70 7BX
**Tel:** 01834 842279 **Email:** tudormerchantshouse@nationaltrust.org.uk

USK CASTLE
Monmouth Road, Usk, Monmouthshire NP5 1SD
**Tel:** 01291 672563 **Email:** info@uskcastle.com

ABERCAMLAIS HOUSE
Brecon, Powys, Wales, LD3 8EY
**Tel:** 07789930064

ABERYSTWYTH CASTLE
Aberystwyth, Ceredigion SY23 2AG
**Tel:** 01970 612125

CANOLFAN OWAIN GLYNDWR
Heol Maengwyn, Machylleth, Powys SY20 8EE
**Tel:** 01654 703336 **Email:** glyndwr.enquiries@canolfanglyndwr.org

GLANSEVERN HALL GARDENS
Glansevern, Berriew, Welshpool, Powys SY21 8AH
**Tel:** 01686 640644 **Email:** glansevern@yahoo.co.uk

GREGYNOG
Tregynon, Nr Newtown, Powys SY16 3PW
**Tel:** 01686 650224 **Email:** enquiries@gregynog.org

**HAFOD ESTATE**

**Pontrhyd-y-groe, Ystrad Meurig, Ceredigion SY25 6DX**
Ten miles of restored walks, the epitome of the Picturesque and Sublime. Set in 500 acres of wood and parkland featuring cascades, bridges and wonderful views.

**Tel:** 01974 282568 **Email:** trust@hafod.org
**Map Ref:** 5:G8 **Website:** www.hafod.org
**Open:** All year - daylight hours. **Admission:** Free.

THE HALL AT ABBEY-CWM-HIR
Nr Llandrindod Wells, Powys LD1 6PH
**Tel:** 01597 851727 **Email:** info@abbeycwmhir.com

THE JUDGE'S LODGING
Broad Street, Presteigne, Powys, Mid Wales, LD8 2AD
**Tel:** 01544 260650 **Email:** info@judgeslodging.org.uk

LLANERCHAERON
Ciliau Aeron, Nr Aberaeron, Ceredigion SA48 8DG
**Tel:** 01545 570200 **Email:** llanerchaeron@nationaltrust.org.uk

POWIS CASTLE & GARDEN
Welshpool, Powys SY21 8RF
**Tel:** 01938 551929 **Email:** powiscastle@nationaltrust.org.uk

TREWERN HALL
Trewern, Welshpool, Powys SY21 8DT
**Tel:** 01938 570243

ABERCONWY HOUSE
Castle Street, Conwy LL32 8AY
**Tel:** 01492 592246 **Email:** aberconwyhouse@nationaltrust.org.uk

BEAUMARIS CASTLE
Beaumaris, Anglesey LL58 8AP
**Tel:** 01248 810361

BODNANT GARDEN
Tal-Y-Cafn, Colwyn Bay LL28 5RE
**Tel:** 01492 650460 **Email:** bodnantgarden@nationaltrust.org.uk

BODRHYDDAN HALL
Bodrhyddan, Rhuddlan, Rhyl, Denbighshire LL18 5SB
**Tel:** 01745 590414

CAERNARFON CASTLE
Castle Ditch, Caernarfon LL55 2AY
**Tel:** 01286 677617

CHIRK CASTLE
Chirk LL14 5AF
**Tel:** 01691 777701 **Email:** chirkcastle@nationaltrust.org.uk

CONWY CASTLE
Conwy LL32 8AY
**Tel:** 01492 592358

CRICCIETH CASTLE
Castle Street, Criccieth, Gwynedd LL52 0DP
**Tel:** 01766 522227 **Email:** cadw@wales.gsi.gov.uk

DOLBELYDR
Trefnant, Denbighshire LL16 5AG
**Tel:** 01628 825925 **Email:** bookings@landmarktrust.org.uk

ERDDIG
Wrexham LL13 0YT
**Tel:** 01978 355314 **Email:** erddig@nationaltrust.org.uk

FLINT CASTLE
Castle St, Flint, Flintshire CH6 5HF
**Tel:** 01443 336000

Wales

GWYDIR CASTLE
Llanrwst, Conwy LL26 0PN
**Tel:** 01492 641687 **Email:** info@gwydircastle.co.uk

HARLECH CASTLE
Castle Square, Harlech LL46 2YH
**Tel:** 01766 780552

PENRHYN CASTLE
Bangor, Gwynedd LL57 4HN
**Tel:** 01248 353084 **Email:** penrhyncastle@nationaltrust.org.uk

PLAS BRONDANW GARDENS, CAFFI & SHOP
Plas Brondanw, Llanfrothen, Gwynedd LL48 6SW
**Tel:** 01766 772772 / 01743 239236 **Email:** enquiries@plasbrondanw.com

PLAS MAWR
High Street, Conwy LL32 8DE
**Tel:** 01492 580167

PLAS NEWYDD
Hill Street, Llangollen, Denbighshire LL20 8AW
**Tel:** 01978 862834 **Email:** heritage@denbighshire.gov.uk

PLAS NEWYDD HOUSE & GARDENS
Llanfairpwll, Anglesey LL61 6DQ
**Tel:** 01248 714795 **Email:** plasnewydd@nationaltrust.org.uk

PLAS YN RHIW
Rhiw, Pwllheli, Gwynedd LL53 8AB
**Tel:** 01758 780219 **Email:** plasynrhiw@nationaltrust.org.uk

PORTMEIRION
Minffordd, Penrhyndeudraeth, Gwynedd LL48 6ER
**Tel:** 01766 772311 **Email:** enquiries@portmeirion-village.com

RHUDDLAN CASTLE
Castle Street, Rhuddlan, Rhyl LL18 5AD
**Tel:** 01745 590777

TOWER
Nercwys Road, Mold, Flintshire CH7 4EW
**Tel:** 01352 700220 **Email:** enquiries@towerwales.co.uk

LUXURY ACCOMMODATION AT ISCOYD PARK

# NORTHERN IRELAND

ANTRIM • ARMAGH • DOWN
FERMANAGH • LONDONDERRY • TYRONE

GIANT'S CAUSEWAY, NORTH COAST OF NORTHERN IRELAND, ©VISITBRITAIN/DISCOVER NORTHERN IRELAND

**COUNTRYSIDE**
Causeway Coast
Mourne Mountains
Lough Neagh

**HERITAGE**
Norman castles
Plantation houses
Game of Thrones locations

**FOOD**
Stout & whiskey
Potato breads
Irish stew

# Baronscourt

## Escape to the Country

When the first Earls of Abercorn came to Baronscourt in the 17th century, Ireland was a land inured in conflict. Four centuries later, today's Dukes of Abercorn live in one of the most tranquil places in the British Isles. If a traditional rural escape is what you want, the Baronscourt Estate is hard to beat. At the heart of the estate is a neo-classical mansion built for the 8th Earl in 1778 and remodelled by Sir John Soane in 1791.

STAY A NIGHT IN THE PEACE OF BARONSCOURT

Although the house is not open, the landscape setting offers plenty of variety for visitors. The pleasure grounds are lapped by forest and the wild heather-clad Sperrin mountains. The estate is renowned for the quality of its sport, rough shooting, winter woodcock shoots and salmon or pike fishing on the River Mourne. If you forgot to pack your tweeds, there is a golf course and gentler walks around the parkland and woodlands, particularly spectacular in Spring for the bluebell, rhododendron and azalea trails. Spot deer, red squirrels and plentiful wildlife or explore the nearby Neolithic tombs which clearly show that people have been drawn to this place from the earliest times. The more adventurous can take a mountain hiking trail on foot or by bike, the estate provides detailed trail maps so there is no chance of getting lost.

AUTUMN AT BARONSCOURT

Cottages in the converted stables, which date from 1819, each accommodate four on a self-catering basis. Visitors are bringing activity back to the stable courtyard which, a century ago, was busy with the family's carriages, horses, ponies, grooms and postilions. The Governor's Lodge was once the billet for the guard assigned to the 3rd Duke while Governor of Northern Ireland in the 1920s though today offers guests considerably more comfort while the upstairs living room of the Clock Tower has far-reaching views over the parkland. ■

THE GOVERNOR'S LODGE, TRANSFORMED INTO A COTTAGE FOR 4

# Northern Ireland

## Top 3 Venues

WEDDING COUPLE WALK IN HILLSBOROUGH CASTLE GROUNDS - GRAHAM CRICHTON PHOTOGRAPHY

### Hillsborough Castle, County Down

Hillsborough Castle is an official residence of the Royal Family in Northern Ireland and is conveniently situated just 20 minutes from Belfast. Choose one of the staterooms and be surrounded by oil paintings from the Royal Collection. For larger gatherings, the Dining Room Terrace and the South Lawn Marquee areas can hold up to 350 guests. The Throne Room, often used by Her Majesty the Queen when she is in residence, may be used for meetings and conferences for up to 120 people seated theatre-style.

BARONS COURT

### Barons Court, County Tyrone

The Carriage House at Barons Court seats up to 60 guests and can be hired for corporate and private events whatever the occasion. It features high ceilings and two stunning open fireplaces at each end of the room which are still in use today. The room is often used for fundraising by local church and community groups as well as being part of corporate Land Rover Experience Days. As its name suggests The Carriage Room was originally used to house the horse carriages for many years before the horse-drawn carriage was replaced by the car.

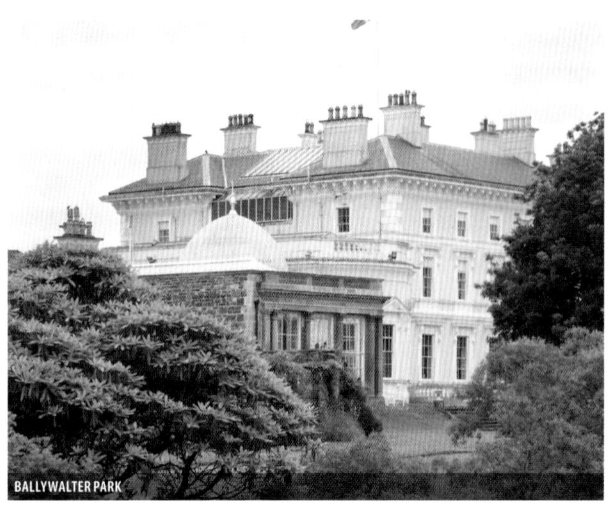
BALLYWALTER PARK

### Ballywalter Park, County Down

Ballywalter Park has played host to royalty on several occasions since its construction in the mid 19th century, most notable to the Duke and Duchess of York (later to become King George VI and Queen Elizabeth) in 1924. The venue is ideal for corporate events, product launches and meetings. Outdoor pursuits can be arranged in the surrounding pleasure grounds. Overnight stays are available in the nine double and two twin en-suite rooms plus one further double with use of private bathroom.

**The Open Championship, Royal Portrush, County Antrim** *14th - 21st July 2019*

**World Senior Snooker Championships, Belfast** *3rd March 2019*

**North West 200 Superbike Races, North Coast** *16th & 18th May 2019*

## Top 3 Annual Events

### Belfast Culture Night, Belfast *September 2019*

On Culture Night Belfast plays host to free events for all the family across the city. There are musical performances, art, comedy and circus events, street performers, cookery demonstrations and choral music. Events take place in the streets as well as on specially constructed stages. The event has been running since 2008 and grows bigger every year.

CULTURE NIGHT BELFAST - BELFAST LIVE

### Titanic Belfast *All Year*

Take a walking tour from the spot RMS Titanic was launched to discover more about the ship and her journey. The Titanic Experience takes you through nine levels of interactive galleries, from the shipyards to the bottom of the ocean. Full-scale reconstructions, dark rides and special effects all add to the journey of discovery. In Hamilton Dock visitors can step aboard SS Nomadic, tender ship to RMS Titanic. SS Nomadic has been restored as she would have been in 1911 and is the last remaining White Star Line ship in the world.

TITANIC BELFAST - VISIT BELFAST

### Game of Thrones Tours, Various Locations *All Year*

Filming for the popular television show has taken place across multiple locations in Northern Ireland and numerous speciality tours are on offer for fans of the show. If an organised tour is not your thing then why not do your own research and design your own route. Among the most popular destinations are Castle Ward in County Down, which doubles as the house of Stark, and Portstewart Strand in County Derry which is shown as the Kingdom of Dorne. Dragonstone is really Mussenden Temple in County Antrim.

GAME OF THRONES TOURS - VISIT BELFAST

# BALLYWALTER PARK

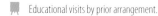

www.ballywalterpark.com

Ballywalter Park was built in the Italianate Palazzo style, by Sir Charles Lanyon for Andrew Mulholland. A Gentleman's wing was added in 1870 for Andrew's son, John Mulholland, later 1st Baron Dunleath. The house has a fine collection of original furniture and paintings, complemented by contemporary pieces.

- No photography indoors.
- Toilet facilities available.
- Accepts Euros.
- By appointment only.
- Parking available.
- Twelve en suite bedrooms available for group tours and corporate events.
- Obligatory.
- Educational visits by prior arrangement.
- Refreshments by prior arrangement.
- Lunches and dinners can be booked by prior arrangement.
- The house is available for corporate and incentive events, lunches and dinners.
- Special events on occasion throughout the year.
- Film and television location.

**CONTACT** Owner: The Lord and Lady Dunleath
Contact: Mrs Sharon Graham, The Estate Office
Tel: 028 4275 8264 Fax: 028 4275 8818
Email: enq@dunleath-estates.co.uk

**LOCATION** Ballywalter, Newtownards, County Down BT22 2PP
Map Ref: 18:P4 Off A2 on unclassified road, 1 km South of Ballywalter village.

**OPENING TIMES**
By prior appointment only; please contact The Estate Office.

**ADMISSION** House or Gardens: £10 per person
House & Gardens: £17 per person Groups: Max 50 people (No group discount) Refreshments by arrangement.

## BARONS COURT

www.barons-court.com

The home of the Duke and Duchess of Abercorn, Barons Court was built between 1779 and 1782, and subsequently extensively remodelled by John Soane (1791), William and Richard Morrison (1819-1841), Sir Albert Richardson (1947-49) and David Hicks (1975-76).

**CONTACT** Contact: The Estate Office Tel: 028 8166 1683
Email: info@barons-court.com

**LOCATION** Newtownstewart, Omagh, Co Tyrone BT78 4EZ
Map Ref:18:M3 - 5km South West of Newtownstewart.

**OPENING TIMES** By appointment only **ADMISSION** Tour of House and/or Gardens: £14 per person Tour inc. tea/coffee/scones: £19 per person Groups max. 50.

No photography. Open all year by appointment. Parking available. Partially accessible. Holiday cottages, 4 star rated by Northern Ireland Tourist Board. Guided tours by arrangement. The Carriage Room in the Stable Yard.

BARONS COURT ESTATE

BALLYWALTER PARK - STAIRCASE

HILLSBOROUGH CASTLE - WEDDING VENUE

# HILLSBOROUGH CASTLE & GARDENS

**www.hrp.org.uk/hillsborough-castle**

From grand family home to Northern Ireland's only royal residence, Hillsborough Castle and Gardens has welcomed the world and witnessed pivotal chapters in British and Irish politics for over three centuries. Enjoy a tour of the elegant State Rooms including the majestic Throne Room and graceful Drawing Room. Outside, explore 100 acres of glorious gardens including peaceful woodland, meandering waterways and picturesque glens.

From spring 2019, visitors can enjoy a new and improved visitor experience, including the newly restored Walled Garden, free carpark, café and shop.

- Toilet changing facilities.
- Baby changing facilities.
- Free parking on site from spring 2019. Check website for details
- Complimentary tickets for adult carers are available to collect on the day of your visit.
- Assistance dogs only.
- Offer reduced admission for group bookings.

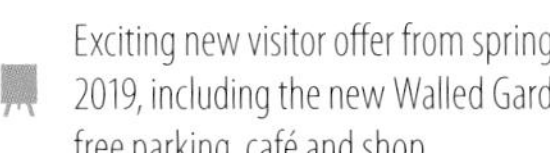

- Exciting new visitor offer from spring 2019, including the new Walled Garden, free parking, café and shop.

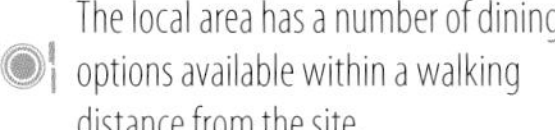

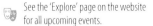

- The local area has a number of dining options available within a walking distance from the site.
- See the 'Explore' page on the website for all upcoming events.

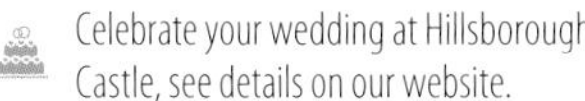

- Celebrate your wedding at Hillsborough Castle, see details on our website.
- Available to host private and corporate dinners, conferences and other celebrations.

**CONTACT** Owner: Historic Royal Palaces Tel: 028 9268 1300 Email: hillsboroughcastle@hrp.org.uk

**LOCATION** Hillsborough BT26 6AG Map Ref: 18:N5

**OPENING TIMES** Gardens open daily, castle tours daily from March 2019 and on specific days before March, check website for details. Closed 24-26 December and 1 January. New visitor facilities opening spring 2019.

**ADMISSION** See website. House by guided tour only, advance booking recommended.

ARTHUR ANCESTRAL HOME
Cullybackey, County Antrim BT42 1AB
**Tel:** 028 2563 8494 **Email:** devel.leisure@ballymena.gov.uk

BELFAST CASTLE
Cave Hill, Antrim Road, Belfast BT15 5GR
**Tel:** 028 9077 6925

BOTANIC GARDENS
Stransmillis Road, Belfast BT7 1LP
**Tel:** 028 9031 4762

GLENARM CASTLE WALLED GARDEN
2 Castle Lane, Glenarm, Larne, County Antrim BT44 0BQ
**Tel:** 028 2884 1305

MONTALTO HOUSE
5 Craigaboney Road, Bushmills, County Antrim BT57 8XD
**Tel:** 028 2073 1257 **Email:** montaltohouse@btconnect.com

NORTHERN IRELAND ASSEMBLY
Parliament Buildings , Ballymiscaw, Stormont, Belfast BT4 3XX
**Tel:** 028 90 521137 **Email:** info@niassembly.gov.uk

SENTRY HILL
Ballycraigy Road, Newtownabbey BT36 5SY
**Tel:** 028 9034 0000

ARDRESS HOUSE
64 Ardress Road, Portadown, Co Armagh BT62 1SQ
**Tel:** 028 8778 4753 **Email:** ardress@nationaltrust.org.uk

BENBURB CASTLE
Servite Priory, Main Street, Benburb, Co Tyrone BT71 7JZ
**Tel:** 028 3754 8241 **Email:** servitepriory@btinternet.com

DERRYMORE
Bessbrook, Newry, Co Armagh BT35 7EF
**Tel:** 028 8778 4753 **Email:** derrymore@nationaltrust.org.uk

GILFORD CASTLE ESTATE
Banbridge Road, Gilford BT63 6DT
**Tel:** 028 4062 3322 **Email:** gilford@irishfieldsports.com

AUDLEYS CASTLE
Strangford, County Down BT30 7LP
**Tel:** 028 9054 3034

BANGOR ABBEY
Bangor, County Down BT20 4JF
**Tel:** 028 9127 1200

BANGOR CASTLE
Bangor, County Down BT20 4BN
**Tel:** 028 9127 0371

CLOUGH CASTLE
Clough Village, Downpatrick, County Down 028 9054 3034
**Tel:** 028 9054 3034

DUNDRUM CASTLE
Dundrum Village, Newcastle, County Down BT33 0QX
**Tel:** 028 9054 3034

GREENCASTLE ROYAL CASTLE
Cranfield Point, Kilkeel, County Down BT34 4LR
**Tel:** 028 9054 3037

GREY ABBEY
9-11 Church Street, Greyabbey, County Down BT22 2NQ
**Tel:** 028 9054 6552

GREY POINT FORT
Crawfordsburn Country Park, Helens Bay, Co. Down BT19 1LE
**Tel:** 028 9185 3621

HELENS TOWER
Clandeboye Estate, Bangor BT19 1RN
**Tel:** 028 9185 2817

INCH ABBEY
Downpatrick, County Down BT30 9AX
**Tel:** 028 9181 1491

KILCLIEF CASTLE
Strangford, County Down
**Tel:** 028 9054 3034

MAHEE CASTLE
Mahee Island, Comber, Newtownards BT23 6EP
**Tel:** 028 9182 6846

MOVILLA ABBEY
63 Movilla Road, Newtownards BT23 8EZ
**Tel:** 028 9181 0787

NEWRY CATHEDRAL
38 Hill Street, Newry, County Down BT34 1AT
**Tel:** 028 3026 2586

PORTAFERRY CASTLE
Castle Street, Portaferry, County Down BT22 1NZ
**Tel:** 028 9054 3033

THE PRIORY
Newtownards, County Down
**Tel:** 028 9054 3037

QUOILE CASTLE
Downpatrick, County Down BT30 7JB
**Tel:** 028 9054 3034

RINGHADDY CASTLE
Killyleagh, County Down
**Tel:** 028 9054 3037

ROWALLANE GARDEN
Ballynahinch, Co Down BT24 7LH
**Tel:** 028 9751 0721 **Email:** rowallane@nationaltrust.org.uk

SKETRICK CASTLE
Whiterock, County Down BT23 6QA
**Tel:** 028 4278 8387

STRANGFORD CASTLE
Strangford, County Down
**Tel:** 028 9054 3034

CROM ESTATE
Newtownbutler, County Fermanagh BT92 8AP
**Tel:** 028 6773 8118

ENNISKILLEN CASTLE
Castle Barracks, Enniskillen, County Fermanagh BT74 7HL
**Tel:** 028 6632 5000 **Email:** castle@fermanagh.gov.uk

FLORENCE COURT
Enniskillen, Co Fermanagh BT92 1DB
**Tel:** 028 6634 8249 **Email:** florencecourt@nationaltrust.org.uk

BELLAGHY BAWN
Castle Street, Bellaghy, County Londonderry BT45 8LA
**Tel:** 028 7938 6812

DUNGIVEN CASTLE
Main Street, Dungiven, Co Londonderry BT47 4LF
**Tel:** 028 7774 2428 **Email:** enquiries@dungivencastle.com

DUNGIVEN PRIORY & O CAHANS TOMB
Dungiven, County Londonderry BT47 4PF
**Tel:** 028 7772 2074

THE GUILDHALL
Guildhall Square, Londonderry BT48 6DQ
**Tel:** 028 7137 7335

MOUNTSANDAL FORT
Mountsandal Road, Coleraine, Co Londonderry BT52 1PE
**Tel:** 027 7034 4723 **Email:** coleraine@nitic.net

PREHEN HOUSE
Prehen Road, Londonderry BT47 2PB
**Tel:** 028 7131 2829 **Email:** colinpeck@yahoo.com

SAINT COLUMB'S CATHEDRAL
London Street, Derry, County Londonderry BT48 6RQ
**Tel:** 028 7126 7313 **Email:** stcolumbs@ic24.net

SAMPSON'S TOWER
Limavady TIC, 7 Connell Street, Limavady BT49 0HA
**Tel:** 028 7776 0307

ANTRIM CASTLE GARDENS & CLOTWORTHY HOUSE
Randalstown Road, Antrim BT41 4LH
**Tel:** 028 9448 1338 **Email:** culture@antrimandnewtwonabbey.gov.uk

BENVARDEN GARDEN
Benvarden, Dervock, County Antrim BT53 6NN
**Tel:** 028 2074 1331

CARRICKFERGUS CASTLE
Marine Highway, Carrickfergus, County Antrim BT38 7BG
**Tel:** 028 9335 1273 **Email:** scmenquiries@communities-ni.gov.uk

CASTLE COOLE
Enniskillen, Co Fermanagh BT74 6JY
**Tel:** 028 6632 2690 **Email:** castlecoole@nationaltrust.org.uk

CASTLE WARD HOUSE & DEMESNE
Strangford, Downpatrick, Co Down BT30 7LS
**Tel:** 028 4488 1204 **Email:** castleward@nationaltrust.org.uk

DOWN CATHEDRAL
Cathedral Office, English Street, Downpatrick, County Down BT30 6AB
**Tel:** 028 4461 4922 **Email:** info@downcathedral.org

DUNLUCE CASTLE
87 Dunluce Road, Portrush, County Antrim BT57 8UY
**Tel:** 028 2073 1938 **Email:** scmenquiries@communities-ni.gov.uk

KILLYLEAGH CASTLE
Killyleagh, Downpatrick, Co Down BT30 9QA
**Tel:** 028 4482 8261 **Email:** gawnrh@gmail.com

LISSAN HOUSE
Drumgrass Road, Cookstown, County Tyrone BT80 9SW
**Tel:** 028 8676 3312 **Email:** lissan.house@btconnect.com

MONTALTO ESTATE & CARRIAGE ROOMS
Ballynahinch, Co. Down BT24 8AY
**Tel:** 028 9756 6100 **Email:** info@montaltoestate.com

MOUNT STEWART
Newtonards, Co Down BT22 2AD
**Tel:** 028 4278 8387 **Email:** mountstewart@nationaltrust.org.uk

SEAFORDE GARDENS
Seaforde, County Down BT30 8PG
**Tel:** 028 4481 1225 **Email:** springhill@nationaltrust.org.uk

SPRINGHILL HOUSE
20 Springhill Road, Moneymore, Co Londonderry BT45 7NQ
**Tel:** 028 8674 8210 **Email:** devel.leisure@ballymena.gov.uk

THE ARGORY
Moy, Dungannon, Co Tyrone BT71 6NA
**Tel:** 028 8778 4753 **Email:** argory@nationaltrust.org.uk

CASTLEDERG CASTLE
Castle Park, Castlederg, County Tyrone BT81 7AS
**Tel:** 028 7138 2204

HARRY AVERYS CASTLE
Old Castle Road, Newtownstewart BT82 8DY
**Tel:** 028 7138 2204

KILLYMOON CASTLE
Killymoon Road, Cookstown, County Tyrone
**Tel:** 028 8676 3514

NEWTOWNSTEWART CASTLE
Townhall Street, Newtownstewart BT78 4AX
**Tel:** 028 6862 1588 **Email:** nieainfo@doeni.gov.uk

SAINT MACARTAN'S CATHEDRAL
Clogher, County Tyrone BT76 0AD
**Tel:** 028 0478 1220

SIR JOHN DAVIES CASTLE
Castlederg, County Tyrone BT81 7AS
**Tel:** 028 7138 2204

TULLYHOGUE FORT
B162, Cookstown, County Tyrone BT80 8UB
**Tel:** 028 8676 6727

# QUICK GUIDES

# PLANT SALES

## LONDON



## SOUTH EAST



## SOUTH WEST



## EAST OF ENGLAND



## EAST MIDLANDS



## HEART OF ENGLAND



## YORKSHIRE & THE HUMBER



## NORTH WEST



## SCOTLAND



## WALES

PLANT FAIR - HOLKHAM HALL

# PLACES TO STAY

ISCOYD PARK STABLE COTTAGES

# ❄ OPEN ALL YEAR

# CIVIL WEDDINGS

## LONDON



## SOUTH EAST



## SOUTH WEST



## EAST OF ENGLAND



## EAST MIDLANDS



## HEART OF ENGLAND



## YORKSHIRE & THE HUMBER



## NORTH WEST



## NORTH EAST

# PRIVATE HIRE

LEEDS CASTLE

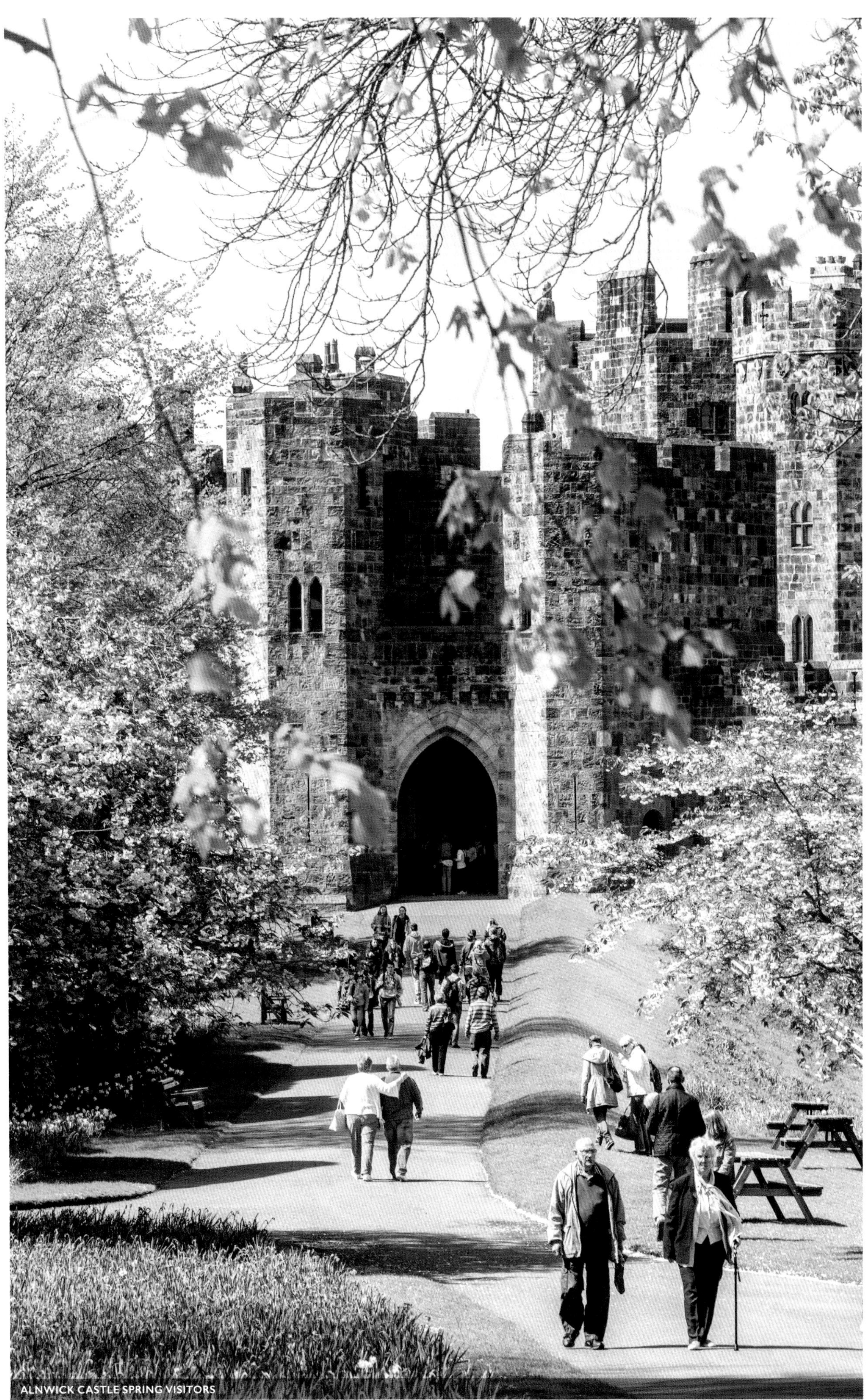

ALNWICK CASTLE SPRING VISITORS

# GUIDED TOURS

## LONDON



## SOUTH EAST



## SOUTH WEST



## EAST OF ENGLAND

# DOGS WELCOME

BRONZE GREYHOUNDS AT CHATSWORTH ©LINNIE FLICKR

## YORKSHIRE & THE HUMBER



## NORTH WEST



## NORTH EAST



## SCOTLAND



## WALES



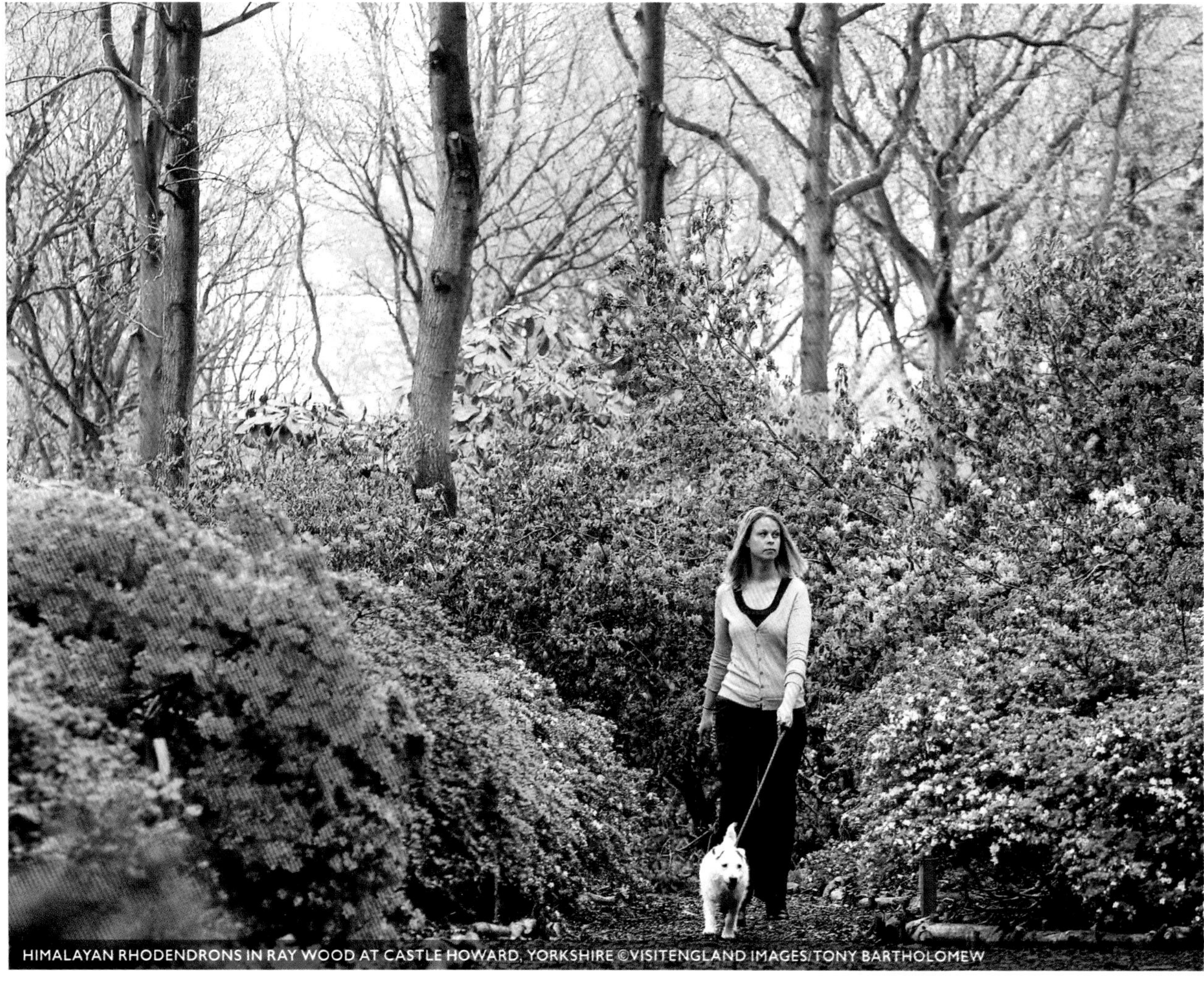

HIMALAYAN RHODENDRONS IN RAY WOOD AT CASTLE HOWARD, YORKSHIRE ©VISITENGLAND IMAGES/TONY BARTHOLOMEW

# IN THE MOVIES

## SOUTH EAST



## SOUTH WEST



## EAST OF ENGLAND



## EAST MIDLANDS



## HEART OF ENGLAND



## YORKSHIRE & THE HUMBER



## NORTH WEST



## NORTH EAST



## SCOTLAND



## NORTHERN IRELAND

BLENHEIM PALACE IS AN OBVIOUS FIT FOR PERIOD DRAMAS.

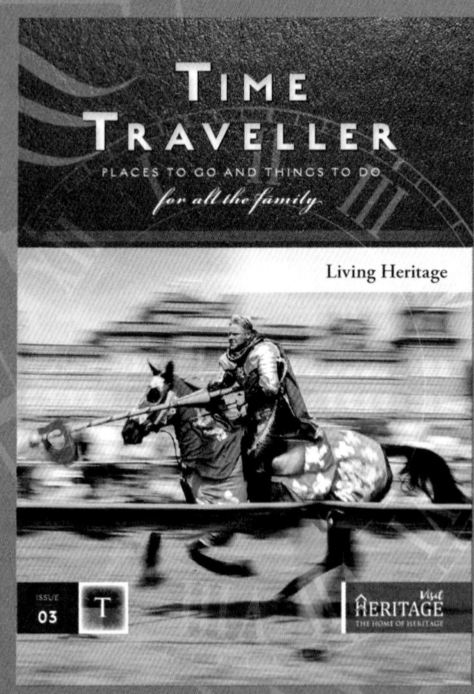

# TIME TRAVELLER

# ENJOY HERITAGE
## BECOME A
# TIME TRAVELLER

**TIME TRAVELLER** is a quarterly publication from Visit Heritage, publishers of Hudsons Heritage Guide, Britain's leading annual guide to historic places for the last 30 years.

Time Traveller brings you interesting and informative articles about Britain's heritage and shows you some of the best places to visit and to stay with a list of up coming attractions. It has fun stuff too, with a heritage quiz, recipe and pages for children to enjoy.

Each issue has a distinct theme; previous issues have focused on Gardens, Living History and Ghosts & Ghouls.

**TIME TRAVELLER** is only available to Time Traveller members - to find out about this and other benefits of joining, go to the Visit Heritage website and click JOIN US.

 020 3880 5059

 sales@visitheritage.co.uk

 www.visitheritage.co.uk

The Signpost Guide celebrates it's 80th edition with a new look and format.
SIGNPOST
SIGNPOST GUIDES
PREMIER SELECTION
2019
80TH EDITION
RRP £10.99
Visit HERITAGE THE HOME OF HERITAGE
LASTINGHAM GRANGE COUNTRY HOUSE HOTEL
UK HERITAGE AWARDS 2019
Visit HERITAGE THE HOME OF HERITAGE
SIGNPOST GUIDES
020 3880 5059
sales@visitheritage.co.uk
www.visitheritage.co.uk
PLACES TO VISIT
PLACES TO STAY

John O'Groats
MAP 15
MAP 16
MAP 17
Western Isles
Highlands & Skye
Grampian Highlands
MAP 12
MAP 13
MAP 14
Perthshire / Fife
West Highlands & Islands
Edinburgh
Greater Glasgow
Borders
MAP 18
North'land
MAP 9
South West Scotland
MAP 10
MAP 11
Tyne & Wear
Co.Durham
Northern Ireland
Cumbria
Isle of Man
Yorkshire
Lancs
MAP 5
MAP 6
MAP 7
MAP 8
Cheshire
Derbys
Notts
Lincs
North Wales
Staffs
Leics & Rutland
Norfolk
Salop
West Mids
Mid Wales
Northants
Cambs
Worcs
Warks
Suffolk
Beds
Herefordshire
Bucks
South Wales
Glos
Oxon
Herts
Essex
MAP 1
MAP 2
MAP 3
MAP 4
London
Berks
Wilts
Surrey
Kent
Somerset
Hants
W.Sussex
E.Sussex
Devon
Dorset
Isles of Wight
Cornwall
CHANNEL ISLANDS
Guernsey
Jersey
Alderney
Sark

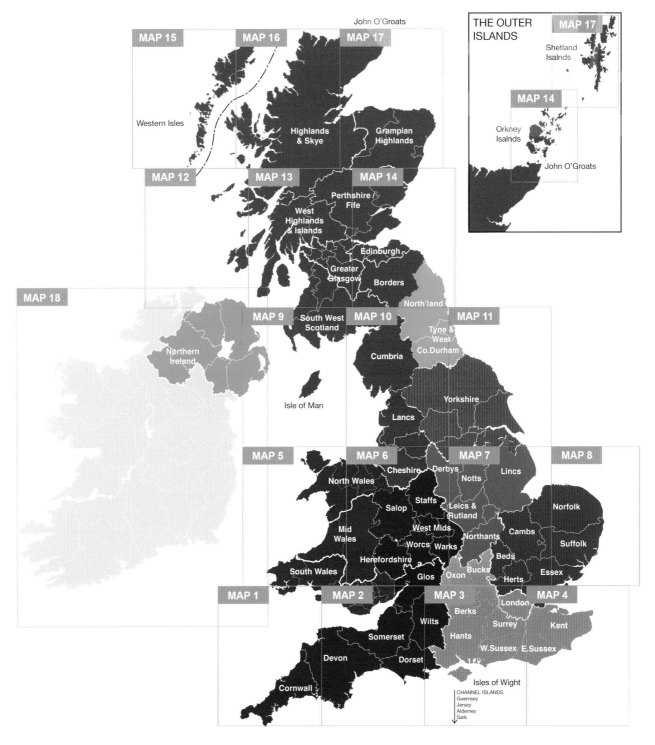

THE OUTER ISLANDS
MAP 17
Shetland Isalnds
MAP 14
Orkney Isalnds
John O'Groats

# MAP 1

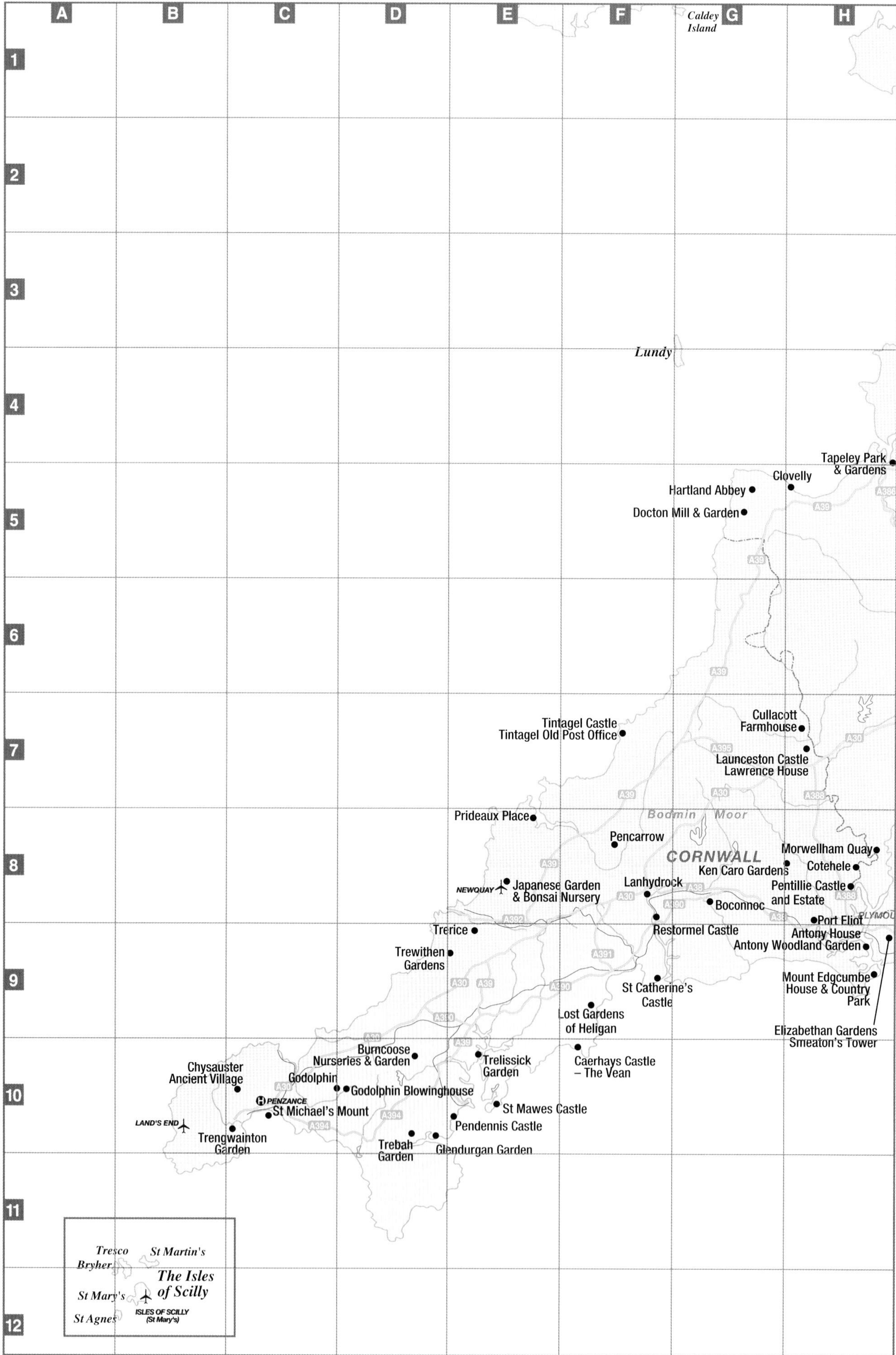

A
B
C
D
E
F
G
H
1
2
3
4
5
6
7
8
9
10
11
12
Caldey Island
Lundy
Tapeley Park & Gardens
Clovelly
Hartland Abbey
Docton Mill & Garden
Cullacott Farmhouse
Tintagel Castle
Tintagel Old Post Office
Launceston Castle
Lawrence House
Bodmin Moor
Prideaux Place
Pencarrow
CORNWALL
Morwellham Quay
Ken Caro Gardens
Cotehele
Lanhydrock
Pentillie Castle and Estate
NEWQUAY
Japanese Garden & Bonsai Nursery
Boconnoc
Port Eliot
PLYMOU
Trerice
Restormel Castle
Antony House
Antony Woodland Garden
Trewithen Gardens
St Catherine's Castle
Mount Edgcumbe House & Country Park
Lost Gardens of Heligan
Elizabethan Gardens
Smeaton's Tower
Burncoose Nurseries & Garden
Trelissick Garden
Caerhays Castle – The Vean
Chysauster Ancient Village
Godolphin
Godolphin Blowinghouse
PENZANCE
St Michael's Mount
St Mawes Castle
LAND'S END
Pendennis Castle
Trengwainton Garden
Trebah Garden
Glendurgan Garden
Tresco
St Martin's
Bryher
The Isles of Scilly
St Mary's
ISLES OF SCILLY (St Mary's)
St Agnes

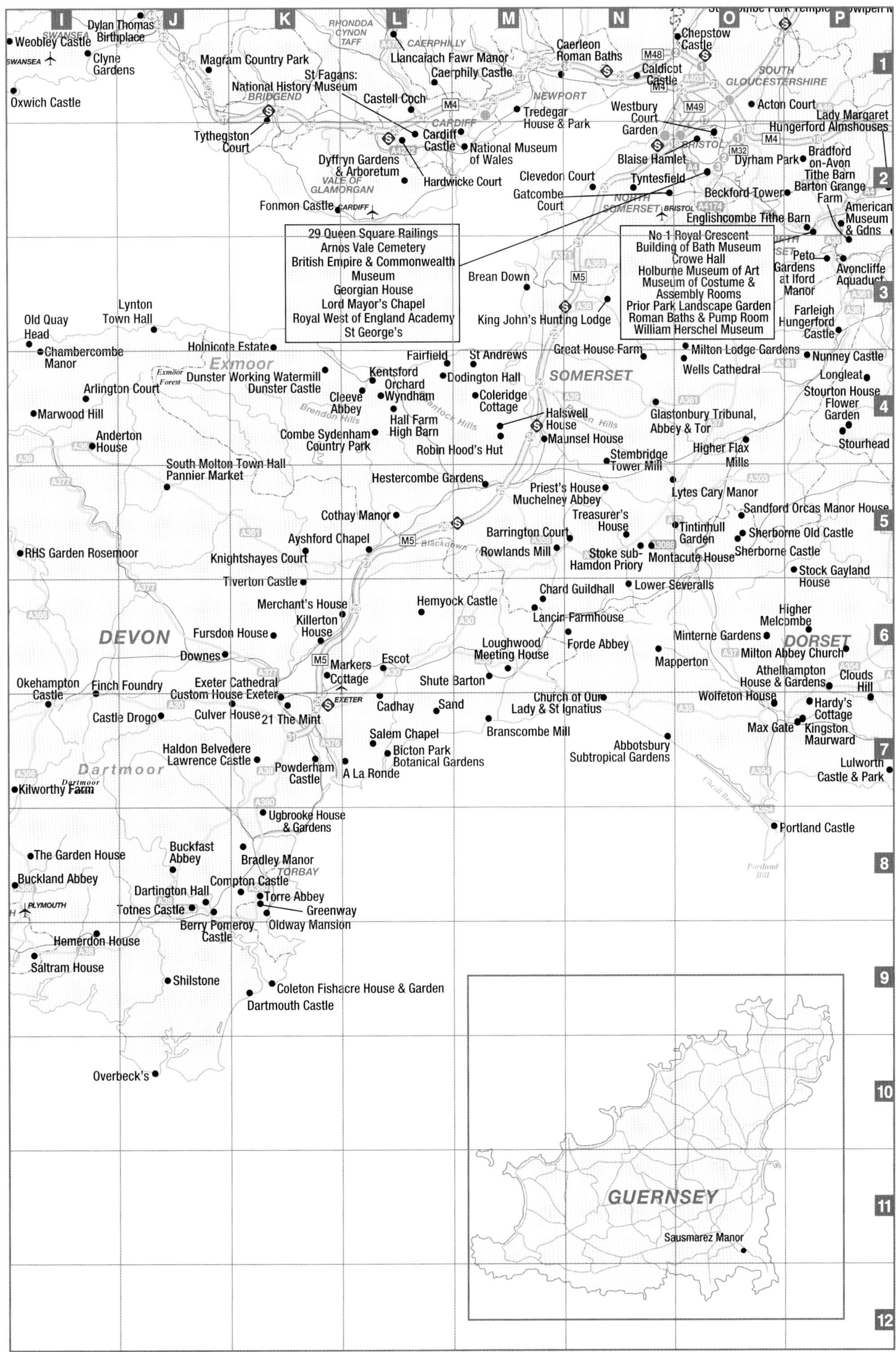

Dylan Thomas Birthplace
Weobley Castle
Clyne Gardens
Oxwich Castle
Magram Country Park
St Fagans: National History Museum
Tythegston Court
Llancaiach Fawr Manor
Caerphilly Castle
Castell Coch
Cardiff Castle
National Museum of Wales
Dyffryn Gardens & Arboretum
Hardwicke Court
Fonmon Castle
Caerleon Roman Baths
Tredegar House & Park
Chepstow Castle
Caldicot Castle
Westbury Court Garden
Blaise Hamlet
Clevedon Court
Gatcombe Court
Tyntesfield
Acton Court
Lady Margaret Hungerford Almshouses
Dyrham Park
Bradford on-Avon Tithe Barn
Barton Grange Farm
Beckford Tower
Englishcombe Tithe Barn
American Museum & Gdns
29 Queen Square Railings
Arnos Vale Cemetery
British Empire & Commonwealth Museum
Georgian House
Lord Mayor's Chapel
Royal West of England Academy
St George's
No 1 Royal Crescent
Building of Bath Museum
Crowe Hall
Holburne Museum of Art
Museum of Costume & Assembly Rooms
Prior Park Landscape Garden
Roman Baths & Pump Room
William Herschel Museum
Peto Gardens at Iford Manor
Avoncliffe Aquaduct
Farleigh Hungerford Castle
Brean Down
King John's Hunting Lodge
Lynton Town Hall
Old Quay Head
Chambercombe Manor
Holnicote Estate
Exmoor
Dunster Working Watermill
Dunster Castle
Arlington Court
Marwood Hill
Anderton House
Fairfield
St Andrews
Kentsford
Orchard Wyndham
Cleeve Abbey
Dodington Hall
Coleridge Cottage
Hall Farm High Barn
Combe Sydenham Country Park
Robin Hood's Hut
Halswell House
Maunsel House
Great House Farm
Milton Lodge Gardens
Nunney Castle
Wells Cathedral
SOMERSET
Longleat
Stourton House Flower Garden
Stourhead
Glastonbury Tribunal, Abbey & Tor
Higher Flax Mills
Stembridge Tower Mill
South Molton Town Hall Pannier Market
Hestercombe Gardens
Priest's House
Muchelney Abbey
Lytes Cary Manor
Sandford Orcas Manor House
Cothay Manor
Treasurer's House
Tintinhull Garden
Sherborne Old Castle
Sherborne Castle
Ayshford Chapel
Barrington Court
Rowlands Mill
Stoke sub-Hamdon Priory
Montacute House
RHS Garden Rosemoor
Knightshayes Court
Tiverton Castle
Stock Gayland House
Chard Guildhall
Lower Severalls
Merchant's House
Hemyock Castle
Killerton House
Lancin Farmhouse
Higher Melcombe
DEVON
Fursdon House
Loughwood Meeting House
Forde Abbey
Minterne Gardens
DORSET
Downes
Mapperton
Milton Abbey Church
Markers Cottage
Escot
Athelhampton House & Gardens
Clouds Hill
Okehampton Castle
Finch Foundry
Exeter Cathedral
Custom House Exeter
Shute Barton
Church of Our Lady & St Ignatius
Wolfeton House
Hardy's Cottage
Castle Drogo
Culver House
21 The Mint
Cadhay
Sand
Max Gate
Kingston Maurward
Salem Chapel
Branscombe Mill
Haldon Belvedere
Lawrence Castle
Bicton Park Botanical Gardens
Abbotsbury Subtropical Gardens
Lulworth Castle & Park
Powderham Castle
A La Ronde
Dartmoor
Kilworthy Farm
Ugbrooke House & Gardens
Portland Castle
The Garden House
Buckfast Abbey
Bradley Manor
Buckland Abbey
Dartington Hall
Compton Castle
Torre Abbey
Totnes Castle
Greenway
Berry Pomeroy Castle
Oldway Mansion
Hemerdon House
Saltram House
Shilstone
Coleton Fishacre House & Garden
Dartmouth Castle
Overbeck's
GUERNSEY
Sausmarez Manor

# MAP 3

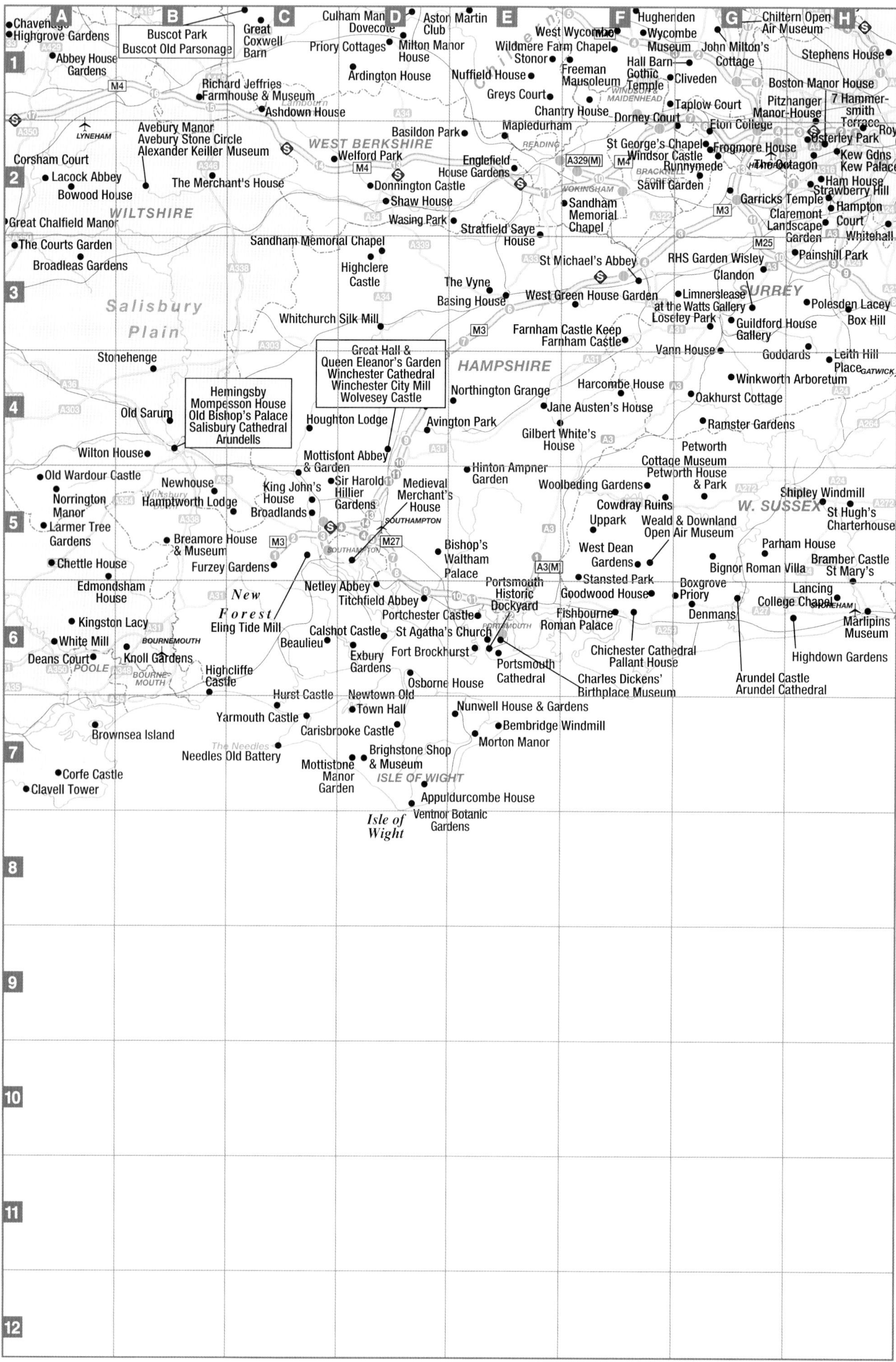

A
B
C
D
E
F
G
H
1
2
3
4
5
6
7
8
9
10
11
12
Highgrove Gardens
Abbey House Gardens
Buscot Park
Buscot Old Parsonage
Great Coxwell Barn
Culham Manor Dovecote
Priory Cottages
Milton Manor House
Aston Martin Club
West Wycombe
Wildmere Farm Chapel
Stonor
Hughenden
Wycombe Museum
John Milton's Cottage
Chiltern Open Air Museum
Stephens House
Richard Jeffries Farmhouse & Museum
Ashdown House
Ardington House
Nuffield House
Greys Court
Freeman Mausoleum
Hall Barn
Gothic Temple
Cliveden
Boston Manor House
Pitzhanger Manor-House
7 Hammersmith Terrace
Taplow Court
Chantry House
Dorney Court
Eton College
Osterley Park
Corsham Court
Lacock Abbey
Bowood House
Avebury Manor
Avebury Stone Circle
Alexander Keiller Museum
The Merchant's House
WEST BERKSHIRE
Welford Park
Basildon Park
Mapledurham
Englefield House Gardens
Donnington Castle
Shaw House
Wasing Park
St George's Chapel
Windsor Castle
Runnymede
Frogmore House
The Octagon
Kew Gdns
Kew Palace
Savill Garden
Ham House
Strawberry Hill
Garricks Temple
Hampton Court
Claremont Landscape Garden
Whitehall
WILTSHIRE
Great Chalfield Manor
The Courts Garden
Broadleas Gardens
Sandham Memorial Chapel
Stratfield Saye House
Highclere Castle
St Michael's Abbey
RHS Garden Wisley
Painshill Park
Clandon
SURREY
Salisbury Plain
The Vyne
Basing House
West Green House Garden
Limnerslease at the Watts Gallery
Loseley Park
Guildford House Gallery
Polesden Lacey
Box Hill
Whitchurch Silk Mill
Farnham Castle Keep
Farnham Castle
Great Hall &
Queen Eleanor's Garden
Winchester Cathedral
Winchester City Mill
Wolvesey Castle
HAMPSHIRE
Vann House
Goddards
Leith Hill Place
Stonehenge
Northington Grange
Harcombe House
Winkworth Arboretum
Hemingsby
Mompesson House
Old Bishop's Palace
Salisbury Cathedral
Arundells
Old Sarum
Houghton Lodge
Avington Park
Jane Austen's House
Oakhurst Cottage
Gilbert White's House
Ramster Gardens
Wilton House
Mottisfont Abbey & Garden
Hinton Ampner Garden
Petworth Cottage Museum
Petworth House & Park
Old Wardour Castle
Newhouse
Norrington Manor
Hamptworth Lodge
King John's House
Broadlands
Sir Harold Hillier Gardens
Medieval Merchant's House
Woolbeding Gardens
Cowdray Ruins
Uppark
Shipley Windmill
St Hugh's Charterhouse
W. SUSSEX
Weald & Downland Open Air Museum
Larmer Tree Gardens
Breamore House & Museum
Furzey Gardens
Bishop's Waltham Palace
West Dean Gardens
Parham House
Bramber Castle
St Mary's
Chettle House
Bignor Roman Villa
Stansted Park
Edmondsham House
New Forest
Eling Tide Mill
Netley Abbey
Titchfield Abbey
Portsmouth Historic Dockyard
Goodwood House
Boxgrove Priory
Lancing College Chapel
Portchester Castle
Fishbourne Roman Palace
Denmans
Kingston Lacy
Calshot Castle
St Agatha's Church
Marlipins Museum
White Mill
Beaulieu
Exbury Gardens
Fort Brockhurst
Chichester Cathedral
Pallant House
Highdown Gardens
Deans Court
Knoll Gardens
Highcliffe Castle
Portsmouth Cathedral
Charles Dickens' Birthplace Museum
Arundel Castle
Arundel Cathedral
Osborne House
Hurst Castle
Newtown Old Town Hall
Nunwell House & Gardens
Yarmouth Castle
Bembridge Windmill
Brownsea Island
Carisbrooke Castle
Morton Manor
Needles Old Battery
Brighstone Shop & Museum
Mottistone Manor Garden
ISLE OF WIGHT
Corfe Castle
Clavell Tower
Appuldurcombe House
Ventnor Botanic Gardens
Isle of Wight

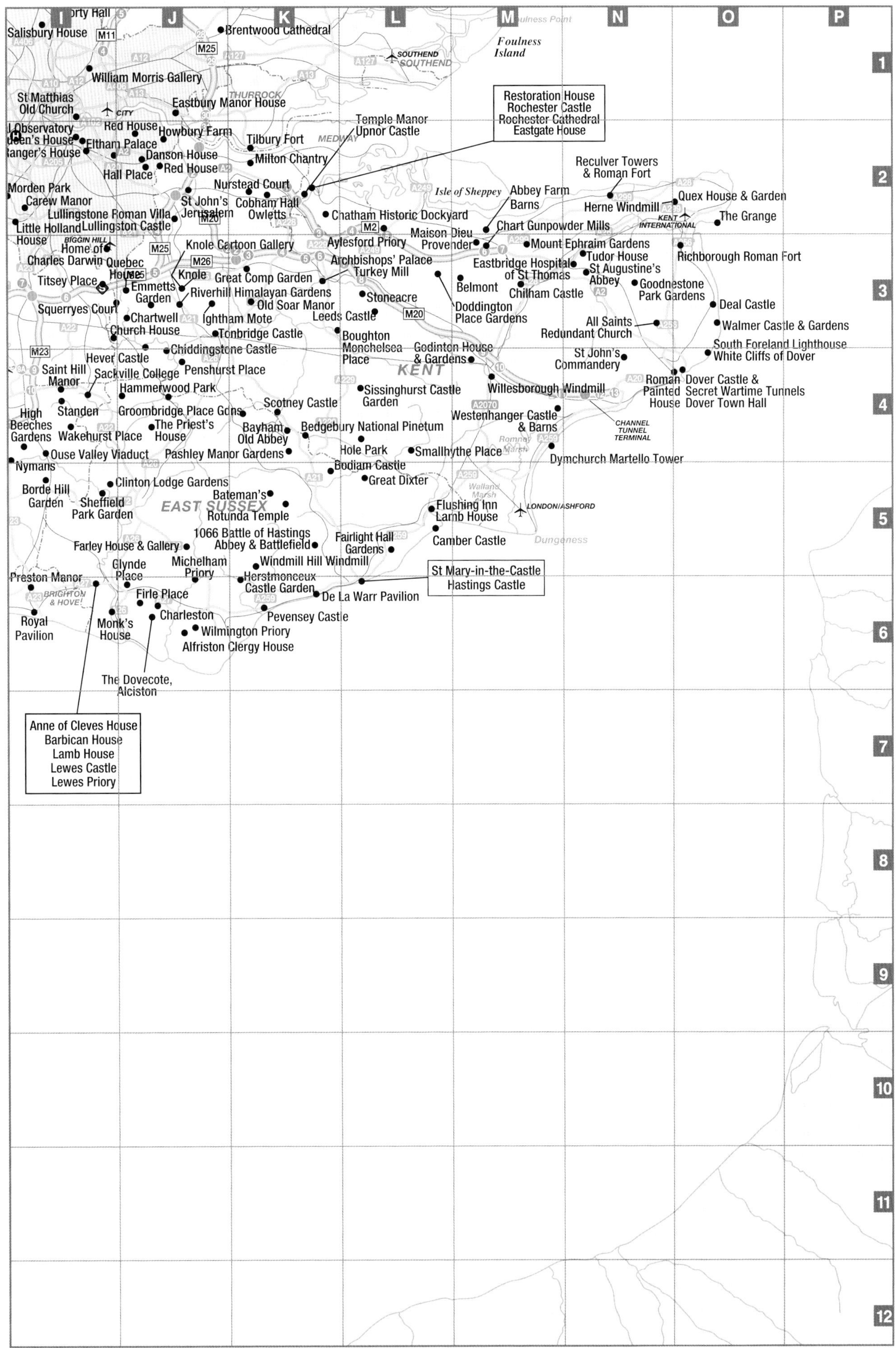

# MAP 5

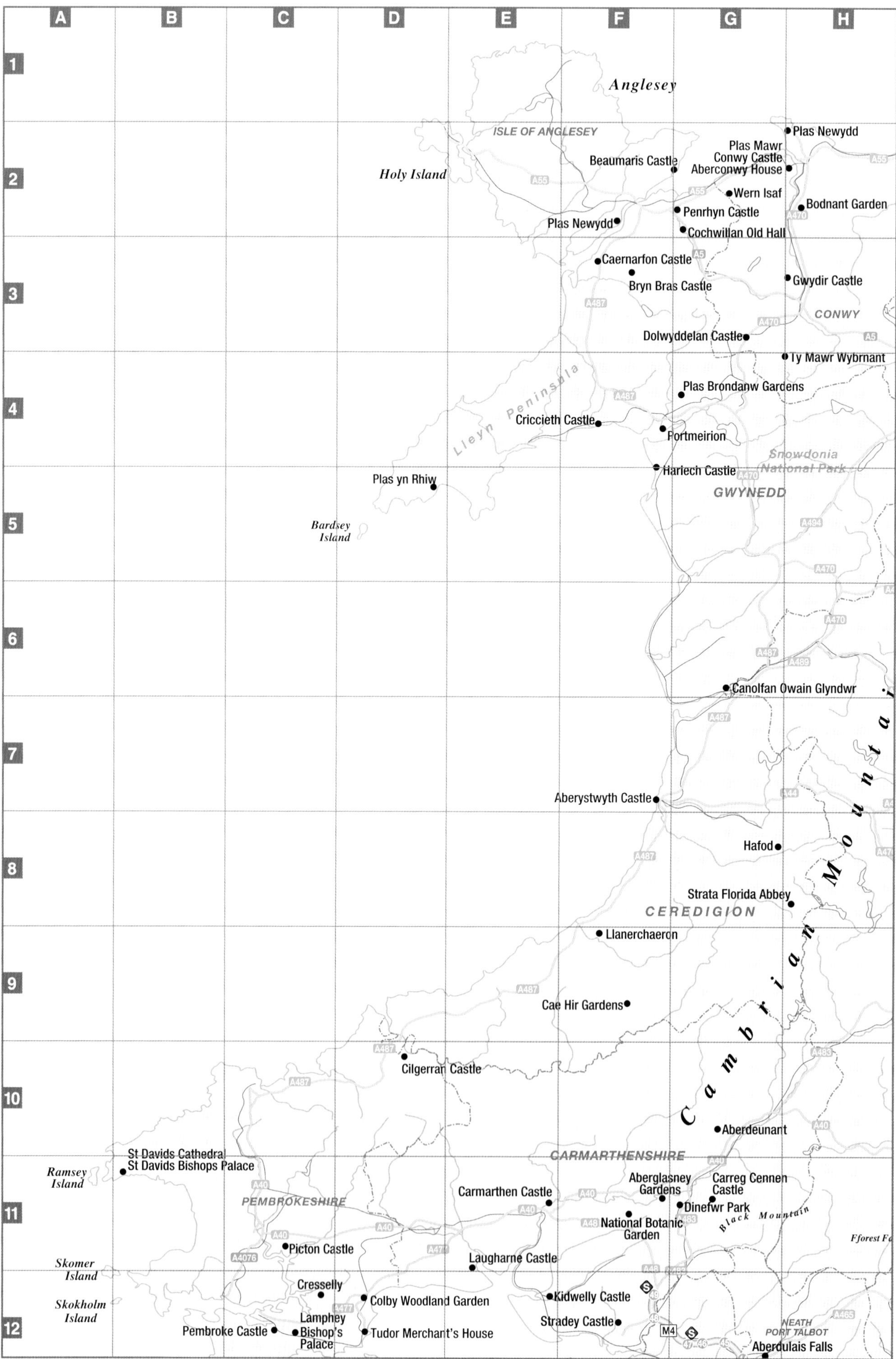

A
B
C
D
E
F
G
H
1
2
3
4
5
6
7
8
9
10
11
12
Anglesey
ISLE OF ANGLESEY
Holy Island
Beaumaris Castle
Plas Newydd
Plas Mawr
Conwy Castle
Aberconwy House
Wern Isaf
Bodnant Garden
Penrhyn Castle
Plas Newydd
Cochwillan Old Hall
Caernarfon Castle
Bryn Bras Castle
Gwydir Castle
CONWY
Dolwyddelan Castle
Ty Mawr Wybrnant
Lleyn Peninsula
Plas Brondanw Gardens
Criccieth Castle
Portmeirion
Snowdonia National Park
Harlech Castle
GWYNEDD
Plas yn Rhiw
Bardsey Island
Canolfan Owain Glyndwr
Aberystwyth Castle
Hafod
Strata Florida Abbey
CEREDIGION
Cambrian Mountains
Llanerchaeron
Cae Hir Gardens
Cilgerran Castle
Aberdeunant
CARMARTHENSHIRE
St Davids Cathedral
St Davids Bishops Palace
Ramsey Island
PEMBROKESHIRE
Carmarthen Castle
Aberglasney Gardens
Carreg Cennen Castle
Dinefwr Park
Black Mountain
National Botanic Garden
Picton Castle
Laugharne Castle
Skomer Island
Cresselly
Skokholm Island
Colby Woodland Garden
Kidwelly Castle
Lamphey Bishop's Palace
Stradey Castle
Pembroke Castle
Tudor Merchant's House
NEATH PORT TALBOT
Aberdulais Falls

I
J
K
L
M
N
O
P
1
2
3
4
5
6
7
8
9
10
11
12
Cathedral of Christ the King
Croxteth Hall
Liverpool Cathedral
Liverpool Collegiate Apartments
Liverpool Metropolitan
The Hardmans' House
West Derby Courthouse
Wallasey Unitarian Church
Sefton Park
The Beatles' Childhood Homes
Grand Entrance, Birkenhead Park
Elizabeth Gaskell's House
The Arches
Former Church of St Benedict
Staircase House
1830 Warehouse
Heaton Hall
Manchester Cathedral
Ordsall Hall
Victoria Baths
Wortley Hall
S. YORKS
MERSEYSIDE
WARRINGTON
HALTON
LIVERPOOL
MANCHESTER
SHEFFIELD CITY
Dunham Massey
Bramall Hall
Speke Hall
Norton Priory
Quarry Bank Mill
Lyme Park
Peveril Castle
Bodrhyddan
Rhuddlan Castle
Bodelwyddan Castle
St Asaph Cathedral
Dolbelydr
Denbigh Castle
Ness Botanic Gardens
Arley Hall
Belmont Hall
Tabley House
Tatton Park
Adlington Hall
Hare Hill
Capesthorne Hall
Gawsworth Hall
Peover Hall
Assembly Rooms
Opera House
St Ann's Hotel
Devonshire Royal Hospital
Pavilion Gardens
Unthank Hall Barn
Eyam Hall
Chatsworth
Peak District
DERBYSHIRE
Haddon Hall
Chester Cathedral
Chester Roman Amphitheatre
Holmston Hall Barn
CHESHIRE
Tower
FLINTSHIRE
Fferm
Hartsheath
Beeston Castle
Bache House Farm
Rode Hall
Little Moreton Hall
Biddulph Grange Garden
Masson Mills
Cromford Mill
Casterne Hall
Hopton Hall Gardens
Tissington Hall
Cheddleton Flint Mill
Woodhey Chapel
Dorfold Hall
Erddig
Cholmondeley Castle & Garden
St Chad's Church Tower
Middleport Pottery
Trentham Mausoleum
Trentham Gardens
STOKE-ON-TRENT
Malthouse
Sudbury Hall
Rug Chapel
DENBIGHSHIRE
WREXHAM
Valle Crucis Abbey
Combermere Abbey
Highfields
Llangar Church
Chirk Castle
Iscoyd Park
Whitmore Hall
Kedleston Hall
Dorothy Clive Garden
STAFFORDSHIRE
The Heath House
The Lyth
Oakley Hall
Barlaston Hall
DERBY
Hawkstone Hall & Gardens
Wollerton Old Hall Garden
Izaak Walton's Cottage
Sandon Hall
Hodnet Hall Gardens
Ancient High House
Sinai House
2/3 Milk Street
Coleham Pumping Station
Old Mansion
Old Market Hall
Shrewsbury Abbey
Shrewsbury Castle
Shrewsbury Museum & Art Gallery
Yeaton Peverey Hall
Stafford Castle
Hamstall Ridware Manor
Catton Hall
Claymills Pumping Station
Moreton Corbet Castle
Jackfield Tile Museum & Factory
Shugborough
Bishton Hall
Doric Screen
10 The Close
Erasmus Darwin House
St Mary's
Ashby de La Zouch Castle
Haughmond Abbey
TELFORD & WREKIN
Lilleshall Abbey
Loton Hall
Sunnycroft
Weston Park
Sir John Moore's School
Longner Hall
Attingham Park
Wroxeter Roman City
John Rose Building
Boscobel House
Chillington Hall
Wall Roman Site
Trewern Hall
Powis Castle & Garden
Cound Hall
Iron Bridge
Tamworth Castle
SHROPSHIRE
Buildwas Abbey
Acton Burnell Castle
Brosely Pipeworks
Moseley Old Hall
Molineux Hotel
Castle Bromwich Hall Gardens
Gregynog Hall
Glansevern Hall Gardens
Wenlock Guildhall & Priory
Benthall Hall
Langley Chapel & Gatehouse
Wightwick Manor
Middleton Hall
Preen Manor Gardens
Dorter House
Upton Cressett Hall
Morville Hall
WOLVERHAMPTON
Big House
Arbury Hall
Walcot Hall
Shipton Hall
Pitchford Hall & Tree House
Red House Glasscone
Kinver Edge
Back to Backs
BIRMINGHAM
St James Church
Clun Forest
Clun Castle
Stokesay Castle
Hopton Court Conservatory
Kinver Edge & The Rockhouses
Hagley Hall
Harvington Hall
Aston Hall
Birmingham Museums
Blakesley Hall
Botanical Gardens
Perrott's Folly
Selly Manor
Soho House
Coventry Cathedral
Bagots Castle
POWYS
Ludlow Castle
Castle House
Mawley Hall
Hartlebury Castle
Baddesley Clinton
Stoneleigh Abbey
The Hall at Abbey-Cwm-Hir
Abberley Hall Clock Tower
St Michael's Ruined Nave & West Tower
Packwood House
Kenilworth Castle
Berrington Hall
Radnor Forest
Witley Court
Hanbury Hall
Lord Leycester Hospital
Warwick Castle
The Judge's Lodging
Hill Close Gardens
Croft Castle
Hawford Dovecote
Mary Arden's House
WARWICKSHIRE
Whitbourne Hall Palm House
Leigh Court Barn
Coughton Court
Charlecote Park
Brockhampton Estate
Greyfriars
Ragley Hall
Hergest Court
Hergest Croft Gardens
Spetchley Park
Anne Hathaway's Cottage
Shakespeare Houses
HEREFORDSHIRE
Hiller Garden
Madresfield Court
WORCESTERSHIRE
Hereford Cathedral
Waterworks Museum
Abbey Gateway
Croome Park
Walker Hall
Kiftsgate Court
Honington Hall
Little Malvern Court
Hidcote Manor
Tudor House
West Banqueting House
Old Campden House
Rotherwas Chapel
Sufton Old Court
Old Sufton
Eastnor Castle
Broadway Tower
Batsford Arboretum
Abbey Dore Court Garden
Hellens
Stanway House
Snowshill Manor
Bourton House
Abercamlais
Black Mountains
Treberfydd
The Laskett Garden
St Mary's Church
Longtown Castle
Ashleworth Tithe Barn
Hailes Abbey
Sudeley Castle
Sezincote
Chastleton House
Trebinshwn House
Brecon Beacons
Langstone Court
Wilton Castle
Cornwall House
Skenfrith Castle
GLOUCESTERSHIRE
Blackfriars
Holst Birthplace Museum
Whittington Court
Tretower Court & Castle
Elmore Court
Llanvihangel Court
White Castle
Goodrich Castle
Gloucester Cathedral
Lodge Park & Sherborne Estate
Cornwall House
Westbury Court Garden
Chedworth Roman Villa
Blaenavon Ironworks
Treowen
Kymin
Forest of Dean
Painswick Rococo Gardens
Minster Lovell Hall
Raglan Castle
MONMOUTHSHIRE
Frampton Manor
Frampton Court
Tanhouse Farm Tythe Barn
Misarden Park Garden
Ablington Manor
BLAENAU GWENT
MERTHYR TYDFIL
TORFAEN
Berkeley Castle
Stanley Mill
Deer Park
Cirencester Park
Baptist Chapel
Usk Castle
Dr Jenner's House & Garden
GLOUCESTERSHIRE
Woodchester Park Mansion
Kelmscott Manor
Tintern Abbey
Stancombe Park Temple
Owlpen Manor
Rodmarton Manor

# MAP 7

Cawthorne Museum
Scawby Hall
Wentworth Woodhouse
Gainsborough Old Hall
Roche Abbey
Westgate House
Lyceum Theatre
Hodsock Priory
Renishaw Hall Gardens
Mr Straw's House
Barlborough Hall
3/3a Vicars Court
Lincoln Castle
Lincoln Medieval Bishop's Palace
Monksthorpe Chapel
St Peter
Clumber Park
Sutton Scarsdale Hall
Bolsover Castle
Doddington Hall & Gardens
Gunby Hall
Hardstoft Herb Garden
Pleasley Colliery
Rufford Abbey
Carlton Hall
LINCOLNSHIRE
Scrivelsby Walled Garden
Bolingbroke Castle
Hardwick Hall
Stainsby Mill
Hardwick Old Hall
NOTTINGHAMSHIRE
Aubourn Hall
Wingfield Manor
Winkburn Hall
Tattershall Castle
Carnfield Hall
Newstead Abbey
Kelham Hall
Lincolnshire Wolds
D H Lawrence Heritage
Papplewick Hall
Newark Townhall
Kiln Warehouse
Leadenham House
Kyme Tower
Sibsey Trader Windmill
Fulbeck Manor
Bennerley Viaduct
Nottingham Castle
Heckington Windmill
Fydell House Gates, Piers & Railings
Elvaston Castle Country Park
Wollaton Hall & Park
Holme Pierrepont Hall
Church of St Mary
Marston Hall
Belton House
Ruddington Framework
Harlaxton Manor
Thrumpton Hall
Ruddington Framework Knitters' Museum
Belvoir Castle
Belvoir Castle Riding Ring
Easton Walled Gardens
Sandringham
Melbourne Hall
Staunton Harold Church
Ellys Manor House
Woolsthorpe Manor
Moulton Windmill
Castle Rising Castle
Calke Abbey
Grimsthorpe Castle Park & Gardens
Ayscoughfee Hall Museum & Gardens
St George's Guildhall
Clifton House
Donington le Heath Manor House
LEICESTERSHIRE
Bearsby Packhorse Bridge
Exton Park
Ruined Chapel of St Peter
Octavia Hill Birthplace Museum
Stoneywell
Bradgate Park
Peckover House & Garden
Sulehay House
The Fens
Oakham Castle
RUTLAND
Burghley House
Kirby Muxloe Castle
LEICESTER
Longthorpe Tower
PETERBOROUGH
Lyddington Bede House
Prebendal Manor
Peterborough Cathedral Minster Precincts
Laxton Hall
Apethorpe Palace
Rockingham Castle
Kirby Hall
Elton Hall
Ely Cathedral
Old Palace
Oliver Cromwell's House
Southwick Hall
Deene Park
Astley Castle
Rushton Triangular Lodge
Lyveden New Bield
Eleanor Cross
CAMBRIDGESHIRE
Stanford Hall
Kelmarsh Hall
Boughton House
Drayton House
Cottesbrooke
Lamport Hall
COVENTRY
Coton Manor Garden
NORTHAMPTONSHIRE
Harrowden Hall Gardens
The Manor, Hemingford Grey
Chippenham Park
Haddonstone Show Gardens
Kimbolton Castle
Island Hall
Denny Abbey & Farmland Museum
Holdenby House
Althorp
Northampton Cathedral
78 Derngate
Bushmead Priory
Anglesey Abbey
Delapre Abbey
BEDFORDSHIRE
Cambridge Botanic Garden
CAMBRIDGE
Turvey House
Compton Verney
Canons Ashby
Cowper & Newton Museum
Wimpole Hall
Farnborough Hall
Stoke Park Pavilions
MILTON KEYNES
Moggerhanger Park & House
Weston Hall
Cecil Higgins Art Gallery
Upton House
Wakefield Lodge
Bromham Mill & Gallery
Swiss Garden
Docwra's Manor Garden
Brook Cottage
Sulgrave Manor
Houghton House
Queen Anne's Summerhouse
Broughton Castle
Old Palace
Stowe House
De Grey Mausoleum
Audley End House & Gardens
Wrest Park
Swalcliffe Barn
Bletchley Park
Woburn Abbey
Deddington Castle
Buckingham Chantry Chapel
Cromer Windmill
Prior's Hall Barn
John Webb's Windmill
Old Church Tower of All Saints
Ford End Windmill
Rousham House
Claydon House
Ascott
LUTON
St Pauls Walden Bury
Benington Lordship
Old Friends Meeting House
Ditchley Park
BUCKINGHAMSHIRE
Shaw's Corner
HERTFORDSHIRE
Saling Hall
STANSTED
Cornbury Park
Boarstall Duck Decoy
Waddesdon Manor
Pitstone Windmill
Knebworth
Woodhall Park
Forge Museum
Gardens of Easton Lodge
Great Dunmow Maltings
Blenheim Palace
Walter Rothschild Zoological Museum
The Golden Parsonage
Hertford Museum
Wotton House
Ashridge
Scott's Grotto
Boarstall Tower
King's Head
Bridgewater Monument
Gorhambury House
Shotover Park
Nether Winchendon House
Hatfield House
Chelmsford Cathedral
OXFORDSHIRE
Berkhamsted Castle
Redbournbury Mill
Cathedral & Abbey Church of St Albans
Copped Hall
Waterperry Gardens
Town Hall
Hylands House
Rycote Chapel
Chenies Manor House
All Saints Pastoral Centre
Folly Arch
Waltham Abbey Gatehouse & Bridge
Hill Hall
Kingston Bagpuize
26A East St Helen Street

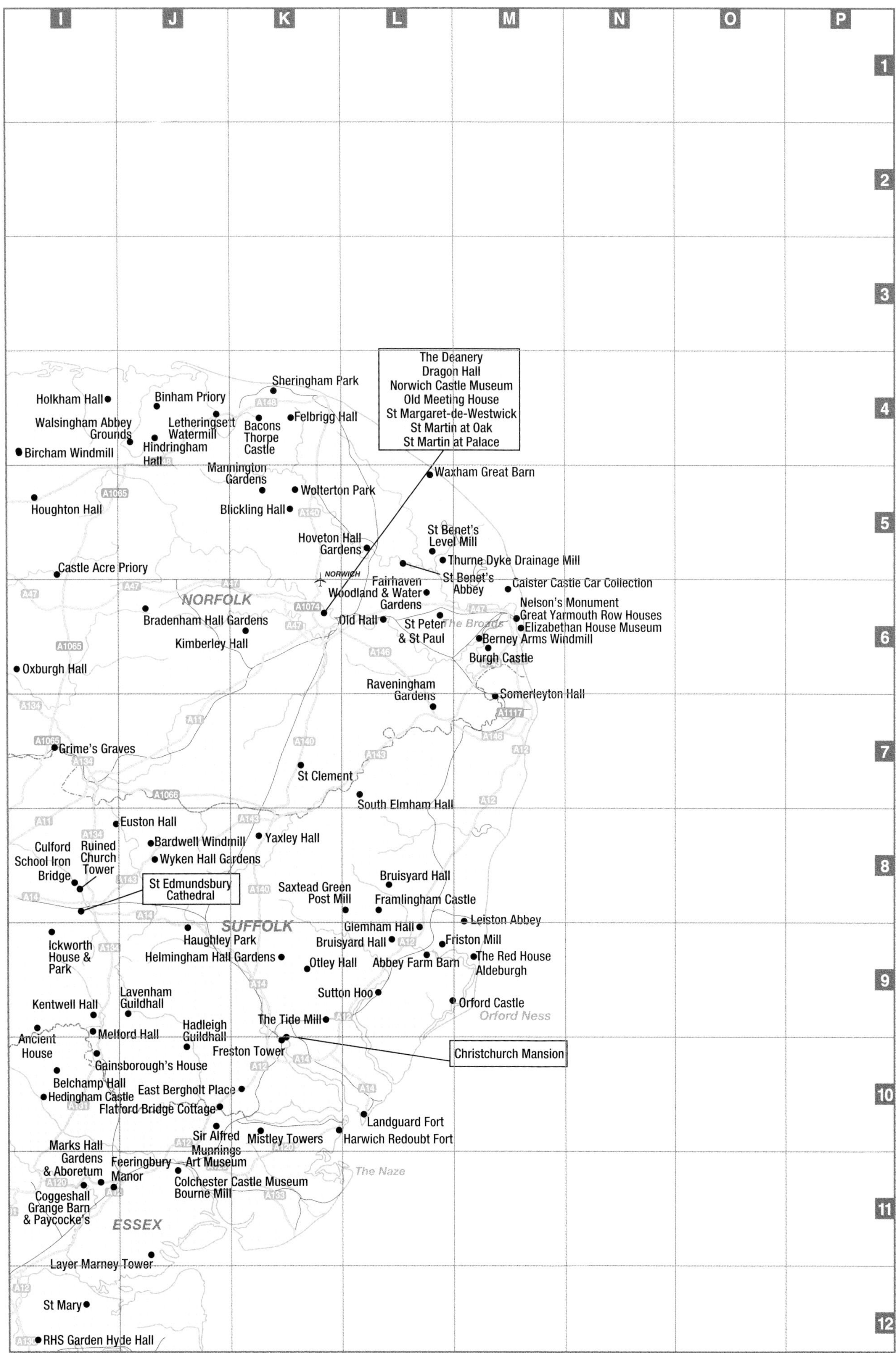

I
J
K
L
M
N
O
P
1
2
3
4
5
6
7
8
9
10
11
12
The Deanery
Dragon Hall
Norwich Castle Museum
Old Meeting House
St Margaret-de-Westwick
St Martin at Oak
St Martin at Palace
Sheringham Park
Holkham Hall
Binham Priory
Walsingham Abbey Grounds
Letheringsett Watermill
Bacons Thorpe Castle
Felbrigg Hall
Bircham Windmill
Hindringham Hall
Mannington Gardens
Waxham Great Barn
Wolterton Park
Houghton Hall
Blickling Hall
St Benet's Level Mill
Hoveton Hall Gardens
Thurne Dyke Drainage Mill
Castle Acre Priory
NORWICH
Fairhaven Woodland & Water Gardens
St Benet's Abbey
Caister Castle Car Collection
NORFOLK
Nelson's Monument
Great Yarmouth Row Houses
Elizabethan House Museum
Bradenham Hall Gardens
Old Hall
St Peter & St Paul
The Broads
Berney Arms Windmill
Kimberley Hall
Burgh Castle
Oxburgh Hall
Raveningham Gardens
Somerleyton Hall
Grime's Graves
St Clement
South Elmham Hall
Euston Hall
Bardwell Windmill
Yaxley Hall
Culford School Iron Bridge
Ruined Church Tower
Wyken Hall Gardens
St Edmundsbury Cathedral
Saxtead Green Post Mill
Bruisyard Hall
Framlingham Castle
Leiston Abbey
SUFFOLK
Glemham Hall
Ickworth House & Park
Haughley Park
Bruisyard Hall
Friston Mill
Helmingham Hall Gardens
Otley Hall
Abbey Farm Barn
The Red House Aldeburgh
Lavenham Guildhall
Kentwell Hall
Sutton Hoo
Orford Castle
Orford Ness
Hadleigh Guildhall
The Tide Mill
Ancient House
Melford Hall
Freston Tower
Christchurch Mansion
Gainsborough's House
Belchamp Hall
East Bergholt Place
Hedingham Castle
Flatford Bridge Cottage
Landguard Fort
Sir Alfred Munnings Art Museum
Mistley Towers
Harwich Redoubt Fort
Marks Hall Gardens & Aboretum
Feeringbury Manor
The Naze
Colchester Castle Museum
Bourne Mill
Coggeshall Grange Barn & Paycocke's
ESSEX
Layer Marney Tower
St Mary
RHS Garden Hyde Hall

# MAP 9

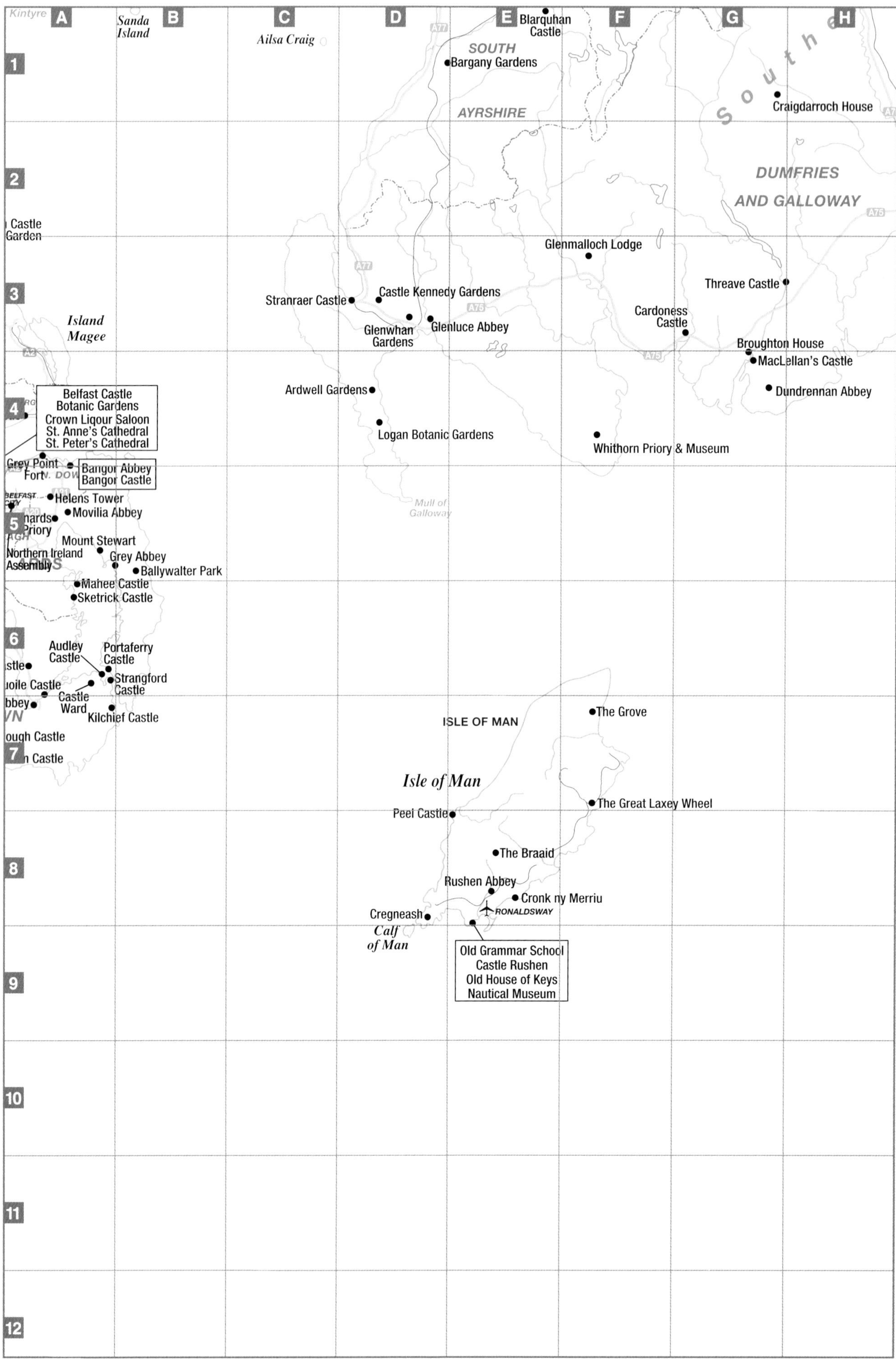

Kintyre
Sanda Island
Ailsa Craig
Blarquhan Castle
SOUTH
Bargany Gardens
AYRSHIRE
Craigdarroch House
DUMFRIES AND GALLOWAY
Castle Garden
Glenmalloch Lodge
Threave Castle
Stranraer Castle
Castle Kennedy Gardens
Glenwhan Gardens
Glenluce Abbey
Cardoness Castle
Island Magee
Broughton House
MacLellan's Castle
Dundrennan Abbey
Ardwell Gardens
Belfast Castle
Botanic Gardens
Crown Liqour Saloon
St. Anne's Cathedral
St. Peter's Cathedral
Logan Botanic Gardens
Whithorn Priory & Museum
Grey Point Fort
Bangor Abbey
Bangor Castle
Helens Tower
Movilia Abbey
Mull of Galloway
Mount Stewart
Northern Ireland Assembly
Grey Abbey
Ballywalter Park
Mahee Castle
Sketrick Castle
Audley Castle
Portaferry Castle
Strangford Castle
Castle Ward
Kilchief Castle
The Grove
ISLE OF MAN
Isle of Man
The Great Laxey Wheel
Peel Castle
The Braaid
Rushen Abbey
Cronk ny Merriu
RONALDSWAY
Cregneash
Calf of Man
Old Grammar School
Castle Rushen
Old House of Keys
Nautical Museum

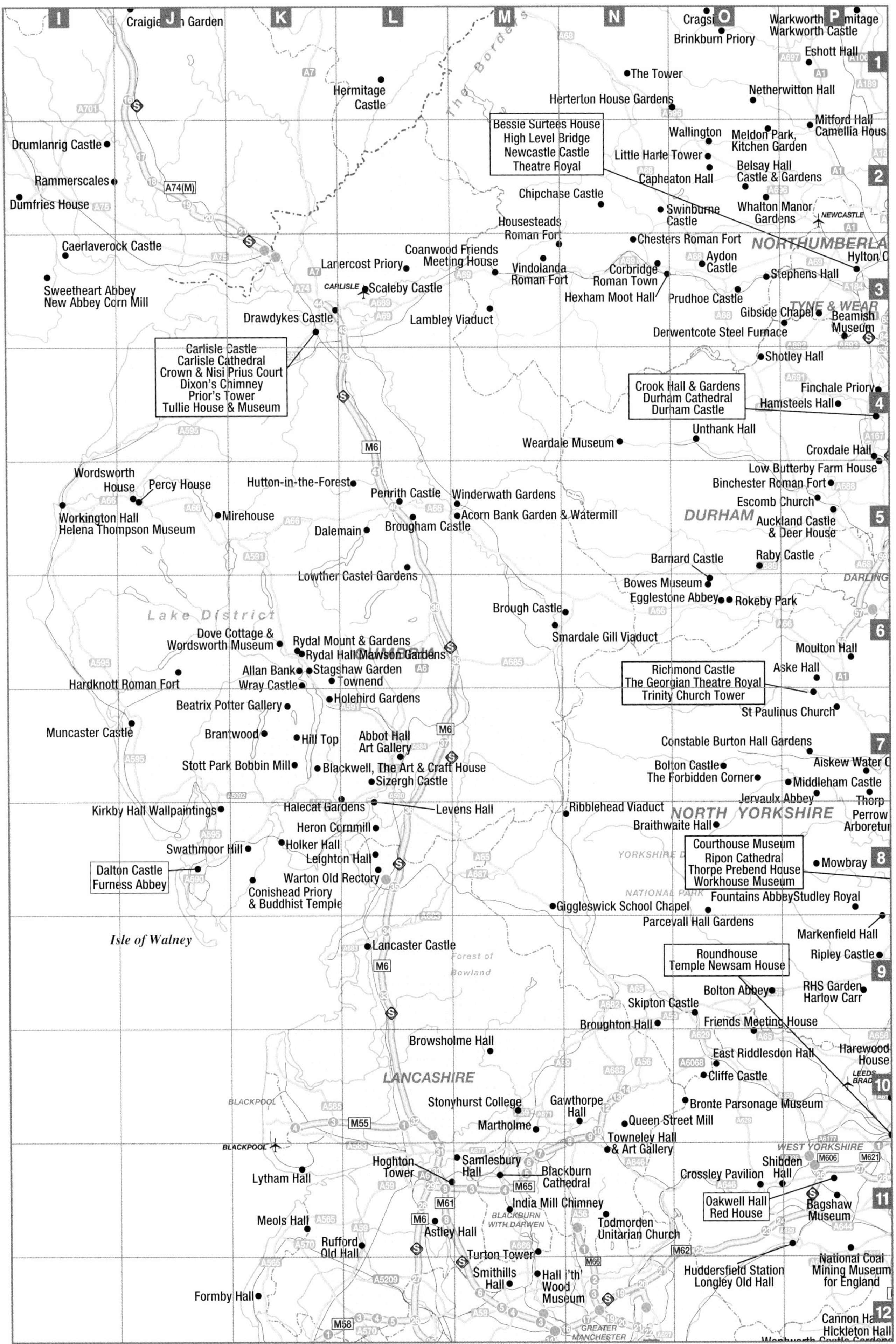

Craigieburn Garden
Hermitage Castle
Drumlanrig Castle
Rammerscales
Dumfries House
Caerlaverock Castle
Sweetheart Abbey
New Abbey Corn Mill
Lanercost Priory
Coanwood Friends Meeting House
Scaleby Castle
Drawdykes Castle
Lambley Viaduct
Carlisle Castle
Carlisle Cathedral
Crown & Nisi Prius Court
Dixon's Chimney
Prior's Tower
Tullie House & Museum
The Tower
Herterton House Gardens
Bessie Surtees House
High Level Bridge
Newcastle Castle
Theatre Royal
Little Harle Tower
Capheaton Hall
Chipchase Castle
Housesteads Roman Fort
Vindolanda Roman Fort
Chesters Roman Fort
Corbridge Roman Town
Hexham Moot Hall
Aydon Castle
Prudhoe Castle
Swinburne Castle
Cragside
Brinkburn Priory
Warkworth Hermitage
Warkworth Castle
Eshott Hall
Netherwitton Hall
Wallington
Meldon Park, Kitchen Garden
Mitford Hall
Camellia House
Belsay Hall Castle & Gardens
Whalton Manor Gardens
NORTHUMBERLAND
Hylton Castle
Stephens Hall
TYNE & WEAR
Gibside Chapel
Beamish Museum
Derwentcote Steel Furnace
Shotley Hall
Crook Hall & Gardens
Durham Cathedral
Durham Castle
Finchale Priory
Hamsteels Hall
Unthank Hall
Weardale Museum
Croxdale Hall
Low Butterby Farm House
Binchester Roman Fort
Escomb Church
DURHAM
Auckland Castle & Deer House
Barnard Castle
Raby Castle
Bowes Museum
Egglestone Abbey
Rokeby Park
Wordsworth House
Percy House
Workington Hall
Helena Thompson Museum
Mirehouse
Hutton-in-the-Forest
Penrith Castle
Winderwath Gardens
Acorn Bank Garden & Watermill
Dalemain
Brougham Castle
Lowther Castel Gardens
Lake District
Brough Castle
Smardale Gill Viaduct
Dove Cottage & Wordsworth Museum
Rydal Mount & Gardens
Rydal Hall
Mawson Gardens
Allan Bank
Stagshaw Garden
Townend
Wray Castle
Hardknott Roman Fort
Holehird Gardens
Beatrix Potter Gallery
Muncaster Castle
Brantwood
Hill Top
Abbot Hall Art Gallery
Stott Park Bobbin Mill
Blackwell, The Art & Craft House
Sizergh Castle
Kirkby Hall Wallpaintings
Halecat Gardens
Levens Hall
Heron Cornmill
Holker Hall
Leighton Hall
Swarthmoor Hill
Dalton Castle
Furness Abbey
Warton Old Rectory
Conishead Priory & Buddhist Temple
Isle of Walney
Richmond Castle
The Georgian Theatre Royal
Trinity Church Tower
Moulton Hall
Aske Hall
St Paulinus Church
Constable Burton Hall Gardens
Aiskew Water C
Bolton Castle
The Forbidden Corner
Middleham Castle
Jervaulx Abbey
Thorp Perrow Arboretum
Ribblehead Viaduct
NORTH YORKSHIRE
Braithwaite Hall
Courthouse Museum
Ripon Cathedral
Thorpe Prebend House
Workhouse Museum
Mowbray
Fountains Abbey
Studley Royal
Giggleswick School Chapel
Parcevall Hall Gardens
Markenfield Hall
Ripley Castle
Lancaster Castle
Forest of Bowland
Roundhouse
Temple Newsam House
Bolton Abbey
RHS Garden Harlow Carr
Skipton Castle
Friends Meeting House
Broughton Hall
Browsholme Hall
East Riddlesden Hall
Harewood House
Cliffe Castle
LANCASHIRE
Stonyhurst College
Gawthorpe Hall
Bronte Parsonage Museum
Queen Street Mill
Martholme
Towneley Hall & Art Gallery
WEST YORKSHIRE
Hoghton Tower
Samlesbury Hall
Blackburn Cathedral
Shibden Hall
Lytham Hall
Crossley Pavilion
India Mill Chimney
Oakwell Hall
Red House
Bagshaw Museum
Meols Hall
Astley Hall
Todmorden Unitarian Church
Rufford Old Hall
Turton Tower
Smithills Hall
Hall i'th' Wood Museum
Huddersfield Station
Longley Old Hall
National Coal Mining Museum for England
Formby Hall
Cannon Hall
Hickleton Hall
GREATER MANCHESTER
BLACKPOOL
CARLISLE
NEWCASTLE
The Borders

# MAP 11

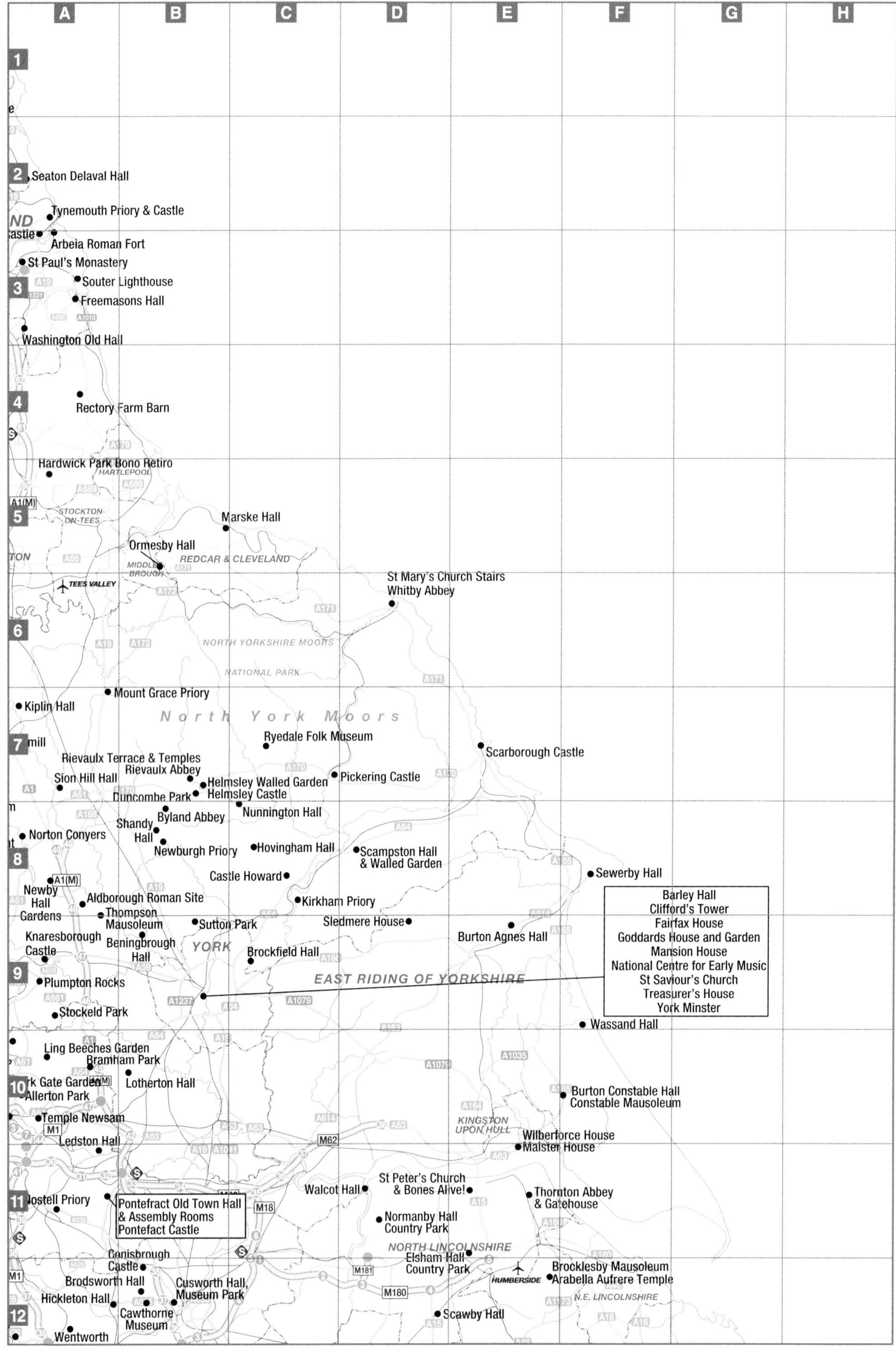

A
B
C
D
E
F
G
H
Seaton Delaval Hall
Tynemouth Priory & Castle
Arbeia Roman Fort
St Paul's Monastery
Souter Lighthouse
Freemasons Hall
Washington Old Hall
Rectory Farm Barn
Hardwick Park Bono Retiro
HARTLEPOOL
STOCKTON-ON-TEES
Marske Hall
Ormesby Hall
REDCAR & CLEVELAND
TEES VALLEY
St Mary's Church Stairs
Whitby Abbey
NORTH YORKSHIRE MOORS
NATIONAL PARK
Mount Grace Priory
Kiplin Hall
North York Moors
Ryedale Folk Museum
Scarborough Castle
Rievaulx Terrace & Temples
Rievaulx Abbey
Sion Hill Hall
Helmsley Walled Garden
Helmsley Castle
Pickering Castle
Duncombe Park
Nunnington Hall
Byland Abbey
Shandy Hall
Norton Conyers
Newburgh Priory
Hovingham Hall
Scampston Hall & Walled Garden
Castle Howard
Sewerby Hall
Newby Hall Gardens
Aldborough Roman Site
Kirkham Priory
Thompson Mausoleum
Sutton Park
Sledmere House
Burton Agnes Hall
Knaresborough Castle
Beningbrough Hall
YORK
Brockfield Hall
Barley Hall
Clifford's Tower
Fairfax House
Goddards House and Garden
Mansion House
National Centre for Early Music
St Saviour's Church
Treasurer's House
York Minster
EAST RIDING OF YORKSHIRE
Plumpton Rocks
Stockeld Park
Wassand Hall
Ling Beeches Garden
Bramham Park
Lotherton Hall
Allerton Park
Burton Constable Hall
Constable Mausoleum
Temple Newsam
KINGSTON UPON HULL
Wilberforce House
Maister House
Ledston Hall
St Peter's Church & Bones Alive!
Walcot Hall
Thornton Abbey & Gatehouse
Nostell Priory
Pontefract Old Town Hall & Assembly Rooms
Pontefract Castle
Normanby Hall Country Park
NORTH LINCOLNSHIRE
Conisbrough Castle
Elsham Hall Country Park
Brocklesby Mausoleum
Arabella Aufrere Temple
HUMBERSIDE
N.E. LINCOLNSHIRE
Brodsworth Hall
Cusworth Hall, Museum Park
Hickleton Hall
Cawthorne Museum
Scawby Hall
Wentworth

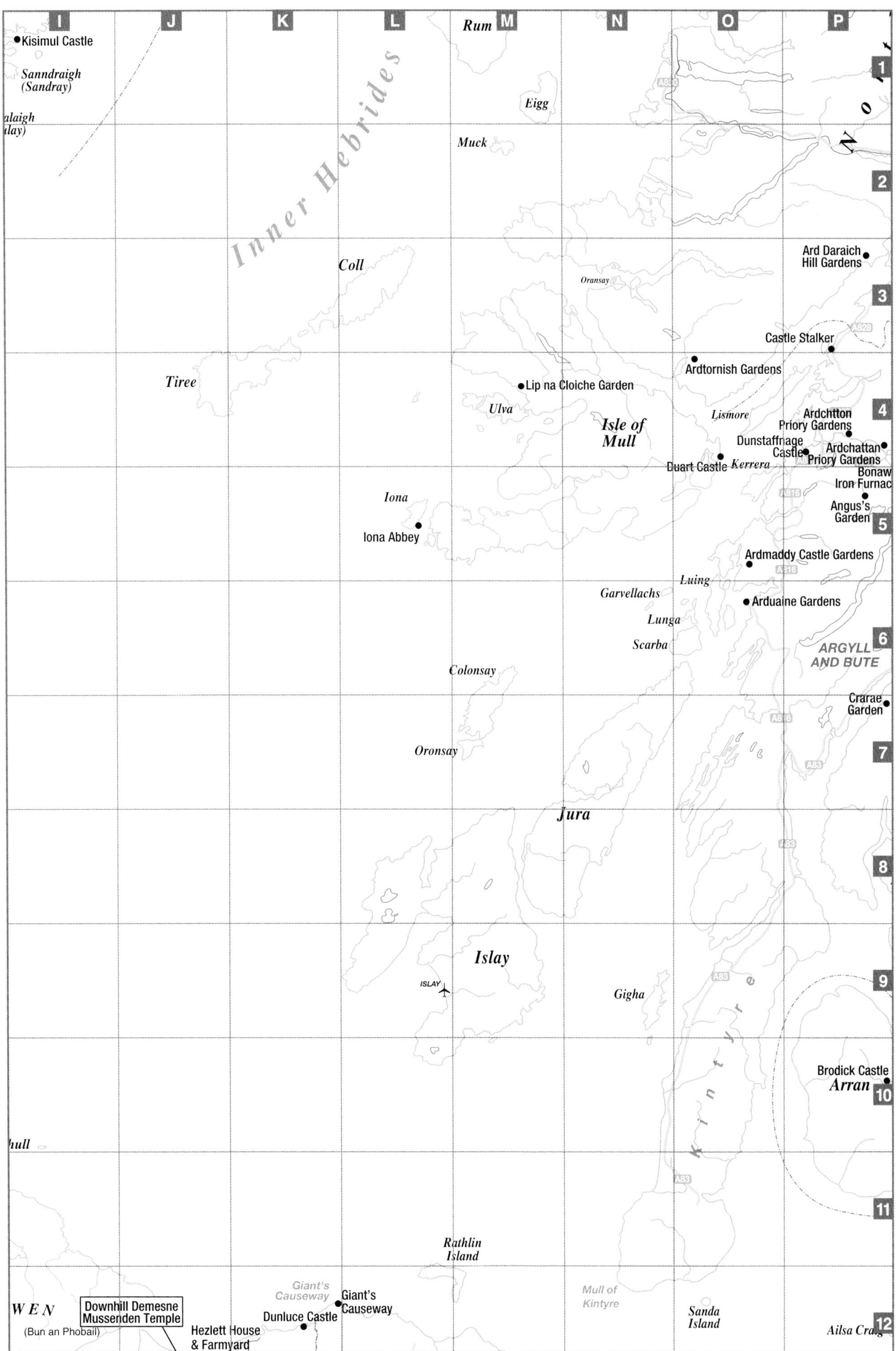
I
J
K
L
M
N
O
P
Kisimul Castle
Sanndraigh
(Sandray)
Rum
Eigg
Muck
Inner Hebrides
Coll
Oransay
Tiree
Ard Daraich
Hill Gardens
Castle Stalker
Ardtornish Gardens
Lip na Cloiche Garden
Ulva
Isle of
Mull
Lismore
Ardchtton
Priory Gardens
Dunstaffnage
Castle
Ardchattan
Priory Gardens
Duart Castle
Kerrera
Iron Furnac
Angus's
Garden
Iona
Iona Abbey
Ardmaddy Castle Gardens
Luing
Garvellachs
Arduaine Gardens
Lunga
Scarba
ARGYLL
AND BUTE
Colonsay
Crarae
Garden
Oronsay
Jura
Islay
ISLAY
Gigha
Kintyre
Brodick Castle
Arran
Rathlin
Island
Giant's
Causeway
Giant's
Causeway
Dunluce Castle
Downhill Demesne
Mussenden Temple
Hezlett House
& Farmyard
Mull of
Kintyre
Sanda
Island
Ailsa Crag
(Bun an Phobail)
1
2
3
4
5
6
7
8
9
10
11
12

# MAP 13

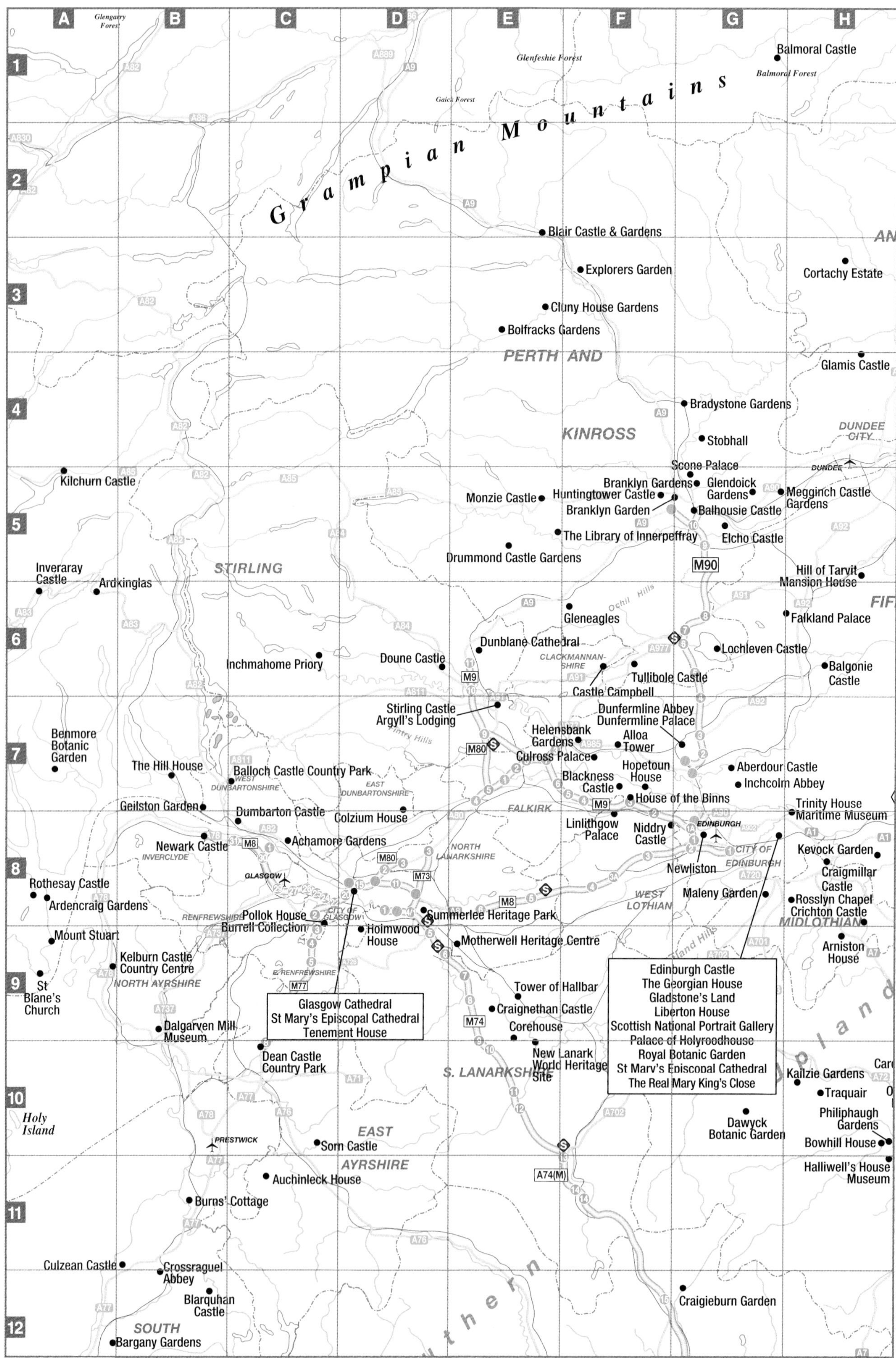

Glengarry Forest
Glenfeshie Forest
Gaick Forest
Balmoral Castle
Balmoral Forest
Grampian Mountains
Blair Castle & Gardens
Explorers Garden
Cortachy Estate
Cluny House Gardens
Bolfracks Gardens
PERTH AND
KINROSS
Glamis Castle
Bradystone Gardens
Stobhall
DUNDEE CITY
DUNDEE
Scone Palace
Kilchurn Castle
Branklyn Gardens
Glendoick Gardens
Megginch Castle Gardens
Monzie Castle
Huntingtower Castle
Branklyn Garden
Balhousie Castle
The Library of Innerpeffray
Elcho Castle
Drummond Castle Gardens
M90
Inveraray Castle
Ardkinglas
STIRLING
Hill of Tarvit Mansion House
Ochil Hills
Gleneagles
FIFE
Falkland Palace
Inchmahome Priory
Doune Castle
Dunblane Cathedral
CLACKMANNANSHIRE
Lochleven Castle
Balgonie Castle
M9
Tullibole Castle
Castle Campbell
Stirling Castle
Argyll's Lodging
Dunfermline Abbey
Dunfermline Palace
Benmore Botanic Garden
Helensbank Gardens
Alloa Tower
M80
Culross Palace
The Hill House
Balloch Castle Country Park
WEST DUNBARTONSHIRE
EAST DUNBARTONSHIRE
Hopetoun House
Aberdour Castle
Blackness Castle
Inchcolm Abbey
House of the Binns
Geilston Garden
Dumbarton Castle
Colzium House
FALKIRK
Trinity House Maritime Museum
Linlithgow Palace
Niddry Castle
EDINBURGH
Newark Castle
M8
INVERCLYDE
Achamore Gardens
NORTH LANARKSHIRE
CITY OF EDINBURGH
Kevock Garden
GLASGOW
M73
Newliston
Craigmillar Castle
Rothesay Castle
Ardencraig Gardens
WEST LOTHIAN
Maleny Garden
Rosslyn Chapel
Crichton Castle
RENFREWSHIRE
Pollok House
Burrell Collection
CITY OF GLASGOW
Summerlee Heritage Park
MIDLOTHIAN
Mount Stuart
Holmwood House
Motherwell Heritage Centre
Arniston House
Kelburn Castle Country Centre
E. RENFREWSHIRE
NORTH AYRSHIRE
Edinburgh Castle
The Georgian House
Gladstone's Land
Liberton House
Scottish National Portrait Gallery
Palace of Holyroodhouse
Royal Botanic Garden
St Mary's Episcopal Cathedral
The Real Mary King's Close
St Blane's Church
M77
Tower of Hallbar
Glasgow Cathedral
St Mary's Episcopal Cathedral
Tenement House
Craignethan Castle
M74
Corehouse
Dalgarven Mill Museum
New Lanark World Heritage Site
Dean Castle Country Park
S. LANARKSHIRE
Kailzie Gardens
Traquair
Holy Island
Philiphaugh Gardens
Dawyck Botanic Garden
PRESTWICK
EAST
Sorn Castle
Bowhill House
AYRSHIRE
Auchinleck House
A74(M)
Halliwell's House Museum
Burns' Cottage
Culzean Castle
Crossraguel Abbey
Craigieburn Garden
Blarquhan Castle
SOUTH
Bargany Gardens

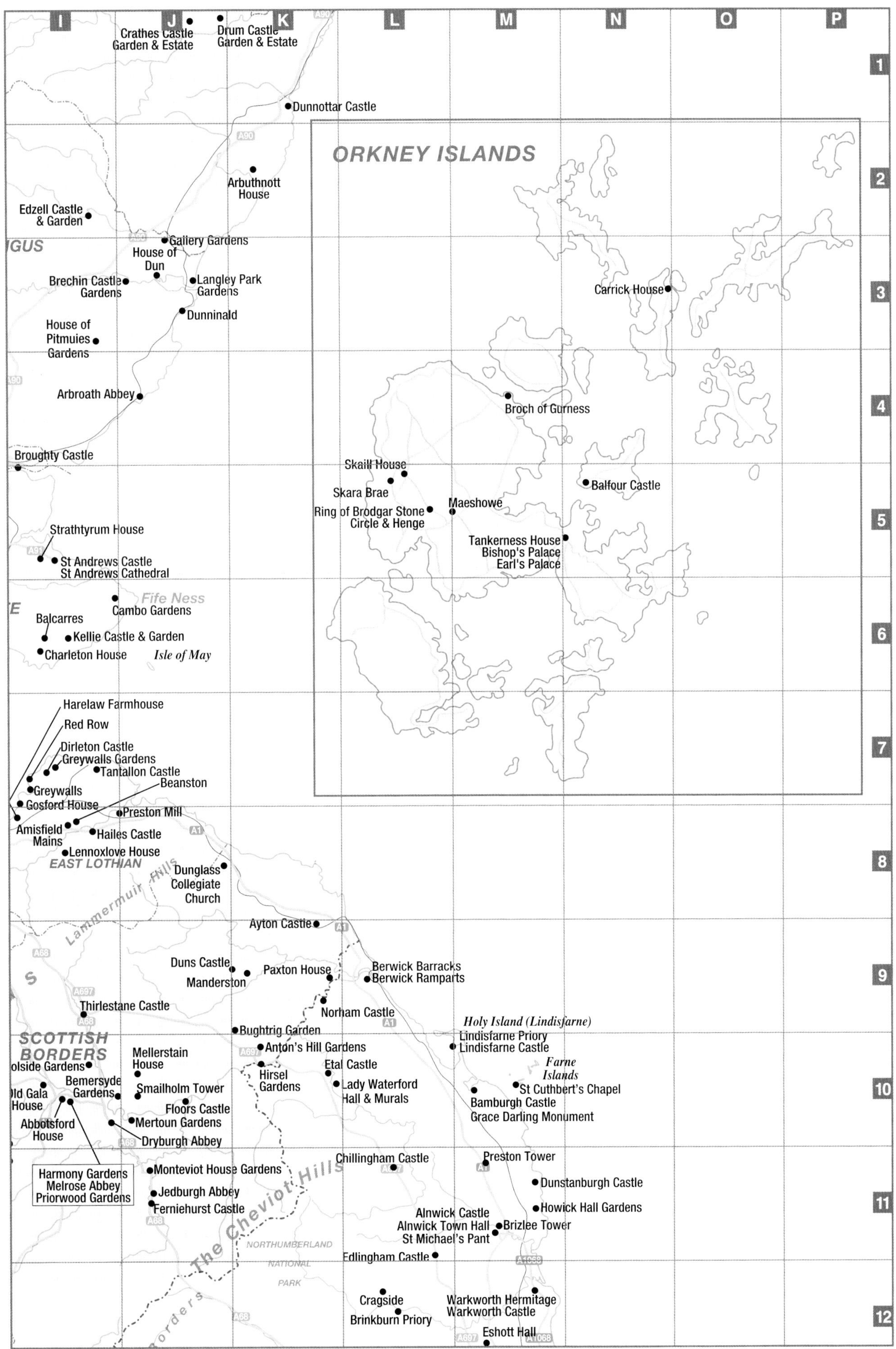
I
J
K
L
M
N
O
P
1
2
3
4
5
6
7
8
9
10
11
12
Crathes Castle Garden & Estate
Drum Castle Garden & Estate
Dunnottar Castle
Arbuthnott House
Edzell Castle & Garden
Gallery Gardens
House of Dun
Brechin Castle Gardens
Langley Park Gardens
Dunninald
House of Pitmuies Gardens
Arbroath Abbey
Broughty Castle
Strathtyrum House
St Andrews Castle
St Andrews Cathedral
Fife Ness
Cambo Gardens
Balcarres
Kellie Castle & Garden
Charleton House
Isle of May
ORKNEY ISLANDS
Carrick House
Broch of Gurness
Skaill House
Skara Brae
Ring of Brodgar Stone Circle & Henge
Maeshowe
Balfour Castle
Tankerness House
Bishop's Palace
Earl's Palace
Harelaw Farmhouse
Red Row
Dirleton Castle
Greywalls Gardens
Tantallon Castle
Beanston
Greywalls
Gosford House
Preston Mill
Amisfield Mains
Hailes Castle
Lennoxlove House
EAST LOTHIAN
Dunglass Collegiate Church
Lammermuir Hills
Ayton Castle
Duns Castle
Manderston
Paxton House
Berwick Barracks
Berwick Ramparts
Thirlestane Castle
Norham Castle
SCOTTISH BORDERS
Bughtrig Garden
Holy Island (Lindisfarne)
Lindisfarne Priory
Lindisfarne Castle
Mellerstain House
Anton's Hill Gardens
Hirsel Gardens
Etal Castle
Lady Waterford Hall & Murals
Farne Islands
St Cuthbert's Chapel
Bamburgh Castle
Grace Darling Monument
Bemersyde Gardens
Smailholm Tower
Floors Castle
Mertoun Gardens
Dryburgh Abbey
Abbotsford House
Harmony Gardens
Melrose Abbey
Priorwood Gardens
Monteviot House Gardens
Jedburgh Abbey
Ferniehurst Castle
The Cheviot Hills
Chillingham Castle
Preston Tower
Dunstanburgh Castle
Howick Hall Gardens
Alnwick Castle
Alnwick Town Hall
St Michael's Pant
Brizlee Tower
Edlingham Castle
NORTHUMBERLAND NATIONAL PARK
Cragside
Brinkburn Priory
Warkworth Hermitage
Warkworth Castle
Eshott Hall
A90
A1
A68
A697
A1068

# MAP 15

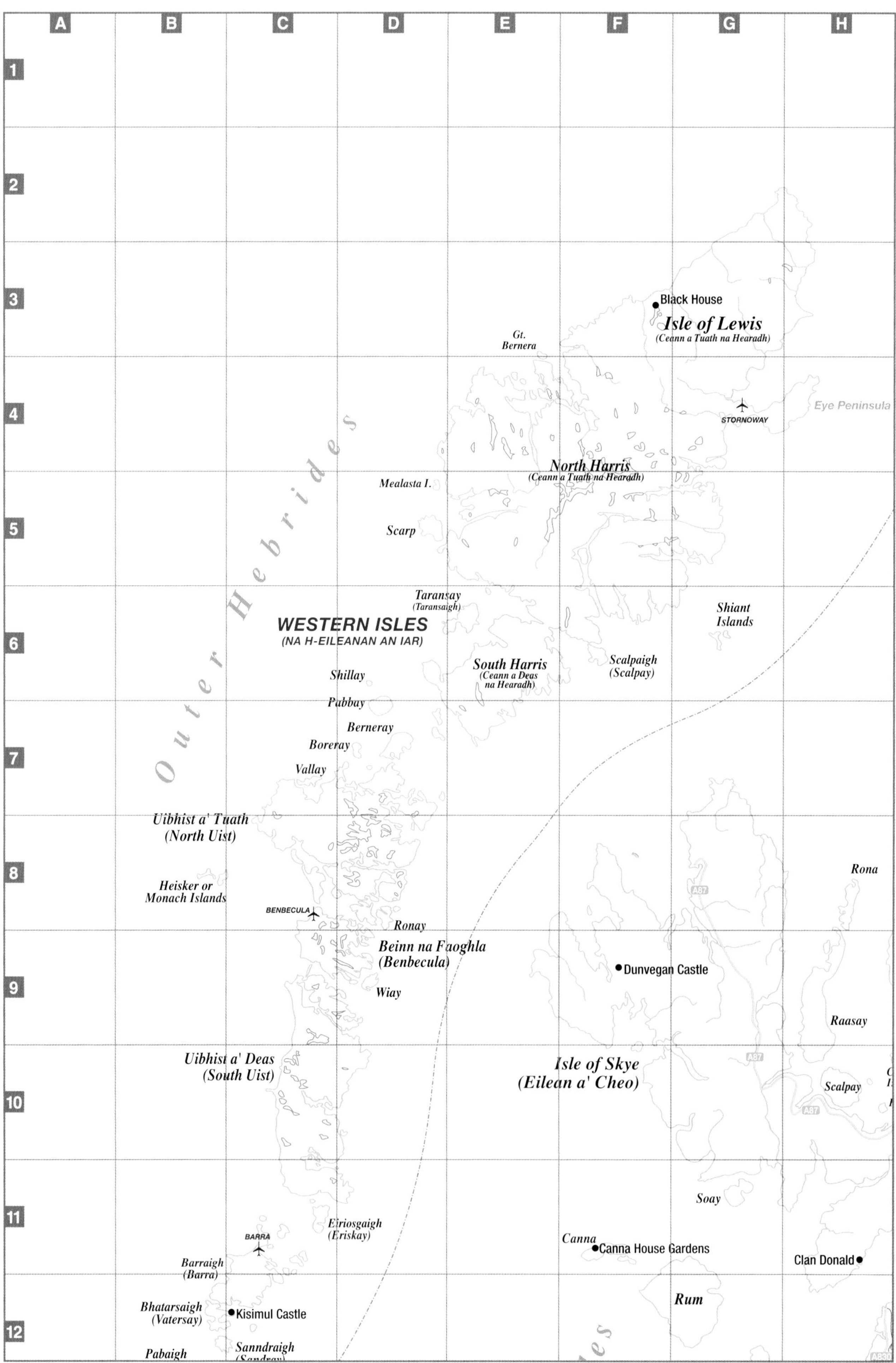
A
B
C
D
E
F
G
H
1
2
3
4
5
6
7
8
9
10
11
12
Black House
Isle of Lewis
(Ceann a Tuath na Hearadh)
Gt. Bernera
STORNOWAY
Eye Peninsula
North Harris
(Ceann a Tuath na Hearadh)
Mealasta I.
Scarp
Outer Hebrides
Taransay
(Taransaigh)
WESTERN ISLES
(NA H-EILEANAN AN IAR)
Shiant Islands
South Harris
(Ceann a Deas na Hearadh)
Scalpaigh
(Scalpay)
Shillay
Pabbay
Berneray
Boreray
Vallay
Uibhist a' Tuath
(North Uist)
Heisker or Monach Islands
BENBECULA
Ronay
Beinn na Faoghla
(Benbecula)
Wiay
Rona
A87
Dunvegan Castle
Raasay
Uibhist a' Deas
(South Uist)
Isle of Skye
(Eilean a' Cheo)
Scalpay
Soay
Eiriosgaigh
(Eriskay)
BARRA
Canna
Canna House Gardens
Clan Donald
Barraigh
(Barra)
Rum
Bhatarsaigh
(Vatersay)
Kisimul Castle
Pabaigh
Sanndraigh

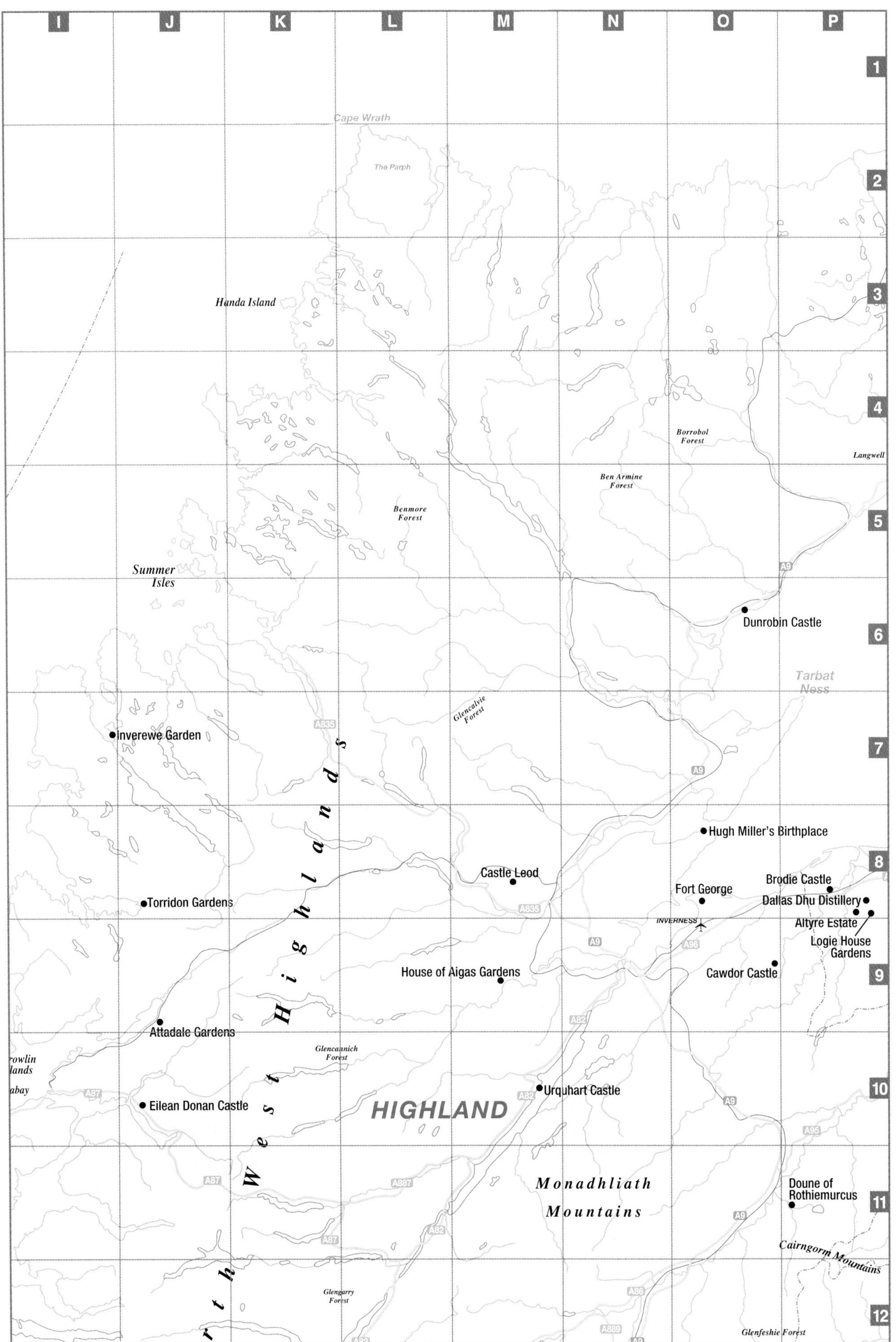
I
J
K
L
M
N
O
P
1
2
3
4
5
6
7
8
9
10
11
12
Cape Wrath
The Parph
Handa Island
Borrobol Forest
Langwell
Ben Armine Forest
Benmore Forest
Summer Isles
A9
Dunrobin Castle
Tarbat Ness
Glencalvie Forest
A835
Inverewe Garden
North West Highlands
A9
Hugh Miller's Birthplace
Castle Leod
Fort George
Brodie Castle
Dallas Dhu Distillery
Torridon Gardens
A835
INVERNESS
Altyre Estate
A9
A96
Logie House Gardens
House of Aigas Gardens
Cawdor Castle
A82
Attadale Gardens
Glencannich Forest
Urquhart Castle
A87
A82
Eilean Donan Castle
HIGHLAND
A9
A95
A87
A887
Monadhliath Mountains
Doune of Rothiemurcus
A9
A87
A82
Cairngorm Mountains
Glengarry Forest
A86
A889
A82
A9
Glenfeshie Forest

# MAP 17

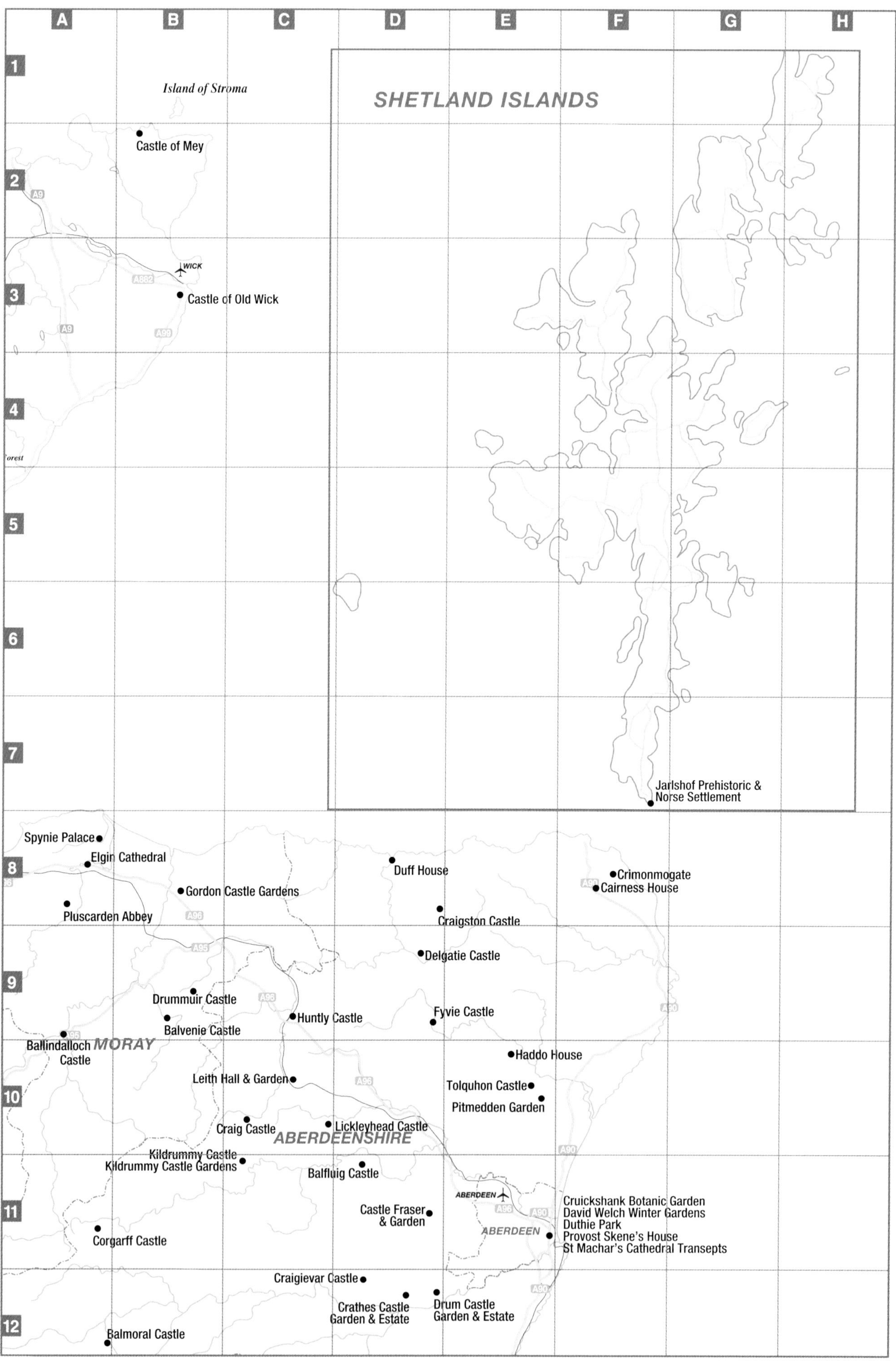

A
B
C
D
E
F
G
H
1
2
3
4
5
6
7
8
9
10
11
12
Island of Stroma
SHETLAND ISLANDS
Castle of Mey
A9
WICK
A882
Castle of Old Wick
A99
Jarlshof Prehistoric & Norse Settlement
Spynie Palace
Elgin Cathedral
Gordon Castle Gardens
Pluscarden Abbey
A96
A95
Duff House
Crimonmogate
Cairness House
Craigston Castle
Delgatie Castle
Drummuir Castle
Huntly Castle
Fyvie Castle
Balvenie Castle
Ballindalloch Castle
MORAY
Haddo House
Leith Hall & Garden
Tolquhon Castle
Pitmedden Garden
Craig Castle
Lickleyhead Castle
ABERDEENSHIRE
Kildrummy Castle
Kildrummy Castle Gardens
Balfluig Castle
A90
ABERDEEN
Castle Fraser & Garden
Cruickshank Botanic Garden
David Welch Winter Gardens
Duthie Park
Provost Skene's House
St Machar's Cathedral Transepts
Corgarff Castle
Craigievar Castle
Crathes Castle Garden & Estate
Drum Castle Garden & Estate
Balmoral Castle

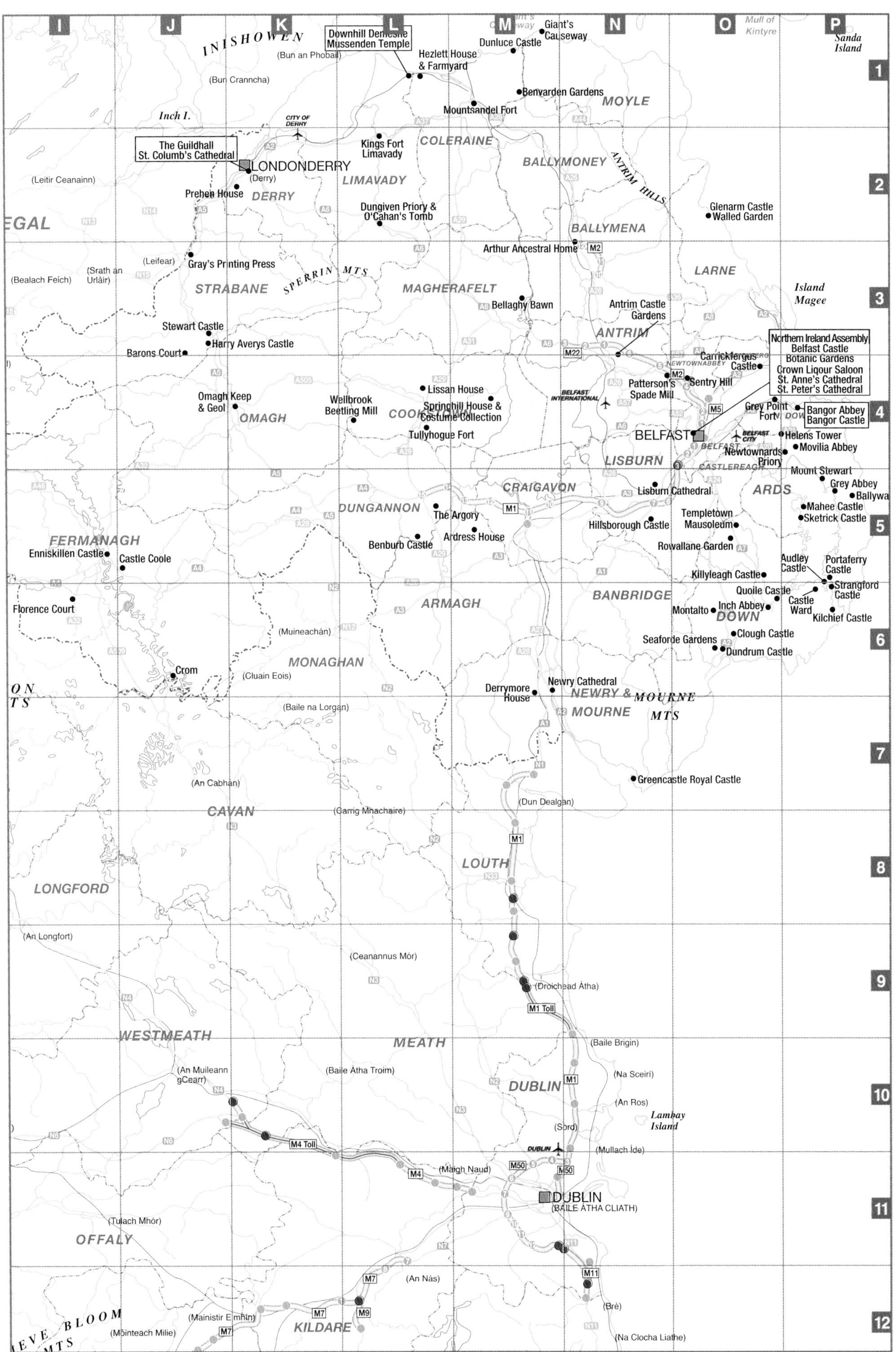
Downhill Demesne
Mussenden Temple
Giant's Causeway
Dunluce Castle
Hezlett House & Farmyard
Benvarden Gardens
Mountsandel Fort
MOYLE
INISHOWEN
Inch I.
The Guildhall
St. Columb's Cathedral
LONDONDERRY
(Derry)
Kings Fort Limavady
COLERAINE
LIMAVADY
BALLYMONEY
ANTRIM HILLS
Prehen House
DERRY
Dungiven Priory & O'Cahan's Tomb
Glenarm Castle Walled Garden
BALLYMENA
Arthur Ancestral Home
Gray's Printing Press
SPERRIN MTS
STRABANE
MAGHERAFELT
LARNE
Island Magee
Bellaghy Bawn
Antrim Castle Gardens
ANTRIM
Stewart Castle
Harry Averys Castle
Barons Court
Northern Ireland Assembly
Belfast Castle
Botanic Gardens
Crown Liqour Saloon
St. Anne's Cathedral
St. Peter's Cathedral
Carrickfergus Castle
Patterson's Spade Mill
Sentry Hill
Lissan House
Omagh Keep & Geol
Wellbrook Beetling Mill
Springhill House & Costume Collection
OMAGH
Tullyhogue Fort
Grey Point Fort
Bangor Abbey
Bangor Castle
BELFAST
Helens Tower
Movilia Abbey
Newtownards Priory
LISBURN
Mount Stewart
Grey Abbey
CRAIGAVON
Lisburn Cathedral
ARDS
DUNGANNON
The Argory
Templetown Mausoleum
Mahee Castle
Sketrick Castle
FERMANAGH
Enniskillen Castle
Castle Coole
Benburb Castle
Ardress House
Hillsborough Castle
Rowallane Garden
Audley Castle
Portaferry Castle
Killyleagh Castle
Strangford Castle
Florence Court
ARMAGH
BANBRIDGE
Quoile Castle
Montalto
Inch Abbey
DOWN
Castle Ward
Kilchief Castle
Clough Castle
Seaforde Gardens
Dundrum Castle
MONAGHAN
Crom
Derrymore House
Newry Cathedral
NEWRY & MOURNE
MOURNE MTS
Greencastle Royal Castle
CAVAN
LONGFORD
LOUTH
WESTMEATH
MEATH
DUBLIN
Lambay Island
DUBLIN
(BAILE ÁTHA CLIATH)
OFFALY
KILDARE
Mull of Kintyre
Sanda Island

# MAP 19

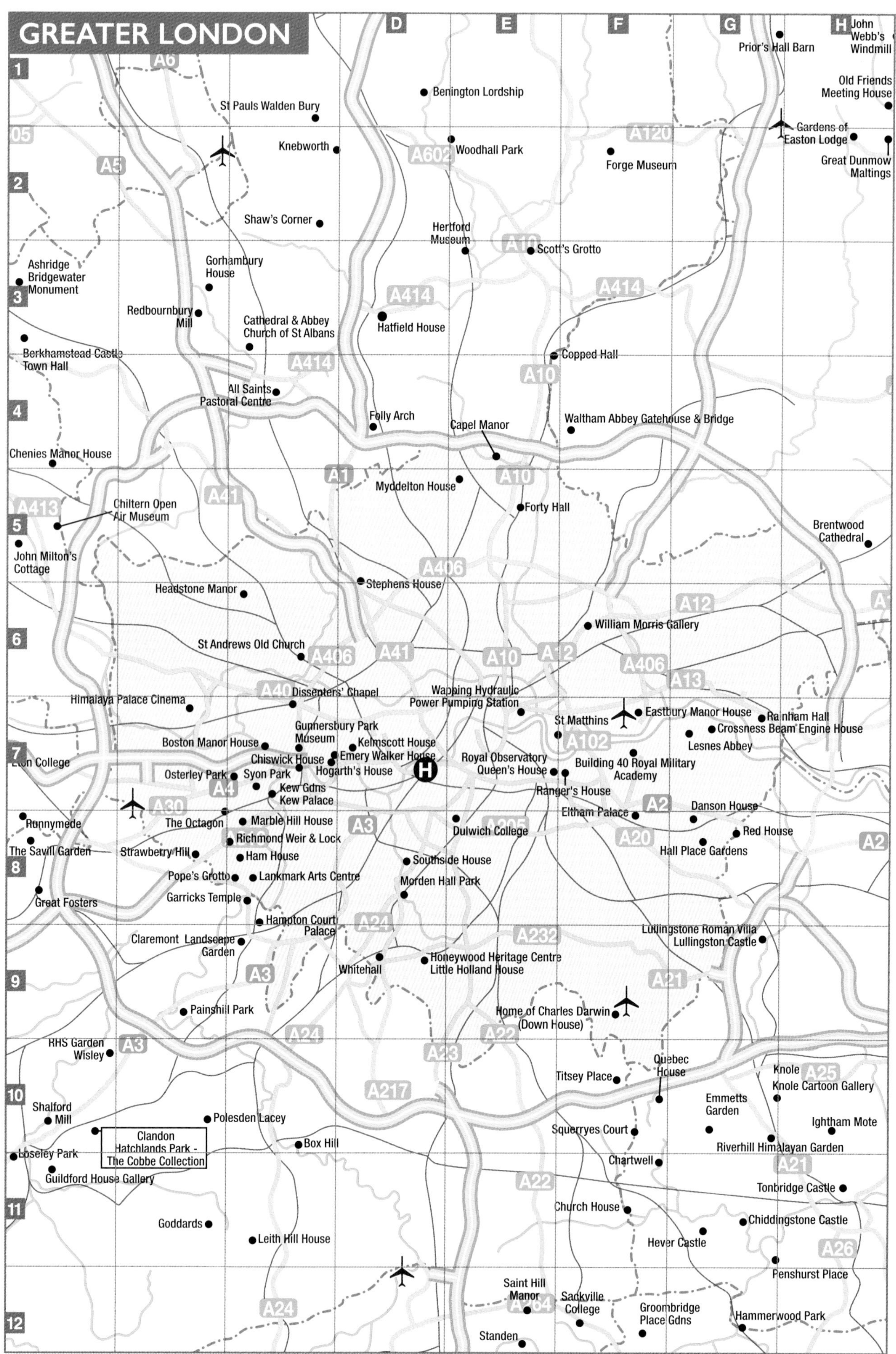
GREATER LONDON
D
E
F
G
H
1
2
3
4
5
6
7
8
9
10
11
12
A6
A5
A602
A120
A10
A414
A1
A41
A413
A406
A12
A13
A40
A102
A4
A30
A3
A205
A2
A20
A24
A232
A21
A23
A22
A217
A25
A26
A264
John Webb's Windmill
Prior's Hall Barn
Old Friends Meeting House
Gardens of Easton Lodge
Great Dunmow Maltings
Benington Lordship
St Pauls Walden Bury
Knebworth
Woodhall Park
Forge Museum
Shaw's Corner
Hertford Museum
Scott's Grotto
Ashridge Bridgewater Monument
Gorhambury House
Redbournbury Mill
Cathedral & Abbey Church of St Albans
Hatfield House
Berkhamstead Castle Town Hall
Copped Hall
All Saints Pastoral Centre
Folly Arch
Capel Manor
Waltham Abbey Gatehouse & Bridge
Chenies Manor House
Myddelton House
Forty Hall
Chiltern Open Air Museum
John Milton's Cottage
Brentwood Cathedral
Stephens House
Headstone Manor
William Morris Gallery
St Andrews Old Church
Dissenters' Chapel
Himalaya Palace Cinema
Wapping Hydraulic Power Pumping Station
Eastbury Manor House
Rainham Hall
St Matthins
Crossness Beam Engine House
Gunnersbury Park Museum
Boston Manor House
Kelmscott House
Lesnes Abbey
Eton College
Chiswick House
Emery Walker House
Royal Observatory
Queen's House
Building 40 Royal Military Academy
Osterley Park
Syon Park
Hogarth's House
Ranger's House
Kew Gdns
Kew Palace
Eltham Palace
Danson House
Runnymede
The Octagon
Marble Hill House
Dulwich College
Red House
The Savill Garden
Strawberry Hill
Richmond Weir & Lock
Ham House
Hall Place Gardens
Southside House
Pope's Grotto
Lankmark Arts Centre
Morden Hall Park
Great Fosters
Garricks Temple
Hampton Court Palace
Lullingstone Roman Villa
Lullingstone Castle
Claremont Landscape Garden
Whitehall
Honeywood Heritage Centre
Little Holland House
Painshill Park
Home of Charles Darwin (Down House)
RHS Garden Wisley
Quebec House
Titsey Place
Knole
Knole Cartoon Gallery
Emmetts Garden
Shalford Mill
Polesden Lacey
Ightham Mote
Squerryes Court
Clandon
Hatchlands Park - The Cobbe Collection
Box Hill
Riverhill Himalayan Garden
Loseley Park
Chartwell
Guildford House Gallery
Tonbridge Castle
Church House
Goddards
Chiddingstone Castle
Leith Hill House
Hever Castle
Penshurst Place
Saint Hill Manor
Sackville College
Groombridge Place Gdns
Hammerwood Park
Standen

CENTRAL LONDON
Kenwood House
Highpoint
Highgate
Archway
Upper Holloway
Finsbury Park
Fenton House
Burgh House
2 Willow Road
Hampstead
Keats House
Stoke Newington
Freud Museum
Swiss Cottage
The Round Chapel
St Paul's Steiner Project
Hackney Empire
Sutton House
Islington
The Roundhouse
Camden Town
Shoreditch
Mappin Terrace Café
Kilburn
St John's Wood
King's Cross
Chapel of the Hospital of St John & St Elizabeth
Regent's Park
Euston
Priory Church
John Wesley's House
Bethnal Green
Maida Vale
Brunswick Square Gardens
The Charterhouse
Foundling Museum
Fitzroy House
St John's Gate
18 St George's German Lutheran Church
Marylebone
Fitzroy House
Bloomsbury
18 Folgate St
Charles Dickens House
19 Princelet Street
Sir John Soane's Museum
Paddington
Whitechapel Art Gallery
Dr Johnson's House
St Paul's Cathedral
Hendrix and Handel
College of Arms
Wiltons Music Hall
Queen's Chapel
Somerset House
St Ethelburga's Centre
Mayfair
Benjamin Franklin's House
Tower of London
Hyde Park
Southwark Cathedral & Footbridge
Tower Bridge Exhibition
Spencer House
Wellington Arch
Banqueting House
Kensington Palace
Albert Memorial
Apsley House
Kensington
Houses of Parliament
Buckingham Palace
Queen's Gallery
Chapter House
Linley Sambourne House
Royal Mews
Blewcoat School
Jewel Tower
St George's Cathedral
Bermondsey
Leighton House Museum
Westminster Cathedral
Elephant & Castle
Sloane Sq
Earls Court
Vauxhall
Pimlico
Carlyle's House
Chelsea Physic Garden
Kennington
Chelsea
Oval
Camberwell
Nine Elms
Brixton Academy
575 Wandsworth Road
Battersea
Stockwell
Fulham
Fulham Palace & Museum
Clapham
Spaniards Rd
Finchley Road
Rosslyn Hill
Kentish Town Rd
Holloway Road
Seven Sisters Rd
Camden Road
Kilburn High Road
Kingsland Road
City Rd
Old St
Euston Rd
Westway
Oxford St
Bayswater Rd
Park Lane
Moorgate
Aldgate
Old Kent Road
Kings Rd

# INDEX

Places listed by name in alphabetical order

## A

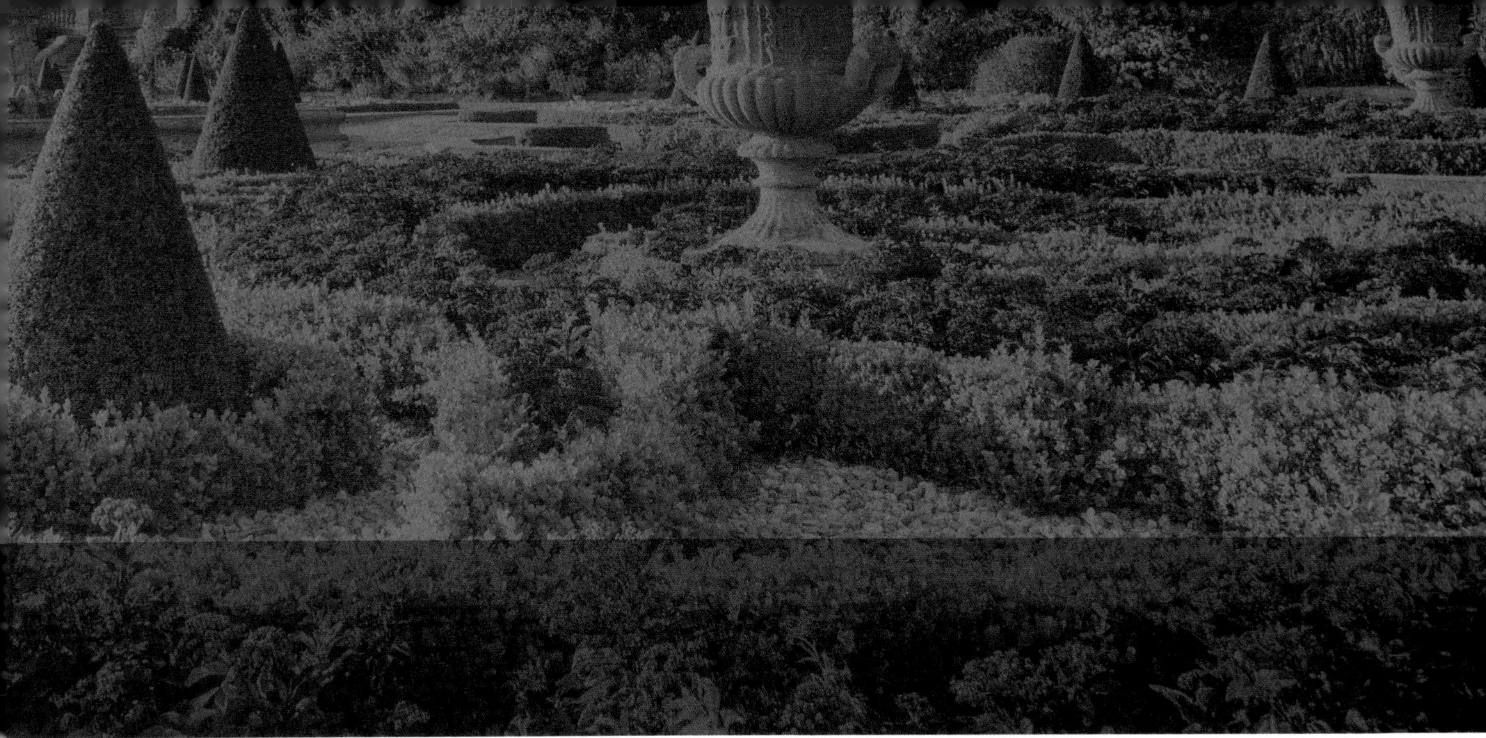



# B

# INDEX



## C

# D

# INDEX

## E



## F



## G



## H

## I



## J



## K

# INDEX



# L



# M

# N



# O



# P

# Q



# R



# S

# T



# U

# INDEX

The Signpost Guide celebrates it's 80th edition with a new look and format.

North Yorkshire Pickering

OPEN ALL YEAR

LASTINGHAM GRANGE COUNTRY HOUSE HOTEL

High Street, Lastingham, Nr Kirbymoorside YO62 6TH
T: (01751) 417345
E: reservations@lastinghamgrange.com
W: www.lastinghamgrange.com

It is easy to see why guests return time and again to this charming hotel situated on the edge of the Moors in the historic village of Lastingham, a peaceful backwater in the heart of the North York Moors National Park. The old, stone-walled country house, built around a courtyard and set within 10 acres of attractive gardens, is owned and personally run by the Wood family. Their charming friendliness and hospitality sets the mood for all guests to feel at ease in this elegant and tasteful country home. The atmosphere is unhurried and peaceful, the south facing terrace providing a tranquil setting in which to relax and enjoy the beautiful rose garden. The welcoming hall, the spacious lounge with its open fire, the comfortable bedrooms with their impressive views,

**BEDROOMS: 12** - Bedrooms are quite traditional, all are tastefully furnished and decorated.

**DINING:** Table d'hôte dinner £42; lunch from £28; Sunday lunch from £32; special diets available; last orders 2030.

Site:
Payment:
Leisure:
Property:
Children:
Catering:
Room:
See front of guide for key to symbols

**MORE INFO:** Activities nearby include riding, walking and golf. The Old Reading Room is located in the heart of the village and is a self catering holiday cottage available year round. Lastingham Grange is open March - beginning of December.

B&B PER ROOM PER NIGHT:
**S: £145.00 - £150.00**
**D: £199.00 - £210.00**

PLACES TO VISIT: CASTLE HOWARD, HOVINGHAM HALL, WHITBY

PLACES TO EAT: CASTLE HOWARD, BLACKSMITHS ARMS

020 3880 5059

sales@visitheritage.co.uk

www.visitheritage.co.uk

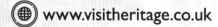